CALCUTTA
OLD AND NEW

CALCULTTA OLD AND NEW

H. E. A COTTON

GYAN

Published by

Gyan Publishing House
5, Ansari Road
Daryaganj, New Delhi-110002
Phone: 011-47034999, 9811692060
E-mail: books@gyanbooks.com

Distribution Network
gyanbooks.com
India, USA, Canada, UK, Australia

ISBN: 978-93-7169-539-8 (PB)

First Published, 1907

2nd Impression 2025

Printed at: Gyan Press, Delhi.

CALCUTTA OLD AND NEW
Author: H. E. A COTTON

CALCUTTA
OLD AND NEW.

A HISTORICAL & DESCRIPTIVE HANDBOOK TO THE CITY.

BY

H. E. A. COTTON,

OF LINCOLN'S INN, BARRISTER-AT-LAW AND ADVOCATE OF THE HIGH COURT
AT FORT WILLIAM IN BENGAL:
SOMETIME SCHOLAR OF JESUS COLLEGE, OXFORD.

CALCUTTA:
W. NEWMAN & CO., 4, DALHOUSIE SQUARE.
1907.

INTRODUCTION.

Full of romantic vicissitudes is the story of Calcutta—a story of strange events, much heroism and not a little of that "blundering through" that has marked British enterprise in all parts of the globe. The very names around us have each their adventure to tell: Fort William called, like its predecessor, after the Dutch King of England, and linked imperishably with the fame of Clive, and the crowning mercy of Plassey: Garden Reach, once studded with the riverside villas of merchant-princes; Park Street, the deer-park of old Sir Elijah Impey, whose name, thanks to Nuncomar and Macaulay, will never be forgotten; Kalighat, the landing-stage of the grim goddess of the city; the Mahratta Ditch, eloquent of wars and rumours of wars; Writers' Buildings, the nursery of pro-consuls; Ochterlony's Column to the honour of an American born Sepoy-General; and latest, but not least, the marble replica of Holwell's monument to his fellow-sufferers in the Black Hole. Other memories of the past have perished, whether from the ravages of time or the incuriousness of those in office. Gone is the forest glade at Belvedere, for all that it deserved to live as the stage whereon Hastings and Francis met in mortal encounter. Nor may posterity gaze upon the great Boytaconnah tree where the founder of Calcutta sat pulling at his hookah and pondering upon the possibilities of a settlement amid the marshes. Wellesley the magnificent lives again in his Government House, but we shall look in vain for the adjutant birds, once a familiar feature of the Calcutta landscape and bold enough to annex even the lion and unicorn on the stately facade. The name of Creek Row is all that is left of the Creek which ran a hundred yards from Dalhousie Square and upon whose banks an Armenian centenarian, who died a few years ago, remembered seeing boats. Not a vestige remains of the old Fort: like the good men and true who defended it against Seraj-ud-Dowlah, it has faded away into nothingness.

And as with men and things, so with manners. Life in Calcutta is no longer what it was in the "good old days." Then the Capuas of "Semlah" and "Whotakamund" had not been invented, and our forbears toiled year in and year out without thought of flitting to the hills or escaping to Europe on privilege leave. Then was the Augustan Age of John Company. Then sahibs were sahibs, veritable lords of creation, and interlopers were interlopers: and the exile in India made the country his home. There are so many sahibs nowadays that they have ceased to be venerable or wonderful: and the baboo has been to England and back again. Could we only shut our eyes and people Calcutta with the denizens of a century and a quarter ago, what a procession of heroes and heroines would file before us. There goes Hicky, the "true-born Englishman," father of the Calcutta Press, hurrying to the coffee house to catch the latest scandal for to-morrow's Gazette. Hard upon his heels there comes into sight portly self-satisfied "Padra" Johnson, rolling in his pocket the gold mohurs he has earned by celebrating a wealthy marriage. He is meditating, no doubt, some soft speech for that great lady, the Begum, who owns him as her fourth husband, for he hardly heeds the salutation of honest Cudbert Thornhill, the eighteenth century Sinbad who is ending his days as Master Attendant of the Port. There speeds to the Assembly-rooms along Tank Square the lacquered palankeen of beautiful Miss Sanderson, the belle of the settlement, escorted by sixteen attendant beaux in her livery colours: there hobnob in Mission Row the triumvirate of East Indian nabobs, Francis, Clavering and Monson. In Bhowanipore the Barwells sit at dinner with the whole house of Chambers, and the ladies are pelting the gentlemen with bread pills *à la mode de Bengale*. Zoffany is at his easel finishing his canvas of the Last Supper and borrowing with impartial hand the features of friend and foe: while his brother artist Hodges is off to "eat the air" in his country-built chariot with the boy-collector Clevland, *dulce decus* of the early civil service. There Macrabie, incomparable diarist and faithful friend, is deep in converse with Charles Weston, the generous and the good, whose portrait hangs to-day in St. John's vestry-room and challenges attention by reason of its strange headgear. There missionary Kiernander, if that sad jade Rumour says true, is "ogling from the pulpit with two rich and fat ladies of his congregation." A hundred other shadows beckon to us across the dim veil of years. We seem to see Dr. Tysoe Saul Hancock with gold cane and snuff-box listening to George Bogle's stories of newly explored Tibet, and Tiretta of Tiretta's Bazar fame drawing his great lottery and praying that he may win the *gros lot* himself. "Bibby" Motte from her house in Post Office Street sends chit after chit to Mrs.

Hastings the " Lady Governess "; and Madam Grand, the goddess of beauty, chats idly with Lawyer Farrer who pleaded in vain for Nuncomar's life before their lordships of the Supreme Court. Nubkissen, heedless of the widow carried off to suttee past his door, is hard at work preparing a nautch for the patricians of Chowringhee and Council House Street. Only here and there a familiar object greets the eye. The long stream of pilgrims on their way to bathe in the sacred river and the Moorman shouting his " Huson-Hawson " at Mohurrum time remind us that we are in the unchanging East. Behind the palaces that fringe the maidan lurk the same bazars and bustees as to-day, " Loll " Bazar and " John " Bazar, with their " boutiques " and " Balasore bearers," " Chowkydars " and coolies. Yet, before we can summon up the ghosts of the succeeding generations, the glare of the present comes swiftly to blind us to the glamour of the past. A new Calcutta is rising in our midst. The talk is all of an Anglo-Indian Haussmann who is to transform the teeming Indian quarter. On every hand the electric car and the electric fan tell of the advent of a new era. Surely, the occasion could not be more opportune for enlisting a patriotic interest in the scenes and sites which confront each one of us in our daily round, from the tourist in his ticca-gharry to the " city-man " in his brougham? And to those who know her, what can there be more fascinating than the City of Palaces? Let us who have lived in Calcutta and learnt to love her, leave to others the sorry pleasure of proclaiming her imperfections upon the house-tops: and let us all be proud of our city, proud of her past and prouder still of her present.

In the ensuing pages an attempt has been made to do justice to Calcutta not only in her bygone but in her modern aspect. There has been no pretence at originality on the part of the writer except, it may be, in the matter of treatment. The chroniclers of the annals of the second city in the British Empire have been many. Each of the stages in the wondrous up-springing of Charnock's modest grain of mustard seed has received tender and expert handling. But it is submitted, without any desire to be presumptuous, that a complete and comprehensive history of Calcutta remains to be written. The threads have still to be gathered and woven into one connected fabric. It is this task which the present writer has with much misgiving ventured to essay. The book has been divided of set purpose into two parts. In the earlier portion the aim has been to recall the historical associations of Calcutta, to remind the citizen no less than the stranger within her gates of her vanished buildings and changed localities, and to commemorate the men who have helped to make the city what she is. The second half of the book is designed to serve as an interesting and informing guide to the Calcutta of to-day. If the writer has not made adequate acknowledgement in the course of the ensuing pages of the debt he owes to the labours of his predecessors, it has been from no unwillingness to admit his obligation. He is deeply sensible that a work of this nature must be at its best little more than a compilation, and he has not hesitated to borrow where the loan was likely to dissipate doubt or assist enquiry. In a bibliography prepared with the assistance of the late Mr. J. Macfarlane, Librarian of the Imperial Library, an attempt (necessarily incomplete) has been made to indicate the names and the books of the principal authors who have selected Calcutta as their theme. To almost all of these the writer has at one time or another referred, as he hopes his readers will: but he must be content in this place with a confession of the main sources of his inspiration. Upon the early history of the city, the minute and valuable researches of Archdeacon Hyde and the late Professor C. R. Wilson have been laid under frequent contribution. Much help has also been obtained from the "Short History of Calcutta" by Mr. A. K. Ray, which forms Part I of the Calcutta Census Report for 1901. Regarding the period of Warren Hastings, it would be hard to find anything that has been unsaid by Dr. Busteed in his incomparable "Echoes from Old Calcutta." But acquisitions of interest have resulted nevertheless from independent examination of hackneyed yet always fascinating contemporary authorities. Nor in this connection has quotation been disdained from that entertaining if sometimes apocryphal description of eighteenth-century Calcutta which goes by the name of "Hartly House": for whether it be written or not by a Grub-Street hack, it is undoubtedly based upon the experiences of an actual sojourner by Hooghly's "hallowed but malarious stream." Considerable use has likewise been made of the well-known articles in the *Calcutta Review* by the Rev. James Long, and of the scattered newspaper contributions of the late Mr. H. James Rainey—honoured pioneers both in the field of local antiquarian investigation, in spite of the verification of which their statements often stand in need. Passing to more modern times, mention must not be neglected of the drafts made upon the ample fund of material in Sir George Trevelyan's "Letters of a Competition-wallah" (that faithful mirror of Calcutta in the fifties and sixties), and Mr. C. E. Buckland's annals of "Bengal under the Lieutenant-Governors." Lastly, the writer's special thanks are due to his brother, Mr. Julian Cotton, of the Madras Civil Service, not only for the two chapters he has contributed, but also for much time and labour ungrudgingly spent in seeing almost the whole of the second half of the book through the press. Acknowledgment must likewise be made of the permission accorded to use extracts from the informing articles from his pen upon "Forgotten India" which have appeared from time to time in the pages of the *Calcutta Review*. The Index has been the work of Mr. E. W. Madge, of the Imperial Library, Calcutta, to whom the writer is also indebted for other valuable assistance always freely and cheerfully given. In many places portions have been incorporated in the text of articles and reviews contributed by the writer to the *Pioneer, Statesman, Englishman,* and *Indian Daily News:* and to the Editors of these journals acknowledgment is due for their courtesy in granting liberty of reproduction.

CONTENTS.

PART I.

PART II.

APPENDIX.

ERRATA.

Page.	*Line.*	*For*	*Read.*
1	third last	fifth	fifteenth
13	21	"A cargo of behars, pepper, and redwood candy"	A cargo of 286 behars and 415 lbs. of pepper and redwood, 268 candy, 15 maunds.
27	4	convey	convoy
32	23	hand	haud
39	22	larger map of 1793	map of 1794
49	18	Mr. Cruttenden	Mr. Edward Cruttenden
,,	18, 19	once Governor of the settlement	once Member of Council
56	4 (footnote)	ship	ships
84	24	Hartley	Hartly
92	26	Nuncomar's place of imprisonment	Nuncomar's, & Hicky's place of imprisonment
,,	27	the country jail	the Birjee or country jail
,,	28, 29	But the jail where Hicky was confined.	the other jail
93	19	south-west corner of Tank Square	north-east corner of Mission Row
108	15	*inten*	*inter*
112	last three	Francis and Clavering ...remained impassive.	But that power lay vested under the Act in the Supreme Court, and not in the majority which Francis commanded. He was compelled to remain impassive.
156	last	grandpré	Grandpré
183	second last	commodius	commodious
201	12	March 3	March 2
203	3	Bruce	Bryce
220	17	1860	1863
235	2	1882	1883
276	19	*of*	*from*
289	4	1844	1846
290	8	1785	1795
298	2	*Resartas*	*Resartus*
299	7	Colonel Kyd	General Alexander Kyd, his relative and heir
302	22	the English	English's
303	2	Rs. 50	Rs. 30
,,	9	father	relative
311	21	Daniel	Daniel
327	1	Palace	Place

Page.	*Line.*	*For*	*Read.*
327	8	J. R. Rainey	H. J. Rainey
336	2	La Bourdounais	La Bourdonnais
341	5	compliment	complement
348	17	South	North
351	6	J. R. Rainy	H. J. Rainy
361	14	neighbouring church	former church of that name
373	5	Speed	Theed
413	21, 22, 24	it is intended to place	there was placed during the current year (1907); and omit in line 24 "which is understood to be approaching completion."
415	25	seventies	eighties
437	5	1863	1883
438	21	outlet	inlet
448	13	Eye	Eyre.
480	15, 19	Blacquire	Blaquiere.
482	1, 2	There was......using	The painter was, it may be noted, only too partial to the habit of using
492	23	plam	plain
494	14	Idea	India
,,	25	Church	Churchyard
495	10, 11	*Omit:* Until the river washed the ruins away a few years ago.	
502	3	Transtead	Stanstead
506	1	Tippo	Tippoo
514	3	headquarter	headquarters
516	24	Macnaughten	McNaghten, *and add*, he was the brother-in-law of Miss Emma Roberts, whose *Scenes and Characteristics of Hindustan*, published in the thirties, contain interesting references to Calcutta.
518	3	her	its
518	3rd last	Mrs.	Miss
520	19	memoirs	echoes
523	3rd last	who......................1843	whose book on Decrees keeps his legal memory green
524	26, 27	the building......Howrah	The building of the Church at the Free School and St. Thomas's Church Howrah.

Page.	*Line.*	*For*	*Read.*
524	27, 28	Seaman's	the Seamen's
537	24	good	poor
541	16	Richard	Richmond
542	28	Nicks, married	Nicks whom he married
550	2	Benjamanis	Benjaminis
552	2	on.......................1711	seven months passed and
553	22	31	(1)
556	19	*Omit :* Governor, and add "and garden" after "mansion"	
569	10	quaeris	requiris
571	6, 7	*Omit :* Thackeray's maternal grandfather.	named on his tombstone as "an honest man."
573	2nd last	Hickey	Hicky
580	11	E. J. Shore	F. J. Shore
583	20	Cotes	Coates
593	3	Friend	Cousin
609	24	Macnaughten	Macnaghten
610	24	add "late" before "Military Secretary"	
612	7	Silchar	Kohima
617	11	Lloyd	Loyd
622	3rd last	and.........1893	Who...........1893 (These words should follow "1878," two lines above, as they refer to General Sir H. E. L. Thuillier and not to Colonel Sir H. R. Thuillier.)
627	17	Ralph Johnson	Edward Ralph Johnson
646	12	Rev. D. Mieklejohn	Rev. Dr. W. H. Meiklejohn
,,	18	Rawdon Street	Bhowanipore
656	18	Babu	Baba
,,	23	and his	His
,,	25		after "Bengal" *Add :* is buried in the Greek Church.
657	5	after	afterwards
668	2nd last	H. M. Locke	H. H. Locke
669	9	Brown	Broun
,,	17	Steel	Steell
,,	19, 20	where it now is. It is intended to remove it	It has now been removed
672	2	*Omit:* of India	
677	2	*Omit:* in 1877	
677	24	Wilson	Willison
686	8	installer	installation

Page.	*Line.*	*For*	*Read.*
687	15, 16	where it now is	whence it has since been transferred to the Victoria Memorial Collection.
689	11	son	brother
,,	16	father	elder
,,	17	son's	younger's
695	11	second Afghan War	first Afghan War
715	4th last	schoolmasters	school fellows
717	4	1771	1774
720	12 & 20	Harrington	Harington
723	19	Jacquement	Jacquemont
725	25, 26	historical trial itself	trial of Nuncomar and Fowke for conspiracy
727	9	Attorney's	Attorneys'
734	17	Taylor	Tayler
750	17	Wyle	Wylie
758	18	*Omit:* "present"	
762	12	1832	1882
769	1	1860	1861
769	9	1888	1898
771	13	*Omit* his colleague	
774	23	After "Calcutta" *insert* (with the exception of Bishop Welldon.)	
777	21	now	late
784	11	Bannerjee	Bonnerjee
,,	18	1880	1890
788	11	James Grant	John Grant
,,	25	Ronald	Ranald
793	8	after "Librarian."	*insert full-stop and add* "A serious loss has befallen the Library by the recent death of the first incumbent of that office, Mr. J. Macfarlane.
796	12	present Librarian	late Librarian
,,	17	Mr. Macfarlane	the Librarian
798	13	are being prepared	have been prepared
809	17	Steel	Steell
814	8	The painter's name i, unknown	add Note :—The India Office have just (April 1907) purchased an engraving of this picture which gives the painter's name as Chinnery.
819	25	father-in-law	brother-in-law
822	4	Sujjum-ud-Dowlah	Nujjum-ud-Dowlah
853	8	continued	contrived

Page.	*Line.*	*For*	*Read.*
879	20	7th August	17th August
880	5	North Park Street	South Park Street
881	11	"Hartley House"	"Hartly House.'
885	5	conjectures	states
894	22	aucion	auction
918	4	*Omit*: Sir, and read C. B. for K. C. B.	
921	15, 16	*Omit:* then Chief Justice of Bengal.	
954	4th last	J. H. Rattray	R. H. Rattray
957	8, 9	*Omit sentence:* The College ... Government.	
958	13	Hodges	Hodge
963	20, 21	L. Schwendler	C. L. Schwendler
971	13	Walter	William
,,	23	fave of	fave et
986	25	east	south
993	11	Miss	Mrs.
996	26	Mogul	Mungul
Appendix,	p 1, last line,	*Omit* name of author of Chowringhee Theatre Librettos.	
,,	p vi.	Bentinck Cavendish	Cavendish Bentinck

CHAPTER I.

THE FOUNDING OF CALCUTTA.

Calcutta is the sixth capital which Bengal has enjoyed within a period of as many centuries. Gour, in the modern district of Maldah, which had flourished for two thousand years, was deprived of her proud position by the shifting of the course of the river, and nothing now marks her past grandeur but a cluster of majestic ruins. To her succeeded in turn Rajmahal, the city of one hundred kings, Dacca, famed from Roman times, Nuddea, for five centuries the Oxford of Bengal, and Moorshedabad, the home of the declining power of the Mahomedan Nabobs of Bengal. The honour has accrued to-day to a city which, by the side of her immemorial predecessors, has but the veriest fragment of history to show.

The English Capital of India has grown up out of the union of a group of river-side places. The three hitherto recognized members of this cluster are the hamlets of Calcutta, Suttanuttee, and Govindpore: but, as the late Dr. C. R. Wilson has pointed out, four others at least must be reckoned among the elementary constituents of the city—Chitpore, Sulkea, the sanctuary of Kalighat, and as the original focus of the trade, Betor, on the west bank of the river, close by the modern Seebpore. At the end of the fifth century, a poem in praise of the Serpent-goddess written by Bipradas, a Bengalee Brahmin, in days when Husain Shah was reigning Sultan of Bengal, gives us our first authentic glimpse of Calcutta. Satgaon or Saptagram, on the right bank of the river, between Tribeni and Bandel, is the great port, and not Hooghly. Lower down the river, Betor, on the same side, is a large market town, where travellers pause to buy provisions and worship the goddess Chandi. Chitpore and Calcutta are neighbouring villages passed just before reaching Betor; Govindpore and Suttanuttee do not exist. Kalighat is a small sanctuary claiming just a bare notice.

When the Portuguese first began to frequent Bengal about the year 1530, the two great centres of trade were Chittagong in the East, and Satgaon in the West. The former was distinguished as the Great Haven or Porto Grande, and under favourable circumstances might have retained the commercial importance which she is now-a-days bent upon winning back—but in an evil hour for her fortunes she became the rendezvous of "Feringi" outlaws and pirates, adventurers and fugitives from Goa and its dependencies. Satgaon, which has now dwindled into an insignificant group of huts in the vicinity of the town of Hooghly, was known as the Little Haven or Porto Piqueno. The river was easily navigable by sea-going ships as far as the Adi-ganga, the modern Tolly's Nullah, which was then the outlet to the sea: but beyond this it was considered too shallow for any but country boats. In Garden Reach, therefore, was the anchoring place of the Portuguese, and at Betor was the mart of thatched huts, erected year by year on the arrival of the ships from Goa, and destroyed as swiftly a few months later, when the last boat had come down from Satgaon and her cargo safely shipped aboard the galliasses.

Here then may be traced the nucleus of the future city of Calcutta, and as time went on the silting up of the river opposite Satgaon still further favoured her fortunes.

Towards the end of the sixteenth century the merchant-princes of Porto Piqueno were one after the other forced to seek another market for their trade. The great majority settled down at Hooghly: but four families of Bysacks and one of Setts determined to profit by the growing prosperity of Betor, and founded the village of Govindpore, on the east bank of the river, just above its junction with the Adi-ganga. They cleared the jungle and built houses for themselves and a shrine for their deity Govindjee: and in a short space of time opened, on the north side of Calcutta, a place for the sale of cloth which was soon to become celebrated as Suttanuttee Hât, the Cotton Bale Market. The Portuguese, however, were not as encouraging to the enterprise as its pioneers had hoped, and went higher up the river in response to the invitation extended to them by Akbar to form a settlement at Hooghly. Here Fitch found them permanently settled when he visited Bengal in 1583. But their neglect to keep the Gulf of Bengal clear of pirates brought the vengeance of Shah Jehan upon them, and in 1632 the town of Hooghly was captured and its entire population transferred as slaves to Agra.

To the Portuguese succeeded the Dutch, who had in 1625 made their way to Bengal and now established themselves at Pipli and Chinsurah. The English were still contenting themselves with trade at Balasore and

Hariharpore in Orissa, and it was not until the days of the great Protector Oliver that they ventured up the river to Hooghly.

Calcutta, meanwhile, was growing in stature and in strength. In the *Ain-i-Akbari,* a work written in 1596 by Abul Fazl, the Prime Minister of the Emperor Akbar, the place is noticed as a district in the Government or Sirkar of Satgaon, which with the districts of Barbakpur and Bakuya paid into the Imperial Exchequer the annual sum of Rs. 23,405.

In the seventeenth century, Betor disappears from history : its name was changed into the village of Mukwah Tannah, and its foreign market transferred to Suttanuttee, where the Setts and Bysacks had been laboriously building up an European connection, and particularly with the English, who had in 1652—thanks to Gabriel Boughton, the Surgeon of the *Hopewell*, and his cure of the Emperor's daughter Jahanara—been permitted to set up their factory at Hooghly, and, like the Portuguese, were using Garden Reach as an anchorage for their sea-going vessels.

He would have been a bold man, nevertheless, who would have prophesied the English Empire in India out of these small beginnings. A despatch, dated the 27th February, 1658, gives an almost complete list of the Councils established in Bengal. The head-quarters of the English merchants lay at Hooghly, where their chief Agent was passing rich on a salary of one hundred pounds per annum. Hard by at Chinsurah, and almost within a stone's throw, the Dutch were striving with them for the custom of the subjects of the Nabob. Still more formidable was the organized opposition of the "interlopers" who were making strenuous efforts to share in the large profits of the trade, and were presently to oust the London Company from its pride of place. Among these "interlopers" or private traders was a notable "young beginner" of the name of Thomas Pitt, "a fellow of a haughty huffying daring temper," destined in after years to be Governor of Fort St. George, to discover the finest diamond in the world, and to be the progenitor of two of England's greatest statesmen. Outside Hooghly a few isolated factories at Dacca, Balasore, Cossimbazar, and Patna, made up the sum total of the English possessions in Bengal. Where Calcutta now greets the world with her amazing medley of Western opulence and Eastern squalor, there stood a cluster of obscure villages: and thirty years and more were yet to elapse before Job Charnock was to establish himself at Suttanuttee after a series of bewildering attempts to settle at Hidgelee, Oolooberriah, and even Chittagong.

The character of the English society of the day in Bengal may be gathered from the private correspondence still extant and enshrined for posterity in the pages of Sir William Hedges' Diary. Their literature was books such as the *Eikon Basilike* or the *Religio Medici,* and it was an amusement of the day to stuff their letters with "Latin saws and elaborate compliments and invocations for Heliconian irrigation" after the manner of good Sir Thomas Browne. Life at Hooghly was regulated after the fashion of a college. The hours of work were from nine or ten till twelve in the morning, and again in the afternoon till about four o'clock if work was pressing. At mid-day there was dinner in the common hall, the seats strictly arranged in order of seniority. The second meal taken together in the hall was supper. At nine o'clock the factory gates were shut. For excursions, they had the English garden, two miles north of the factory: for exercise, shooting at the butts or sport in the country around: and for entertainment, they had themselves and their Dutch neighbours. The chief and second had a palanquin each when they went abroad, and the rest of the Council with the Chaplain were allowed to have large umbrellas borne over them in solemn state: but not so the rank and file. In the diary of Streynsham Master, Governor of Fort St. George, who came to the Bay in 1676 on a tour of inspection, investigation and correction, we find the following: "There being an ill custom in the ffactory of writers having roundells carried over their heads.........it is therefore ordered that noe person in this ffactory shall have a roundell carried over them, but such as are of the Councell and the Chaplain." There was a good deal of hard drinking. Arrack-punch and Shiraz wine were the main beverages, European wine and bottled beer being great luxuries. In matter of dress, they strove to imitate their brothers in Europe, but at a respectful distance, as needs must be. In 1658 a good cloth coat with silver lace was all the fashion, and was considered to be the badge of an Englishman. Great personages, such as the Right Worshipful the Agent and His Reverence the Chaplain, no doubt, wore the ample wig, but perukes were as a rule at a discount, for those who consulted comfort and made terms with the climate "entered into the Moors' fashion" and cut their hair short. Of English ladies, there were sadly few, and most of the merchants had Indian wives and fell largely into Indian ways. When away from the factory they took their meals lying on carpets and wore the Indian dress. No one stirred abroad without a number of orderlies. Foibles and faults they had in plenty: but to their credit be it said, they adhered to their obligations in the dealings with the people, and were rewarded in kind by the faithfulness of the Hindoo merchants to the Company's interests. They were not exactly such as wear soft raiment and dwell in King's houses. But their lives and morals were not so dark as some would paint them.

The years 1686 to 1690 were a stormy crisis in the fortunes of the Bengal factories. The hostility of the Nabob's Foujdar at Hooghly led to a sharp skirmish, and after a gallant defence, Job Charnock, who was now the Company's chief Agent, was compelled to withdraw "all ye Right Honourable Company's concerns and our own." On the way down the river, he halted at Suttanuttee (upon which even then he had cast his eye) and negotiated in vain for peace. But the Nabob's troops came nearer and nearer: and while Charnock did what he could to hinder their progress by demolishing all the forts within his reach, Captain Nicholson was sent to take possession of the island of Hidgelee, a low deadly swamp at the mouth of the river. Here the English threw up a hasty encampment and gallantly withstood its siege by "Abdul Summud, the Nabob's buxy." In three months one half of Charnock's troops were dead, and the remainder in miserable plight. Overtures were made by Shaista Khan, the Nabob, and the English returned to Suttanuttee: but the arrival of reinforcements from England put an altogether new face upon the situation. The Court of Directors, in answer to Charnock's appeals for help, had sent out a "capricious and futile feather-brained" sea-captain of the name of Heath, with orders to set up the Factory at Chittagong, which they fancied he would find somewhere "up the great Ganges." The treaty was disallowed, and this was followed by the embarcation of the Agent and his officers on the ships, the bombardment and burning of Balasore, and finally the forcible transportation of the entire English settlement in Bengal to Madras by Captain Heath, whose six months' mad cruise around the Bay in search of a site to take the place of Hooghly reads more like a romance than like a statement of sober fact. For fifteen weary months Charnock sat eating out his heart at Fort St. George, until the offer by Ibrahim Khan, the new Nabob at Dacca, of Rs. 60,000 by way of compensation for the goods plundered enabled him to start back to Bengal with the faithful remnant of his followers.

There exists at the India Office a series of eleven volumes, extending to 1706, the first of which is entitled "Diary and Consultation Book for affairs of the Rt. Hon'ble English East India Company kept by the Rt. Worshipfull the Agent and Council, beginning July 16, 1690." Here may be read, in the words of Charnock, the story of how on the 24th August, 1690, the English occupied the deserted village of Suttanuttee for the third and final time: and here, too, is the record of the first "consultation" held four days later by the restored Bengal Council. There were present "the Rt. Worshipfull Agent Charnock, Mr. Francis Ellis, and Mr. Jere (miah) Peachie:" and "in consideration that all the former buildings here are destroyed, it is resolved that such places be built as necessity requires and as cheap as possible......these to be done with mudd walls and thatched till we get ground whereon to build a factory." Thus "with the rain falling day and night," and "the factors forced to betake themselves to boats which, considering the season of the year, is very unhealthy," was set up amid ruin and desolation the city of Calcutta.

Enough, perhaps, has been said to indicate some, at any rate, of the reasons which induced Charnock to select "this very small spot of rising ground on the east side of the river" for the permanent settlement of the English in Bengal. But the subject cannot be dismissed without reference to a time-honoured legend. If tradition is to be believed, Charnock first conceived the idea in days when Suttanuttee was the halfway house of the foreign merchants, and he was wont to sit and smoke a meditative hookah under the shade of a spreading peepul tree, which stood at the junction of what is now Bow Bazar Street and Lower Circular Road. The spot went by the name of Boytaconnah (boitak-khana) or resting-place, and for years it continued to be a favourite rendezvous. "Here the merchants met to depart in bodies from Calcutta to protect each other from robbers in the neighbouring jungle, and here they dispersed when they arrived at Calcutta with merchandise for the factory." The historic tree was removed by the Marquess of

Hastings in 1820, in pursuance of his schemes for the improvement of the city, but not without lament and prophecy of evil from the superstitious.

Captain Alexander Hamilton, an "eighteenth century Sinbad," who traded and travelled by sea and land between the Cape and India and Japan from 1688 to 1723, has left a characteristic account of the foundation of Calcutta, which is not without interest, for it indicates how strong at the time was the tradition of the famous Boytaconnah tree.

"Mr. Job Chaunock"—so spelt by Hamilton—"being then the Company's Agent in Bengal, he had the liberty to settle an emporium in any part on the river's side below Hooghly, and for the sake of a large shady tree chose that place, though he could not have chosen a more unhealthy place, on the river, for three miles to the north-eastward is a salt-water lake that overflows in September and October, and then prodigious numbers of fish resort thither, but in November and December, when the floods are dissipated, those fishes are left dry, and with their putrefaction affect the air with thick stinking vapors, which the north-east winds bring with them to Fort William that they cause a yearly mortality."

Hamilton bore no love for the English factors, whose restrictions upon private trade were not at all to his taste. But he does not overdraw his picture of the unhealthiness of early Calcutta: and from the beginning the most formidable obstacle was invariably supplied by the climate.

In spite of the favour shown them by Ibrahim Khan,

whom the English in their gratitude styled "the most famously just and good Nabob," the situation of the factors at Suttanuttee was at first comfortless in the extreme. An Imperial Order issued in 1691 authorized them to "contentedly continue their trade" in Bengal, on payment of Rs. 3,000 yearly by way of all dues. But the fever-haunted swamps behind the river bank exacted a terrible toll, and the shadow hung over them of the war which William the Third was waging against the French, and which compelled them to keep an anxious eye upon their fellow-merchants at Chandernagore. We can little realise in these days the miseries which the rugged pioneers with their English habits of eating and drinking must have suffered in the stifling cabins and fore-castles of their sloops and country-boats and in the mat hovels which too often formed their sole shelter ashore. Charnock died in 1693 and left this new settlement in strange disorder. His many hardships seem to have sapped his energy and his strength of will. He made scarcely any attempt at government, and did not even mark out the premises of a factory. The only conspicuous masonry building he acquired, in addition to the "Portuguese mass-house," which was destroyed after his death, was the cutcherry of the Mojumdar family who were the local jagirdars: and here were lodged the Company's official staff and the records. Every one was allowed to enclose lands, dig tanks and build houses where and how they pleased. Violence, waste, and vice ruled in the little colony; and the Chief, and Hill, the Captain of his guard, set their subordinates fighting duels. Hill was permitted to "keep a punch-house and billiard table gratis while others paid for it." Charnock himself, as tradition has it, developed a savage temper, and flogged his servants for the most trivial offences, the execution being "generally done when he was at dinner, so near his dining-room that the groans and the cries of the poor delinquents served him for music." Equally famous is the story also told of him that he turned heathen and sacrificed a cock on his Indian wife's grave. But with all his faults and failings, it can never be forgotten that Charnock, and Charnock alone, founded Calcutta. It was he who deliberately and wisely chose it as the foundation-stone of the British Empire in India—and it was through no merit of his Hon'ble Masters that the establishment at Suttanuttee was acquiesced in, for they did not countermand only because they "could not now help it."

CHAPTER II.

THE EARLY DAYS OF THE SETTLEMENT.

CHARNOCK's immediate successor was Francis Ellis, his second in Council, a man of little character or ability, who had ten years before suffered dismissal at the hands of Sir William Hedges and been reinstated by President Gyfford. But in August 1693 there arrived in Calcutta, bent on reorganization and reform, Sir John Goldsborough, "Commissary Generall and Admirall of the East India Fleet" and "Chief Governour of the Right Honorable English East India Company's Affaires." The reins were taken out of the listless hands of Ellis, and Charles Eyre, Charnock's son-in-law, of whom there was little to complain "except that he was addicted to the country habits and customs," was summoned to Suttanuttee to assume charge of the settlement. His was a character of a different stamp to that of Ellis: and under his management, the situation began to mend. During the first year of his rule there occurred the memorable catastrophe which has given a name of world-wide fame to one of the most dangerous quicksands on the river. The *Royal James and Mary* had arrived from Sumatra in August, 1694, with "a cargo of behars, pepper, and red-wood candy," which she took in at Madras: but coming up the Hooghly on the 24th September, she struck upon the fatal shoal, turned over immediately, and broke her back. With the memory of Eyre must also be linked the building of the massive octagonal mausoleum where, within the precincts of St. John's Churchyard, the Father of Calcutta sleeps undisturbed amid the dust and din of the town he called into existence.

Calcutta had now been nearly ten years in existence: but beyond the laying out by Goldsborough of the lines for a fort, the settlement remained unfortified and unprotected. The opportunity came in 1696, while Eyre was still Agent. The insurrection of Rajah Subah Singh, who seized Hooghly and Moorshedabad, and advanced in December of that year upon Suttanuttee, extorted from the unready Nabob Ibrahim Khan at Dacca the long-delayed permission to the English to "defend themselves." The settlement was secured from the attack of Subah Singh by means of the guardships, which lay at anchor in the river: and fortifications were hurriedly run up and rapidly pushed on after the withdrawal of the danger. A bastion and a walled enclosure were completed by January, 1697, and we find the Company's servants at Calcutta writing to Madras for ten guns to arm the points.* In the following year (1698) confidence had been so far established that a vigorous attempt was made to gain a definite status in the eyes of the "Country Powers" by obtaining from Azim-ush-shan, the grandson of Aurangzebe, who was then Viceroy of Bengal, certain privileges of trade as well as permission to rent the three villages of Suttanuttee, Govindpore and Calcutta. Unhappily Aurangzebe himself

---

* A full description of old Fort William will be found in the second part of this book.

and Murshed Kuli Khan, his Dewan in Bengal, had little liking for the foreign merchants. The Mogul believed that they were in some manner connected with the pirates who infested the Arabian Sea and plundered the pilgrims on their way to Mecca: and he would have driven them altogether out of India, except for the consideration that his commerce and revenue would suffer in consequence. The Dewan, on his part, resolved that, if the strangers remained, they should be made to contribute heavily to the Imperial Exchequer. He prevented the local zemindars from selling the three villages to the Company, and kept the factors in a constant state of uncertainty and alarm by assuming an attitude first of hostility and then of friendliness and again of hostility. When Aurangzebe had in 1702 given orders to seize and confine every European in his dominions, the President at Fort William, John Beard, had said boldly enough that force and a strong fortification were better than an ambassador. But his colleagues held a different view, and were for ever sending vakeels with presents of money and rich merchandise to placate the Dewan and obtain from him *perwannahs* and *sunnuds* which were not worth the paper they were written on. The Company had, however, sufficiently secured their position in Bengal by 1699 to entitle them to receive from their honourable masters the distinction implied in the elevation of their factory to the rank of an independent Presidency: and the name of Fort William was in the following year conferred upon its rising fort in commemoration of the reigning King.

The death of Aurangzebe in 1707 opened the gates to a flood of civil war and anarchy, which threatened to react seriously upon the Company's trade. A "hot-headed phousdar" at Hooghly took advantage of the disordered situation to stop the saltpetre boats and imprison the servants of the Company: and an attack on Fort William seemed imminent. Only the north-east and south-east bastions had up to this time been erected within the walled enclosure: and the opportunity was taken to add two more bastions on the river-side. But the storm blew over, and the Council set to work to secure from the new Emperor Shah Alam a renewal of their privileges of trade. After much haggling and blustering, the *perwannah* was obtained on payment of forty-five thousand rupees: and the superintendent of the royal treasury, who was pleased to visit Calcutta in October, 1709, was "received very civilly" and placated with a present of one thousand rupees value.

From 1711 to 1713 there ruled over the settlement a grandson of Oliver Cromwell, in the person of John Russell, the son of a Cambridgeshire baronet and of the Protector's youngest and favourite daughter Frances. Three years before his appointment to the governorship, Henry Frankland, who was the second son of his sister Elizabeth, arrived in India, and later on, from 1726 to 1728, himself occupied the chief place in Council. Yet another scion of the Protector's stock was Nicholas Morse, Governor of Madras at the time of its surrender to De la Bourdonnais in 1746, and the irony of fate was never better exemplified than when it condemned the descendant of Cromwell and Ireton to march with the members of his Council in humiliating procession through the streets of Pondicherry. Another Russell, the grand-nephew of Governor John, and the sixth baronet of the family, was Chief at Cossimbazar in 1728, and again in 1741, and Member of Council at Fort William in 1731. Less fortunate than his relative, who lived on in England to a green old age, and lies buried in Bath, Sir Francis Russell died in Calcutta in 1743. He will reappear later in these pages as the chronicler of the famous storm of 1737. His widow was among those who took refuge at Fulta after Seraj-ud-daulah's capture of Calcutta and must have died there, for her will, dated August 24, 1756, was proved in the Mayor's Court in 1757. Of Governor John Russell himself, we catch more than one interesting glimpse in Dr. C. R. Wilson's *Early Annals of the English in Bengal.* His first wife was the sister of Sir Charles Eyre, Governor of Fort William from 1695 to 1707, the husband of Job Charnock's daughter Mary, and the builder (as we have recorded in its place) of the monument in St. John's Churchyard. Madam Russell, as she is termed in the consultation-books, died at Chandernagore in 1713, and we read that she was buried in Calcutta. Her eldest daughter, Frances, left India with her father in the following year, and became in after years bed-chamber-woman to the Princess Amelia, daughter of George the Second, Horace Walpole's Princess Amelie, who died unmarried in 1786 at her house in Cavendish Square. Of her Dr. Wilson preserves an excellent anecdote. She was on a thirtieth of January in the Princess' room adjusting her mistress' dress, when the Prince of Wales, coming into the room, took occasion to observe, with more freedom than courtesy, "Ah! Miss Russell, why are you not at church to endeavour to avert the judgement of heaven from falling upon the nation for the sins of your ancestor Oliver?" "Is it not humiliation enough," replied the Governor's daughter with spirit, "for a descendant of the great Cromwell to be pinning up your sister's tail?" It is pleasant to see that even the degenerate atmosphere of the eighteenth century could not stifle the spirit of the grim Protector. Yet we wonder what Miss Russell and her redoubtable forbear alike would have said, if they could have seen the style of the letters addressed by Governor John to the Emperor Furruckseer? "The request of the smallest particle of sand, John Russell, president for the English East India Company," so runs one of the epistles transcribed by Dr. Wilson, "with his forehead at command rub'd on the Ground, and reverence due from a Slave among those that make their request to your Throne which is the Seat of Miracles, you're the Lord of the World and the present age, a Support and a shade to all that inhabite the world, you equallize the great Darius, your Throne Resembles that of Solomon's, you're a second Cyrus, a Conquerour of Countrys, a Strengthner of the root of justice, and an eradicator of violence and oppression."

There was some method, however, in this self-abasement. For in spite of the concessions purchased from the representatives of the Mogul, Murshed Kuli Khan, their old enemy, continued to press the Company hard. This remarkable man, who was the son of a Dekhani Brahmin, had been in 1701 appointed to the *dewanny* of Bengal by Aurangzebe and was rapidly increasing his power and influence at Moorshedabad, whither he had removed his capital from Dacca, and where he reigned until his death in 1725. His exactions became so grievous that it was determined in 1715 to send an Embassy to Delhi to represent the grievances of the Company to the Emperor Ferokhshah (Furruckseer).

The Mogul had already shown sympathy with them by issuing orders to Murshed Kuli Khan in January of the preceding year to cease his intérference with the English trade: and the event had been celebrated in Calcutta with a *feu-de-joie* and the drinking of the healths of Queen Anne and King Furruckseer with fifty-one guns to each health. The Embassy consisted of John Surman and Edward Stephenson, two of the ablest factors in the service: a wealthy Armenian merchant, named Khojah Serhaud, who acted as interpreter, and William Hamilton, a surgeon on the establishment at Fort William. They carried presents for the Mogul and his court valued at £30,000, and arrived at Delhi on the 8th July, 1715, after a march of three months, having on the way proclaimed His Majesty King George the First "with all the ceremony they were Masters of" before Agra on the 17th June. But it was not until January, 1716, that they could gain permission to present their petition: and they might even then have returned empty-handed, had it not been for a happy circumstance which recalls the time-honoured tradition of Surgeon Gabriel Boughton's cure of the daughter of Shah Jehan.

The Emperor had been ill, and having been persuaded to allow Hamilton, the Surgeon of the Embassy, to attend him, was restored to health. "He was pleased to reward Mr. Hamilton for his care and success," wrote Surman to the Council at Calcutta, by presenting him with a "vest" or robe of honour, an elephant, a horse, two diamond rings and five thousand rupees: but his gratitude was such that he asked the doctor to name any other reward which he could confer upon him. Hamilton at once besought the Emperor to concede to the English Embassy the object of their mission, and finally, after further tedious delay and with the aid of a little "well-timed bribery," a *firman* was handed to Surman, granting to the Company the privilege of free trade and also permission to purchase thirty-seven villages adjacent to the three already acquired in 1698 and extending ten miles south of Calcutta along the bank on either side of the river Hooghly. The Embassy returned in triumph after a stay of exactly two years at the Court of the Mogul. Surgeon Hamilton, whose "memory ought to be dear to this Nation for the credit he gained the English," did not live to receive the rewards of his countrymen. He died in Calcutta on December 4, 1717, barely a month after his arrival,* but the fruits of his success were not long in making themselves apparent. The purchase of the thirty-seven villages was not, in fact, effected, owing to the opposition of Murshed Kuli Khan, who used all his authority to prevent the zemindars from making over the lands: but the privileges of free trade and the other facilities and immunities bestowed upon the Company more than

* His tombstone is among those in the Charnock Mausoleum in the old burying-ground adjoining St. John's Church.

compensated for any accession of territory. "The inhabitants of Calcutta," says Stewart, in his history of Bengal, "enjoyed after the return of the Embassy, a degree of freedom and security unknown to the other subjects of the Mogul Empire; and that city increased yearly in wealth, beauty, and riches. Success produced new adventures, and besides a number of English private merchants licensed by the Company, Calcutta was, in a short time, peopled by Portuguese, Armenian, Mogul, and Hindoo merchants, who carried on their commerce under the protection of the British flag: thus the shipping belonging to the port, in the course of ten years after the Embassy, amounted to ten thousand tons, and many individuals amassed fortunes without injury to the Company's trade, or incurring the displeasure of the Mogul Government."

The land actually held by the English at Calcutta at this time amounted, says Dr. C. R. Wilson, to about 5,077 bighas or 1,861 acres, that is, about one-third of the present area of the Town. It was about three miles in length and about a mile in breadth, its inland boundary being the modern Chitpore Road, which afforded access to the famous Kalighat Temple. "The Company's Colony," says Captain Alexander Hamilton, who visited it in 1710, "contain in all about 10,000 or 12,000 souls, and the Company's revenues are pretty good and well paid. They rise from Ground-rents and Consulage on all goods imported and exported by British subjects; but all natives besides are free from taxes."

The three villages may be said, roughly speaking, to have extended along the river from Coolie Bazar, where the buildings of the Commissariat now stand in the vicinity of Prinsep's Ghât, to Chitpore: but the English settlement proper was a very small affair indeed. It was confined to the locality between Baboo Ghât, hard by the modern Eden Gardens, and a point about a hundred yards north of Clive Street. Surrounding it was the native portion of "Dhee" Calcutta, and to the north was Suttanuttee. On the south stood Govindpore, high on the river-bank and covered with thick jungle. The total amount of inhabited land was only about 840 bighas, or one-sixth of the territory conveyed by the sanad of Azim-us-shan: and of this 204 bighas was absorbed by the Settlement itself, and 400 by the great Bazar to its immediate north. In Colonel Mark Wood's Map of 1784, published in 1792 by Mr. William Baillie, Suttanuttee is described as extending from Chitpore in the north to what is designated in the map as Jora Bagan Ghât, a little below Nimtollah Ghât. Thence commenced the northern boundary of "Dhee" Calcutta, and that village proceeded south as far as Baboo Ghât. Here Govindpore began and ended at the Govindpore Creek, afterwards called Surman's Nullah and later "Tolly's Nullah."

CHAPTER III.

THE CALCUTTA OF QUEEN ANNE.

We have more than one picture from contemporary hands of the Calcutta of Queen Anne and King George the First. The pivot of the settlement must be sought in what is now Dalhousie Square, but was then known as the Lall Bagh or Park. In the centre was the Lall Dighi, or great Tank, which had been in existence before the coming of Charnock within what was once the enclosure of the cutcherry of the former zemindars. It was deepened and lengthened in 1709 and converted from a dirty pond full of weeds and noxious matter into a much needed reservoir of sweet water. The greater part of the western or riverside edge of the Park was given over to the Fort, which lay between the points now demarcated by Fairlie Place and Koila Ghât. It was now strong enough to ward off any attack by the "country powers," but the buildings within it had been erected very leisurely. Of the new Factory House only one storey had been finished when the United Council came into power in 1704. The consultation book shows us Sir Edward Littleton calling in Calcutta on his way up the river Hooghly, and sitting down at the head of the Council-table to discuss where he is to live. "He thinks that a house in the town will be most convenient to him, there being but few good rooms being finished in the Fort." There was no Strand Road, and the waves of the Hooghly lapped the ramparts of the Fort. To the south, there extended from Koila Ghât to Chandpal Ghât the mouth of a creek, navigable for large boats, which passed along Hastings Street and made its way through Creek Row and Wellington Square to Balliaghatta near the Salt-lakes. On the other side of this creek were bushy trees (which were afterwards removed by degrees), thatched hovels and pools of fetid water which rendered anything but inviting the path that led across it past the burial-ground and the hospital to the Govindpore fields, where the modern Fort William stands. Beyond the purely European buildings lying around the Fort were four villages of mud and bamboo, all of which were included in the zemindary limits of the original settlement. These villages were the original three with the addition of Chowringhee, which was in 1717 a hamlet of isolated hovels, surrounded by water-logged paddy-fields and bamboo-groves and separated from Govindpore by a tiger-haunted jungle where expands the grassy level of the maidan. The Esplanade was a jungle not yet cleared, interspersed with a few huts and small plots of grazing and arable lands. Beyond the Chitpore Road, which formed the eastern boundary of the settlement, lay more pools, swamps and rice-fields, dotted here and there with the straggling huts of fishermen, falconers, wood-cutters, weavers and cultivators.

The English inhabitants lived principally in the immediate neighbourhood of the Fort and the Park. "The town, rising about this old Fort," says Captain Alexander Hamilton, "like one about a baronial castle in the medieval times, was built without order, as the builders thought most convenient for their own affairs, every one taking what ground best pleased them for gardening, so that in most houses you must pass through a garden into the house: the English building near the riverside and the natives within land." Price in his "Observations" has much the same tale to tell: "Round their little fort and close to it, by degrees they built themselves very neat, useful, if not elegant, houses, a church, a court-house and the like, laid out walks, planted trees, and made their own little district neat, clean and convenient." The houses, however, were without flues, venetians, glass windows, or punkhas: they had panelled doors only, and frames with a net work of cane for windows. "Carriages they had none, for there were no carriage roads in the country then, nor for many years after."

The majority of English residences were to be found to the north of the Fort, in what is to-day Clive Street, and was then, as now, the main thoroughfare leading to the great native mart or Burra Bazar. There was no Court-house Street on the east of the great Tank, and the green expanse of the Park stretched right up to the Rope-walk which modern Calcutta calls Mission Row. From the south-western corner of the Park, a road ran past the Company's warehouses and gave access to the hospital and burial-ground, which with the powder-magazine occupied the site of St. John's Church and the adjoining buildings in Hare Street and Church Lane.

North of the Park and immediately fronting the Fort, on the site of the present Bengal Legislative Council Chamber, stood the Presidency Church of St. Anne in its compound, its lofty spire forming a principal object in every view of the town. It had been completed in 1709 and solemnly dedicated in compliment (no doubt) to the royal lady, whom, according to Pope, three realms obeyed, and who "sometimes counsel took—and sometimes tea." From the east gate of the Fort, passing the church and forming the northern boundary of the Park, ran out the great Eastern road to the Salt-lakes, now known as Lall Bazar and Bow Bazar Streets, crossed at a little distance by the principal highway of the native traffic, the immemorial pilgrim path to Kalighat, disguised to-day under such various names as Chitpore Road, Cossaitollah Gully (or Bentinck Street) and Chowringhee Road. At the cross-roads was the spot, appropriately marked by the Police Court of to-day, where criminal justice was publicly meted out to offenders. Along this great Eastern road and its bisecting thoroughfare, the garden houses of the wealthier of the Company's merchants, and of the opulent native traders, were beginning to become numerous. Of these latter, the famous Punjabi Omichand was just beginning a career in which he amassed prodigious wealth by almost monopolizing the intermediary trade between the Country and the Company, until the system was in 1753 abolished in favour of that of rural Collectors. Somewhere in the neighbourhood of, and possibly not far from, what is now Middleton Street, lay the "Company's garden"—"a pretty good garden," Hamilton calls it, "that furnishes the Governor's table with herbage and fruits; and some fish ponds to serve his kitchen with good carp, calkops and mullet."

The Governor had his official residence within the Fort; and within the Fort also were "convenient lodgings for factors and writers" in what was known as the Long Row. The collegiate system was still in force, and only the married men were permitted establishments of their own. The garrison of Fort William generally consisted of two or three hundred soldiers, "more," according to Hamilton, "for to convey their fleet from Patna with the Company's saltpetre, and piece-goods, raw silk, and some opium belonging to other merchants, than for the defence of the fort."

There was little thought of territorial power or aggrandisement in the minds of the factors of those days. The very names of the offices held by the members of Council at the Presidency betoken the peaceful cause of their presence in the East. The Honourable the President was, of course, the Chief in Council. The Worshipful the Second was usually Chief at Cossimbazar, and the Fourth was also ordinarily up-country in charge of the subordinate factory at Dacca. The Third Member performed the duties of Accomptant, the Fifth was Export Warehouse-keeper, the Sixth Import Warehouse-keeper, the Seventh Buxey, or Paymaster, the Eighth Zemindar, or, as we now call him, Collector of Calcutta (of whom we are presently to hear), and the Ninth Secretary. The consultation books kept by this last-named functionary are full of side-lights on the life and manners of the time. They were not always flush of cash. "Having demands on us to a great amount for ready money, and almost no cash in the house," runs the entry for January 17, 1713, "agreed that we endeavour to borrow at interest 100,000 rupees to satisfy those merchants who are pressing for their money."

The scale of salaries was of the most modest kind. The

President and Chaplain were paid £100 a year each. Members of Council were fain to be content with £40. These salaries were "to be paid in the Country, as the Court and the Managers direct, at two shillings and sixpence to the rupee." Surgeon Hamilton, we discover from a list of salaries paid to the covenanted servants of the Company in 1712, was considered to be sufficiently remunerated with a pittance of £36 a year. Diet and house-allowance was fixed at Rs. 30/- a month for those that lived outside the Fort. The rest of the Company's servants messed together at a common table, but the church-burdars, or caterers, exacted a merciless rate of *dustoorie*, and the butlers and mussaulchees were "not less faulty in the destruction of table linen, dishes and plates," so that one day in May 1713, a solemn meeting of the Council at Fort William was held to review the situation. The matter was considered of sufficient gravity to be recorded in *extenso* in the consultation book: and the upshot of the deliberation was the placing of all the "gentlemen of the Company" at the Presidency on board wages, the Council to receive Rs. 40/- a month each, and "all other merchants, factors, and writers, and the doctors," Rs. 20/-

Social life, whether at Calcutta or at the factories up-country, was much the same in character. "Most gentlemen and ladies in Bengal," says Hamilton, "live both splendidly and pleasantly: forenoons being dedicated to business and after dinner to rest, and in the evening recreate themselves in chaises or palanquins in the fields, or to gardens, or by water in their budgeroes, which is a convenient boat that goes over swiftly with the force of the oars. On the river sometimes there is the diversion of fishing or fowling, or both; and before the night they make friendly visits to one another, when pride or contention do not spoil society, which too often they do among the ladies, as discord and faction do among men." Books were scarce: and out-door games rare. The factors' wildest excitement was to sit in Mistress Domingo Ash's parlour sipping arrack punch and listening to the news brought by the latest ship, or the causes which led to the explosion in the Powder Mill, and the latest quarrel among "the dignities." The Council met at nine o'clock in the morning at the beginning of each week: and we may picture them, dressed in muslin shirts, pyjamas, and starched white caps, sitting in the consultation-room of the newly-built house within the Fort, with a case-bottle of good old arrack and a goglet of water on the table, which the secretary with skilful hand converted into punch when the occasion arose, and penning their interminable protests and petitions. There was always the show of religion and decorum which characterized the early half of the eighteenth century. The chaplain read the prayers in the Factory every morning and evening, and there was a solemn procession to church on Sundays, headed by the Governor. When there was no chaplain, the prayers were read and the sermon preached by a Member of Council, "who having provided Black Apparrell for that Service, agreed that we gave him a gratuity of one hundred rupees." When they fell ill, they took a run up the river to Nuddea: and when they died, their last will and testament was solemnly recorded in the consultation books.

Private trade was, of course, largely indulged in as a means of eking out the petty official stipends, but the factors did not believe in doing unto others as they would be done by. "Although," to quote Hamilton once again, "the conscript fathers disagreed in many points among themselves, yet they all agree in oppressing strangers who are consigned to them, not suffering them to buy or sell their goods at the most advantageous markets, but of the Governor and his Council, who fix their own prices, high or low, as seemeth best to their wisdom and discretion. The colony has very little manufactory of its own; for the Government being pretty arbitrary, discourages ingenuity and industry in the populace; for by the weight of the Company's authority, if a native chances to disoblige one of the upper-house, he is liable to arbitrary punishment, or corporal sufferings." The Company's servants took full advantage of their exclusiveness: and if a man were only lucky enough to escape laying his bones within the confines of the Mahratta Ditch or in the burying-ground which lay hard by the hospital, he might count upon returning to Europe in easy circumstances. The odds were, however, greatly against his ever leaving Bengal. The settlement literally reeked with malaria. Mortality was so extraordinarily high, that death literally overshadowed every soul. Hamilton says that in one year, out of the twelve hundred English in Calcutta, no less than 460 died between August and the following January. There was no hospital until the autumn of 1707, and up to August 1705 only one doctor. Of this hospital the observant Captain has no very cheerful account to give. "The Company," he says, "has a pretty good hospital at Calcutta, where many go in to undergo the grievance of physic, but few come out to give account of its operation." There were certainly more attractive places in the world than Calcutta in the opening days of the eighteenth century: and there was little change for the better as the years went by, in spite of the encomium of the old annalist who speaks of 1737 as "a period when we had opulent merchants, in days when gold was plenty, labour cheap, and not one indigent European in all Calcutta."

In 1726, being the thirteenth year of the reign of George the First, four courts were constituted in Calcutta by Royal Charter. The first of these was the Mayor's Court. This was a Court of Record, consisting of a Mayor and nine Aldermen, seven of whom, together with the Mayor, were required to be natural-born subjects. The remaining two might be foreign protestants, the subject of any state in amity with Great Britain. Their duty was to deal with the more important civil disputes in which the English inhabitants were concerned. Their decisions were not final, but might be referred to the Court of Appeal, which consisted of the Governor and Council. The Governor and Council formed the Court of Quarter Sessions, which was also a Court of Record, "of Oyer and Terminer and Gaol Delivery," as the quaint phrase went, for trying and punishing of all offenders and offences, with the exception of high treason only. The Fourth Court was the Court of Requests, composed of twenty-four Commissioners selected by the Governor and Council from among the inhabitants of Calcutta, who determined summarily all suits, the subject-matter of which did not exceed five pagodas or forty shillings.

The Council's revenue was derived from three main sources—ground-rents, fines and forfeits, and customs and tolls, and out of the money so collected they had to meet the expenses of the settlement, and the yearly rent of Rs. 1,281-8-0 payable to the Mogul Government. It was at first a matter of difficulty with them to pay their way. And so in April 1704, the Zemindar, Mr. Benjamin Boucher, was instructed to measure every one's compound to see that they had no more than they paid for, and "to send into the Council a particular account of what each man pays." We have here a glimpse of a very important personage indeed, to whom the real internal administration of the settlement was entrusted. The office of zemindar is said to date from 1720, but the consultation books show it to be nearly as old as Calcutta itself. When the Factory was elevated to the rank of a Presidency in 1699, the Zemindar became a member of the Council. In 1700 the post was held by Ralph Sheldon, whose tombstone in the old graveyard declares him to have been "illustris Sheldoniani stematis hand indigna proles," but who was, as a matter of fact, not related to the great Archbishop whose benefactions to the University of Oxford are commemorated by the great Theatre which bears his name. He was the first Magistrate and Collector in British India, and the double function was cast upon him of gathering the revenues of the three villages and keeping them in order. As Magistrate he controlled the native inhabitants —hearing and deciding cases, civil as well as criminal in the zemindary or foujdary cutcherry. He had under him a police force consisting of one chief peon, 45 peons, two chobdars and twenty sepoys. Petty disputes between Europeans were settled in early days by a Committee of three, who sat for this purpose every Saturday from nine to twelve in the morning: and the more difficult and important cases were heard in full Council, or referred to Madras. In August 1706 we get a glimpse of the methods by which justice was administered. A number of thieves and murderers having been recently caught, it was ordered that they be branded on the cheek and "turned on the other side of the water." The Zemindar was a collector of revenue as well as a judicial officer; and it is on record that it was part of his duty to "make roads and repair drains." In his capacity as revenue officer he held what was known as the Collector's cutcherry, where "the farmers and tenants under his jurisdiction who are backward in their payments are confined, whipped, and otherwise punished independently of the other Courts in Calcutta." The President and Council, or "any three of them, the President being one," were empowered to hold a court in revenue cases, but the real power lay with the Zemindar, and, it may be added, with his Indian deputy, who went by the name of the "Black Zemindar." This office was filled during the whole of the period from 1720 to 1756 by the famous Gobindram Metre (Mitter), of whom John Zephaniah Holwell, Zemindar of Calcutta from 1752 to 1756, wrote that by reason of the many changes in the headship of the office, "a power in perpetuity devolved on the standing deputy who was always styled the 'Black

Zemindar,' and such was the tyranny of this man and such the dread conceived of him in the minds of the natives that no one durst complain or give information." It need hardly be said that Gobindram accumulated vast wealth during his tenure of power: and he is said to have built in 1731 a magnificent "nine-jewel" temple on the Chitpore Road, the loftiest pinnacle of which was higher than the Ochterlony Monument, and the smallest cupola of which still exists. The main building was overthrown in the terrible cyclone and earthquake of 1737.

A contemporary account of this famous storm is contained in a letter from Sir Francis Russell, a member of the Calcutta Council, and is dated the last day of the year 1737. The letter speaks of "the dreadful hurricane we had here the 30th September at night," and continues:—

"Such a scene of horror as that night was I never saw or heard off. Such Terrible gust of wind like the loudest thunder and torrents of rain that I expected every moment the house I live in which is I believe the Strongest in the town would have fallen on my head. The noise was so violent above Stairs that myself and family was obliged to go down and stay below till morning with poor Mrs. Wastell and her children who had fled to our house for shelter the doors and windows of hers being burst from the walls. But good God what Sight was the town and river in the morning; not a ship but the Duke of Dorsett to be seen in the river were (*sic*) the evening before was above twenty-nine sails of vessels great and small many being drove ashore. Some broke to pieces and others founder'd and this which is Scarse creditable in a river hardly a mile wide, there was no ebb tide for near twenty-four hours. Our church steeple was blown down as also eight or ten English houses and numbers belonging to the black Merchants. The whole town looked like a place that had been bombarded by an enemy. Such a havoc did it make that 'tis impossible to find words to express it. All our beautiful shady roads laid bare which will not be the like again this twenty years."

This may be taken to be an accurate, if incoherent, account of the occurrence: but a remarkable tradition has grown up in connection with the mishap to the church. *Asiaticus,* writing in 1803, gives what purports to be an extract descriptive of the storm, from the "Gentleman's Magazine" of 1738. It contains this extraordinary statement:—"The high and magnificent steeple of the English church sank into the ground without breaking." And the following note is added, as if by way of corroboration:—"Mr. Charles Weston, the son of the Recorder of the Mayor's Court, was born in Calcutta in 1731, in a house then opposite to where the Tiretta Bazar now stands. He recollects the great storm and inundation of 1737, as it compelled his family to quit their house. The steeple of the Church he states to have fallen prostrate, a more probable position to have fell in than that stated in the 'Gentleman's Magazine.'"

There is, however, no allusion to the church steeple in the "Magazine," as will be seen from the actual extract, which is as curious of its kind as the narrative of Russell:—"On September 30th last, happened a furious hurricane in the Bay of Bengal, attended with a very

* *

heavy rain which raised 15 inches of water in 5 hours, and a violent earthquake which threw down abundance of houses and as the storm reached 60 leagues up the river, it is computed that 20,000 ships, barks, sloops, boats, canoes, etc., have been cast away. A prodigious quantity of cattle of all sorts, a great many tigers and several rhinoceroses were drowned, even a great many caymans were stifled by the furious agitation of the waters and an innumerable quantity of birds were beat down into the river by the storm. Two English ships of 500 tons were thrown into a village about 200 fathoms from the bed of the river Ganges, broke to pieces, and all the people drowned pell-mell amongst the inhabitants and cattle. Barks of 60 tons were blown 2 leagues up the land over the tops of high trees. The water rose in all 40 feet higher than usual. The English ships which drove ashore and broke to pieces were the Decker, Devonshire and Newcastle, and the Pelham is missing. A French ship was drove on shore and bulged: after the wind and waters abated they opened the hatches and took out several bales of merchandise, etc., but the man who was in the hold to sling the bales suddenly ceased working nor by calling him could they get any reply, on which they sent down another but heard nothing of him, which very much added to their fear so that for some time no one would venture down; at length one more hardy than the rest went down and became silent and inactive as the two former to the astonishment of all. They then agreed by lights to look down into the hold which had a great quantity of water in it and to their great surprise they saw a huge aligator staring as expecting more prey. It had come in through a hole in the ship side and it was with difficulty they killed it, when they found the three men in the creature's belly."

The inaccuracy of *Asiaticus* stands sufficiently exposed: but what of the tradition? Archdeacon Hyde supplies possibly the best explanation, when he conjectures that the deluge of mud and wreckage washed over the settlement by the 40 feet tide, when the ebb of the Hooghly had been forced back for four and twenty hours, may have partially concealed the prostrate spire, and so have originated the story that it sank into the ground. The more, however, we investigate, the more we increase our bewilderment. The "Gentleman's Magazine" would have us believe that an earthquake accompanied the cyclone. But in the official account of this famous castastrophe in the "Consultations of the Fort William Council," there is no mention of an earthquake, and we only read as follows:—

"On the 30th September, there was a great storm which drove several ships ashore. The Mohanna flag-staff at Balasore was blown down."

The razor which is so ruthlessly applied to the official reports of modern India would find it difficult to justify its existence, in face of this eminently colourless and laconic record.

CHAPTER IV.

THE MAHRATTA DITCH AND THE PALISADES.

FIVE years after the great storm of 1737, the monotony of life in Calcutta was again broken. Janojee, the son of Raghujee Bhonsla, chief of Nagpore and the "Bounceloe" of contemporary chroniclers, burst into Bengal in 1742 at the head of a Mahratta horde, and it needed all the skill and the energy of the Nabob Ali Verdi Khan to keep him in check. The country was laid waste from Balasore to Rajmehal: Mukwah Tannah Fort, which stood on the site of the house now occupied by the Superintendent of the Botanical Gardens, was taken, and finally Hooghly was captured and Orissa surrendered. "Crowds of the inhabitants of the Country on the western side of the river came and implored the protection of the English, who in consequence of the general alarm, obtained permission from Ali Verdi to dig an intrenchment round their territory. This work, had it been completed, would have extended seven miles. In six months three miles of it were finished, when the inhabitants, finding that the Mahrattas did not approach Calcutta, desisted from their works." Such is the account given by Stewart in his History of Bengal of the origin and the history of the famous Mahratta Ditch. As a matter of fact, the original scheme was to plant seven batteries in different parts of the town. This was actually done, and the Ditch was an afterthought. But while the batteries vanished, the Ditch continued for years to be as prominent a landmark of

Calcutta as the Boytaconnah tree. The earth excavated was so disposed on the inner or townward side as to form a tolerably high road, along the margin of which was planted a row of trees, and this constituted the most frequented and fashionable resort of the town. In 1802 we find an old writer declaring that "on the Circular Road of Calcutta the young, the sprightly, and the opulent during the fragrance of morning, in the chariot of health, enjoy the gales of recreation." The element of imagination must have entered very largely into this picture: for when the Ditch was filled up about this time by order of the Marquess of Wellesley, it had been for forty years and more the receptacle of all the filth and garbage in Calcutta: and the "gales" wafted from it to the "chariot of health" must have been the reverse of fragrant or recreative.

The Ditch is clearly shown in a plan to a scale of four inches to one mile of "the territory of Calcutta, as marked out in the year 1742, exhibiting likewise the Military Operations at Calcutta when attacked and taken by Seraj-ud-Dowlah on the 18th of June, 1756." It will be found inserted by Upjohn in a corner of his larger map of 1793, and is apparently the plan, upon a larger scale, to which Archdeacon Hyde refers in his *Parochial Annals of Bengal* as having been seen by him in the British Museum. Except for a detour on the north-east at Halsibagan, to enclose the garden-houses of Gobindram Mitter, the "black zemindar," and of Omichand, it follows the modern Circular Road from Perrin's Point, at the north-western extremity of Suttanuttee, where the Chitpore creek meets the river, down to a spot near the present Entally corner. It was intended in the first instance to extend it to the southern part of Govindpore, but in the plan a considerable space, over a couple of miles, is left blank to the southward and is inscribed "this part not executed." Hindoo tradition has it (says Mr. A. K. Ray in his *Short History of Calcutta*) that the ditch existed also on the south of Govindpore up to the edge of the river, and that the big open drain on the town side of the Bhowanipore bridge over Tolly's Nullah, which still goes by the name of the Mahratta Ditch, is a portion of it, and further that the drain across the Maidan through which tidal water used to reach this drain, marks its site on the south of Govindpore. It is, however, certain, that the southern portion, if at all made, was not a continuation of the historic Ditch which enclosed the northern and eastern sides of the town alone and stopped about the corner of Corporation Street (Jaunbazar) and Lower Circular Road.

Revealed also by this plan of 1742 is the interesting fact that the "Settlement," within which alone resided the Christian population—English, Armenian and Portuguese—was at one time surrounded by a complete ring-fence of palisades. A point in the plan is thus marked: "the extensions of the palisades to the northward from whence they go all round the town till they meet those at the southward." And not only was the circle complete and the fence continued along the river face and the edge of the creek (which skirted the southern wall of the old burying-ground), but every road issuing from the town and each of the ghats at the foot of the principal streets leading to the waterside was guarded by a gate. Archdeacon Hyde has worked out the circuit of streets around which this stockade ran, and his description may be briefly summarized, for an excellent idea can thereby be had of the extent of the Calcutta of the day.

In order, however, to beat the bounds with accuracy, we must keep well in mind the alterations which have been wrought in the physical features of the city. The Strand Road, as we now see it, did not exist at this period: it has nearly all been reclaimed from the river. All that there was of it in 1742 was north of the Fort (which stood, be it remembered, between Koila Ghât Street and Fairlie Place), a narrow roadway of very uneven line, bordered all along by the garden walls of bungalows, and a few warehouses. Beyond the Fort it was broken by ship-building slips or small docks. There is no Hastings Street, we must remind ourselves, and its place is taken by the creek, to which reference has already been made, and which was navigable for large boats, and ran out towards the Salt Lakes through Creek Row, where a ship is said to have been wrecked during the storm of 1737. On the river-side edge of this creek, at the corner of Church Lane and what is now Hastings Street, stood a square earthwork sustaining a pair of bastions, whence guns pointed up the creek and down the river. The creek took a half-turn round this battery and crept eastwards beneath three gated bridges. The first opened from the burying-ground, occupied then, as now, by the mausoleum of Charnock and with many another massive pyramid and obelisk that have been swept away. The second crossed the creek at the spacious gunpowder-yard with its great bell-shaped magazine of masonry. At the third bridge (where Fancy Lane opens into Wellesley Place) the fence sharply swerved from the natural boundary of the creek, for the reason, as Mr. Hyde suggests, that "Fancy" is a corruption of the native *phansi,* and that here stood a gallows-tree. However this may be, Fancy Lane was the entrance to the Bailey which encircled the whole town within the palisade. Crossing Wellesley Place, the circuit may be traced along Larkins' Lane and British Indian Street, known to our grandfathers as Rana Madda Gully, and the scene of a "frenzied fight" during Seraj-ud-Dowlah's attack on Calcutta. In Upjohn's map the name of this street is given as Rana Madda Lane, clearly showing that the derivation, as he understood it, was not from any queen of huckstresses (Ranee Moodee) as Mr. Hyde seems to imagine. Thence through Barretto's Lane and a portion of Mangoe Lane the palisades passed into Mission Row, once the Rope-walk and the witness of another hard-fought struggle. Here, at Lall Bazar, the palisades ran up the road to a gate at the cross-roads where the cutcherry was and the Police Court still is: but the line of the Bailey branched off at Radha Bazar, connecting with Ezra Street by a crooked alley. From this point it continued northward along Amratollah Street, keeping clear of the crowded pilgrim path to Kalighat, and the hamlets of the butchers, oilmongers and scavengers and basket-makers, which are kept alive to-day by such street appellations as Cossaitollah (the old name of Bentinck Street), Colootollah, and Doomtollah. Crossing Murghihatta Street, or Canning Street, to give it its modern title, the Bailey entered the Portuguese quarter, and hard by where the Greek Church was built in the days of Hastings, zigzagged riverwards to Armenian Street by a lane which local usage still terms Hamamgullee, although Turkish baths have long ceased to exist in Calcutta. Near the modest brick chapel which had served the Portuguese since 1700 as a place of worship, and which made way in 1799 for the Murghihatta Cathedral Church of Our Lady of the Rosary, the fences, according to the plan, were thrown out at an angle, by extending the Armenian Street line until they met the road running past the church. The palisades next turned round the Armenian burying-ground, within which had been erected in 1724 their Church of St. Nazareth: and thence the Bailey ran in and out down to the river by Durmahatta and Khengraputty (the streets of the sellers of reed mats and scouring brushes) and the tail of old China Bazar now known as Bonfield's Lane. The northernmost limit of the river face was in the present Rajah Woodmunt's Street, a few yards south of the Hooghly Bridge.

As Calcutta became settled, Suttanuttee was gradually abandoned by the English as a place of abode. There remained, indeed, near its northernmost corner, where Bag Bazar (the Bazar in the *bag* or garden) now stands to perpetuate the name, Perrin's Garden, a pleasure resort, where once it was the height of gentility for the Company's covenanted servants to take their ladies for an evening stroll or moonlight fête. But it began to be little frequented about 1746, and by 1752 it was altogether out of use and repair, and was sold for Rs. 25,000.

It was named after Captain Perrin, the owner of several ships, among which was the *Sceptre*, seized by the Company in 1707 for the alleged liabilities of the Captain to Thomas Pitt of Diamond fame and others, but released on receipt of evidence from Madras that the ships no longer belonged to him. In 1755, it was in the possession of Colonel Caroline Frederick Scott, Commandant of the garrison, and father of Warren Hastings' first wife. For a time it was transformed into a gunpowder factory, and on Colonel Scott's death it returned in its new character into the hands of the Company. As late as 1793, its memory stood preserved in Upjohn's map by Old Powder Mill Bazar and Road, the latter marking the starting point of the embankment alongside the Mahratta Ditch. The glory of Perrin's was usurped by Surman's garden, which lay at the other extremity of the settlement, at the upper end of Garden Reach, probably not far from Cooly Bazar, the modern Hastings. Surman, it will not have been forgotten, was the leader of the eventful Embassy to Delhi in 1717 and seems also at one time to have owned both Belvedere House and garden, which were sold in 1780 by Warren Hastings to Captain Tolly of nullah fame. This nullah, which followed the silted-up bed of the Adiganga and branched off from the river Hooghly at the old pillar-stone which marked the boundary of Govindpore, was excavated originally by Surman. It bore for some time his name: but was deepened in 1773 by Tolly and henceforward became Tolly's Nullah.

An interesting picture of the dimensions and appearance of the English settlement, as distinguished from the portions within the palisades set apart for the Armenians and the Portuguese, can be obtained from a study of the Plan of "Fort William and part of the city" prepared in 1753 by William Wills, "Lieutenant of the Artillery Company in Bengal." The plan is drawn to a scale of 100 feet to the inch, and the various houses are ticketed with their owners' names and exhibited with clearness and precision. The English quarter is shown as situated between the modern Canning Street on the north and Hastings Street (then the creek) on the south, Mission Row (or as it is called the Rope-walk) on the east, and the river on the west. Within these limits, which are likewise those of the plan, no less than 230 structures of brick and mortar may be counted. Most of the houses are surrounded by spacious compounds, and many have tanks, large and small, within their enclosures. None of the streets and lanes are distinguished by names: but it is possible with an effort to identify nearly all of them. In the centre of the plan is the familiar Park with the "large tank or canal" in its midst. To the north-west of the tank lies the Fort, and adjoining the Fort on the south are the export and import warehouses built in 1741 on the outside of the south curtain. Between the warehouses and the "Company's house" is a road leading to the Killah or Fort Ghat on the river side, nowadays by a mistaken analogy misspelt Koila Ghat. Immediately fronting the northern section of the Fort, we may still see the Presidency Church of St. Anne. Eastwards, skirting the church and one side of the park, runs as before, the great avenue which intersects the well-worn pilgrim track from Chitpore to Kalighat.

The Court-house is at the north-east corner of the Park, on the spot covered by St. Andrew's Church. Between it and the Church four building sites are shown where Writers' Buildings now stand. The Court-house compound covers also the space occupied nowadays by the road to the west of the church which affords access to Lyon's Range. Behind the Court-house is a large tank. Old Court-House Corner can be traced, and also Radha Bazar Street. Separated from the Court-house by another tank is the cutcherry, a little nearer the square than its modern successor, but still in Lal Bazar. At the junction with Bentinck Street was the Jail. The block of modern buildings on the eastern face of the square are non-existent, and there is no sign of the old-fashioned bungalow at the north-east corner tenanted in the forties by Colesworthy Grant, and now replaced by the West End Watch Company's premises. Facing the cutcherry and at the corner of Mission Row and Lal Bazar is the play-house, not to be confounded with the later play-house erected to the rear of Writers' Buildings. It was turned into a battery by the "Moors" in the siege of 1756. Next to the play-house are indicated the houses of Mr. Brown and Lady Russell, the widow of Sir Francis Russell, whose descent from Oliver Cromwell has already claimed our notice. Lady Russell's house is almost exactly upon the spot now occupied by the Mission Church, and the site of Mr. Brown's may be identified with that of the house in Mission Row in which General Clavering died. Mangoe Lane is there: but Old Court-House Street will be looked for in vain, and in its Place are large houses at the south-eastern corner of the Park, belonging to Colonel Scott, the purchaser of Perrin's garden, and Mr. Matthew Collet, Seventh in Council, who was to have the disagreeable task a few years later of delivering up the Cossimbazar Factory to the Moors. The southern boundary of the Park is taken up by a large tank and a range of buildings facing it which are consecrated to "the calico printers." Between them they fill the space now allotted to the Central Telegraph Office. Next to the calico printers we see the spacious compound of Chaplain Bellamy, the largest shown in the plan. His house stands upon the frontage of what is now Government Place, and its site may fairly be identified as that of the house of the Military Secretary to the Viceroy, while the gardens extend right down to Dalhousie Square along the whole length of what is now Wellesley Place. There is a sort of small open space or *cul-de-sac* between Mr. Bellamy's compound and the Company's stables: and the adjacent houses stand at the junction of the square and a street which is identical with the modern Council House Street. The hospital offers itself next to view, along the frontage of what is now Hare Street. Behind it to the south is the Powder Magazine and, conveniently enough, the burying-ground lies handy to the west. Opposite the magazine-yard at the southern end of Council House Street may be seen with its compound wall running flush with the creek, the house of Mr. Culling Smith, a servant of the Company, who achieved a baronetcy in his seventieth year, lived until 1812, and was the maternal grandfather of Mr. H. C. E. Childers, Mr. Gladstone's colleague in so many Liberal Governments. There is a tank in the Magazine-yard, where St. John's parsonage has been built of recent years: and another tank wedged in between the hospital and the burying-ground and connected by a channel with the creek which runs from the river bank along the course of what is now Hastings Street. Holwell's name is affixed to two houses. One of them is the south-easternmost of the block of buildings contiguous to the Company's house on the south, and standing as nearly as may be upon the site of the Small Cause Court at the corner of Bankshall Street. The other is at the corner of what is now Church Lane and Hastings Street: but it was in those days bounded upon the south as we have seen by the creek. It stands upon the spot afterwards occupied by the old Mint and nowadays by the Stationery Office and the premises of Messrs. Ahmuty and Co. Behind it, on the site of the Metcalfe Hall, is a house owned by Ramkissen Seat, or Sett, the Company's chief broker, and rented by Mr. Peter Amyatt, a senior merchant who escaped the Black Hole by flight to Fulta, and met his death in 1763 at the hands of Meer Kasim near Moorshedabad.

To the north of the Park and behind the Church is a thick cluster of masonry buildings. The house of Mr. Edward Eyre, Tenth of Council and Store-keeper, who was one of those to perish in the Black Hole, is on the site of Messrs. Finlay, Muir and Co.'s offices: but was then immediately opposite the north-east bastion of the Fort. After the recapture of Calcutta by Clive and Watson, we find the Theatre of the settlement transferred to this spot. There are three houses adjoining in what we now call Lyon's Range: those of Omichund, of Mr. Coates or Coales, a senior merchant, and another victim of the Black Hole, and of Mr. John Knox, perhaps the assistant surgeon of that name who escaped from the Fort in the confusion following the surrender. Immediately to the east of Omichund's enclosure runs a lane which bears the name of Theatre Street in Upjohn's map of 1793, and may be traced nowadays in that portion of New China Bazar Street which connects Lyon's Range with Old China Bazar Street. Clive Street is shown in its present position, but the remainder of New China Bazar Street, which leads into it at right angles, is altogether wanting. Secretary Cooke, who survived the Black Hole and supplied Orme with materials, has a house here, just behind Mr. Eyre's compound: and next to him is Mrs. Beard, widow of the Charles Beard, son of President John, whose tombstone may be seen among those around the Charnock mausoleum. On the site occupied by their buildings, Clive and Philip Francis lived after them, and the Royal Exchange now stands. The enclosure of Mr. Cruttenden, once a governor of the settlement, faces the northern wall of the Fort. The main portion of the house looks out upon the river, and judging from its dimensions in the plan, it must have been one of the finest and most imposing of the buildings in the settlement. With its spacious compound, it occupies the whole of what is now the northern road-line of Fairlie Place. Behind it to the north is the more modest residence of Mr. William Tooke, who has left posterity an account of the "Troubles" which culminated in the Black Hole tragedy. Further north again, and on the same western side of Clive Street, we come to the saltpetre godowns, which may be located on the site of the premises shared by Messrs. Bird and Co. and the

Allahabad Bank. In rear of them and built right upon the water's edge is a house bearing the name of Mr. Watts, Second in Council and chief at Cossimbazar, who deserves remembrance as one of the many husbands of the famous Begum Johnson, and as the grandfather of the Earl of Liverpool, who was Prime Minister from 1812 to 1827. At the point where Clive Street turns to the left and narrows, the building now connected with the firm of Messrs. Graham and Co. is indicated clearly enough as Mr. Griffiths' house. Gillander House is represented by a building to which is attached the name of Captain Wills, who may be the maker of the plan, but is more probably a "country captain." There is no Clive Row, although a sort of alley is seen which leads to the residence of Mr. William Mackett, Ninth in Council and Buxey, of whom Holwell relates that having escorted his sick wife on board the ships just before the desertion of Drake and Minchin, he was carried away to Fulta against his will.

We have singled out only a few of the more prominent names appearing upon the houses in the plan: but enough has been said to demonstrate how compact and exclusive was the quarter formed by the Company's servants for themselves. Omichand and the Setts are the only Indians whose names appear as house-owners, and the Englishmen are all either factors or merchants or officers of the garrison. The Portuguese and Armenians were relegated, as we have already seen, to the neighbourhood of their churches in Moorghihatta: while the demarcation between the "white" and "black" towns was even sharper. The people of the country were indispensable to the prosperity of the factory: but they were not permitted within the palisades. Outside the stockaded two hundred and twenty acres, which comprised Christian Calcutta, there had therefore sprung up to the north and east a large and flourishing "native town" within the wider contour of the Mahratta Ditch. Its importance and extent were materially increased by the influx of population from the western bank of the river, which accompanied the Mahratta scare of 1742. Along the riverside it stretched from Burra Bazar and Roeyhattah (as Upjohn has it in his map of 1793), the great cotton-mart, which lay about half a mile north of the old Fort, to Bagbazar, on the edge of the Chitpore creek, where the Ditch began. Inland it sprawled in a succession of hamlets over the tract between the Ditch and the Kalighat Road, from Hogulkuria on the north with its jungle of elephant grass, to the salt-workers' huts in Collingah on the fringe of Chowringhee. The names of many of these hamlets survive in the designations of police-stations and municipal wards in the Indian quarter. Some recall the occupations of the original settlers. Koomartolly was the quarter of the potters, Moocheepara of the cobblers, Colootollah, as we have already noticed, of the *kalus* or oil-pressers. Others derived their appellations from prominent natural objects. The fame of a spreading banian-tree is perpetuated by Burtollah; the beauties of a tank full of flowering water-lilies by Puddopookur. So too the *simul* or cotton-tree gives its name to Simla, and Entally recalls the time when all that portion of Calcutta was a tidal swamp, for the *hintal* is a species of date-palm growing only in such localities. There was neither uniformity nor symmetry in the arrangement of the houses in these hamlets. The rich Bengalees of the day had no eye for the advantages of a wide street or an open compound. The dense jungle which surrounded their houses were full of dacoits and thieves, as names such as Chorebagan still testify by their situation and their name: and his first object was to guard against their attack and secure the privacy of his purdah. The frontage of the house he would let, therefore, to artisans who paid him a substantial rent and might serve as a defence in time of need: and access to the double quadrangle was only had by a narrow and winding lane, which could be barricaded at a moment's notice and at the same time was always cool and shaded in the hottest weather. Hundreds of mansions with surroundings such as these may be seen to this day, and the legacy of congestion and insanitation, which they represent, has been the despair of municipal reformers since the time of Wellesley.

In the midst of the "native town," the Faujdari Balakhana at the corner of Lower Chitpore Road and Colootollah, serves to remind us of days when the Faujdar, or military governor, of Hooghly had his official residence in Calcutta in the "lofty mansion" which once stood there. It was the prerogative of this functionary to adjudicate if he was so minded upon the quarrels of the native inhabitants of Calcutta, and from 1700 onwards he received a handsome annual bribe from the Council at Fort William in consideration of his foregoing its exercise. As late even as May, 1742, the Consultations contain the significant entry: "The Hugly Phousdar, demanding the usual annual present due in November last, amounting to current rupees two thousand seven hundred and fifty :—agreed that the President do pay the same out of the cash." Fourteen years later, the Faujdar of Hooghly, Manick Chand, entered upon the performance of his long deferred duties and dispensed justice for a few months in Calcutta as the lieutenant of the conquering Nabob. The tale of the one great humiliation suffered by the English at Fort William must be left, however, to be told in a chapter of its own.

CHAPTER V.

THE "TROUBLES" OF 1756.

In 1756 there died Aliverdi Khan, who had in 1740 ousted the son of Murshed Kuli Khan by force of arms from the musnud of Bengal, and had permitted the English to excavate the Mahratta Ditch in 1742. His successor was his grandson Seraj-ud-Dowlah, a youth of twenty, whom posterity has agreed to describe as cruel and profligate and full of hatred for the English. The action of Roger Drake, the Governor of the Settlement, in giving shelter to Kishen Das, the son of Rajah Rajbullab, Governor of Dacca, whose wealth he coveted, gave the new Nabob a pretext for hostilities. He demanded the surrender of Kishen Das and the destruction of the fortifications of Calcutta: and upon neither of these demands being complied with, he, in the month of June, 1756, marched upon Fort William with an army which is said to have consisted of 50,000 men. The English were wholly unprepared to meet any organized attack. Colonel Scott, the Commandant, in 1754 elaborated a plan for "securing the Settlement from any attack of the country forces," but, wrote the Council to the Court of Directors, "his death put a check upon our pursuing it," and "we were cautious about laying out much money." Consequently, the fortifications had been utterly neglected, and warehouses had been built up to the edge of the ramparts. The Fort was commanded by the church and adjoining houses and was unprotected by any ditch or outwork. The terraces were so shaky that the lightest guns could not be used upon them, and the parapets were too low to admit of the effective employment of musketry. Heavy fire was restricted to the bastions and the main gate, but even here the embrasures were dangerously wide. To ventilate the chambers against the east curtain, several windows had been made, "so many breaches for the enemy." The supplies were as inadequate as the defences. There was not sufficient powder, and what there was, was not good. Hardly a carriage would bear a gun, and hardly a shell would fit. Holwell in his narrative states that the "garrison consisted of 145 men of the battalion and 45 of the train,* officers included, and in both only 60 Europeans. There were not five that had ever seen a musket fired in anger. From the Militia about 65, chiefly Europeans, most of them covenanted servants, entered as volunteers in the battalion. In the last struggle, the number engaged on our side did not exceed 170 men, of whom 25 were killed and about 70 wounded." Orme's estimate of the

* Buckle in his memoirs of the Bengal Artillery says that in 1756 the Bengal Company of Artillery was commanded by Captain Lawrence Witherington, with headquarters at Fort William, and detachments at Dacca, Balasore, Cossimbazar, Patna, etc. On the siege of the Fort only 45 Artillery-men were in the garrison, and all perished in the Black Hole with their Commander. They belonged to No. 1 Company of the 1st Battery, Bengal Artillery, now 2nd Mountain Battery, R. G. A. An entry in the Battery-record reads: "A portion of this company perished in the Black Hole at Calcutta: the remnant at Plassey." (See a letter in the *Pioneer* of August 17, 1902.)

defending forces is slightly discrepant in detail, but of similar purport. According to him, the regular garrison was composed of 264 men, and the inhabitants serving as Militia added another 250, making in all 514. "Yet only 174 of this number were Europeans, and of these not ten had ever seen any other than the service of the parade: the rest were topasses,* Armenians, and Portuguese inhabitants, on whose faith or spirit no reliance could be placed." Captain George Minchin, who had succeeded Colonel Scott as commandant, and his senior officers, with the one exception of Captain John Buchanan, Scott's son-in-law, were entirely deficient in military experience,† and the troops were almost undisciplined.

It was known in Calcutta on the 1st of June that Cossimbazar was threatened, but it was not until six days later that authentic information arrived that the Factory had fallen without striking a blow, and that an immediate descent on Fort William was to follow. Urgent calls for help were sent to Madras and an appeal made to Chandernagore and Chinsurah. But the Dutchmen begged to be excused, and the French proposed that the English should join them at Fort Orleans. It was clear that neither

* By Topasses are meant Portuguese half-castes, generally employed, even by the "Country powers," as gunners.

† There were indeed two Engineers, of whom the one, Charles O'Hara, went on board the ship with Drake, and the other, Colin Simson, perished in the Black Hole: but they can have been little better than amateurs, for they were constantly oscillating between a writership and their purely military duties.

were inclined to be friendly. Left to themselves, the inhabitants of Calcutta mustered their forces and put their defences in whatever order they were able. The buxerries, or Indian matchlock-men, were increased to 1,500, on the news of the Nabob's advance. Earthworks were hastily thrown up. All the narrow passes leading to the town were blocked by ditches: and intrenchments were begun across the park, and a ravelin to defend the main gate of the Factory, but there was no time to finish them. Nevertheless, three principal batteries were constructed and mounted; one across the "avenue leading to the eastward, in advance of the great gateway of the Fort and having the Mayor's Court on its left and the Park on its right," which may be located near the spot now occupied by the Scotch Church: a second on the river bank at the foot of the modern Clive Ghât Street described in the topography of the time as "close to the Saltpetre godown on the cross road that passes behind the Fort and leads by way of the Strand to Chitpore"; and the third "some three hundred yards to the south of the Fort, at the corner of the burying-ground and commanding one of the principal roads," which may be placed at the junction formed to-day by Hastings Street, Council House Street, and Government Place. There was, in addition, towards the north at Chitpore at the junction of the Mahratta Ditch with the river, an outlying redoubt at Perrin's Garden.

Here the enemy, under Meer Jaffer (who was hereafter to reign at Murshidabad as Clive's nominee), came into contact with the English on Wednesday, June 16th. The little garrison under Ensign Piccard met them with vigour, repulsed the first attack and made a night-sortie in which they spiked four of the enemy's guns. Encouraged by the retreat of Meer Jaffer upon Dum-Dum, the English spent the following morning in burning the bazars in front and to the south of the Fort as far as Govindpore. The "white houses" were, by an arranged signal, vacated, and the European women and children crowded into the Fort, where, writes Governor Drake, the former "diligently employed themselves in making cannon cartridges." On Friday, the 17th, the enemy reappeared in force, but the attack was delivered from the east, and no longer from the north. In the afternoon, they set fire to the Burra Bazar, which lay within half a mile from the Fort on the north-east, and swarmed all round the Settlement. The Portuguese and other "black Christians" now flocked inside the defences, to the number of 2,500, but they rendered little or no assistance to the garrison, and were on the contrary a source of much inconvenience and hindrance.

The English outposts were driven in on the following morning, the 18th, the most resolute assault being made on the battery to the eastward (which we have already located on the site of St. Andrew's Kirk) and its outposts in the jail close to it. This portion of the position was partly held by a detachment of Militia commanded by John Zephaniah Holwell, who had joined the Company's service as a Surgeon, but was now Eighth of Council. We have already encountered him in the capacity of Zemindar, and he was still holding that office. "The post was in a very exposed position," writes Dr. Busteed in his admirable *Echoes from Old Calcutta,* "and was very stubbornly defended. So heavy was the fire brought to bear upon it that only the men necessary to work the guns were at last allowed to remain in it, the rest being ordered under cover within the Mayor's Court close by, ready to take the places from time to time of those who were shot down." At length Captain Clayton, the military officer in charge, directed Holwell to go to the Fort and report the critical situation of affairs. On Holwell's return, however, with orders to withdraw and spike the cannon, he found the outpost in the utmost confusion and on the point of being abandoned. The principal guns, two 18-pounders, were so ineffectually disabled that they were re-mounted by the enemy and used against the Fort with most damaging results.

The loss of this post led to the precipitate recall of the other batteries the same evening. After much gallant but irregular fighting in the streets, notably in those now known as Mission Row and British Indian Street, which needlessly divided the small force, a general retreat was made to the shelter of the Fort. Small parties were hastily thrown into the houses which most closely commanded the ramparts, such as St. Anne's Church, where the Bengal Legislative Council Chamber now stands, Mr. Cruttenden's house on the northern side of what is to-day Fairlie Place, and the Company's House on the south of the Fort, these being at a distance of only thirty or forty yards. At eight o'clock in the evening, the party in the Company's House were dislodged by a strong fire from a house further south where the enemy had installed themselves, and which may well have been the building which bears Holwell's name in Wills' plan. The position was now recognized as desperate, although the Moors attempted nothing further after nightfall beyond a half-hearted escalade of the "new godowns."

A Council of War was held, and it was resolved to send the women and children on board the vessels lying off the Fort. The embarkation was so hurriedly carried out, and with so little order, that several women, the Governor's wife among them, were obliged to remain until next day for want of boats. Some few, including Mrs. Carey, the wife of a sea-captain, elected to remain with their husbands to the end. Manningham, the Third of Council and Export Warehouse-keeper, and Frankland, Sixth of Council and Import Warehouse-keeper, escaped, says Holwell, at this juncture under pretence of escorting the ladies. The ships remained at anchor during the night of the 18th: and on the following (Saturday) morning Mapletoft, the Junior Chaplain, and Mackett, the Ninth of Council and Buxey, who had been working without intermission in "cutting open the bales of cotton and filling it in bags to carry upon the parapets," obtained permission, with other gentlemen, to repair on board the ships to bid farewell to their wives and children and deposit their goods and valuables in their care. While they were so engaged, the panic and disorder on shore was rapidly reaching its climax. The enemy had been since daybreak playing upon the church and factory from the two 18-pounders they had captured at the eastern battery. "They fired with wall-pieces and small arms from every hole and corner, and all our efforts to dispossess them of the houses proved ineffectual." By nine o'clock in the morning, the small parties occupying the church and Mr. Cruttenden's house on the north were nearly cut off, and were ordered inside the Fort, after setting fire to the latter buildings. The despatch on board the ships of the remainder of the European women was followed by the departure of one of the vessels to a situation three miles lower down the river to "avoid the fire-arrows." Several other vessels did the same, and this was the signal for a general stampede. The cry went round that the means of escape were vanishing, and the terror and confusion among the "black Christians" became uncontrollable. At half past ten o'clock the only two remaining boats at the wharf were manned by Drake, the Governor, Minchin, the Commandant, and others, who rowed to the ships in all haste, and representing that the Fort was abandoned and the rout general, persuaded the captains to cast off their moorings and drop down to a safe distance with the ebbing tide.

The story of this cowardly flight is an ignoble one. As Voltaire took occasion to say in his most biting words, the quaker governor was of a very different stamp from the doughty admiral of his name who fell in Nombre de Dios Bay. But it is the first and only instance of its kind in the history of British India, and need not be recalled, except it be by way of contrast to the courage of those who remained behind to uphold the honour of the British flag. After their base desertion, the command of the poor remnant of the garrison was by common consent placed in the hands of Holwell. He personally had every opportunity of escape, but he resolved to remain and defend the Fort until either the disappearing vessels might return, or the *St. George,* the last remaining ship which was at Perrin's Redoubt, might drop down to enable them to make a general retreat. But no vessels came back on the flood, as they might easily have done. Morris, the Pilot of the *St. George,* lost his head, and the ship ran aground and was seized and burnt by the enemy. Nothing now remained but to resist to the last with diminished strength and failing ammunition. The enemy obtained possession of the church and opened a galling fusillade from it. At dawn on Sunday, the 20th of June, a vigorous effort was made to carry the northern curtain, but it was as vigorously repulsed, and the little garrison continued to hold its own until late in the afternoon. There were by that time less than eighty unwounded men left, and all were worn out. Holwell, yielding to their importunities, ceased firing and began to parley, whereupon the enemy swarmed in, and by six o'clock in the evening Seraj-ud-Dowlah was in possession of the Fort. To say, as Macaulay does, that "the Fort was taken after a feeble resistance," is to cast an unmerited slur upon Holwell and his slender force. As a matter of fact, the Fort was fiercely defended for some thirty hours, and the enemy's own list of killed and wounded entirely negatives the assertion. By the confession of Seraj-ud-Dowlah's own men, over 5,000 of their troops, together with "80 jemadars and officers of consequence," were killed in the attack upon the Fort from first to last.

In the confusion which followed the surrender, about twenty of the garrison ran to the north-west bastion and dropped from the embrasures, "where some escaped along the slime of the river." Among these (according to one account) was Paul Richard Pearkes, Fifth of Council and Accomptant. He had resigned to Holwell the command to which he was entitled by seniority after the defection of Drake, and a letter of protest from him against Holwell's colourless report of his surrender of authority is to be found in the proceedings of March 1757, with a note by the copying clerk to the effect that "P. R. Pearkes was a poltroon." Still he was one of the very few who remained at his post, and the censure may be far more fitly directed against those who deserted their comrades while there was still hope. The remainder were surrounded and taken prisoners. Holwell was summoned before the Nabob, and reproached for his audacity in defending the Fort, but received the assurance that no harm should be done to the prisoners. As evening came, however, the whole of the captives, some 146 in number, were crammed into a wretched dungeon in the Fort, "a cube of 18 feet," with two small grated windows only, which had been used as the prison of the garrison and was called the Black Hole. They were of all ranks and classes, senior merchants and factors, writers who had only been a year or two in the country, sea-captains and mariners, military officers and their men, and humble artisans of the Company. There was even a "lawyer," and, it is to be feared, more than one woman and child. Besides Holwell, the more prominent included two members of Council, Eyre and Baillie, respectively Tenth and Eleventh, Gervas Bellamy, the Senior Chaplain to the Settlement, and an old man of 66, John Cooke, the Secretary to the Board, Captain

John Buchanan, whose widow became the first wife of Warren Hastings, and Robert Byng, a young writer, nephew of the unfortunate Admiral. Of these, Secretary Cooke alone survived.

The night was one of the hottest of the most sultry season of the year, and the prisoners soon became frantic with insufferable thirst and suffocating want of air. As the night wore on, they sank one by one and died: and when the door was opened in the morning, only twenty-three, among whom was one woman, Mrs. Carey, came out alive. Holwell, Ensign Walcott, a senior merchant named Richard Court, and Burdett, a writer, were placed in irons and sent to Murshidabad in a country-boat. The rest were suffered to escape, and the experiences of two of them may be taken as typical of all. Mills, a sea-captain, who gave up his place at one of the windows to Holwell, records how he, accompanied by three others, walked to Surman's (in the vicinity of the modern Prinsep's Ghât) after their release from the "Hell in miniature," and thence back to Govindpore, where Fort William stands to-day. Here they stayed for three days in a native hut and eventually found their way to the camp of Drake and the other refugees near the "despicable village" of Fulta, some 30 miles down the river. So, too, Henry Lushington, a young writer, was allowed to make his way down to the ships and to earn a place in History as the man who, under the orders of Clive, forged the name of Admiral Watson on the Red Treaty (loll coggedge*) which was

* Lall Khagaz.

intended to deceive Omichand and trick him out of his reward for betraying Seraj-ud-Dowlah. He was killed in 1763 in the massacre at Patna.

Meanwhile the plight of the fugitives at Fulta was becoming pitiable in the extreme. While Seraj-ud-Dowlah was disporting himself at Alinagur, the name by which he had ordained that Calcutta should henceforth be known, Drake and his forlorn company were living in the utmost destitution and discomfort, partly on board the shipping and partly in tents and straw hovels ashore. Had it not been for Nubkissen, the Company's *moonshee* or interpreter, and the charity of the Dutch at Chinsurah and Fulta itself, they must have starved for want of provisions.

The mortality during the rains and the trying months of September and October was very heavy. Under any circumstances, the place was extremely unhealthy, in spite of its being the site selected for a Dutch Settlement: and the great number of persons now crowded together on board the vessels and on shore, sleeping on deck and under imperfect cover, and exposed to the rains without so much as a change of clothes, caused a serious epidemic of disease. "About two-thirds of the men died of fluxes and fevers," says a contemporary account, "the European ladies held out the best of all: for few or none of them died, which was surprising, as they scarce had cloathes to wear." Surgeon Ives, of Admiral Watson's flagship the *Kent,* who saw them at the end of the year 1756, writes no less tragically of their condition: "They were crowded together in the most wretched habitation, clad in the meanest apparel, and for almost five months had been surrounded by sickness and disease, which made strange havoc among them."

During the whole of this period, the "consultations" of the Committee of Government were carried on, sometimes "on board the *Phœnix* schooner" and at other times "on board the *Grampus* sloop." The fortunes of the Company in Bengal were at their lowest ebb. Warren Hastings, writing from Cossimbazar, where he was living in a species of surveillance, does not hesitate to say that "the English at the Court of Moorshidabad are never mentioned except with pity and contempt." The party at Fulta had received a small reinforcement in the shape of 230 Europeans, who had been hastily despatched under the command of Major Kilpatrick from Madras, when information had come to hand about the middle of July of the fall of the factory at Cossimbazar. This little force had arrived in August, but it was too weak to attempt any serious hostilities against Manick Chand, the Nabob's governor of Calcutta. It suffered grievously from the necessity of taking up its quarters in swampy ground, by reason of the want of room on board the ships, and Clive and Watson found fully four-fifths of them dead, and "of the rest not more than ten fit for duty."

The avenging force did not reach Fulta, however, until the end of 1756 was near at hand. News of the capture of Calcutta and of the tragedy of the Black Hole was received at Fort St. George on August 16. Pigot, the Governor, afterwards in a second term of office to be the victim of an audacious arrest and imprisonment, immediately summoned Clive, who had only just assumed office as Deputy Governor of Fort St. David. As it chanced, there were both troops and means of transport available. Admirals Charles Watson and George Pocock had been despatched with a fleet to the Coromandel Coast during the year 1755, in anticipation of hostilities with France. In February 1757, Clive had been assisting them in the destruction of Gherriah, the stronghold of the pirate Angria on the Bombay coast: and the ships had returned in triumph and were lying in the Madras roads. They had brought out on board from England the King's Thirty-Ninth Regiment of Foot, and had landed them at Fort St. George in January, 1756:—*Primus in Indis,* as the proud motto on their colours still testifies. The regiment is now known territorially as the 1st battalion of the Dorsetshire Regiment: and was at first known as Colonel Adlercron's Regiment, from the name of its commander. Among its officers was a young captain of thirty years of age, named Eyre Coote, the future opponent of Hyder Ali. Although originally raised for service as marines on board the East India fleet, they were being kept in readiness to march against Bussy who had established himself with a French garrison near Hyderabad. But the bad news from Bengal altered their destination. An expedition was quickly equipped and sailed on October 16th, 1756. But it was not until the middle of December that the English at Fulta descried the sails of the *Kent* and the *Tyger* and the *Cumberland.*

CHAPTER VI.

THE WORK OF CLIVE AND WATSON.

CLIVE and Watson lost no time in setting to work. The fort of Budge-Budge, which blocked the way, was taken almost at once, and on January 2nd, 1757, Calcutta and Fort William once more fell into the hands of the English.* A week later, the town of Hooghly was stormed by Coote. Seraj-ud-Dowlah, who had retired to Murshidabad, marched towards Calcutta, masking his purpose by a show of listening to peaceful overtures from Drake and his colleagues, who had taken the earliest opportunity of re-installing themselves in office. Clive, grown impatient of delay, made a determined assault on the Mogul camp on February 4th. The Nabob hastily withdrew his troops: and five days later concluded a treaty which restored to the English all their former privileges of free passage of goods by land and water, placed them once more in possession of their factories and stolen properties, and permitted the fortification of Calcutta and the establishment of a Mint. He also stipulated he

* The earliest Judges of the Supreme Court at Fort William based the right of the English to Calcutta upon conquest as a result of this achievement. In 1782, we find Mr. Justice Hyde (Sir Robert Chambers concurring) laying down the following dictum from the Bench: "We say the inhabitants of this town are all British subjects, because this town was conquered by Admiral Watson and Colonel Clive, but that does not extend to subordinate factories."

would allow the zemindars to grant to the Company the villages in the vicinity of Calcutta given by Ferokshah's firman, but "detained from them by order of the Soubah." The treaty, however, was never carried into effect. War having broken out between England and France, Clive and Watson attacked Chandernagore and captured Fort Orleans on March 22nd, after a nine days' siege.

An open rupture followed with Seraj-ud-Dowlah who was professing to assist the French. Clive wrote a peremptory letter, demanding satisfaction for all injuries, among which, strangely enough, the Black Hole tragedy found no place. The Nabob by way of reply instantly set his army in motion, but Clive was already advancing. On the 17th June, the English concentrated at Chandernagore their little force of about 900 Europeans, including the 39th and 50 sailors from Watson's ships, 200 men of mixed Portuguese and "Country" blood who served with the Europeans, a small detail of lascars, and 2,100 Sepoys, accompanied by eight six-pounders and two small howitzers. Kutwa was seized on the 16th by a detachment under Major Eyre Coote, but a severe storm compelled a halt on the following day. Here Clive received a letter from Meer Jaffer, the Nabob's *buxey* or principal officer, on whose support he was counting, telling him he had feigned a reconciliation with Seraj-ud-Dowlah, and had taken an oath not to assist the English, but adding that "the purport of his convention with them must be carried out." On the 20th Clive heard from Watts, the Company's chief at Murshidabad, that Meer

Jaffer had denounced him to the Nabob's emissaries as a spy and threatened to destroy the English if they attempted to cross the Bhagirathi and attack the capital.

The memorable Council of War was thereupon called which decided against immediate action in spite of the protests of Eyre Coote and six other officers. Clive, however, almost immediately began to doubt the wisdom of his decision, which, as he admitted afterwards, would, if persisted in, have "caused the ruin of the East India Company." At this very juncture a reassuring letter from Meer Jaffer reached him, and he determined to fight. He issued his orders accordingly, crossed the river on the 22nd June, and moving forward in spite of a heavy storm, reached the historic field of Plassey at 1 A.M. on the 23rd. Here they lay down to rest in a mango-tope within a mile of Seraj-ud-Dowlah's army, which occupied an entrenched position in a loop of the river. The odds were great: for to Clive's small force were opposed an army of 50,000 infantry, 18,000 horse and 53 guns, mostly thirty-two, twenty-four and eighteen pounders, mounted on wheeled platforms drawn by oxen and elephants. But the most efficient portion of the Nabob's force was a small party of forty or fifty Frenchmen, commanded by M. St. Frais (or Sinfrey, as the contemporary documents have it) who had formerly been one of the Council at Chandernagore. This party had with it four light field pieces. The Nabob took the offensive, and made an enveloping attack supported by a heavy artillery fire. But the British force found cover in the mango-tope and in the grounds of an adjoining "hunting bungalow": and about noon the enemy drew off and returned to camp, having suffered far more heavily than their antagonists. Clive held another conference at which it was resolved to hold on to their position until nightfall and then attack Seraj-ud-Dowlah's camp. A heavy storm now burst over both armies, and the Nabob, thinking Clive's powder must be wet, charged the mango-tope, but was driven back with serious loss, his principal supporter, Meer Muddun, being killed. Up to this point Meer Jaffer had not declared himself, and his nephew, the Nabob, casting his turban at his feet, urged him to remain faithful to his oath. He gave his promise, but at once sent to Clive begging him to press his attack at once or at latest by nightfall. Another traitor, Rajah Durlabh Ram, besought the Nabob to seek safety in flight, and yielding to his persuasions Seraj-ud-Dowlah ordered his troops to retire into their entrenchments and fled to Murshidabad, accompanied by 2,000 horsemen. This decided the fate of the day, but severe fighting was not yet over: for the Frenchmen held out in a redoubt at a corner of the entrenchment until the open defection of Meer Jaffer's detachment enabled Clive to push forward in force. The native levies dispersed, and St. Frais, "deeming it wiser to preserve his handful of Europeans for another occasion," fell back as the clock struck five, leaving his guns behind him. His resistance was the last opposition offered to the English.

The loss of Clive's little army was remarkably small, only seven being killed and 13 wounded among the Europeans: among the sepoys 36 were killed and the same number wounded. Not a single officer was killed and only two were wounded. The enemy's casualties amounted to about a thousand, including many officers. More than 120 years after the event, the Bengal Government erected on the field a simple obelisk with the equally simple and significant inscription: "Plassey: erected by the Bengal Government in 1883." The famous mango-tope has disappeared, but it is only ten years since the downfall of the last survivor of the old trees. So also the loop in the river, which was the scene of Seraj-ud-Dowlah's entrenchment, has been eaten away by the stream, but the deserted river-bed can still be discerned and is a favourite snipe ground for sportsmen from Calcutta. The tank still exists from which Sinfrey's cannon played upon the English, and the mound, the capture of which carried the day, still rises bare and bleak over the plain.

Clive's triumph was complete. He entered Murshidabad in triumph, and installed Meer Jaffer on the guddee of Bengal, Behar and Orissa; while the unhappy Seraj-ud-Dowlah being seized at Rajmehal in his flight, was brought back to his capital and assassinated by Meerun, the son of Meer Jaffer, with his own hand. The new Nabob was now called upon to fulfil the engagements he had made with his allies. But first of all it became necessary (as Clive put it) to "undeceive" Omichand. This man had been playing a deep game from the beginning. He was willing to betray Seraj-ud-Dowlah whose ear he possessed, but demanded thirty lakhs of rupees as the price of his secrecy and his assistance. Clive had been unable to dispense with his services, for the whole success of his plans depended upon the silence of the man, who held the thread of the intrigue in his hands. He professed to acquiesce in the demand, but determined to punish him with his own weapons. Two treaties were prepared for submission to Meer Jaffer. The one on red paper, to which the forged signature of Watson was attached, contained an article touching Omichand's claims. In the other, which was on white paper, and which was the genuine document, no such stipulation was inserted. A conference was held at the house of Juggut Set, the great banker, at Murshidabad. The white treaty was produced and read: and Omichand was informed that the red treaty, which had been previously shown him, was a trick. Well might Watson exclaim, when told on his death-bed of the use made of his name, that, as there was so much iniquity among mankind, he did not wish any longer to remain among them.

By the treaty now concluded, Meer Jaffer agreed to grant to the Company the land within the Mahratta Ditch and six hundred yards without the Ditch: and engaged further that the land lying to the south of Calcutta as as far as Culpee should be under the Zemindari of the Company, who were to pay the revenue in the same manner with other Zemindars. The revenue of this Zemindari was fixed at Rs. 2,22,958: and as it included twenty-four pergunnahs or local divisions, it gave its name to the district around Calcutta which is still known as the district of the Twenty-four Pergunnahs. In considera- tion of the losses sustained by the capture and plunder of Calcutta by Seraj-ud-Dowlah, one crore of rupees was paid: and another sum of nearly eighty lakhs was promised by way of compensations for the losses sustained by the English, native and Armenian inhabitants of the Settlement. The perwannah of the Nabob to the landholders and officials of the granted lands ends with these quaint words: "Know then, ye Zemindars, Choudhrys, Talooqdars, Mucuddems, Recayahs, Morsawreans, and Mootawettawahs of the Chuckla of the Hooghly and others situated in Bengal the Terrestrial Paradise, that ye are dependents of the Company, and that ye must submit to such treatment as they give you, whether good or bad, and this is my express injunction."

According to treaty, the English inhabitants of Calcutta recovered fifty, the Hindoo and Mahomedans twenty, and the Armenians seven lakhs of rupees, "restitution-money." On the 6th July, 1757, a year after the sack of Calcutta, there arrived from Murshidabad nearly seventy-six lakhs of rupees of coined silver, packed in 700 chests and laden in 100 boats. Never before did the English nation obtain such a prize in solid money. Before another six weeks, forty lakhs more of coined silver arrived in Calcutta, to meet the losses sustained by the Company. The treaty permitted the Company to establish a mint, from which the first coin was issued on the 19th August, 1757. The coins were, however, struck in the name of the Emperor of Delhi. It was not till the reign of William IV, that the Company commenced to strike rupees with the King's head and an English inscription.

When Clive and Watson re-took Calcutta in 1757, seven months after the sack, they found most of the best houses of the English demolished or damaged by fire. St. Anne's lay in ruins: but the Armenian and Portuguese Churches seem to have escaped. Everything of value belonging to the inhabitants had been removed. In the native town, many houses lay in ruins. The Burra Bazar had been burnt down. In the middle of the Fort, a mosque had been erected with the material of several buildings which had been pulled down to make room for it. Of the inhabitants of the native town, most of whom had fled at the approach of Seraj-ud-Dowlah, about 50,000 are said to have afterwards returned. They were, however, mostly of the lower classes, as the rapacity of Manick Chand, whom Seraj-ud-Dowlah had left as Governor of Calcutta, deterred such as were known to have property from trusting themselves within his reach. The greater part of the merchandise belonging to the Company, which was stored up in the Fort, was found untouched, for this part of the plunder had been reserved for the Nabob.

Immediately after the receipt of the "restitution-money," a Committee of the most respectable inhabitants was appointed to distribute it. They executed the office with much minuteness, if not also with discretion and equity. Commerce revived; the destroyed houses were re-built; in fact, we may date modern Calcutta from 1757.

The remaining stages in the consolidation of British rule in Bengal followed with startling swiftness upon the heels of Plassey. In 1758 Behar was invaded by Mahomed Gohur, the son of the Emperor Alamgir the Second, who was afterwards as Shah Alam the Second to put himself and his tinsel sovereignty under Lake's protection in 1803. Patna was besieged: and Clive marched to its relief. The terror of his name was sufficient, and the Shahzada's army had entirely dispersed before he reached the City. As a reward for this service Meer Jaffer granted Clive the quit-rent amounting to about 3 lakhs of rupees which the Company had agreed to pay for the Zemindari of Calcutta. By a subsequent sanad of the Nabob, dated 23rd June, 1765, and a firman of the Emperor, dated 30th September of the same year, this grant was continued to Clive for ten years from May 16, 1764, after which, or at the death of Clive, if it occurred before the expiry of this term, it was to revert to the English Company as an unconditional jagir or assignment and a perpetual gift..

In 1760 there was another invasion of Behar by the Shahzada, who had now assumed the title of Emperor on the assassination of his father by Ghazi-ud-din, the Commander-in-Chief, who had put him on his throne in 1754. But he was defeated by Colonel Calliaud in February of that year and again by Major Carnac early in 1761. Meer Jaffer was deposed by Vansittart, who was now Governor at Fort William, and his son-in-law, Meer Kasim, placed on the guddee in consideration of his assigning to the Company the three districts of Burdwan, Chittagong and Midnapore, which yielded about one-third of the entire revenue of Bengal. Peace was concluded with the Emperor, who invested Meer Kasim with the soubahdari at Patna. But disputes broke out between the new Nabob and the English regarding the right of the Company to trade duty free. He captured the English Factory at Patna and its leading officers, but was immediately defeated and fled to Oudh. Before his departure he issued an order for the murder of the English prisoners in his hands. The Nabob's own officers declined to do such butcher's work, but he found a ready instrument in Walter Reinhardt, a Swiss renegade, who, by reason of his swarthy complexion, was nicknamed Sombre—an appellation which his Indian associates transformed into Sumroo. The victims numbered no fewer than 150. They were surprised at dinner and fought desperately to the last with bottles and plates, in default of the knives and forks of which they had been treacherously deprived by their infamous executioner. The news of the massacre created a deep sensation in Calcutta, and in addition to a public sermon of commemoration, a fortnight's general mourning was ordered, and a day of universal fasting. Meanwhile, justice was being swiftly meted out to the author of the wrong. A few weeks only were suffered to elapse before Patna was stormed by Major Adams: Meer Jaffer was reinstated, and in 1763 confirmed the cession of Burdwan, Midnapore, and Chittagong. In the following year Shuja-ud-Dowlah, the Nabob Vizier of Oudh, who had invaded Oudh in the cause of Meer Kasim, was completely routed at the battle of Buxar by Major Munro. He threw himself on the mercy of the English, who took Allahabad and Korah from him and handed these over to the Emperor of Delhi, receiving in return the perpetual grant of the Dewanny of Bengal, Behar and Orissa, by a treaty dated August 12, 1765. The firman conveyed to the English the military government of the three provinces, the right to administer civil justice, and the entire control of the finances, subject to a payment of 20 lakhs to the Emperor and to provision of the expenses of administering criminal justice and maintaining the police. Meer Jaffer had died in the preceding January, at the age of seventy-six: and it was an easy matter to obtain the confirmation of the Imperial gift from his son and successor Najjam-ud-dowlah, who was a mere boy and of the weakest possible character. "I shall now have as many dancing-girls as I like," was the careless saying with which he bartered away for an annual stipend of 53 lakhs the last shreds of power which his father left him. The titular attributes of sovereignty were permitted to remain with him, and as late as 1780 we find Warren Hastings writing officially to the Nabob at Murshidabad and recommending the conferment of titles of honour upon such and such deserving persons "as the Governor-General never bestows titles upon anybody." But these were matters of the merest form, and all the essentials of rule in Bengal were henceforth in the hands of the Company.

Clive had sailed for England after Plassey, to receive, at the age of thirty-four, fresh honours from his admiring countrymen. He returned to Calcutta in May, 1765, as Lord Clive, Baron of Plassey, and Governor and Commander-in-Chief of the Company's possessions in Bengal. One of his first acts was to obtain the treaty, to which reference has just been made, and which formally endowed the English with the government of twenty-five millions of people and the control of a revenue of four millions sterling. But he had also to render the English in India worthy of the Empire he had won for them. The Company's servants were in the habit of eking out their small salaries by all manner of indirect and illicit means. "The people under their dominions," wrote a native chronicler of the times, "groan everywhere, and are reduced to poverty and distress." Nearly the whole of the inland trade passed through the hands of the Council at Fort William and their subordinates: and no one was safe from their cupidity. The sums of money that were amassed are almost incredible. It is related "that one private company, which consisted of 10 shareholders, divided a clear profit of eleven lakhs in two years." To opportunities such as these were added the boundless possibilities revealed by the victory at Plassey. As Clive himself said, there had been no limit to his own acquisitions but his moderation. Others were not so scrupulous. The tale of Meer Jaffér's "transactions" with Vansittart and Spencer during the year 1763 is one long record of greed and extortion. From ten lakhs the demand was raised to forty, and no sooner was the deed of assignment of the forty lakhs executed than further contributions were called for in a manner which could not be mistaken until another thirteen lakhs had been paid over during Vansittart's governorship and ten during that of Spencer. Twenty more lakhs of rupees from the exhausted treasury at Murshidabad were distributed among the nine principal members of Council in Calcutta as the price of their agreeing to set up the feeble-minded Nujjum-ud-dowlah on the throne. The "Nabob" became a notorious and not too well-beloved a figure in English politics and society. His was the purse that controlled the rotten boroughs; his the senseless and vulgar extravagance which furnished a butt for the playwright and the humourist. Nor did the natives of the country neglect to profit by the opportunity and the example. The Governor's dewan, Ram Chand, and Nubkissen, the Company's moonshee, who enjoyed in succession the complete confidence of Clive and of Hastings, realized enormous fortunes in the course of ten years. The former at his death in 1767 left a fortune of 12½ millions of rupees, says a Mahomedan writer in the *Tarikh-i-munsuri*, and Nubkissen could afford to spend nine lakhs on the occasion of his mother's death, although in 1757, such men had been in receipt of a monthly salary of sixty rupees. Clive mourned over the eclipse of his country's fame and declared in honest scorn that "there were not five men of principle left at the Presidency." But he had gone out to India once more determined to "destroy these great and growing evils, or to perish in the attempt:" and he set himself to the work. In less than two years, his task might be said to have been fairly accomplished. When in 1767 he sailed down the Hooghly for the last time, he had completed his achievements by the introduction of a series of sweeping reforms, carried through in the midst of obloquy and intrigue and open resistance. The taking of presents from natives of the country was forbidden under stern penalties, and private trade by officials put down. The temptation to grow rich by stealth could only be removed, as Cornwallis removed it, by the payment of an adequate salary: but Clive strove to keep it under control by reserving to the Company's servants the salt, betel-nut and tobacco monopoly, the proceeds of which each was to receive in proportion to his rank.

It is melancholy to reflect that this measure, which at least succeeded in uprooting the worst abuses of a faulty system, should have been in later years charged against its author as the most heinous of his offences.

CHAPTER VII.

CALCUTTA AFTER PLASSEY.

THE year 1757, distinguished by the victories of Clive and Watson and the re-establishment of British power in Bengal, was also marked by a terrible epidemic. Ives, who was surgeon on board Watson's flagship the *Kent*, furnishes the following instructive statistics which sufficiently show the terrible unhealthiness of the settlement and help us to understand why the Hospital was removed in 1768 to its present site on the southern edge of the Maidan. "Between February 8th and August 8th of that year (1757)," he records, "1,150 patients recovered: of these, 54 were for scurvy, 302 bilious fevers, and 56 bilious colic: 52 men buried. Between 7th August and 7th November, 717 fresh patients were taken in: of these, 147 were in putrid fevers and 15 in putrid fluxes: 101 were buried." Among the victims was Admiral Watson himself, who died on the 16th of August, 1757, and lies buried in the old churchyard adjoining St. John's, where his monument may still be seen. Within eight months he had delivered Calcutta, captured the strongholds of the French and the "country powers" higher up the river, and turned the great sea-entrance to Bengal once and for ever into a British highway. And he had done more even than this. For by virtue of his "King's commission" it was he, and not Clive, who was in command of the relieving expedition, and, like Outram a hundred years later, he proved his patriotism by waiving his rights, and so averted a deadlock between the sea and the land forces. *Exegit monumentum aere perennius:* but how many Englishmen, who visit his tomb in Calcutta or pass by the memorial erected in his honour in Westminster Abbey, realize what a debt they owe to him?

In 1762 another epidemic ravaged Calcutta and is said to have swept away 50,000 "blacks" and 800 Europeans. There was yet another grievous famine and pestilence in Bengal in 1770 which carried off, according to Hickey's Gazette, no less than 76,000 souls in the town of Calcutta, between the 15th July and the 10th September. It was of this terrible year that Macaulay wrote that "the very streets of Calcutta were blocked by the dying and the dead": and the mortality among Europeans alone was returned at 1,500. Small wonder, therefore, was it that sailors of the day, by an odd distortion of the name of Gholghat, the old English factory-house at Hooghly, spoke of Charnock's city as another Golgotha. Such grotesque perversions were common enough: and perhaps the palm may be given to Jno. Gernaete, which appears in a manuscript of 1680 as a substitute for Juggernath. But in the case of Calcutta the sinister corruption had a foundation in fact as solid as it was tragic. The rains were the deadly time in Calcutta, particularly for the new arrivals. The crews of ships in the river died in appalling numbers from "exposure to the night-fogs": while those on land fared little better. The fact was, that Calcutta was nothing more or less than an undrained swamp, in the immediate vicinity of a malarious jungle. The Mahratta Ditch was simply an open sewer, and the river-banks were strewn with the dead bodies of men and animals. The ditch to the east of the old fort, into which the bodies of the victims of the Black Hole had been flung, was no less a cause of offence: it was the receptacle for all manner of abomination, and although it was in the very centre of the settlement, it was not filled up until 1766. Doctors were few and badly paid. Fever and ague, "barbers," a disease common to the lower class of Europeans, "bilious or putrid fluxes," exacted every year a heavy contribution for the burying-ground.

So insecure was the tenure of life that the European inhabitants of Calcutta were long accustomed to meet each year on the 15th November, and to congratulate themselves on their escape from the perils of the rains and the effluvia from the pestilential Salt Lakes. The crowded charnel-house in the heart of the city gave way as early as 1767 to a new cemetery at the eastern extremity of Park Street, which appears in Upjohn's map of 1793 under the melancholy name of Burying Ground Road. Down it would file many a sad company of mourners from April to October. "The departed one of whatever rank," we read in "Hartley House," a lively collection of contemporary letters, "is carried on men's shoulders (like your walking funerals in England) and a procession of gentlemen equally numerous and respectable from the genteel connexions, following." So frequent was the spectacle that special precautions were taken not to harrow the feelings of the fair sex. "All funeral processions are concealed as far as possible from the sight of the ladies, that their vivacity may not be wounded." We may smile at the quaint conceit of the expression, but the precaution was only too necessary. Death followed with startling rapidity upon attack. Patients were commonly carried off after a "cold stage" of twelve hours: and it was no unusual occurrence to sup with your host and leave him in perfect health, and be summoned to attend his funeral on the following morning. The result was that, of course, every Englishman who was able avoided the plague-stricken air of Calcutta by residing in garden-houses outside its boundaries. Clive lived at Dum-Dum, Sir William Jones at Garden Reach, Sir Robert Chambers had a house at Cossipore and another at Bhowanipore "far out of the town" in those days, but well within sight of the present Cathedral. In 1763 Warren Hastings obtained permission to build a suspension bridge over the Kalighat Nullah, on the way to his garden-house at Alipore. Here also, in the modern Collector's residence, Philip Francis had his country seat, and close by was Barwell's mansion at Kidderpore, known to-day as the Military Orphan Asylum. "The banks of Garden Reach," wrote Mrs. Fay in 1780, "are studded with elegant mansions, called garden-houses, surrounded with groves and lawns which descend to the water's edge, and present a constant succession of whatever can delight the eye, or bespeak wealth and elegance in the owners."

To the east and west of the Mahratta Ditch, but principally to the east, were also to be found many of these pleasant adjuncts to life in old Calcutta; and the name of

Boytaconnah Road, borne in Upjohn's map of 1793 by the Circular Road which ran alongside the Ditch, is referred by many to the presence of these *baitakkhanas*, or garden-houses, rather than to the historic tree at the Sealdah end of the "road and avenue leading to the eastward." Two at least of these gardens preserved memories of the times of storm and stress through which the city had just passed. Allusion has already been made to the garden at Halsibagan on the north-east, which was the property of Omichand, who amassed more than a crore of rupees out of the Company's contracts for the placing of their investments, and who was certainly in a position to stipulate for the reward of thirty lakhs for betraying Seraj-ud-Dowlah, out of which Clive tricked him. To this garden-house, then the head-quarters of the Nabob's army, were brought Holwell and his fellow-captives on the day after the terrible scene in the Black Hole, and left all night in a three-foot tent, exposed to torrents of tropical rain. The connection of the second with the "Troubles" was perpetuated still more directly. Hatibagan, which must be sought further south in Entally, was the place where the Nabob's elephants were kept during the siege: and its name has survived until to-day.

Of Calcutta at the period at which we are now arrived—that which succeeded the departure of Lord Clive in 1767—a graphic description is found in the Letters of Mrs. Kindersley :—

"I think I have never given you any account of the town of Calcutta," she writes in June, 1768, "indeed, after Madras, it does not appear much worthy describing; for although it is large, with a great many good houses in it, it is as awkward a place as can be conceived; and so irregular that it looks as if all the houses had been thrown up in the air, and fallen down again by accident as they now stand. People keep constantly building; and every one who can procure a piece of ground to build a house upon, consults his own taste and convenience without any regard to the beauty or regularity of the town. Besides, the appearance of the best houses is spoiled by the little straw huts, and such sort of incumbrances, which are built up by the servants for themselves to sleep in: so that all the English part of the town, which is the largest, is a confusion of very superb and very shoddy houses, dead walls, straw huts, warehouses, and I know not what.

"The most like a street is the *Buzar,* the name they call every place by where anything is to be sold: the *Buzar* is full of little shabby-looking shops, called Boutiques: they are kept by black people.

"The English seldom visit these places themselves, but depend on their Banians and other servants, for the purchase of everything: indeed, if they do it is much the same, for at all events they are sure to be cheated.

"About the middle of the town, on the river's edge, stands the old fort, memorable for the catastrophe of the Black Hole, so much talked of in England. It was in one of the apartments in it that the wretched sufferers were confined. The fort is now made a very different use of; the only apology for a church is in some of the rooms in it, where divine service is sometimes performed.

"In a distinct part of the town reside the Armenians;

and the people called the Portuguese. Each of these have their own churches; and the Portuguese keep up the processions and pageantry of the Romish Church, as far as they are permitted; but are obliged to perform it all within their own walls. The chief connection we have with these people is, employing some of the women as servants, or the men as writers, or some times cooks.

" Here is not, as at Madras, a black town near for the servants to reside in; therefore Calcutta is partly environed by their habitations, which makes the roads rather unpleasant; for the huts they live in, which are built of mud and straw, are so low that they can scarcely stand upright in them; and, having no chimnies, the smoke of the fires with which they dress their victuals comes all out at the doors, and is perhaps more disagreeable to the passenger then to themselves.

" The new fort, an immence place, is on the river side about a mile below the town. If all the buildings, which are intended within its walls are finished, it will be a town within itself; for besides houses for the engineers and other officers who reside at Calcutta, there are apartments for the Company's writers; barracks for soldiers, magazines for stores, etc.

" The Town of Calcutta is likewise daily increasing in size, notwithstanding which, the English inhabitants multiply so fast, that houses are extremely scarce. Paper or wainscot are improper, both on account of the heat, the vermin and the difficulty of getting it done; the rooms are therefore all whited walls, but plastered in pannels, which has a pretty effect, and are generally ornamented with prints, looking-glasses, or whatever else can be procured from Europe. The floors are likewise plaster, covered all over with fine matt, which is nailed down; for although carpets are manufactured in some parts of the country, they are such an addition to the heat, that they are seldom made use of. The rooms are few, but mostly very large and lofty; many of the new built houses have glass windows which are pleasant to the eye, but not so well calculated for the climate as the old ones, which are made of cane.

"Furniture is so exorbitantly dear, and so very difficult to procure, that one seldom sees a room where all the chairs and couches are of one part; people of the first consequence are forced to pick them up as they can, either from the Captains of European ships, or from China, or having some made by the blundering carpenters of the country, or send for them to Bombay, which are generally received about three years after they are bespoke; so that these people who have great good luck, generally get their houses tolerably well equipped by the time they are quitting them to return to England.

"Beds, or as they are always called cotts, are no very expensive part of furniture; the wood-work which is exceedingly slight, is made to take in pieces; the furniture is either gauze or muslin, made to put on all at once; and people sleep on a thin matress or quilt; one sheet, and two or three pillows, complete the bedding; so that when it is taken in pieces the whole lays in a small compass and is easily removed from one place to another: whenever people travel, they always carry their beds with them.

"A little out of the town is a clear airy spot free from smoke or any encumbrances called the *corse* (because it is a road the length of a *corse* or two miles) in a sort of ring or rather angle made on purpose to take the air in which the company frequent in their carriages about sunset, or in the morning before the sun is up."

The new Fort William, of which Mrs. Kindersley speaks as an "immence place," was commenced in 1758 upon lines traced by Clive and completed about 1773. The site chosen was on the river-bank, but considerably south of its predecessor and in the centre of what was then the populous flourishing village of Govindpore. A portion of the "restitution-money" was spent in compensating the inhabitants, who were given lands in other parts of the town, notably Toltollah, Kumartooly and Sobhabazar. In the last named quarter a large grant was made to Nubkissen, Clive's Munshee, and it began at once to rise rapidly in buildings and population. In Govindpore itself great improvements also were effected. The tiger-haunted jungle which cut off the village of Chowringhee from the river was cleared, and gave way to the wide grassy stretch of *Maidan* of which Calcutta is so proud. The formation of this airy expanse and the filling up of the creek, which had cut off the settlement on the south, led the European inhabitants to gradually forsake the narrow limits of the old palisades. The movement towards Chowringhee had already been noticeable as early as 1746, for we find Holwell referring to the locality as "the road leading to Collegot" (Kalighat): but it was very slow and deliberate. The new cemetery was considered such a distance from the settlement that the Council in 1768 granted the chaplain a special allowance for palkee-bearers. Sir Elijah Impey's house (it is true) stood upon the site now occupied by the Loretto Convent at the end of Middleton Row, and was surrounded by an extensive deer-park lying between, though not quite up to, Camac Street on the one side and Russell Street on the other. But Wood's map of 1784 shows the *gol-talao* or round tank still in existence where the Catholic Church dedicated to St. Thomas now stands. The present Middleton Row was a leafy avenue which led through the Park to the mansion from Burying-ground road. And Sir Elijah was looked upon as living quite outside the town. Palkee bearers in his day still charged double fares for going so far afield: and servants returning home of an evening would form large parties "leaving their good clothes behind" for fear of the rascally characters who infested the Maidan. When Grandpré visited Calcutta in 1789, Tank Square was still the centre of fashion. "As we enter the town," he writes, "a very extensive square opens before us, with a large piece of water in the middle for the public use. The pond has a grass plot round it, and the whole is enclosed by a wall breast-high, with a railing on the top. The sides of this enclosure are each nearly five hundred yards in length. The square itself is composed of magnificent houses, which render Calcutta not only the handsomest town in Asia, but one of the finest in the world. One side of the square consists of a range of buildings occupied by persons in civil employments under the Company, such as writers in the public offices. Part of the side towards the river is taken up by the old fort, which was the first citadel built by the English after their establishment in Bengal."

The old Council House, where Stanlake Batson struck

Hastings in the face in 1763, was in close proximity to the Old Fort. When it was purchased for the Company's use in 1758, it was the dwelling-house of Richard Court, who after surviving the Black Hole and the added horrors of the journey in chains to Moorshedabad, had been drowned in the Hooghly that year. There is no house with Court's name in Wills' map of 1753: but its situation can be guessed, for the Council discarded it in 1764 as being "from its vicinity to the public office very ill-calculated for conducting the business of the Board with that privacy which is often requisite." Its successor which was not pulled down until 1800, stood on the western portion of the modern Government House compound, whence the name of the street that ran past it. Hastings' second wife, the "beautiful Mrs. Imhoff," held her *salon* in a house in the street which already bears his name in Wood's map of 1784. Francis, when in town, lived in the house in Clive Street where the Royal Exchange now stands, and where Clive had dwelt before him; Clavering and Monson in Mission Row—one and all in the heart of the business quarter of to-day. The house occupied by Sir Eyre Coote, while Member of Council from 1779 to 1783, is now included in the Treasury Buildings. Mr. Justice Hyde resided on the site of the modern Town Hall. Le Maistre, his colleague, had a house upon the spot where the Free School now stands in the Street of that name. Nuncomar's place of imprisonment was the "country jail," which is represented to-day by the Presidency Jail upon the Maidan. But the jail in which Hickey was confined was in Lall Bazar, opposite the modern Police Office. And at the cross-roads, where Lall Bazar and Bow Bazar met the pilgrim path to

Kalighat, was the pillory, one of whose involuntary occupants was said to have been alive as lately as 1852. The other associations of old Lall Bazar are more pleasant. For next door to the jail was the Harmonic Tavern, whose renown still rings down the dim vista of years as the scene of all the gaiety and revelry of old Calcutta. The London Tavern, which was not far off, was another fashionable resort of our great-grandfathers. "Vauxhall and Fireworks at Cossinaut Baboo's garden in the Dhurrumtollah," is the head of an advertisement in the Gazette of December 4, 1788, which lets us into the secret of yet a third. The Bread and Cheese Bungalow hard by the Boytaconnah tree was also a favourite haunt in 1780: and if more luxurious fare were demanded, it might be had at the emporium which Sir Elijah Impey's late steward and Sir Thomas Rumbold's late cook were advertising in that year at which "turtle were dressed, gentlemen boarded, and families supplied with pastry." The old play-house at the south-west corner of Tank Square had vanished, and its place was taken by the Theatre at the north-west end of what is now Lyon's Range which has already found mention in these pages. It was built in 1775 by public subscription, and in the list of subscribers may be seen the names of Hastings, Barwell, Monson, and Impey and his brethren of the Supreme Court. But there was no church until St. John's was consecrated in 1787. Philip Dormer Stanhope, writing in 1774, comments upon the deficiency: "There is a noble play-house, but no church, the want of which is supplied by a spacious apartment in the old Fort, adjoining to the room so well known by the name of the Black Hole."

Mrs. Kindersley dismisses this "apology for a church" with the barest possible notice in 1767. It meets with no more complimentary treatment from Sophia Goldborne, who sets down her impressions of Calcutta some fifteen years later in "Hartley House." The edifice, we are told, "dignified at present with the appellation of church, "does not deserve notice." But, if we are to credit her prattle, there were few better methods of obtaining a picture of the Anglo-Indian Society of the time than by paying a visit to the Chapel of St. John in the Old Fort. "I have been to church, my dear girl," she writes, "in my new palanquin (the mode of genteel conveyance) where *all* ladies, are approached, by sanction of ancient custom, by *all* gentlemen indiscriminately, known or unknown, with offers of their hand to conduct them to their seat: accordingly, those gentlemen who wish to change their condition, (which between ourselves are mostly old fellows, for the young ones either chuse country-born ladies for wealth, or having left their hearts behind them, enrich themselves in order to be united to their favourite dulcineas in their native land) on hearing of a ship's arrival, make a point of repairing to this holy dome and eagerly tender their services to the fair strangers: who, if this stolen view happens to captivate, often without undergoing the ceremony of a formal introduction, receive matrimonial overtures and, becoming brides in the utmost possible splendour, have their rank instantaneously established, and are visited and paid every honour to which the consequence of their husband entitles them." Nor was the Calcutta Coelebs in search of a wife less importunate on week-days. "You are liable," she declares elsewhere, "to be plundered of your consent any evening of your life : and without time to collect yourself much less to retract, by the Padra's being one of the company may be induced to give him a claim to twenty gold mohurs before he takes his leave : and so being married in haste, left to repent at leisure."

We may supplement the gossip of this vivacious young lady with a few jottings from contemporary official records. And, inasmuch as a ready transition offers from housewives *in posse* to households *in esse,* a beginning may be made with the servant question—that subject of never-failing interest to the memsahib. In 1759, in consequence of the "insolence and exorbitant wages exacted by the menial servants of the Settlement," it was ordered at a meeting of the "Quorum of Zemindars" that a regular monthly scale of wages should be fixed and observed. Some of the names in the list are strangely unfamiliar and many have not even survived. *Chobdars* no longer carry silver sticks before us : *sontabardars* and *hurkarus* are content nowadays with the designation of peon ; and the *abdar,* or water cooler, has been elbowed out of existence by the Calcutta Ice Association. Gone, too, are the *hookah* and the *hookah-burdar,* once the inseparable companions of every dinner-party in Calcutta. Mr. and Mrs. Warren Hastings, inviting their friends in October, 1779, to a concert and supper at "Mrs. Hastings' house in Town," beg that no servants be brought "except a *houccabardar.*" By 1784, however, *hookahs* would seem to have been banished from Calcutta ball-rooms, for the advertisements regarding such festivities generally intimate that "no *hookahs* will be admitted upstairs." Still, the habit died hard. Eighty years ago, nothing was more ordinary than for the *hookah* to be introduced with the dessert. Behind each diner would stand his *hookah*, with its respective *hookah-burdar* feeding the *chillum* and keeping up the red fire of the *gool*. A *hookah* rug constituted one of the carpet-work fancies of the young ladies of the day; and sometimes they took a turn at the hubble-bubble themselves. "The rage for smoking," wrote Grandpré in 1789, "extends even to the ladies; and the highest compliment they can pay a man is to give him preference by smoking his *hookah*. In this case it is a point of politeness to take off the mouthpiece he is using, and substitute a fresh one, which he presents to the lady with his *hookah*, who soon returns it. The compliment is not always a trivial importance; it sometimes signifies a great deal to a friend, and often still more to a husband." We do not know how long these tender associations may have clung around the *gool* and the *chillum*. Certain it is that it was not until 1840 that the practice of *hookah*-smoking by Europeans began to fall into disuse: and even in the seventies it still had its votaries

Along with their fellows have also disappeared the comprador, who bought the table-supplies, and the crutch-purdar, who relieved his master of the trouble of making actual payments. These two individuals were clearly believers in hiding their light under a bushel, for they figure low in the Zemindar's list, where their pay is stated to be only three and four rupees a month respectively. But, like the servants of John Company Bahadur, they made up with the left hand for the deficiencies of the right. Others of seemingly less importance had apparently fewer opportunities, for they were paid better. A khansamah, "whether christian, Moor or gentoo," a head cook and a coachman were rated at Rs. 5, a head bearer and a khitmagar at Rs. 3, a washerman at the same figure if he worked "for a family," and half of the amount if he worked for a single person, a mussalchee, who was in those days primarily a torch-bearer, at Rs. 2, a "shaving barber or wig-barber" at Rs. 1-8-0, and a house tailor at Rs. 3. The last named was ordered to attend at seven o'clock in the morning during the hot season, and eight o'clock in the cold weather months, "on pain of corporal punishment, if complaint is made and proved before the court of Zemindary." Any servant refusing to comply with these rules was declared liable to sequestration of his landed possessions or imprisonment: but he was assured on the other hand that he would be released from his service, if he could adduce satisfactory evidence of ill-usage by his master. And an individual of the name of Marshall Johnson was fined in 1763 for striking a servant and committed in default of payment to prison, from whence he petitions Governor Vansittart for release, urging that he had been for three months "rotting in a loathsome jail, having not the wherewithal to pay the fine nor even to provide the common necessaries."

Between 1759 and 1787, the rates of wages had risen to nearly three times the sum which were deemed sufficient by Richard Becher and Holwell: and we find "consumahs" receiving Rs. 25, cooks and coachmen Rs. 20, and khitmagars and head bearers Rs. 10 a month. The rise in wages would not appear, however, to have been accompanied by any reduction in the quantity of servants that inexorable custom deemed necessary. "One hundred and ten servants to wait upon a family of four people!" writes Macrabie, the Secretary and brother-in-law of Francis, in comic despair, "and yet we are economists! Oh monstrous! Tell me if this land does not want weeding!" In addition to this horde of paid servants, many Anglo-Indians kept slaves. These were usually negroes, and went by the name of Coffrees. They were habitually offered for sale, and the local records are full of advertisements of the kind. Four hundred rupees was deemed a good price for a man who understood the business both of butler and cook: others were in demand on account of their musical skill, and their dexterity in shaving and dressing and waiting at table. Nor were the slaves all Africans. Many were the children of poor parents who had sold them from their inability to support them. There was, it is to be feared, a good deal of ill-usage of these unfortunate creatures, and it comes as a shock to realize that no measure for the abolition of slavery found a place on the statute-book until the year 1842. The fact was, that the services of the slave were a great deal too convenient to be dispensed with. He performed all the menial duties which a hired servant would not do for fear of demeaning himself: and if he ran away, the summary methods of the police were always available for capture and chastisement.

These overgrown establishments were not at all to the liking of the Court of Directors. While the "Quorum of Zemindars" directed their attention to the servants, the "Chairs" at the India House were never weary of inculcating the virtues of the simple life upon the masters. As early even as 1725, we come across letter after letter full of remonstrance and reprobation. The President, John Deane, had charged "Rupees eleven hundred for a chaise and pair" to the public account. This sum he is ordered immediately to refund. "If our servants," say the Directors, "will have such superfluities, let them pay for them." Despite of reprimands, however, habits of luxury continued, and in 1731, we find "the foppery of having a set of music at his table, and a coach and six with guards and running footmen," made a matter of reproof against both the President and "some of inferior rank." And by way of adding insult to injury, it is broadly hinted that "wherever such practice prevails in any of our servants, we shall always expect that we are the paymasters in some shape or other."

As time goes on, the grievance assumes a different aspect. It is no longer the unauthorized expenditure of the Company's money that forms the burden of complaint: but the writers must not spend their own salaries as they think fit. In 1754 it is laid down "as a standing and a positive command that no writer be allowed to keep a pallackee (palanquin), horse or chaise during the term of his writership," under pain of dismissal. After the "Troubles," the Directors were induced to relent and after much inveighing against "expenses about cookrooms and gardens lately observed on the face of the bills," permission was accorded to the writers to use a palanquin during the hot weather and rains "on account of the distance of some of their houses from the offices they belong to." But the indulgence was accompanied with the warning that "when the citadel is finished and apartments for the Company's servants are built contiguous to the public offices, there will be no occasion for the expense of a palanquin, and we shall then oblige them to lay it aside." The "gentlemen writers" would appear, however, to have taken an ell instead of the inch allotted to them, and in 1767, during the Governorship of Verelst, the Court insist on the need of "a thorough change of manners in the Settlement," and demand the enactment of a stringent code of sumptuary laws. "The turbulent factious conduct of these young men" (of the Civil Service), they write, "is of so alarming a nature that we are determined to quell it, and if they cannot be brought to a sense of their duty, they are unworthy our service and must not be suffered to continue in India." By their direction a Committee of Inspection was appointed, and the following regulations were made and circulated with an intimation that "impilcit obedience" was expected to the directions thereon conveyed. "1st.—With respect to the servants necessary to be kept by a writer without a family, the Committee are of opinion that they should be allowed two, and a cook;—one for the immediate care of his house and charge of his effects, and another to attend him when he goes out, or to assist in the charge of his house and effects in case of the sickness of the other. 2nd.—It is recommended that an order be issued that no writer shall be allowed to keep a horse without the express permission of the Governor; or be permitted either of himself or jointly with others, to keep a garden house. 3rd.—It is further recommended that the writers be enjoined to wear no other than plain cloaths."

We may extend or not, as we please, our sympathy to the "young men," whose households and wardrobes were thus sought to be placed under supervision. But if they were "factious or turbulent" they were after all no worse than their seniors in the service. There was little restraint placed upon language even in the highest quarters. Mr. Gray, a civilian dismissed from Maldah, writes officially to Lord Clive and informs him that his language is "more calculated for the meridian of Grub Street or Billingsgate than for the Records of the Hon'ble Board." Another official, no less a person than the Collector of Calcutta, on being invited to discontinue a practice which is prohibited by the orders of the Company, rejoins in the following remarkable words:—"Lord Clive in his minute assumes his usual stile of affected superiority and contempt for those of different sentiments from himself. Although I do not feel myself hurt by his contumelious manner, yet as the appearance of submission may encourage him to a continuance of it, I will here without scruple treat his Lordship with that freedom of sentiment and expression of which he has set me the example."

With these thunderclaps ringing in our ears, we may appropriately pass on to the memorable battle royal which has linked the history of Calcutta so inseparably with the names of Hastings and Francis.

CHAPTER VIII.

HASTINGS AND FRANCIS.

In the year 1773 Calcutta became for the first time the official capital of British India. Parliament determined to interfere "for the better regulation of the British territories in the East Indies," and, while renewing the Charter of the Company, enacted a variety of important changes in its constitution. Warren Hastings, who had in May, 1772, succeeded John Cartier as "President in the Bay" and Governor of Bengal, was elevated to the rank of Governor-General, not of India, but of the "Presidency of Fort William in Bengal," and invested with supreme authority over all the British possessions in India. This great, if sometimes erring, statesman had first sailed for India in 1750 at the age of eighteen. At the time of the capture of Calcutta, he was Fifth at Cossimbazar and escaped the clutches of the Nabob by his absence at the *aurungs* or up-country factories. The talent and power of successful negotiation displayed by him during the "Troubles" won for him the notice of Clive, and he was placed in 1757 in the difficult post of Resident at Moorshedabad. In 1760 he became a member of Council at Fort William, where his great abilities and his upright dealing stood out in sharp relief against the shortcomings of profligate or blundering colleagues. Returning to England in 1764, with a good name and a poorly stocked purse, he went out five years later as second member of Council at

Fort St. George. While he was doing his best there to relieve the financial disorders consequent on the war with Hyder Ali, he found himself appointed President of the Calcutta Council. The change in his fortunes which now befell him was not quite all that it appeared upon the surface. His salary as Governor-General was fixed at the princely figure of two and a half lakhs of rupees, but his powers were crippled by the appointment of a Council of four members with equal authority to himself at the board. A Supreme Court of Judicature was established at the same time in Calcutta, to consist of a Chief Justice and three puisne Judges.

To the seats in Council were nominated Richard Barwell, a senior member of the Civil Service, Philip Francis, an ex-clerk in the War Office, whose appointment may be held by those who will to have been hush-money to secure the silence of Junius, and General John Clavering and Colonel George Monson, two military officers of distinguished reputation and powerful connections.* Of these, Barwell was alone in India: and when his colleagues landed at Fort William in the month of October, 1774, they were accompanied by their Lordships of the Supreme Court—

* Clavering was colonel of the 52nd Foot, and was brigadier at the attack on Guadeloupe in 1759, where he led the British troops in person. According to Horace Walpole, he was "the real hero of Guadeloupe," and came home "covered with more laurels than a boar's head." Monson, who was the third son of the first Lord Monson, served in the Carnatic wars and was severely wounded at the siege of Pondicherry by Eyre Coote in 1761. He also took part in Sir William Draper's capture of Manilla in the following year. Orme awards him honourable mention for his bravery.—(*Busteed.*)

Sir Elijah Impey, John Hyde, Robert Chambers, the friend and correspondent of Dr. Johnson, and Stephen Cæsar Le Maistre—who had sailed from England at the same time as themselves, but in a different ship. Dr. Busteed in his *Echoes from Old Calcutta* has reproduced in the inimitable language of Macrabie, the brother-in-law and private secretary of Francis, the famous story of the landing and the "Royal Salute" that was expected and was not accorded. From the first the executive and the judicial had been at cross-purposes: and thorny questions of rank and etiquette threatened to create a breach before the voyage had proceeded further than Madeira. But the injured pride of the new Councillors had been mollified by the great pomp with which they were received at Madras, "like fallen angels in a little hell of our own," as Macrabie puts it: and in spite of their jealousy of the Supreme Court who were "sailing better than we do and their Charter gives them precedence," they were prepared to forget their annoyances in view of the triumphal entry into Fort William which was awaiting them. The vessels arrived at Hidgelee at the mouth of the river on the 12th October, 1774: and the next six days were spent in journeying up the river in budgerows. Anchor was cast three miles below the city hard by the spot where the Botanical Gardens now stand: and on the 19th, at ten o'clock, the distinguished passengers, with the members of their staff, were conveyed on the Commodore's barge to the "Swallow" sloop, where they were joined by their rivals of the Supreme Court. "Exactly at noon, a comfortable season for establishing the etiquette of precedency," writes Macrabie, "the whole party are safely disposed in three boats, and both courts safely landed at the capital of their jurisdiction. The procession to the Governor's house beggars all description: the heat, the confusion, not an attempt at regularity. No guards, no persons to receive or to show the way, no state. But surely Mr. Hastings might have put on a ruffled shirt. The ceremony of introduction gone through, the audience broke up, and we changed the scene, but not the climate. At two the whole party, increased by this time to one hundred and fifty, met again at the Governor's house to dine. In such a company little order can be expected. We eat and drank and endeavoured at society, but even wine in ale glasses cannot remove suspicion. At four everybody retired to sleep or meditation. At six rose to tea, dress and go visiting. We welcome all our fair companions to Calcutta."

Calcutta tradition names Chandpal Ghât, to the immediate east of the present High Court, as the scene of the historic landing which Macrabie describes in such picturesque and entertaining fashion: and all the details suggest a procession on foot to Hastings' official residence on the Esplanade. This must not be sought where Government House now stands, although a Government House was then in existence on the eastern portion of the site: but on the plot opposite at the corner of Esplanade Row and Old Court House Street, now occupied by the premises of Messrs. R. Scott Thomson and Company, the chemists.*

* If we are to accept the authority of the late Dr. Ferris, who lived for many years in the house, the initials of Hastings were, until recently, to be seen scratched on a pane of glass in one of the windows.

The installation of the new Government was followed by a brisk interchange of official correspondence between Hastings and the Council. "King Francis the First" (as Calcutta gossips were soon to nickname him) and his colleagues had expected a salute of twenty-one guns from the batteries of Fort William. Hastings accorded them seventeen, and in his despatch to the Court of Directors, he demonstrates clearly enough that his action was in strict compliance with the orders they had given. We may fail, perhaps, to agree with Macaulay when he traces in this personal difference the commencement of "that long quarrel which, after distracting British India, was renewed in England, and in which all the most eminent statesmen and orators of the age took active part on one or the other side." But the fact remains that the skirmish upon the question of the salute was the prelude to a bitter campaign between Hastings and Francis. Barwell, as a rule, supported Hastings in Council: but the votes of Clavering and Monson were pertinaciously cast against him: and the new Governor-General found himself harassed and thwarted at every turn. The differences between the members of Government divided Calcutta into two camps. "Majority" and "Minority" became expressions in common use to denote the partisans. People spoke of their arrival in India as having occurred a very little while before or after "the majority came." Macrabie writes in January, 1776, "Mr. Barwell was at the Governor's last night: 'and pray,' says he, 'what brought you here: coming over to the mincrity, I suppose?' 'Without doubt, Sir,' replied I, 'I breakfasted at your house this morning.'"

It is easy for posterity to sit in judgment after the

lapse of a century and to apportion the blame to this side and that. But if we transport ourselves to the Calcutta of the day, the marvel for consideration is surely not that its inhabitants quarrelled so much, but that they were ever good-tempered at all. "Dulce est desipere," it will be said, has always been the motto of Calcutta even with the thermometer at 104 degrees in the shade. Yet what shall be said of pleasure pursued amid conditions which called for the following outspoken "Guides to health" in the hot weather?:—"Our good friends and readers have been so often told that the weather is very hot, that we shall spare the information, and confine ourselves to some general advice which we presume to offer for the preservation of their health. The gentlemen are particularly entreated not to eat above four pounds of solids at a meal, or drink above six bottles of claret; and to refrain from riding between the hours of ten and four in the day. Dancing will be extremely fatal to the ladies, if taken more than three times a week, and they are positively forbid to wear full dresses of either satin or velvet, until the 1st of November." So far the *Calcutta Gazette* of October 9, 1788, in jest: but the reality is grim enough that lurks behind. To swelter through September and October is deemed a penance by the modern Ditcher, in spite of the alleviations afforded by ice and electric fans. Hastings and Francis hardly knew the luxury of ice, and were denied even the doubtful solace of a swinging punkha. Grandpré found the latter in use in 1789, but they were unknown to Sophia Goldborne, who had the priority of him by seven years. When that sprightly young lady dined out in Calcutta—and the dinner hour, be it remembered, was at two o'clock, when the sun was at its hottest,—she was fain to be content with boys with flappers and fans and to imagine that their exertions produced a "tolerably comfortable artificial atmosphere." There was, moreover, no means of escape from the miseries of the climate. "This bile is the devil," writes Macrabie in September, 1775, tormented by the heat and the heavy suppers and late nights: yet where was he to go? The High Court Judges of to-day think nothing of their annual trip to England: Sir Elijah Impey, and after him Sir William Jones, had to console themselves with a holiday snatched at Chittagong. Francis never moved a hundred miles out of Calcutta, and had no refuge except Barwell's hunting lodge at Baraset, where the draughts were as deep and the play as high as at the Alipore villa *inten paludes*. Hastings sought refreshment in the sea-breezes at Beercool, near Midnapore. For the ordinary man a trip to Chinsurah, or if he were really ill, to Monghyr, had to suffice. Amid such surroundings, the Governor-General and his Council might be excused if they turned to strife as the only galvanizer of their sluggish energies.

We need not follow the historic quarrel through its long and devious course. But there is one incident which cannot be passed over. Closely connected with Calcutta, it furnished in after years one of the principal grounds of accusation against Hastings, and continues to arouse after the lapse of a century the fiercest difference of opinion. It has pleased Burke and Mill and Macaulay to represent Nuncomar as the victim of a judicial murder. Impey, the Chief Justice (Macaulay does not hesitate to say), misused his office to put a man unjustly to death to serve a political purpose: Hastings, struggling for fortune, honour, liberty, stooped to the employment of a false charge to rid himself of an unforgiving and unprincipled enemy. But the cooler judgment of Fitz James Stephen and Malleson has arrived at a very different verdict upon the facts: and the case of Nuncomar stands revealed in its true colours.

Maharajah Nuncomar, or more correctly Nanda Kumar, was a Brahmin of the highest rank. His abilities and address procured for him the confidence of the Moorshedabad Durbar by whom he was ennobled and promoted to important office: and we find him in 1758 recommended to Clive as a suitable person to act as their agent in the collection of the revenues of the districts of Burdwan, Nuddea, and Hooghly, which had been assigned by Meer Jaffer to the Company after Plassey. But he could not resist the allurements of intrigue, and on the accession of Mobaruck-ud-Dowlah, a boy of twelve, as fifth Nawab Nazim, in 1770, he strove to bring about the ruin of the two most powerful officials at Moorshedabad, Mohammed Reza Khan, the Naib Subah, or head of the Native administration in Bengal, and Rajah Sitab Roy, his Hindoo colleague in Behar. Both were dismissed from office by Hastings in 1770. But the misdeeds alleged against them wholly failed to stand the test of an enquiry: and Nuncomar gained nothing beyond the appointment of his son as treasurer of the little Nabob's household. He was himself completely ignored. The real government of Bengal and Behar was handed over to the acknowledged servants of the Company: and the seat of rule, together with the Treasury and the Courts of Justice, finally transferred from Moorshedabad to Calcutta. For the moment he was defeated: but the advent of Francis in 1774 gave him the outlet for revenge for which he was seeking. On the 11th March, 1775, Francis laid before the Board a formal letter addressed to the Governor-General and Council by Nuncomar. In this document a direct charge was laid against Hastings of accepting bribes from Munny Begum, the widow of Meer Jaffer, Mahomed Reza Khan, and others. Two days later, Nuncomar in another letter offered to appear before the Board and give his evidence, oral and documentary. The majority were in favour of accepting the offer. Hastings declared the Council dissolved and quitted the room with Barwell, protesting against acts of the Council during his absence as illegal and unwarranted. Francis and the other two thereupon voted themselves a Council, put Clavering in the chair, went into the charges preferred by Nuncomar, and declared Hastings guilty of having amassed forty lakhs of rupees in two and a half years by all manner of underhand means.

The entire accusation was afterwards proved to be a wilful falsehood founded on letters forged by Nuncomar himself. But the recollection of the episode alone has survived while its attendant circumstances have been forgotten: with the result that a connection has been forced between it and the trial and execution of Nuncomar upon a charge of forgery, which followed close upon it. There is no ground, however, for imputing the initiation of this prosecution to Hastings, or for accusing Impey of acting as his tool. It is true that Hastings lodged a charge of conspiracy and false swearing against Nuncomar, by way of reply to his attempt to use the Council against him. But the matter never came to a hearing, and for this reason. "There had been a litigation of long standing," says Sir J. F. Stephen, "in which the imputation of having forged certain bonds had been cast upon Nuncomar. His antagonist decided to prosecute him criminally and tried to do so many months before the Supreme Court was established, but was unable at that time to get the necessary materials. When the Supreme Court was established, the application was renewed and succeeded: and as soon as the forged document was obtained Nuncomar was brought before the magistrates and committed for trial in the ordinary course." With this case, which related entirely to Nuncomar's private affairs, Hastings cannot be shown to have had any concern. As for Impey's share in the transaction, it need only be stated that the preliminary enquiry was held entirely independently of him and by two of the puisne Judges, Hyde and Le Maistre, who sat, according to the inconvenient procedure of the time, as Justices of the Peace: while the trial was held before the whole Court of four Judges and a Jury, which was not empanelled until Nuncomar had exhausted eighteen out of the twenty challenges allowed him by the law.

Pending the erection of a new court-house on the Esplanade, where its successor stands now, the sittings of the Supreme Court were held in the spacious ground-floor room of the Old Court House, which stood, as we already know, on the site of St. Andrew's Church. Here Nuncomar was arraigned in the summer of 1775. The proceedings were conducted throughout in the most solemn and decorous fashion. The Court sat for eight consecutive days, the intervening Sunday included, from eight in the morning until late at night. There was no adjournment, one of the Judges always remaining in the Court-room or in a room opening out of it, and the jury retiring under charge of the Sheriff's officers to an adjoining room. It was the first week of a Calcutta June, and the heat must have been unbearable. The Judges were arrayed in their red robes and heavy full-bottomed wigs: and calmness and impartiality might well have been deemed at a discount, under the distressing condition in which their Lordships must have found themselves from their heads to their trickling fingers. The invective of Macaulay would rank Impey in the same category as Scroggs and Jeffreys: but the Chief Justice's allocution to the Jury was of the fairest possible character and in striking contrast to many a contemporary summing up of Mansfield and Loughborough in England. The verdict which was returned at four o'clock in the morning of June 16, was an unanimous one of guilty, and, in the opinion of those experts who have studied the evidence, was amply justified. The punishment of death was no abuse of judicial authority, but inflicted in accordance with the law as it then stood and as Sir Elijah Impey and his brother-judges were bound to administer it.

The condemned man petitioned the Council for a respite. Francis and Clavering and Monson, by virtue of the majority they commanded, had it in their power to save his life. But they remained impassive: and on August 5,

1775, Nuncomar was hanged at Cooly Bazar "within a few paces off Fort William," and close to the modern Hastings Bridge. The distasteful duty of attending him to the scaffold devolved upon Macrabie, who had in that year been appointed first Sheriff of Calcutta: and the account of the execution, which he wrote immediately after the event, and which may be read *in extenso* in Dr. Busteed's admirable *Echoes from Old Calcutta,* is interesting reading from the circumstances that he has not a word to say regarding the horror and consternation of the assembled multitude upon which so much imagination was expended by Macaulay, and in earlier days by the first Lord Minto when moving, as Sir Gilbert Elliot, for the impeachment of Impey in 1782. It is certainly likely that the masses of the Hindoo population were shocked by the hanging of a conspicuous Brahmin, and equally probable that those who witnessed it betook themselves to the Ganges to wash out the pollution they conceived had been put upon them by the sight. It may also be that many families of Brahmins forsook the soil of Calcutta and settled in protest at Bally Khal and Utterpara, on the opposite side of the river. But the fact remains that a hundred of the leading Hindoo inhabitants joined in an address to Impey in which they expressed their entire confidence and satisfaction in the Chief Justice and Judges of the Supreme Court.

Hastings held charge of his high office for eleven years: and outlived or outstayed all his three opponents. Monson, who was forty-four when he had left England, enjoyed hardly a day's good health from the time he set foot on Indian soil, and was soon forced to fly to sea to save his life. Two years after his arrival, he resigned his office, sorely stricken with disease: but before he could escape, death clutched him, and he died at Hooghly in September, 1776. Sixteen months of the Calcutta climate had already proved too much for his wife, Lady Anne, and she had been lying since February in the South Park Street burying-ground, when they placed him beside her.* No inscription marks their graves: but Clavering, whose tomb is hard by, has been more fortunate. His turn was not long in coming. He died in August 1777, a month or two after receiving the red ribbon of the Bath. "After a delirium of many hours he expired at half past 2 P.M., and was buried at eight. The Governor ordered minute guns." Such is the entry in the melancholy record headed "Dates of Facts," in which Francis has methodically set down the deaths among those who had accompanied him to Calcutta. He himself left India at the end of 1780, but not before the tension between him and Hastings had culminated, a few months before his departure, in a duel in the Alipore fields. "I do not trust to Mr. Francis's promises of candour, convinced that he is incapable of it," wrote Hastings in a minute read in Council and recorded on the consultations of Government, "I judge of his public conduct by his private, which I have found to be void of truth and honour." After the Council had risen, Francis took the

* Lady Anne Monson was the daughter of Henry Vane, first Earl of Darlington, and through her mother, Lady Grace Fitz Roy, could claim descent from royalty, for her grand-father, the first Duke of Cleveland, was son of Charles the Second by Barbara Villiers (Lady Castlemaine). She must have been at least forty-five when she arrived in India.—(*Busteed.*)

Governor-General into a private room and put into his hands a written challenge, which was immediately accepted. They met on August 17 and Francis was shot in the right side, but not dangerously. He resigned his appointment in the following December and returned to England to enter the House of Commons and to prepare for the next and greater phase of the struggle between them.

It may not be unjust to set down Philip Francis as one of the ablest, fiercest, wrongest-headed and most rancorous of the public men of his day. Yet if, as John Bright has put it, statesmanship consists in foreseeing no less than in doing, he must be adjudged to have earned a high place in Indian history. "The waste of spirits in this cursed country," we find him crying aloud in the bitterness of his heart, "is a disease unconquerable, a misery unutterable." But from the first he determined not to give way to it. "I hate the thought of dying of the spleen, like a rat in a hole. If I had given way to it hereto fore, I should now have been stretched alongside of Clavering, Monson and Le Maistre with a damned *hic jacet* upon my heart. I have many reasons for not wishing to die in Bengal.' Perverse Calcutta has remembered only the personal aspects of his career, and if he lives at all in her memory, it is as the implacable foe of Hastings and the hero of the escapade with the fair and frail Madam Grand,*

* Dr. Busteed has disentangled with untiring diligence the adventures of this eighteenth century Rhodopis. Born in 1762 at the old Danish Settlement of Tranquebar on the Coromandel Coast, she was the daughter of Pierre Werlée, a native of Mauritius, who rose to be master attendant at Chandernagore. She was married in 1777, at the age of 15, to a Company's servant of the name of Grand, and

which cost him fifty thousand rupees in 1779—"siccas, siccas, brother Impey," as his lordship Mr. Justice Hyde was careful to insist. But he has far more solid pretensions to fame. Within a short time after his arrival in Calcutta, he sketched out in a letter to the Prime Minister a plan for the Government of India which was not appreciated for many years, but which was adopted in its main features nearly a century later. Later on, while the tatlers of Calcutta credited him with striving to overcome the mental and physical stagnation of Indian exile with cards and wine, he was in 1775 drawing out and sending home a land-revenue scheme for the permanent settlement of Bengal, which was in all its essentials carried out eighteen years later by Lord Cornwallis. Posterity has elected to associate with the name of that Governor-General the great remedial measure which has secured the prosperity and the happiness of the people of Bengal. But to Philip Francis belongs the credit of its conception and its earliest official advocacy.

His great opponent remained at the head of the Government until February, 1785. The victory was at last his, which for so long had seemed beyond his grasp. "Within

---

speedily became the belle of Calcutta. After the famous night of the 8th March, 1778, when Francis was discovered in her house at Alipore ("at night the *diable à quatre* in the house of G. F. Grand, Esq," as he puts it in his diary) she was established by her "protector" at Hooghly, under a species of chaperonage by Lady Chambers. In December. 1780, she left for Europe, and after an interval of silence reappears in Paris as the wife of Talleyrand, whom she married in 1802. She died in 1835 and lies in a nameless grave in the Montparnasse cemetery.

three years after Francis landed under the guns of Fort William, confident that he held the reversion of India, death had stripped him of the last of his allies, and he stood at bay, alone. It was the memory of those Indian graves and of the bullet which he put into Francis' right side, that stirred Hastings to his stern summary of the struggle: 'My antagonists sickened, died, and fled.'" The later years of his rule were comparatively tranquil: and Calcutta received some share of the attention which he never grudged but which he had been unable to give her. The project for providing the settlement with the church of which she had so long been in need, found in him a hearty supporter. He accepted the office of President of the Building Committee, and from the first busied himself in the matter of obtaining a suitable site. In December, 1783, he was able to inform them that he had been successful, and that he had received from Maharajah Nubkissen a formal gift of the old powder magazine yard, which adjoined the disused burying-ground and now forms the eastern portion of the enclosure of St. John's Church. A week before he resigned the office of Governor-General, he formally conveyed the land to the Building Committee. With characteristic modesty he disclaimed all praise. "It will be sufficient to inform you," he wrote from "Baugulpoor," on February 27, 1784, in a letter which is still to be seen in the Vestry records, "that I have no other share in the appropriation of the ground destined for the new church than in the slight suggestion of it to Maharajah Nubkishon, the proprietor of it, who with a liberality of sentiment which reflects equal Honor on his character and the principles of his Religion, most cheerfully adopted it." His absence up-country did not allow of his laying the foundation stone in the April following the date of this letter: but his exertions were not forgotten, and the stone fitly proclaims for the information of posterity that it was "laid under the auspices of the Hon'ble Warren Hastings, Esquire, Governour of India."

It was under the auspices of Hastings also, that in January of the same year (1784), the Asiatic Society of Bengal embarked upon its honourable career. "That distinguished body," says Macaulay, "selected him to be its first President, but with excellent taste and feeling, he declined the honour in favour of Sir William Jones," who had succeeded jovial card-playing Le Maistre as a judge of the Supreme Court in October, 1783. He contented himself with the office of Patron, and until his death in 1818 his name remained upon the Society's books. The Mahomedan Moulvi and the Brahmin Pundit who stand upon either side of his statue in the Town Hall are indications that his interest in the languages of the East was not simulated. In Persian and Arabic literature he was a recognized proficient: and although he had no personal acquaintance with Sanskrit, he was the first foreign ruler who overcame the jealous distrust of the priestly caste and induced them to reveal the mysteries of Hindoo theology and jurisprudence.

But Hastings possesses yet higher claims upon the gratitude of Calcutta than either the Old Cathedral or the Asiatic Society can exhaust. During the perilous crisis through which England had been passing from 1770 to 1785, the only quarter of the globe in which she had lost nothing was India. Her thirteen colonies in America had cut themselves adrift: she had been compelled to cede Minorca and Florida and other fruits of her victories in former wars. But neither Fort William nor Fort St. George had opened its gates to a hostile army. Those days of humiliation were over: and the credit must be wholly awarded to the skill and resolution of Hastings. The English in India never allowed themselves to forget it, and had it not been for the zeal of Burke and Sheridan and the malevolence of Francis, there was no reward he might not have claimed from his countrymen at home. He left Calcutta in the full blaze of popularity. "On the day on which he delivered up the keys of office," says Macaulay, "a crowd of friends and admirers formed a lane to the quay where he embarked." As many more escorted him down the river. "He would have taken leave of his friends at Diamond Point," we read in *Hartly House,* "but they would not hear of such a thing—their bugeros (budgerows) were well stored with provisions and every requisite, so with pendants flying and bands of music, to the last man and instrument to be found in Calcutta, they attended him to Sawger, the extremity of the river." A very different reception was preparing in England. The curtain had only rung down upon the first act of the drama with the discomfiture and departure of Francis: and when Hastings landed at Plymouth in June, 1785, it was to endure the suspense and the crushing burden of a long-drawn-out impeachment.

CHAPTER IX.

FROM CORNWALLIS TO WELLESLEY.

The successor of Hastings in the office of Governor-General was Charles Earl Cornwallis, who had already played a prominent, if not a glorious, part in the war of American Independence, and was afterwards to suppress the Irish rising in 1798. But he did not arrive in Calcutta until September, 1786: and during the twenty months which immediately followed the departure of Hastings, the government was administered by John Macpherson, the senior member of Council, and a typical "Nabob." He had come out originally to Madras in 1767 as the purser of an East Indiaman, and gained admittance to the Company's service at Fort St. George three years later. Attaching himself to Wala Jah, the Nabob of the Carnatic, he shook the pagoda-tree at Chepauk Palace with such success that when he returned to England in 1776, he proceeded at once to purchase a seat in Parliament. In 1781 he obtained from Lord North the place in Council resigned by Barwell and now found himself in his fortieth year in occupation of the chair. He fully expected the permanent appointment, but had to rest content with a baronetcy. The remaining thirty-three years of his life he spent in England, where he became a close friend and confidant of the Prince Regent. He figures in Hicky's Gazette as The Thane, and being of great stature and of "rare bodily graces," earned also the nickname of the

"Gentle Giant." His administration of Bengal was uneventful, but it was far from edifying, in spite of his boast that he had reduced expenditure by two and a half lakhs. Cornwallis had a very poor opinion of his abilities and principles, and in a letter to Dundas he characterized his methods of government as "a system of the dirtiest jobbery."

The Directors, mindful of the factions which the disagreements of Hastings and Francis had produced, empowered Cornwallis to disregard the votes of his Council: and he was accordingly able to bend all his energies towards the work of reorganization and reform which Pitt had prevailed upon him to undertake. His first task was the removal of the corruption which was rife in all branches of the public service. The efforts of Clive had not been without success, but the scale of official salaries was still entirely inadequate, and the Company's servants availed themselves as freely, as of old, of the opportunities of amassing wealth by every species of official depredation. Cornwallis assigned to each officer of Government a salary sufficient to banish all manner of excuse for private trading and every temptation for increasing his fortune by illicit means. Abuses were put down with a firm hand, fraud was steadily punished, and jobbery and crooked dealing were met with a courage and consistency which soon awakened a wholesome change. The purity of the Indian services rapidly became, and has continued to be, as conspicuous as their venality had been notorious.

The laudatory inscription upon Cornwallis' statue in the Town Hall must be left to tell of his victories over Tippoo and the Mahrattas, and the measures of internal organization which have secured him fame as the author of the Permanent Settlement and the creator of a settled and intelligible code of civil and criminal procedure. With Calcutta his connection was necessarily fitful, owing to his prolonged absence at Fort St. George during the Mysore campaign. And it must be confessed that he does not seem to have loved her overmuch. He writes to his son Lord Brome at Eton that life in the City of Palaces was mere clockwork. "I get on horseback just as the dawn of day begins to appear, ride on the same road and the same distance; pass the whole forenoon after my return from riding in doing business and almost exactly the same portion of time every day at table; drive out in a phæton a little before sunset, then write or read over letters or papers on business for two hours; sit down at nine with two or three officers of my family to some fruit and a biscuit and go to bed soon after the clock strikes ten. I don't think the greatest sap at Eton can lead a duller life than this." But though Calcutta may have seemed a Sleepy Hollow to Cornwallis, he did not fail in his duty by her. It is on record that he presided over the first vestry-meeting of the new church of St. John in 1787, and he was present in state at the formal consecration of the building in June of that year. The minutes tell us further of "two handsome windfalls which accrued to the Church under the favour of Lord Cornwallis," in the shape of the proceeds of certain confiscated goods and of the melting of certain bullion belonging to a State pavilion which had been destroyed by fire. In the north gallery of St. John's Church there stands to this day a bust of the Governor-General bearing an inscription which testifies to his close association with the foundation and consecration of the Old Cathedral.

The administration of Lord Cornwallis witnessed also the disappearance of one of Calcutta's most prominent landmarks. From the date of their arrival in 1775, the Judges of the Supreme Court had sat in the Old Court House which stood at the foot of the street of that name on the site of St. Andrew's Kirk. Wood's map of 1784 shows, however, that their Lordships had migrated by that year to the "New Court House" on the western Esplanade on the spot now occupied by the High Court: and the Old Court House was finally pulled down in 1792. Many were the memories surrounding the vanished building. *Asiaticus,* writing in 1802, traces its origin to the liberality of Robert Bourchier, second in Council at Fort William and Master Attendant of the Port in 1731, and later, from 1750 to 1760, Governor of Bombay, who gave it to the Company to be used for a charity school. Another tradition, preserved in the minutes of St. John's Vestry as late as 1787, connected it with the name of Omichand, and credited the famous Sikh millionaire with bequeathing its rent to the charity fund, which supported and educated the children of British subjects in indigent circumstances and was the parent of the Free School of to-day. But Omichand died in 1763, and the letters of Gervas Bellamy, the gallant old chaplain who perished in the Black Hole, prove that the house had been built by public subscription thirty years before. Erected in the first instance to serve as a charity school it certainly was: but it was rented at an early stage of its existence by the authorities of the Mayor's Court, which was established by statute in 1727: and in Wills' Map, drawn in 1753, it figures under the familiar name of the "Court House." Here for a quarter of a century the predecessors of Impey and Hyde administered justice: the Mayor sitting in full official dress on a velvet cushion, and the nine Aldermen arrayed in all the glory of red taffety gowns. Orme, writing of it in 1756, describes it as "a very spacious house of one floor in which the Mayor's Court and assizes used to be held." If this description is correct, it must have been rebuilt after the "Troubles." For an excellent representation of the House, as it appeared in 1786, may be seen among Thomas Daniell's Views, and it is there pictured as a fine two-storeyed building with a portico running along its whole length and surmounted by a wide verandah. The lower floor was used as the Court-room. Of the upper floor, Stavorinus, the Dutch Admiral who visited Calcutta in 1770, has left a description: "Over the Court House are two handsome assembly rooms. In one of these are hung up the portraits of the King of France and of the late Queen, as large as life, which were brought up by the English from Chandernagore, when they took the place." There is no mention, it will be noticed, of the busts of the Twelve Cæsars, which also were at one time among the ornaments of the Court House Assembly Room, and have accompanied the pictures to Government House. They must be of later date, if the generally accepted explanation of their presence in Calcutta be correct, which declares them to have been a present from the French King to the Nizam of Hyderabad, and to have been captured on the high seas along with the ship that was conveying them. The reference of Stavorinus is of course to the capture of Fort Orleans in March, 1757, when the dreams of Dupleix were shattered by Clive and Watson, and the French Settlement razed to the ground in reprisal for Lally's destruction of the English factors' houses at Fort St. David.

Old Chandernagore never recovered from the merciless punishment meted out to her. Captain Brohier, the English Company's Engineer, carried out his masters' mandate so thoroughly that "only a few indigent widows' huts" were left standing in what had once been a city of a hundred thousand inhabitants. Yet with the breaking out of the Revolution in France, she was able once again to excite a momentary flutter of anxiety in the breasts of her English neighbours at Calcutta. The Republic of Chandernagore sounds almost as absurd as the principality of Monaco or the independent state of Andorra: but the political antics of the colony, after the receipt of the news of the taking of the Bastille, recall the worst excesses of communards and pétroleuses. A ragamuffin rabble, headed by a broken-down advocate and a bankrupt merchant, plundered the town, made a bonfire of the public records and indulged themselves freely with the madeira in the Governor's cellars. De Montigny, the Governor, retired to Gyretty, the famous country-house built on the ruins of the palace of Dupleix and described by Grandpré as the finest building in India. Here he fortified himself with a dozen families, to whom the cry of liberty and equality did not appeal. But the mob, on hearing that Louis the Sixteenth had been brought in triumph from Versailles to Paris, determined that they would not be behind time, and took their Governor by force from his entrenchment and shut him up in the jail at Chandernagore with all his officers.

It may be imagined that this state of anarchy did not fail to excite the liveliest anxiety at Calcutta. Lord Cornwallis sent a demand for the instant release of De Montigny. The defiant sansculottes, deterred only from repeating the September massacres by the fear of the neighbouring Nabob whom Madame la Répubique could not afford to offend, loaded their prisoners with chains and sent them down the river in a pilot brig for conveyance to the Isle of France. The Governor-General stopped the vessel as it passed Fort William and released the captives. Chandernagore meanwhile continued in a perpetual state of ferment. A new President was elected every fortnight, and a descent upon the bazars of Chinsurah and even of Calcutta was threatened repeatedly. It became necessary to end the " reign of terror " : and on the breaking out of hostilities between England and France in 1793, a detachment of British troops marched into Chandernagore. For the next twenty-two years the Union Jack floated over the spot upon which Dupleix had dreamed of founding an Eastern Paris : and it was not until 1816 that the Settlement was handed back to the representatives of King Louis the Eighteenth. The glory of the Settlement was now finally departed : and for nearly a century an administrateur and twenty-five cipahis have represented the only remnants of French power left in Bengal.

Lord Cornwallis resigned in 1793, and was followed by

Sir John Shore, a Bengal Civilian of long standing and integrity, and a recognized expert in revenue matters, who was, a few months before his retirement in 1798, elevated to the Irish peerage as Lord Teignmouth.* An important stage in the history of Calcutta was reached in the year after his assumption of the reins of government. The time-honoured office of Zemindar, which had for seventy years been charged with the "care of public order, convenience and health," not only in Calcutta but in the suburbs, was relieved of its municipal authority in 1794. Justices of the Peace were appointed under a statute of King George the Third and entrusted with the management of the Town. In the next year the first regular assessment was made, and a system of organised municipal government was for the first time attempted.

By another provision of the same statute, the duty was enjoined of accurately defining the boundary between the Town proper and the suburbs: and by a proclamation dated the 10th September, 1794, the lines of demarcation were

---

* Shore was an intimate friend of Warren Hastings, who addressed to him a set of verses in imitation of the *otium divos* of Horace. The stanzas, which were written during Hastings' last voyage to England in 1785, are of an indifferent order: but one of them will bear quotation from the personal note it strikes:—

"No fears his peace of mind annoy
"Lest printed lies his fame destroy,
"Which labour'd years have won:
"Nor pack'd committees break his rest
"Nor avarice sends him forth in quest
"Of climes beneath the sun."

laid down. The limit of Calcutta on the west was declared to be a line drawn at low-water mark along the western side of the Hooghly river, "but excluding the ghauts of Ramkissenpore, Howrah and Sulkea," and extending as far as "the brook called Chitpore Nullah or Bag Bazar Nullah," which formed the northern boundary. On the east, the dividing line was provided by the Mahratta Ditch and the Lower Circular Road, or, as it was then called, the Boytaconnah Road, as far as the turning into Ballygunge Circular Road, "thereby including the Protestant burying-ground, Chowringhee, and the land thereto belonging to Dhee Birjee," which is the district lying between Park Street and Theatre Road, Chowringhee being to the north of it. The southern boundary began from the point in the Boytaconnah Road, where the eastern boundary ended, and ran along that road skirting Birjee talao, the great tank near the Cathedral of to-day, and the Presidency Jail, but excluding the General Hospital and "Dhee Bowanipore," until Alipore or Belvedere Bridge was reached, when it followed the southern bank of Tolly's Nullah to the river past Surman's Bridge, which we have ungratefully named Kidderpore Bridge. Outside these boundaries lay the "Suburbs," made up of the Panchannagram or fifty-five villages which lay beyond the Ditch, and had been added to Calcutta out of the Twenty-four Pergunnahs granted by Meer Jaffer in 1757. For revenue purposes they formed part of Calcutta, but their legal existence was separate and distinct. The boundaries of the town, as laid down by this Proclamation, have remained in force ever since as the limits of the jurisdiction, first of the old Supreme Court, and, from 1862, of the original side of the High Court, which has taken its place: but, so far as the municipal limits are affected, they ceased to exist in 1888. They will be found clearly given in the reproduction made by Baillie in 1792 of Wood's map of 1784, as well as in the map published by Upjohn in April, 1794, although both are prior in date to the proclamation.

An inspection of these maps will reveal other features of interest as illustrating the growth of Calcutta. Many of the streets are now named, and there is quite an imposing array of references in the key plan. In the earlier maps it had been deemed sufficient to indicate the principal thoroughfares as the "road to the Court House," the "avenue leading eastward," the "road to Surman's," the "northern road to Perrin's Garden," or the "Jorabagan road," the last named being so called because it led from the river to the twin garden-houses of Omichand and Govindram Mitter. We now come across a host of names, familiar and unfamiliar. Hastings Street has taken the place of the Creek which once shut in the English quarter of Calcutta on the south. From Chandpaul Ghaut, hard by the New Court House on the riverside, Esplanade Row runs into Dhurrumtollah in a straight line past the Council House and Government House, then standing side by side, for we have still five years to wait before the laying of the foundations of the "new Government House." To the north of the modern Government House compound is Wheler Place, which runs into Old Court House Street, but has no outlet towards Hastings Street. There is no Wellesley Place, and access to Larkins' Lane and Fancy Lane is obtained by a narrow tortuous gully which bears the appropriate name of Corkscrew Lane. Neither the Eden Gardens nor Baboo Ghaut are in existence, and the Maidan is strangely treeless. But on the south of Esplanade Row is the Esplanade, a wide expanse of grass stretching to the new Fort and "a favourite promenade of elegant walking parties on moonlight evenings." Between Chandpaul Ghaut and Colvin's Ghaut, then called Cucha-goody Ghaut, from the fact that country boats were used to be hauled up on the banks of the neighbouring creek, is King's Bench Walk with a row of trees separating it from the riverbank. This was also a fashionable resort, and was exclusively reserved for the English inhabitants from 5 to 8 o'clock every evening, sentries being posted "near the sluice-bridge" to prevent the entrance of natives. Old Court House Street cuts Esplanade Row at right angles then, as it still does, and its prolongation across the Maidan to Kidderpore Bridge past the new Fort is clearly visible. The Red Road has not come into existence as a name, and "The Course" is indicated as occupying the site of the Race-Course to the west of the Jail. The river is shown flowing close up to the walls of the Fort. A flourishing industry was being carried on at Kidderpore at Colonel Watson's ship-building yard, which was just outside the limits of the town of Calcutta. Burying-ground Road, which we have more euphoniously termed Park Street, connects Chowringhee Road with the English burying-ground on the edge of Lower Circular Road and the adjoining Short's Bazar, which survives to-day in Short Street. At its junction with Chowringhee Road, it is continued past the "New Tank," which still exists, to meet the Road across the Maidan to Kidderpore, at the point where Lord Dufferin's statue now stands. Sir Robert Chambers is now Chief Justice: but Impey's mansion with its wooded Park on the site of the "Company's garden" of Queen Anne's day is still a conspicuous feature on the southern side of Burying-ground Road, amid the general absence of trees on the Maidan which obtrudes itself so forcibly upon the modern observer.

The "west end" is rapidly coming into existence. Camac Street, Russell Street, Middleton Street, Harington Street, and Theatre Road, are all depicted, but unnamed. Both sides of Circular Road are studded with houses, and a most remarkable alteration is noticeable along Chowringhee Road. This thoroughfare, singularly enough, bears no designation in Upjohn's map, and the reason is not far to seek. Chowringhee is in reality the name of a locality or village and denotes properly "The Square," bounded by Colinga on the north, by Park Street on the south, by Circular Road on the east, and by the Maidan on the west. In Colonel Mark Wood's map of 1784, this is made quite plain by the marking of that part of the existing Chowringhee road from Dhurrumtolla to Park Street as the "Road to Chowringhy." The quarter was then quite out of town, and its houses were called "country houses." And as lately as 1852, there was alive an old lady in Calcutta, Mrs. Ellerton, the friend of Bishop Wilson, who was able to assure the Rev. Mr. Long, that she "recollected when there were only two houses in Chauringi." Her statement finds corroboration in a map of Calcutta drawn in 1757, in which there are only a couple of houses shown in what we know as Chowringhee

Road, the one at the corner of Dhurrumtollah and entered from that street, the other a little distance from it, with an entrance facing the Maidan. For Mrs. Ellerton to have seen them, these houses must have continued in isolation until the last twenty-five or thirty years of the century. By the time at which we have now arrived, however, a complete transformation had taken place. Between Corporation Street, or Jaun Bazar Road, as it was then called, and Park Street, forty European residences, mostly with large compounds, are depicted in Upjohn's Map in "Colingah and Chouringhy" and an equal number may be counted in Dhee Birjee, the quarter immediately south of Park Street. The care with which this new European quarter has been mapped out, is apparent. "In this part of the town," notes Mr. Beverley in his census report for 1876, "the streets are laid out with perfect regularity, very different from the rest of the town, which presents a network of lanes and bye-lanes, the irregularity of which shows that they arose spontaneously out of the necessity of the times without any regard to public convenience and apparently without the slightest control on the part of the authorities."

In the centre of Old Calcutta there is much to puzzle the visitor of to-day. There is no Bank of Bengal on the Strand Road: it commenced its career in 1806 as the Government Bank of Calcutta, and did not receive its charter and present name until 1809, when Lord Minto had been Governor-General for two years. The Mint stands in Church Lane opposite St. John's Church, on the site of the Stationery Office, where Gillet's ship-building establishment had once utilized the creek. It was not removed to its present quarters in the Strand Road, beyond the Hooghly Bridge, until 1832, during the Government of Lord William Bentinck. The Post Office must be sought in the street of that name, now crowded with barristers' chambers and solicitors' offices. But it cannot have been there very long, for in 1789 we find Mrs. Eliza Fay, the authoress of the *Original Letters from India,* representing to the Vestry of St. John's that four years previously she had purchased "the house at the south-western corner of the old burying-ground" (and therefore at the corner of Hastings Street and Church Lane) "which was formerly the Post Office," and complaining that the new boundary wall of the churchyard blocked the light from her lower windows. Hare Street does not appear to have been opened out, and the Marine House or "Bankshall" stands in place of the Small Cause Court. Just about the site of the Metcalfe Hall there are the words "new dock," marking the location at Bankshall Ghaut of the first dry dock in Calcutta, built by Government in 1790, and removed in 1808. Koilah Ghaut Street figures as Tackshall Street, running, as it still does, at right angles to Bankshall Street, and is so named from the Custom House or "Tackshall" at the south-western corner of the Old Fort, which cumbers the whole of the western side of Tank Square. There is no Fairlie Place, but to the north of the Fort is the Old Fort Ghaut, and that part of Dalhousie Square which leads into Clive Street and is now called Charnock Place, is named Old Fort Street. St. Anne's Church has disappeared long since from the north-western corner of the Square. For twenty years after the

"Troubles" the site, together with the land intervening between it and the Old Court House, remained waste: and in 1776 it was conveyed by the Council to Thomas Lyons. The fruit of the transaction may be seen in Writers' Buildings, pictured by Daniell in 1780 as a long three-storied bungalow of the plainest possible construction, and in Lyons' Range which is immediately in rear of them. On the south side of the Square stood a little later Lord Wellesley's short-lived College for the Company's newly-arrived writers, which was intended to make the establishment of Haileybury unnecessary, but which closed its doors in 1828 after a life that began with the century. At the western end of Lyons' Range is the Theatre, where the door-keepers are Europeans, for "the black people, in an office of that nature, would have no authority with the public," and Theatre Street, now merged in New China Bazar Street. Along the river bank, the attention is arrested by the large number of ghauts. There are no less than thirty-six of them between Chandpaul Ghaut, the southernmost, and Old Powder Mill Ghaut, in the extreme north; some, like the last named with its memories of Perrin's Redoubt and Colonel Scott's magazine, recall the past; others are named after individuals, English and Indian, and one after a lady, Mrs. Ross.

The purely Indian quarter of the town, as shown in these maps, is thickly populated. Rajah Nubkissen, who had died in 1791 at the age of 66, is the only Indian whose name stands affixed to any building. His home on the road leading to Shambazar and Halsibagan is the identical house occupied by his great-grandson Rajah Rajendra Narayan Deb in very recent years. Beyond the Mahratta Ditch and the Chitpore Creek, and almost opposite Sulkea, was the palace of another Indian dignitary. The Chitpore Nawab, Mahomed Reza Khan, was once Naib-Subadar and Naib Nazim of Bengal, with supreme control over the revenues and police of the province. After his deprivation of authority by Warren Hastings in 1772, and his acquittal of the charges brought against him by Nuncomar, he lived here in great state. That well-informed young lady, the authoress of "Hartly House," elevates him to the height of "Viceroy to the Mogul, in like manner with your Lord Lieutenant of Ireland, and the representative of his most sublime master." The commanding officer of his guard, which consisted of a whole battalion of black troops, was an Englishman, the "younger brother of an ennobled family, who paid Rs. 80,000, acquired in this world of wealth, for the appointment." The buildings and gardens were sumptuously furnished and laid out in English style. "The exterior of Chitpore in some degree bespeaks the grandeur of its owner," continues Miss Sophia Goldborne, "but I am apprised that few things exceed the magnificence of its interior architecture and ornaments. The apartments are immense, the baths elegant, and the seraglio, though a private one, suited in every particular to the rest of the building: nor must the gardens be unmentioned, for they not only cover a wide extent of ground but are furnished with all the beauties and perfumes of the vegetable kingdom." The Chitpore Nawab, as he was styled, lived on terms of intimacy with the "powers" of the day and was accounted by them a personage of the first rank. The foreign Governors—Danish, French and Dutch—on their visits to Calcutta from Serampore, Chandernagore and Chinsurah, made it the practice to halt at Chitpore, where a deputation received them, and they then rode in state to Government House, mounted on the Nawab's splendid elephant and attended by his guard-of-honour.

It was perhaps just as well for the owner of the glories of Chitpore that they were displayed at a distance of some four miles from Fort William. For in the month of May, 1798, the office of Governor-General was assumed by Richard, Earl of Mornington and Marquess Wellesley. The "Akbar of the Company's dynasty" was not the man to tolerate two kings in Brentford: and if he neglected to reap the field close at hand, it was because his scythe was busy during the seven years of his rule with the taller poppies that reared their heads outside the confines of British territory. How narrow were the limits of Bengal as he found them, two examples will serve to demonstrate. When Richmond Thackeray, the novelist's father, was posted in 1800 as Assistant to the "Chief" of Midnapore, the Mahrattas were still in possession of Orissa. The Company's factory on the frontier was the scene of many an "act of violence" and "depredation," and it was not until 1803 that Cuttack and Balasore were annexed by Wellesley to British India. Towards the north the treaty of Lucknow in 1801 rendered the English masters of the heart of Rohilkhand. Yet, when Lord Valentia paid his visit to the "Ceded Provinces" in February, 1803, he notes, after leaving Jaunpore, that he had "passed the boundaries of the East India Company's territory, and entered that of His Excellency the Nabob Vizier." Allahabad had in those days just been promoted to the position of frontier-depôt till then occupied by Monghyr, and the most stringent regulations as to traffic were in force at Buxar. No one was permitted to visit the Upper Provinces without a pass; and all vessels passing up or down the Ganges, as well as every traveller by land, were detained and sent back to the place from whence they had come, if their papers were not strictly *en règle*. Lord Valentia had intended to visit Agra and Delhi, and had received "very polite invitations from Colonel Perron and the Begum Soomroo to stay some time with them on the way;" but "the changeable conduct of Scindiah made it doubtful from the first" whether their hospitable offers could be accepted. Not only was the expedition abandoned, but the journey from Lucknow to Futtyghur and Kanauj was declared impossible without the escort of a company of sepoys of the 10th Native Infantry and twenty sowars.

The mere recital of an itinerary such as this is sufficient to indicate the nature of the task which Wellesley set before him. He brought to bear upon it an imperious will and an authority no less ample: and he succeeded. *Monumentum si quaeris, circumspice.* We have only to unroll the map of India of to-day and to compare it with the map as it stood at the dawn of the nineteenth century, in order to realise how full and how complete has been the development and the fulfilment of Wellesley's policy during the past hundred years.

CHAPTER X.

CALCUTTA A HUNDRED YEARS AGO.

WITH the advent of Wellesley, the time approaches when we must take our leave of the Calcutta of "beauties balloon'd and powder'd beaus," in which Englishmen pulled at *hookahs* and lived in Oriental state, and fortunes were still to be made by shaking the pagoda-tree. But it is hard to resist the temptation of a sentimental journey into this land of dreams, before we bid a final farewell. Wonderful as the transformation in the political aspect of the country has been, the alteration in our social manners and customs has been even more striking. Let us linger awhile and attempt to throw upon the canvas a representation of the lives our forefathers led in Calcutta a hundred years ago.

There is, perhaps, nothing in which we differ more remarkably from them than in the distribution of our time. In the early days of Calcutta, the midday dinner and the afternoon siesta were recognised institutions. "The dinner hour here is two," wrote Mrs. Fay, the wife of a Calcutta barrister in the days of Warren Hastings, who was so unwise as to quarrel with his Chief Justice, "and it is customary to sit a long while at table; particularly during the cold weather. During dinner a good deal of wine is drank, but very little after the cloth is removed, except in bachelors' parties, as they are called; for the custom of reposing, if not of sleeping, after dinner is so general that the streets of Calcutta are, from four to five in the afternoon, almost as empty of Europeans as if it were midnight. Next come the evening airings on the course, where everyone goes, though sure of being half-suffocated with dust. On returning thence, tea is served, and universally drank here even during the extreme heats. After tea, either cards or loo fill up the space till ten, when supper is usually announced. Formal visits are paid in the evening; they are generally very short, as perhaps each lady has a dozen calls to make, and a party waiting for her at home besides. Gentlemen also call to offer their respects, and if asked to put down their hats, it is considered as an invitation to supper." Begum Johnson, the grandmother of the Earl of Liverpool, who died in Calcutta in 1812, at the age of 87, and who had been the wife of a Member of Council in the days of Colonel Clive and the Black Hole, prided herself on keeping up these old usages to the last. She would dine in the afternoon at three or four o'clock, take her siesta after dinner, and then her airing in her carriage. On her return home, her house in Clive Street would be lit up and thrown open for the reception of visitors until ten o'clock at night. All who were on visiting terms were expected to come without invitation, and a few who had been previously invited stayed to supper and cards.

With such a daily programme to fulfil, it may be supposed that Calcutta arose betimes in the closing years of the eighteenth century; and as a matter of fact, the work was all performed in the cool hours of the morning, in order to leave the remainder of the day free. The modern tiffin does not make its appearance until the new century; when the dinner hour, which had gradually been growing later and later, found itself suddenly thrown back to the evening, and the forenoon visits took the place of the evening call between eight and nine o'clock. Lord Valentia, who visited Calcutta during the Governor-Generalship of Lord Wellesley, tells us that it was "usual in Calcutta to rise early, in order to enjoy the cool air of the morning, which is particularly pleasant before sunrise. At twelve they take a hot meal, which they call 'tiffing,' and they generally go to bed for two or three hours. The dinner hour is commonly between seven and eight; which is certainly too late in this hot climate, as it prevents an evening ride in the proper time and keeps them up till midnight or later."

Anglo-Indians are nothing if not conservative: and it is curious to notice how little they had altered their methods of spending the day when Mrs. Fenton, wife of a subaltern and first cousin to the famous Lawrence brothers, came to jot down her impressions of India as she found it in 1827, in the days of Earl Amherst of Arracan, whose title tells the tale of the main achievement of his reign. The voyager of to-day considers himself mightily aggrieved if he is not brought alongside the jetties within twelve hours of sighting the pilot-brig at the Sandheads. He would learn to possess his soul in patience, if he were condemned to make his entry into Calcutta after the manner of Mrs. Fenton and those of her generation. For on arrival in the Hooghly the Company's ships lay off Kedjeree, which was, up to 1824, quite a populous town, and boasted of several taverns, where passengers were accustomed to stay for several days on landing from the outward bound Indiamen, or while waiting for the sailing of the vessels in which they had taken their passage. The sea has now-a-days washed away all vestige of these buildings; and all traces have likewise disappeared of the "Great Eastern" of the day, which was established at Fulta in 1800 for the accommodation of "families and single ladies" who had to embark and disembark at that uninviting spot on account of the wind and tide. Mrs. Fenton's Indiaman, following the fashion of its kind, cast anchor at Kedjeree, and her passengers were left to make their own way up the river by boat. No stay was made at Fulta: but a halt was called, just before reaching Calcutta, at the house of Mr. Cleland at Garden Reach; and here the new-comer was left while her husband went on ahead to report his arrival. Her first introduction to Anglo-Indian surroundings is described with much humour. The ladies of the family are discovered at breakfast, and she notes with amazement that they quietly light up their cheroots at the end of the meal. Her bedroom is another source of sad perplexity to her. "'My powers!' thought I, 'who could sleep in a room where four doors and four windows all stand open?'" As she tries to do so without a mosquito-curtain, the attempt is not very successful. At twelve, she sallies out for tiffin and comes upon the hostess and her friend bargaining with the "boxwaller" and flinging his wares at his head, because he demands too high a price. Of tiffin, she records the curious detail that "it is no other than a small dinner, excepting that the dishes are placed on the table without a cloth, which at first had an unpleasant appearance." After lunch, the ladies subject their guest to a searching cross-examination as to the last English fashions, "length of waists and shape of sleeves and shoes." At two o'clock the questions cease and everyone goes to sleep: and at four comes the evening ride or drive. The master of the house arrives from Calcutta at seven, and at eight dinner is announced, "a long tedious formal meal." More cheroot smoking is indulged in, "by all present but myself:" and after tea has been served in the drawing-room, the yawns of the household speedily lead to retirement for the night, or at all events, for part of it. For, at four o'clock in the morning, "while it is yet utterly dark," there is an universal stir throughout the house, much talk of horses, hats, whips and coffee; and a voice at the door enquiring whether a ride or a drive will be preferable. After the outing, bed is naturally enough the popular refuge until eight o'clock, when the bewildering round recommences with "breakfast and cheroots."

Of the prevailing tone of Anglo-Indian Society in her day, Mrs. Fenton does not paint a very attractive picture. The man who came out to India when the nineteenth century was young, had to make up his mind to live there for an indefinite period: and the absence of comforts, which we regard as indispensable, combined to produce languor, gloom and disgust. Nor was the country as healthful to Europeans as we find it to-day. Sudden death forms the groundwork of many of Mrs. Fenton's anecdotes and stories. But her reminiscences are not all so melancholy or so tragic. Heber was then touching the close of his episcopate, and there is a reference to his wife in quite another vein. "The other evening," runs the entry in the diary, "I heard Mrs. Heber's name frequently repeated, and rather with some terms bordering on censure. There was something she had done which was pronounced 'not consistent with strict propriety.' I was considerably relieved to find it was some particular trimming omitted on her bonnet."

The eight o'clock dinner, in spite of Lord Valentia's warning and Mrs. Fenton's depreciation of its length and its tediousness, has survived to this day. But the afternoon siesta is a thing of the past, and along with it the "pucka fever," which used to attack the sleeper, and result in the invitation of those, who had dined with him at noon, to his funeral before supper time. In the matter of drinks, the days of Hodgson and Bass were yet to come and go, and the favourite liquors, Lord Valentia tells us, were claret and madeira, "the latter, which is excellent, during the meal, the former afterwards;" the claret, he adds, being medicated for the voyage, is too strong and has little flavour. Those with a more slender purse, and especially the young military men, indulged in sherbet and punch. The latter indeed, whose very name betokens its Indian origin and its five ingredients, seems to have been the first beverage to which Englishmen in India addicted themselves—and in many cases it was certainly the last. But the days were slipping by of hard-drinkers and of men whose "lives were not worth two monsoons." By the beginning of the century, the change had become sufficiently marked to call for the comment of visitors to Calcutta. People continued to flock to the East in search of a fortune, but they no longer considered that the only alternative lay in dying of a fever.

Yet, if they were more temperate, they were not less extravagant than the Nabob of the days of Holwell and Francis. There was no question then of saving up for the three months' privilege leave to Europe: and the money was more freely spent in India itself. The number of servants kept was as astonishing as ever: and Macrabie's satire upon them had lost none of its point after the lapse of thirty years. Lord Valentia's constant concern during his travels in India was the enormous *suwarry* or retinue, which his high rank and dignity were held to require. "We had eight elephants, eleven camels, four horses, ten bullocks of our own, besides *tattoos* (ponies) and bullocks belonging to our servants." Such is Mountstuart Elphinstone's description of the cavalcade which accompanied him and Edward Strachey across India in 1801. And the men were as numerous as the animals. "We had twenty sepoys and from one hundred and fifty to two hundred servants and coolies." A Governor-General suffered naturally in proportion. When the Marquess of Hastings started in 1814 upon his progress up-country, his fleet consisted of no less than four hundred boats. "I drive out almost every evening," writes Lord Minto in 1807, "but the formality of these airings is uncomfortable to a degree that I cannot at all accustom myself to. Four syces with flyflappers ran alongside of the horses until I positively rebelled against this annoyance. It is still worse with a palanquin. Thirty people go before in two lines, which extend a great way forward. They carry gold and silver maces and halberds and embroidered fans, and cows' tails to keep the flies off. All these run on foot at a round trot, some of them proclaiming my titles: which, as the proclamation is rather long, I imagine must be Hindustanee for Gilbert Elliot, Murray of Melgund and Kynynmound of that ilk." This was, it is true, rather a relic of old times, when, as a gentleman assured Heber, he had himself heard at the dinner-party of one of the Company's civil servants, a herald proclaiming aloud all the great man's titles; but even in the twenties, each functionary had quite a regiment of servants attached to him. Even children were not suffered to escape. "A Lady told us," writes Heber in 1824, "that she had seen a little boy of six years old paraded in a pony phæton and pair, with his *ayah* or nurse, coachman, *chattah-burdar* or umbrella-bearer, a *saees* on each side, and another behind, leading a third pony, splendidly caparisoned, not in case the young sahib should chuse to ride, he was too young for that—but, as the *saees* himself expressed it, 'for the look of the thing.'"

Mrs. Fenton is quite as entertaining when she tells us of her numerous household. The *khansama,* who demands meekly on entering her service to know "whether mem-sahib is very passionate," claims it as his privilege, not only to charge commission at the rate of two annas in the rupee on his bazar, but to "carry in the first dish, the soup, and standing behind his lady's chair to superintend." "The mission in life of the durwan is to search the persons of your friends' *khidmutgars* whenever you give a *burra khana,* in order to make sure that none of your spoons and forks are disappearing along with them." To the *mussulgee* is assigned the duty of holding the lanthorn, "which none of the bearers will do, as perchance it might have been made of a cow." The "Balasore" bearers of the day were, in fact, a troublesome class. They refused to touch a washing-basin: and in one of Sir Charles D'Oyly's series of water-colour drawings representing the life of an European in India, the bearer is seen holding a towel ready to dry his master's foot as soon as a servant of lower caste has washed it. Perhaps it is the multiplicity of servants, with their prejudices and their fancies, that leads Mrs. Fenton to remark mournfully that "the times are for ever gone when people made a fortune in India."

But, however true this might be of the days of Amherst, there was a rich harvest of mohurs to be made under Cornwallis and Wellesley. It was no longer merely John Company's servants who amassed money. The lawyers, thanks to the Supreme Court, had overtaken them in the race. "A man of abilities and good address in this line, if he has the firmness to resist the fashionable contagion, gambling, need only pass seven years of his life at Calcutta to return home in affluent circumstances." Physic, as well as law, was "a gold mine for its professors to work it at will." Nor was the Church without its opportunities. "Weddings," we are told, "are very joyous things for all parties: especially, I should suppose, to the Padra, who frequently receives twenty gold mohurs for his trouble in performing the ceremony."

Whether for business or pleasure, the palanquin was the usual method of conveyance a hundred years ago (as Lord Minto has just reminded us) and so gilded and covered with brocade was it, that three thousand rupees often only barely represented its cost. Carriages were not very common, although Lord Valentia notes that "most gentlemen" kept them. The fact was, there was little to invite the pleasure of a drive. The streets were unmetalled and there were other discomforts, not to say dangers. In 1805 we read of a family returning home one evening and encountering an elephant on Esplanade Row opposite the tank at the corner of Dhurrumtollah with the result that "the horses got wild and ran the carriage on to the drain close to Mr. Brady's house, and upset it." There was no Strand Road in those days, and in the time of Heber it was still unfinished. The only drive was the Course, so called according to Mrs. Kindersley, who wrote in 1768, because the length was a *koss,* or two miles; and judging from all accounts, it seems to have been dusty and very crowded. According to the old poem, one swallowed ten mouthfuls of dust for one of fresh air; but it was the place to which every one flocked of an evening and was "the scene," we are assured, "of various gradations of equestrian grace and charioteering excellence, the very Rotten Row of our Eastern emporium."

"Sedate they quit the ruminating chair,
"And breathe abroad the evening dust and air,

"As dips the sun, of dazzling splendour shorn,
"When the wide Fort resounds the evening horn,
"Full many a soddened form, in jacket white,
"Wings on the thronging course his airy flight,
"Borne on the steed, or perched, with whip and reins,
"In a dear specimen of Steuart's pains."*

There was one peculiar accompaniment of the evening drive which we shall look for in vain to-day. "The *mussalchees,*" says Lord Valentia, "when it grows dark, go out to meet their masters on their return, and run before them, at the rate of full eight miles an hour, and the numerous lights moving along the Esplanade produce a singular and pleasing effect." The alternative to the drive on the dusty course was boating "in the delightful boats and upon the pleasant waves of the Ganges." Gentlemen kept their mourpunkeys, or snake-boats, and trips to Sook Saugor or to Chandernagore were often made. These "snake-boats" were very long and narrow, not more than eight feet in breadth and often upwards of a hundred in length. They were paddled by thirty or forty men, and steered by a large paddle from the stern, which was either in the shape of a snake, a peacock, or some other animal. "In one part of the stern is a canopy supported by pillars, on which are seated the owner and his friends who partake of the refreshing breezes of the evening." Lord Valentia came

* The firm of Steuart and Co. will still be found plying their coachmaker's business in an old house in Old Court House corner behind St. Andrew's Church. The poem from which the extract is taken is entitled "Calcutta in 1811."

up the river in 1803 in Lord Wellesley's state barge, which was evidently a boat after this pattern. His journey in it reminded him, he says, of the fairy tales. "It was very long in proportion to its width; richly ornamented with green and gold: its head, a spread eagle gilt; its stern, a tiger's head and body. The centre would contain twenty people with ease, and was covered with an awning and silk curtain; forward were seated twenty natives dressed in scarlet habits with rose-coloured turbans, who paddled away with great velocity."

Twenty years later, Heber was equally struck with the magnificence of Lord Amherst's state barges. "Of these," he writes, "there are two: the largest is called the *Sunamookee,* and is a splendid but heavy gilt and painted barge rigged like a ketch with a dining-room and a bed-room. The other is the *Feel Churra,* elephant bark, from having its head adorned with that of an elephant, with silver tusks. It is a large, light and beautiful canoe paddled by twenty men, who sit with their faces towards the head, with one leg hanging over the side of the boat, and the great toe through a ring fastened to its side. They keep time with their paddles, and join occasionally in chorus with a man who stands in the middle, singing what I was assured were verses of his own composition, sometimes amatory, sometimes in praise of the British nation, the Company Sahib, and the Governor-General. In the fore-part of the boat is a small cabin, very richly ornamented, like the awnings in English barges, but enclosed with venetian blinds; and between this and the head the mace-bearers of the

Governor-General stand." In Miss Eden's time the *Soona-mookie*, as she spells it, was still to the fore; and when Lord Northbrook visited the Surma Valley in 1874, it was in a house-boat of the same name, which has now passed into the possession of the Lieutenant-Governor of Eastern Bengal and Assam. Needless to say, its gorgeousness (although not its comfort) has become a thing of the past.

The reign of the snake-boat and the palanquin are over to-day: and we are content to "eat the air" in a modest victoria or a dogcart. Gone, too, are the days of the magnificent buildings, with vestibules eighty feet in length and twenty in width, and verandahs to match. Our forefathers, who spent money as royally as they made it, delighted to live in their own mansions and scorned boarding establishments and lower flats. But rents were even then calculated on the basis of a King's ransom, and the weaker vessels were already being driven in 1800 to "the Parsee fashion of having a suite of rooms in a house." Still, no matter whether they lived in a palace or only in a part of it, people amused themselves pretty much in those days as we do, a century later. There was even a St. Andrew's dinner in full swing in 1794, and Scotsmen will be interested to know that the subscription in 1805 was fixed at fifty rupees a head. The Golf Club is an institution of later creation, but we come across it in 1839, with a Captain in the person of Lord Ramsay, elder brother of Lord Dalhousie, the great Governor-General, and at the time aide-de-camp to his father, then filling the office of Commander-in-Chief in India. Pending its arrival, there were other recreations. Hog-hunting could always be had at Buckra, only fifteen miles away: and there were still leopards in the suburbs of Calcutta to tempt the *shikarree*. Billiards and cards were then as now favourite pastimes, and "the sums won and lost must keep the blood in a perpetual fever." Selby's Club was a famous resort for gamblers, until Lord Cornwallis put down the public playing of games of hazard with a high hand. Racing was always popular in old Calcutta. The Bengal Jockey Club came into being in 1803, and not even Lord Wellesley's disapprobation could extinguish the ardour of the Anglo-Indian sportsman. Lord Valentia notes that "on Lord Wellesley's arrival in the country he set his face decidedly against horse-racing and every other species of gambling. Yet at the end of November, 1803, there were three days' races at a small distance from Calcutta." These must have been run, in all probability, on the course which existed at the end of Garden Reach, on the site of what was afterwards the Akra Farm. Still, it was many years before Calcutta racing altogether revived from the shock, and it was not until March, 1816, that the races again commenced under the patronage of the Marquess of Hastings. On each of the three days, two races were run; and as the events were decided in the morning after the fogs had disappeared, it must have been warm work for both horses and on-lookers. The first notice we can find of cricket in Calcutta is that of a grand match, played on the 18th and 19th of January, 1804, between the Etonian civilians and all other servants of the Company resident in Calcutta. The Etonians, it is related, scored 232, while their opponents, who had two innings to their one, were not able to total more than 80.

In the matter of theatres Old Calcutta was well supplied, but their quality does not seem to have kept pace with their quantity. The authoress of "Hartly House" grows enthusiastic over the old play-house in Lyons' Range and declares that it "equals the most splendid European exhibitions." But we may agree to differ with Mrs. Fay, who did not think very highly of it and considered that a gold mohur was "really too much to bestow upon such a temporary gratification." The farces and other plays announced from time to time in the *Calcutta Gazette* are of the most mediocre description, and one learns without surprise that the theatre soon fell into debt. It had more than one rival. In 1795 it is notified that by permission of the Governor-General Mr. Lebedeff will open a theatre in Doomtullah, the lane leading out of China Bazar which is nowadays disguised under the name of Ezra Street. Three years later, we hear of another in Wheler Place, a forgotten locality, which we have already identified as a portion of Government Place, North. Last, but not least, there was the private theatre in Chowringhee of Mrs. Bristow, the wife of a senior merchant. She returned to England in 1790 and (to quote Dr. Busteed) "for long Calcutta refused to be comforted." When the play-house in Lyons' Range was finally closed in 1808 and its buildings converted into the New China Bazar, its successor was placed in the locality where she had achieved her triumphs. This theatre which, like the earlier, was the fruit of public subscription, stood in Chowringhee at the corner of the thoroughfare which has ever since been styled Theatre Road, and was opened in November, 1813. Notwithstanding the fact that it was crowned with a dome, it did not escape the indignity of description as a "clumsy old edifice": but, such as it was, it was admittedly an improvement upon the theatre it supplanted, and we find it at the zenith of its popularity in Lord Amherst's time. It was burnt down in May, 1839, and was not rebuilt, fashion having apparently once more decreed that theatres were better situated in the Dhurrumtollah region. For the Athenæum which was opened in 1812, was in Circular Road, and in 1824 we come across the "Boytaconnah Theatre" which was "a little below the Portuguese Church."

State functions were more frequent in Lord Wellesley's day than they are now, and were always held in the morning. When Sir Alured Clarke took his seat as Deputy Governor of Fort William during the Governor-General's absence in Madras to direct the operations against Tippoo, it was officially notified that he would hold a levée at his house at Chowringhee every Wednesday morning at 9 o'clock, until further notice. Lord Wellesley's levées were also weekly, on Tuesdays at 10 o'clock; and on October 23rd, 1800, we find the following interesting notification in the Gazette :—"The Most Noble the Governor-General will give audience to-day from 10 until 12 o'clock." In the hot weather, the grand ball and supper, on such ceremonial occasions as the King's birthday and the anniversary of the Capture of Seringapatam, were very sensibly replaced by a breakfast at the theatre in Lyons' Range at half past six o'clock, to which "all gentlemen belonging to the Civil and Military services of His Majesty and of the East India Company," were invited by notification in the

Gazette. The public breakfast was abolished by Lord Cornwallis: but the distinctions of rank were continued. It was not until the time of Lord William Bentinck that invitations to Government House were extended to those who were neither civil or military grandees; and the innovation was not effected without much murmuring on the part of the twiceborn. In Lord Auckland's day, it was the fashion for the hostess at Government House to personally receive her callers of both sexes. "The visits," says Miss Eden, "are not long; but I hope they will not compare notes as to what we have said; I know some of my topics served many times over."

Calcutta has always been famous for her hospitality, and her traditions in this respect were upheld by Wellesley in characteristic fashion. Lord Valentia was much struck by the magnificence of the entertainments at Government House, which had just been finished at the time of his visit, and with which he was greatly impressed. "The fêtes given by the Governor-General," he writes, "are frequent, splendid, and well-arranged," and Calcutta evidently appreciated them. For Calcutta was nothing, if not gay, a hundred years ago. "Hardly a day passes," we are told, particularly during the cold season, "without a reception or a dance or a dinner party. The convivial hospitality, which prevails upon these occasions, would render them extremely pleasant, were they more limited; but a small and quiet party is unknown in Calcutta." Breakfast is described as the only *dégagé* meal. Dinner, tea, and supper were regular state functions. Dancing was an amusement which was kept with great zest; and if we are to credit Lord Valentia, the belles of the time paid dearly for their devotion. "Consumptions," he writes, "are very frequent among the ladies, which I attribute in great measure to the incessant dancing, even during the hotest weather. After such violent exercise they go into the verandahs, and expose themselves to a cool breeze and damp atmosphere." Things were the same in Lord Auckland's day. "They danced away," says Miss Eden, in describing her first ball, in March, 1836, "as if they were not in a furnace, and instead of resting between the dances, they walked round the room in pairs. There were few young ladies, but some young brides, and they all seemed to dance on to a most respectable old age. Several mothers of grown-up daughters never missed a quadrille or a waltz. It cannot be such a bad climate, or the old gentlemen who were figuring away at the ball, would not be so active."

Our respect for our ancestors' powers of endurance is increased when we remember that the costume of that day was anything but suitable for such feats of agility. The heat must have been terrific. A coat was a rare sight during the hot season, to be encountered only at formal parties, where decorum was held to require a temporary sacrifice of comfort. Lord Cornwallis, however, who had a character for disregarding these petty distinctions, saw no reason for burdening his guests at Government House with superfluous clothing, and it was his habit, on sitting down at table, to give the word of command, "off coats!" So commonly, indeed, were these articles of attire dispensed with, that gentlemen habitually wore an upper and a lower waistcoat, both of white or alpaca, and the former with sleeves. Hanging punkhas had, it is true, come in with the century as we have already noted: and we are told that "to stride these aerial fans has been the frolic of many a bacchanalian party." But they do not appear to have been in general use up to 1808, for they are advertised in May of that year as a special attraction to a course of lectures on Mechanics, "to which some ladies and gentlemen have decided to subscribe on account of the warmth of the season." *Tempora mutantur.* By the year 1908 punkhas bid fair to be as much a thing of the past as their predecessors, the "kittesol boys," whose business it was to wave large fans or chowries of palm leaves behind their master's chair.

Nor was the climate the only obstacle to enjoyment. The mosquito, like the poor, is still with us, but somehow or other age (or shall we say sanitation?) has improved his manners, and he does not torment us as much as he did our forefathers. Time was when his ravages earned for him the respectful tribute of the poet:

> " With many a drowsy nod
> " I paid dull homage to the sleepy god:
> " But nought the sofa's easy length availed,
> " A ceaseless hum my listening ears regaled:
> " Musquitoes swarmed around, a thirsty throng,
> " Raised the red bump, and tuned the hollow song."

But that was in 1811, and the reign of the petty tyrant is all but over to-day. We no longer resort for immunity to the singular expedient, of which grandpré tells us, of wrapping pasteboard round our legs, if we have to stay in-doors for any length of time. Nor was this the only subterfuge of suffering Anglo-Indian humanity. "You should always contrive to have some blooming youth fresh from England to sit next to you: they are sure to go to him": was the advice given to Lord Minto by "Bobus" Smith, his Advocate-General, who combined with that office the higher distinction of being the brother of the famous Sydney. As for the ladies, poor souls, they thought nothing of three weeks' confinement as the result of mosquito-bites. Miss Eden, in her entertaining letters from India, speaks of such an event as quite an ordinary occurrence. "Nobody can guess what these animals are till they have lived among them," she writes in March, 1836, a few days after Lord Auckland had been sworn in as Governor-General, "many people have been laid up for many weeks by their bites on their first arrival." A week later there is another entry in her diary: "Sir Charles Metcalfe, who has been here for thirty years, says they bite him now, as much as they did the first day; and many people seem to be confined for months after they first arrive, from the inflammation of the bites." No less a scourge was the prickly heat, if we are to credit Lord Minto. "To give you a notion of its intensity," he writes from Madras, where he stayed with the Bentincks on his outward journey to Calcutta in 1807, "the placid Lord William has been found sprawling on a table on his back: and Sir Henry Gwillim, one of the Madras Judges, who is a Welshman, and a fiery Briton in all senses, was discovered by a visitor rolling on his own floor roaring like a baited bull." We have only to compare the recital of these agonies with the boast of many a tough old qui-hye of to-day who will tell you that mosquito-curtains are an unknown luxury to him, and that prickly heat is never suffered to disturb his equanimity; and we shall find ourselves beginning to wonder how people ever lived in Calcutta at all a hundred years ago.

CHAPTER XI.

THE MAKING OF MODERN CALCUTTA.

CALCUTTA played no prominent part in the events which have so inseparably linked the names of Wellesley and Wellington with the history of the English in India. But her inhabitants came forward time after time with voluntary contributions "for the support of His Majesty's Government in Europe," which was then engaged in its long struggle against Revolutionary France. Nor were the successes of our army in India forgotten. The fall of Seringapatam on May 4th, 1799, was celebrated by the firing of a Royal Salute from the ramparts of Fort William: and its anniversary was observed with due solemnity in succeeding years. In 1800, a general day of thanksgiving was appointed on the 6th February by a characteristic proclamation. "We, the Governor-General in Council," ran the preamble, "entertaining a deep and devout sense of the happy deliverance of His Majesty's dominions in Europe, as well as of the British possessions in India, from the destructive designs of the enemy, and taking into our most serious consideration the indispensable duty which we owe to Almighty God for the interposition of His good Providence, manifested by the blessing recently bestowed on the energy and valour of the naval and military forces of His Majesty and of His allies in various parts of the globe: as well as by the prosperous issue of the late just and necessary war in Mysore, by the conclusion and settlement of peace in the Peninsula of India, and by the ultimate establishment of the tranquillity and security of the British possessions subject to our superintendence, direction and control: have thought fit to issue this proclamation." The service was held at "the New Church in Calcutta" before His Lordship, and the sermon preached upon the occasion by the Rev. Claudius Buchanan was ordered to be printed. When peace was finally concluded in 1803, a solemn *Te Deum* was sung on the 18th January at the new Church of St. John, "His Excellency proceeding in his carriage from the new Government House to the Church through the new street leading from the north portico," which we may identify as Government Place, North, and "followed by all the public officers, civil and military." Three royal salutes were fired, the first on the Governor-General's setting out, the second during the celebration of the *Te Deum,* and the third on His Excellency's return. Extra *batta* or rations were served to the European troops, and the colours remained hoisted through the day. A week later, "a most splendid entertainment was given to about eight hundred ladies and gentlemen at the new Government House in honour of the general peace." The ramparts of the Fort, the shipping in the river, and all the principal buildings fronting the Esplanade, were brilliantly lighted: and "an extensive illumination, interspersed with a variety of beautiful transparencies, was at the same time exhibited in the environs of the new Government House." After holding a durbar in the northern verandah for the "vakeels from the foreign native courts" and the Indian gentlemen, Lord Wellesley entered the Ball-room and took his seat on a chair of state placed on a carpet which had formed one of the ornaments of Tippoo Sultan's throne. Dancing was carried on until twelve o'clock, and the company then "dispersed them-selves through the several porticos, corridors and apart-ments fronting the Esplanade of this spacious mansion," in order to view a special display of fireworks executed by artificers sent from Lucknow and Moorshidabad. Dancing was renewed at half past two and continued until near four o'clock, "at which hour His Excellency retired."

The "new Government House," which was the scene of this royal display, is of course the present imposing building which had just then been completed, and which constitutes Wellesley's chief monument in Calcutta. The centenary of the "most splendid entertainment" which signalized its inauguration was celebrated by Lord Curzon on the 26th January, 1903, by a ball, in every way as magnificent, in the costume of the period, the Viceroy himself impersonating his great predecessor.

It is not difficult to discern in the glowing contemporary accounts of the many elaborate ceremonials of Wellesley's reign, the love of pomp and magnificence which formed so distinguishing a feature of his character. But if he was something of an Oriental Sultan in his administration of India, he was certainly the most benevolent of despots in his relations with Calcutta. He designed to make her the Queen of the East, and his schemes for her regenera-tion have furnished the model for all succeeding ones.

The Justices appointed under the statute of 1794 had set to work with a will, and we find them in 1799 busy with the metalling of Circular Road which they describe as "the road forming the eastern boundary of the town, commonly called the Boytockunah Road, and commencing from the Russapuglah Road at the corner of Chowringhee and terminating at Chitpore Road." In 1801 also we discover them advertising for tenders for the supply of eighty-five pairs of bullocks "with the proportional numbers of drivers, for the use of carts employed under the scavengers for cleaning the streets and drains." But their powers were limited. Although empowered by their act to collect revenues, they were restricted to expenditure principally on "repairing, watering and cleaning the streets." Something more thorough and systematic was called for, if the condition of the town was to be effectually remedied. This was supplied by Lord Wellesley. Realizing the importance of thoroughly arousing public interest and attention, he appointed a series of Committees to investigate and report. The first of these Committees was nominated in 1803 by the famous Minute, in which the improvement of drains, roads, streets and buildings was strongly urged, and the need of public markets, slaughter-houses and burial-grounds pointed out. The Governor-General's indictment does not err on the side of comprehensiveness. He notes that the construction of the public drains and watercourses is extremely defective, and that they neither answer the purpose of cleaning the town nor of discharging the annual inundations occasioned by the rise of the river or by the excessive fall of rain. He observes that no general regulations exist regarding the situation of public markets or slaughter-houses or burying-grounds, and he urges that steps should be at once taken to forbid irregularity of building, and to ensure the construction after an order systematic fashion of streets and lanes, "which have hitherto been formed without attention to the health, convenience, or safety of the inhabitants." Thirty of the leading citizens of Calcutta were selected to form a Town Improvement Committee, and to carry the Governor-General's scheme into execution. Extensive enquiries were set on foot, and improvements as extensive were sanctioned. But the project suffered, as did so many of the projects of Wellesley, from the magnitude of the scale upon which it was designed: and when he quitted India in August, 1805, his dream of an Empire City was still very far from realization.

His measures of municipal reform were inaugurated however none too soon. In outward appearance, indeed, the European quarter of Calcutta was as palatial and imposing as could be described. Lord Valentia, who honoured the city with his presence in 1803, was much impressed with its general aspect. "The town of Calcutta," he writes, "is at present well worthy of being the seat of our Indian Government, both from its size and from the magnificent buildings which decorate the part of it inhabited by Europeans. The citadel of Fort William is a very fine work, but greatly too large for defence. The Esplanade leaves a grand opening, on the edge of which is placed the new Government House, erected by Lord Wellesley, a noble structure, although not without faults in the architecture, and, upon the whole, not unworthy of its destination. On a line with this edifice is a range of excellent houses, chunamed and ornamented with verandahs. Chowringhee, an entire village of palaces, runs for a considerable length at right angles with it, and altogether forms the finest view I ever beheld in any city." The noble viscount is less enthusiastic, however, when he comes to treat of the purely Indian quarter. "The Black Town," he continues, "is as complete a contrast to this as can well be conceived. Its streets are narrow and dirty; the houses, of two stories, occasionally brick, but generally mud, and thatched, perfectly resembling the cabins of the poorest class in Ireland." And, if we are to credit other observers, he would have had much the same picture to draw of the English Settlement if he had chosen to probe below the surface. According to William Mackintosh, who published his "Travels in Europe, Asia and Africa," in 1782, there was "not a spot where judgement, taste, decency and convenience are so grossly insulted, as in that scattered and confused chaos of houses, huts, sheds, streets, lanes, alleys, windings, gutters, sinks and tanks, which jumbled into an undistinguished mass of filth and corruption, equally offensive to human sense and health, compose the capital of the English Company's Government in India. The very small portion of cleanliness which it enjoys is owing to the familiar intercourse of hungry jackals by night, and ravenous vultures, kites and crows by day. In like manner it is indebted to the smoke raised in public streets, in temporary huts and sheds, for any respite it enjoys from mosquitoes, the natural production of stagnated and putrid waters." And he proceeds incontinently to recommend its removal to the "cleanly and salubrious" atmosphere of Chandernagore. Mackintosh might, it is true, have paused, before penning this formidable indictment, to reflect that nothing could have been filthier or more insanitary than London itself at the period of which he was writing.

But he was not alone in his condemnation of Calcutta. Grandpré, who visited it in 1790, is no less emphatic. The roads, he says, were "merely made of earth: the drains mere ditches between the houses and the sides of the road, the receptacle for all manner of abomination." Dead carcases were flung into any tank or open space that offered, and left to putrefy. The only scavengers were the jackals and birds of prey, and the plague of flies was insupportable.

The painful confession must be made that the strictures of Grandpré and Mackintosh continued to be deserved as late as 1820. The improvements sanctioned by Wellesley seventeen years before remained unexecuted. With four or five exceptions, the streets were still unmetalled, and the air continued to be polluted by the noisome "open canals" by the roadside which had so disgusted the French traveller. Nevertheless, although the progress was slow, and the results produced may have seemed slight, many important works were, as a matter of fact, undertaken and carried through, during the administration of the first Lord Minto, who reigned at Government House from 1807 to 1813, and of his successor the Marquess of Hastings, who ruled over India from 1813 to 1823, and who until the year 1816 was known as the Earl of Moira.

In 1814 Lord Wellesley's Improvement Committee ceased to exist, and its funds and records were transferred to the Lottery Commissioners, who were empowered to raise funds by lotteries for the accomplishment of municipal improvements. This method of obtaining money for public objects had first come into vogue in Calcutta in 1784 in connection with the building of St. John's Church, when a special Lottery Commission of nine gentlemen were appointed to carry the scheme into execution. In 1793 we find the "Commissioners for the Bengal Lottery" issuing ten thousand tickets at thirty-two rupees each, and offering ten per cent. of their takings to the Committee of the Native Hospital, which was then situated in the Foujdari Balakhana at the corner of Chitpore Road and Colootollah, to which reference has already been made in an earlier chapter as the official residence in Calcutta of the Nabob's representative at Hooghly. The offer, it is true, was declined, and the money was eventually devoted to the relief of insolvent debtors. But the practice became a favourite one, and between 1805 and 1817 a portion of the proceeds of lotteries was regularly set aside for public purposes. With the funds so procured, many tanks were dug, the Town Hall, which had been begun under the auspices of Wellesley, was completed in 1813 in the time of Lord Minto, the Belliaghatta Canal was constructed and numerous roads were made. Among these last was Elliot Road, which was named after John Elliot, the President of the Boards of Police and Conservancy, who was in 1813 presented by the merchants of the city with an "accommodation boat" in recognition of his exertions in the suppression of the gang robberies or dacoities then so prevalent in Calcutta.

The Lottery Commissioners held office for three years. To them succeeded in 1817 the famous "Lottery Committee," which under the authority of Government took over the balance of the previous seventeen lotteries aggregating four and a half lakhs of rupees. This Committee looked after the affairs of the town until the year 1836, the only department not under their control being the conservancy which remained, as before, in the hands of the Board of Justices. To them Calcutta is indebted for a long catalogue of improvements: and they may justly claim to be held in grateful remembrance as her second founders. Roads and paths were run across the Maidan and the familiar balustrades set up. Numerous tanks were excavated in all parts of the town from Short's Bazar to Soortibagan, which preserves the memory of the *Surti* or lottery prize that resulted in its purchase. The Strand Road was completed in 1828, but it made its way to Hastings behind and not in front of Prinsep's Ghât, which was erected some twenty years later. The handsome roadway, which traverses the city from north to south under the names of Cornwallis Street, College Street, Wellington Street, Wellesley Street and Wood Street, may be signalled out as another notable illustration of the Committee's vigour and activity. Under their supervision were constructed also the fine squares, each with a large tank in the centre, which lie along its course. The improvement effected was immense. The site of Cornwallis Square was long of evil repute on account of the numerous murders committed there. Wellington Square swept out of existence a mass of wretched huts inhabited by lascars, who made the place a mass of filth and dirt. As late as 1826, the district in the neighbourhood of College Square, was notorious as a rendezvous of thieves and rogues: and "no native for love or money could be got to go this way after sunset." In other quarters of the town, the same policy was pursued. The group of streets which commemorate the various titles of Lord Hastings and his wife, who was Countess of Loudoun in her own right, are also the work of the Lottery Committee, and were designed to afford access to the Panchkotee, or five mansions, which will be found surrounding Rawdon Street, Moira Street, Hungerford Street and Loudoun Street (as it should be properly spelt). During the Government of Lord Amherst, who ruled from 1823 to 1828, the street was laid out, which bears his name and connects Bow Bazar with Manicktollah Street. Other streets were opened, straightened or widened, such as Free School Street, Kyd Street, Hastings Street, Creek Row, Mangoe Lane and Cossaitollah, the last being renamed Bentinck Street, in honour of Lord William Bentinck, Governor-General from 1828 to 1835. To the same period must also be referred the building of Baboo Ghaut on the riverside and the construction to its southward of the Respondentia Walk, which has long since disappeared, but which in its day furnished the pretext for many a moonlight ramble. Nor was the activity of the Committee confined to the making of new thoroughfares. A systematic plan for metalling the roads was also taken in hand, and a quarter of a lakh of rupees ordered to be yearly set aside for the purpose.

Schalch's Map of 1825 affords ample testimony of the progress that was being made. Old Calcutta now appears thickly populated, the streets being mostly lined by continuous rows of houses. In the southern quarter especially, there has been a marked increase of masonry buildings since 1794. It is worth noting, however, that the English inhabitants were still chiefly to be found where their fathers had lived before them. Colonel Sleeman, writing of Calcutta in the year 1810, speaks of the residences of the Europeans as lying mainly between Dhurrumtollah and China Bazar; and the great tank, in what is now Dalhousie Square, was in the middle of the Belgravia of his day. It was small wonder that the Colonel congratulated himself upon the compactness of the settlement, which made the toil of visiting much lighter. Twenty years later, things were much the same. St. John's Church was the Cathedral of Calcutta's first Bishop, Middleton, and of three of his successors, and Wellesley's discarded Government House in the Fort served Heber as a Palace for a while until he migrated to Russell Street in 1825. The Police Office in Lall Bazar was the mansion of John Palmer, the son of Warren Hastings' secretary, and a king among merchant princes. Moore's Assembly Rooms, where Calcutta gave its farewell ball to Lord Minto in 1813, were in Dacre's Lane—quite a fashionable locality at the time. Chowringhee was, even so late as 1824, regarded as a suburb, and Miss Eden calls it the Regent's Park of Calcutta. The *John Bull* newspaper of August, 1822, finds, as Colonel Sleeman had done, the "most thickly inhabited European part of Calcutta" in "the division between Dhurrumtollah and Bow Bazar." The lower or southern division is described as "thinly peopled: the houses of the Europeans widely scattered, and Colinga, which is a part of it, chiefly inhabited by natives." To the district between Bow Bazar and Machooa Bazar is assigned the "most dense part of the population": but the upper division to the north of

Machooa Bazar is, "comparatively speaking, but sparsely covered with dwellings, presenting towards the north and east, extensive gardens, large tanks, and ruinous buildings." Tanks and pools of water are, not however, confined to any particular locality. In Schalch's map an enormous number are noticeable all over the town, "almost every square inch containing two or more of them."

The Lottery Committee succumbed in 1836 to the force of public opinion in England which condemned the method of raising money for municipal purposes. In its place sprang up the Fever Hospital Committee, appointed by Lord Auckland, who reigned as Governor-General from 1836 to 1842, and to whose sisters Calcutta is indebted for the Eden Gardens. Its scope was much larger than its name implied, and it was presided over by the very man for the post, Sir John Peter Grant, Puisne Judge of the Supreme Court from 1833 to 1848, and father of the Lieutenant-Governor of Bengal of the same name. Sir John Peter had already, when Judge of the Bombay Court in 1829, been the hero of a memorable conflict of executive and judicial authority with Sir John Malcolm, the Governor: and it was of him that Lord Ellenborough, then President of the Board of Control, wrote recommending that two colleagues should be appointed to sit with him in order to "keep him in check like a wild elephant between two tame ones." Under the supervision of this restless and energetic personality, the Fever Hospital Committee enquired and reported in every conceivable direction. Their first report (which was followed by two others) dealt with an enormous number and variety of questions affecting the city: and their recommendations ranged from drainage and conservancy and water-supply to the establishments of Hospitals and Dispensaries and the improvement of the system of collecting and appropriating the taxes of the town. The information collected by them, no less than the suggestions offered, have had a most important influence on subsequent municipal action, but their researches and deliberations produced no immediate practical results of consequence except one. The multiple administration of the town by Committees, Justices of Peace, and Magistrates was resulting in friction and disorganization: and in 1840 Lord Auckland attempted what was then deemed the bold experiment of dividing the town of Calcutta into four divisions, and empowering the Government, on the application of two-thirds of the rate-payers in any division, to entrust to them the assessment collection and management of the rates on a scheme to be approved by Government. Not a single application in Calcutta was, as a matter of fact, made under the Act, and the idea *pro tanto* proved a failure. But it is nevertheless worthy of commemoration, for it marks the beginning of modern Municipal Government.

Lord Ellenborough and Lord Hardinge, who filled the gap between the departure of Lord Auckland in March 1842 and the arrival of the Earl of Dalhousie in 1848, were too busy with schemes of military glory and conquest to devote either time or energy to the embellishment or improvement of Calcutta. An attempt was made, however, to persevere with Lord Auckland's scheme of partially representative administration of municipal affairs: and Act

XVI of 1847 constituted a Board of Seven Commissioners for the improvement of the Town, three of whom were to be Government nominees, while the selection of the remaining four was left to the rate-payers. In this Board were vested the Conservancy functions of the Justices, and they were empowered to apply municipal funds towards the relief of congested areas and the opening out of new streets. The experiment was an interesting one, but there were not wanting those who lamented the passing away of the days when a captain of engineers had had sole charge of municipal arrangements, and the Lottery Committee had been busy transforming the face of the City: and it was said, that the Board, of whom four were Englishmen and three Indians, talked a great deal, wrote more, and did very little that was good.

The advent of Lord Dalhousie was the signal for reforms of a far-reaching character. He was quick to recognise that one of the chief needs of Calcutta was pure water, that it was no less important that means should be taken to introduce a proper system of sewerage and drainage, and that a survey of the town was urgently required for the purpose of ascertaining its manifold defects. One of his first measures was the passing of an Act which contained provisions for the carrying into execution of these pressing reforms by the Board of Commissioners, and ordered the survey to which we owe Simms' Survey Map and report of the condition of the town in 1850. A further step was taken in 1852, when the number of Commissioners was reduced to four, who received a monthly salary of Rs. 250, and the four districts into which Lord Auckland had divided

Calcutta in 1840, were merged in two—the Northern and Southern Divisions, which are still used for police purposes. Finally, in 1856, a very elaborate Act was passed which constituted a new Board of three paid Commissioners, nominated by Government, for the conservancy and improvement of the town. This was quickly followed by two other Acts in the same year, by which the Commissioners were declared to be a Corporation, with the municipal funds under their control, and with power to raise funds for the drainage and lighting of the town. For seven years this Corporation of three continued in office, and they speedily justified their existence by inaugurating in 1859 the great scheme of under-ground drainage, which took sixteen years to complete, and which owes its initiation to Mr. Clark, the Secretary and Engineer to the Commissioners.

There will be those, no doubt, by whom these details of municipal development will be voted dull. In these breathless days forecasts of the future are all the fashion, and memories of the past are thrust into the background. But if modern Calcutta has ever a thought to give to the citizens who have made her what she is, she will find many a name worthy of honour among those who recognized Moira and Bentinck and Auckland and Dalhousie as king in turn.

CHAPTER XII.

BETWEEN THE TWENTIES AND THE FIFTIES.

ALTHOUGH material of much interest has accumulated with regard to the topography of Calcutta of a century or even a century and a half ago, a period almost as attractive has been strangely neglected. How little are the present generation acquainted with personalities and events which absorbed public interest during the decades immediately preceding and succeeding the Mutiny! We speak of the changes which have transformed the "Land we Live in" during the period of our own brief sojourn of fifteen, twenty and even thirty years: but what of the momentous years which witnessed the all-pervading energy of Dalhousie and the wise statesmanship of Canning? Let us by the selection of three epochs in the career of a single great Anglo-Indian endeavour to realize how complete is the divorce between the Bengal of ourselves and our fathers, and still more of our grandfathers.

In the year 1854 the lower provinces of Bengal were constituted a separate subordinate government, and Sir Frederick Halliday, to give him the belated title conferred upon him after his retirement, was appointed the first Lieutenant-Governor. When he had landed in June, 1825, as a young writer on the banks of the Hooghly, Lord Amherst had been for two years Governor-General at Fort William. Assam had just been wrested from the Burmese: and Sir Archibald Campbell was forcing the arrogant King of Ava to purchase peace by the cession of Arracan and Tenasserim. An attempt to reach Manipore by the Cachar route, which Lord Curzon traversed in perfect security in 1901, had not long before been utterly baffled by the hardships of a march through an unbroken succession of steep hills and hollows, covered with pathless forests and beset with deep quagmires. The impregnable fortress of Bhurtpore, which had defied the assaults of Lake, was, in the course of a few months, to open her gates to Combermere, the *beau sabreur* of the Peninsular War. Lahore, Rangoon, Nagpore and Kurrachee stood sullenly outside the confines of British territory. Sir Thomas Munro, still remembered in Southern India as the father of the people, was Governor in Madras, and Mountstuart Elphinstone, in Bombay. A year had still to run before Reginald Heber was to meet his death in the fatal swimming bath at Trichinopoly. John Lawrence was a cadet at Haileybury, and Henry Havelock a subaltern in a marching regiment. The Prime Minister of England was Lord Liverpool, whose grandmother had been the wife of a member of Council and a prisoner of Seraj-ud-Dowlah at Moorshedabad in the days of the Black Hole. Darjeeling was unknown, and when Dr. Campbell took charge of the district thirty years later, it contained only twenty families. Simla, acquired at the close of the Goorkha War in 1816, was boasting of her first permanent house: and it was not until 1829 that Lord Amherst spent the summer there and set the example which Sir John Lawrence stereotyped in 1864. Calcutta was in the hands of the indefatigable Lottery Committee. Her merchant-princes were at the zenith of their prosperity: and the shadow was still distant of the terrible years between 1830 and 1834, which witnessed the collapse of the great banking-houses of the city, with liabilities exceeding sixteen millions sterling and involved in one gigantic ruin the military and civilian families of Bengal. The Governor-General was in fact, as well as in name, the immediate ruler of the Presidency of Fort William. Belvedere, which Halliday was to occupy twenty-nine years later, was the residence of Sir Edward Paget, the Commander-in-Chief: and the office of Deputy Governor of Bengal, which served as a half-way house to the Lieutenant-Governorship, was not thought of until 1833.

In these days of rapid travel, when the journey from Bombay to Brindisi can be completed in less than a fortnight, it is difficult to realise that there was a time when the voyage to India was an undertaking which was not to be lightly attempted. Yet so it was. Sir John Shore would not allow his wife to accompany him to India so impressed was he with the difficulties and dangers of the long circuit round the Cape. And as the new century succeeded the old, there was not much improvement to show. Heber, who left England on June 16, 1823, was thought to have done remarkably well, in reaching Saugor Roads on October 3. When Lord Auckland and his sisters came out in 1836, they were five months on the high seas; and Miss Eden writes in the most matter-of-fact way: "We are now within 200 miles of the Sandheads, but we may be a week reaching them. I was telling George (her brother) last night that when children learn their Indian History, they will come to 'Sir C. Metcalfe began to reign in 1835, preceded by George of Auckland, who was surnamed the Navigator, from the very remarkable fact that he never made land during the five years his government lasted.' " Let those who grumble because the round voyage from London to Calcutta occupies them thirty days, be thankful that they live in less leisurely times. But there was even a time when five months was regarded as a quick passage. Lord Valentia spent from June to the following January on his voyage out in 1802. "Seven months and a half have now elapsed since the date of the latest advices from Europe," is the despairing exclamation of the editor of the *Calcutta Gazette* on the 4th May, 1809. Twenty years earlier, the arrival is chronicled, on the 24th March, 1789, of a Dutch East Indiaman, which had taken fourteen months to come from Amsterdam to Bengal. The amount of time wasted on the journey was extraordinary. A month or more would be spent before the ship fairly put out to sea. She would stay twenty days at Gravesend, and another twenty in the Downs. At Madeira there would be a halt of four or five days, two or more would be spent at St. Helena, and at least a week, if not longer, at the Cape. If contrary winds were met with, the journey from the Cape to the Bay of Bengal might occupy another couple of months, for the ship was often driven out of her course so far south as the latitude of King George's Sound. After 1830, however, more rapid voyages began to be made, and in the course of a few years it became the ordinary thing for a sailing ship to make the entire trip from Portsmouth to Calcutta in seventy-nine and even seventy-seven days.

The annoyances of tedious and laborious locomotion by no means vanished on arrival in India itself. It was necessary to make the most elaborate preparations before taking a journey overland. "I have, through my friend Mr. Graham, purchased three palanquins, in which Mr. Salt, I, and my English servant, proceed by dawk;" writes Lord Valentia from Calcutta in 1803, when on the point of starting for Secrole, the English cantonment of Benares in order to begin his tour in Upper India, "my luggage goes chiefly by the Ganges in a small boat, escorted by two sepoys and under the care of two of my native servants. We take with us, indeed, in six *bangys* (wicker baskets slung on man's shoulders) sufficient changes of linen until the others arrive, which from the lowness of the water, will probably not be for three months, as the Cossimbazar river is closed, and they are obliged to proceed by the Sunderbunds." The ideal of rapid transit had evidently still to be attained in 1817, as witness the following extract from a Calcutta newspaper of the day: "It may give some idea of the rapidity of the stream at this season of the year (September) if we may observe that a gentleman has recently arrived in Calcutta who was only nine and a half days on his passage from Cawnpore. His Lordship the Governor-General (the Marquess of Hastings) may be expected to reach Cawnpore about the 15th, making the voyage in about two months. On the 1st of September, he had arrived at Allahabad." Not many years later, in the days of Heber, the river was still the principal method of locomotion. The worthy Bishop was three weeks on his journey from Calcutta to Dacca and more than a month from Dacca to Benares. And if we wish to realize how closely the tragedies of life were sometimes brought home to the travellers of the time, we have only to take up once again the diary of Mrs. Fenton. She relates, for instance, how she goes driving one morning at Chinsurah and on her way home notices a budgerow near the ghaut wearing a peculiar air of disarrangement. *Khidmatgars* and a *dhobee* sit smoking on the roof, and it is only the presence of a number of articles of baggage that denote the existence of an inhabitant. Enquiry elicits the reply: "The boat belongs to Dundas Sahib: he died yesterday near Santipore." The unfortunate man had left Berhampore on sick leave, intending to proceed to Europe, and found himself overtaken by death in the lonely reaches of the river, when care and companionship might perhaps have saved him. We turn over a few pages, and read of Colonel and Mrs. Chalmers of the 41st Regiment returning with their daughter to Bangalore from a visit to a distant station. The father and mother are attacked simultaneously with cholera, and the poor girl is left alone in a tent with the dead bodies of her parents, deserted by her servants, and far removed from European aid. Hardly less pitiful is the story told to Mrs. Fenton by her own brother. Travelling in Madras through some remote country he comes up with a palkee, on the ground, without bearers. He alights from his conveyance and draws back the door to find a young man lying within dead.

Under circumstances such as these, the balance of disadvantage seems evenly struck between a voyage by water and a journey on land. But it was a case of Hobson's choice, as far as Bengal was concerned. Roads were officially regarded as a superfluity in that province: and it was upon one occasion solemnly placed upon record by the

Hon'ble Court of Directors that the development of commerce in the province and the convenience of the people, were amply provided for by the many navigable waterways to be found in all directions throughout the year. In his amusing sketch of life in India which he has called *Peregrine Pulteney,* Sir John William Kaye has many a gibe to cast at the badness of the roads in Calcutta and its neighbourhood in the year 1844. "What are the people to do in an unpicturesque country," he says, "if they have no holes and ruts to swear at by the way?" Nowadays, how many sahibs are there who trouble their heads over the manner in which the Public Works Department look after the highroads? No one on the Bombay side or anywhere else has ever heard of the monument erected to commemorate the opening of the Bhor Ghât to wheeled traffic. We whirl along in our first-class carriages, write to the newspapers to complain if our train is an hour late, and give never a thought to the old marching routes, trodden by so many of our soldiers. And yet it is only since 1871 that Bombay has been in direct communication with Calcutta and Madras; and the East Coast branch of the Bengal-Nagpore Railway is the creation of the past few years. We think nothing of sending a deferred telegram a thousand miles for four annas, and we expect, as a matter of course, to be able to send a letter from one end of the Peninsula to the other for half an anna. Yet it is only since the days of Lord Dalhousie that we have been able to do the one or other. Still more wonderful, if possible, has been the cheapening of the rates of postage between England and India. The curious may still read, in the *Bombay*

Courier of the 4th January, 1798, the official announcement that letters will be transmitted monthly from that Presidency to Great Britain, *viâ* Bussorah, at a charge per single letter of ten rupees per quarter tola. One penny is all that is needful to-day to carry a letter from Peshawar to Cape Town, from Mandalay to Dublin, from Dibrugarh to Quebec; nor is the time far distant when an even more modest coin may suffice to frank a letter from Macaulay's New Zealander to the gentleman whom he imagines to be in charge of the ruins of London town.

There is something very strange and outlandish to us of a later day about these old-world surroundings of the twenties and thirties. Yet shall we find ourselves on more familiar ground if we transport ourselves back into the year 1848,—the year of Lord Dalhousie's arrival in India? The Punjab and the Central Provinces are still independent of John Company's rule. Vans Agnew and Anderson, whose epitaph from the pen of Macaulay may be read upon the walls of the Calcutta Cathedral, have just been murdered at Mooltan and the second Sikh War is in progress. Suttee and thuggee have been abolished by Lord William Bentinck, the freedom of the Press has been bestowed by Lord Metcalfe, and an attempt made to promote steam communication with England by way of Suez. But communications in India itself are still so bad, that even so great an artery of traffic as the Grand Trunk Road must be patrolled at frequent intervals by a force of sowars and police numerically equal to a regiment of infantry. Railways, telegraphs, cheap postage, are blessings yet to come. Berhampore, Chittagong and Midnapore are military stations: the districts of Nuddea and Jessore are studded with the hospitable homes of prosperous indigo-planters: Burdwan has not yet been robbed by malaria of the reputation as a sanitarium it enjoys along with Bhagalpore and Monghyr. In Calcutta there is no University, no Provincial Legislative Council, no Indian Museum in Chowringhee, no Corporation, no Port Trust, no Hooghly Bridge. The Volunteer movement awaits the Mutiny to call it into existence. There are no Penal and Procedure Codes, and no Evidence Act: and the Company's and the Queen's Courts are distinct. Before the civilian judges of the Sudder Dewanny Adawlut and their native law officers at Bhowanipore, pleaders and moonshees are arguing abstruse questions of Hindoo and Mahomedan law in Persian. In the Court House on the Esplanade Sir Henry Seton and his colleagues of the Supreme Court administer the laws of England in English and exercise a separate jurisdiction over all who reside within the limits of the Mahratta Ditch.

And what of the aspect of Calcutta itself? We are fortunate enough in this respect to be able to assure ourselves, if we will, by personal conversation with an eye-witness.* For there is yet living in Calcutta, hale and hearty, an honoured citizen whose memories date back to

* Mr. Robert Belchambers, known to three generations of judges and lawyers as an indispensable and indefatigable official and a valued friend, must forgive the writer if he here acknowledges the kindness and courtesy with which his enquiries were met and answered. It is not given to many Englishmen in India to serve the State faithfully and continuously for fifty-one years, and to be as vigorous and capable of work after retirement from a laborious office, as Mr. Belchambers proves himself to be.

this very year 1848. In his person a host of bygone associations and forgotten traditions are enshrined. He can carry his recollection back to the time when the Bishop's Palace had only just been removed from Russell Street to Chowringhee, when St. Paul's Cathedral was in the first year of its existence, when Garden Reach did not belie her name and was still famous for spacious mansions and shady gardens, and when Lord Dalhousie might be seen personally superintending the planting of the trees which are the glory to-day of the Maidan. There are no footpaths in the streets. Adjutant birds perch on every roof and pinnacle or stalk about assisting the jackals and the Board of Commissioners in the scavenging of the town. Most of the houses in the European quarter stand in their own compounds with high walls around them. Durwans sit guarding the pillared gates and watching the stream of palkees in which Englishman and Indian alike are lying stretched but not at ease, as far as the former are concerned. Chowringhee, where the first footpath in Calcutta was made in 1858 by the filling up of an open drain, is one long street of such houses: and there is not a single shop upon it. At the corner of Dhurrumtollah is an untidy bazar. An equally ill-kept lane represents the wide street leading to the Municipal Office of to-day. The old High School, transplanted in 1863 to Darjeeling under the name of St. Paul's School, stands in place of the Indian Museum. Since the departure of Macaulay in 1838, his house had sheltered, as it still does, the Bengal Club: but in those days it lacked its present second storey, and was not the commodius building which a series of additions have made it to-day.

The Supreme Court occupied only the western portion of the plot now appropriated by the High Court. It was not an imposing building externally: but its interior held compensations for its outer insignificance. On the upper floor was the Grand Jury Room, adorned with pictures of Judges and with Chantrey's statue of Sir Edward Hyde East, Chief Justice from 1813 to 1822, whose exertions in the cause of education in India stood thus honourably commemorated. On the ground floor was the Court House in which their Lordships sat together to dispense justice. Wigs had wisely been discarded since the days of Nuncomar's trial, when in spite of the lack of ice and of swinging punkhas, the Judges insisted upon sitting on the Bench in full-bottomed wigs and paid the penalty by retiring three or four times daily to change their linen. But in other respects, the traditions of Impey and Hyde and Chambers were worthily maintained. Sepoys mounted guard at the outer gates which opened to the Maidan: and a Crier ushered their Lordships into Court with stately formality. The remainder of the site now absorbed by the High Court was given over to private houses. Next door to the Supreme Court building on its east and facing the Maidan stood the house of Longueville Clarke, the distinguished advocate whose name appears at the head of every public movement of the day from the Ice House and the Metcalfe Hall, to the Education Commission, of which Macaulay was the brain. Round the corner in Old Post Office Street was the residence of Sir James Colvile, who after seven years' service as Puisne Judge succeeded to the dignity of Chief Justice in 1853. Sir Lawrence Peel, his predecessor in that office, preferred the suburbs, and lived, first at Cossipore as Sir Robert Chambers had done, and then at Garden Reach in a house since swallowed up in the extensive establishment of the ex-King of Oudh. Sir Barnes Peacock, who began his distinguished career in 1852 as Law Member of Council and followed Sir James Colvile as Chief Justice in 1859, resided in Russell Street, hard by the house assigned by tradition as the home of Rose Aylmer and another Chief Justice, her uncle Sir Henry Russell.

The Sudder Dewanny Adawlat, the Court of Appeal from the decisions of Judges in the mofussil, stood on the Lower Circular Road on the edge of Bhowanipore. A fine pile with a colonnade frontage of great length, it was originally built as a military hospital but as soon as it was completed Lord William Bentinck annexed it for the accommodation of the Company's Court. On the creation of the High Court in 1862, the building reverted to its original use, and as the Station Hospital for British troops it survives to this day. If we walk along the Circular Road to the west and make for the river bank, we shall find the Hooghly flowing right up to the steps of Prinsep's Ghaut, as indeed it did until well on into the sixties. It is crowded with vessels, but the sailing ships are three times as numerous as the steamers. "A hundred and fifty ships and fifty steamers constantly occupy the berths and moorings:" and the Indiaman did not yield her pride of place without a gallant struggle. For it is only a matter of three years since the famous Hooghly Pilot Service boasted as its senior member, one who could recall the time when the bulk of the trade of the port was carried in sailing-vessels, and when a tall hat and lavender kid gloves were considered almost an indispensable adjunct to the working costume of a Hooghly pilot.

Neither the dome of the Post Office nor the octagon of the Bengal Council Chamber are to be seen in the Tank Square of the forties. The handsome façade of Writers' Buildings which we admire to-day, will be looked for equally in vain. But some attempt had been made to clothe the gaunt nakedness of the huge barrack-like whitewashed structure, and it had been since 1821 ornamented with three pediments in front, supported on colonnades which formed wide verandahs. The Dalhousie Institute is represented by its entrance portico alone, with its statue of Lord Hastings. Towards the south, however, the Metcalfe Hall, which is completing the fourth year of its existence, serves in some measure to dispel the atmosphere of unfamiliarity. But there are no warehouses or ungainly godowns along the Strand Road to obstruct the river-view of its graceful proportions. And almost opposite in Hare Street, to the west of the modern Small Cause Court building, the eye rests in surprise on the odd-looking and squat outlines of the Ice House wherein the whole stock of Calcutta ice is stored.

The memory of Calcutta is proverbially short, and the Ice House has passed into the category of forgotten things. But in its day it was one of the institutions of the city, and there were not wanting those who placed it upon the pedestal of the public benefactor. "I cannot in this place omit noticing an illustration—called to mind by that all-engrossing verb 'to cool' which I have just employed—of the very singular wants which the climate and habits of a country may induce upon its inhabitants. The services of two ships, each of 5 or 600 tons burthen, are retained by an American speculatist for no other purpose than that of supplying the people of Calcutta yearly, with *common ice,* and the people of Calcutta, that is, the richer portion of them, not only receive it with joy, but have built a house of a very peculiar construction, for its preservation and reception, from whence the public obtain their daily supplies at the rate of three annas per seer. With those, therefore, who avail themselves of the ice, saltpetre, patent refrigerators, and all foreign contrivances are discarded for the more simple and efficacious material of nature's own preparing, by aid of which wine, beer, or drinking water can be reduced from a state positively tepid to a degree nearly that of zero. I will not talk of nectar or elysium, but I will say that if there be a *luxury* here, it is this—it is this!"

To the Anglo-Indian of to-day who looks upon a cheap and plentiful supply of ice as an ordinary and obvious accessory to his sojourn in the East, this rhapsody will appear overdone. But at the time Colesworthy Grant wrote the words in 1849, in the delightful letters to his mother which he calls an *Anglo-Indian Domestic Sketch,* the "bad old days" were still within measurable recollection, when ice was a luxury reserved for the few, and often unattainable even by them. As late as 1834, the ice-supply of Calcutta was dependent on the whim of certain speculative individuals at Hooghly, who manufactured as much as they thought fit, whenever the weather permitted it. In that year, however, an enterprising American, who had been an apothecary, brought some 40 tons of ice from Boston to Calcutta. A block of pure ice weighing two maunds was a sight Calcutta had never before seen. The sensation was great: and it speedily took a practical shape. A number of subscribers, headed by Bishop Wilson, presented the adventurous apothecary with a silver cup as a stimulus to further exertions. The gentleman honoured, so the story goes, promptly converted the cup into dollars and set up as a boarding-house keeper and dentist: but Calcutta was not content to leave the matter there. It had become a great fact that twenty-two thousand miles of sea was no hindrance to the importation of ice from Boston, where it could be obtained so easily, to Calcutta, where it was needed so badly. And the idea occurred to Mr. Longueville Clarke that as American ships came to the Hooghly in ballast, the cost of freight would be so trivial and the article itself could be sold so cheap, that if the inhabitants of Calcutta would provide an Ice House for the use of an importer, ice might be procurable in Calcutta all the year round at half the price it sold in London. We may let the father of the scheme tell the rest of the story in his own words:*

"Acting on this belief, I wrote to Mr. Frederick Tudor, the great Boston ice-importer. He accepted the terms and I then called a meeting at the Town Hall. The idea of

* The writer is indebted to Mr. Patrick McGuire, of Messrs. Markby and Co., for this interesting MS. account by Mr. Longueville Clarke of the establishment of the Ice House, written, as its opening words indicate, for the information of Lord Dalhousie.

having the purest ice at three halfpence a pound during the whole year, instead of having the Hooghly slush for six weeks at fourpence the pound, was irresistible. In three days the Government gave us a grant of land on the river-side and the inhabitants subscribed Rs. 25,000. A committee was nominated by the subscribers who appointed me their president." The first members of this committee included Sir Edward Ryan, Chief Justice of the Supreme Court from 1833 to 1843; General Forbes of the Bengal Engineers, the architect of the new Mint and St. Paul's Cathedral; James Pattle, Member of the Board of Revenue, and famous as the father of the "beautiful Miss Pattles," of whom the best known became Mrs. Julia Margaret Cameron, the wife of Macaulay's colleague on the Indian Law Commission; and last, but not least, James Prinsep, Deputy Assay Master at the Mint, whose civic virtues stand commemorated by the ghât which bears his name.

"The Ice House," continues the narrative, "was built, the ice imported, but the accommodation was too small. The success of the experiment had, however, been established, so I called another public meeting, obtained another Rs. 25,000 and a further grant of ground from Government. On the occasion of granting the second piece of ground, Lord Auckland, accompanied by Mr. Thoby Prinsep, came to the premises and formally delivered them to me as President of the Committee, in presence of Sir Edward Ryan. Let me here mention, as an interesting anecdote, a circumstance under which an additional sum was obtained. Twenty-two medical practitioners in Calcutta had sent into Government their separate certificates, that ice was among the first of remedies in the hospitals. One of our committee men and the great ornament of his service, Henry Meredith Parker, seized hold of this: he wrote an inimitable address to the women of Calcutta to support the importation of ice for the benefit of the sick, beginning with the well-known lines: 'Oh! woman in our hours of ease.' The address succeeded. The Miss Edens headed the subscription and in two days the women of Calcutta subscribed Rs. 3,000. On the arrival in Calcutta of the first cargo of Mr. Tudor's ice, seven hundred tons were safely landed, and the committee delivered possession of the ice-house to Mr. Bacon, the agent. The regularity of the supply has been twice interrupted, one ship having been wrecked at the Sandheads and another burnt at sea; but for the last nine years there has not been any interruption."

When these words were written, the forties were slipping away, the Marquess of Dalhousie was Governor-General, and the Ice House was in the heyday of its career. To-day the visitor will search in vain in Hare Street for the strangely-shaped globular building which stood perched on the summit of a flight of steps and challenged the attention of every passer-by. It was razed to the ground in 1882, and even the memories of the murder committed within its walls have faded away. Madras still preserves the shell of her ice-house. Calcutta has been more iconoclastic, and not a vestige remains of the once familiar structure in which for nearly fifty years she hoarded her precious frozen blocks from Wenham Lake.

The temptation is great to linger over these reminiscences of vanished Calcutta: but we must hasten on to the third of our pictures. Here, standing in his father's shoes, the modern enquirer may begin at last to find himself more at home. For we shall select the year 1859, the year of Sir Frederick Halliday's departure from India after a five years' tenure of his office of Lieutenant-Governor. Universities at Calcutta, Madras and Bombay are an accomplished fact. A settled form of municipal self-government is on its trial in Calcutta. The Hindoo College, founded by Sir Edward Hyde East and David Hare in 1817, has been transformed into the Presidency College: and in spite of the check administered by the Mutiny, a candle lighted for the benefit of generations to come which can never be put out. Civil appointments are no longer to be obtained on the nomination of Mr. Goldmore, the East India Director: and competition-wallahs have come to oust the men of Haileybury from their monopoly of place and preferment. A beginning had been made with the vast network of railways and waterways which intersect the length and breadth of the Bengal of to-day. The East Indian Railway, which in the Mutiny year had ended impotently at Raneegunge, was resolutely pushing on towards Delhi and by the end of 1862 could claim to have penetrated as far as Benares. The Ganges Canal had been opened and a Public Works Department called into being. Cheap postage and telegraphs had come into the daily life of all. A great stir had been created by the announcement that the tea-plant had been discovered by Mr. Bruce growing wild in the far-off province of Assam. Large parts of land had been applied for, and a service of steamers organized which wound their leisurely way once a month through the reeking tiger-infested Sunderbund jungles to Narain-gunge, in those days the home of a solitary Scotsman. Thence the tedious journey lay past Seraigunge, which was just springing up into a jute mart, to Gowhatty and Tezpore and Dibrugarh, one and all rising settlements in the midst of the jungle, where the forcible entry of a wild elephant into the dining room of the bungalow or the sight of a tiger asleep on the grass-grown road after nightfall was no surprising occurrence. In the outer world of India, annexation had been the order of the day. Pegu, Nagpore and, finally, Oudh, had been added to the British dominions. The Sikh Wars had come and gone: and those whom Lord Gough and Sir Harry Smith had found it so hard to defeat at Aliwal, Sobraon and Chillian-wallah, had been the foremost to rally around us in our hour of need in 1857. The last of the Moguls was ending his days in exile at Rangoon: John Company Bahadur had given way to Queen and Parliament, and the Union Jack was floating, the more proudly for its recent eclipse, from every fortress between Peshawar and Tuticorin.

CHAPTER XIII.

CALCUTTA DURING THE MUTINY.

THE Sepoy rebellion of 1857 did not touch Calcutta nearly, but the city shared, nevertheless, in all the feelings of alarm and suspense which were the common lot of Englishmen in India during that terrible year. There were ominous threatenings of trouble in the winter of 1856 at Barrackpore, sixteen miles from Calcutta, which was the head-quarters of the Presidency Division of the Bengal army, and included four regiments of native infantry among its garrison. The storm burst towards the end of February at Berhampore, a hundred miles away. The 19th Native Infantry refused to receive their ammunition, but were quieted down and ordered to march to Barrackpore, where they were publicly disbanded and disarmed on March 31. Two days earlier, however, the first blood of the mutiny had already been spilt at that station by Mungul Panday of the 34th Regiment, and a serious outbreak had only been averted by the courage and presence of mind of General Hearsey, the Brigadier. Mungul Panday was hanged after trial by court-martial, and the seven companies of the 34th, which were at Barrackpore, were disarmed. These punishments were followed by a lull, which completely deceived both civil and military authorities. It was deemed sufficient to bring over the 84th Regiment from Burmah and quarter them at Barrackpore. Allahabad and Delhi, the two chief fortresses and arsenals in the North-Western Provinces, were left without the protection of a British garrison, and no steps were taken to secure the prompt movement or mobilization of British troops. The awakening came rudely and suddenly. On the 3rd May the 7th Oudh Irregulars mutinied at Lucknow and were disarmed by Sir Henry Lawrence. Seven days later, the sepoys at Meerut rose in revolt and were unaccountably permitted to escape, after murdering their officers. On the eleventh of May the English in Delhi were lying dead in the Fort or in the streets, and the King of Delhi was proclaimed Emperor of India. The rebellion spread like wild-fire over Oudh: yet up to the end of May the Government at Calcutta seemed strangely unwilling to admit the gravity of the position.

"Everything is quiet within six hundred miles of the capital: the mischief caused by a passing and groundless panic has already been arrested: and there is every reason to hope that in the course of a few days tranquillity and confidence will be restored throughout the Presidency." Such was the reply sent on the 25th of May by the Home Secretary, Mr. Cecil Beadon, to the French Consul and other French residents of Calcutta who had offered their services. But as May faded into June, and June into July and August, the Calcutta journals began to chronicle a very different tale. The fortified city of Delhi remained in the hands of the rebels: Lucknow was closely invested: and there was no news from Cawnpore, where Sir Hugh Wheeler's little force had been holding out against overwhelming odds since the beginning of June. Every *cossid*, or messenger, from the North brought tidings of massacre and misery, of English women and children dragged along under a burning sun in hourly expectation, and soon in hourly hope, of death, of Judges and Magistrates and officers pelted to death with brickbats or murdered, after a mock trial, by those in whom they had placed implicit confidence.

In Calcutta, the situation was fast developing serious possibilities. On the night of the 6th June, the 6th Native Infantry at Allahabad, which had on the previous day been thanked by Government for its professions of unswerving loyalty, mutinied and murdered nearly all its officers. The catastrophe promised to repeat itself at the Presidency. There were three and a half sepoy regiments at Barrackpore in full possession of their arms and seething with disaffection. The 84th Regiment, which had been watching them, was on its way up-country: and their place had been taken by a wing of the 35th. There was another regiment of sepoys in Fort William, and against them and the battalions at Barrackpore there was nothing to oppose but a weak wing of the 53rd Foot (now the Shropshire Light Infantry) and the artillerymen of the English field battery, which had come up from Ceylon under the command of Captain Cornwallis Maude, in response to the urgent appeal of Lord Canning. The only complete regiment of English troops in the neighbourhood of Calcutta was the 78th Highlanders at Chinsurah, some 25 miles up the river. Had the sepoys been disarmed, this force might have sufficed: but this obvious precaution had not been taken. Nor were these the only elements of danger. As Mr. John Peter

Grant, the second Lieutenant-Governor of Bengal, who was then a member of the Supreme Council, graphically put it in a minute recorded early in June, the Government had other enemies besides the regiments at Barrackpore and in the Fort, "one and a half of which are the very worst type we know: one, two, three (for no one knows) thousand armed retainers of the King of Oudh at Garden Reach, or available there at a moment: some hundred armed men of the Scinde Ameers at Dum-Dum: and all the blackguards of all sorts of a town of six hundred thousand people. There is no reason to expect real help in real danger from the native police. My conviction is that even a street-row at the capital would give us an awful shake, not only in Bengal, but in Bombay and Madras, at this moment."

Such was the condition of affairs in Calcutta when on Sunday, the 14th June, the news arrived, just after the conclusion of morning service, that the native regiments at Barrackpore had mutinied and were in full march on the capital. The intelligence was happily untrue in fact. The secret had been betrayed, and the sepoys had given up their arms without resistance to the Highlanders, who had hurried down from Chinsurah. But the earlier report remained uncontradicted, and the public agitation was increased by the rumbling sound of heavy material moving out of the Fort. A sudden and uncontrollable panic seized hold of the European and East Indian population. Its details have been set down in the famous "Red Pamphlet" by Colonel Malleson, who was himself an eye-witness, and who twenty years later wrote in his history of the Sepoy Mutiny, that "as an accurate picture of the events of that afternoon, it is irrefutable: there is not a comma to add, nor is there a comma to be withdrawn."

He paints the scene in the following vivid colours: "It has been said by a great writer that there is scarcely a more undignified entity than a patrician in a panic. The veriest sceptic as to the truth of this aphorism could have doubted no longer, had he witnessed the living panorama of Calcutta on the 14th June. All was panic, disorder, and dismay. It was all but universally credited that the Barrackpore brigade was in full march on Calcutta, that the people in the suburbs had already risen, that the King of Oudh with his followers, was plundering Garden Reach. Those highest in office were the first to give the alarm. There were secretaries to Government running over to Members of Council, loading their pistols, barricading their doors, sleeping on sofas: Members of Council abandoning their houses with their families and taking refuge on board the ships in the river. Crowds of lesser celebrities, impelled by these examples, having hastily collected their valuables, were rushing to the Fort, only too happy to be permitted to sleep under the Fort guns. Horses, carriages, palanquins, vehicles of every sort and kind, were put into requisition to convey panic-stricken fugitives out of the reach of imaginary cut-throats. In the suburbs, almost every house belonging to the Christian population was deserted. Half a dozen determined fanatics could have burnt down three parts of the town. A score of London thieves could have made their fortunes by plundering the houses in the neighbourhood of Chowringhee which had been abandoned by their inmates." Dr. Mouat, another eye-witness, compares the scamper across the Maidan to "what might have been if a modern Herculaneum had been evacuated in broad daylight on the approach of a visible eruption from a neighbouring volcano." He adds, in the account which he furnished to Sir John William Kaye, "the whole of the ghauts was crowded with fugitives, and those who could find no shelter on the ships, took refuge within the Fort, of which the squares, the corridors, all the available space everywhere, indeed, were thronged by many, who passed the night in their carriages."

Both Colonel Malleson and Dr. Mouat bear testimony, however, to the courage and steadfastness displayed by the members of the commercial and trading community, which, says the former, "nothing could exceed." There was no time for concerted action, and little was done in the way of arranging a rendezvous. The Light Horse had then no existence, and the day before Panic Sunday only had witnessed the issue of a notification calling into being a corps of Volunteer Guards, of which Lieutenant (afterwards Sir) Orfeur Cavenagh was appointed commandant, and which was ordered to consist of a battery of four guns, five troops of cavalry, and seven companies of infantry. As matters stood, each man was left perforce to his own resources: and many and various were the devices for defence adopted by those who declined to abandon their houses. In one instance it was said that a much-respected tradesman in Dalhousie Square barricaded his entrance-hall and awaited the enemy at the head of the stairs with a loaded weapon, serviceable if old-fashioned, which is still preserved on the premises, and a plentiful supply of molten lead and boiling water. In other cases, the roof was selected as the most suitable place for an entrenchment, in the hope that the old smoothbores of the mutineers would not be able to carry so far, and that in the hurry of attack and the pleasurable anticipation of loot they would forget to bring their artillery with them.

As time wore on and no sepoys were either seen or heard, the tension slackened, and that portion of Calcutta which had not completely lost its head, began to recover composure, if not confidence. The Town Major sought out the refugees in the fort and on the ships, and endeavoured to induce them to return to their houses. But alarm was again aroused when at half-past four in the afternoon a column of European troops was seen to emerge from the Plassey gate of the Fort. All manner of speculation was indulged in as the detachment marched across the Maidan and past Government House and Loudon-buildings (where the Imperial Secretariat now stands) into Government Place North and thence into Wellesley Place. Here the men were halted before a small barrack occupied by the company of sepoys which furnished the official guard : and it became evident to the crowd of Europeans which had assembled that nothing more formidable was afoot than the disarmament of this body. The sepoys were ordered to pile arms, which they did without demur, and they were then marched away to a sufficient distance, while the English soldiers, who were gunners from Maude's battery, drew out the ramrods and stacked muskets and bayonets in bullock-carts for conveyance into the Fort. It had been with the greatest difficulty that Lord Canning had been induced to sanction this proceeding. At length he had been overcome by the persuasions of Sir Frederick Halliday, who had left Belvedere and was living in rooms opposite the Governor-General's official residence, in order that his frequent and close communication with his chief might be uninterrupted. But he persistently refused to disarm his body-guard, and it was not until the end of the following August that he could be prevailed upon to substitute European for Sepoy sentries at Government House.

The remainder of "Panic Sunday" passed uneventfully away. The Great Eastern Hotel, which was then in fact, as it still is in the language of the *thika gariwallahs*, Wilson's Hotel, became the rallying place of the European community. Fifty stand of arms were requisitioned from the Fort and at once supplied: and a patrol of about forty Englishmen was organised. These formed into two squads, and paraded the streets in the native quarter of the Town for over an hour in the evening. An extraordinary state of terror was found to be prevailing, especially among the poorer Eurasian classes, who had come to the conclusion that their only chance of safety lay in a frantic and aimless fusilade with blank cartridge, which continued for hours, and was checked with the utmost difficulty. The patrols were finally dismissed shortly after midnight, and when the city awoke upon the following morning, it learnt that all the native troops at Barrackpore and elsewhere in the neighbourhood had been successfully disarmed, and that the ex-King of Oudh with his late Prime Minister were prisoners in the Fort. Recovered from their panic, the European residents set about soldiering with a will, and when the Calcutta Volunteer Guards were disbanded on the 1st June, 1859, their services were publicly acknowledged by the Viceroy, who thanked them, in the name of the Government of India, for the "cheerful and hearty manner in which they had performed their duties at a great sacrifice of time and convenience."

There was a repetition of the scene of Panic Sunday on March 3, 1858. The rebellion had been all but crushed, but the slightest cause was still enough to produce excitement and alarm. A telegram from Barrackpore reached Calcutta to the effect that the sepoys of the two native regiments stationed there were deserting in bodies of ten and twelve and were making their way to the capital. No one stopped to reflect that the sepoys had been disarmed, or that the Volunteer Guards would be more than a match for them if they ventured to put in an appearance. The news was received with consternation, and the inhabitants of the suburbs in particular, consisting principally of Eurasians, gave way to the most exaggerated fears. Pickets of infantry Volunteers were promptly posted at the points supposed to be threatened: the streets were patrolled by the Volunteer cavalry, and the guns manned by the Volunteer artillery. The regular troops in the Fort stood to their arms. But no enemy appeared, and the panic evaporated even more speedily than it had arisen.

No picture of Calcutta during the Mutiny can be deemed complete without a sketch of the Homeric contest between the Press and the Government which centred around the Gagging Act of 1857. The Press had now been free for twenty-one years. But until the administration of Sir Charles Metcalfe, its liberator, in 1836, it had been kept strictly under control. The first newspaper to appear in Calcutta was Hicky's *Bengal Gazette*, which was published on Saturday, January 29th, 1780, eight years before the birth of *The Times* in London. It grew so scurrilous, however, that in the following November Warren Hastings prohibited its circulation through the channels of the General Post Office "on account of its lately having been found to contain several improper paragraphs tending to vilify private characters and to disturb the peace of the settlement": and Hicky ended his Indian career in the Jail in Lall Bazar. Other journals followed between 1781 and 1786, but most of these were shortlived. By the end of the century, Calcutta boasted of no less than eight: of which the best-known were the *Asiatic Mirror* and the *Bengal Hurkaru,* now merged in the *Indian Daily News.* Their existence was of the most chequered description. Both Lord Wellesley and Lord Minto were extraordinarily sensitive to newspaper criticism. A rigid censorship was instituted in 1799. Every copy of a newspaper was required to be submitted before publication to the inspection of the Government Secretary, under penalty of immediate deportation to England in default: and the blue pencil was freely applied. Many were the warnings and rebuffs conveyed to Calcutta editors during the period from 1799 to 1813. While Wellesley was at Madras directing the campaign against Tippoo, we find him commanding Sir Alured Clarke, his deputy at Fort William, to embark Mr. Bruce, the editor of the *Asiatic Mirror*, on the first ship which might be sailing for Europe, and adding that if the editors of the other papers could not be "tranquillized," their journals were to be suppressed by force and their persons deported. In 1808 the editor of the *Calcutta Gazette* was censured by Lord Minto for having omitted during several weeks to submit proofsheets of his paper for inspection. Three years later, the Missionaries who had established a printing press at the Danish Settlement of Serampore, were called upon to remove within British jurisdiction and to cease publication of their "extremely scurrilous" attacks upon the beliefs of Hindoos and Mussulmans.

Lord Hastings endeavoured to alleviate the burden of this irritating thraldom. The censorship was abolished in 1818, the year which witnessed the foundation of the *Friend of India* as a monthly Magazine by the elder Marshman at Serampore: and nothing but certain regulations, which became a dead-letter, and the power of deportation remained. The latter was employed in startling fashion in 1823, during Mr. John Adam's tenure of office pending the arrival of Lord Amherst, when Mr. Silk Buckingham, the editor of the *Calcutta Journal*, was actually deported for his outspoken comments upon official acts and personages. A storm of indignation was aroused in Calcutta, but the time was not yet ripe for complete emancipation. Lord William Bentinck hesitated to formally proclaim the liberty of the Indian Press: and it was not until his retirement that on September 15th, 1836, the boon was granted by Sir Charles Metcalfe, who was in temporary charge of the government, acting entirely on his own motion and responsibility and largely fortified by the advice and support of Macaulay. The Court of Directors reprimanded Metcalfe for his action, and recorded their opinion that the passing of the Act, XI of 1835, without a reference to the Home authorities, was "indefensible": but they abstained from disallowing it, and Metcalfe was acclaimed upon all hands as the "Liberator of the Indian Press." Henceforth the *Englishman,* which absorbed the older and moribund *John Bull* in 1833 and first appeared in that year under the name of the *Englishman and Military Chronicle,* bore a motto to that effect upon one side of its title. Upon the other side were displayed the well-known lines from Milton: "This is true liberty when free-born men, having to advise the public, may speak out."

It must be acknowledged that both the *Englishman* and its rival Calcutta Journal, the *Bengal Hurkaru,* availed themselves fully of the right of free speech they had obtained. "People may preach to us of the beauty of brotherly love as long as they like," writes the *Englishman* upon one occasion, "but, Lord bless us, where is the man who having a press at his command, can at all times resist a jest at the expense of his opponent?" Yet, if those jests "sometimes displayed themselves in a manner more gratifying to an editor's personal feelings than instructive to the public," it was not altogether the fault of the Press. There was no lack of literary talent in the Calcutta of that day. Charles Thackeray, the uncle of the novelist, who sank about 1846 into an obscure grave, was among the leader writers of the *Englishman,* and during the eight years which preceded his death, he and John Farley Leith and more than one other clever advocate of the Supreme Court were frequent contributors to its columns. Their great difficulty, however, was the want of news upon which to exercise their wits. The mails from Europe were few and far between. Once a month, or even at longer intervals, a ship would come in, and then there would be a flood of cuttings from the London papers and of caustic and shrewd observations. But on the days which were not red-letter ones, what was the journalist to do, if he did not indulge in "any of the excruciating delights which spring from a good hearty dislike of a rival"?

The trouble unfortunately in 1857 was that the Calcutta newspaper world did not content itself with the interchange of editorial amenities after the fashion of Mr. Pott and Mr. Slurk. In times such as ours when the Presidency Chambers of Commerce are credited with so large a controlling influence over the actions of Government, it requires an effort to realize the bitter animosity between officials and "interlopers" as the non-officials in irony named themselves, which marked the forties and fifties of the nineteenth century. We are sufficiently habituated nowadays to the free expression of our thoughts and our grievances through public channels to regard newspaper criticism as a necessary, if sometimes unduly acid, corrective to the vagaries of constituted authority: and not even the Viceroy can claim immunity from censure if he elects to run counter to the sentiments of any portion of the community. But a glance through the files of the *Englishman* and the *Hurkaru* during the Mutiny year will reveal a want of self-control and a wealth of invective upon which the official mind might well be pardoned for looking with misgiving at a time when the power of the English was trembling in the balance and John Company's Raj seemed tottering to its fall. There never was greater need for a cool head and calm judgment: and the Calcutta Press made not the slightest attempt to keep the one or to cultivate the other.

Their tone was, frankly speaking, deplorable. Utter blindness before the event was followed by demoralization so complete as to be almost incredible. Sir George Trevelyan has collated in his *Letters of a Competition-wallah* a number of extracts from the Calcutta papers of the year. Those of the spring reserve their choicest shafts of ridicule and sarcasm for the "croakers of evil," the few observant men who read aright the signs and portents which seem so plain to us of a later generation. The sepoy was every thing that could be desired. Faithful and docile, his prejudices were to be respected, and his calumniators snubbed. "Even Cromwell's Ironsides," we read, "would have mutinied if they had been forced to hear the Common Prayer read." While the air was full of dim prophecies and ghastly rumours, and the mysterious chupatties were passing from hand to hand and from village to village, the Calcutta papers filled their columns with the trifles of Anglo-Indian society small-talk. Amateur theatricals, abuse of the municipal board for their neglect to water the Course, thorny questions of precedence and etiquette—such are the topics which interested Calcutta. The *Lucknow News* in May, 1857, consists chiefly of complaints regarding the badness of the road from Cawnpore. "Soft blankets should be provided in the dawk carriages, and plenty of them." The people of Delhi have no thought for anything but the conduct of a peppery colonel who at a station-ball, for some fancied insult to himself from a civilian, had turned his band out of the room and stopped the dancing. There is no other news to give. "All is quiet and dull" on the fifth of that same month of May, only six days before the troops from Meerut were hunting down and butchering every Christian in the capital of the great Mogul. "Truly, there is an irony in history, surpassing in depth the irony of Sophocles."

But as autumn set in, the style alters. "What a pity it is," wrote an officer of the 65th Native Infantry in February 1857, "that Europeans abusing a corps cannot be strung up." A few months, and it had become necessary to double the guards at Fort William, in order to prevent the soldiers from sallying out at nights to avenge the atrocities committed in Oudh and Rohilcund upon syces and palkee-bearers. The residents at a station in Behar, declares one of them in unblushing print, would be "all right and merry, if we could only get a few people to hang." A gentleman at Raneegunge gives details of a "picturesque gallows," which he is anxious to construct and which would "accommodate sixteen of the largest size without inconveniencing each other." At Allahabad, the Judicial Commissioners, whom Lord Canning sent later into compulsory private life, are reported to be "doing good service in tucking up and scratching the backs of rebels." Soon afterwards a correspondent from the same place recommends torture as the best method for dealing with "respectable Mahomedans." The editorial columns teemed with deliberate propositions to raze entire cities to the ground, to depopulate whole provinces, to put to the edge of the sword all the women in Delhi and Cawnpore. Nor were the vials of wrath left unemptied upon those who chose to remember that righteousness exalteth a nation. It stands eternally to the credit of Lord Canning that in spite of the vituperation and obloquy poured upon him, he never faltered in his policy nor suffered the passions of the moment to gain the mastery over him. "I will not govern in anger," he wrote to Lord Granville, "justice, and that as stern, as inflexible as law and might can make it, I will deal out. But I will never allow an angry and undiscriminating act or word to proceed from the Government of India, as long as I am responsible for it." Unhappily, his motives were totally misconstrued. There was nothing too unworthy to be alleged against him because he would not follow the gospel of wholesale hangings and burnings preached by a panic-stricken community and a frenzied Press. Towards the end of 1857 the European public of Calcutta and Bengal addressed a petition to the Queen, in which they prayed for the Governor-General's recall. The "language of rage in which the indictment was framed reached its climax in the concluding sentences which declared in so many words that the "only policy by which British rule and the lives, honour and property of Your Majesty's Christian subjects in this country can in future be secured, is a policy of vigorous repression and punishment." And if the Governor-General was despicable for the humanity which forbade him to visit the sins of an ill-organized, spoilt and misgoverned mercenary army upon the people at large, Sir Frederick Halliday and Sir John Peter Grant, the men that kept the bridge with him, merited, so it was said, the contempt of every right-thinking individual because they loyally stood by their chief and uniformly exercised their great personal influence over him on the side of justice and moderation. Lest these words of condemnation be deemed strong, they shall be fortified by contemporary authority. "Barring humanity-pretenders, To Hell of none are we the willing senders," wrote some wretch in the "poet's corner" of the *Englishman*, "But if to sepoys entrance must be given, Locate them, Lord, in the back slums of Heaven."

It is impossible to avoid a feeling of shame and humiliation as we read extracts such as these and strive to appreciate the melancholy fact that they represent the smallest portion of the invective and calumny in which the newspapers of Calcutta permitted themselves to indulge during the year of blood. Yet a few quotations are not without their value, in view of the contumely and blame showered upon Lord Canning for his interference with a liberty which had degenerated into the most dangerous license. On the 13th of June, 1857, the day before Panic Sunday, and a fortnight before the massacre at Cawnpore which has stamped the name of the Nana Sahib with infamy, Lord Canning himself introduced a Bill into the Legislative Council, which put the

14

Press once more into the leading strings from which Metcalfe had released it. It was passed on the same day without a dissentient voice and became Act XV of 1857. The duration of the Act, which prohibited the keeping or using of a printing press without a license, was limited to one year, and its application extended over the whole of India and embraced not only the English newspapers, but also native journals, of which there were by this time not a few. This want of discrimination was bitterly resented by the Anglo-Indian community, who conceived that the same restrictions were not required for the *Englishman* and the *Hurkaru* as for the *Samachar Sudhabarshan.* A perfect tornado of angry passion burst forth: but the Government remained unmoved. It is sadly indicative of the temper of the times that one of the first papers to come under the operation of the Act was the *Friend of India.* During the editorship of the younger Marshman, who transformed it into a weekly journal in 1835, its influence during the thirties and forties had been of the most beneficial and elevating kind, and under its modern daily garb of the *Statesman,* it has forfeited none of its early reputation. Nevertheless, on the 29th of June, 1857, Lord Canning's Secretary found it necessary to warn its publisher against a "repetition of remarks of the dangerous nature" contained in an article on the centenary of Plassey. Certain native editors were brought to trial before the Supreme Court on a charge of publishing seditious libels, and the grand jury returned a true bill: but the charge was not pressed on the tender of an expression of contrition and an undertaking not to offend for the future. To such a pitch, however, did public feeling run, and so unrestrained was the language employed, that on the 18th September, the *Hurkaru* was after a warning suppressed: and its license was not restored until an apology had been received from the proprietor. The excitement was heightened by the action taken by Sir Frederick Halliday in the well-known case of Mr. William Tayler, the Commissioner of Patna. The controversy on the propriety of Mr. Tayler's conduct in ordering his district officers to abandon their posts and to fall back upon Dinapore, has filled many volumes: and the present is not the occasion for raking up the embers of this famous feud. But it is hard to deny our sympathy to a man whose cause has evoked the advocacy of historians of the calibre of Sir John William Kaye and Colonel Malleson, and harder still, perhaps, to escape the thought that personal dislike to Mr. Tayler was not without its influence on the Lieutenant-Governor's inflexible attitude towards him. The Calcutta Press after the removal of its muzzle in June, 1858, made full use of the weapon which was thus afforded: and it is only fair to add that the *Hurkaru* was not the only or by any means the worst offender, and that if it did not repent with its betters, it certainly sinned with a great many of its elders.

CHAPTER XIV.

ON THE THRESHOLD OF TO-DAY.

WITH the passing of the cloud of mutiny and massacre which hangs over the year 1857, we emerge into the history of our own times. Calcutta, as we know it to-day, has literally grown up within the memory of many who are still among her citizens. "It is not too much to say," wrote Sir George Trevelyan of the Calcutta of 1863, "that there is nothing here which answers to a public office in London. The business of the State is transacted in private houses hired or bought for the purpose. The lobby of the Treasury is a dirty closet with a whitewashed wall, daubed with specimens of native art, and opening into an untidy back-yard. Out here the Horse Guards would be regarded as an elegant and commodious pile of architecture and the National Gallery as the model of a chaste and classic style." The gibe is out of date, but it is not so very long ago that it might still have been reckoned to be deserved. A glance at the Calcutta Directory of 1870 will reveal how very new is the splendid group of public offices which surrounds Government House. The foundations of the High Court were laid, it is true, in 1864, but it was not completed until 1872: and meanwhile the Original Side of the Court sat in the Town Hall and the Appellate Benches in the Court house of the old Sudder Dewanny Adawlat on the Lower Circular Road. The offices of the Government of India were here, there, and everywhere: the Home Department was in Chowringhee and the Public Works Department in the Strand Road. The Treasury Building (the subject of Sir George Trevelyan's ire) stood where it now does, but its present shape was assumed between 1877 and 1882 : and the same period witnessed the construction of the Imperial Secretariat behind it, which stands on the site of what was once known partly as Loudoun Buildings and partly as Spence's Hotel. The General Post Office was opened to the public as far back as 1868 : but the Central Telegraph Office was in Clive Street in 1869 and in Fancy Lane in 1870, and the existing building was not commenced before 1873.

To the seventies, that is to the energetic Lieutenant-Governorship of Sir Richard Temple, must equally be assigned the Indian Museum in Chowringhee, which was declared ready for occupation in 1875. The Small Cause Court was to be found in Mangoe Lane in 1870. Its modern habitation at the corner of Bankshall Street and Hare Street was erected four years later, and may be deemed quite an ancient landmark by the side of its neighbour, the Military Account Department's offices. The Bengal Secretariat led a nomadic existence for years. In 1854 it started its career at 1, Council House Street : two years later it had been transferred to Somerset Buildings, at the corner of Hastings Street and Strand Road : and during the seventies it occupied two houses, one in Chowringhee on the site of the present School of Art, and the other in Sudder Street. It was not until 1880 that a permanent home was found in Writers' Buildings, and the East Indian Railway Company compelled to seek quarters elsewhere.

The imposing façade was added in 1882, and the Bengal Council Chamber which obscures the memory of the old Church of St. Anne, was first used in the cold weather of 1883. The Board of Revenue, which since the last few months has been located in the newly-built northerly wing of Writers' Buildings, was in Russell Street in the twenties, whence it migrated to the premises in Bankshall Street, now handed over to the Imperial Department of Commerce and Industry. The Collector of Calcutta, lineal descendant of the Zemindar of olden days, has wandered all over the city in search of a resting-place. In 1783 his office was on the southern side of Lall Bazar, with the old jail to the east and Kiernander's Mission Church to the north. By 1820 it had been removed to a house at the junction of Chowringhee and Park Street. Thence in the thirties it journeyed to the old Mint premises in Church Lane (on the site of the present Stationery Office), and fifty years later it had found its way to a house in Bankshall Street, opposite to the premises just quitted by the Board of Revenue. The block of buildings in Charnock Place, in the north-western corner of Dalhousie Square, which accommodate the Collector and the Presidency Commissioner to-day, were erected in the nineties during the Lieutenant-Governorship of Sir Charles Elliott. The modern Custom House (the third of its race) likewise dates from 1899: and the Municipal Office in Corporation Street and the Military Secretariat, which has swept away the once familiar Belattee Bungalow on the Esplanade to the east of Government House, are the work of the present year.

As with public offices, so it has been with private dwellings. When the King, then the Prince of Wales, visited Calcutta in the winter of 1875, the untidy bustis and dirty dwellings which still mark the entrance to the city from the Howrah Bridge extended all the way down to the Eden Gardens. The space between the present inhabited portion of the Strand and Dalhousie Square was covered with native dwellings of the very worst type, for that was a time when the Hughli was a real forest of masts and the lascar had only just begun to appear on the scene. The drinking shops of Radha Bazar now only remain to testify to the manner in which the European sailor of the sailing ships which lay in the port for months at a time was catered for, but Kipling's ballad of "Fulta Fisher's Boarding House" brings before us clearly enough the conditions which obtained with regard to the port of Calcutta. Recent improvements made by the Bengal-Nagpore Railway at Garden Reach have removed a famous drinking tavern of the class at one time greatly resorted to by sailors. The original proprietor of the tavern, a low class Bengali, met with a terrible death during the Mutiny. Thirty or forty sailors belonging to a ship of war, lying in the Hughli at the time, were taken mysteriously ill. The men suspected that an attempt had been made by the keeper of the tavern to poison them, and a party of sailors stole ashore during the night, seized the unfortunate man, and hanged him from Kidderpore Bridge. An enquiry was held, but the actual perpetrators of the crime were never discovered.

If the name of the first Lieutenant-Governor of Bengal recalls little but Mutiny memories, it is even more difficult to conjure up a picture of the times of his successor which is not deeply tinged with indigo. The gravity of the crisis produced by the struggle between Sir John Peter Grant and the powers of the indigo world was such that even the calm, dispassionate mind of Lord Canning was forced to admit that it "caused him more anxiety than he had felt since the fall of Delhi." Of the bitterness of feeling engendered between officials and planters, and of the uproar in particular created in Calcutta by the famous *Nil Durpan* case, the contemporary press, as in the case of the Mutiny, will be our best interpreters: but it would be hard to pen a description more graphic than that contained in the pages of the *Competition-wallah*, which have already been so freely laid under contribution, and which are a perfect mine of wealth to all who desire to gain a knowledge of the manners and customs and politics of India in the sixties. *Nil Durpan*, or the "mirror of indigo," was in its origin a drama in Bengalee depicting the indigo-planting system as viewed by the natives of the country. It was translated into English by the Rev. James Long, a missionary who was a few years later to add to his fame as one of the most prominent members of the Indian Record Commission. If his name were not already immortalized by his connection with *Nil Durpan*, he would be amply remembered by his "Selections from the Unpublished Records of Government" and his articles in the *Calcutta Review*, which cast a flood of light upon the early history of the English in India and have furnished the starting point for all subsequent enquirers. Extracts from Mr. Long's translation of *Nil Durpan* may be found in the *Competition-wallah*, and they read harmlessly enough after the lapse of five and forty years. But the planting community and their organs in the Press chose to regard the *brochure* as an insult and a libel levelled against their whole class. Mr. Long was brought to trial in the Supreme Court on the 19th of July, 1861, and indicted upon two counts: first for having libelled the *Englishman* and the *Bengal Hurkaru* in his preface, and secondly for having libelled "the general body of planters," in the play itself. Evidence of the "wrong" done to them was given by Mr. Walter Brett and Mr. Alexander Forbes, the editors of the two papers, which were at the moment attacking Lord Canning and Sir John Peter Grant with such virulence that they came to be known in common parlance as the "factory journals." An extraordinary and fiercely discussed summing-up by the Judge, Sir Mordaunt Wells, which must be acknowledged not to have erred on the side of impartiality, resulted in a verdict of guilty from the jury: and Mr. Long was sentenced to a month's imprisonment and a fine of one thousand rupees which was immediately paid by a rich Hindoo gentleman. The sympathy of the public with Mr. Long was not, however, confined to the Hindoo community. During the four days of his trial the Court-room was filled to suffocation by Europeans and Indians, and the crowd was so great that it was remarked that "there could be nobody left to carry on the business of Calcutta." After his conviction, his "apartments in the common jail," we read in a friendly journal of the time, "were thronged by members of the Civil Service, as well as of the Uncovenanted Service, by Chaplains and Missionaries, by gentlemen of the Press and native gentlemen of every degree. Never was a person declared guilty by the highest Court of India for whom so much sympathy was excited as for Mr. Long." The native inhabitants of Calcutta, under the presidency of the grandson of Nubkissen, Rajah Sir Radha Kanta Deb, demanded in public meeting the recall of Sir Mordaunt Wells, "in consequence of his frequent and indiscriminate attacks on the characters of the natives of the country with an intemperance inconsistent with the calm dignity of the Bench, as also his repeated and indiscreet exhibitions of a strong political bias and race prejudice which are not compatible with the impartial administration of justice." Even the Bishop of Calcutta, Dr. Cotton, could not remain silent. "The charge of Sir Mordaunt Wells," he wrote, "is a melancholy instance of the opposition which may be sometimes observed in the world between legal and moral justice. Passages which the Judge described as foul and disgusting, are in no way more gross than many an English story or play turning on the ruin of a simple hunted rustic which people read and talk about without scruple."

There was much truth in these words of the Bishop. The position, as it was pointed out at the time, was exactly as if the French clergy had prosecuted Molière or the Yorkshire schoolmasters the creator of Mr. Squeers: and the triumph of the planters was in the end to profit them nothing. Lord Canning stood loyally by his lieutenant, and Sir Charles Wood, the Secretary of State, never wavered in his support. The ultimate result of the struggle may be seen in the ruined and desolate factories which confront the traveller in Nuddea and Jessore: and however unfortunate it may be deemed, it must be conceded to have been inevitable. Still, the victory of the moment rested with indigo, and its champions were not slow to take advantage of it. Mr. Seton-Karr, Secretary to the Government of Bengal, by whose sanction the unlucky pamphlet was circulated, was assailed with hostile criticism from all sides and compelled to resign his office: but he was afterwards made a Judge of the High Court and (such were the methods of those days) ended his official career as Foreign Secretary to the Government of India. He was not the only Civilian attacked. The planters roundly declared that the object of the official was to ruin the industry and expel the "interloper" and the "adventurer" from the country. Every Magistrate suspected of the smallest leaning towards the side of the raiyats was mercilessly gibbeted in the *Englishman* and the *Hurkaru*. All the weapons of invective employed during the Mutiny year were brought once again into requisition. "Mr. Grant may now be said to be reaping. It is manufacturing season with him just at present. He sowed perwannahs, he ploughed with minutes, he harrowed us with Lushingtons and Herschels, and he is now reaping blood."* Poetry of a sort found as usual a place among the wares with which the journalistic Billingsgate was stocked. A choice specimen, though by no means of the strongest brand, may be borrowed from the *Hurkaru*. "Governor Grant," we are told, "is a terrible man, As he reigns in Alipore Hall, A compound of

* Mr. E. H. Lushington was the Commissioner of the Nuddea Division, the centre of the indigo disturbances, and Mr. (now Sir William) Herschel, the Magistrate and Collector of Krishnagar, the headquarters station of that district.

Ghengis and Kublai Khan, Tamerlane, Nadir and all." And, as he sits upon his throne, " Says J. P. Grant, sez he, Drive me the planters into the sea."

Lampoons were followed by more litigation, and the Lieutenant-Governor was actually sued for libel by an indignant indigo-planter. The case was heard by Sir Barnes Peacock, who judiciously devoured the oyster and handed each party one of the shells: for how else shall his finding be interpreted that the defendant had published defamatory matter without legal excuse, but without " malice in fact," and his award of the sum of one rupee without costs to the plaintiff who had been able to show no damage upon his part?

In the midst of all the excitement and ferment produced by these incidents, matters of more real and permanent importance to the city were not suffered to be neglected. In 1860 the Calcutta Rifle Corps was officially constituted. Its entire strength, including volunteers from Serampore and Alipore, totalled some 160 men, and it was placed under the command of Colonel (then Captain) G. B. Malleson, the historian of the Indian Mutiny. A commission was appointed in the following year, on the representation of the Trades' Association, to enquire into the perennial problem of municipal administration. Their report stated their conviction that the inadequacy of the conservancy arrangements of which complaint was so loud, was due to want of funds: and a recommendation was submitted for the constitution of a central Municipal Board consisting of 6 members, with the Commissioner of Police as President, and 6 local boards. The scheme fell through, however, like so many of the sort, only to be revived in our own day as an entirely new project under the guise of Borough Councils. Another measure which may be said to have been of direct interest to Calcutta was the establishment on the 18th January, 1862, of a Legislative Council of 12 members for the Bengal Division of the Presidency of Fort William: and the first Council which met on the 18th February, 1862, consisted of officials and non-officials and Indians in equal proportions. During the earlier years of its existence the Council assembled in the building behind the Town Hall which is now occupied by the Legislative Department of the Government of India. A few months after the first meeting of the provincial legislature, the Judges of the newly constituted High Court at Fort William took their seats in the Court House on the Esplanade, and the separate jurisdictions of the Supreme Court and the Sudder Adawlat ceased to exist. The Queen's and the Company's courts were henceforth one: and barristers and members of the Civil Service administered justice side by side.

The shadow of the Orissa famine of 1866, which fills so large a part of the period of office of Sir Cecil Beadon did not fall upon Calcutta. She was more concerned with the new municipal constitution with which she was presented in 1863 shortly after the new Lieutenant-Governor's installation at Belvedere: and which vested the Government of the town in a Corporation consisting of an official Chairman and of the Justices of the Peace, whether for the province or the city. The provincial Justices soon dropped out, and the scheme thus amended remained in operation for nearly fourteen years. The insanitary condition of Calcutta at this time was a matter of serious moment, if we are to accept Sir John Strachey as an authority. Writing in March, 1864, in his capacity of President of the Sanitary Commission for Bengal, he did not hesitate to declare that "the state of the capital of British India, one of the greatest and wealthiest cities in the world, is a scandal and a disgrace to a civilized government. The condition of the city is such that it is literally unfit for the habitation of civilized men. The state even of the southern division of the town, which contains the fine houses of the principal European inhabitants, is often most offensive and objectionable, while with regard to the northern or native division of Calcutta, which contains some hundred thousand people, it is no figure of speech, but the simple truth, to say that no language can adequately describe its abominations. In the filthiest quarters of the filthiest towns that I have seen in other parts of India or other countries, I have never seen anything which can for a moment be compared with the filthiness of Calcutta. This is true, not merely of the interior portions of the town, or of the byeways and places inhabited by the poorer classes, but it is true of the principal thoroughfares anl of the quarters filled with the houses of the richest and most influential portions of the native community. If a plain unvarnished description of the streets of the northern division of Calcutta, bordered by their horrible open drains, in which almost all the filth of the city stagnates and putrefies, were given to the people of England, I believe that they would consider the account altogether incredible. The condition of the river upon the banks of which Calcutta stands is as abominable as that of the city itself. I need only mention one fact regarding it. More than five thousand human corpses have been every year thrown from Calcutta into the river which supplies the greater part of the inhabitants with water for all domestic purposes, and which for several miles is covered with shipping as thickly as almost any river in the world. Fifteen hundred corpses have actually been thrown into the river in one year from the Government hospitals alone. That such things should be true seems really to be hardly credible."*

Whether this picture be overcoloured or not, it must be set down to the credit of the Justices that they had a long list of improvements and reforms to exhibit when they laid down their office in 1876. A Health Officer and Engineer were for the first time appointed for the city: and in obedience to the dictum of Sir John Strachey, that "the municipality should rule the police, and not the police the municipality"—a dictum now discredited—the Chairman of the Justices became also Commissioner of Police for the town of Calcutta. A numerous public body has been officially declared now-a-days to connote inefficiency, and the Justices varied in number from 129 to 153. But the drainage works of Calcutta became a reality under their auspices, and the water-supply, which in 1863 was obtainable only

* The quotation is taken from Mr. C. E. Buckland's *Bengal under the Lieutenant-Governors*—a book which is well worth consultation by the student of modern Indian history, in spite of the long caravan of official documents which straggles unattended across its pages.

from foul and insanitary tanks, and was rarely sufficient in quantity, was made both pure and constant. The "horrible open drains," which had disgusted Sir John Strachey as they had Grandpré and Mackintosh, were filled in, and their place taken by 38 miles of brick sewers under main streets, and 37 miles of pipe-sewers along the alleys. Not less remarkable was the arrangement, still in operation, by which the sewage of the town was daily carried off by steam pumps through a high level sewer to the Salt Lakes, there to contribute to the raising and transformation into a fertile tract of the swamps which had once been a standing menace to the health of Calcutta. The Municipal Railway along Lower Circular Road, which transports the street and house sweepings to the same locality, and which incinerators should before long relieve of its duties, was constructed between 1865 and 1867. The New Market, which was built between 1871 and 1874, is another monument to the energy of the Justices which the ordinary citizen of Calcutta probably feels better able to appreciate. In the matter of the water-supply infinite tact and patience were required to meet the initial difficulty occasioned by the prejudices of religion. Orthodox Hindoos debated whether they could, without loss of caste, drink water that had come through infidel pipes. But their scruples were gradually overcome. The claims of conscience were met halfway by the mingling of a little of the muddy but holy Ganges water with the pure fluid from the municipal standpost: and finally they were ignored altogether. All Calcutta to-day contentedly draws its supply from the waterworks at Pulta, two miles from Barrackpore, where everything that filtration can accomplish is employed to render her water pure and wholesome. Services to the city as real, although upon a more modest scale, were rendered in the direction of making and widening streets. Beadon Street and Beadon Square and Grey Street (called after Sir William Grey, the successor of Sir Cecil Beadon) owe their existence to the Justices. Moorgheehatta Street, renamed in honour of Lord Canning, was improved and widened and continued to meet Jackson Ghât Street. The congestion in Clive Street was sought to be met by the opening out of Clive Row to afford an outlet into Canning Street: and Free School Street was extended as far as Dhurrumtollah. To these achievements may be added the lighting of 105 miles of streets by gas, the establishment of slaughter-houses, and the making of footpaths along the side of nearly the whole of the principal thoroughfares—and enough will be deemed to have been said to justify the generous acknowledgment of the services of the Justices which was placed upon record by Sir Richard Temple in 1876, when he replaced them by a more representative municipal body. No less than two crores of rupees were expended on the improvement of Calcutta between 1858 and 1876, and not one anna can be charged to have been wasted.

CHAPTER XV.

THE LAST FORTY YEARS.

THE year 1864, which was the one immediately following the incorporation of the Justices, was likewise a memorable one for Calcutta. It witnessed the formal inauguration of the Simla exodus which for eight months each year deprives the capital of the presence of the Viceroy and the members of the Supreme Government. Lord Amherst had spent the hot weather of 1829 at Simla: but his successors were content with Barrackpore as a summer residence until the advent of Sir John Lawrence. It witnessed also the speculativé mania over an unlucky scheme for the reclamation of the Sunderbunds, of which nothing remains but the deserted wharves of Port Canning, but which resulted in ruin to many. Finally, the autumn of the year was marked also by a cyclone of unprecedented violence, which burst over Calcutta on the 5th October. There are still living eye-witnesses of the havoc and disaster caused in every quarter of the town. The force of the wind is described as extraordinarily great: so strong was it that over a hundred masonry houses were destroyed and the walls of the stoutest brick buildings quivered under the gusts. The full weight of the storm was felt between ten o'clock in the forenoon and four o'clock in the afternoon. About midday a noise like that of distant thunder gave warning, and in an incredibly short space of time the hurricane fell upon the town. It was accompanied by torrents of strong driving rain which flooded the streets, and by a storm-wave which devastated the country at a distance of eight miles inland on either side of the river, carrying away entire villages and rising in some places to a height of thirty feet. In the northern division of the town, the native huts were blown down in great numbers, about forty thousand being ruined or injured. The distress in the southern quarter was almost as great: and many an English residence in Elysium Row and Camac Street was turned into a refuge for the homeless inhabitants of bustees which had been levelled with the ground. Some seventeen persons were officially reported as killed in the town, and thirty-two in the suburbs. Hundreds of birds were dashed to the ground, and lay gathered into great heaps on the Maidan on the following day. Business was completely arrested: the only two attendants at the Court House were Sir Barnes Peacock, the Chief Justice, and Mr. Belchambers, the Registrar, the latter earning the distinction of being the first arrival. The roof of St. Paul's Cathedral was torn off, and a similar fate overtook the minarets of the great mosque at the corner of Dhurrumtollah and the roof of the Free School. The noble avenue of trees which led up to the "Governor's house" in Fort William, and the avenues in the Botanic Gardens and on the Barrackpore Road vanished utterly.

On the river, the devastation was even greater. There were 195 vessels within the limits of the Port of Calcutta on the 5th of October. They withstood the wind: but the storm-wave was too much for them. One ship after another slipped her moorings. Ten vessels and six tug steamers were lost, and 145 ships driven ashore. The *Govindpore,* a new ship of 1,200 tons, capsized off the Custom House. The Burmah mail steamer foundered at the Sandheads with nearly all hands: the P. & O. Company's mail-boat *Bengal* stranded on the Howrah side of the river, but was got off without damage, and their hulk, the *Hindostan,* broke loose and went down off Garden Reach. Two river-steamers were blown ashore, one on the top of the other. At six o'clock in the evening the Strand Road was breast high in water at places. There had been severe storms in Calcutta in 1842 and 1852, but the cyclone of 1864 was by common consent declared to have surpassed them in intensity.

Three years later, Calcutta was visited by another hurricane on the 2nd November, 1867, which, occurring as it did in the small hours of the morning, was productive of even greater injury and loss of life than its predecessor. The returns showed a death-roll of over a thousand persons in the town and suburbs: and the destruction of over a hundred and fifty masonry buildings and nearly thirty thousand huts was reported. The damage on the river was of a serious character. There was no storm-wave, and the ships in the river were generally able to ride out the cyclone: but the number of cargo boats lost was so great that the business of the Port was seriously interfered with for a time.

In the year 1870, Calcutta was honoured by a visit from the Duke of Edinburgh, who landed from H. M. S. *Galatea* at Prinsep's Ghat, according to time-honoured custom, on the 22nd December, and remained at Government House until the 7th of January, as the guest of the Viceroy, the Earl of Mayo. The city was then able to boast of an Italian opera, and a gala performance was the prelude to a fortnight of ceremonial and festivity. In the Town Hall may be seen a picture commemorating the installation of Prince Alfred as an extra Knight Grand Commander of the Star of India during the period of his stay.

It fell to the lot of Sir George Campbell, who ruled at Belvedere from 1871 to 1874, to witness, during his term of office, the assassination of a Chief Justice and the murder of a Viceroy. On the morning of the 20th September, 1871, Mr. John Paxton Norman, who was officiating as Chief Justice pending the arrival of Sir Richard Couch, was mortally wounded by a Mahomedan fanatic, as he was ascending the steps of the northern portico of the Town Hall, which was then in temporary use as a High Court building. He was placed in a *palki* and carried into the shop of Messrs. Thacker, Spink & Co., where he was laid on a couch in a back room and his wounds examined. Dr. Fayrer and three other doctors were speedily in attendance, but the injuries he had received were fatal and he died shortly after midnight on the same day. There was an extraordinary demonstration of public feeling on the occasion of his funeral. All the public offices in the city were closed, the standard at Fort William and the flags of the ships in the river hung at half mast, every shop was shut and business entirely suspended. The murderer, who was promptly secured and subsequently convicted and executed, was supposed by some to be connected with the

Wahabees, a truculent and seditious Muhammadan sect, which had been of late causing trouble. But the closest enquiry failed to show any grounds for such suspicion: and the author of the crime died on the scaffold without giving any clue to his motives.

Four months later, on the 8th of February, 1872, the Viceroy, Lord Mayo, was fatally stabbed at Port Blair, the capital of the penal Settlement in the Andaman Islands, by a Punjabee convict of the name of Shere Ali, who was under sentence of transportation for life for murder. The news reached Calcutta on the 13th, and on the 17th the late Viceroy's remains, which had been brought up the river in H. M. S. *Daphne,* were landed at Garden Reach and conveyed to Government House over Hastings Bridge and along the Strand Road. At the grass plot opposite Prinsep's Ghat, where the statue of Lord Napier of Magdala now stands, the European residents in Calcutta joined in the funeral procession. The coffin lay in state in the Throne-Room at Government House for two days, and after a funeral service had been performed by Bishop Milman on the north grand staircase on the morning of the 21st, it was taken on board a ship of war for despatch to Ireland, in accordance with Lord Mayo's special directions in his will. As in the case of Chief Justice Norman, the motives of the murder remained a mystery: and it was found, as before, impossible to trace any communication between him and the Wahabee leaders in India. The profoundest sensation was caused in Calcutta by this quick succession of calamities: and for some time it was feared that the Lieutenant-Governor and other high officials had been marked down as the next victims. Sir George Campbell records, however, in his Memoirs that he was convinced that the two assassinations were only unhappy coincidences, and he took no precautions. He proved to be in the right: but it was some time before even the toughest nerves in Calcutta ceased to feel the strain put upon them by the double tragedy.

In the winter of 1875, the Prince of Wales, whom we now know as King Edward the Seventh, followed the example set by his brother Prince Alfred, and visited the capital of his future Empire. The procedure followed was on very similar lines, and will bear record, in view of the visit of another Prince of Wales which marks so auspiciously the opening of Lord Minto's Viceroyalty. The *Serapis*, with the Royal party on board, arrived near Diamond Harbour on the evening of the 22nd December, and the then Lieutenant-Governor of Bengal, Sir Richard Temple, went down the river and met His Royal Highness. On the following day the *Serapis* anchored off Calcutta, and the Prince of Wales landed at Prinsep's Ghat, where he was welcomed by the Viceroy (Lord Northbrook), and the public, both official and non-official, with every demonstration of loyalty. He received an address at the Ghat from the city, and was conducted in grand procession by way of the Ellenborough course, the road being lined with troops and crowded with spectators, to Government House, where he took up his residence as the guest of the Viceroy. A series of ceremonies and festivities in honour of the Prince ensued. Addresses, illuminations, fireworks, State Banquets, a State Ball, receptions of the principal Chiefs and return visits, and a Levée, by no means exhausted the list. A Ball at the Town Hall was given by European Society, and an Indian entertainment at the famous Belgachia garden house that had once been Lord Auckland's country retreat. Visits were paid to Barrackpore, Chandernagore, and the Botanical Gardens, and the Races duly attended. Room was found also for a garden-party and dinner at Belvedere, a Chapter of the Order of the Star of India (the Prince acting as High Commissioner), the unveiling of Lord Mayo's statue, a polo-match between Calcutta and Manipuri-players, a State performance at the theatre with Charles Mathews, the famous comedian, as the principal attraction, a display of native horsemanship, and the investiture of the Prince with the Degree of Doctor of Law by the University of Calcutta. On Christmas Day, the Prince attended Divine Service at the Cathedral. All public offices were closed throughout Bengal from the 23rd December to the 3rd January.

It was also the privilege of Sir Richard Temple to attend the Durbar at Delhi on New Year's Day, 1877, at which Queen Victoria's assumption of the title of Empress of India was publicly proclaimed. But the period of his three years' Lieutenant-Governorship deserves remembrance in Calcutta, not so much by reason of his participations in these historic events, as for the number of additions to the amenities of the city of which he is the author. He was the founder of the Zoological Gardens at Alipore, and their inauguration was one of the many functions undertaken by King Edward during his visit. The

Art Gallery, which started its career in Bow Bazar under the auspices of Lord Northbrook, is another of Sir Richard Temple's creations. The floating bridge over the Hooghly, which Calcutta still considers adequate for the ceaseless stream of traffic that pours along the Strand Road to Howrah, was opened to the public in the first year of his administration. The Botanical Gardens at Seebpore, which had suffered much from the cyclone of 1864 and 1867, were enlarged and improved with the aid of a liberal grant: and the Economic Museum, which Sir George Campbell had tentatively established in Hastings Street, was developed side by side with a special Statistical Department in the Government Secretariat.

The constitution of the Municipal government of Calcutta on an elective basis must, however, be reckoned the most important of Sir Richard Temple's achievements. By Act IV of the Bengal Council for the year 1876, the Justices handed over their administrative functions to a Corporation consisting of seventy-two Commissioners, of whom two-thirds were elected and the remaining third appointed by Government. In 1888, the jurisdiction of this body was extended over a large portion of the suburbs, and various modifications were introduced into the law. The number of Commissioners was raised to 75, out of which 50 were allotted to the 25 wards into which the city was now divided: the nomination of 15 was retained by Government, and of the rest, the Chamber of Commerce and the Calcutta Trades Association were permitted to return four each, and two were given to the Port Trust, which had come into existence in 1870. But with these exceptions, the local administration of Calcutta remained substantially unaltered for the next quarter of a century. The Commissioners, in their review of the work done by them during the twelve years from 1876 to 1888, claimed to have completed the whole of the original drainage scheme, to have doubled the supply of water, to have filled up 240 foul tanks and opened out five new squares, and to have taken large conservancy works in hand. The tramway service, which has substituted electric for horse traction during the last few years, was inaugurated in 1880 with a line between Sealdah and Hare Street running through Bow Bazar, Lall Bazar and Dalhousie Square. The Mayo Native Hospital, which had since 1798 stood on "the open and airy road of Dhurrumtollah," was transferred to its present site on Strand Road North in Jorabagan, and enlarged and re-named as a memorial of the murdered Viceroy. In Colootollah, a large bustee was cleared away to give place to the Eden Hospital: and in Colingah, Duncan's bustee in Wood Street made way for the Surveyor-General's Office. Barrackpore was supplied for the first time with filtered water: Chitpore Road was widened: and nearly twenty-eight lakhs of rupees was expended upon the opening out of the great central thoroughfare from Sealdah Railway Station to the Howrah Bridge, upon which the name of Harrison Road was bestowed in honour of Sir Henry Harrison, then Chairman of the Corporation, and one of the best and most energetic Calcutta has ever known.

During these twenty-four years of municipal expansion, Calcutta passed through the whirlpool of another political controversy. This is not the place in which to discuss the rights and the wrongs of the agitation aroused in 1882 by the proposal of Lord Ripon, who had succeeded Lord Lytton as Viceroy three years earlier, to amend that portion of the Criminal Procedure Code which confined the office of Justice of the Peace outside the Presidency Towns to European British subjects. The suggestion emanated shortly before the conclusion of his term of office as Lieutenant-Governor, from Sir Ashley Eden, who had taken over charge of Bengal from Sir Richard Temple in January, 1877; and in the Statement of Objects and Reasons the anomaly was also pointed out by Mr. Ilbert, the Law Member, of admitting natives of India to the Covenanted Civil Service, and permitting them to discharge the highest judicial duties in the High Court and elsewhere, while restricting their jurisdiction over European British subjects outside the Presidency Towns of Calcutta, Madras and Bombay. The Bill which sought to effect the change, was greeted, however, with the fiercest opposition on the part of the Anglo-Indian community. Some idea of the ferment and the turmoil which an unpopular measure can create in Calcutta has lately been afforded by the agitation against the partition of Bengal. But the campaign against the Ilbert Bill, as it came to be called, possessed this important difference that it found its general in Sir Rivers Thompson, the newly appointed Lieutenant-Governor of Bengal, and its lieutenants in the most influential men in the legal and commercial world of the city. No attempt will here be made to rake up old animosities or to stir up the smouldering embers of race-feeling. Those who have an inclination to rummage in the mouldy records of the past will find that Mr. Buckland has in his annals of "Bengal under the Lieutenant-Governors" anticipated their every wish: for he has reproduced *in extenso* minutes and speeches, inflammatory and otherwise, and has not forgotten to relate how the Viceroy was personally insulted at the gate of Government House and threatened even with forcible deportation. It will suffice to record that the battle ended in a compromise, secured mainly through the efforts of Sir Griffith Evans, a distinguished advocate of the Calcutta High Court: and that the most abiding, although perhaps the most unlooked for, result of the agitation has been the formation of the Indian National Congress which meets yearly at various provincial capitals in the capacity of an organised and crystallized body of native public opinion.

We may pass more rapidly over the events of the succeeding years. In 1890, the late Prince Albert Victor visited Calcutta during the Viceroyalty of Lord Lansdowne and the Lieutenant-Governorship of Sir Steuart Bayley: and, like his father, landed, according to established precedent, at Prinsep's Ghat. A year later Calcutta had the honour of welcoming the present Czar of Russia. The opening of the Kidderpore Docks and the completion of the series of stately Government offices which are so conspicuous a feature of the European quarter, remains as evidences of the vigorous rule of Sir Charles Elliott. The Lieutenant-Governorship of Sir Alexander Mackenzie, who governed Bengal from 1895 to 1898, was marked by the outbreak of plague in Bombay in 1896, the great famine of 1898, and the disastrous earthquake of 1897 which laid Shillong in ruins and shook Calcutta to its foundations. But it may be questioned whether even these tragedies of nature produced as great an upheaval as the complete remodelling of the Municipality upon lines largely denounced as retrograde. The cardinal principle of the much-discussed Bill, which eventually became law in 1899, was that the ordinary everyday work of a city sheltering nearly a million souls could not be adequately performed unless it were concentrated in the hands of one man, and that man a member of the Indian Civil Service. The Corporation was not extinguished as a body, but its numbers were reduced, the percentage of elected Commissioners diminished, and many of its powers either largely curtailed or else transferred to a General Committee in which the elected Commissioners are in a minority. It is too early as yet to speak of the success of this latest experiment in municipal politics: but of its unpopularity at the time of its introduction, ample proof was afforded by the simultaneous resignation of their seats by twenty-eight of the most public spirited and influential of the elected Commissioners of Indian nationality.

The history of the Viceroyalty of Lord Curzon must be left to be written by other hands. In matters of minor importance it may be said at once that the obligation of Calcutta to the late Viceroy stands in need of no reservation. The restoration of the Holwell Monument, the transformation into a pleasant garden of the "No Man's Land" to the east of Government House, the establishment of the Imperial Library, the purchase of Hastings' historic house at Alipore as a State guest-house, and the conception of the "snow-white fabric" of the Victoria Memorial Hall, which will before long supplant the unsightly Jail building on the southern extremity of the Maidan—these are marks of interest and appreciation which the citizens of the Imperial capital of British India have not been slow to acknowledge. But, where larger questions are at issue, the public demands time for reflection. It is always a trifle forced and often a trifle defiant to attempt to anticipate the verdict of posterity regarding the men and measures of yesterday. The gigantic Calcutta Improvement Scheme which looms in the immediate future, has not passed beyond the pale of controversy, and it has yet to justify the welcome which is officially demanded on its behalf. We must content ourselves in a final chapter with an effort to depict for the benefit of the generations to come which will pass judgment upon us, who and what manner of men we are that claim to be "citizens of no mean city" and inheritors of the labours of Charnock and Holwell and Clive and Hastings.

CHAPTER XVI.

"CITIZENS OF NO MEAN CITY."

"TAKE your map of India, and find, if you can, a more uninviting spot than Calcutta. Placed in the burning plain of Bengal, on the largest delta of the world, amidst a network of sluggish, muddy streams, in the neighbourhood of the jungles and marshes of the Sunderbunds, and yet so distant from the open sea as to miss the benefits of the breeze which consoles Madras for the want of a cold season and a permanent Settlement—it unites every condition of a perfectly unhealthy situation. The place is so bad by nature, that human efforts could do little to make it worse: but that little has been done faithfully and assiduously." Such was the unflattering picture of the capital of British India drawn by Sir George Trevelyan in days gone by. But forty-two years have elapsed since the words were written: and it may be said without any boasting that the Calcutta of 1905 is a much better place to live in than the Calcutta of 1863 seems to have been. It is to be feared that the humid and enervating climate has remained the same, and not even the most enthusiastic admirer of the City of Palaces can conscientiously give it unalloyed praise upon that score. But in all else, in healthiness, in outward beauty, in the amenities of civilization, there has been a marked improvement: and the Englishman who is condemned by fate to dwell in the East, will on the whole find it hard to discover pleasanter quarters than Calcutta will provide him.

In one sense Calcutta may not be the metropolis of the Empire. She cannot claim to be the earliest possession of the English in India: nor has she inherited any of the traditions that linger around the audience-chambers of the great Mogul. But for a century and a half she has been the central seat of the English Government. Circumstances have made her the pivot of the administration, and it cannot be denied that she is nobly symbolical of her high position. There are other cities in India with magnificent associations. Delhi with her imperial memories and Agra with her majestic monuments, may vaunt a beauty and a grandeur to which the smoky and steamy city by the banks of the Hooghly can never aspire. The splendid architecture of Bombay and the green and white freshness of Madras, that city of historic renown—and of distances—may be held by those who will to constitute their own peculiar charm. It may even be that Calcutta is destined, as the outcome of Lord Curzon's insistence upon the division of Bengal, to be shorn of her commercial crown by the superior natural advantages of Chittagong. The time may perhaps come when the restoration of the old-world glories of Dacca will have robbed her of a portion of the political prestige she enjoys as the focus of educated Indian opinion. Rivals she has in plenty, but one and all among them lack that which is possessed by the city set among the marshes, the *urbs inter paludes* of old Job Charnock.

There is everything in Calcutta to remind her citizens and to impress upon the stranger within her gates that she is the capital of the British Raj—Wellesley's stately

Government House, the statues of past Governors-General upon her vast expanse of emerald-green *maidan*, the massive blocks of Government offices, the long array of palaces upon Chowringhee, the rows of warehouses and jetties and docks, the swift flowing Hooghly with its multitude of masts, the hum and bustle of the restless mercantile quarter, the large European colony, whose counterpart, whether in numbers or influence, will be sought in vain in the other Presidency towns, the signs upon every hand of opulence and prosperity. Yet Calcutta is not dependent upon the glamour of imperialism for the meed of recognition and appreciation which she courts. We may condemn as inartistic the straggling outlines and uneven frontages of our city : we may inveigh against the stifling dust of her streets and the stucco pretence of her buildings : we may be appalled by the squalor of her crowded slums, but we cannot deny the vague and tantalizing charm with which she carries off all her imperfections and vanquishes all her detractors. The cool green foliage with which her tanks are fringed refreshes the eye under the fiercest sun : there are few sights which can challenge comparison with the *maidan* when it is ablaze with the scarlet splendour of the blossoming gold mohur trees. "In the gorgeous hues of her sunsets, Calcutta is wholly beautiful, and never lovelier than in the chill of some misty winter's evening, or at the close of a sullen monsoon day, when the crimson clouds are piled over Hastings like the reflection from some giant conflagration, and the silent river rushes along, black and unfathomable, faintly illumined by the twinkling lights of Howrah and the Strand. Another witching mood is hers when she lies sleeping in the white enchantment of the Indian moonlight, which turns her stucco to rubies, her plaster to pearls, and pours out its flood of silver upon her dark waters."

But Calcutta is withal a Queen of two faces: a city of startling contrasts, of palaces and hovels, of progress and reaction, of royal grandeur and of squalor that beggars description. Captains of ships at anchor in the Hooghly no longer (it is true) send one of their crew every morning to remove dead bodies from the cables. The adjutant bird no more patrols our streets and haunts our roofs. The goodwill of a rainy season has ceased to be worth half a lakh of rupees to an undertaker. Naked faquirs have given over parading the streets of Calcutta; nor may human sacrifices be witnessed at Kalighat. But the electric tramcar rumbles along Old Court House Street side-by-side with the ramshackle antediluvian unspeakable ticca gharry. Ten minutes' walk from Dalhousie Square will land the seeker after sensation in a labyrinth of narrow unpaved winding lanes, polluted with odours that put those of Cologne to shame and swarming with humanity, where the scavenging carts are the rarest of visitors and the ghostly glimmer of an occasional and inadequate gas-lamp furnishes the solitary illumination. Not a thousand yards from Government House, troops of jackals may be heard after sunset sweeping through the deserted streets and making night hideous with their fearsome howls.

Other cities hide their rags and tatters: why does Calcutta flaunt hers unabashed? Let us be just, and recognise that she is still standing at the parting of the ways. She is the creation of the West. The ideals and the civilization of the West are luring her on: and the spirit of advancement is abroad. There are those among her Indian citizens who in point of intellectual culture can hold their own with any Englishman. Not least among the marvellous changes wrought in India during the sixty years of Queen Victoria's reign has been the spread of English education. But the East is the East, and the West is the West. The prejudices and the customs of a religion which is half as old as time are not to be discarded in the twinkling of an eye. The marvel in Calcutta is not what remains to be done, but what has been done. The Oriental is leisurely and may not be hurried: and the Anglo-Indian is so accustomed to look upon Calcutta as an European city that he is apt to forget that she is set among the tropics and that the European is the merest drop in the ocean of her inhabitants.

An air of mystery long hung over the question of the population of Calcutta. There have been repeated enumerations, but the extraordinary discrepancies and fluctuations which they reveal have invested with uncertainty the solution of a problem that should be of the simplest. The difficulty has been mainly caused by the fetish which succeeding generations have chosen to make of Holwell's so-called "census" of 1752. In his capacity as Zemindar he computed the areas under his jurisdiction, and "agreeably to his exactest judgement" arrived at the conclusion that they sheltered 409,506 "constant inhabitants" without reckoning "the multitude that daily come in and return but yet add to the consumption of the place." His calculations have been carefully checked, and upon his own estimate of eight persons to what he terms a "house," it has been shown that the figure, "agreeably to the best information he had acquired," should stand at 117,744 for the 3,085 acres and 14,718 "houses" which then comprised the Settlement. We may be content to moderate Holwell's inflated estimate accordingly, ignoring the fantastic guesses with which it inspired Grandpré and Sir Edward Hyde East, and passing over the later efforts at accurate enumeration which it still did its best to mystify. The contrast will not suffer. For the present area of Calcutta proper, by which is intended the twenty-five municipal wards, the Fort and the "water tract" covered by the Port and the Canals, is 13,237 statute acres, according to the census of 1901, and its population consists of 847,796 souls, of whom 562,596 are males and 285,200 females. Its boundary on the north and east is the circular canal, which separates it from the suburban municipalities of Cossipore-Chitpore and Manicktollah. Lower down on the east it marches with the district of the Twenty-four Pergunnahs, its most easterly wards being Ballygunge and Tollygunge. The southern boundary is supplied by the Garden Reach Municipality: and on the west the river Hooghly flows along its entire length. If these three minor municipalities, which are all that was left of the old "Suburban Municipality" by the Act of 1888, and are, strictly speaking, "outside the town," are included within the limits of Calcutta, an addition of 101,348 to the population must be made, and the final numbers will then stand at 949,144 persons, of whom 624,855 are males and 324,289 females.

The bulk of this population is Hindoo. Out of the total of well-nigh a million, 615,491 are Hindoos, 286,576 are Muhammadans, and 38,515 are Christians, 14,663 of the last-named being Eurasians and 8,943 native converts. By far the most numerous among the 180 Hindoo castes is that of the Brahmans, who supply one-seventh of the total Hindoo community and all but ten per cent. of the entire population. Among the Muhammadans, 7,586 are Sayyids or descendants, whether actual or reputed, of the Prophet. The Christians, exclusive of those of mixed and Indian parentage, are divided into 31 nationalities. There are 8,460 Englishmen, 1,648 Irishmen, 1,181 Scotchmen, and 76 Welshmen, making a total of 11,425 natives of the United Kingdom. In view of the remarkable vitality displayed by the Scotchmen of Calcutta and their predominance in almost every walk of life in the city, there may be some incredulity in accepting the statement that they are numerically inferior to the Irishmen. It may, indeed, be questioned whether some of the "census" Irishmen are not of the "Baroda Highlander" class, and whether Eurasians of Irish descent (who are undoubtedly common) have not in certain cases preferred to return themselves as of the whole rather than of the half blood. The rest of the British Empire contributes 53, and the domiciled Armenians, who may also be reckoned as subjects of King Edward, number 777. There are, in addition, 222 Germans, 205 Americans, 198 Frenchmen, 178 Portuguese, 145 Austrians, 122 Greeks, 103 Belgians, 71 Swedes, 67 Russians, 49 Norwegians, 37 Dutchmen, 35 Spaniards, 20 Danes, and 13 Hungarians.

Among minor religions in Calcutta, four only, besides

those named, have more than 1,000 adherents. The Buddhists (mainly Burmans, Chinamen and Mughs from Chittagong) claim 2,903, the Jews (of whom the best families come from Bagdad) 1,889, the Brahmos or Hindoo "Protestants," 1,799, and the Jains, who are chiefly merchants, 1,241. The only others deserving of mention are the Parsees, the Confucians, who are principally the Chinese bootmakers, carpenters and cabinet-makers of Bentinck Street, and the Sikhs, who are mostly durwans and employés of the electric supply companies. But they contribute the merest handful, accounting for 290, 178, and 153 persons respectively.

In the matter of education, the Census of 1901 discloses that less than one-fourth of the total population of Calcutta and suburbs are able to read and write. But among those returned as illiterate, many are, of course, children: and the number of literate persons above 20, which is 50,805, forms, as a matter of fact, a little more than 70 per cent. of the total literate population. The percentage of literates is highest, as might be expected, among Christians, both male and female, and lowest among Mahomedans. With regard to knowledge of English, the percentage among Hindoos is 14, among Parsees 68, and among Mussulmans only about 2½. There are fifty-seven languages spoken in Calcutta, 41 of which are Asiatic and 16 non-Asiatic. The mother-tongue, however, of the greater portion of the population is either Bengalee or Hindustani, which absorb between them 80 per cent. The three languages coming next in order are Ooriya, English, and Urdu.

According to the returns, the number of married men in the city amounts to 358,336. But the total of married women is only 131,816, and it would appear therefore that there are no less than 226,520 husbands living in Calcutta without their wives. This high proportion of males to females is no novel element among the distinctive features presented by the population of Calcutta. There has been, it is true, a large increase, in these days of rapid and comfortable transit, in the number of Englishwomen who take up their residence in India: and it is no longer true to assert that "the European women to be found in Bengal and its dependencies cannot amount to two hundred and fifty, while the European male inhabitants of respectability, including military officers, may be taken at about four thousand." But the fluctuations of the English population pass unnoticed in Calcutta. The reason for the disparity of the sexes must be sought in the habits and customs of the people of the country. The poorer classes whom the inducement of high wages attracts to the city, rarely bring their women with them: and the cost of living, and especially of accommodation, is so high that necessity combines with prejudice to curtail very largely the existence of anything of the nature of family life among them.

The question of occupation is one of considerable interest. Nearly the entire non-agricultural labouring population are either Hindoos or Mahomedans. As regards the former, it is well-known that each of the numerous castes into which they are separated have a traditional occupation or profession assigned to them. It would be useless, however, to attempt to classify after any rigid system the occupations of the modern Hindoo world by the castes to which they belong. Caste avocations, it will be found upon examination, have largely given way in Calcutta before the wider outlook afforded by education. There are Deputy Magistrates of the barber caste and Brahmans who do not shrink from the contamination of a bone-mill. The profession of the law is almost entirely absorbed by the higher castes, but Sadgops, whose traditional occupation is cultivation, are to be met with in professorial chairs, and Sunris, or wine-sellers, in the postal and telegraph departments. Still, the general observation is subject to the qualification that the lower castes have not emancipated themselves as completely as the higher. The mass of Dhobas still wash clothes, although one-fourth of them have adopted other pursuits, and some have made their way into Government service. The Chatri or soldier caste supplies most recruits to the police, and many are durwans or doorkeepers. The Malo is usually a boatman like his ancestor. So, too, the Dome and the Hari, who are among the most degraded classes, are employed principally in the scavenging occupations of their caste. But two-fifths only of the Kahars carry palanquins which, be it noted, are being fast elbowed out of existence in Calcutta by the electric tram and the third-class hackney-carriage. Bengalee Moochees still make boots and shoes: but Behari Chamars or leather-sellers are beginning to take to other occupations. The Lalbegis, or disciples of Lal Beg, the God of the Broom, are by no means all sweepers. Kaiburtas (cultivators), Tantis (weavers), and Telis (oil-sellers) have very largely given up their traditional callings. Subarnabarnicks (gold-smiths) have turned to money-lending and banking: and the majority of the Kayasthas, or writers, have laid aside the pen for commerce and service. The Vaidyas, whose pursuit should be that of medicine, are now chiefly to be found in Government and mercantile offices and as teachers in schools. Among Brahmans, only 13 per cent. follow the traditional callings of their caste, that is to say, are priests, religious preceptors, pundits, or cooks, the last named occupation being obviously dictated by the law which prohibits a Hindoo from accepting food prepared by a man of inferior caste.

Upon the general question, it may be observed that certain occupations emerge as specially favoured by Hindoos, and others by Mahomedans. Thus, Hindoos as a class would appear to avoid employment as building artificers, ships' crews, boatmen, watermen, syces, drivers and dress-makers. If they have a preference, it is to carry on the business of general merchants and traders, and to act as menial servants and general labourers. They supply 96 per cent. of the cowkeepers and milksellers, 88 per cent. of the workers and 92 per cent. of the dealers in percious metals and stones, 95 per cent. of the workers and 92 per cent. of the dealers in brass, copper and bell-metal, and 88 per cent. of the workers and 85 per cent. of the sellers of hardware. On the other hand, 81 per cent. of the butchers are Musulmans, and 82 per cent. of the masons and builders. Musulmans figure largely also as lascars and boatmen, bheesties or water-carriers and cart-drivers, coachmen and syces or grooms, tailors and duftries, although the last named have largely exchanged the mending of quills for the binding of books. They contribute also 32 per cent. of the general labourers: but they seem to dislike shop-keeping, except in the matter of making and selling glass and China ware, and are averse to the vending of vegetable food. Householders will perhaps learn with surprise that they do not enjoy the monopoly of domestic service in European and other Christian families. They are, as of old, the table-servants, but Madrasis and low-caste Hindoos are supplanting them as cooks to a considerable extent. Ooriyas can no longer earn a monotonous living as punkha-pullers in a city where electric fans have passed into the category of ordinary Anglo-Indian necessaries: but they are still first favourites as gardeners and house-servants, their familiar appellation of bearer showing clearly enough the manner in which the good graces of the sahib were won, in days when palkees were an essential accompaniment of Anglo-Indian life, and none but the Governor-General and the senior member of Council kept carriages.

Among the many communities that inhabit Calcutta, the most powerful and influential is, unquestionably, the European community. In its composition it does not differ essentially from that of other large cities, excepting in the almost entire absence of the European artizan, who forms so important an element in the population of English towns. The few British mechanics in Calcutta are not actual labourers in their crafts at all, but merely supervisors of the work, which is almost entirely performed by natives. The official element is very strong, by reason of the presence of both the Supreme and Local Administrations, but Law and Medicine and other learned professions are well represented. Of Merchants there is, nominally, a goodly list; but a large proportion of them are, more properly speaking, commission agents. The Tradesmen, for extent and variety of stock, will compare favourably with the same class at home, and if the prices seem at first sight somewhat startling to the newly-arrived Londoner, it must be remembered that the rupee with which payment is made has come to occupy much the same position as the shilling in England. Satirists have divided the English in India into the three great castes of the Hindoos: the ruling caste who, like the Brahmans of old, reserve to themselves in perpetuity all situations of authority and emolument under the State: the military caste, who keep alive the tradition that India is held by the sword: and the mass of non-officials, who, as a rule, are too absorbed in their professions and pursuits to concern themselves with abating the exclusive pretensions to place and power of the civilian and the soldier. There is, nevertheless, a strong body of English public opinion in Calcutta which does not fail to make itself felt when it conceives its interests to be affected. Time was when a number of brilliant advocates of the Supreme Court, under the leadership of men like Longueville Clarke and Dickens, controlled and directed the current of feeling which frequently ran in direct opposition to the main stream of Government policy. The mantle is now worn by the Bengal Chamber of Commerce, and there have not been wanting memorable occasions during the last ten years when the Viceroy has been compelled to acknowledge defeat at their hands.

The term *Eurasian* was invented by the Marquess of Hastings, and is now applied generically to the progeny or descendants of European fathers and Hindoo or Mahomedan mothers. Many of them bear names which once stood high in the Anglo-Indian world. There are not a few who have attained, and still hold, high official rank and positions of trust in mercantile and other offices. But it is to be regretted that in the majority of cases their opportunities and, it must be added, their energies have proved insufficient to enable them to carve out for themselves a distinguished or a successful career in life.

Among Eurasians are now generally classed the *Kintals*, who as a distinct and individual type, are fast disappearing from among the peoples of Calcutta. Closely allied at the present day to the natives in race, and possessing little to differentiate them beyond their religion and their names, they are nevertheless the descendants of the Portuguese, the first conquerors of India, who during the sixteenth century, held the absolute monopoly of the trade between the East and the West. The Portuguese language was once the *lingua franca* of Calcutta, and Captain Alexander Hamilton declares that "it is the language the Europeans must learn to qualify themselves for general conversation with one another, as well as the different inhabitants of India." But those days are also long since past, and few of those who speak of castes and topees, ayahs and almirahs, imagine that they are employing the flotsam and jetsam of the "universal language" of two centuries ago. The history has not been dissimilar of the derelict DeSouzas and DeCruzes and D'Almeidas of Calcutta. In origin the Kintals are the offspring of those Portuguese soldiers who established the first European settlement in

Bengal at Hooghly, and set up the famous shrine at Bandel to bear witness to their robust piety, if not to the freedom with which they intermarried with the people of the country. As the star of Calcutta rose, the fortunes of Hooghly waned, and the Kintals migrated in the first years of the eighteenth century to the new city. Here a separate quarter was assigned to them within the palisades, and by reason of the fact that they were then the only people that kept fowls, was named Moorghihatta. They were not all of Portuguese descent, and in many cases were natives converted to the Roman Catholic faith by the Portuguese clergy and endowed with Portuguese descent. Holwell speaks of them as the "black mustee Portuguese Christians residing in the Settlement," and describes them comprehensively in 1755 as "Feringys." No less than 2,000 sought refuge in the Fort during the "Troubles" of the following year, and were a serious incumbrance to the garrison. As "topasses" they figure largely in the early military chronicles of the English in India, and until their slovenly and careless methods brought down upon them the wrath of the Court of Directors, they were the *keranis* or clerks of the Settlement. For many years they were a law to themselves: and they crop up in all manner of unconventional and disreputable stations in life—as slaves and even as bandits and pirates in the Sunderbunds. In twentieth century Calcutta the women seek employment as ayahs and the men essay the more modest occupations of clerks, printers and even cooks. "They cherish the improvidence, the religion and the generous moral latitude of the early Portuguese," says a writer who has had the advantage of studying them closely, but they have forgotten the language and discarded the ancient costume. Of recent years, they have fallen between the two stools of absorption and disintegration. Ten years ago, says the same observer, the Kintals "swarmed from Boitakhana to Dhurrumtollah: to-day search must be made for odd remnants in the secluded parts of Chuna Gully, Khyroo Mehter's Lane and Gooreeamah's Lane." And he attributes the rapid extinction of the community to the spread of cheap education on the one hand, which has transformed many a Kintal into an "Eurasian," and the marriage on the other hand of Kintal women with the Chinese shoemakers and cane-workers of Bentinck Street. Genuine specimens of the Portuguese stock are still to be found: but even among these pure Kintals nothing survives of the old senhors of Hooghly beyond the names they bear, the religion they profess, a few ancient images on the domestic altar, and certain dishes and sweets they much affect at their feasts. "No wedding or christening or celebration of the high festivals of the church is complete without a plentiful supply of Bindaloo, Foogath, Plantifrith, Bollcomardo and Mel de Rose." But the Goanese musician looks down with superior contempt upon the falling away of the weaker vessel from ancestral traditions: and the Calcutta "Protag" himself in the majority of cases indignantly repudiates the ascription.

The Armenians form another community, which, although numerically small, is of extreme interest from a historical point of view. They were among the earliest traders to India, coming from the Persian Gulf to Khorasan, and thence by way of Kandahar and Kabul to Delhi, Benares, Patna and Bengal. About 250 years ago they formed a settlement at Saidabad (in the environs of Cossimbazar), and when the Dutch settled at Chinsurah in 1625, they were followed by the Armenians. It would seem also that they were already trading at Suttanuttee before the coming of Charnock, for an inscription exists over a grave in the Armenian churchyard at Calcutta which bears date the 11th July, 1630. After the founding of Calcutta they followed the example of the Portuguese and settled at the northern extremity of the Settlement, where "Armani-tola," Armenian Ghât and Armenian Street still recall the days when the locality was in their exclusive occupation. They were from the outset looked upon with peculiar favour by the Company by reason of the services they were able to render as agents and interpreters. Their Church of St. Nazareth in Calcutta, which derives its name from Aga Nazar, its donor, was built in 1724, but as early as 1717, we find Coja Serhaud accompanying Surman's embassy to Delhi as interpreter. Forty years later, when Calcutta was captured by Seraj-ud-Doulah, two Armenians, Coja Petrus Aratoon and Abraham Jacobs, carried on communications between Drake and his Council at Fulta and Omichand in Calcutta. The Armenian community has always been a rich and thriving one: and by dint of ability and perseverance they have gained for themselves the highest positions not only in the commercial world, but in the learned professions.

The Greeks, like the Armenians, owe their association with Calcutta to the allurements of commerce. The first eminent Greek settler in Calcutta was Hadjee Alexios Argyree, a native of Philippopolis, who came to Bengal in 1750 and earned his living as an interpreter. Among Asiatic communities mention must not be omitted of the Arabs and the Marwaris. The Arabs are chiefly traders with the Persian and Arabian Gulf and one great item of their traffic lies in Arab horses. They own several large ships, which trade regularly to this port. In the northern quarter of the town they take high rank as influential and respected members of the Mahomedan community. The Marwaris may be readily distinguished by their neat brightly-coloured head-dresses and their handsome intelligent faces. Technically speaking they are not British subjects, for they are inhabitants of Marwar or Bikaneer in the north of the Peninsula : but many of them have settled permanently in Calcutta, and it is not many years since a prominent member of their community filled the responsible and honourable office of Sheriff. They are not the only Indian traders of non-Bengalee origin, for there are many Gujeratis and Mahrattas from the Bombay side and men of Madras and the Punjab who can boast both of substance and business capacity. But in the hand of the Marwaris is the trade in opium, Manchester piece goods, and country produce. Shrewd men are they at a bargain and by their enemies declared to be not overparticular. Burra Bazar is their stronghold : and they will be found congregated in Harrison Road and Cotton Street, and in the neighbouring lanes and gullies in squalid and crowded tenements, which are in bewildering contrast to the enormous wealth of which they are the masters.

With this attempt to unravel the tangle of her castes and creeds, we may be content to leave the history of Calcutta. It is the fashion among some of her citizens of to-day to rail at her unhealthiness and to cry out upon her manifold imperfections. But enough has surely been set down in the foregoing pages to clear the City from the charge of having stood still while all others, whether in the East or in the West, have resolutely pressed forward. Very different is the Calcutta of to-day from the "Golgotha" of our forefathers, inhabited, as the quaint words of the Mahomedan chronicler have it, by a tribe of Englishmen. No longer a precarious trading settlement battling in rivalry with French and Danes and Dutch and Ostenders she has grown to be the metropolis of the English in India. Through evil report and good report, through famine, siege, and pestilence, the foothold foundation of Charnock has scattered all its enemies and put all its rivals to shame. There is not a stone in Calcutta which does not breathe out its story of British courage and endurance and energy. And she has come rapidly to her own. The last twenty years have witnessed such sweeping changes that the swampy settlement has awakened almost in a night to find herself the third largest city in the British Empire. It is a sluggish imagination that is not stirred by the thought. But how many of the critics of Calcutta realize the full extent of what has been actually accomplished? Few of them, we may venture to affirm, ever cast back their thoughts to the time, only two hundred and twenty years ago, when the entire site of Calcutta was "a place of mists, alligators, and wild boars," when a dense jungle ran up to where Government House now stands, when the south wind, the only mitigation of the fierce tropical heat from May to October, blew over steaming rice lands and tidal marshes on its way to the city, and heaps of putrid dead fish, left in the salt-water lakes by the receding waters during the dry season, made of the easterly breeze a veritable blast of death. It may be the sad truth that the English drama in India is played amid a bustle of exits and entrances and a hurried scene-shifting which allow time for nothing but the present. Migratory Calcutta may take knowledge only of the people with whom it dances and dines, and regard all others with an unconcern quite goodnatured but absolutely complete. Yet, even if we elect to occupy ourselves with the present, let us be just also to the past. As Sir William Hunter has finely reminded us, "to these poor predecessors of ours, who lived and died at their work, and to whom fame was always half disfame, we owe no small debt. They found Calcutta a swamp, and they created on it a capital." Bombay may boast that she is *urbs prima in Indis*—the first city of the English in India, in point of time. But the motto of Calcutta is an even prouder one, for it tells of a victory over the forces of nature and of an Empire reared amid every surrounding of disadvantage and difficulty. *Per ardua stabilis esto.* As she has been in days gone by, so may she be in the days to come.

PART II.

CHAPTER I.

TWENTIETH CENTURY CALCUTTA.

CALCUTTA, the chief city of Bengal, the seat of the Supreme Government, and the Metropolis of India, stands in Lat. 22° 33′ N., and Long. 88° 23′ E. It is situated about 100 miles from the sea on the left bank of the western branch of the Ganges, called by Europeans the *Hooghly* and by the people of the country, who reverence it as a holy stream, "Mother Ganges" or the *Bhagiratti*. The main stream of the Ganges has, as a matter of fact, long since deserted this part of its delta, and now reaches the sea through the *Hurringotta* and the *Megna*, far to the eastward. But according to native tradition, the *Hooghly* was once the sacred stream, and an old temple which, till a few years ago, stood near the tank to the south of the Alipore Jail, and was believed to be 600 years old, is said to have been built on the bank of the Ganges, which at that time followed the line of Tolly's Nullah past Kalighat. The width of the Hooghly at Armenian Ghat is about 600 yards, but at other parts it widens to nearly a mile. Calcutta occupies a space along the bank of the river of about 4½ miles, estimated from Chitpore on the north, to Kidderpore on the south, and with an average width of a mile and a half from east to west, that is, from the river bank to the Circular

Road, which forms the eastern boundary. The area may be put at seven square miles, and the length of roads in the town is about 120 miles.

The ground on which Calcutta is built is a part of the alluvial deposits of the Gangetic delta, and is elevated not more than 16 or 18 feet above the mean sea level. Excavations that have been made for tanks and foundations shew that to a depth of about 40 feet the surface formation is an alternation of sand and clay beds. A band of vegetable matter, which appears to indicate an old land surface, is met with at about 20 feet (and therefore below the actual level of the sea), and from this down to 30 feet the stumps of *soondri* trees, with their roots attached in the position of their growth, are frequently found; all of which indicate that the site of Calcutta was once occupied by marshy islands, flooded by the tides, and in the condition of the outer Sunderbuns of the present day; and that, since that time, the old land surface has sunk some 18 or 20 feet, and has been afterwards covered and raised by silt gradually deposited from the river waters. At a depth of about 40 feet a bed of semi-fluid quicksand is met with; the existence of which renders it difficult to erect heavy and massive piles of masonry in Calcutta. Indeed, many of the large buildings, such as the High Court and the Indian Museum in Chowringhee, have suffered more or less by unequal sinking and alarming cracks are by no means uncommon. The general slope of the ground surface is slight, and, as is usually the case in river deltas, away from the river bank. The natural drainage of the land therefore tends towards the salt lakes, and not into the Hooghly: and the admirable system of artificial drainage designed by Mr. W. Clark follows the same direction.

Being situated almost at the limits of the torrid zone, and within a degree of the tropic of Cancer, the climate of Calcutta is less uniform than that of Madras and other places nearer the equator. At the same time, owing to her maritime position, she is far from presenting those strong contrasts of season that are felt by residents of Northern India and generally in the interior. Three seasons may be distinguished—the hot season, lasting from the middle of March to the setting in of the rains in June; the rains, which usually set in about the middle of June and last till the end of September, or, in favourable years, to the middle or latter part of October; and the cold season from November to the early part of March. The average temperature of the whole year is 77·9, that of the hot weather months 83·3 (of May 85·7), that of the rains 82·5, and that of the cold weather 68·3. According to the careful records kept at the Alipore Observatory, there have been no less than 62 occasions when a maximum of over 100° has been registered in the month of May, and 20 occasions when the same figure has been reached in June, since the year 1877. The record is held by the 11th June, 1901, when the maximum in the shade reached 108·2, and it is by no means certain that it has not been surpassed during the terribly trying summer through which Calcutta passed in 1905. On the 11th June, the maximum temperature in the shade was returned at 106·1 degrees, and since that date even higher figures were shown. In May, 1867 and 1874, temperatures of 106° were recorded, and the opposite extreme is supplied by January, 1899, when a thermometer exposed under a thatched shade registered as low as 44·2. During the hot weather months, however, Calcutta enjoys the advantage of a sea breeze, which sets in late in the afternoon and blows for some hours after sunset. The intensity of the heat at this season is also mitigated by the occasional occurrence of a north-wester, a storm which, as its name imports, comes up from the west or north-west more frequently than from any other direction, and is preceded by violent gusts of wind and clouds of dust, blowing outwards in advance of the storm. The lightning in these storms is sometimes very vivid, and a season rarely passes in which houses are not struck.

The annual rainfall of Calcutta has been known to rise as high as 93 inches and to fall as low as 43, but its average may be reasonably put at 60 inches. The greater part of this falls between June and October, during which time the temperature varies not more than about 8° during the twenty-four hours; the air is very damp, and rain is heavy and frequent, but not continuous. Clothes and books become mouldy if not frequently opened out and aired; and the heat, though less intense than in April and May, is more oppressive, producing a feeling of lassitude, which is very inimical to mental and bodily activity. To Europeans, the latter part of the rains is the most unhealthy season of the year. It is at the beginning and close of the rainy season, namely, in May and June, and again in October and the early part of

November, that Calcutta is most frequently visited by cyclones. These dreaded storms originate in the Bay of Bengal, sometimes as far down as the Nicobars and the Andaman Islands; and after gathering strength for two or three days, with but little change of place, they move forward in a direction between north and west, becoming fiercer and more destructive as they advance. The nature of these storms is now well understood. The winds blow spirally round and into a central region (the eye of the storm) where a perfect calm prevails. When the centre of such a storm passes over any place the wind blows steadily from the same quarter (in Calcutta from the East or E. N. E.) with increasing violence. There is then a complete calm, which lasts from a few minutes to an hour or more; and this is followed by a sudden renewal of the storm, with its maximum violence, from the opposite quarter of the compass. Calcutta has not been traversed by the *centre* of a severe cyclone since the 3rd June, 1842; but the storms of the 5th October, 1864, and 31st October, 1867, when the centre passed a few miles to the west of the city, were not less destructive, the whole shipping of the river being carried away from its moorings, and a great part wrecked and stranded. Since their occurrence, a system of storm signals has been established, and whenever the weather appears threatening these are exhibited, both in Calcutta, and at two or three stations on the river below.

The conventional divisions of the city are two, *Northern* and *Southern*; Bow Bazar Street, continued in a line from the Circular Road to the river, forming the boundary. The Northern portion, with the exception of the business portion to the north-west of Dalhousie Square, is almost exclusively occupied by the people of the country. The streets, like those of most oriental towns, are narrow, and in some parts, the houses are lofty. A large portion of the northern area is occupied by bustees or native villages, covered with mud or straw huts. Placed on the bare damp ground and crammed together without ventilation or drainage, these bustees are usually grouped round a tank or pond which as often as not receives most of the domestic refuse, and is at the same time used for washing if not for cooking purposes. The houses of the better classes are brick-built, from two to three stories high, and flat roofed. Many of the larger ones consist of a double quadrangle: and as a rule, they are built in the form of a hollow square, which, on the occasion of Hindoo festivals, is covered in and lighted up. On the northern side is the *Thakoor-ghur* where the presiding deity is placed. The upper floor contains the living apartments, with verandahs, which always face inwards towards the quadrangle. Many of the older houses have also wooden verandahs or balconies facing the street. There are a few really fine mansions belonging to wealthy Indian gentlemen, but as a rule, the native architecture presents a mean and dilapidated appearance. The main streets in the northern division, running north and south, are the Strand Road, which commences just above the Nimtollah burning-ghat; Durmahatta (the "street of the sellers of reed-mats") which beginning about the same point, is prolonged through Clive Street to Dalhousie Square; the Chitpore Road, which traverses the entire length of the town under various names, and is the immemorial pilgrim-path from Chitpore to Kalighat: the equally long road, known as Cornwallis Street, College Street, Wellington Street and Wellesley Street, which connects Sham Bazar and Bag Bazar in the extreme north with Park Street in the south: Amherst Street, isssuing from Manicktolah Street, to the south-east of Cornwallis Square, and running south to Bow Bazar Street: and finally, Circular Road, which envelopes the town on the East, and represents the old boundary of the Mahratta Ditch.

From east to west, we may notice starting from the south, the "avenue to the eastward," which is termed firstly Lall Bazar until it intersects the Chitpore Road, then Bow Bazar from that point until it meets College Street, and (popularly) Boytaconnah for the remainder of its length until it reaches the Circular Road at Sealdah at the point where the Boytaconnah tree formerly stood. Next in order, running from the river to the Circular Road, are Colootollah, with its extension to the west once known as Moorghihatta and now called Canning Street, and prolonged to the east past College Street under the name of Mirzapore Street: the Harrison Road, which connects the Sealdah and Howrah Railway Stations: Machooa Bazar, a narrow street continued to the east towards the gas works, and to the river under the name of Cotton Street; Banstollah and Mooktaram Baboo's Street connecting Durmahatta and Cornwallis Street: Rutton Sircar's Street, also issuing from Durmahatta and running through to the Circular Road under the name of Baranosee Ghose's Street and Sukeas Street: Beadon Street, leading from Nimtollah Street to the Circular Road, with a fine square about its centre: Grey Street named like Beadon Street after a Lieutenant-Governor of Bengal, and a prolongation in the same direction of Sobha Bazar Street one of the oldest streets in Calcutta: and finally Sham Bazar and Bow Bazar Streets, the one running in a north-easterly direction towards the suburb of Belgachia, and the other closing in the northern boundary of the Town.

The principal *Bazars* in the Northern Division are the *Radha Bazar*, the Old and New *China Bazar*, the *Burra Bazar* and *Tiretta's Bazar*. In the two former, liquors, oilman's stores, furniture, clothing, and an immense variety of other goods may be obtained at moderate prices, provided the purchaser has all his wits about him, and remembers that there is always what is called an "asking price," which is generally from one to two-thirds in excess of the price that will be taken. Tiretta's Bazar is the haunt *par excellence* of the dealer in birds and other live stock. In the Burra Bazar will be found piece-goods, Cashmere shawls, jewellery, precious stones, and hardware of every description, drugs and medicines, both indigenous and imported. The visitor will hardly know whether to wonder most at the large stocks of goods which he may inspect, or at the wonderful dens in which they are stowed away.

The business part of the city, that is to say, the European portion of it, must be sought in the Southern Division of the city, and is centred in Clive Street and Clive Row, Hare Street, Hastings Street, The Esplanade, Government Place, Old Court House Street and Dalhousie Square. Speaking generally, the western portion is chiefly occupied by the merchants, and the south-eastern by tradesmen. The principal shops—and there are some very fine ones—are to be found in Dalhousie Square, in Old Court House Street, and in Government Place.

The district lying between Bow Bazar and Dhurrumtollah and bounded on the west by Bentinck Street, is a district inhabited chiefly by East Indians, Portuguese, and Europeans of the poorer class, together with a considerable number of natives. Candour compels the admission that the quarter presents features as unpleasant as any part of Calcutta. Full of tortuous and narrow lanes, badly drained, and reeking with foul odours, thickly populated, and miserably housed, nothing but grinding poverty could induce Christian men to take up their abode in such a locality. In this district, on the north side of Dhurrumtollah, is the Bazar called *Chandney Chowk*, a labyrinth of ill-kept passages, lined with shops, in which may be found a wonderful collection of sundries, from a door nail to a silk dress. Very similar shops and stalls may now be found, but under conditions infinitely more advantageous and comfortable, in the Municipal Market in Lindsay Street, off Chowringhee.

South of Dhurrumtollah, commencing at Bentinck Street, runs the noble *Chowringhee Road,* nearly two miles long and eighty feet broad. The eastern side is lined by handsome houses, facing the fine grassy *Maidan* which lies between them and the river. They are generally ornamented with spacious verandahs to the south, that being the quarter from which, in the hot weather, the cool evening breeze blows.

Parallel with Chowringhee Road runs *Wellesley Street*, the fine broad thoroughfare which has already claimed our notice under its northern designation of Cornwallis Street. Along its course are situated *Wellesley Square*, the north side of which is occupied by the *Madrassah*, or great Mahomedan College, and *Wellington Square* which contains the Great Reservoir and the Pumping Station of the New Water Works. To the east of Wellesley Street, and bounded on the north by Dhurrumtollah, on the south by Collinga, and on the east by the Circular Road, is the district called *Toltollah*, chiefly peopled by Mahomedan khalassies and lascars. *Park Street*, and the districts to the south of it, are almost entirely inhabited by Europeans, and contain some of the best residences in the city. Within the last-half century this quarter has been considerably extended, a large number of new houses having been erected, and new streets and squares formed, on sites formerly occupied by native bustees. There are also some good houses in the Circular Road, which has been drained and greatly improved by the construction of foot-paths, and the planting of avenues of trees.

The great *Maidan*, or plain, presents a most refreshing appearance to the eye, the heavy night dews, even in the hot season, keeping the grass green. Many of the fine trees with which it was once studded were blown down in the cyclone of 1864. But they have not been allowed to remain without successors, and the handsome avenues across the Maidan still constitute the chief glory of Calcutta. Dotting the wide expanse are a number of fine tanks, from which the inhabitants were content in former days to obtain their water-supply.

The oldest road on the Maidan is the *Course*. It is described in 1768 as being "out of town in a sort of angle, made to take the air in." Although an old song tells us that those who frequented it "swallowed ten mouthfuls of dust for one of fresh air," it is still one of the airiest and pleasantest drives in Calcutta, extending from the "Cocked Hat" on the north to the Kidderpore Bridge. The broad gravelled walk on the west side of that portion of it which is known as the Red Road, is called Secretary's Walk, and was constructed in 1820. To the south of the Fort is the *Ellenborough Course*, a fine raised and turfed ride for horse exercise; and towards the east, the *Race Course*, commenced in 1819.

The Suburbs of Calcutta environ the city on the north, east, and south sides of the Circular Road, the remaining boundary being formed by the River Hooghly. Under this designation is included the greater portion of the *Punchannogram*, or the 55 villages purchased by the old East India Company in 1717, and comprised to-day within the Magisterial and Revenue Jurisdictions of the Twenty-four Pergunnahs. They are spread over an area of 23 square miles.

At the extreme north is the village of *Cossipore* (Kasipur) where are the Government Gun Foundry, the Snider and Rifle Shell Factories—originally constructed by Colonel Hutchinson, of the Engineers, after he had ransacked England and Europe for the best models. Now-a-days, few guns are cast there; but a vast amount of useful and necessary work is carried on. Very many improvements have been introduced, and the factory has become a great local assistance to Government, rendering it, in many respects, quite independent of Home indents. Here are also extensive Sugar Mills, and Jute Screw Houses. The Cossipore reach is one of the finest on the river, and is lined by a number of handsome villa residences.

To the south is the village of *Chitpore,* which appears to have been in existence 300 years ago. It was then written Chittrupoor, and was noted for the temple of Chittru, or Kalee, renowned for the number of human sacrifices formerly offered at her shrine. Here were the house and garden of the Chitpore Nawab, Mahomed Reza Khan, to whom the whole administration of Bengal was entrusted for several years after the Company had obtained the Dewanee.

Adjoining are the suburbs of *Paikpara* and *Belgachia,* both favourite haunts of the wealthy Indian inhabitants of Calcutta. The famous Belgachia Villa was once the country house of Lord Auckland and passed at a later date into the possession of Dwarkanath Tagore, known by his contemporaries as Prince Tagore. It is now the property of the Paikpara Raj family, and is celebrated in local history as the scene of the Indian entertainment offered to King Edward the Seventh on the occasion of his visit to the city in the winter of 1875.

At Chitpore the *Circular Canal* falls into the Hooghly. A large new lock and tidal basin has been constructed at the mouth of the Canal, which is crossed by a girder bridge and a lifting bridge at the entrance. Crossing

Chitpore Bridge, and passing southwards, we come to *Narkaldungah,* where are the extensive works of the Oriental Gas Company.

East of the Circular Road, is *Halsi Bagan,* formerly the garden-house of Omichand [Amin Chand], "the Rothschild of his day,"—the great Sikh millionaire who lives in history by reason of his deception at the hands of Clive.

Sealdah, which was described in 1757 as a "narrow causeway, several feet above the level of the country, leading from the east," comes next. Here is the Terminus of the Eastern Bengal State Railway, by which access is had to Darjeeling and the jute and tobacoo-producing districts of Eastern Bengal. There are also several jute screw houses and the offices and depôts of various Labour and Emigration Agencies. Here too is the old Pauper Hospital,—now called the "Campbell Hospital and Medical School" and set apart among other uses for the reception of small-pox cases. To the east of Sealdah stretch the *Salt Water Lakes,* a broad tract of low country, regularly submerged by the tide. Reclamation and the natural process of silting are constantly diminishing their area, and they have long ceased to exercise their former maleficent sway over the climate and the health of the city.

Proceeding still further south, we arrive at *Entally,* an extensive district intersected with numerous tortuous roads and lanes. It contains a large number of European residences, some of them fine buildings in extensive grounds. But the amenities of life in the locality are not improved by the proximity of a number of necessary but not attractive civic institutions. Here are the Municipal Foundry and Workshops, the Municipal Slaughter-houses and the Pumping Station of the Drainage Works, where the whole sewage of the city is pumped into a high level sewer and conveyed to the Salt Water Lakes, whence an open channel conveys it to within reach of tidal influence. The Municipal Railway runs along the side of the Lower Circular Road and the Lakes by way of Sealdah and conveys several hundred tons of sweepings daily which are employed to raise a square mile of land which has been bunded off from the lanes for the purpose. South of Entally is the fine Volunteer Rifle Range, constructed in 1877.

Ballygunge lies to the east of the Circular Road, beyond Entally. Here there is a fine maidan, adjoining which are the Barracks and Exercise Ground of the Governor-General's Body Guard. Around this maidan, and lining some of the adjoining roads, are many very fine European residences standing in extensive grounds, and presenting great attractions to those who are kept by business during the day in the hot and dusty town.

Bhowanipore is a populous native place, inhabited chiefly by Hindu artizans in metals who work for the houses in town. The quarter is also a very favourite one for the large community of pleaders and attorneys who practice in the High Court and at Alipore. The London Missionary Society's Institution is in Bhowanipore, and also the Lunatic Asylum. Bhowanipore is on the road to Kalighat, the great Hindu temple—great not from any structural beauty, but as the shrine at which all good Hindus worship when they leave their own "Thakoor Bari." There is a constant stream of traffic to and fro. Kalighat is thickly populated; the principal houses belong to the Haldars, the priestly family attached to the temples. The present temples are of modern construction and were erected by the Chowdhry family in 1809. Kalighat should be seen by all visitors. Further to the south is *Tollygunge*, a station of the Church Missionary Society, near which is a group of handsome Hindu temples erected in 1796. Beyond is *Russapugla,* the residence of the Mysore family, the descendants of Tippoo Sultan.

To the eastward of Bhowanipore, crossing the Tolly's Nullah, we come to *Alipore*, the residence of the Lieutenant-Governor of Bengal, the Head-quarters of the "Presidency Division" and of the 24-Pergunnahs, and also a Military station for a Native regiment. Here also are the great Jail of the District, the Army Clothing Agency, the Government Telegraph Store Yards and Workshop. In the last century, Warren Hastings had his favourite villa at Alipore, which still bears his name. There are many European residences in this locality, and its reputation for healthiness is good. A tract of land on the banks of Tolly's Nullah, formerly thickly covered with huts, has been cleared, and laid out, principally at the cost of Government, as a *Zoological Garden.*

Kidderpore, which lies to the west of Alipore, is extensively populated, principally by natives. But it includes nevertheless within its boundaries, the Military Orphan

School, a Church, the Mazzuchelli Bazar, and the Government Dockyard. Here, in 1780, Colonel Henry Watson whose name survives in the adjoining Watgunge, and who acted as second to Francis in the historic duel with Hastings, established wet and dry docks, and a marine yard for repairing and equipping vessels of war and merchantmen. The next year he launched the *Nonsuch* frigate of 36 guns, and in 1788, the *Surprise* frigate of 36 guns. For eight years he devoted his time and fortune to this national undertaking, by which time he had sunk ten lakhs of Rupees in his enterprise, and was obliged to abandon it, his resources being exhausted. According to Sophia Goldborne it was a pleasant place of resort in Watson's day. "Watson's Works," she writes in *Hartly House*, "a place for building bugeros and small sloops (the road to which lies across the Esplanade, to the river, in an oblique direction) is some miles from Calcutta,—and to Watson's Works, in order to see the launching of a large bugero, built on a new construction, we repaired yesterday, after taking our tea: and do but conceive the éclat of half-a-dozen, or more of the eastern barges all freighted with elegant parties gliding down the stream together the oars beating time to the notes of the clarinets and oboes." The docks afterwards fell into the hands of the two East Indian sons of Colonel Kyd, an enterprising European, the Chief Engineer on the E. I. Company's Military Establishment. In 1818, they launched from the dock the *Hastings*, a 74 gun ship. Between 1781 and 1800, thirty-five vessels were launched; from 1781 to 1821, the total was 237, at a cost of more than two millions sterling. At Fort Gloucester, the site of flourishing jute mills at the present day, about 5 miles below, on the opposite side of the river, 27 vessels were built between 1811 and 1828 : and there was also a dockyard at Titaghur, near Barrackpore, at which, in 1801, a vessel of 1,445 tons, the *Countess of Sutherland*, was built. Kyd's dockyard is now the Government dockyard, but for many years, no vessels of any size have been built there.

In the east part of Kidderpore is the *Military Orphan School*, established in 1783, by Major William Kirkpatrick. It was the mansion of Richard Barwell, the colleague and supporter of Hastings in Council, and the hero of the "bring more curricles" story. The fine Ball-room in this building calls to mind the state of society in former days, when European ladies were afraid to face the climate of India, and when in consequence, Kidderpore was a harbour of refuge, where men in want of wives made their selection, travelling often a distance of 500 miles to attend the balls given expressly on that behalf.

North of Kidderpore, and separating it from the Maidan, flows *Tolly's Nullah*, or canal, excavated by Colonel Tolly in 1775, at his own expense. It was formerly known as the Govindpore Creek, and was, in fact, part of the old bed of the Ganges. It now runs into the Circular Canal, which again communicates with the Hooghly, north of Chitpore, forming the great inlet for country boats bringing produce from the Sunderbunds and the eastern districts of Bengal.

The Nullah is here spanned by a bridge, once known, as the nullah was, by the name of Edward Surman, the head of the Embassy to Delhi in 1717, but now called the Kidderpore Bridge. It is traversed by the Calcutta Tramways, which run from here direct to the Esplanade Junction at the corner of Dhurrumtollah.

Proceeding in a westerly direction after crossing the bridge, we find ourselves in *Hastings*,—a Government colony, consisting chiefly of warrant officers and conductors of the Ordnance and Commissariat Departments, and also officers connected with the Harbour Master's Department of the Port Commissioners. Here also the Commissariat Godowns are situated. It was here that Nunda Kumar, Dewan to the Nawab of Moorshedabad, was executed, August 5th, 1775, the first Brahman hanged by the English in India. The old name of the place was Cooly Bazar, and it is said that it owes its origin to the numerous workmen and coolies employed in building the Fort who are said to have formed a regular village to the south. In connection with this place we snatch a paragraph from Dr. Busteed's *Echoes of Old Calcutta* relating to the treatment of native servants in 1778. A Colonel Watson prosecuted one Ram Singh as an impostor for receiving pay as a carpenter when actually nothing more than a Baboo. "Ordered fifteen rattans, and to be drummed through the Coolie Bazar to Colonel Watson's gates."

To the westward of Hastings Tolly's Nullah is once more crossed by the Hastings Bridge. This was originally a fine suspension bridge erected by public subscription to commemorate the administration of the Marquis of Hastings, but it collapsed suddenly in 1874, probably from the granulation of the iron resulting from continual vibration, and was replaced by a substantial girder bridge. From Hastings Bridge, the fine broad Strand Road and its offshoots extend north along the banks of the river, forming the evening promenade. The Port Commissioners' railway now runs along the river bank straight into the new Kidderpore Docks, crossing the Nullah on an exceedingly handsome iron bridge, the roadway of which is elevated by hydraulic power when it is necessary for vessels to pass under it.

Crossing the Hastings Bridge and proceeding to the southward, we arrive at *Garden Reach,* the oldest and best known suburb. The river bank, for a distance of two miles, is lined by beautiful houses standing in large compounds. Erected between the years 1768 and 1780, these were formerly the residences of fashionable Calcutta Society: but the character of the place was materially altered by the settlement in 1857 of the late ex-King of Oudh and his swarm of followers in 1857, in the beautiful house and grounds formerly occupied by Sir Lawrence Peel, Chief Justice of the Supreme Court from 1848 to 1855. Much of the adjoining property was bought up by the King, and, as a consequence, this beautiful suburb became less popular as a residence for Europeans. Within the last thirty years, still greater changes have taken place in Garden Reach and Kidderpore. The opening of the Suez Canal necessitated the removal of the head-quarters of the Peninsular & Oriental Steam Navigation Company to Bombay. Garden Reach has become the centre of the foreign coolie emigration agencies and the head-quarters of the offices of the Bengal-Nagpore Railway Company. The death of Wajid Ali Shah, the last King of Oudh, was followed by the sale of his properties to a Syndicate, and the dispersion of his enormous establishment of followers, male and female. Their departure has been the signal for the erection of Jute Mills and the construction of the enormous Tidal Docks and their connected wharves and works, with the result that a complete transformation has taken place in the aspect of Kidderpore and the upper end of Garden Reach, and the memories of the past have been altogether obliterated.

CHAPTER II.

HISTORIC HOUSES AND FAMOUS LOCALITIES.

It has always been a slur upon the Anglo-Indian that he is bound by so slight a tie to the country in which he welters through the best years of his life. He is so occupied with the amassing of money, so engrossed by his profession and his pleasures, that he casts hardly a thought behind him. Too little honour is paid by the Calcutta of to-day to the Calcutta of the past. And yet there is many a spot, hallowed by classic associations and rich with memories of Hastings and Francis, Clive and Watson, and even of Job Charnock himself, *conditor urbis.* The fault is not so much, perhaps, with the sojourner within the walls, as with those who sit in authority over him. In London and in most of the large towns in England, a terra-cotta medallion informs the passer-by that the quiet unpretentious house on his right hand or on his left, was once the abode of Milton, or Franklin, or Reynolds, and a whole host of thoughts and fancies is at once awakened. Until a year ago the adoption of a similar method of commemoration was unthought of in modern Calcutta: and the visitor was left to make his sentimental journey unassisted and uninformed. To-day he may discern, as he drives or walks through the streets, that many a house stands distinguished by a mural tablet inscribed with the name of the occupant that has made it famous. Lord Curzon has never concealed his interest in the bygone associations of the historic capital of British India: and if the sin of omission may in this respect be no longer laid at the door of the City of Palaces, it is to the late Viceroy that her acknowledgments are due. Modern Calcutta lives and thrives upon the labours of the illustrious dead, and it behoves her to frankly acknowledge the debt she owes to the race of Englishmen who have gone before, and to discard the magnificently selfish policy of obliterating every record of the great grave-yard of the past.

Let us begin our pilgrimage by entering *Chowringhee Road* from the south where it meets the Lower Circular Road. We are now on the main thoroughfare from Chitpore to the famous shrine at Kalighat: and the name of Chowringhee is attached only to that portion, a mile and five furlongs in length, which extends from the junction made with Circular Road to Dhurrumtollah. The "road to Chowringhee" has always been a prominent landmark of Calcutta, and in the days of Holwell we find mention made of it as "the road leading to Collegot." Some derive the name Chowringhee, which appears in early records as "Cherangi," from the legend of Kali's origin by being cut up with Vishnu's disc. But there is a simpler alternative, already indicated in these pages, to hold that the name in Hindustani signifies "The Square." According to the old maps, Chowringhee is a locality, not a road.

In Colonel Mark Wood's map of 1784, which was republished in 1792, this is made quite plain by the marking of that part of the existing Chowringhee Road from Dhurrumtollah to Park Street as the "Road to Chowringhee": and the name "Chowringhee" is there given to the quarter immediately south of Park Street. But in Upjohn's map of 1794, this district is named Dhee Birjee, and the boundaries of "Chowringhee" appear as Circular Road on the east, Park Street on the south, Colingah on the north, and a portion of Chowringhee Road on the west. The populous district to the east of the road is entirely of modern creation, and the wide expanse of Maidan was once a dense jungle, infested with wild boars and tigers and dacoits. Its clearance dates from 1757, the year in which the erection of the present Fort was commenced. But tradition has it that Warren Hastings hunted with elephants in the forest where the Cathedral now stands, and the traveller was long deemed a truly adventurous spirit who ventured to cross it alone and unarmed. The Cathedral indeed is only just over half a century old. Both it and the Palace which faces it on the east are associated with the name of Bishop Wilson. The former will be sought in vain in any of the maps of Calcutta before the time of Lord Dalhousie, but the early history of the Palace is connected with William Wilberforce Bird, whose picture hangs in the Town Hall, and who signed the act abolishing slavery in India while officiating as Governor-General in 1844.

At the corner of Chowringhee and *Theatre Road* was the Theatre of Calcutta from 1813 to 1839. The male characters used to be taken by amateurs, the female by ladies who received monthly salaries and resided on the premises. Here Mrs. Leach, the "Indian Siddons," made her bow to a Calcutta audience as Lady Teazle on July 27th,

1826. She was then barely seventeen, and for many years she continued to be the idol of the theatre-going public. In the early morning of the last day of May, 1839, the Chowringhee Theatre was destroyed by fire. The wooden dome blazed fiercely, and the glare of the conflagration was seen in the remotest parts of the town. In an hour the entire building was gutted. It was not rebuilt, and the site is now occupied by a house which was once the residence of Sir William Markby, a judge of the High Court from 1866 to 1877, and is now a boarding establishment.

The next turning to the east beyond Theatre Road is *Harington Street,* named after John Herbert Harington, once a Judge of the Sudder Adawlut, and later a member of the Supreme Council, who was a prominent resident in the locality in the twenties. At No. 4, in the street, lived Sir Richard Garth, Chief Justice of Bengal from 1875 to 1886. No. 3, was the residence of Heber, after his short stay in the Governor's House in Fort William (now used as the Outram Institute). He had been careful before leaving England to obtain the promise of a free residence, but did not like this house in Harington Street. It was too small for his family and his books, and too far from St. John's Cathedral and the Free School. Impey's old house in Park Street pleased him as little: and a palace was finally provided at No. 5, Russell Street, which we shall presently encounter as we continue our survey.

There are two houses in Chowringhee between Harington Street and Middleton Street, the next turning to the east. At No. 43, lived Sir Comer Petheram, Chief Justice of Bengal from 1886 to 1896, and the house next door (No. 42) was the residence in the sixties of Sir Joseph Fayrer, then professor of surgery at the Medical College Hospital. Adjoining is the Calcutta house of the Maharajah of Durbhunga which is numbered as the first house in Middleton Street. At the opposite corner is the imposing pile of the Army and Navy Stores. The stranger may well be forgiven if he mistakes it for the University or the offices of some Government Department: but if he will snatch a moment to glance at the "crimson pavilions" which lie to the south-west of the Cathedral in Circular Road, he will speedily appreciate the manner in which the æsthetic sense of the Public Works Department expresses itself under stereotyped official formulæ. The names of *Middleton Street* and *Middleton Row* (the latter lying further to the east and approached from Park Street), are attributed by some to Dr. Thomas Fanshaw Middleton, the first Bishop of Calcutta (1814 to 1822), but it is a question whether they do not commemorate a local celebrity of much lesser rank. Mr. Samuel Middleton was a member of the Civil Service who owned considerable property in the neighbourhood and who flourished in the time of Cornwallis and Wellesley. He acted for a time as Police Magistrate and figures in the *Calcutta Gazette* of December 6th, 1792, upon appointment as "Commissioner in the Sunderbands for suppressing depredation of dacoits, in the room of Mr. William Hyndman, deceased." Middleton Street is not marked in Colonel Mark Wood's map of 1784: but it appears, along with Harington Street, in Upjohn's map of 1794, although neither are distinguished by any name.

Continuing along Chowringhee, we pass numbers 37 and 36 in the order named, the latter associated with the name of Sir Arthur Macpherson, Judge of the High Court from 1865 to 1877, and the former with that of Sir James Fitz-James Stephen, Law Member of Council from 1869 to 1872. A little further on, we find ourselves at the Bengal Club House (No. 33), where a tablet at the gate informs us that the house was once the residence of Thomas Babington Macaulay, Law Member of the Supreme Council from 1834 to 1838. On the Friday of every week, Sir George Trevelyan in the life of his uncle tells us, a chosen few would meet round Macaulay's breakfast table and sit far onwards towards noon until an uneasy sense of accumulating despatch-boxes drove them one by one to their respective offices. There was much to argue in those days. When discussion had been exhausted of the progress which the Law Commission had made in its labours, there always remained material for debate in the *pros* and *cons* of the great education campaign which was to decide whether the Eastern mind was to find emancipation by the well worn high road of Arabic and Sanskrit learning or the untried avenue of English instruction. The duel between the Orientalists and the Occidentalists was fought with much bitterness. Henry Thoby Prinsep the elder, and Macaulay, "butted one another like two bulls": but Macaulay carried the day, and time has shown both his wisdom and his foresight.

At the back of the Bengal Club House runs *Russell Street,* so named after Sir Henry Russell, Chief Justice of the Supreme Court from 1806 to 1813, who built the first house in the street in the closing years of the eighteenth century. Tradition assigns the site to the one now occupied by the large house and compound that go by the name of "Golightly Hall." Here it was that Rose Aylmer spent her short Indian life; and it was from its gates that she was carried to her grave in the South Park Street Cemetery in March, 1800. The houses numbered as 12 and 13 are associated with the name of three Chief Justices, Sir Barnes Peacock, Chief Justice from 1859 to 1870, Mr. John Paxton Norman, who was assassinated in 1871 when acting as Chief Justice, and Sir Richard Couch, who held the office from 1871 to 1875. At No. 5, on the opposite side of the road, is the house which served as the Bishop's Palace from 1825 to 1849. Heber was its first occupant from 1825 to 1826. A tablet commemorates the fact and records also that the house was the official residence of Bishops Turner, James and Wilson. Turner died here on July 7th, 1831. The episcopal residence of Middleton, the first Bishop, was originally in Council House Street in one of the houses opposite the Old Cathedral, and subsequently in Chowringhee, but neither building has been accurately traced.

Russell Street is met at its northern end by *Park Street*, a fine thoroughfare, seven-and-half furlongs in length, running from Chowringhee Road to Circular Road. At the corner of Chowringhee and Park Street is the Asiatic Society's house, built on a plot of ground granted by the Government. The Society was founded on the 15th January, 1784, its first patron being Warren Hastings and its first President Sir William Jones. Most of the Society's fine collection of pictures have been lent to the Trustees of the Victoria Memorial Hall, and are to be seen in the temporary home allotted to them in the Indian Museum, pending the completion of the Hall. Park Street is not shown in any map earlier than 1760, and the name of Burying-ground Road which it bears in Upjohn's map of 1794, clearly indicates that it came into existence as a means of access to the new cemetery at the southern corner of Circular Road which was consecrated in 1768. The name by which it is now known, as well as its native appellation of Badamtollah or Almond grove, were bestowed upon it from the fact that it led to Sir Elijah Impey's mansion and Park. Time was when it was customary for wayfarers to form into large parties before braving the terrors of Burying-ground Road: and a guard of sepoys paraded nightly to scare away the dacoits and protect my Lord Chief Justice's person and property. The site of Impey's house, now the Loretto Convent, will be found at the end of Middleton Row, the first turning to the right as the visitor proceeds down Park Street from Chowringhee. On the wall to the right of St. Thomas' Church, and at the entrance to the Convent, has been affixed a tablet which states that "This house was the garden house of Mr. Henry Vansittart, Governor of Bengal, 1760-64. It was occupied by Sir Elijah Impey, the first Chief Justice of the Supreme Court, Calcutta, 1774-82, and also by Bishop Heber for a few months in 1824." In Impey's day the house stood in a large park, which stretched from Russell Street in the west to Camac Street on the east, and the principal entrance to it was from Park Street through Middleton Row which was then an avenue of trees. The large house numbered 6 in Park Street, is now the property of Mr. W. C. Bonnerjee, the distinguished advocate of the High Court. It was once in the possession of Sir John Peter Grant, Lieutenant-Governor of Bengal from 1859 to 1862, who is said to have exerted his influence to procure the purchase of the house as the official residence of the Lieutenant-Governors of Bengal, but without success, the mansion at Alipore, which goes by the name of Belvedere, being selected in preference.

Associations of a pathetic character linger around the building further east on the same side of the road, which is occupied to-day by St. Xavier's College, the great educational institution of the Jesuit Fathers. It was once the Sans Souci Theatre, and it was here that Mrs. Esther Leach, the "Queen of the Indian stage," met her death. We have already come across her name in connection with the Chowringhee Theatre. When that theatre was destroyed by fire in 1839, she was in England. But on her return, she was aided by Mr. Stocqueler of the *Englishman*, to collect funds for the erection of a new playhouse. Lord Auckland contributed Rs. 1,000, and in May, 1840, the Sans Souci Theatre was completed. The formal opening took place on March 8th, 1841, under the patronage and in the immediate presence of the Governor-General and suite. Sheridan Knowles' play "The Wife" was enacted, and Mrs. Leach who took the part of Mariana, recited a metrical prologue written for the occasion by Sir John William Kaye. Her company comprised both amateurs and professionals. Among the former were Mr. H. W. Torrens, a versatile Bengal Civilian, and his son-in-law Mr. James Hume, afterwards a Magistrate of Calcutta. Mr. Stocqueler had also imported some actors from England. One of them, a Mr. Barry, had a capricious voice which was given to deserting him at the critical moment and reducing him to the necessity of winding up in dumbshow. Among the leaders we hear of a Mrs. Deacle, who had, as Miss Darling, made a "gorgeous Cleopatra" at the Adelphi in London, and according to Stocqueler, "had not her devotion to Bacchus interfered with her attention to the rites of Thalia and Melpomene, she might have been valuable." There was also Miss Cowley, regarding whom Miss Eden after a night at the play, wrote in her *Letters from India,* "A little Miss C—is one of the best comic actresses I have seen, and had great success. She is very ugly." The catastrophe which cost Mrs. Leach her life occurred on the 2nd November, 1843. Mr. James Vining, an actor of English reputation, had made his first appearance in India as Shylock to an overflowing house: and the afterpiece was a farce in which Mrs. Leach was playing. As she stood waiting for her cue at the upper right hand entrance to the stage, her dress caught fire from an oil-lamp, one of a row placed on the floor. She rushed on the stage calling for help just as the audience had arisen in the greatest excitement under the impression that the house was on fire. She was instantly thrown down and the flames extinguished, but not before she had been severely burnt. Her residence, now the Archbishop's Palace, adjoined the Theatre, and she was carried there without delay: but the shock had been too great and after rallying once or twice she died on November 18th, at the age of 34. Her grave in the military cemetery at Bhowanipore has been levelled, but a tablet to the memory of an infant daughter who died in 1828, may be seen preserved in a square of masonry. After her death, the theatre was leased out to a French company: but the days of the Sans Souci were numbered. It was sold in the year 1844 to Archbishop Carew, and entered upon a new career as St. John's, and subsequently, St. Xavier's College. There have been considerable additions and alterations in the buildings: but the handsome portico and fine flight of steps are still in existence.

The district bounded by Park Street, Circular Road, Theatre Road and Chowringhee, was known in former days (as a glance at Upjohn's map will remind us) as Dhee Birjee, a name still recalled by the Birjee Talao, the tank to the south of the Cathedral. A number of streets in the locality are identified with eminent names. *Loudoun Street,* (which should not be deprived of its second "u") *Rawdon Street, Hungerford Street, Moira Street,* attempt to exhaust the various titles enjoyed by the Marquess of Hastings, Governor-General at the time of their construction in 1820, and his wife who was Countess of Loudoun in her own right. *Robison Street,* persistently mis-spelt "Robinson" Street, is named after Charles Knowles Robison, Police Magistrate of Calcutta in the forties, and architect of the Metcalfe Hall and other public buildings.

Camac Street stretches from Park Street to Lower Circular Road. Its name is derived from William Camac, a senior merchant of the days of Cornwallis and Wellesley, who owned a large number of houses in the locality a century and a quarter ago. In the *Calcutta Gazette* of March 6th, 1788, he advertises one of them for sale in the following terms: "For sale, that small upper-roomed garden house with about five biggahs of land, on the road leading from Chowringhee to the burial-ground, which formerly belonged to the Moravians. It is very private from the number of trees on the ground, and having lately received considerable additions and repairs, is well adapted for a black family." William Camac, according to the Directory of 1785, was judge of Tipperah and subsequently of Dacca. The name of Camac is a well-known one in the Indian Civil and Military Services. Major Jacob Camac defeated Scindia in 1781 and retired in the following year with the rank of Colonel. Malleson, Gleig, Trotter and Forrest, in their lives of Warren Hastings, all make mention of his exploit, but more than one of them do him an injustice in the matter of his name and record it as "Carnac." Burges Camac was aide-de-camp to Lord Wellesley in 1804, and in Dodwell and Miles may be seen the names of two other Camacs, George and Turner. Camac Street is known to the natives as Duncan bustee-ka-rasta, "the road of Duncan's bustee." It has no existence in Wood's map of 1784, and although it is shown in Upjohn's map, it bears no name. Since the demolition of the bustees in Theatre-road within the last few years, it has become one of the pleasantest streets in the English quarter.

Wood Street is named after Mr. Henry Wood, who on the 13th July, 1848, brought to the notice of the Lottery Committee "the inadequate manner in which the establishment entertained for the purpose performs its duty in removing the filth"—a complaint which has lost little of its justice by the lapse of years. In a house at the corner of Wood Street and Theatre Road, formerly occupied by the Eye Infirmary, lived Colonel Stuart, commonly known as Hindoo Stuart, from his conformity to "idolatrous customs." He was one of a class, now passed away, who looked with almost equal regard on the worship of Christ and Krishna. His tomb in the south Park Street burial-ground is worthy of the man whose grave it covers. It is constructed of elaborately carved black stone, which once formed part of a Hindu temple, and the recesses on each side of the door-way are occupied by ancient sculptured figures of "Bhagiruth" and "Prithi Devi," the incarnation of the Ganges, and the goddess of the earth, and fairies and sunyassies, while the bust of an elaborately decorated Hindu goddess crowns the whole.

Free School Street was a bamboo jungle in 1780, which people were afraid to pass at night. It now proceeds in a northerly direction from Park Street until it reaches Dhurrumtollah. Its name is due to the Free School which was established in 1789, and merged with the older charity school in 1800. The building which it occupies is said to have been erected on the site of the house of Mr. Justice LeMaistre, the colleague of Impey, Hyde and Chambers in the Supreme Court from 1774 to 1777. It was before Le Maistre that the famous charge of forgery against Nuncomar was first exhibited. He at once requested the attendance of his brother Hyde, who attended with him the whole day until ten o'clock at night, "when, no doubt remaining in the breast of either of us upon the evidence on the part of the Crown," a commitment was made. It was represented to the Judges that Nuncomar "was a person of very high rank and of the cast of Brahmins" and ought not to be confined in the common jail. Whereupon their Lordships waited upon the Chief Justice, to take the benefit of his advice, with the result that the following missive was despatched to Mr. Samuel Tolfrey, the Under-Sheriff: "Upon consultation with the Lord Chief Justice, we are all clearly of opinion that the Sheriff ought to confine his prisoner in the common jail upon this occasion.—S. C. Le Maistre." And Nuncomar was committed accordingly to the "Country Jail" which we name to-day the Presidency Jail, and which stood then as it does now to the south of the Maidan. The life of LeMaistre in Calcutta was a short one, but he seems to have made the most of it. He was a great card-player and *bonvivant*. "LeMaistre kept us laughing for two hours," is the pictrue drawn of him by a contemporary. "These lawyers are always in court, dispute, contention, cavil, upon the most ordinary topics." Before coming to India, he had been recorder of Rochester, and there were those who said he owed his judgeship to the fact of his being a protégé of the notorious Lord Sandwich. Another building in Free School Street possesses historical associations, if tradition is to be believed. Thackeray, the novelist, is popularly supposed to have been born on July 18th, 1811, in the house now numbered 39 and occupied by the Armenian College (not Convent, as so many writers assert). His father, Richmond Thackeray, was at the time Secretary to the Board of Revenue, but was six months later appointed Collector of the 24-Pergunnahs, and when we come to pay our visit to Alipore, we shall find his name prominently associated with the house which had been "The Lodge of Philip Francis."

Mott's Lane, a turning out of Free School Street, preserves the memory of Mr. Motte, a "free merchant," whose name often occurs in the private correspondence of Hastings. In 1766, he undertook a journey to the diamond mines in Orissa by direction of Clive and wrote an account of it. He afterwards lived at Benares and moved thence to Chinsurah, where the Hastings used frequently to visit him and his wife, who is constantly alluded to as "Bibby Motte" in the Governor-General's letters to his "dearest Marian." For some time he held a police appointment in Calcutta, but seems about 1781 to have fallen into financial difficulties, if we may judge from an advertisement which appears in the *Gazette* of that year calling a meeting of his creditors. Among the Impey manuscripts in the British Museum (says Dr. Busteed), there is a petition from Mr. Motte written from the Calcutta Jail in 1783, in which he begs that his creditors will assent to his release from prison on the score of humanity. Mrs. Motte accompanied Mrs. Hastings to England in 1784. "The whole place is engaged in adieus," writes the author of *Hartly House*, "and Mrs. H—— will be accompanied to England by a Mrs. M——, who has been presented with 500 gold-mohurs (a thousand pounds) in return for her complaisance in making the voyage with her. Two black girls, and a steward, are Mrs. ——'s attendants: and the state cabin and roundhouse will be entirely devoted to her use."

Royds Street commences from 41, Free School Street, and proceeds as far as Elliot Road. It is, according to usage, spelt Royd Street without the final letter to the proper name: but incorrectly so, for it is called in honour of a former resident in the quarter, Sir John Royds, puisne judge of the Supreme Court from 1787 to 1816. Sir James Watson, his predecessor, held office only from March 1st to May 2nd, 1796: but he was more fortunate. His house is said to have stood on the site of what is now the Doveton College. He died in 1816, at the age of 65, and lies buried in the South Park Street burial-ground. The tombstone upon his grave records that "he conscientiously discharged his important duties with honour to himself and with advantage to the public, while he benefited and advanced the society in which he lived by the benevolence of his disposition and the accomplishments of a scholar and a gentleman." He may be credited with presiding at one of the shortest sessions on record in Calcutta. On the 9th June, 1804, he held "the first session of Oyer and Terminer and General Gaol delivery" and disposed of the cases in the calendar, which were only two in number, at a single sitting. In a report of the proceedings, published in the *Calcutta Gazette* of June 21st, 1804, His Lordship in his charge to the Jury, is reported to have paid a high compliment to "the system and energy of the well-regulated police which we enjoy in this settlement." Appropriately enough, the street into which Royds Street leads to the east recalls the memory of the man to whom Calcutta owed it that the compliment so paid was not idle or unmeaning.

Elliot Road is named after John Elliot of the Bengal Civil Service, who was, in the early years of the last century, President of the Boards of Police and Conservancy in Calcutta, and effected great and important reforms in the administration of the city. As chief of the Police he was largely instrumental in putting down the dacoits, a gang of robbers who were one of the principal pests of the Calcutta of the day: and the "Dacoit's Song" celebrated his prowess in the following lines:—

> "Here a health to the jolly Dacoits,
> "Who are hung in the Law's fatal chain!
> "Here's a health to John Elliot whose daring exploits
> "I never shall witness again!"

This vigilant Magistrate and thief-catcher survived Sir John Royds by two years and died in Calcutta on the 28th January, 1818, at the age of 53. A handsome monument stands over his grave in the North Park Street burying-ground, and the inscription upon it records that it was "erected by a voluntary association of persons who were long and intimately acquainted with his merits and character, and who were desirous of evincing by a lasting memorial their sentiments of esteem and regard." The road is shown in the map of 1784, but under the name of "Ahmed Jamadaur's Street."

Roberts Street, once known as Sibtollah Lane, takes its present title not from Lord Roberts, but from John Blessington Roberts, Chairman of the Justices from 1862 to 1871 whose portrait hangs in the Municipal Office. He commenced his remarkable career as a constable in the police force, and from being Tyler, rose to be Deputy District Grand Master of Bengal.

Ripon Street, Ripon Lane, Marquis Street, and *Marquis Lane,* which are in the immediate vicinity, are named after the Viceroy who governed India from 1880 to 1884, and who is now (1906) a member of Sir Henry Campbell-Bannerman's government. Their earlier names were less euphonious: South Colinga Street, Anis Barber's Lane, Joratalao Lane (from twin-tanks which once stood in the neighbourhood) and Misser Khansamah's Lane. We may feel surprised at the early naming of these streets after insignificant persons. But at the time the appellations were bestowed, the streets were no better than narrow gullies, and barbers, khansamahs, duftries, tailors (ostagurs), and carpenters were the principal residents. A few of the old names still survive. Panchee Dhobany Gully commemorates a laundress, Chidam Mudee's Lane a grocer, and Shama Bai's Gully a dancing girl: but in Colinga and the European quarter they have all but vanished. At No. 9, Ripon Street, resided John William Ricketts (1791-1835), the "East Indian Patriot," who founded the Doveton College in 1823, under the name of the Parental Academy and was deputed in 1829 to present to Parliament a numerously signed petition on behalf of the East Indian community. He was examined at the bar of the House of Lords by the select Committee on Indian Affairs: and also by the Lower House. An important result of his deputation may be found in the clause in the Charter Act of 1833, which proclaimed that all persons without disqualification of birth or colour, were eligible for civil and military employment under the government of India.

Retracing our steps up Park Street, and reserving the

Doveton College and Free Masons' Hall for consideration in another chapter, we find ourselves once more in Chowringhee. The tank on the maidan to the south of the Outram Statue may be noticed. In Upjohn's map of 1794, it bears the name of the "New Tank." Dr. Simon Nicolson, Lord Dalhousie's physician, who from 1820 to 1855 enjoyed undisputed pre-eminence as the most celebrated doctor in India, lived in the building at the corner of Park Street and Chowringhee, which until a few months ago was the home of the United Service Club: and the avenue leading across the Maidan past where the Mayo Statue now stands, is said to have been made to enable him to have direct access from Chowringhee to Government House. A portrait of Dr. Nicolson hangs in the rooms of the Asiatic Society a few paces away. Another resident of Chowringhee we may single out for mention is Sir Arthur Buller, Judge of the Supreme Court from 1854 to 1859, the pupil of Carlyle and brother of the Charles Buller to whose early death and loveable character there is an affecting allusion in Thackeray's "Doctor Birch and his young friends," and whom Bulwer Lytton eulogizes in his poem of "St. Stephens"—"Farewell, fine humourist, finer reasoner still, Lively as Luttrell, logical as Mill." The mother of the Bullers was the daughter of Colonel William Kirkpatrick the Orientalist, and had been the belle of Calcutta of a previous generation. Even so critical a genius as John Leyden made her the theme of his verse, as befitted one who was known on the banks of the Hooghly as Titania, and had been compared for her stately beauty to Madame Récamier. Carlyle found her in 1822 "a graceful, airy and ingeniously intelligent person of the gossamer type." Charles Buller the elder, who appears in *Sartor Resartas* as Count Zähdarm and will be remembered for his quizzical Latin epitaph, was a Company's servant, and it was at his house in Chowringhee that James Achilles Kirkpatrick, the Hushmat Jung of Hyderabad history, died in October, 1805.

Just beyond Dr. Simon Nicholson's former dwelling, and separating it from the United Service Club's new and imposing mansion, is *Kyd Street*, which proceeds in an easterly direction to Free School Street. During the last century it was known as "Chowringhee Tank Street," and it is so marked in Wood's map of 1784. The tank itself will be found indicated as early as 1742 in the maps of Calcutta, and is now situated within the compound of the house of the Superintendent of the School of Art on the northern side of the street, which is known in native parlance as "Janjiri-talao-ka-rasta" or "Sieve Tank Street." The significance of the name will be readily appreciated after an inspection of the water-gate which may be seen from the road just beyond the United Service Club and which effectually prevents the entering of the tank by those who may come to draw water. The modern designation bestowed upon the street commemorates a well-known resident of Calcutta of the last century—Lieutenant-Colonel Robert Kyd, Military Secretary to the Government of Bengal, and a distinguished botanist, who is said to have lived in the house we have just associated with Dr. Nicolson. He was mainly instrumental in the establishment in 1787 of the Calcutta Botanical Gardens, and until his death in 1793, he zealously performed the duties of Superintendent without any remuneration whatsoever. A handsome marble bust, by Banks, stands opposite the orchid-house to keep alive the memory of the "Father of the Gardens": and the Agri-Horticultural Society possesses a most curious portrait of him in coloured chalks which it is hoped they may present to the Victoria Memorial Hall. The son of Colonel Kyd was the famous James Kyd, the shipbuilder after whom Kidderpore, where his dock was situated, is said by some to have been named. The dock was, however, of older date, and had been established in 1780 by Colonel Henry Watson, who acted as second to Francis in his memorable duel with Hastings; and Kyd did not come into possession until 1807. James Kyd was universally recognised as "the head of the East Indian Class, to which he belonged, *quando ullum invenient parem?*" He died at Kidderpore on the 26th October, 1836: and, it is said, left a pamphlet behind him in which he set out the incidents of his career with a view to benefit youths "of his own class" and induce them to "imitate his example and betake themselves to handycraft more generally than they were wont to do."

The next turning to the East is *Sudder Street*, which issues from Chowringhee to the north of the Museum building and proceeds as far as Free School Street. It bore in former days the name both of Ford Street and Speke Street. It appears under the former title in Wood's map of 1784. The latter designation is derived from the occupation by Mr. Speke, Member of Council from 1789 to 1801, of the house in the centre of the Museum compound, which is now the residence of the Superintendent. The house was built in 1790, and the grounds extended to Kyd Street, including the "Sieve Tank," which we have just been noticing. It was the scene of an exciting occurrence in 1798, when a young Sikh, whose petition was refused by Mr. Speke, killed one of his servants and took refuge on the roof where he was finally shot dead by a party of sepoys. Subsequently it was rented by Mr. Speke to Government, and was for some years used as the Sudder Court—a circumstance which readily suggests the reason for its present appellation. From the time, however, of Lord William Bentinck (1828-1835), the Sudder Court sat in the present Military Hospital at Bhowanipore: and in late years the building was utilised by the Bengal Government as a Secretariat.

We are now approaching the quarter once known as Colinga. The tank which stands on the Maidan, opposite Messrs. Johnston and Hoffmann's premises, will give us our clue: for in Upjohn's map of 1793, we find it named as "Colinga Tank."

Beyond Sudder Street, and leading to the Municipal Market is *Lindsay Street.* The eponymous hero of the Street is in all probability the Hon'ble Robert Lindsay (1754-1836), whose adventurous career in the Company's service may be found related by himself in the "Lives of the Lindsays." His house in the locality in thus advertized for sale in the *Calcutta Gazette* of September 27th, 1804:—"The house at Chowringhee, belonging to the Hon'ble Robert Lindsay, at present occupied by William Trower, Esq., on leave for twelve months from the 5th July last, at Rs. 250 a month and the taxes." Lindsay was the second son of the fifth Earl of Balcarres, and was sent out as a writer to India by Henry Dundas, Lord Melville. He landed in Calcutta in September, 1772, and after spending some years at Dacca, succeeded William Holland as Collector of Sylhet in 1777. Those were times when the Company's servants did not live by the bread alone of their official salaries. The elder William Makepeace Thackeray, grandfather of the novelist, had been the first Collector of Sylhet a year or two before Lindsay's arrival. His chief sources of income were the destruction of tigers and the capture of elephants: and his name survives to this day as a mighty hunter. In Lindsay's day the supply of elephants for the Company's troops still yielded a good profit, and the bag of tigers was as plentiful, for he was able to account for sixty or seventy yearly, upon all of which the Government allowed liberal rewards. But he devised other methods of money making in addition. "Thrown on his own resources he assumed by turns, as circumstances minister to occasion, the character of soldier, magistrate, political agent, elephant-catcher, tiger-hunter, shipbuilder, lime-manufacturer, physician and surgeon." The revenue, he found, was collected in cowries. A fleet of armed boats was maintained to convey the annual accumulation of 700 millions of these little shells to Dacca "at a loss of no less than ten per cent. exclusive of depredations on the passage down." Lindsay conceived the idea of remitting the value of the cowries in limestone, for which he held the contract, and keeping the revenues of Sylhet in payment. It was, says Sir William Hunter in his *Thackerays in India*, only the unfortunate limit to the demand for mortar in Calcutta that prevented the whole land tax of the district from passing into his pockets. He also created a shipbuilding trade from the timber of the Sylhet forests after some Crusoe experiences of being unable to get his craft down the river owing to their large size. He wrote an account of his enterprise to his mother, Lady Balcarres. "Your talents in this line I do not dispute," replied the Countess, "but I have one favour to ask of you, which is that you will not come home in a ship of your own building!" "I implicitly followed her advice" adds the sagacious Robert. He left India in 1787, the purchase of the barony of Leuchar in Fife having established him as a landed proprietor while still in the Company's service: and lived for nearly fifty years in enjoyment of the large fortune he had amassed. Two of his grandsons, Sir Coutts Lindsay and the late Lord Wantage, are well known to the present generation. He married the daughter of Sir Alexander Dick in 1788, having, as he said, "marked her for his own before he went to India."

In Lindsay Street is the Opera House, a wooden building which hardly comes up to the expectations created by its title. It was once known as the English Theatre, and it was here that Charles Mathews on New Year's night, 1876, played the part of Adonis Evergreen in his own comedy, *My Awful Dad,* before King Edward the Seventh, then Prince of Wales. "On that occasion," says Mr. E. W. Madge in an excellent article on the Theatres of Calcutta which has already been laid under contribution, "with the view, no doubt of reserving the place for Indian Noblemen, the following prices of admission were asked: upper tier boxes, six seats, Rs. 1,000: lower tier boxes, six seats Rs. 500: Stalls, Rs. 50/- each."

Madge's Lane, which leads out of Lindsay Street close to the Opera House, is named after a well-known East Indian family who at one time owned landed property where the New Market and Opera House now stand. James Madge, who was head assistant in the office of the Chief Engineer, Bengal, was one of those who signed the farewell address to Lord Minto in 1813. His father, Captain E. H. Madge, of the 19th Regiment, commanded at Fort MacDowall, Kandy, in 1803. Worthy representatives of the family may be found in Calcutta to-day in Mr. W. C. Madge, Secretary to the European and Anglo-Indian Defence Association, and his son, Mr. E. W. Madge, Superintendent of the Reading Room of the Imperial Library.

The modern name of *Corporation Street,* which comes just before Dhurrumtollah, needs no elucidation. It extends from Chowringhee to Circular Road, covering a distance of exactly a mile: and the offices of the Corporation of Calcutta may be discerned a few yards from its Chowringhee end. The street is clearly shown in Colonel Wood's map of 1784, and bore the designation of Jaun Bazar until a few years ago. Holwell in his Indian Tracts speaks of "Dhee Calcutta including John Nagore," and the name was probably conferred upon it because it led to that locality. It has been lately widened, and when the contemplated improvements are carried out along its entire length, it will make one of the finest streets in the city.

Dhurrumtollah (properly Dharmtala) commences at the

north end of Chowringhee. It is commonly held to derive its name Dharamtola or Holy Street, from a large mosque which stood on the site of Messrs. Cook and Company's livery stables. But Dr. Hoernle discerns in the name a reference to Dharma, one of the units in the Buddhist Trinity, and points to the Buddhist Temple in Jaun Bazar hard by, in confirmation of his theory. The fine Musjid which now stands at the corner of Dhurumtollah and Chowringhee was erected and endowed in 1842 by Prince Gholam Muhammad, K.C.S.I., a son of Tippoo Sultan, who was a pensioner of the British Government and resided at Tollygunge. In the last century, Dhurrumtollah is described as a "well raised causeway, raised by deepening the ditch on either side," with wretched huts on the south side. It was shaded with trees on both sides. The land in the vicinity was owned by a jemadar named Jaffer in the employ of Warren Hastings. Dhurrumtollah Bazar was established in 1794. It was formerly called Shakespear's bazar, and was one of the sites thought of for the present Town Hall. It was purchased by the Justices, shortly after the establishment in the seventies of the Municipal Market, which was suffering from its competition.

Just north of Dhurrumtollah, a creek formerly ran from Chandpal Ghat to Balliaghatta near the Salt Lakes. The creek passed through *Wellington Square* and *Creek Row*, and was navigable for large boats. Dinga Bhanga, the native name of Creek Row, is said to have its origin in the wrecking at that place of a ship which, during the terrible cyclone of 1737, had been driven up by a storm wave from the river. The Creek is represented in an early view copied in Howitt's History of England. It issued from the river Hooghly at Colvin's Ghat, formerly known as Cutcha Goodee Ghat, at the foot of Hastings Street, and proceeding along that street, skirted the old burying-ground on the south. At the south-west of St. John's Church it was crossed by a bridge, and in Wills' map of 1753, the mouth of this Creek is plainly shown, together with a second bridge at the corner of what is now Hastings Street and Council House Street. Mr. Blochmann, the distinguished Principal of the Calcutta Madrassa, who died in 1878, and whose bust by Roscoe Mullins adorns the rooms of the Asiatic Society, has in an interesting lecture on old Calcutta spoken of the Creek as "running from Chandpal Ghat to Ballia Ghat near the Salt Lakes." Orme describes it as "a deep miry gully." Wellington Square contained a tank made upon the bed of this creek which the Calcutta Water Works have annexed for a reservoir. From a map of Calcutta drawn in 1774, it appears that Dinga Bhanga was a division of the town not to the north of Dhurrumtollah, where Creek Row is situate, but to the south of it, and bounded by Jaun Bazar (Corporation Street) to the south, Chowringhee to the west, and Circular Road to the east. Neither Wellington Square nor Creek Row were in existence at the time. Both were the work of the Lottery Committee. In the *Calcutta Gazette* of August 9th, 1821, Wellington Square is referred to as "the new square in the Dhurrumtollah," which "with the street passing along its western side to the Bow Bazar" and now called Wellington Street, "must be as favourable to the salubrity as they are ornamental to the appearance of that part of the town," and it is added that "a great deal has been at the same time effected with the direct object of removing nuisance and purifying the atmosphere in confined places which is not equally apparent to common observers, who may not be aware of the many noxious tanks that have been filled up in almost every quarter."

Bentinck Street is the modern designation of *Cossaitollah* the quarter of the *Kasai* or butchers. It must therefore have been a hateful street for the Hindoos to pass through, and yet it lay on their direct road from Chitpore to the shrine at Kalighat, being in fact that portion of the immemorial pilgrim path which stretches from Lall Bazar to the junction of Dhurrumtollah and the Esplanade. In the earliest maps it is clearly marked and all its eastern side appears to have been a mass of jungle, for it is shown covered with trees. Only a single house at the north-west corner (where it meets Lall Bazar) appears to have existed in 1757: and in subsequent maps three only are indicated. Even as late as 1780, it was declared to be almost impassable from mud in the rains. Nevertheless several houses in and about the "Cossaitollah Bazar" are advertised in the *Calcutta Gazette* from 1784 to 1788: Mr. J. Trenholm's Tavern, "adjoining Mr. Meredith's stables": Mr. John Palmer's undertaking establishment, "near Mr. Oliphant's the coachmaker's": the Union Tavern at No. 44: and Mr. Mackinnon's School. Its modern name is derived from Lord William Bentinck, who was Governor-General from 1828 to 1835. The house now occupied by Messrs. Llewellyn & Co., is asserted to have been used as a Government House in the time of the first Earl of

Minto, Governor-General from 1807 to 1813. The arches and pillars of the Throne Room, Council Chamber and Reception room are still standing as originally built; no alterations whatever (it is said) have been made therein. The house proper, with out-offices and stables, remain intact as they were in the year 1807.

We are now in fact approaching the heart of old Calcutta. Many of the lanes about Bentinck Street and Dalhousie Square had the same names a century ago as at the present day, such as Grant's, Meredith's, Weston's, Zig-zag, Imambari, Sooterkin's, Chandney Choke, Cooper's, Mangoe, Dacres', Crooked, Fancy, and Larkins' Lanes. Until recently it was possible to place Raneemoody Gully in the same category, but it has now been called British Indian Street, in compliment to the British Indian Association, which has its offices there.

Grant's Lane issues from Bentinck Street and is one of the oldest streets in Calcutta. In the map of 1784, it is marked and is shewn as inhabited by Europeans. The name it bears is that of the pious and benevolent Charles Grant, whose residence was "the first house on the right-hand side from Cossaitollah" (Bentinck Street). In his time there were only two or three houses in the street. It must not be confounded with Grant Street which is a modern road running in a southerly direction from Dhurrumtollah to the offices of the City Corporation, and is named after Sir John Peter Grant, Lieutenant-Governor of Bengal from 1859 to 1862. Charles Grant belonged to the Civil Service of an earlier generation. He served in India for over twenty years, and after his retirement in 1790, became a director of the Company and Chairman in 1808, 1809 and 1815. His favourite place of worship was the Old Church in Mission Row: and when the seal of the Sheriff of Calcutta was placed upon its door on the insolvency of John Zachariah Kiernander whose private property it was, he came forward and purchasing the building for Rs. 10,000, made it over on the 31st October, 1787, to trustees for the benefit of the Christian public. A tablet in the Church bears witness to his munificence. He died in London on October 31st, 1823, at the age of 78. His son became a prominent figure in English politics. He was Secretary of State for the Colonies from 1834 to 1839, and was raised to the peerage as Lord Glenelg in 1835.

Meredith's Lane, which issues likewise from Bentinck Street and terminates at Chandney Choke Lane, derives its name from one of the first livery stables in Calcutta which was owned by a certain Mr. Meredith. The locality seems to have been a favourite one for the trade in olden times: for we find Mr. Massey and Messrs. Dexter and Lane with their places of business in Cossaitollah. The former advertises in the *Calcutta Gazette* of March 25th, 1784, for "two postillions of light weight." In Cossaitollah also (as we have just seen) was the shop of Mr. Oliphant "Coach-maker" and rival of Messrs. Steuart and Co., then as now of Old Court House Corner.

Weston's Lane runs out from Bentinck Street and proceeds as far as Zig-Zag Lane. It bears the name of one of the oldest and most respected citizens of Calcutta in his day—Charles Weston, who was born in 1731 in a house which existed opposite Tiretta Bazar. He was the son of the Recorder of the Mayor's Court and seems to have been of mixed parentage. There is a monument over his grave in the South Park Street cemetery which tells part of his life's history. It records that he died on the 25th December, 1809, in the 78th year of his age, and proceeds:— "A life protracted to unusual length he marked by an unostentatious life of benevolence and charity seldom equalled and never yet exceeded in British India. By the wise economical management of a fortune far from enormous (the product of his own industry, secured by the divine blessing), he was enabled to pour forth streams of bounty and mercy. He manifested a grateful mind, by cherishing in his old age his former employer and benefactor, the late Governor Holwell, and after being the friend of the destitute, the support of the widow and fatherless, an ornament to the British name, and a blessing to mankind, he descended to the tomb amid the tears of the indigent, and the lamentations of surviving friends. Reader! this stone is no flatterer: go, and do thou likewise." The details of Weston's career which have survived do not belie these encomiums. In early life he served his time as surgeon's apprentice to Holwell and accompanied him on one occasion to Europe. On Holwell's appointment as a covenanted civilian, he also changed his pursuits. During the siege of Calcutta he took his turn of duty as a militiaman and escaped the Black Hole by having been sent on the river to look after Holwell's baggage boats on the day before the Fort was taken. He does not appear to have gone to Fulta, but to have taken refuge with the Dutch at Chinsurah. When Holwell left India in 1760, he gave Weston 2,000 rupees and lent him another 5,000. With this capital he made a large fortune, chiefly by agency business: and was lucky enough to win the Tiretta Bazar in the lottery of 1791, which gave the big prize to the drawer of the last ticket. The rents and profits of the Bazar he applied to his own use: but the interest upon the rest of his wealth, which was invested in Government securities, was distributed by him in charities. The lakh of rupees which he left at his death, says Dr. Busteed, was the smallest of his benefactions. He served as a juror at the trial of Nuncomar in June, 1775: and lived to see the Governor-Generalship of Lord Minto. There is a portrait of him in the vestry of St. John's Church.

Returning to Chowringhee end of Bentinck Street we may now proceed westwards towards Government House along *Esplanade Row*. The street, which is styled by its present name in the map of 1784, is divided nowadays by the Gardens of Government House into Esplanade Row West and East: but before 1800, it ran without interruption from Chandpal Ghat to Dhurrumtollah, passing on its way, the Council House and Government House which stood side by side facing the Maidan, the one on the west and the other on the east. Hastings appears not to have cared to live at Government or Buckingham House as it was then called, and tradition points out his Calcutta residence at No. 4, Esplanade Row, East, the house at the corner of Old Court House Street. It is evidently the house referred to in an advertisement in the *Calcutta Gazette of September* 6th, 1787, in which a reward of 2,000 sicca rupees is offered for the recovery of an "old black wood bureau" which was "about the time of Mr. Hastings' departure from Bengal either stolen from his house on the Esplanade or by mistake sold at the auction of his effects," and the loss of which was evidently keenly felt by him. After his marriage with the Baroness Imhoff, he went to live at her house in Hastings Street where we shall in due course find a commemorative tablet.

The Esplanade was the old name given to the portion of the maidan now absorbed by the Eden Gardens and the grounds of Government House. It stretched as far as the glacis of the Fort and formed in the days of Hastings a favourite promenade for "elegant walking parties" on moonlight evenings. The five principal streets of Calcutta abutted on it, says Miss Sophia Goldborne who wrote in 1780. To the south was the maidan, then covered with jungle, while "the course" led the ladies down to see an occasional launch at Watson's works at Kidderpore. Both Daniell and Baillie give us a picture of the Esplanade, as it appeared in the closing years of the eighteenth century. The old Government House and the Council House are conspicuous objects in each drawing, and Daniel presents us with an unfamiliar addition to the view in the shape of a couple of elephants perambulating the street with a crowd of attendants.

Dacres Lane is an exceedingly short road issuing from Esplanade Row, East, and proceeding to Waterloo Street. Its entire length is only a furlong: but it is one of the ancient streets of Calcutta. The individual after whom it is named was Philip Milner Dacres, Collector of Calcutta in 1773 and afterwards a member of Council. He deserves remembrance as one of those who in a petition, dated December 15th, 1757, "To the Hon'ble Roger Drake, Esq., President and Governor in Council" prayed for the establishment of a corps of militia by the name of the "Patriot Band." Dacres appears to have been at the time a writer on the monthly salary of Rs. 20. The street was once a fashionable locality. In it were situated Moore's Assembly Rooms where the English citizens of Calcutta entertained Lord Minto at a farewell banquet in December, 1813.

Waterloo Street has no existence in Upjohn's map of 1794, and the period of its construction is indicated with sufficient clearness by its name.

From the corner of Esplanade Row, East, there runs down into Dalhousie Square the broad and magnificent thoroughfare which goes by the name of *Old Court House Street.* It will not be found in maps of Calcutta of date anterior to the Black Hole: Mission Row then forming the eastern boundary of Tank Square. In Wood's map of 1784, it is shown as issuing from the Old Court House from which it took its designation, and which stood upon the site of St. Andrew's Kirk, but the latter portion of its length is now known as Dalhousie Square, East. As a matter of fact it extends across the maidan as far as "Surman's Bridge" at Kidderpore, and the Red Road is merely a continuation of it. It was constructed about 1781 when the finishing touches were put to the present Fort William, and is linked with the name of Colonel Henry Watson to whom Calcutta owes many improvements including not only the completion of the citadel itself, but also the laying out of the surrounding Esplanade. Writing in 1782 to Hastings upon the matter, he "offers his best services" to render the "great road leading to Surman's Bridge both durable and commodious for a moderate sum," and points out that "the intentions of the Board to keep the Esplanade clean and free from Incroachments can never be fulfilled without enclosing it with some sort of Pailing or Fence." At the corner of Old Court House Street and Waterloo Street, upon the site of the premises which is now known as Ezra Buildings and occupied as to the ground floor by Messrs. Cuthbertson and Harper the saddlers, Mrs. Leach opened a temporary theatre in June, 1839, on the destruction of the Chowringhee Theatre. It was known at that time as St. Andrew's Library and was owned by Messrs. W. Thacker & Co. The lower flat was little better than a godown, but Mrs. Leach transformed it into a theatre capable of holding 400 persons. It was supplanted in 1840, by the Sans Souci Theatre in Park Street. Mr. Long allots the site to Sir John Clavering's house. However this may be, the General died at 8, Mission Row, and if he lived here also, it must have been a very temporary habitation, for his life in Calcutta lasted only three years.

The northern side of Government Place was formerly known as *Wheler Place*. The name commemorates the senior member of Council who laid the foundation-stone of St. John's Church in April, 1784, in the absence of Warren Hastings in Upper India. He died in Calcutta in the following October, after sitting in Council for ten years, and so lost by a few months the honour which accrued to John Macpherson, the "gentle giant," of acting as Governor-General on Hastings' departure. According to the inscription on his tombstone, Edward Wheler was the third son of Sir William Wheler, Bart., of Leamington Hastings in the country of Warwick, grandson of Sir Stephen Glyn, Bart., of Bicester in Oxfordshire, and great-grandson of Sir Edward Evelyn, Bart., of Long Ditton in Surrey. His first wife, whose maiden name was Harriet Chicheley Plowden, arrived in Bengal in December, 1777, and survived the climate only seven months. Francis writes of her; "She appeared in public for the first time at our ball in wonderful splendour. At sight of her hoop all our beauties stared in envy and admiration. I never saw the like before."

Larkins' Lane is a very small street connecting Old Court House Street on the west with Wellesley Place. It is, however, an old one, for it appears in Wood's map of 1784. William Larkins, after whom it was called, was a leading citizen of Calcutta in his day, a churchwarden of St. John's Church and an intimate friend of Warren Hastings, in whose correspondence his name frequently occurs. He was for a time after Hastings' departure Accountant-General and, having previously been in charge of the moneys received by Hastings from native princes and others on behalf of the Company, was called at the Trial to give evidence on the charges relating to presents. He finally retired from India in 1793 and died in 1800. John Pascal Larkins, who was presumably the son of William, was a prominent Calcutta citizen in the twenties. In a list of subscribers "towards the erection of a statue to Warren Hastings at Calcutta," which bears the date September 14th, 1820, and the signature as chairman of Mr. J. P. Larkins, we find the following names, which will give us a glimpse of his contemporaries in Calcutta, and the measure of their liberality :—Marquess of Hastings, Rs. 1,000 : Sir Edward Hyde East (Chief Justice), Rs. 300 : Sir Francis Macnaghten, Rs. 100 : Sir Antony Buller (the second puisne judge and not to be confounded with Sir Arthur Buller, who administered justice thirty years later), Rs. 200 : C. T. Metcalfe, Esq. (Lord Metcalfe), Rs. 500 : Sir Charles D'Oyly, Rs. 500 : Lieutenant-General Sir J. Macdonald, K.C.B. (whose tomb in the South Park Street cemetery records that he died in 1824, "after an honourable and faithful service of half a century"), Rs. 500 : Mr. John Fendall, Member of Council from 1820 to 1825 (who lies buried near him), Rs. 500 : and Mr. John Palmer (the "Prince of Merchants"), Rs. 500. The total amount obtained is Rs. 41,493, and Larkins himself is among the donors of Rs. 500. There are a large number of Indian subscribers, the Rajah of Benares contributing no less a sum than Rs. 5,000. Larkins was also a prominent Free Mason, and in the capacity of "Deputy Grand Master in and over the whole of India" and "acting by delegation" from Lord Hastings, the officiating "Grand Master of India," laid the foundation-stone of St. Peter's Church in the Fort on July 24th, 1822.

We may leave Dalhousie Square for the present and make our way through Larkins' Lane into *Fancy Lane*, which meets it on the other side of Wellesley Place. Archdeacon Hyde traces the derivation of Fancy Lane to the *phansi* or gallows which he places in this locality in the early days when Calcutta was surrounded by palisades and the southern boundary was shut in by the creek which flowed along the course of what is now Hastings Street. *Wellesley Place* has succeeded Corkscrew Lane, a narrow winding gully which ended abruptly about the point where Spence's Hotel now stands and afforded no outlet to Dalhousie Square. Its name is sufficiently indicative of the period of its origin.

Fancy Lane emerges on the west into *Council House Street,* the home of the principal Banks, and containing also the Foreign Office (now in process of rebuilding) and the offices of the Private Secretary to the Viceroy and the Administrator-General of Bengal. It derives its name from the Old Council House which was pulled down in 1800 and stood on the western portion of the present Government House enclosure. The southern end of the street where it runs between Government House and what was once Loudoun buildings and is now the India Secretariat, is known to-day as Government Place, West, but in earlier times Council House Street as such continued until it joined with Esplanade Row. On June 22nd, 1758, "there being at present no proper places for the public offices from which circumstance many inconveniences arise in carrying on the business of the settlement, and as it will be proper likewise to have a room to hold our Councils in contiguous to the Secretary's and Accountant's offices, it was agreed at a consultation that the dwelling-house of the late Mr. Richard Court be purchased for the Hon'ble Company and appropriated to the above uses." Court will be remembered as the senior merchant who survived the Black Hole and was sent in chains to Moorshedabad with Holwell. He had been drowned in the Hooghly in May, 1758, just a month before the purchase of his house. It was in this building that Stanlake Batson, one of the Members of Council, on June 9th, 1763, struck Warren Hastings in the face during a Council Meeting. "Mr. Batson making some unbecoming reflections on the Governor," writes Hastings in his official representation, "I replied thereto, and I appeal to the Board whether in any indecent or provoking terms, upon which Mr. Batson gave me the lie and struck me in the presence of the Board. I leave them to take such notice as they may think proper of the indignity offered to themselves by this step of Mr. Batson's. For my own part I cannot think of sitting any longer at a Board where I am subject to such insults." Batson was in the result suspended, and on his making a full apology the majority in Council voted for his restoration to office: but the President (Vansittart) refusing to sit with him, it was decided that the minutes of each Council were to be submitted to him in his own house. Where was this Old Council House? Long says vaguely that it was in Council House Street: but this is not of much assistance, and Wills' map of 1753 is still less helpful, for Court's house is not shown in it at all. It was probably in Clive Street, but it is impossible to speak with authority. In any case it was not the Council Chamber in which Hastings and Francis carried on their warfare of words during the year 1775 and 1776. For in the "proceedings" of the Board in Calcutta of the 15th October, 1764, there occurs the following paragraph: "The present Council Room being from its situation greatly exposed to the heat of the weather and from its vicinity to the public office very ill-calculated for conducting the business of the Board with that privacy which is often requisite, it is agreed to build a new Council-room at a convenient distance from the offices." Popular tradition associates this new Council House with a number of buildings in Calcutta, including among others that occupied by the office of the Private Secretary to the Viceroy in Council House Street. Long places it "in the house which still stands, between Mackenzie's and Hollings' offices:" but he does not state where these offices were. According to the Bengal Directory for 1813, John Mackenzie and William Hollings, "Merchants and Agents," had their offices in Lall Bazar, and this would seem to be the locality indicated: for in 1852, the year in which Long wrote, the name of Hollings has long disappeared from the Directory, and the offices of Mackenzie and Co., are in Pollock Street, near the Armenian Church. But in any case, Long's topography would appear to be as inaccurate as it is slipshod. No greater consideration (it is to be feared), must be paid to the strong tradition in Calcutta which connects the Secretary's working room in the Legislative Department's office behind the Town Hall with the Council Chamber of Warren Hastings and Francis. The maps of 1784 and 1794 by Colonel Mark Wood and Upjohn disclose that a building resembling the office of the Legislative Department in general appearance already existed on the site now occupied by that office. But they show also that the Council House was situated on the other side of Council House Street, which is shown by other indications not to have materially altered its position, on a portion of the area now appropriated to Government House. This is confirmed by a contemporary woodcut representing the frontage of Government House with the Council Chamber, which certainly resembled the Legislative Office in general structure, at a short distance to the left. There was, however, a time when the Legislative Secretary's room did fulfil the purpose tradition has assigned to it. The Public Works Department is in possession of a record showing steps taken to adorn the room in order to render it suitable for a Council Chamber, when legislative authority was conferred upon the Lieutenant-Governor of Bengal in the early sixties: and the meetings of the Bengal Legislative Council were held in this room for a number of years.

To the south of Council House Street runs *Hastings Street.* At No. 7, in the house now occupied by Messrs. Burn and Co., lived the "beautiful Mrs. Imhoff," who became in 1777, the second wife of Warren Hastings. For some three years after his marriage, Hastings appears to have lived in this house, and to have used the old Government House, or Buckingham House, as it was then called, only for official purposes. A tablet appropriately recalls the fact and reminds the passer-by of the great Governor-General after whom the street takes its name. But the house has been entirely modernized and it cannot be truthfully declared that its new dress of red brick recalls many memories of the past: although a few solitary relics of its old magnificence are preserved within in the shape of ancient punkah-frames gorgeously painted in crimson and gold. Hastings once more made the house his head-quarters after his return from up-country in November, 1784, and lived here until he sailed for England in February of the following year. "On the 4th of this month, Mr. Stables called at Sooksaugor and passed," he writes to his wife on November 20th, 1784, referring to one of his colleagues in Council, "I followed him the same morning, and arrived at your gloomy mansion in Calcutta between 6, and 7, after an absence of eight months and eighteen days." But he continued to make of Alipore his "Saturday and Sunday residence" until he could "find a purchaser or leave the country:" for (he tells his wife in the same letter) "I find it a relief to my mind, and my health is certainly the better for it."

At the corner of Church Lane and Hastings Street stood the original Post Office, which was afterwards the house of Mrs. Fay. A later Post Office was located in *Old Post Office Street*, the street running to the south, in a house nearly opposite the High Court. Once a residential quarter, the street is now entirely given over to solicitors' offices and barristers' chambers. At the southern end of Old Post Office Street we emerge into the western portion of Esplanade Row: and on our left we shall perceive the Town Hall, which occupied the site of the residence of Mr. Justice Hyde. He is said to have paid rent for it at the rate of Rs. 1,200 a month, but the modern citizen of Calcutta with his experience of Chowringhee house rents, will elect to receive the statement with caution. Hyde was a married man and with his wife was a great favourite in Calcutta society. "Mrs. Hyde, after her return from the country, sees life in all the forms," writes Macrabie, "Lady I—sits with her though they hate each other like poison." We learn from Mrs. Fay that "on the first day of every term the professional gentlemen all met at a public breakfast at Mrs. Hyde's house, and went thence in procession to the Court House," which after 1784, stood where the High Court now strives to reproduce the grandeur of the Town Hall of Ypres.

To the west of the Esplanade runs the *Strand Road*, which in its modern shape extends from Prinsep's Ghat to Hatkhola Ghat in the extreme north of the Town. It was formerly a low, sedgy bank, and the river near it shallow, the deep channel being on the Howrah side: but owing to the formation of the Sumatra sand, by the sinking of a ship of that name, opposite Prinsep's Ghat, the shallow water has shifted to the west. The present road dates from 1823, and is one of the many undertakings successfully carried through by the Lottery Committee. It has undergone great improvements of late years in the neighbourhood of Prinsep's Ghat, a considerable portion of the river-bank having been reclaimed and thrown into the roadway.

A little to the south of the High Court, and at the end of an avenue to which the name of Auckland Road has lately been given, stands *Baboo Ghat*, a handsome colonnade of the Grecian Doric order. It bears the following inscription:—"The Right Hon'ble Lord William Cavendish Bentinck, Governor-General of India, with a view to encourage public munificence to works of public utility, has been pleased to determine that this Ghât, erected at the expense of Baboo Rajchunder Doss in 1838, shall hereafter be called Baboo Rajchunder Doss' Ghât." The Baboo whose generosity is here commemorated was the husband of the well known Rani Rashmoni of Jaun Bazar.

Opposite Baboo Ghât and immediately south of the Esplanade Road are the Eden Gardens, for which the inhabitants are indebted to the liberality and taste of the Misses Eden, sisters of Lord Auckland, Governor-General of India, whose statue by Weekes at one time stood in the gardens, and was subsequently placed on the road to the north near the High Court. A large space has been turfed and is well patronised by hundreds of citizens who may be seen taking their evening exercise on the green sward. On the western side of this promenade a band-stand has been erected, where the Town Band, or the band of one of the Regiments stationed in the Fort, play every evening. The gardens themselves are laid out with winding paths and artificial water, interspersed with a profusion of flowering trees and shrubs. A pleasanter place for a morning or evening stroll cannot be found. The portion devoted to promenading is well illuminated with the electric light. In the gardens is a fine Burmese Pagoda, removed from Prome after the war in 1854, and re-erected here in 1856. Adjoining the gardens is the ground of the Calcutta Cricket Club, on the west side of which is a pavilion. Round the whole is a broad grassy ride for equestrians, enclosed by shady walks and plantations.

The *Respondentia Walk* extended a little below Baboo's Ghat. It was the resort of those fond of moonlight rambles, and of children, with their train of servants. Its position was no doubt indicated by the row of fine trees which stood south of Baboo Ghat, but most of these were destroyed in the cyclone of 1864.

Close adjoining and immediately to the west of the High Court is *Chandpal Ghat,* which we find in existence in 1774 on the southern boundary of "Dhee Calcutta." It derives its name from a certain Chunder Nath Pal, who kept a moodee's shop hereabouts "for the refreshment of pedestrians and boatmen" in days when the maidan was a dense forest interpersed with a few weavers' sheds, and the river was scarcely frequented. When the New Fort was erected and the intervening space had been converted into the Respondentia Walk, Chandpal Ghat became the spot where India welcomed and bade farewell to her rulers. "Here, it was that Governors-General, Commanders-in-Chief, Judges of the High Court, Bishops, and all who were entitled to the honors of a salute from the ramparts of Fort William, first set foot in the Metropolis. To enumerate all who have landed at these stairs would be to recount the most distinguished men of the last seventy years. It is not noticed in the map of 1756, but it was certainly in existence in 1774. For it was here that Francis and his companions counted one by one the guns which boomed from the Fort, and found to their mortification that they did not exceed seventeen, whereas the expected number was nineteen. And it was at Chandpal Ghat also that upon the same day in 1774, the first Judges of the Supreme Court first landed in India. It was here too that the Chief Justice, as he contemplated the bare legs and feet of the multitude who crowded to witness their advent, exclaimed to his colleagues, "See, brother, the wretched victims of tyranny. The Crown Court was not surely established before it was needed. I trust it will not have been in operation six months before we shall see all these poor creatures comfortably clothed in shoes and stockings."

The old Ghat has been recently removed to make way for the new embankment and the Port Commissioners' railway. An elaborate landing stage has been erected a few yards further south, but arriving and departing Viceroys prefer nowadays to come and go by railway, and enter and leave Calcutta by the Howrah bridge, or if they are desirous of approaching or quitting their capital in the time honoured way, the spot selected is Prinsep's Ghat.

Proceeding north up the Strand Road, we come once more to *Hastings Street,* at the river end of which stands *Colvin's Ghat*, formerly called *Cutcha Goodee Ghat,* or the "place for collecting country boats." They were hauled up in olden days on the banks of the Creek which ran along what is now Hastings Street to the Salt Water Lakes on the east. It was on the banks of this creek, on the spot now indicated by the corner of Council House Street that the southern battery was thrown up in 1756. The present name of Colvin's Ghat is borrowed from the once celebrated firm of Colvin Cowie and Co., which still has its office in Hastings Street.

Turning out of Hastings Street towards the north and connecting it with Hare Street, is *Church Lane.* This street derives its name from the old Cathedral which has since 1784, furnished its eastern boundary: but as a matter of fact it was in existence long before. In Wills' map of 1753, it is shown as leading to the creek, which was crossed by a bridge at the point where Hastings Street is met by the present road. The name appears as Church Lane in Wood's map of 1784: and the buildings numbered as 4 and 5, the western side of which was then on the river-bank, are indicated as the Old Mint. In later years No. 4 was used as the office of the Superintendent of Stamps and Stationery, and No. 5 as the Calcutta Collectorate. Both buildings are now occupied by the Stationery Department. At No. 3, was the office of the well known firm of Moran & Co., as late as 1870, and their Indigo sales were advertised in consequence as held at the "Old Mint Mart."

Hare Street may be described as a prolongation of Dalhousie Square south towards the Strand Road. It was the work of the Lottery Committee in the twenties: and towards the west it supplanted a narrow lane which led from the river-bank to an open space lying between the modern Small Cause Court and St. John's Churchyard. Its name is derived from David Hare, the watchmaker philanthrophist and father of native education in Bengal, whose residence in the house at the corner of Church Lane is duly commemorated by a tablet. In Hare Street are situated the office of the *Englishman* newspaper, the Metcalfe Hall, which is entering upon a new lease of life as the Imperial Library, and the Small Cause Court. The last named obscures the memory of two buildings of olden time—the Ice House, which was swept away in 1882 to make way for its extension on the west, and the Marine House and Master Attendant's Office, which occupied the remainder of the site at the corner of Bankshall Street. Before the "Troubles" of 1756, the Marine House had been the mansion of the President outside the Fort and went by the name of the Company's House. The river flowed in those days immediately to the west, and the gardens appear to have extended from the water's edge to Tank Square. After the recapture of the city by Clive and Watson, the house was converted into a marine yard or "Bankshall," as it was named after the Dutch word of similar signification, and at the Ghat in front of it (now represented by the Police Ghat), a dry dock was constructed for the repairs of pilot-vessels, which was not dismantled and filled up until 1808. To the south of this "New Dock" was Gillet's Dockyard, which stood upon the spot once occupied by the Old Mint and now by the Stationery office, as we have noted when passing through Church Lane.

To the east of Church Lane, and to the north of the old Churchyard, is a cul-de-sac opening out of Hare Street, which is known as *Garstin's Place*. The name perpetuates the memory of Major-General John Garstin, the architect of the Town Hall, and of the great *golah* or granary at Bankipore, the doors of which by some strange oversight are constructed to open inwards. His death took place in Calcutta in 1820, and he lies buried in the South Park Street burying-ground. He is said to have built the houses in the Place with some of the materials of the Old Court House which was demolished in 1792.

Almost opposite the entrance to Garstin's Palace is *Bankshall Street*. The derivation of this street, which connects Hare Street and Koila Ghat Street, has already been more than hinted at: but the word Bankshall has been a puzzle to many. John Clark Marshman traced it to a Portuguese word. The Rev. James Long took a literal view and held it to mean "a hall on the banks of the river, and so a Bank Hall." According to the late Mr. J. R. Rainey, it is probably a hybrid, being a compound of the English "bank" and the Sanskrit *sala,* "house", or in the alternative traceable to the Bengalee *bank,* a "bend", and the Sanskrit *sala.* But it seems simpler to refer the word to the Dutch for a Marine House, which stood, as we have seen, at the corner of Bankshall Street and what is now Hare Street. In any case the name first occurs as early as 1700, when the Court of Directors ordered a *Bankshull* or marine yard to be built at Kedgeree, where ships of 400 tons burden and over could anchor, all vessels of less tonnage being directed to proceed up the river to Calcutta.

Koila Ghat Street runs from the western end of Dalhousie Square to the Strand Road, along what was once the southern side of the *killa* or Old Fort. The *Killa Ghat,* or Fort Wharf, became corrupted (it is said) into *Koila Ghat*, on account of its large traffic in coal in the early years of the nineteenth century, and hence its present name. In Upjohn's map of 1794 it figures as Tankshall Street by an error in printing: for the word should correctly be *Tackshall,* the Dutch for the Custom House, which then stood at the south-west angle of the Fort on the river bank, to the east of the "New Wharf."

Turning to the right up Koila Ghat Street we find ourselves once more in Dalhousie Square just by the General Post Office.

Tank Square (now called *Dalhousie Square*), was last century, "in the middle of the city." It covers upwards of 25 acres of ground. "It was dug," says the Dutch admiral Stavorinus who visited the settlement in 1770, "by order of Government, to provide the inhabitants of Calcutta with water, which is very sweet and pleasant. The number of springs which it contains makes the water in it almost on the same level. It is railed round, no one may wash in it." Its first name was "The Green before the Fort." In early days when the Maidan was a mass of jungle, it was the place of recreation for the Company's factors, and in the middle of last century it was the scene of many a moonlight saunter of young people, and elderly ones too who amused themselves on the banks of the "fish pond in the park," (as it was then called), inhaling the evening breezes, and talking of the friends of whom they had heard nine months before. The tank was formerly more extensive, but was cleansed and embanked completely in Warren Hastings' time. It has always been esteemed the sweetest water in Calcutta, and until the introduction of the municipal water supply, was the chief source of supply of drinking water to the European community.

The western side of Dalhousie Square has within the last five or six years been named *Charnock Place* in honour of the Father of Calcutta. It is almost entirely taken up with public offices, but until the closing years of the eighteenth century it was disfigured by the derelict remains of the Old Fort and adjoining warehouses. A portion of the ruins was pulled down in 1819, to make way for the Custom House, and the remainder was removed in 1856 to make way for the new General Post Office. The masonry was of such strength that pick-axe and crow-bar were of no avail, and blasting by gunpowder had to be resorted to. A section of the old wall is still visible. It is enormously thick and strong. The old builders of India, like the Romans, preferred tiles to bricks for walls. The walls of the Old Fort extended to the site of the Port Commissioners' Office in Koila Ghat Street, in digging the foundations for which, fortifications of great strength were disclosed. Similar discoveries were made when constructing the new East Indian Railway offices at the corner of Fairlie Place.

In the north-west corner of Lyon's Range, stood the *Theatre*, on a large plot of ground now occupied by the offices of Messrs. Finlay Muir and Co. This theatre, which served the settlement from 1775 to 1808, was generally graced by amateur performers, and a ballroom was attached, which was the scene of many a gay gathering. In the days of Cornwallis and Wellesley, the State receptions and "public breakfasts" were habitually held here.

Writers' Buildings, which fills the whole of the north side of Dalhousie Square, is so called from having been in the first instance erected for the residence of the writers, or junior servants of the Company. To the west upon the spot now covered by the Bengal Legislative Council-Chamber stood the first Church of Calcutta, called St. Anne's. This church is said to have been perfect in composition; its steeple was very lofty and uncommonly magnificient. It was built in 1716, when "gold was plenty and labour cheap; chiefly by the pious contributions of seafaring men." The steeple fell in the earthquake of 1737, and the church itself was demolished in the siege of 1756.

Thereafter for many years the site as well as the adjoining plot remained waste until in October, 1776, both "parcels" were granted to Mr. Thomas Lyon "for the purpose of erecting a range of buildings for the accommodation of the junior servants of the Company." The original *pottah* relating to the transaction was discovered by the late Mr. R. C. Sterndale, during his tenure of office as Collector of Calcutta in the eighties, and it is reproduced in the interesting "History of the Calcutta Collectorate" published by him in 1885. Lyon is of course, the name-father of the Range which runs immediately behind Writers' Buildings: but it would seem that he was merely the ostensible purchaser and was acting on behalf of Richard Barwell, the solitary supporter of Hastings in Council and hero of the famous command to "bring more curricles." For when the building was, after its completion, taken over in 1780 by Government on a five years' lease, Barwell and not Lyon appears as the owner. "Mr. Barwell's house taken for five years by his own rate at 31,720 current rupees per annum to be paid half-yearly in advance," writes Francis in his diary under date, February 29th, "Mr. Wheler and I declare we shall not sign the lease." A few days later after the accomplishment of this highly satisfactory bargain, Barwell retired and Francis received a step in seniority in Council—

both events being announced with a salute of seventeen guns. For years the Buildings remained appropriated to the purpose for which they were erected: but gradually the collegiate system of living was abandoned, and the nineteen sets of apartments drifted into the hands of merchants and private individuals. To Sir Ashley Eden is due its modern transformation. A handsome new frontage has been added to the range of buildings which, with the extensive new blocks erected in Lyon's Range, accommodate all the offices of the Bengal Government.

The *College of Fort William,* on its establishment in 1800, was located on the southern side of the square in the premises at the corner of Council House Street subsequently occupied for many years by Messrs. Mackenzie Lyall & Co., and known as the Exchange. The house is now tenanted by the Bengal-Nagpore Railway Company. Another building opposite (soon to be demolished), was also appropriated by the College, and the two were connected by a gallery across the street. As we linger at this corner of th Square and muse upon what might have been if Wellesley had been permitted to cary out the scheme which was to find fruition in a splendid college at Garden Reach, we must not forget to recall that we are treading upon what was until the early days of the nineteenth century the Parade-ground of the settlement. Here Minchin exhibited his incapacity to command in days when the siege and sack of Calcutta were still undreamt of: and here too the "Patriot Band" mustered and drilled after Clive and Watson had recaptured Fort William for the English. In one of Daniell's Views of Tank Square painted about the year 1788, a narrow strip of the Parade-ground on the southern side of the Tank may be seen with quaint figures of Militia men in the foreground.

There is quite an interesting history attached to the premises No. 4 on the eastern side of Dalhousie Square, now in the occupation of Messrs. W. Newman & Co. By a pottah granted on September 5th, 1780, the land upon which it stood is described as "one biggah and 16 cottahs of the Honourable Company's 'camar' or untenanted land situate in Dhee Calcutta," and is granted to Charles Weston, the benefactor of the poor of Calcutta and friend of Holwell in his old age, with a condition that "no house, wall or other erection of any kind whatsoever shall be built upon the ground excepting a palisade, fence or railing," and "on failing of this condition, the ground shall revert to the Company." In 1795, Weston sold the land for Rs. 6,000, with the prohibition attaching thereto: and in 1799 it passed to the Barrettos. It remained waste for the next nine years, and one of the pictures of old Calcutta which hang on the staircase of the Metcalfe Hall shows the bare expanse of land between Tank Square and Kiernander's Church in Mission Row. The restriction was finally removed on the 8th May, 1806, by virtue of a certain "letter bearing date, Council-Chamber the same day, under the signature of Thomas Brown, Secretary to the Government of Fort William in Bengal in the Public Department." A house was thereupon built, and between 1830, when it was in the occupation of Messrs. Alport and Co., and 1833, it passed into the possession of the Bengal Club. It was sold for Rs. 82,000 in 1836 by the assignees of the insolvent firm of Cruttenden Mackillop and Co., to James William Macleod: and retains its designation of the "Club House" in a letter of August, 1841, in which a proposal of purchase for Rs. 95,000 is made by Messrs. Jenkins Law and Co., to Thomas DeSouza and Co. In 1882, the premises were purchased by the late Sir Walter DeSouza for Rs. 1,80,000 and were sold by him a few years later for Rs. 3,50,000—a figure nearly sixty times as great as that which honest Charles Weston was glad to name in 1795. The present occupants date their possession from 1882. In 1870, the tenants of that day elected to be known as "Bodelio's Emporium of Fashion."

Vansittart Row is a short cul-de-sac issuing from Dalhousie Square South, and will be found immediately to the west of Wellesley Place. It is shown in both the maps of 1784 and 1794, and there can be little doubt that it is named after Henry Vansittart who succeeded Holwell as Governor of Bengal in 1760 and held the office until 1764. His appointment was due to the recommendation of Clive and was much resented by the Council at Fort William who were all senior to him. On December 29th, 1759, they addressed a protest to the Directors who replied in January 21st, 1761, by dismissing Holwell and the other signatories from their official places. During Vansittart's administration occurred the overthrow of Meer Cassim and the massacre at Patna in October, 1763, when 150 Englishmen were murdered by the renegade Sumroo. After being relieved of the Government by John Spencer, Vansittart sailed for England and became member of Parliament for Reading and a Director of the Company:

but in 1769, he was sent out to India by the Court as one of the three Commissioners appointed for the purpose of reducing expenditure and checking abuses. His fellow-Commissioners were both remarkable men. Colonel Francis Forde, the capturer of Rajahmundry and Masulipatam from the French in 1759, became Clive's second in command in Bengal. He was ready to assist Clive in his operations against the Dutch at Chinsurah in 1766, and it was to him that Clive wrote his famous note on the back of a playing card "attack at once: will send order in Council afterwards." Forde did attack and won a complete victory. In the following year, he returned to England with Clive, and it was mainly Clive's advocacy of his claims that brought about the historic quarrel with the Sulivan party in the India House. Luke Scrafton, the third Commissioner, was the junior merchant who had by Clive's command told Omichand that the Red Paper given to him was a trick and that he would gain nothing by the treaty with Meer Jaffer. They were accompanied by William Hirst, who had been Chaplain in the Bay from 1762 to 1764, and preached the sermon in commemoration of the massacre at Patna. Hirst was quite one of the most accomplished men who have belonged to the Church in Bengal. He had visited Lisbon after the earthquake of 1755– "Georgius Secundus was then alive, Snuffy old drone from the German Hive"—and made a careful study of the ruined city. While staying at Government House, Madras, in June, 1761, he was able to observe a transit of Venus of which he transmitted a full account to the Royal Society: and posterity is also indebted to him for descriptions of the two violent earthquakes which convulsed Bengal in 1762. The party embarked in September, 1769, on board the frigate *Aurora*: but the vessel was never heard of again after leaving the Cape: and it is supposed she must have foundered at sea with all hands on board. Among the crew was William Falconer, author of "The Shipwreck" who was purser on board. Vansittart was made the victim of a peculiar practical joke during his Governorship of Bengal. Upon the death of an eccentric individual of the name of David Martinett, it was discovered that by clause four of his will, he had bequeathed "To Governor Henry Vansittart, as an opulent man, the discharge of all such sum or sums, the whole not exceeding 300 rupees, that I shall stand indebted to indigent persons in the town of Calcutta." And it is on record that "Governor Vansittart, with great good nature and humanity, very faithfully complied with the will of the deceased." Vansittart's youngest son was Chancellor of the Exchequer during the first portion of the long administration of the Earl of Liverpool, which lasted from 1812 to 1827, and was raised to the peerage as Lord Bexley in 1823, dying in 1851 at the age of 85. In the *Bengal Obituary*, mention is made of the monument in the South Park Street burying ground of Vansittart's eldest son, Henry, who died in Calcutta in 1786 at the age of 32. Mention also occurs of another Vansittart: Arthur Hastings Vansittart, Esq., of the Bengal Civil Service, died on the 19th February, 1807, aged 33 years: who may have been the son of this Henry. In his youth, Governor Vansittart was a member of the graceless Medmenham revellers who went by the name of the Hell-Fire Club. He married the daughter of Nicholas Morse a descendant of

Oliver Cromwell, who was Governor of Fort St. George, when it was captured by La Bourdounais in 1746, and who died at Madras in 1772 at the age of 72.

Lall Bazar stretching from the north east corner of Dalhousie Square to "Boytaconnah" (which we shall presently investigate) was said in 1768 to be the best street in Calcutta. It was called in early days the "Avenue to the eastward" and in Thomas Lyon's pottah of October, 1776, which we have just been considering in our survey of the history of Writers' Buildings, it is described as "the great road leading from Holwell's monument by the south front of the Court House to the Salt Water Lake and known by the name of Great Bungalo Road." The modern Police Office was the residence of John Palmer, one of the "merchant princes" of Calcutta. His father was secretary to Warren Hastings. He was noted for his hospitality, and on one occasion entertained two Governor-Generals. On the opposite side of the street, stood the old Jail of Calcutta, of which we get a glimpse in a report of a select committee of the House of Commons, published in 1782. It was said to be "an old ruin of a house, formerly the residence of some black native." In the centre of the enclosure was a tank where everyone "promiscuously bathed and washed their clothes." European prisoners were generally permitted to erect small bamboo mat-huts near this tank: but it was impossible to exist for any length of time in the foul, poisonous atmosphere. There was no jail allowance and no infirmary, and many died from sheer want of the necessaries of life. The house next to the Police Office, formerly the Sailors' Home, but now pulled down and replaced by the Magistrate's Court, was the famous *Harmonic Tavern,* the handsomest house of its day in Calcutta. Mrs. Fay writes of it in 1780—"I felt far more gratified some time ago when Mrs. Jackson procured me a ticket for the Harmonic, which was supported by a select number of gentlemen, who, each in alphabetical rotation, give a concert, ball and supper, during the cold season, I believe, once a fortnight." There were many other hotels and houses of entertainment in the street, at one of which, "the London," entertainments were furnished at a gold-mohur a head, exclusive of dessert and wines. At the coffee houses, a single dish of coffee cost one rupee.

The road from Lall Bazar to Mangoe Lane, called *Mission Row,* was formerly named the *Rope Walk,* and was the scene of hard fighting at the time of the siege of Calcutta in 1756. Two houses in this street have been distinguished by tablets. No. 8, was the house of General Sir John Clavering, colleague of Hastings and Francis in Council and he died there on August 30th, 1777. No. 1, was the residence of Colonel the Hon'ble George Monson, Francis' second faithful supporter, who died at Hooghly in 1776. The street derives its present name from the old Mission Church, established by John Zachariah Kiernander in 1770. The house at the corner of Mission Row and Lall Bazar stands on the site of what was the play house of the settlement, in days before the Black Hole. The eastern side of Dalhousie Square did not then exist, and the "Rope Walk" formed the boundary of the great Tank in that direction. A few doors from the play house was the residence of Lady Russell, widow of Sir Francis Russell, sixth baronet of Chippenham in the county of Cambridge, who was a member of Council at Fort William in 1731 and succeeded to the title in 1738. After her husband's death at Calcutta in 1743, she appears to have married a merchant of the name of Thomas Holmes in the following year: but to have retained her former style. We find her among the refugees at Fulta after Seraj-ud-Dowlah's capture of the Settlement, and she must have died there, for her will, dated August 24th, 1756, was proved in the Mayor's Court in 1757. The family was closely connected with Oliver Cromwell, whose favourite daughter Frances was the grandmother of Sir Francis Russell and mother of John Russell, Governor of Fort William from 1711 to 1713.

The name of *Mangoe Lane* tells its own tale. The street is plainly shown in Wills' map of 1753, running in winding fashion (as it still does) from the Rope Walk to Bentinck Street. At No. 25, where Messrs. Lyall Marshall & Co., now have their office, and Messrs. Carlisles Nephews and Co., preceded them in the seventies, was formerly located the great banking firm of Barretto & Co., which failed in 1827. The house was one of the few that had a treasure vault. *Barretto's Lane* which commences at No. 4, Mangoe Lane and connects with British Indian Street, commemorates one of the merchant princes of the firm. Joseph Barretto, who died in 1824, was not only a man of large wealth, but could in addition lay claim to being a good Persian scholar. He largely helped in the erection of the Roman Catholic Cathedral in Moorghihatta, of which the foundation was laid in 1797: and a tablet under the portico of the grand entrance perpetuates the memory of his munificence. The Portuguese cemetery at Boytaconnah, just beyond Sealdah Railway Station, was also purchased by him for eight thousand rupees and presented as "an asylum for departed Roman Catholics" in the year 1785. Another member of the family, John Barretto, who died towards the close of the forties, bequeathed no less than five lakhs of rupees for distribution among various religious and charitable institutions. The family is one of ancient Portuguese origin: a Barretto was Viceroy in 1558 of the Portuguese possessions in India. In the maps of 1792 and 1794, the street is called *Cross Street*; and Barretto's Lane appears as the name given to what is now a disused private lane leading through No. 39, Strand Road, while Armenian Ghat which is close by, is named Barretto's Ghat. There is a Cross Street in modern Calcutta but it is in the Burra Bazar.

Clive Street commences from the north-western corner of Dalhousie Square and extends in a northerly direction until it meets Durmahatta, the "street of the makers of reed-mats." The origin of its name is self-evident. It has always been the great commercial thoroughfare in Calcutta. In early days we find it described as "the grand theatre of business, and there stood the Council House and every public mart in it," the reference being to the first Council House, which was discarded in 1764. Much of the street is on ground reclaimed from the river, and with Chitpore Road and the "avenue leading to the eastward," it takes rank among the oldest streets in the city. The building now known as the Royal Exchange was once the residence of Clive. To him succeeded Philip Francis, who would seem to have divided his time between the "house in town" and the villa at Alipore, where Richmond Thackeray came after him. "Here I live," writes Francis to John Burke, son of the orator, "master of the finest house in Bengal, with a hundred servants, a country house, and spacious gardens, horses and carriages, yet so perverse is my nature that the devil take me if I would not exchange the best dinner and the best company I ever saw in Bengal for a breakfast and claret at the Horn and let me choose my company." Of the exact whereabouts of the "finest house in Bengal," we are afforded an indication by the evidence of a witness in the famous "action for criminal conversation with the wife of the plaintiff" brought by the husband of Madam Grand against Francis in February, 1779. Meerun, Grand's khidmatgar, identifies the man he saw at his master's house as "Mr. Francis, the Counsellor, who lives behind the playhouse." This is of course, the new play house which we have already located at the corner of Lyon's Range on the site of Messrs. Finlay Muir and Company's fine offices. A tablet on the Royal Exchange building apprizes the stranger of the historical associations it possesses: but somewhat unaccountably the Bonded Warehouse opposite remains undistinguished. It was the home of the famous Begum Johnson, whose tomb in St. John's churchyard commemorates her four marriages and the eventful history of her life.

Fairlie Place, which runs from Clive Street to the Strand Road, immediately to the north of the East Indian Railway Company's offices, owes its name to William Fairlie, a distinguished Calcutta merchant of the time of Wellesley. In the *Calcutta Gazette* of April 25th, 1799, he appears as a candidate for a contract for "supplying and feeding elephants and camels for the service of the Army in the Bengal Presidency." The full compliment of elephants maintained appears to have been 200, and of camels 90: while the charge for the keep and feed of a single animal is set down, for elephants Rs. 30/ to Rs. 40/- a month, and for camels Rs. 11/- to Rs. 13/- a month. Fairlie's name occurs frequently as one of the "Gentlemen of the grand jury": and on December 5th, 1805, he had the privilege as foreman of presenting the address to Sir John Anstruther, the Chief Justice, in which permission was asked for the placing in the Town Hall of the portrait which now hangs in the High Court. He appears to have been a senior member of the firm of Fairlie, Gilmore and Co., and his name heads the list of the Commissioners of the Calcutta Exchange Lottery advertised in the *Gazette* in 1799. Fairlie Place figures in Upjohn's map of 1794 as a passage without name leading to the Old Fort Ghat. Here stood prior to 1756, Mr. Cruttenden's mansion and spacious grounds which were burnt down on the second night of the siege of the Fort by Seraj-ud-Dowlah.

Clive Ghat Street is the second of the turnings to the west which connect Clive Street with the Strand Road. The riverside Ghat at its western end was formerly known as Blythe's Ghat from a ship builder of that name, and it is so marked in Wood's map of 1784. The vernacular name of the street is *I'Smith Ghat-ke-rasta*: and preserves the name of Captain Matthew Smith of the Company's

Navy, who upon his retirement after a long period of service started iron-works and a shipbuilding business at Howrah. He died in 1822, at the age of 54, and his tomb is among those in the South Park Street burial-ground.

Bonfield's Lane commencing from No. 33, Clive Street, is an old street. It will be found in Wood's map of 1784, and probably owes its name to a well-known auctioneer of the day of Warren Hastings who had his premises here. The following advertisement appears in the *Calcutta Gazette* of August 5th, 1774: "On Thursday, the 2nd September next, will be sold by public outcry by Mr. Bonfield at his auction room, if not before sold by private sale, that extensive piece of ground belonging to Warren Hastings, Esq., called Rishera (Ishara) situated on the western bank of the river two miles below Serampore consisting of 136 beghas, 18 of which are lakherage land or land paying no rent." A commemorative tablet identifies this house at Rishera which is now included within the compound of the Hastings Jute Mills.

Canning Street, which commences from No. 28, Strand Road, and runs through to the Chitpore Road at right angles to Clive Street, is named, of course, after the first Viceroy of India. Its olden name of Murghihatta still clings to it in the vernacular and was bestowed upon it, because it was the quarter in which the Portuguese inhabitants of Calcutta lived and held a "fowl market." It figures in Wood's map of 1784. From No. 100, in the street issues *Portuguese Church Street* which proceeds in a southerly direction as far as Armenian Street. This is also an old Calcutta Street: and the old Portuguese

Church from which it derives its name and which was succeeded in 1797 by the present Roman Catholic Cathedral, is shown in Orme's map of Calcutta 1756-57 and also in the map of 1784.

Making our way down Canning Street to the Strand Road, we shall, if we turn our steps to the north, soon find ourselves at Armenian Ghat,—still known by that name in spite of the handsome mansonry structure on the river bank which bears an inscription to the effect that it is Mutty Lall Seal's public bathing ghat. The Indian millionaire, to whom it owes its present substantial appearance, has also given his name to a small street leading off Corporation Street. He began life as a supplier of military stores in a humble way, and by collecting and speculating in empty bottles and corks, laid (it is said), the foundation of an enormous fortune. When he died in 1854, he was *banian* to three of the leading European mercantile firms in the city, and was one of the richest men in Calcutta.

Mullick's Ghat, another handsome masonry structure immediately to the north of the Howrah Bridge, dated from 1855. It is named after its builder, Ram Mohan Mullick, son of Nayan Chand Mullick of Burrabazar, who made a large fortune in the eighteenth century by speculation in salt and land, and left a crore of rupees at his death. The name of "Nain Mullick" appears in the "Abstract of the Thirteen Native Commissioners' Restitution Money Account" published in the Consultation of September 18th, 1758. He claimed Rs. 43,922 and "deducted" Rs. 5,922.

Rajah Woodmunt's Street which branches off to the east

from Strand Road between Armenian Ghat and Mullick's Ghat, is named after Raja Udwanta Singh, nephew of the famous Maharajah Debi Singh who was appointed Dewan of Bengal in 1773 on the formation of the Provincial Councils in that year. Udwanta Singh was a man of great wealth and large commercial dealings. The British Government being compelled to take up arms against the Rewah Rajah, requested Udwanta to join his "troops" with those of Government. He was for some time Dewan of Ali Jah, Nawab Nazim of Bengal from 1810 to 1821. The present representative of the family which has its seat at Nashipore in the Moorshedabad district is Rajah Ranajit Singh Bahadur.

Proceeding north along the Strand Road past the Mint, we pass many Ghats of little or no note until we arrive at the Baug Bazar Ghat, which formerly bore the name of *Roghoo Mitter's Ghat* after the son of Govindram Mitter, the Black or Deputy Zemindar, one of the most wealthy and influential natives of Calcutta, one hundred and forty years ago.

Nimtollah Ghat in the extreme north is the burning-ghat, where Hindoos of all ranks cremate their dead. The process has much to commend it from a sanitary point of view, but the visitor is not advised to make any close personal acquaintance with its details. *Doorga Charan Mookerjee's Ghat* to the north of Baug Bazar Ghat was built by a Brahmin Dewan of the Opium Agency at Patna who gave it his name.

Above Nimtollah and between Beniatollah and Sobhabazar Ghats lurks forgotten the traditional landing place of Job Charnock and his companions. *Mohunton's Ghat* is said to cover the site of the old "Sootalooty Ghat," whereby access was had to the village of weavers at Sootalooty or Chuttanutty, whose industry is said to have attracted the English factors to the spot. At Chuttanutty Point there stood in olden days a "great tree" which served as a sea-mark to pilots and has been identified by some as the famous Boytaconnah tree under which the Father of Calcutta sat and mused.

Retracing our steps until we arrive once more at Howrah Bridge, we find a broad thoroughfare on our left. This is the *Harrison Road* which runs straight from the Howrah Bridge to the Sealdah Railway Station. It is of the uniform breadth of 75 feet and is named after Sir Henry Harrison, the Chairman of the Corporation, by whom the scheme was inaugurated and matured. Begun in December, 1889, it was completed in 1892, and many an overcrowded tenement and narrow festering lane has been swept away by its construction. It was lighted throughout by electricty; but gas has now been substituted. We are now in the heart of the purely Indian quarter. Many of the streets are called after the occupations of the former residents and date from the period when Holwell under the Directors' orders, allotted "separate districts to the Company's workmen." Of such are *Suriparah* (the place of the wine sellers, *Maidaputty* (the flour-market), *Colootollah* (the place of oil men), *Chuttarparah* (the place of carpenters), *Chunam Gully* (Lime lane), *Molunga* (the place of the salt-works), *Aheeritollah* (cowherds' quarter),

Coomartolly (potters' quarter). Other street and localities again are named after Hindoo Deities, or from prominent natural objects. In the former category may be placed *Charakdanga* (the place of the hookswinging festival of Siva), and according to some *Burrabazar* (from *bura*, old man, as Siva is often called by his devotees). To the latter must be assigned names such as *Nimtollah*, *Nebutollah*, and *Amratollah*, which are all intended to recall the particular trees which were once conspicuous in these localities. In many others, the name of prominent residents in early days are commemorated, as in the case of the streets in the European quarter.

Meeting the Harrison Road at right angles, is the *Chitpore Road* which remains materially unaltered after the lapse of more than a century. It received its name from the goddess *Chiteswari* who had a splendid temple here, erected by Govindram Mitter, where human sacrifices were formerly offered. The lofty dome of the temple which went by the name of the Nabarutna or Shrine of the Nine Jewels, fell with a crash in the earthquake of 1737 and it is now in ruins. This great thoroughfare, which commencing in the extreme south, assumes the various names of Russa Road, Chowringhee Road, Bentinck Street, Chitpore Road, and Barrackpore Trunk Road, forms a continuation of the Dum-Dum Road and was the old line of communication between Moorshedabad and Kalighat. It is said to occupy the site of the old road made by the Savarna Chowdhrys, the old Zemindars of Calcutta, from Barisa, where the junior branch resided, to Halisahar beyond Barrackpore, which was the seat of the senior branch. "The road from Kidderpore to Barisa in the last century," says Mr. Long in his article in the 18th Volume of the Calcutta Review, "presented a picturesque appearance, being planted with shady trees on both sides—a fine old practice." The introduction of the Tramway into Chitpore Road, and the consequent increase of traffic, has rendered the widening of the street imperative, and the proposal is understood to form an important part of the new Calcutta Improvement Scheme.

Tiretta Bazar Street and Lane are on the east of Lower Chitpore Road, and close to Lall Bazar. They are so called from their proximity to an extensive Bazar in the locality well known to all bird and beast fanciers in Calcutta. The walls of the street are hung with the cages of canaries and parrots, and inside the shops may be seen dogs, monkeys and rabbits, with an occasional sambhur and even a leopard cub. It is now the property of the Maharajah of Burdwan, but the name it bears is that of a Venetian named Edward Tiretta. Mr. Long has put the date of its establishment in 1788, but it is described in Wood's map of 1784 as "Tiretta's Bazar," and it is probably much older. In a prospectus of a lottery issued in 1788 and advertized in the *Calcutta Gazette* of that year, the "First Prise" is represented to be "that large and spacious Pucka Buzar or market belonging to Mr. Tiretta, situated in the north central part of the Town of Calcutta, which occupies a space of nine biggahs and eight cottahs of ground, surrounded with a colonnade verandah, and the whole area of the square is divided into commodious streets with pucka stalls, valued at sicca rupees 1,96,000."

It produced a monthly income of sicca Rs. 3,500: and the public are informed that "with proper attention and management it is capable of yielding a much larger monthly income." The lucky winner of the "first prise" was Charles Weston, the benefactor of Holwell in his old age, who has himself given his name to Weston's Lane, a turning off Bentinck Street. Other properties are also set out in the advertisement and are valued in the prospectus at Rs. 3,20,000: from which it would appear that Mr. Tiretta had divers avenues of emolument open to him besides his official appointment of "Superintendent of Streets and Houses" under the Municipal Committee. He appears to have continued to reside in Calcutta after the drawing of the lottery in 1791, but seems not to have died here. His wife's grave is in the cemetery which bears his name and is situated in Park Street to the west of the South Park Street burying-ground.

Opposite the site of the *Tiretta Bazar* stood the house of Charles Weston, who was born there in 1731. The house was evidently surrounded by a large garden. In 1770, we find advertised in *Hicky's Gazette* a house near the Baitakkhana situated to the southward of Mr. Charles Weston's Garden.

Hurrinbaree Lane issues from 22, Tiretta Bazar Street. The name signifies "deer park" and was sarcastically given to the locality, because of the proximity of the Old Jail in Lall Bazar, in which Hicky was confined. "A piece of ground known by the name of Hurring Berry, in front of the public road leading to Chitpoor" is advertized as the second prize in the Tiretta Bazar lottery, and from the description given, it was evidently then in use as a "general grain market." The lane appears in Wood's map of 1784 as Old Harınbaree Lane. At the cross roads, where Lall Bazar, Bow Bazar, Chitpore Road and Bentinck Street meets, was the place of execution, and at a later date a pillory was erected there. The Rev. Mr. Long states in his article in the Calcutta Review (which was written in 1852), that "there is a man still living in Calcutta who underwent the punishment of the pillory there." The stocks were also held *in terrorem* over the law breakers of the day, but of a certain class only, for, we find the following quaint rule regarding them: "If any person of no substance use force or strike any person in dispute about land, he is to be one whole day in the stocks." One is left wondering what the punishment might be for the man "with substance" who committed the same offence.

Bow Bazar Street is the continuation of Lall Bazar, the old "avenue to the eastward", from the point where it meets the Chitpore Road and Bentinck Street: and it extends as far as Sealdah, in an easterly direction, absorbing Boytaconnah Street as it approaches the Circular Road. The derivation of the name is a little puzzling. Bow Bazar is commonly said to be a corruption of Bahu Bazar, the "Bride's Bazar:" but Mr. A. K. Ray in his Short History of Calcutta says he has "failed to trace the Bahu or daughter-in-law of Biswanath Matilal to whose share the bazar is said to have fallen and to whom the name is said to be due."

Boytaconnah Street, (Baithak-khanah) leading from Lall Bazar and Bow Bazar to the Circular Road, received its name from the famous old tree which stood at its eastern extremity and formed a "Boytaconnah," or resting place for the merchants who traded to Calcutta, and whose caravans rested under its shade. Job Charnock is said to have chosen the site of Calcutta for a city, in consequence of the pleasure he found in sitting and smoking under the shade of a large tree. Posterity loved to connect his name with the Boytaconnah tree which is shown in Upjohn's map of 1794, at the corner of Circular Road upon the southern-most portion of the ground now appropriated by Sealdah Station. It finds no place in Wood's map of 1784. We read, however, in *Hicky's Gazette* in 1781 of "a Garden-house situate at Bread and Cheese Bungalo, opposite the great tree, and forms the angle of the two roads." In the same year Mr. Henry Cowen set up a school at the "Bread and Cheese Bungalo or Boytacannah,": and in January, 1802, "that well-raised lower-roomed house and garden" is announced for sale without reserve. In the map of 1784, the whole length of the road from Lall Bazar as far as what is now known as Circular Road is named "Boytaconnah," and also a portion of the Circular Road itself. Its dimensions have been gradually shrinking, for it has no separate existence to-day in the Calcutta Directory, but locally the designation is applied to the quarter bounded by College Street and the Circular Road. The Calcutta Madrassa, established by Hastings in 1782, was originally located on the southern side of Boytaconnah Street, and appears in the map of 1784 as "Madrassah or Persian College."

The Circular Road itself, which stretches from the junction of Cornwallis Street and Sham Bazar on the north to Kidderpore Bridge on the south-west, forms, as we have already learnt, the old boundary of the town. In the vernacular, it is still known as the *Bahar Sarak* or "Outer Road." It is by far the longest road in the City of Palaces: Mr. J. R. Rainey giving its measurement as six miles from its northern extremity to the point where its meets Chowringhee Road by the Cathedral. In its original form it extended no further to the south than the Mahratta Ditch, which was not excavated much beyond the eastern end of Corporation Street. But the map of 1784 indicates that the road had been completed by that date, and in Upjohn's map it bears its present form, with its sharp curve to the west at the turning into Ballygunge. The large two-storeyed building standing on the eastern side of Lower Circular Road, to the south of the road leading to Entally, and numbered 155, is the birth place of Henry Louis Vivian Derozio, the gifted Eurasian poet and teacher, who died in 1831, at the age of twenty-three. His verses are now forgotten, but they were in their day the subject of much admiration: and as a schoolmaster, he was the oracle of Young Bengal, and has found no successor in their affections.

Bolts' Lane, a *cul-de-sac* opening out from Circular Road to the east, immediately opposite the mouth of Ripon Street, may detain us a moment. William Bolts was a Company's servant of Dutch extraction, who being censured by the Court of Directors for his private trading under the Company's authority, resigned the service in 1766, and was two years later forcibly deported as an interloper. In

1772, he published his "Considerations on Indian affairs," in which he vigorously attacked the Bengal Government: and followed this up with another book in 1775. He subsequently entered the Austrian service and founded stations in India for an Austrian Company: but these came to nothing, and he eventually ended his days in Paris in 1808. His claim to inclusion among the worthies of Calcutta, rests, however, upon different grounds. In September, 1768, a paper affixed to the door of the Court House and other public places informed all and sundry that Mr. Bolts "took this method" of bringing to their notice that "the want of a printing press in this city being of great disadvantage in business, he is ready to give the best encouragement to any person or persons who are versed in the business of printing to manage a press, the types and utensils of which he can produce." In the meantime, he begged leave to add that "having in manuscript many things to communicate, which most intimately concern every individual, any person who may be induced by curiosity or other laudable motives, will be permitted at Mr. Bolts' house to read and take copies of the same." Six years had only to elapse from the date of this primitive attempt at public advertisement to the establishment of the Supreme Court and the appointment of Hastings as Governor-General. But Bolts was before his time, and his "manuscripts" were evidently inconveniently full of official secrets. The publication of the notice was rapidly followed by his deportation, and *Hicky's Gazette*, the first Calcutta newspaper, did not make its first appearance until January 29th, 1780.

Coming now to the purely Indian quarter in the north,

we find ourselves at once in an unfamiliar atmosphere. It is one of the inevitable results of a foreign occupation that the history of modern India as written by Englishmen—and no one else has cared to write it—takes little account of the Indian helper whose aid has been essential, and whose advice and knowledge has been invaluable, to the men who have built up the fabric of English rule. Nowhere, perhaps, is this reticence of history more marked than in the case of Maharajah Nubkissen, the friend and counsellor of Clive and Hastings who beginning life as the Persian tutor of the latter, rose to be the Company's interpreter and crowned his career as their political *banyan*. Mill makes no reference to him: Orme does not mention him, and his name is absent from the pages of Sir John Malcolm. Yet he was no ordinary man, and the influence and power wielded by him during the thirty years which preceded his death in 1797 was extraordinarily large. The quarter around Sobhabazar where he lived, is intimately associated with his name, and the family is well represented in the street nomenclature of the locality, principally in Ward 1 (Shampookur). The spacious road connecting Upper Chitpore Road with Upper Circular Road is said to have been constructed by Nubkissen himself and named with his own name. But the latter half of the street is now merged in Grey Street: and the former is known as Sobhabazar Street: while Nubkissen's name has been given to a smaller street just to the north of it. He left two sons, one adopted and the other of his own begetting. The former, Rajah Gopee Mohun Deb, was famous among his countrymen for his musical tastes. He has a street and a lane in Ward 3 called after him: and a similar honour has been accorded to his son, Rajah Sir Radha Kanta Deb, K.C.S.I., and his three grandsons, Rajah Rajendra Narain, Rajah Mahendra Narain, and Rajah Debendra Narain. Nubkissen's natural-born son was Rajah Rajkrishna, who was the father of eight distinguished sons, prominent among whom were Rajah Bahadur Kali Krishna, Maharajah Kamal Krishna, and Maharajah Bahadur Sir Narendra Krishna, K.C.I.E. All these have streets named after them, and the distinction is shared also by Rajah Bahadur Harendra Krishna, the son of Rajah Kali Krishna.

Rajah Rajbullub's Street in Ward 1 recalls historical associations of no less interest, for it is named after the famous naib, or deputy governor of Dacca, whose relations with the English served as a pretext for Seraj-ud-Dowlah's descent upon Calcutta in 1756. During his long administration of the eastern province, he had become enormously rich, and was called upon by the Nabob to render an account, failing which he was placed under strict surveillance at Moorshedabad. Of subsequent events, two explanations are possible. The first is that Rajbullub, to escape from his difficulties and yet save his property, proposed to Seraj-ud-Dowlah to trick the English into sheltering his son, Kissen Das, at Fort William, and then to seize upon their property as punishment for the offence. The second explanation is that Rajbullub, having had much to do with the English and having been enabled to render some service to them, was actuated purely by his own present interests in requesting Drake to admit his son to the English Settlement while on his way with his women and valuables to the shrine of Juggernath in Orissa. This reception of a man under the Nawab's displeasure could not, of course, happen without its being reported to him by his spies, and the incident completed the measure of unfriendliness with which he was already regarding the English. Be the explanation what it may, it was from this event that sprang the siege and capture of Calcutta and the tragedy of the Black Hole.

Bag Bazar Street commences from Bagh Bazar Ghat, once known as "Rogo Meeter's Ghat" from the son of Govindram the "Black Zemindar," and continues in an easterly direction for exactly half a mile until it reaches the northern extremity of Upper Circular Road. Its name has nothing to do with a *bagh* or tiger, although it is sometimes so spelt, but signifies "Garden Buzar Street" and must be referred to Perrin's Garden, the favourite haunt of the Company's servants in days before the capture and sack of Calcutta, when Clive was a writer at Fort St. George, and Hastings was beginning his apprenticeship to the Company's service at Cossimbazar. Baug Bazar occurs in Holwell's account of Calcutta in 1752: and three years earlier, in 1749, it is mentioned as having been farmed out. In the map of 1757, which is published along with volume IV of the Selections from the *Calcutta Gazette*, the street is shown surrounded by a number of trees: and in Wood's map of 1784 it appears as "Baug Bazar," but its length was then limited to a quarter of a mile or two furlongs. A Redoubt was erected at Bag Bazar in 1755 "at a cost of Rs. 338-6-9," and a small force of sixty European and native soldiers stationed there under Ensign Piccard gallantly repulsed the advance-guard of Seraj-ud-Dowlah's army on the 16th June, 1756.

Shambazar Street (also in Ward 1) runs from Rajah Nubkissen's Street, close to Upper Chitpore Road, to the Circular Road where it meets Cornwallis Street and Bag Bazar Street and is continued over the canal towards Belgachia. The name is derived from a large bazar or mart which Holwell calls Charles Bazar. Its present designation was conferred upon it by Sobharam Bysack, one of the wealthiest native inhabitants of Calcutta in the eighteenth century, in honour of Sham Roy (or Govind) the attendant of the goddess Kali. The Bysacks and the Setts who were well-to-do traders at Satgaon, the earliest factory above Hooghly, were among the first to settle at Suttanuttee. They are said to have cleared much jungle, and there can be little doubt that it was chiefly through them that Govindpore and Suttanuttee became a flourishing colony of weavers and a cotton-mart of sufficient importance to attract the English factors. Sobharam Bysack, who has a street in Ward 5 (Jorabagan), and two lanes in Ward 8 (Colootolloh), named after him, figures after the Black Hole and recapture of Calcutta as a "native commissioner for the distribution of the restitution-money." His own demand was for some 4½ lakhs of rupees out of a total of 12½ lakhs, and his "deduction" amounted to Rs. 66,000.

Nandaram Sen's Street in Ward 2 (Coomartolly), is named after the "black deputy" or "General Supervisor" who assisted Ralph Sheldon in his duties on his appointment as first Collector of Calcutta in 1700. He fell under suspicion when Benjamin Bowcher succeeded Sheldon and was summarily dismissed. In 1707, the post remained vacant for several months during which Nundoram again acted as assistant to the Collector. When he was displaced it came out that he had been guilty of extensive peculation. He fled to Hooghly but was given up by the Governor of that place. For a long period he was imprisoned by order of the Council: and was not released until he had refunded the money due by him. He built a bathing Ghat on the river called the Rathtollah Ghat (Rath being the car of Jagannath).

Abhoy Charan Mitter's Street in the same ward is named after the grandson of Raghoo Mitter ("Rogo Meeter"), who was himself the son of Govindram, the "Black Zemindar" of Holwell's time. Abhoy was Dewan of the Collector of the twenty-four Pergunnahs and is reputed to have given a lakh of rupees to his Gooroo or Spiritual Preceptor. Govindram was dismissed by Holwell from his office in 1752 for "heavy frauds," but he had sufficient influence with the majority in Council to procure his re-instalment on his refunding the amount of Rs. 3,397 embezzled by him.

Kalee Prosad Dutt's Street in Ward 3 (Burtollah) is named after the son of Churamoni Dutt, who was the great rival in wealth of Nubkissen, and always fretted for want of his power.

Sukeas Street gives its name to Ward 4. It is named after Peter Sukeas, an Armenian merchant of great wealth, who owned a celebrated garden-house at the "Boytaconnah."

Brindaban Mullick's Lane in this ward deserves notice

by reason of the fact that Pundit Ishwar Chundra Vidyasagar whose statue stands outside the Sanskrit College (1820-1891), had his residence at No. 25. Raja Rajendra Lala Mitra, the great scholar and antiquarian, resided at 6, Manicktollah Road in the same ward.

Rutton Sircar's Garden Street in Ward 5 (Jorabagan), commences from Durmahatta Street and runs in winding fashion right through to the Circular Road. It becomes Baranosee Ghose's Street at its crossing with Chitpore Road, and when it meets Cornwallis Street further on, it takes the name of Sukeas Street. It is so named from the garden-house, once situated here, of Rutton Sircar, an illiterate man, who made a large fortune under the "protection" of Nundoram Sen. Another Rutton Sircar is connected with a well-known incident. In 1679, the *Falcon,* with Captain Stafford in command, came up the river and anchored off Garden Reach. Being in need of an interpreter, the Captain, using the Madras word, asked the villagers to bring him a *dubash.* Not understanding the phrase, they sent him the village *dhoby* or washerman, one Rutton Sircar. As chance would have it, he was an intelligent man and so satisfied his new employer that he was taken into the Company's service as English interpreter and rose to great wealth in the course of a few years.

The great Tagore family have given their names to a number of streets in the Indian quarter. Durponarain Tagore, who has a street and a lane after him in Ward 5, was the son of Joyram Tagore who removed on the building of the New Fort William to Pathuriaghatta from Govindpore where the family had originally settled towards the end of the 17th century. From him are descended the many Tagores whose history is so closely connected with that of the city. He amassed a large fortune as a merchant and was Dewan to the French Government at Chandernagore. Prosunno Coomar Tagore, the founder of the Tagore Professorship in the University, Dwarkanath Tagore, known to his contemporaries as "Prince" Tagore, and Hara Coomar Tagore, the father of the present Maharajah Bahadur Sir Jotendro Mohan Tagore, K.C.S.I., are all similarly name fathers of various streets.

Rajah Gooroo Das's Street, in Ward 6 (Jorasanko), brings back memories of the historic trial of Nuncomar. Gooroo Das was Nuncomar's son and was Dewan to Mobaruck-ud-Dowlah, the fifth Nawab of Bengal.

Mooktaram Baboo's Street, another street in Ward 6, which runs from Banstollah to Cornwallis Street, derives its name from Mooktaram Dey, who held the office of Dewan of the Supreme Court for many years and retired only when the High Court came into existence under the Charter of 1862.

Boloram Ghose's Street in Ward 1 (Shampooker), *Baranosee Ghose's Street* in Ward 6 (Jorasanko), and *Hurree Ghose's Street* in Ward 3 (Burtollah), are named after members of the same family. Boloram was Dewan to Dupleix in the palmy days of Chandernagore. Baranosee was Dewan to Francis Gladwin, Collector of Calcutta from 1788 to 1789. Hurree, or more properly, Srihari, became Dewan of the East India Company at Monghyr. His reputation lives as a man of large generosity and extraordinary simplicity. The story goes that a friend of his took advantage of his want of guile and appropriated all his property, with the result (says Mr. A. K. Ray in his *Short History of Calcutta*), that his last days were clouded with pecuniary difficulties and were spent at Benares.

Cotton Street is the thoroughfare immediately to the north of Harrison Road and forms the northern boundary of Ward 7 (Burrabazar). It runs from Durmahatta Street to the Chitpore Road, and from thence to the Circular Road under the name of Machua Bazar, which like Nikasiparah recalls the time when fishermen tied up their boats in the creeks in the locality and lived upon the banks. There have been members of the Cotton family connected with Calcutta for over a century: but although a Commander-in-Chief, a Bishop, and a Chief Secretary to Government are included in the list, the street is not called after any of them. The old appellation of Roeyhattah indicates clearly enough its origin. It was here in fact that the great cotton-mart was held in days before Charnock dreamed of the foundation of Calcutta: and it is still the gathering-place of the Marwari merchants. Suttanuttee, the old name of the village, is referred by some to the same source and is held to mean "Cotton bale."

Phear's Lane in Ward 8 (Colootollah), is one of the few streets in the Indian quarter which are named after Englishmen. Sir John Budd Phear, who died as recently as 1905, was a puisne Judge of the Calcutta High Court from 1864 to 1876, and served the office of Chief Justice of Ceylon from 1877 to 1879. He was a man of large sympathies, and his attitude of encouragement towards the ideas and aspirations of the educated Indian community, won for him the highest esteem and respect. At No. 59, Bhowani Charun Dutt's Lane, in this ward is the birth-place of Keshub Chunder Sen, religious reformer and Brahmo leader (1838-1884). A tablet commemorates the fact, and the house known as Lily Cottage and numbered 78 in Upper Circular Road, where he resided for many years, has been similarly distinguished.

Amherst Street, a fine wide street opened out by the Lottery Committee, traverses both Wards 4 and 9, and runs from Bow Bazar Street to Manicktollah Street. Its length is recorded as one mile and two furlongs. At its southerly end it connects with St. James's Street (so-called after the neighbouring church) which carries it down to Dhurrumtollah. The house numbered 85 in this street was the family residence of the famous Hindoo religious reformer, Rajah Ram Mohan Roy. From 1814 to 1830, however, he lived at 113, Northern Circular Road, where a tablet recalls the fact. He was born in 1772, and died at Bristol in 1833. The Amhersts have left their mark upon Indian nomenclature in more than one direction. Lady Amherst gave her name to the *Amherstia nobilis*, the magnificent tree which rises to the height of forty feet and is so resplendent an object with its gorgeous blossoms of scarlet and gold covering its pendulous branches. The name was bestowed by Dr. Wallich, Superintendent of the Botanical Gardens. A species of golden pheasant, known to Zoologists as Thaumalea Amherstiae, is also indebted to Lady Amherst for its scientific title. As regards this Calcutta Street, the Governor-General whose rule it commemorates, is justly honoured: but it is impossible not to feel regret that the bestowal of his name upon the road has thrust out of sight the vernacular designation which happily perpetuates the long connection with Calcutta of the Revd. James Long. *Padre Long Sahib-ka-Girja-ka-rasta* is a long title, although it correctly reproduces the principal feature in the street which is the church where Mr. Long officiated for many years: but Long Street should not be deemed impossible for a street appellation in the vicinity.

Long is not the only missionary whose memory is kept alive in the vicinity of Amherst Street. Issuing from No. 32, is *Carey's Church Lane,* which commemorates the famous Serampore missionary. His career was a remarkable one. Bred up as a cobbler, he took to preaching the gospel, and with eleven others established the Baptist Missionary Society in 1792. In the following year, he came out to India with his wife, their four children, his sister-in-law, and a fellow-missionary Thomas. The pittance of Rs. 50 which was all they received from the Society was altogether insufficient for the support of himself and his family, and he was reduced to the necessity of settling at Hussanabad in the Sunderbans, where he attempted to earn a living by cultivating the soil with his own hands. The experiment was of course a failure, and he was glad to accept a post under an indigo-planter named Udney in the Maldah Districts. Here he was placed in charge of the Madnabutti out-factory, and devoted his leisure hours to preaching and translating the Scriptures. In 1799, William Ward and Joshua Marshman reached

India, and the three founded the famous Mission at Serampore. In 1807, Carey was appointed Professor of Bengalee to the College at Fort William which had been founded by Wellesley. He survived until the year 1834, when he died at the age of 74 and lies buried in the mission cemetery at Serampore.

Antony Bagan Lane in Ward 9 (Moocheeparah), commemorates the famous "Antony Sahib," agent of the "proprietor of Calcutta" in the days of Charnock, by whom tradition has it that he was horse-whipped. The tank in the centre of our Dalhousie Square was then within the enclosure of the Zemindar's cutcherry. Vidhyadhur Roy Chowdhry, the senior member of the Majumdar family in whose jagir the "three villages" lay, had allowed the English to acquire his own Zamindari Cutchery building for the protection of their records:* but the worship of the Hindoo god Govind or Sham Roy (who had given his name both to Govindpore and Shambazar) was still celebrated within the enclosure as of old, in spite of the removal of the image to Kalighat. Portuguese Antony's offence lay in his endeavouring to prevent some English factors from entering the enclosure during the *Holi* festival of the god. After the assault he went and took up his abode in his master's house at Kanchrapara, where the sites of

* Vidhyadhar's descendant, Bhairab, is stated in a genealogical table given by Mr. A. K Ray in his Short History of Calcutta, to have been born in 1757 (the year of Plassey), and to have died in 1857 (the Mutiny year). The three "villages" were sold to the Company in November 10th, 1698, by Vidhyadhar's son Ram Chand, and four other members of the family.

"Antony Sahib's" building and hât are still known. His grandson, also known as "Antony Sahib," was famous throughout Bengal, says Mr. A. K. Ray, as the best "Kabi-wallah" or minstrel of his time.

Rai Bankim Chunder Chatterjee Bahadur, the famous Bengalee novelist, who was also a distinguished member of the subordinate executive service, lived at 5, Protap Chunder Chatterjee's Lane in Ward 9.

Bonomali Sircar's Street in Ward 2 (Coomartolly), and *Husooree Mull's Lane* in Ward 11 (Puddopookur), may be taken together. For with the famous Omichand and Govindram Mitter, they are immortalized in a Bengalee proverb as the most prominent inhabitants of the Indian quarter in the days when Holwell ruled as Zemindar. Each man is distinguished by his own special attribute.

"Banmali Sarkarer bari
Govindram Mitrar chari
Amir Chander dari
Huzuri Maler kari,
Ke janen na?"

The allusion to Govindram's *chari* or stick was no doubt well appreciated by Holwell, when he reported to his colleagues in Council upon the oppression of the "Black Zemindar." Bonomali Sarkar's magnificent *bari* or residence in Coomartolly was built during the years 1740 to 1750. He was a cultivator (Sadgope) by caste and was at first Dewan to the Resident at Patna and subsequently Deputy Trader to the East India Company at Calcutta. Omichand's *dari* or beard has not obscured his fame as the victim of Clive's trick upon him with the two treaties. But he did not die from chagrin at the deception and lived on to see the Company established as the real rulers of Bengal. He has made a frequent appearance in these pages, and his career need not be further recapitulated in this place. As for Huzoori Mull's *kari* or wealth, the mere list of his acts of public beneficence is sufficient to show that it was no empty description. He excavated a large tank at Boytaconnah which went by his name until it was filled up. He constructed the Ghat immediately to the south of Howrah Bridge which was known in 1793 as Barretto's Ghat and goes now-a-days by the name of Armenian Ghat. He built the steeple of the Armenian Church and gave away several bighas of land at Kali Ghat where he constructed a pucka ghat near the Temple. And finally he is said to have rendered valuable service to the English at the battle of Buxar in 1761. His friendship with Omichand appears to have been of a close character: and he administered his estate on his death in 1767. In the proceedings of the Board at Fort William, dated March 30th of that year, we find that "Huzzoora Mal, administrator to the estate of the late Omichand, requests he may be indulged with two sets of bills on the Hon'ble the Court of Directors for Rs. 1,500 each, one payable to the Treasurer of the Foundling Hospital and one for the same given to the Magdalen. Ordered that they may be granted to him and that the sub-accomptant be directed to prepare them accordingly." These must be the London institutions of the name: and if so, the bequest is a striking tribute to the large-heartedness and catholicity of Omichand's disposition.

To the south of Ward 11 runs Dhurrumtollah, a reminder that we are arriving at ground we have already trodden, and that it is time to bring our sentimental journey to a close. The chapter has been a long one, but it does not venture on that account to seek recognition as exhaustive. The utmost merit to which it can lay claim must consist in the effort it has made to preserve from oblivion some of the footprints of the past which a matter-of-fact municipality and a busy heedless population have as yet forgotten to effface.

CHAPTER III.

THE STATUES AND MONUMENTS OF CALCUTTA.

CALCUTTA is proud of her statues and her monuments Whatever may be the faults imputed to her inhabitants by their critics, it cannot, at any rate, be laid to their charge that they have neglected to do honour to those to whom honour is due. There is probably no city in the Empire so plentifully adorned with statues of public men erected by subscription. Outram, the Bayard of the East; Mayo, struck down in the midst of a beneficent and patriotic career; Hardinge, the Hero of Albuera and Victor of Moodkee, Ferozeshuhur, and Sobraon; Bentinck, the wise, upright and paternal administrator; William Peel, the "handy man" of the Sepoy Mutiny; "Clemency" Canning, Napier of Magdala, Roberts of Kandahar and Pretoria; Dufferin the courtly and accomplished; John Lawrence, the Assistant Magistrate, who rose to be Viceroy—the memory of these and of many another is for ever kept green by a grateful people upon the wide expanse of Calcutta's historic maidan. Others again there are whose effigies in marble and bronze do not greet our eye as we dash past of an evening in our victorias and our buggies. Warren Hastings, the first Governor-General of Bengal, and Cornwallis, the author of the Permanent Settlement and conqueror of Tippoo Sultan, stand within the precincts of the Town Hall. Chantrey's masterly statue of the Marquess of Hastings adorns the portico of the Dalhousie Institute, and hard by is the marble presentment of James Wilson, the Finance Minister, who died while doing his duty. A brave list, in truth, and yet surely not without its notable omissions. There is more than one maker of history for whom we seem to look in vain. Wellesley, that King of men, is no longer enshrined in the Government House which owes its existence to him, and which is so apt a symbol of the Empire he created. The Marquess of Dalhousie, the greatest of modern Governors-General, as Lord Curzon has fitly characterized him, now occupies no place of honour in the Institute which bears his name. Calcutta, neverthless, has not forgotten them. In the course of a few years, these memorials of the illustrious dead will find a fit resting-place in the Victoria Hall, the "Twentieth century Taj," which will rear its graceful head upon the spot now made hideous by the Presidency jail. For the present they must be sought in their temporary home at the Indian Museum. Nor is the situation unworthy of them. For they stand upon either side of the young Queen whom the one was proud to serve and the other lived to greet: while surrounding them are the effigies of Neill and Havelock and Nicholson and Outram, and heroes of peace such as Rennell and Metcalfe.

On the Maidan.—The visitor cannot better begin his survey of the monuments on the Maidan than by driving to the southernmost extremity of the Strand Road.

Prinsep's Ghat.—Just above the suburb of Hastings, under the south-west angle of the fort, his attention will be arrested by a handsome structure in the Grecian Ionic style of architecture, standing boldly conspicuous on the eastern side of the Strand Road. This is none other than the famous Prinsep's Ghat, erected by the citizens of Calcutta in the forties to perpetuate the memory of JAMES PRINSEP, "one of the most eminent men of his day, who, after a short and brilliant career, fell a sacrifice to his ardour in the pursuits of science." Victor Jacquemont, in his Travels in India, from 1828 to 1832, writes thus of him :—"He devotes his mornings to architectural plans and drawings, his days to assaying at the Mint, and his evenings to musical concerts."

James Prinsep was the younger brother of Henry Thoby Prinsep whose bust stands in the Town Hall, and seventh son of John Prinsep, founder of the indigo industry in Bengal and introducer into the province of the process of printing cotton fabrics. He was born in 1799, and was at the age of 20, appointed Assistant Assay Master at the Calcutta Mint. His chief was Dr. Horace Hayman Wilson, afterwards Boden Professor of Sanskrit at Oxford, and for many years Librarian at the India House. On Wilson's retirement, he became Assay Master and succeeded him also in the Secretaryship of the Asiatic Society. Owing to failing health he was compelled to leave India in 1838, and died in England in 1840, at the age of 41. He was a man of many parts. His skill as an architect was shown by his construction of a bridge of five arches over the river Karamnassa which divides Benares from Behar. It was he also who took down and restored the minarets of the mosque of Aurungzebe. In Calcutta, he completed the canal begun by a brother of his in the Bengal Engineers, which connects the Hooghly with the navigation of the Sunderbunds. To his exploits as an archæologist, the Indian Museum bears abundant testimony. The Asiatic Society's Rooms contained until recently a bust erected by its members in his honour: it has now been transferred to the Victoria Memorial Hall collection at the Indian Museum.

The historical associations of Prinsep's Ghat are many. She can no longer claim to stand upon the river-bank, but she retains nevertheless her position of pride as the landing-place of every distinguished visitor who approaches the City of Palaces by sea. King Edward in 1875, and the Prince of Wales in the closing months of 1905, have adhered strictly to time-honoured custom: and have at this spot received in turn the loyal greetings of the citizens of Calcutta. The days when the prerogative was exclusively enjoyed by Chandpal Ghat have long since departed, and she has even been deprived of the privilege of bidding farewell to her rulers. For it is from Prinsep's Ghat also that the Viceroy and Governor-General sets out upon his homeward voyage, and Lord Curzon is the first of his line who has transgressed precedent by embarking, as he arrived, at the rival port of Bombay.

Lord Napier of Magdala.—To the east of Prinsep's Ghat, on a circular grass plot looking towards the riverside, is the noble bronze equestrian statue of Lord Napier of Magdala by Sir Edgar Boehm, R.A., a replica of which stands in the centre of Waterloo Place in London. The figure is clothed in military uniform, and in one hand is placed a pair of binoculars with which the Field-

Marshal is pointing to some distant object to which he desires to draw the attention of a companion-in-arms. The polished red granite pedestal bears the simple inscription—"Napier of Magdala."

Robert Cornelis Napier, Baron Napier of Magdala, whose title recalls the Abyssinian Campaign of 1867, filled the offices of Military Member of Council from 1861 to 1865, Commander-in-Chief in Bombay from 1865 to 1870, and Commander-in-Chief in India from 1870 to 1876. He was subsequently Governor of Gibraltar and Constable of the Tower of London and died in 1890, at the age of 80. He officiated as Governor-General from November to December, 1863, on the unexpected death at Dharmsala of the eighth Earl of Elgin, and pending the arrival of Sir William Thomas Denison, the Governor of Madras. In 1838, as a subaltern in the Bengal Engineers, he laid out the settlement at Darjeeling, and constructed the road from the plains, seven thousand feet below. During the Mutiny, he served as Military Secretary to Outram and Chief of the Adjutant-General's Department.

THE GWALIOR MONUMENT.—Proceeding up the Strand Road in a northerly direction, we next reach the GWALIOR MONUMENT erected by the Earl of Ellenborough, Governor-General of India, in 1847, in memory of the officers and men who fell in the Gwalior Campaign of 1843 under the leadership of Sir Hugh Gough. The structure, which was designed by Colonel H. Goodwyn of the Bengal Engineers, is built of brick faced with Jeypore marble, and is surmounted by a metal dome or cupola supported by columns made from guns captured from the enemy. The height is 58 feet 6 inches. In the centre is a sarcophagus on which is engraved the names of the "officers, non-commissioned officers and men of Her Majesty's and the Hon'ble Company's service who fell in the victorious actions of Maharajpore and Punniar on the 20th December, 1843." The regiments commemorated are the 2nd and 3rd troops, 2nd brigade, Horse Artillery, 2nd and 3rd troops, 3rd brigade, Horse Artillery, the 16th Lancers, the 1st, 4th, 8th, and 10th Regiments of the Company's Light Cavalry, the 4th Irregular Cavalry, the 1st company, 1st battalion, and 4th company, 4th battalion of the Company's Artillery, "the 1st company, Artillery, Scindia's Contingent," the Buffs, the 39th Foot (now the Dorset Regiment), who had fought at Plassey, the 40th and 50th Foot (now the South Lancashire and the Royal West Kent Regiments), the 2nd (Grenadiers), 14th, 16th (Grenadiers), 39th, 43rd and 56th Native Infantry, and the "Regiment of Kalat-i-Gilzie." Among the officers whose names find place in the inscription are Major-General C. H. Churchill, C.B., and Lieutenant-Colonel E. Sanders, C.B., of the Headquarters Staff, and Major G. A. Crommelin, C. B., of the 1st Light Cavalry. Some of the surnames of the English soldiers are noticeable by their uncommonness: Casebow, Epalett, "Kernon Troy," Homer, Bumevin, Fishlock. Equally striking is the spelling of the native names: Twangerally being quite unrecognisable, although Peer Baccus is not. The campaign in which they fell is now forgotten, although the barony conferred upon Gough tells the tale of his achivement: but its results were not unimportant, for they included the formation of the Gwalior Contingent of 10,000 men under the command of picked English officers, which was to be the source of such anxiety to "Redan" Windham and Colin Campbell at Cawnpore in 1857.

SIR WILLIAM PEEL.—At the corner, facing the main entrance to the Eden Gardens, is the marble statue by Speed of SIR WILLIAM PEEL. The third son of the great Sir Robert Peel by the daughter of General Sir John Floyd, the Murat of the Mysore campaigns and the most dashing cavalry officer of his day, William Peel chanced to be in the year 1857 in Indian waters in command of Her Majesty's frigate *Shannon*. Hastily despatched to the front with his blue-jackets, he led the Naval Brigade to the walls of Lucknow with the relieving force of Sir Colin Campbell. At the bombardment of the Martinière he was exposing himself with his usual indifference under fire, and thinking only of the effects of his shot against the breach he was making, when he was wounded in the thigh. When Lucknow had been captured, and the time came for the Naval Brigade to rejoin the *Shannon*, one of the King of Oudh's carriages was prepared for him. The ship's carpenters painted it, lined it with blue cotton, made a rest for his feet, and painted H. M. S. *Shannon* over the royal arms of Lucknow. But when Peel saw it, he declined to use it, saying that he would prefer to travel in a doolie like one of his blue-jackets. Unhappily the litter in which he was placed had been used by a small-pox patient. He caught the disease at Cawnpore and died in that city of mournful memories on April 27th, 1858. As unconcerned in the midst of danger as if at an evening party, his comrades have told us that to be classed with him was as high an honour as could be wished. "With a jest he won his sailors' hearts, and his singular serenity in the darkest hour of battle raised their hopes and gained their sure trust. He was their natural leader, because he was their own ideal of a perfect sailorman."

LORD AUCKLAND.—If the visitor will now walk through the Eden Gardens past the Burmese Pagoda and out at the northern gate, he will find on the opposite side the effigy by Weeks of George Eden, second Baron and first and only EARL OF AUCKLAND, Governor-General of India from 1836 to 1842. The pedestal upon which it stands displays the following panegyric by way of inscription:—

"To George, Earl of Auckland, Governor-General of India. This statue was erected by men, of whom some were the instruments of his government, of whom many knew that government only by its benign effects, all of whom agreed in the affectionate desire to perpetuate the memory of the six years during which he ruled the destinies of British India—for this just reason that, throughout the whole course of those years, he laboured earnestly and unremittingly to make security from rapine and oppression, freedom of internal trade, the medical science of Europe, the justice which is blind to distinctions of race, and the moral and intellectual affluence which it opens, a common and perpetual inheritance to all the nations who inhabit this Empire. 1848."

This statue, like that of Sir William Peel, was once within the Eden Gardens, for which Calcutta is indebted to the liberality and taste of the Misses Eden, the Governor-General's sisters.

Despite the character of the inscription upon the pedestal, the fates have ordered that Lord Auckland's administration shall be historical by reason of war and disaster. His resolution to support Shah Shujah against Dost Mahomed brought on the first Afghan Expedition (1839-42), and the fatal retreat from Cabul which added little glory to the British arms, redeemed though it was by Sale's heroic defence of Jelalabad and the prowess of Pollock and Nott. Yet he deserves commemoration upon grounds far other than these. His good fortune gave him Macaulay as his colleague, and advisers such as Sir Edward Ryan, then Chief Justice of Bengal, Sir Benjamin Heath Malkin, the able judge and ripe scholar whose short Indian career ended in a grave in St. John's churchyard, John Russell Colvin, whose destiny it was to die sick and weary in the darkest hour of the Mutiny, and Marshman, the wise and far-sighted editor of the *Friend of India*. Under the auspices of Dalhousie, the harvest sown by these men and those who thought with them was reaped in a series of beneficent reforms. Lord Auckland, who was raised to the Earldom in 1839 and died unmarried in 1849, resumed in 1846, after his return to England the office of First Lord of the Admiralty under Lord John Russell which he had previously held under Lord Melbourne in 1834.

LORD NORTHBROOK.—At the other end of the road and immediately facing the Judges' entrance to the High Court is Sir Edgar Boehm's full length statue of Thomas George Baring, second Baron and first EARL OF NORTHBROOK,

Viceroy and Governor-General of India from 1872 to 1876. The granite pedestal bears an inscription on its four sides in English, Bengalee, Persian and Hindi.

Lord Northbrook survived his return from India for nearly thirty years, his death at the age of 78 not taking place until the autumn of 1904. He was created an Earl in 1876, and from 1880 to 1885, was First Lord of the Admiralty in Mr. Gladstone's second administration. Before coming to India he had had the advantage of twice serving as Under-Secretary at the India Office, from 1859 to 1861, and again from 1861 to 1864. His Viceroyalty was signalized by the terrible famine in Bengal of 1873-74, and more happily by the visit to India of King Edward, then Prince of Wales, in the winter of 1875. While the famine was raging, he declined to go to Simla, and spent the hot weather in the plains, visiting, among other places, Hazaribagh and Shillong, stations never before and never since honoured by the presence of a Viceroy.

THE MACDONELL FOUNTAIN.—At the head of Old Post Office Street there comes next into view a memorial fountain erected in honour of MR. WILLIAM FRASER MACDONELL of the Civil Service, who won the Victoria Cross for conspicuous gallantry in 1857, in the sadly mismanaged attempt made from Patna to relieve the gallant garrison of the Little House at Arrah, and who later on filled the office of Judge of the High Court at Calcutta from 1874 to 1886. He died at Cheltenham in 1894. The visitor will look in vain for the portrait medallion which would have added so greatly to the interest of the memorial. But there is an inscription on the side facing the High Court, which pays a deserved tribute, not only to "his personal bravery in action, which won for him the highest distinction his sovereign had to bestow," but also to "his manly rectitude and kindly disposition which gained for him throughout his long service the respect and affection of all who knew him, setting always an honourable example to his colleagues and his countrymen." The exploit which won for MacDonell the Cross of Valour is thus described by Sir George Trevelyan in the *Competition-Wallah*: "On reaching the banks of the nullah, the soldiers who had now lost presence of mind, self-respect, subordination, everything but the unbridled desire for safety, threw themselves into the water, and swam and waded to the boats into which they crowded with all the unseemly hurry of an overpowering terror. As they struggled with the current, floundered in the mud, and scrambled over the gunwales, the sepoys plied them with shot at pistol range, directing their especial attention to a barge which was prevented from effecting its escape by a rope twisted round the rudder. The men inside crouched at the bottom of the boat, not daring to show their heads above the bulwarks as a mark for a hundred muskets. Nothing could have averted the capture and destruction of the whole party, had not a young volunteer, MacDonell by name, climbed out over the stern and unfastened the rope amidst a hail of bullets."

A second Victoria Cross was earned for the Civil Service, during that same retreat of brave men inefficiently led, by Ross Mangles, son of the Chairman of the Court of Directors for the year, who carried a wounded soldier of the 37th Regiment on his back for six miles, "laying him down tenderly from time to time when the enemy came too close to be pleasant." Mr. Mangles retired from India in 1883, as a member of the Board of Revenue and died so recently as March, 1905.

Sir Edward Hyde East.—Crossing over to the High Court, and entering by the principal public entrance, the visitor will find at the head of the main staircase, a handsome memorial marble statue by Sir Francis Chantrey, R.A., of Sir Edward Hyde East, Baronet, Chief Justice of the Supreme Court at Fort William from 1813 to 1822. In former days the statue stood in the grand jury-room of the old Supreme Court which stood on the same site as the present building. The inscription upon the pedestal records that he was "a principal founder of the Hindu College for promoting liberal education in India," and that "the native inhabitants of Calcutta caused this statue to be raised A. D. 1821." Sir Edward Hyde East was created a baronet in 1823, on his return to England, and after sitting in Parliament for some years, was, in 1830, appointed a member of the judicial committee of the Privy Council. He died in 1847. His predecessor as Chief Justice was Sir Henry Russell, the uncle of the ill-fated Rose Aylmer: while his two immediate successors, Sir Robert Henry Blosset and Sir Christopher Puller, who both lie buried in St. John's Churchyard, deserve commemoration from the melancholy coincidence that they held the office for barely a month each.

Lord William Bentinck.—To the east of the High Court and opposite the south entrance of the Town Hall is a fine statue in bronze of Lord William Bentinck, Governor-General of India from 1828 to 1835. Upon the front of the pedestal is a bas-relief representing a *suttee*. Both bas-relief and statue are from the chisel of Sir Richard Westmacott, R.A. On the back of the pedestal is an inscription, rapidly, alas! suffering effacement, from the eloquent pen of Macaulay, who was for eleven months Bentinck's colleague as Law Member of Council:—

"To William Cavendish Bentinck, who during seven years ruled India with eminent prudence, integrity and benevolence: who, placed at the head of a great empire, never laid aside the simplicity and moderation of a private citizen; who infused into Oriental Despotism the Spirit of British Freedom; who never forgot that the end of Government is the welfare of the governed; who abolished cruel rites; who effaced humiliating distinctions; who allowed liberty to the expression of public opinion; whose constant study it was to elevate the moral and intellectual character of the nation committed to his charge."

Lord William Henry Cavendish Bentinck, G.C.B., G.C.H., was the second son of the third Duke of Portland. He had previously filled the office of Governor of Madras from 1803 to 1807, but had been recalled together with Cradock (afterwards Lord Howden), the local Commander-in-Chief, in consequence of the outbreak of the mutiny at Vellore. As Governor-General he was content with but one annexation, that of Coorg, of which he proudly asserted that it was effected "in consideration of the unanimous wish of the people." But, as Macaulay's inscription testifies, his administration was made memorable by the victories of peace. For it is to him that India owes the introduction of steam communication, the abolition of *Suttee,* and the suppression of Thuggee, the appointment of the Law Commission which drew up the Penal Code, the drawing up of Macaulay's famous scheme of English Education, the foundation of the Medical College, the admission of educated Indians to the higher offices of state and the abandonment of all restrictions on trade. Two great qualities are said to have distinguished him in a marked degree—perfect indifference to popular applause and high moral courage. "The man who perhaps does most honour to Europe in Asia is he who governs it," writes Victor Jacquemont in his entertaining account of his travels in India, "Lord William Bentinck on the throne of the Great Mogul thinks and acts like a Pennsylvanian Quaker. You may easily imagine that there are people who talk loudly of the dissolution of the Empire and of the world's end, when they behold their temporary ruler riding on horseback plainly dressed and without escort, or on his way into the country with his umbrella under his arm." Lord William Bentinck was the first Governor-General of India, properly so called. Until November, 1834, when he formally assumed charge of that office, the correct designation of himself and his predecessors had been that of Governor-General of the Presidency of Fort William in Bengal: although the practice had been to speak of them as Governors-General of India. On his return to England, he was returned to Parliament as Liberal member for Glasgow at the General Election of 1837, and retained the seat until a few days before his death. He died in Paris in 1839 at the age of 65, having previously been offered and refused a peerage.

WARREN HASTINGS.—Across the road, and within the south portico of the Town Hall, which immediately faces the effigy of Lord William Bentinck, the visitor will next perceive the statue of WARREN HASTINGS. It is one of the finest efforts of Sir Richard Westmacott: and it would be impossible to find two more striking pieces of sculpture than the figures of the Brahman pundit and the seated Mussulman upon either side of the pedestal. But in its present position, half-obscured by pillars and brickwork, and all but invisible from the roadway, the beauties of this splendid group are completely lost. Nor are incongruity and obscurity the only disadvantages from which it suffers. The dust lies thick upon the pedestal, and idle and irreverent hands have not shrunk from defacing the marble with their scribble.

The invective of Burke and Macaulay and the memories of the long-drawn-out impeachment at the Bar of the House of Lords, have conspired to envelop the name of Warren Hastings in an obloquy which the more sober judgment of posterity will be slow to accord. He is no longer the captain-general of iniquity for whose crimes no adjective can be immoderate, and no form of condemnation inappropriate or undeserved. Yet it may be doubted whether justice has even to-day been completely awarded to him. How many Englishmen adequately realize that it was he who, during the eleven years of his rule in Bengal, securely laid the foundations of the British power in India? And if his successors have accomplished much, it is to him that they owe the opportunity and the possibility. Macaulay, with all his bias and his love of picturesque exaggeration, has borne nevertheless outspoken testimony to the work of Hastings as an administrative organizer and a statesman:

"His internal administration with all its blemishes, gives him a title to be considered as one of the most remarkable men in our history. He dissolved the double government of Nabob and Company. He transferred the direction of affairs to English hands. The whole organization by which justice was dispensed, revenue collected, peace maintained throughout a territory not inferior in population to the dominions of Louis the Sixteenth or the Emperor Joseph, was formed and superintended by him. He boasted that every public office, without exception, which existed when he left Bengal, was his creation. The just fame of Hastings rises still higher when we reflect that he was not bred a statesman: that he was sent from school to a counting-house: and that he was employed during the prime of his manhood as a commercial agent, far from all intellectual society. Nor must we forget that all, or almost all, to whom, when placed at the head of affairs, he could apply for assistance, were persons who owed as little as himself or less than himself to education. His own reflection, his own energy were to supply the place of all Downing Street and Somerset House. It must be added that, while engaged in this most arduous task, he was constantly trammelled by orders from home and frequently borne down by a majority in Council. The preservation of an Empire from a formidable combination of foreign enemies, the construction of a government in all its parts, were accomplished by him, while every ship brought out bales of censure from his employers, and while the records of every consultation were filled with acrimonious minutes by his colleagues. We believe that there never was a public man whose temper was so severely tried. But the temper of Hastings was equal to almost any trial."

And it is this distinguishing feature in his character which has been singled out for commemoration above the picture of Hastings which hangs in the Council Chamber at Government House hard by. *Mens æqua in arduis* runs the legend: and whether he was facing the angry minority in his Council or his judges and accusers in the House of Lords, his aspect was always self-possessed and serene. "He looked like a great man," admits his great critic, "and not like a bad man." His rewards from his countrymen were few, whether during his life or after his death. First among the Governors-General, he stands out among the brilliant throng of his successors as Castlereagh appeared at the Congress of Vienna—undecorated and undistinguished by riband or badge of honour. He was, it is true, made a Privy Councillor, and when in 1813 the charter of the East India Company came before the House of Commons for renewal, the members paid him tardy reparation for their seven years' persecution of him by rising in their places and cheering him when he entered and uncovering as he withdrew. But the half-promised peerage was never conferred, and it was as plain Warren Hastings that the great pro-consul died peacefully at Daylesford in 1818. The statue before us, as the inscription shows, was not erected until the year 1830. In the India Office there has been placed at the foot of the grand staircase another by John Flaxman, R.A., which was completed in 1823, and formerly stood in the general court room of the East India House in Leadenhall Street. And in the north transept of Westminster Abbey is a third statue in his honour, the work of Bacon the younger.

LORD CORNWALLIS.—If Calcutta has been ungrateful to Warren Hastings in the matter of the placing of his effigy, the plight of Charles, second Earl and first MARQUESS CORNWALLIS, father of the Civil Service and tamer of the "Tiger of Mysore," is still more cruel. At the west end of the lower floor of the Town Hall, the great Governor-General stands in silent wonder at the recompense meted out to him by posterity. Not more than a year or two ago the visitor to the Town Hall might well have been forgiven if he left the building wholly ignorant of the existence of this statue. Hidden behind frowsy book-shelves and partitions, and surrounded by the Baboos of the Municipal Engineer's Office and the Water Works Department, it was immured in a veritable oubliette. The very existence of Cornwallis seemed forgotten: and the Municipal clerks used the steps of the pedestal as a receptacle for their bundles and their files. To-day the litter and lumber have been removed: but unsightly wooden and iron props have taken their place and seriously obstruct the view. Yet, even in its sordid environment, and in spite of the dust and the cobwebs and the darkness, the magnificent beauty of the monument is apparent to the most casual of observers. The work of the sculptor, John Bacon the younger, is seen at its best. Dressed in Roman costume of the classic age with a laurel branch in his hand, Cornwallis confronts us in a majestic attitude which even the incongruity of his garb cannot destroy. On either side sits a female allegorical figure; the one grasps a mirror, the other a serpent: and both are of superb workmanship and exquisite design. The whole is placed upon a marble platform, to which access is given by a flight of three steps. Upon the back of the pedestal is a laudatory inscription which is in jarring contrast to the actual reality of the scene. "In honour of the Most Noble Marquis Cornwallis, K.G., Governor-General of India from September, 1786 to October, 1793, who by an administration uniformly conducted on the principles of wisdom, equity, and sound policy, improved the internal resources of the country, promoted the happiness of its inhabitants, conciliated the friendship of the native powers, confirmed the attachment of the allies of the Company, and established the reputation of the British name in Hindustan for good faith and moderation. By fixing in perpetuity the public demand for the landed revenue, he gave to the proprietors of the soil for the first time a permanent interest in it, and by the formation of a code of regulations for every department of the Government, he bestowed on the natives of India the benefit of a constitution and a security before unknown in the enjoyment of their rights and property. Forced into a war by the unprovoked aggression of Tippoo Sultan, his eminent military talents in the conduct of it were no less conspicuous than his moderation in victory. As a lasting memorial of these important services and as a testimony of their respect and esteem for a Governor-General under whose administration public spirit was encouraged and merit liberally rewarded, this statue was erected by the British inhabitants of Bengal, A.D. 1793."

Such is the epitome of Lord Cornwallis' first administration. But he enjoys the distinction of having twice been Governor-General of India. On the departure of Lord Wellesley in 1805, he was prevailed upon to resume his former post at the urgent prayers of the India House. He was in his sixty-fifth year: and prudence might well have dictated refusal. Since his return to England in 1793, he had been Lord-Lieutenant of Ireland, with Lake as his right-hand man, while the great rebellion of 1798 was at its worst: and in 1802, he had performed what he might have been excused for regarding as his last public service by acting as one of the signatories to the peace of Amiens. The Directors, however, were importunate: and he resolved to essay the task. He arrived at Calcutta in July 1805 with the avowed intention of turning back upon the footsteps of his bolder predecessor. The prevailing "frenzy of conquest" was to be subdued: and the Company's treasury saved from utter exhaustion. But the climate of Bengal played havoc with the old man's weakened frame: and he died at Ghazipore, on his way up-country, before he had been ten weeks in office.

The gratitude of his countrymen was liberally bestowed during his lifetime as after his death: and Calcutta's tribute is only one of several. In Madras his statue by Banks occupies the centre of the barrack-square of Fort St. George, opposite the Secretariat. Bombay has done honour to his glorious memory by erecting yet another statue which adorns the Elphinstone Circle.* Installed in a niche on the great staircase of the India Office, and keeping company with Wellesley and Coote and Wellington, is a third statue by the elder Bacon, similar in pose and costume to the Calcutta memorial, which is in fact a copy of it, although on a larger scale and completed by the younger Bacon after his father's death in 1799. A fourth by Rossi may be seen on the eastern side of the south transept of St. Paul's Cathedral, opposite the Nelson monument: and his portrait by Copley hangs upon the walls of the Guild Hall of the City of London.

To those who believe in the injunction to "praise famous men" so familiar at every University and College Commemoration, it will afford some consolation to learn

* Regarding this Bombay statue, there is a curious note in Colonel Colin Mackenzie's well-known book of reminiscences which he entitles *Sunshine and Storm of a Soldier's Life.* "On January 10th, 1843," he writes "we arrived at Bombay. The old practice of worshipping the statue of Lord Cornwallis is still in high value among the natives of Bombay. Little did he anticipate divine honours being paid him after death. Many of the statues of our deceased great men all over India are reverenced in the same way by the superstitious natives."

that the penance of Warren Hastings and his companion in misfortune is likely hereafter to last only so long as the building of the Victoria Memorial Hall upon the Maidan is in progress. The Corporation have offered both statues to the Trustees for inclusion in the sculpture-gallery in the Hall: and Calcutta's tribute of admiration and respect will before long be fittingly, if tardily paid.

We may leave until the occasion of a future visit to the Town Hall, the description of the many interesting busts and portraits which are placed about the upper floor and the northern vestibule.

LORD CANNING.—Returning to the Bentinck Statue, we proceed towards the western gate of Government House and skirt the enclosure until we reach its south-west corner. Here upon a grass plot stands a bronze equestrian statue of EARL CANNING, Governor-General of India from 1856 to 1862, and first Viceroy. It was modelled by J. H. Foley, R.A., and completed by T. Brock, R.A.

Charles John Canning, second Viscount and first Earl Canning, was the third son of George Canning the statesman. His two elder brothers having died, he succeeded his mother in 1837 in the peerage conferred upon her after her husband's death, and became Viscount Canning of Kilbrahan in the County of Kilkenny. In 1841, he was appointed by Peel to be Under-Secretary for Foreign Affairs, and held the office for five years, when he was appointed First Commissioner of Woods and Forests. He joined Lord Aberdeen's Government in 1853 as Post-master-General: and in his management of the Department established a reputation for administrative ability which foreshadowed the qualities which were to distinguish his Indian Viceroyalty—unremitting industry, the habit of careful enquiry into the facts of each case, and caution sometimes perhaps carried to excess. But, whatever his merits as a worker, he did not shine as a speaker. Sir Mountstuart Grant-Duff has recorded in his *Notes from a Diary* the account given him by Lord Dufferin (who was present) of the catastrophe of his first appearance. "Lord Canning after uttering two or three sentences in his maiden speech, put his hands before his face, and said, 'My Lords, I cannot go on,' thus ruining his career as a parliamentarian, though not as a public man."

In 1858, he was nominated to succeed Lord Dalhousie as Governor-General of India and held the office until March, 1862. It was the fate of Lord Canning, who had said at his farewell banquet in London that he earnestly desired a policy of peace, to meet the greatest crisis that has threatened the British Empire in India. "I wish for a peaceful term of office," he had told the Court of Directors who had met to do him honour, "but I cannot forget that in the sky of India, serene as it is, a small cloud may arise no larger than a man's hand, but which, growing larger and larger, may at last threaten to burst and overwhelm us with ruin." Never were words more prophetic or a blow more sudden. "India is quiet throughout," announced the *Bombay Gazette* on May 1st, 1857. Nine days later, the sepoys at Meerut broke into open mutiny: and for twenty months, the English were at bay. The history of Lord Canning's administration, however, is only half told with the tale of the Sepoy Mutiny. On the 18th November, 1858, the Government of India was transferred to the Crown, and the Company's Governor-General became the first Viceroy of Hindustan. In 1861, the Indian Councils Act sanctioned the addition of non-official members to the Supreme and Provincial legislatures. An era of progress and internal reform succeeded that of bloodshed and rapine. But great as were the boons Lord Canning conferred in the prosecution of his policy of expansion and development, he rendered India a yet greater service by the unruffled equanimity and strict impartiality with which he confronted the darkest hour of peril. The epithet of "Clemency Canning" conferred on him by his countrymen in derision, is now remembered only to his honour and his praise.

The last months of Lord Canning's stay in India were clouded by the death of his wife, who died at Barrackpore in November, 1861. She had visited Darjeeling for a brief change, while the Viceroy was on tour in Upper India, and on her way down through the malarious Terai was attacked by jungle fever, which rapidly proved fatal. The loss told severely upon him. He was created an Earl in 1859, and a Knight of the Garter on his retirement. But he survived his return to England only a few weeks. He died in London in June, 1862, and lies buried in Westminster Abbey. "A very mirror of honour, the pattern of a just, high-minded, fearless statesman, kind and considerate and without personal bias against his opponents." Such are the words in which his character has been summed up by Bishop Cotton, who was on terms of close intimacy with him: and the verdict of posterity seeks neither to modify or to disturb the generous appreciation.

LORD LAWRENCE.—Facing the south entrance to Government House is a full length bronze statue of LORD LAWRENCE. John Laird Mair Lawrence, "the saviour of the Punjab" during the Mutiny, is one of the very few members of the Covenanted Civil Service who have filled the office of Governor-General, and the last of those who have done so. Under his administration, measures were taken to reform the finances so as to relieve them from the heavy burden laid upon them by the Sepoy Rebellion. The chief incidents of his rule were the removal of the summer head-quarters of the Government of India to Simla, the Bhutan War, which was followed by the annexation in 1864 of the Dooars (now honeycombed with tea-gardens) and the terrible Orissa famine and commercial crisis of 1866. Created a baronet in 1858, he received a peerage in 1869 on his return to England, and was the first Chairman of the London School Board. The statue, which is the work of Thomas Woolner, R.A., stands upon a large and imposing base to which access is had by steps in front and rear, and bears the following inscription on three sides of the pedestal: "John Lawrence, born 1811: died 1879: Viceroy of India 1864 to 1868." Another statue, which must be described as ineffective, has been erected in his honour at Lahore, where it stands on the Mall between the Cathedral and the Chief Court. A third effigy by Boehm may be seen in London, where the great "Jan Larens" holds silent vigil in Waterloo Place with Colin Campbell and John Franklin.

LORD HARDINGE.—At the south-east of Government House on a triangular plot called "The Cocked Hat" and facing the Red Road, is a fine bronze equestrian statue of LORD HARDINGE, Governor-General of India from 1844 to 1848. It was modelled by J. H. Foley, R.A., and is undoubtedly one of his masterpieces. On the granite pedestal is the following inscription:—

"The statue was erected by the inhabitants of British India of various races and creeds to Henry Viscount Hardinge, in grateful commemoration of a Governor who, trained in war, sought by the acts of Peace to elevate and improve the various Nations committed to his charge, and when re-called to arms by unprovoked invasion, at Moodkee, Ferozeshuhur, and Sobraon, maintained the reputation which, in youth, he won by turning the tide of victory at Albuera."

The campaign which this inscription commemorates was as short as it was sharp. In 1845, the Sikhs crossed the Sutlej. Within three weeks from their invasion of British territory the four pitched battles of Moodkee, Ferozeshuhur, Aliwal and Sobraon had been fought, Lahore surrendered, and the Jullunder Doab annexed to the Company's dominions. The Governor-General was created Viscount Hardinge of Lahore as the reward of his achievement: and on his return to England filled successively the offices of Master-General of Ordnance and Commander-in-Chief of the Forces. In the latter he was succeeded in 1856 by the late Duke of Cambridge and died the same year at the age of 72, having been created a Field-Marshal a twelvemonth earlier. When he left India he ventured upon the anticipation that "it would not be necessary to fire a gun again there for seven years to come:" but his successor, Lord Dalhousie, had spent barely six months in the country when the murder of Vans Agnew and Anderson at Mooltan set the Punjab once more ablaze. Lord Hardinge, who could boast of having been present at sixteen general engagements, lost his left hand at the battle of Ligny, but those who seek to discover the deficiency in the statue will find themselves baffled by the ingenuity of the sculptor.

THE LATE QUEEN-EMPRESS.—Across the road, to the east of the statue of Lord Lawrence and the northern end of the Red Road, has been erected as a temporary measure, the statue of the late QUEEN-EMPRESS VICTORIA, which it is intended, on the completion of the Victoria Memorail Hall, to place at the entrance, at the head of a high flight of stairs with an arch or canopy over it. The statue is the work of Mr. George Frampton, R.A., and possesses a special interest from the fact that her late Majesty commanded the sculptor to submit a sketch model personally to herself at Osborne, allowed him one or two sittings, and suggested certain alterations and improvements in the design, finally expressing her entire satisfaction with the completed model. The figure is cast in light bronze. The Queen-Empress is seated on a throne of striking design, and wears the robes of the Order of the Star of India. In her right hand is borne the sceptre, and in the left the orb of State, surmounted by a figure of St. George. A crown and a wreath of laurels are on the head, and support is given to the shoulders by a cushion.

At the back of the chair the lion of Great Britain and the tiger of India are represented in relief side by side, and above them is the "sun that never sets." Allegorical figures symbolizing Art and Literature and Justice surmount the back of the chair. The base or pedestal is of rich Irish green marble, bearing in front two figures of Goorkha sepoys, supporting a shield with the royal arms encircled by the palm of peace. A decorative design is carried round the pedestal, and the side view of the robes flowing in graceful folds from the shoulder to the ground offers a pleasing contrast to the severe architectural proportions of the chair. The statue, which was the outcome of a public subscription to commemorate the sixtieth year of Her Majesty's reign, was unveiled by Lord Curzon with fitting ceremonial on the 19th March, 1902.

As we proceed up the Red Road, "the Lady's Mile" of Calcutta, we come within view of the bronze equestrian statues of Lord Roberts and Lord Lansdowne, which face one another at the centre of the thoroughfare.

LORD ROBERTS.—The statue of LORD ROBERTS, who is represented in an Afghan "poshteen," and riding his favourite charger, was cast in one piece, the metal being obtained from fourteen guns provided by Government for the purpose. It is supported by allegorical figures at either end of the marble pedestal, the one facing the Fort symbolizing "War" and the other confronting the Red Road "Victory." Around the base of the statue and forming the upper portion of the pedestal is a frieze intended to commemorate the companions in arms of the late Commander-in-Chief in India. In front are Sikhs, to the right is a battery of Horse Artillery, to the left Highlanders and Goorkhas, and at the back a detachment of Native Cavalry, all representatives of corps with which Lord Roberts has been historically connected and designed more especially to recall the famous march from Kabul to Kandahar.

The inscription on the north face of the pedestal runs:—"General Lord Roberts, V.C., G.C.B., G.C.S.I., G.C.I.E., Commander-in-Chief of Her Majesty's Forces in India, November, 1885 to April 1893; Field-Marshal, 1895." On the south face is the following record of Lord Roberts' campaigns and of his valedictory message to the Indian Army: "Kabul to Kandahar, Delhi, Lucknow, Agra, Khodagunge, Umbeyla, Abyssinia, 1867, Lushai, Afghanistan, 1878 to 1880, Peiwar Kotal, Shutar Gardan, Charasiah, Sherpur. I now bid farewell to the army of this country, both British and Native."

The statue is the composition of the late Mr. Harry Bates, R.A., and in the opinion of sculptors of eminence is one of the finest equestrian statues of modern times. The frieze and the allegorical figures which adorn the pedestal were not included in the original design and were generously added by Mr. Bates, at his own cost, for Calcutta's permanent benefit and in fulfilment of the artist's sense of beauty. The statue was unveiled by Lord Elgin on March 2nd, 1898.

The briefest review must suffice of the career of this distinguished soldier whose forty-one years in India are so aptly commemorated by this beautiful work of art. Sir

Frederick Roberts (to give him the name by which he is best known in this country) was born at Cawnpore in 1832. His father, Sir Abraham Roberts, G.C.B., was commanding at Peshawar when he returned to India in 1851, with a commission as Lieutenant in the Bengal Artillery. He won the Victoria Cross in the Mutiny by conspicuous gallantry at Khodagunge. Thereafter he was almost continuously engaged in a succession of wars: of one of these, Vonolel, the name of his favourite charger, is a memory—recalling as it does the Lushai Expedition of 1871, undertaken to rescue Mary Winchester and to exact retribution for a long series of raids upon the tea-gardens of Cachar. After his successful conduct of the Afghan campaign of 1879, he was appointed Commander-in-Chief in Madras. This office he held for five years, and from 1885 to 1893, he was Commander-in-Chief in India. In 1895, he became Commander of the Forces in Ireland, and in 1899 was despatched to South Africa to take the supreme command in the field against the Boers. To the list of engagements commemorated on the pedestal of his statue must be added the battle of Paardeberg, the relief of Kimberley, and the capture of Pretoria. On his return, he obtained the highest office open to an English soldier, and from 1901 to 1904 was Commander-in-Chief. He was made a baronet in 1879, elevated to the peerage as Baron Roberts of Kandahar and Waterford in 1892, and in 1901, was created Earl Roberts at the conclusion of the Boer War, receiving also the Order of the Garter and a substantial money grant from Parliament.

LORD LANSDOWNE.—Upon the opposite side of the road

was placed in January, 1901, the companion statue of the MARQUESS OF LANSDOWNE, Viceroy and Governor-General of India from 1888 to 1894. Like that of Lord Roberts, it was cast from eleven guns contributed by the Government of India. The commission was also entrusted to Mr. Bates, but his lamented death occurred before the pedestal was finished, and the completion of the sculptor's conception was supervised by the late Mr. E. Onslow Ford, R.A., who generously gave his services without any professional fee.

The statue is neither so striking or so artistic as that of Lord Roberts. The horse is an admirable piece of work, but the helmet on the rider has the appearance of being too large for the head and the figure does not sit easily in the saddle. The allegorical figures for which Calcutta is indebted to Mr. Onslow Ford are symbolical of Wisdom joining the hands of India and Great Britain, and of Justice and Law supported by the State.

Lord Lansdowne has had a long and distinguished public career, and comes of a long line of soldiers and statesmen. His grand father held office as Lord President of the Council during the thirties and forties in the Ministries of Grey, Melbourne and Russell: and his mother's father, the Comte de Flahault, was a French general and diplomatist, who married the Baroness Keith and Nairne. In addition to his marquessate, he is the holder of three earldoms, three viscounties and five baronies. Succeeding his father as fifth Marquess in 1866 at the age of twenty-one, he was from 1869 to 1872 a Lord of the Treasury, and from 1872 to 1874, Under-Secretary for

India. In 1883, he was appointed to succeed the Marquess of Lorne as Governor-General of Canada and held that office until 1888, when he followed Lord Dufferin to India. His Viceroyalty was marked by the taking of the first step in currency reform by closing the mints to the free coinage of silver, the reconstitution of the Legislative Councils by the admission of elected members, and, less happily, by the outbreak in Manipore which resulted in the murder of Mr. Quinton, the Chief Commissioner of Assam, and other British officers. Since his return to England, Lord Lansdowne, who is now (1906) in his sixty-first year, has taken an active part in political life, and after having been Secretary of State for War was, in 1900, appointed Secretary of State for Foreign Affairs, an office which he has recently resigned, upon Sir Henry Campbell-Bannerman's accession to power. As a diplomatist, he is in his element. Years ago, it is said that a member of one of Mr. Gladstone's Ministries summed him up in the following words: "He has all the qualities, a tact which never fails, a memory that never slips, a temper which the man is not yet born who can ruffle."

LORD DUFFERIN.—At the head of the Red Road and standing in the centre of the four roads which converge at the south end of Secretary's Walk, is Sir Edgar Boehm's statue of the MARQUESS OF DUFFERIN AND AVA, Viceroy and Governor-General of India from 1884 to 1888; and the predecessor of Lord Lansdowne in the office. The ex-Viceroy is represented in full official uniform, wearing the collars of five orders of Knighthood (St. Patrick, the Bath, St. Michael and St. George, the Star of India, and the Indian Empire), and with a mantle thrown back from his shoulders. The attitude is a characteristic one and the likeness happy, although the art of the sculptor may be thought by some to be a trifle meretricious in style.

The annexation of Upper Burma and the delimitation of the North-Western frontier of Afghanistan remain as the political landmarks of Lord Dufferin's Viceroyalty. With his rule is also indelibly associated the establishment of the Fund which bears the name of his accomplished wife and which has done so much to alleviate the sufferings of the women of India.

The four years of Lord Dufferin's government of India were, however, the veriest fragment of a career of extraordinary brilliancy and distinction. While yet a boy of fifteen, he succeeded his father in the Irish barony of Dufferin: and to the advantage of title and position which was thus secured to him, he added the legacy of wit and *savoir-faire* which he inherited from his mother, the beautiful and gifted grand-daughter of Richard Brinsley Sheridan. The first forty-six years of his life did not bring him very prominently before the public, and his chance did not come to him until 1872, when he accepted the Governor-Generalship of Canada, after an unsuccessful attempt to secure the Viceroyalty of India, which went to Lord Northbrook. But he had already been created an English peer in 1850, and promoted to an earldom in 1871, besides filling a variety of minor ministerial appointments. After six years at Ottawa, he tried his hand at diplomacy, and was successively Ambassador at St. Petersburg and at Constantinople. Then followed his mission to Egypt, and the second great chance of his life when he succeeded the Marquess of Ripon in 1884 as Viceroy of India. Upon his retirement he became once more an Ambassador, first at Rome and latterly at Paris. In 1888, he was advanced to a marquessate by the style and title of Marquess of Dufferin and Ava and Earl of Ava, in commemoration of the acquisition of Upper Burma. Apparently he did not regard as his most signal achievement the transformation of Theebaw's palace-enclosure at Mandalay into Fort Dufferin: for it appears from Sir Alfred Lyall's recently published biography that when he was offered the marquessate, his first wish was to associate with his title the city of Quebec, whose old city walls he had saved from destruction. And it was at the special wish of the late Queen that the name was selected of the ancient capital of the Burmese Kings. He died in 1902, his last years being clouded by financial troubles brought on by the collapse of the Whitaker Wright Companies, and the death of his eldest son, Lord Ava, during the siege of Ladysmith.

SIR JAMES OUTRAM.—Turning to the right, we make our way down the avenue past the Calcutta Golf Club pavilion towards Chowringhee. Here on a grass plot opposite the entrance to Park Street stands the spirited bronze equestrian statue by J. H. Foley, R.A., of SIR JAMES OUTRAM, which was unveiled in 1874 with great ceremony by Lord Napier of Magdala, the then Commander-in-Chief, who had in 1865 succeeded Outram in the office of Military Member of Council. The statue is placed on a lofty granite pedestal and represents Outram in the act of reining in his charger and looking behind him, as if to encourage his men. It bears the following inscription :—

"Sir James Outram, Lieutenant-General, G.C.B., Baronet. His life was given to India: in early manhood he reclaimed wild Races by winning their hearts. Ghazni, Khelat, the Indian Caucasus, witnessed the daring deeds of his prime. Persia brought to sue for peace; Lucknow relieved, defended, and recovered, were fields of his later glories. Faithful servant of England, large-minded and kindly ruler of her subjects; in all the True Knight, The Bayard of the East. Born 29th January, 1803, died 11th March, 1863."

The story of Outram's self-sacrifice during the Mutiny and his surrender to Havelock of the glory of relieving the beleaguered Residency at Lucknow, needs no recapitulation. It was another Napier, Sir Charles James, the conqueror of Sind, who in 1842 at a public banquet to Outram, toasted him as the "Bayard of India, *Sans peur et sans reproche*" and the epithet will always remain linked with his name. It is the sole inscription upon his grave in the centre of the nave of Westminster Abbey. His iron nerve and sagacity were proverbial on the Bombay side, where the saying went that "a fox was a fool and a lion a coward by the side of James Outram." In early life he won the confidence of the wild Bheels in Khandesh by living among them unarmed and trusting to their rough sense of justice and honour. "What do I care for the clawing of a cat?" was the remark with which on one occasion he quieted them when they rescued him from a wounded tiger that was mauling him, and the speech was rife among the Bheels for many years afterwards. He was created a baronet in 1858, and was one of the first Knights of the Star of India on the foundation of the order in 1861. When ill-health compelled him to leave India in 1865, he was publicly entertained in Calcutta. His friends in Bombay presented him with a silver shield designed by Mr. H. H. Armstead, R.A., and now on exhibition at the South Kensington Museum. He died at Pau in 1863. A marble bust by Matthew Noble, R.A., was erected to his memory by order of the Secretary of State over the doorway on the south side of the nave in Westminster Abbey: and a statue of him by the same sculptor stands on the Thames Embankment in London.

Lord Mayo.—We now turn to the left and take the road which runs across the Maidan direct from Park Street to Government House. At the junction which it makes with the long avenue leading from Corporation Street to Kidderpore Bridge, stands a bronze equestrian statue of the Earl of Mayo, which was unveiled by King Edward VII on December 31st, 1875, on the occasion of his visit to India as Prince of Wales. The following inscription appears upon its pedestal:—

"To the honoured and beloved memory of Richard Southwell, 6th Earl of Mayo, K.P., G.M.S.I., Humane, Courteous, Resolute and Enlightened, struck down in the midst of a Patriotic and Beneficent career on the 18th February, 1872, by the treacherous hand of an assassin; the People of India, mourning and indignant, raise this Statue. Born 21st February, 1822, assumed the Viceroyalty, 12th January, 1869."

Lord Mayo's administration is associated with a period of much material progress. An Agricultural Department was created, and the system of provincial finance inaugurated. Roads, railways, and canals sprang up on all sides: a network of State railways was put in hand, and new schools and colleges founded in every province. The horror of his assassination at the convict settlement of Port Blair in the Andamans was augmented by the fact that Mr. John Paxton Norman, the officiating Chief Justice of Bengal, had been murdered barely six months before as he was ascending the steps of the Town Hall which was then in use as a High Court. Lord Mayo's remains were conveyed from India to Dublin where they were received in state by the Lord Lieutenant, and buried in the family vault at Johnstown. Another statue of Lord Mayo will be found in the public gardens at Jeypore.

THE OCHTERLONY MONUMENT.—Upon the Maidan to the right of the Mayo Statue, and facing the eastern portion of the Esplanade, towers the OCHTERLONY MONUMENT which for a long series of years has been the most prominent landmark in Calcutta. It was erected by public subscription in 1828 in honour of Sir David Ochterlony, Bart., G.C.B., Resident in Malwa and Rajpootana, and conqueror of Nepaul. It is a fine column, 152 feet in height, and a splendid panoramic view of the city and neighbourhood may be had from its summit. The cost of erection is stated to have been Rs. 35,000. The design of the structure was taken from Moslem architecture. The upper part of the column is the reproduction of one in Syria, to which is added a base which is pure Egyptian, and the dome which has a metallic cupola is Turkish. The column itself is of brickwork, and the circular staircase within (by which access is had to the two galleries which encircle the column from outside) is constructed of Chunar stone. It rests on a massive pedestal of brickwork and stone, and bears a circular disc of white marble with the following inscription:—

"Sir David Ochterlony, Baronet, Grand Cross of the Military Order of the Bath, Major-General in the Army of Bengal, died at Meerut on the 15th July, 1825. The people of Bengal, natives and European, to commemorate his services as a statesman and a soldier, have in grateful admiration raised this column."

The foundation is said to be an artificial one, made by driving eighty-two sâl logs, each twenty feet long into the ground, their heads being eight feet below the surface level. "Over them a strong teakwood frame was laid, and over that eight feet of solid masonry before the lowest step was begun." There is a story that just before the Monument was completed a dinner party was held on the top of the shaft which was then 3 feet above the floor of the second gallery, at an elevation of 145 feet above the plain. The seats were disposed around the gallery, and a secure temporary railing provided for the occasion. Old chronicles describe the party as an "unique and hilarious function" which did not terminate until "the unusual hour" of nine o'clock at night.

It was Ochterlony who, in 1804, gallantly defended the

citadel of Delhi against Holkar's twenty thousand men and 100 guns, until the advance of Lake's army raised the siege. No action of the war with the Mahratta powers deserves greater commendation than this brave and skilful defence for ten days of an almost untenable position. Twelve years later he was entrusted with the command of the campaign against the Goorkhas, which earned for Lord Moira the Marquessate of Hastings and enabled him to add the hill-stations of Naini Tal, Mussoorie and Simla to the possessions of the English. For his services, Ochterlony was created a baronet, and was granted by the Prince Regent an augmentation to his coat-of-arms by which the conquest of Nepaul was specially commemorated. His death at the age of sixty-eight at Meerut, where he had gone for "change of air" from Delhi, was caused by grief at the censure passed upon him by Lord Amherst for the measures taken by him to preserve tranquillity at Bhurtpore, the wisdom of which was amply demonstrated by the war which broke out a few months later and was only ended by Lord Combermere's capture of the fortress.

Ochterlony was one of the few officers still in harness in the twenties who had seen service under Sir Eyre Coote. "For fifty years a soldier, he had served in every Indian War from the time of Hyder downwards." He was a typical specimen of the class of servant of John Company to whom India was no land of temporary sojourn but a home for good and all. The son of an American loyalist, he came to the East without friends and literally fought his way to notice. When he shook hands with Heber in the heart of Rajputana, he had not left India for fifty-four years: and, as he told the Bishop, who could wonder that he clung to the only place in the world where he could feel himself at home?

THE PANIOTY FOUNTAIN.—At the corner of Explanade Row, East, and Old Court House Street, there has been erected, "as a tribute to faithful and assiduous service, extending over a period of 42 years, by the Viceroy and Private Secretaries who gratefully remember it," a Jeypore marble fountain in memory of Mr. Demetrius Panioty, C.I.E., a highly-respected member of the domiciled Greek Armenian community who filled for many years the office of Assistant Private Secretary to the Viceroy and died in 1895 at Simla. Over the arch on the west side is the inscription: "A good name is rather to be chosen than great riches."

LADY CURZON'S FOUNTAIN.—A little further to the East along Esplanade Row, there will (it is understood) be shortly placed upon the grass plot which immediately faces the new Military Secretariat Buildings, the fountain presented by Lady Curzon to the citizens of Calcutta in token of her gratitude for the sympathy so widely extended to her during the dangerous illness which so nearly put an end to her life during the summer and autumn of 1904. The whole of this portion of the Maidan which was formerly as untidy as it was unsightly has been newly laid out with plants and lawns, and it will be seen that the arrangement of footpaths takes the form of a Union Jack.

IN THE CITY.—We have now completed our view of the

statues and public monuments on the Maidan: but there remain several elsewhere which deserve our notice.

LORD HASTINGS.—On the south side of Dalhousie Square facing the entrance to Wellesley Place there stands within the portico of the Dalhousie Institute a fine marble statue by Sir Francis Chantrey, R.A., of the MARQUESS OF HASTINGS, Governor-General of India from 1813 to 1823. This entrance portico was originally erected in 1824, and the Institute building is an addition of subsequent years, its foundation stone not having been laid until 1865.

Francis Rawdon Hastings, second Earl of Moira, in the peerage of Ireland, and Baron Hastings and Hungerford, was in 1816 created Marquess of Hastings and Earl of Rawdon in the peerage of the United Kingdom. His wife was Countess of Loudoun in her own right: and their joint connection with Calcutta has been perpetuated in the various streets which recall their titles and dignities. Lord Hastings enjoyed the intimate friendship of the Prince Regent, but this did not save him on his return to England from the censure of the Court of Proprietors in connection with his interference with the financial complications of the Nizam and the famous Hyderabad banking firm of Palmer & Co., in which the Rumbolds were partners. Calcutta, however, will always remember him with gratitude, for it is to his appointment of the famous "Lottery Committee" that she owes the Strand Road, the paths and avenues across the Maidan, and many broad streets and shady squares. Under his administration the finishing touches were put to the conquests of the English in Western India, and the map of Hindostan drawn by him remained substantially unchanged until the reign of Lord Dalhousie. He died in 1826 at Malta, where he was holding the office of Governor at the time. Lady Hastings survived until 1840.

JAMES WILSON.—In the great hall of the Dalhousie Institute, stands a fine full-length statue in white marble by Sir John Steell, R.S.A., of the Right Honourable JAMES WILSON, Financial Member of the Viceroy's Council from November 1859 to August 1860. The Institute was erected "as a monumental edifice to contain within its walls the statues and busts of great men" and for thirty-five years after its formal opening in 1870 by Lord Lawrence, it strove to fulfil the object of its existence. Until a few months ago there might have been seen ranged around the hall a number of busts of Mutiny heroes: and in the south-western corner, opposite the effigy of Wilson, was placed Sir John Steell's statue of Lord Dalhousie, which stood originally in Government House facing that of Lord Wellesley. But both Mutiny heroes and Governor-General have now been removed to the Indian Museum, pending their final transfer to the Victoria Memorial Hall. For some obscure reason, James Wilson has not been permitted to follow them. It is to be hoped that the omission will be rectified in the near future, for there is no denying the forlorn and forgotten aspect of the present situation of the memorial. James Wilson was the third son of a wealthy woollen manufacturer in Scotland and was born at Hawick in 1805. His rare mental gifts found scope in the realms of political economy and finance. He became a moving spirit in the anti-corn Law agitation and in consultation with Cobden founded in 1843, the *Economist*, still the leading monetary organ of London. Entering Parliament as member, first for Westbury and subsequently for Devonport, he became successively Secretary to the Board of Control (1848-1852), Financial Secretary to the Treasury (1853-58), and Vice-President of the Board of Trade and Paymaster-General in 1859, when he was also sworn of the Privy Council. He rapidly acquired a reputation in Parliament as an authority on financial questions, and the highest distinctions lay within his grasp, but he abandoned his prospects of office in England at the request of Lord Palmerston, who saw in him the only man who could restore equilibrium to the Indian exchequer after the Mutiny. The story is told that when the late Queen was informed by the Prime Minister of his intention to appoint Wilson as the first Finance Member of the Viceroy's Council, her first words were " But what will become of the *Economist?"* An admirable Editor was found, however, in Wilson's son-in-law, Walter Bagehot, and Wilson set out for Calcutta where he arrived in November, 1859. He died in less than a year at the age of fifty-five, spent with toil in an uncogenial and exacting climate: but not before he had during his nine months' tenure of office left an enduring mark upon Indian Finance. To him is due the imposition of an Income-tax, the creation of a Government paper currency and the remodelling of the whole system of accounts. The dictionary of National Biography describes Wilson as " very active in temperament, fertile in ideas, lucid in exposition. To the last hour of his life he was of a sanguine disposition. His memory was marvellous, his judgment remarkably keen. In society his vivacity of conversation was noteworthy." He was an extremely hard worker and his whole manner gave an impression of massive power and firm determination. There is a bust of Wilson in the national gallery at Edinburgh and his portrait hangs in the Town Hall of Hawick. Three years after his death, his nephew, William Wilson Hunter, landed in Calcutta to carry on the intellectual traditions of the family and to carve out a reputation for himself as brilliant and as enduring.

MAHARAJAH OF DURBHUNGA.—Proceeding down the south side of Dalhousie Square towards Hare Street, the visitor will next see at the south-west corner the white marble statue of the late MAHARAJAH OF DURBHUNGA, which is of interest, as the last work of the eminent sculptor Mr. E. Onslow Ford, R.A. It was unveiled by Sir Andrew Fraser, Lieutenant-Governor of Bengal, on the 25th March, 1904, and is the latest addition to the statues of Calcutta. The Maharajah is represented seated upon his *guddee* or chair of State, with a scimitar in the right hand and a shield in the left, and wearing the ancestral head-dress of his family and the robes and chain of a Knight Grand Commander of the Order of the Indian Empire.

Maharajah Sir Lakshmishwar Singh Bahadur, G.C.I.E., of Durbhunga, who was only in his forty-third year at the time of his death in 1898, was in every sense the best type of the Indian nobleman and landlord. He was the leading zemindar in Behar, where he owned no less than 2,152 square miles with a net yearly rental of 30 lakhs, and was the recognized head of the orthodox Hindoo community. His philanthropy and his munificent contributions to all public movements won for him the esteem of all classes and creeds. He took an active part in public life and enjoyed a high reputation as a progressive and liberal-minded statesman. With but slight interruptions he was a member of the Supreme Legislative Council from the year 1883 until his death, and latterly he sat in that body as the elected representative of the non-official members of the Bengal Council. Few Asiatics have combined more successfully in themselves the apparently incompatible characteristics of East and West.

Sir Ashley Eden.—In the north-west corner of Dalhousie Square and immediately opposite to Writers' Buildings is a seated marble statue by Sir Edgar Boehm of the Hon'ble Sir Ashley Eden, K.C.S.I., C.I.E., Lieutenant-Governor of Bengal from 1877 to 1882, and subsequently Member of the Council of India from 1882 until his death in 1887. The statue formerly stood on the site occupied by the Holwell obelisk.

The career of Sir Ashley Eden is one which the Indian civilian of to-day can scarcely hope to emulate. He was the younger son of the Bishop of Bath and Wells, who succeeded to the barony of Auckland on the death of his brother, the first Earl of that name and Governor-General of India from 1836 to 1842. With these natural advantages he was able to champion lost causes and advocate unpopular beliefs without inflicting injury upon his prospects or erecting an obstacle to his advancement. "There is not," it was said of him, "in the whole Indian Civil Service one who has been more emphatically a public man, regarding whom more facts are known or more lies told, or who has been the happy recipient of more rapid promotion." At 29 years of age he was Junior Secretary to the Board of Revenue, at 31, Secretary to the Government of Bengal, at 42, Chief Commissioner of British Burma, and at 46, Lieutenant-Governor of Bengal. And yet as a junior he had been the right-hand man of Sir John Peter Grant in his unpopular crusade in the sixties against the Indigo planters in Lower Bengal: and as a senior he was the real author of the Bill which fell upon Anglo-India in the eighties like a bombshell and has been fathered upon Sir Courtenay Ilbert. "The devil is loose." was the remark made in Calcutta when the news was received by telegram that Ashley Eden was to succeed Sir Richard Temple as Lieutenant-Governor of Bengal. But his tenure of the office was as orderly and peaceful and uneventful as it might be expected not to have been: and he will be best remembered as the beautifier and second creator of Darjeeling, which has borne testimony to his labours and her gratitude by the erection of a memorial fountain on the Chowrasta.

SIR STEUART BAYLEY.—In the opposite or north-eastern corner has been erected the white marble statue by W. Hamo Thorneycroft, R. A., of SIR STEUART COLVIN BAYLEY, K.C.S.I., C.I.E., Chief Commissioner of Assam from 1878 to 1881, Member of the Supreme Council from 1882 to 1887, and Lieutenant-Governor of Bengal from 1887 to 1890. In the last-mentioned year he was appointed to be Secretary in the Political Department at the India Office, and in 1897, a member of the Council of the Secretary of

State, an office which he has resigned during the year 1905. The statue is strikingly *négligé* in pose, and the spectacles give the appearance of blindness: but there is no denying the faithfulness of the resemblance to the original. Upon the pedestal is a lengthy inscription, which concludes by recording that the statue has been "erected by public subscription as a tribute of respect to a just and wise administrator whose generous sympathies endeared him to the people of Bengal." Sir Steuart Bayley, who passed out from Haileybury in 1855, is the youngest son of Mr. William Butterworth Bayley, who officiated as Governor-General of Bengal from March to July, 1828, during the interregnum between the departure of Earl Amherst and the arrival of Lord William Bentinck, and was subsequently a Director of the Company from 1833 to 1858, filling the office of Chairman in 1840. The statue stood until quite recently upon the grass plot in front of the Treasury Buildings, and was removed to Dalhousie Square in September 1905.

SIR JOHN WOODBURN.—Between these two statues and in the centre of the northern side of the Square it is intended to place Mr. George Frampton's equestrian statue of the late SIR JOHN WOODBURN, K.C.S.I., Lieutenant-Governor of Bengal from 1898 to 1902, which is understood to be approaching completion.

Meanwhile, we have only one more public memorial in Dalhousie Square to examine: and in many respects it will be adjudged to be among the most interesting of those that Calcutta has to offer to the gaze of the visitor.

THE HOLWELL OBELISK.—At the north-western corner of the Square, where a bewildering network of overhead wires marks the junction of the tramway lines opposite the Bengal Legislative Council-Chamber, there now stands once again the obelisk inscribed with the names of those who perished in the Black Hole on the 20th June, 1756. The monument was originally erected at the expense of John Zephaniah Holwell, one of the few survivors of the tragedy, who left India for good in 1760. It marked the site of the ditch of the unfinished ravelin outside the eastern curtain of the Fort, an earthwork hurriedly thrown up to defend the main gate. Here the corpses were flung without ceremony on the following morning: and it was not until 1766 that this "Ditch round the Old Fort," as it is termed in the Proceedings of the Council, was ordered to be filled up.

There is no lack of pictorial representation of the former monument. Upjohn's map of 1793 shows the obelisk as facing the eastern curtain of the ruined Fort, which was still cumbering the western side of Tank Square in its day. Daniell, who saw it in 1786, has introduced it into two of his *Views of Oriental Scenery*, both of which may be found reproduced in Dr. Busteed's *Echoes from Old Calcutta:* and in Fraser's Views of Calcutta, published in 1824, there is another illustration of it. The obelisk in the last named engraving looks at least 50 feet high and is not surrounded with any railings. It seems in consequence to be the lounging place for lower class loafers of all sorts who gossip squatting around and against it. A barber is seen plying his craft in the favourite posture of these Eastern experts. His back is to the base of the monument, while overhead is stretched his outspread cloth between the upper ledge of the pedestal and three or four stakes let into the ground a couple of yards off. The tent thus improvised shelters the operator and a few of his customers. All this unsightliness may explain why the historic structure had a few years before the date of this engraving, disappeared from the City of Palaces, after, as tradition says, it had been struck by lightning. It was taken down in 1821 under the orders of the Marquess of Hastings, but there is no foundation for the surmise that the step was dictated by the Governor-General's extreme sensibility which led him to consider the retention of this relic of the past politically undesirable as likely to wound the feelings of Indians and to recall at the same time memories of a disaster to the English arms.

From this time onward for some eighty years Calcutta remained without even a sculptured tablet to the memory of the hundred and twenty-three of her citizens whose fate will always be so closely associated with her name. It was reserved for Lord Curzon to repair the wrong: and under his directions, a white marble replica of the original brick and plaster monument was erected on the spot, the statue of Sir Ashley Eden which had been set up on the site in the seventies being removed to Dalhousie Square. In his speech at the unveiling of the memorial on December 19th, 1902, His Excellency related how his interest in the restoration of this landmark of Calcutta was first awakened by his reading on his way out to India of Dr. Busteed's delightful *Echoes from old Calcutta.*

The tablet on the original obelisk bore the following inscription written by Holwell himself :—

To the Memorys of

Edward Eyre and William Baillie, Esqs.; the Revd. Jervas Bellamy; Messrs. Jenks, Revely, Law, Coates, Valicourt, Jeb, Toriano E. Page, S. Page, Grub, Street, Harod, P. Johnstone, Ballard, N. Drake, Carse, Knapton, Gosling, Dod, and Dalrymple; Captains Clayton, Buchanan, and Witherington; Lieutenants Bishop, Hays, Blagg, Simson, and J. Bellamy; Ensigns Paccard, Scot, Hastings, C. Wedderburn, and Dumbleton; Sea-captains Hunt, Osburne, and Purnell; Messrs. Carey, Leech, Steavenson, Guy, Porter, Parker, Caulker, Bendal and Atkinson;
Who, with sundry other inhabitants, Military and
Militia, to the number of 123 persons, were by
the tyrannic violence of Suraj-ud-Dowlah,
Suba of Bengal,
Suffocated in the Black Hole Prison of Fort William,
on the night of the 20th day of June, 1756,
and promiscuously thrown the suc-
ceeding morning into the Ditch of
the ravelin of this place.
This monument is erected by their surviving fellow
sufferer,
J. Z. Holwell.
This horrid act of violence was as amply as deservedly
revenged on Suraj-ud-Dowlah, by His Majesty's
arms, under the conduct of Vice-Admiral
Watson and Colonel Clive, Anno 1757.

In the list which Holwell gives in his published account of the Tragedy* four additional names are given: three Sergeants of Militia, Abraham, Cartwright and Bleau,

* See Holwell's Tracts.

and a gentleman in the Civil Service of the name of "Bing," identified by Dr. Busteed as a nephew of the ill-fated Admiral, an order for whose arrest went from England to Gibraltar in this very month of June, 1756. There is no explanation as to why these names were omitted from the epitaph on the monument. Dr. Busteed suggests an oversight on the part of the sculptor.

Lord Curzon has, however, introduced material alterations in this and in other respects in the inscription affixed under his orders. The bitter reference to the personal responsibility of Suraj-ud-Dowlah for the tragedy was not, in his opinion, wholly justified by our fuller knowledge of the facts, and has been accordingly struck out. Furthermore, whereas the original inscription only gave the few names that Holwell could remember and gave some of them inaccurately, a completer and more correct list has been compiled by careful examination of contemporary records, lists and registers, conducted by Lord Curzon himself in conjunction with Mr. S. C. Hill of the Indian Record Department, now Director of Public Instruction at Nagpore. The result is that the new monument records not only Holwell's 50 names, but 20 additional ones of those who died in the prison. There are in all six tablets, two of the sides of the pedestal being left blank. Not only are all those enumerated, who perished in the Black Hole itself, but a list is added of those who are known to have been killed or to have died of their wounds during the siege, and who either did not survive to enter the prison or afterwards succumbed to its effects. Among these last are John Francis Pickard

(Paccard) and Thomas Purnell whose names appear in Holwell's list among those who died in the Black Hole.

The following are the various inscriptions upon the tablets, beginning with the side which faces the buildings in Charnock Place, and walking round the obelisk from left to right. The last inscription is on the south-west :—

I.

This monument
Has been erected by
Lord Curzon, Viceroy and Governor-General of India,
In the year 1902
Upon the site
And in reproduction of the design
Of the original monument
To the memory of the 123 persons
Who perished in the Black Hole Prison
Of Old Fort William
On the night of the 20th June, 1756.
The former memorial was raised by
Their surviving fellow-sufferer
J. Z. Holwell, Governor of Fort William,
On the spot where the bodies of the dead
Had been thrown into the ditch of the ravelin.
It was removed in 1821.

II.

To the Memory of
Edward Eyre, William Baillie,
Revd. Jervas Bellamy, John Jenks,
Roger Reveley, John Carse, John Law,
Thomas Coles, James Valicourt,
John Jebb, Richard Toriano,
Edward Page, Stephen Page,
William Grub, John Street,
Aylmer Harrod, Patrick Johnstone,

George Ballard, Nathan Drake,
William Knapton, Francis Gosling,
Robert Byng, John Dodd,
Stair Dalrymple, David Clayton,
John Buchanan, and Lawrence Witherington,
Who perished in the Black Hole Prison.

III.

The names inscribed on the tablet
On the reverse side of this
Are the names of those persons
Who are known to have been killed
Or to have died of their wounds
During the Siege of Calcutta
In June, 1756,
And who either did not survive
To enter the Black Hole Prison
Or afterwards succumbed to its effects.

IV.

The names of those who perished
In the Black Hole Prison,
Inscribed upon the reverse side
Of this monument,
Are in excess of the list
Recorded by Governor Holwell
Upon the original monument.
The additional names, and
The Christian names of the remainder,
Have been recovered from oblivion
By reference to contemporary documents.

V.

To the Memory of
Peter Smith, Thomas Blagg,
John Francis Pickard, John Pickering,
Michael Collings, Thomas Best,
Ralph Thoresby, Charles Smith,

Robert Wilkinson, Henry Stopford,
William Stopford, Thomas Purnell,
Robert Talbot, William Tidecomb,
Daniel Macpherson, John Johnson, and
Messrs. Whitby, Surman, Bruce,
Montrong, and Janiko, who perished
During the Siege of Calcutta.

VI.

To the Memory of
Richard Bishop, Francis Hayes,
Colin Simson, John Bellamy,
William Scott, Henry Hastings,
Charles Wedderburn, William Dumbleton,
Bernard Abraham, William Cartwright,
Jacob Bleau, Henry Hunt,
Michael Osborne, Peter Carey,
Thomas Leach, Francis Stevenson,
James Guy, James Porter,
William Parker, Eleanor Weston, and
Messrs. Cocker, Bendall, Atkinson, Jennings,
Reid, Barnet, Frere, Wilson,
Burton, Lyon, Hillier, Tilley, and Alsop,
Who perished in the Black Hole Prison.

The site of the Black Hole itself lies immediately behind the Monument to the west: but we may conveniently postpone our pilgrimage to the historic spot until a future occasion, when we shall endeavour, by means of the tablets erected under the directions of Lord Curzon, to picture to ourselves the various localities within the Old Fort as it stood in the year of the tragedy. In the same chapter will be found collected a few stray notes which will not be without interest regarding the more prominent of those who stand here commemorated upon the site of their rude grave.

IN THE NORTHERN QUARTER.—Proceeding northward into

the quarter of the town in which the Indian element is predominant, we shall find several memorials to eminent public men which still await inspection.

Our most convenient method of visiting them will be to take a Shambazar tram from Dalhousie Square and to request the conductor to drop us at College Square. Here are grouped together the Senate House, the Presidency College, the Hare School and the Hindoo School and Sanskrit College. in each there are interesting monuments to be examined.

Prosunno Coomar Tagore.—In the portico of the Senate House has been placed a fine marble seated statue of the Hon'ble Baboo Prosunno Coomar Tagore, C.S.I., founder of the Tagore Professorship of Law in the University of Calcutta. The inscription upon the red granite pedestal records that he was born on the 21st December, 1801, and died on the 30th August, 1868. In his threefold capacity of lawyer, public man, and author, Baboo Prosunno Coomar Tagore was the most conspicuous man of his day. He was the first native of India to be appointed to the Viceregal Legislative Council, and he was twice nominated to a seat in the Bengal Council. His professional income at the Bar is said to have averaged two lakhs of rupees a year, but he was a man of private means and retired from practice while still in the prime of life, in order to devote himself to public matters. At his death it was found that he had left no less than six and a half lakhs of rupees by way of legacies and bequests for religious, charitable and educational purposes. The largest of these was the sum of three lakhs which forms the endowment of the Tagore Professorship of Law. His son, Ganendra Mohun Tagore, enjoys the distinction of being the first Indian called to the English Bar. He was admitted as an advocate of the Supreme Court in March, 1860. Having become a convert to Christianity, he was excluded from inheritance by his father who left his vast landed estates to his nephew, the present Maharajah Bahadur Sir Jotendro Mohun Tagore, K.C.S.I. Long and expensive litigation ensued, and under the modifications introduced into the will by the Privy Council, the estates will revert to the heirs of the disinherited son on the death of the Maharajah Bahadur.

DAVID HARE.—In the adjoining enclosure of the Hare School, there stands facing College Street, a statue of DAVID HARE, watchmaker, philanthropist, and father of native education.

The inscription upon the statue, which was formerly surmounted by a dome, runs as follows:—

"In honor of David Hare, who by steady industry having acquired an ample competence, cheerfully relinquished the prospect of returning to enjoy it in his native land in order to promote the welfare of that of his adoption. To the close of his irreproachable and useful life, he made the improvement, intellectual and moral, as well as the condition, in sickness no less than in health, of the native youth of Bengal, the object of his constant care and unwearying solicitude, and they, in token of gratitude and veneration for the memory of their constant, generous and most disinterested benefactor, have erected this statue."

On the southern side of College Square stands a grey-painted masonry tomb. Here are deposited the remains of Hare, who succumbed in twenty-four hours to an attack of cholera in 1842. The tomb is still an object of veneration to students, and it will always be found decorated with flowers upon the first of June, the anniversary of his death. The monument, which was erected by the rupee subscriptions of the Indian community, bears the following inscription, which is eloquent of the feelings entertained by them towards him:—

"This tomb, erected by his native friends and pupils, encloses the mortal remains of David Hare. He was a native of Scotland, and came to this city in the year 1800, and died 1st June, 1842, aged 67 years. After acquiring a competence by probity and industry in his calling as a watchmaker, he adopted for his own the country of his sojourn, and cheerfully devoted the remainder of his life with unwearying zeal and benevolence to one pervading and darling object, one for which he spared not personal trouble, money or influence, namely, the education and moral improvement of the natives of Bengal, thousands of whom regarded him in life with filial love and reverence, and lament him in death as their best and most disinterested friend, who was to them even as a father."

Hare's labours were not confined to the establishment of the Hindoo College. He spared no pains to increase the usefulness and popularity of the Medical College in the early days of its struggle against prejudice and ignorance. Prior also to 1817 he spent much time in conjunction with Rajah Sir Radha Kanta Deb of the Sobhabazar family, in improving the vernacular schools, by the deputation of inspecting pundits and the grant of printed books. In public matters he was equally energetic and enlightened. He strenuously advocated the introduction of trial by jury for civil cases, and was an ardent champion of the emancipation of the Press and a vigorous opponent of the cooly traffic. Of him it might truly be said that he was the friend of the poor, and few Englishmen of non-official rank have attained so important and influential a position in purely Indian Society.

The Hindoo School and Sanskrit College, founded in 1817 on land made over to Government by David Hare as a free gift, stands opposite upon the northern side of College Square. It was the first institution of its kind in Calcutta, where the only English Schools hitherto had been charitable institutions or private academies.

Pundit Ishwar Chandra Vidyasagar.—Under a canopy in front of the building, which is entered from a turning off College Street, there has been placed a full-sized seated statue of Pundit Ishwar Chandra Vidyasagar, C.I.E., who, as the inscription upon the pedestal relates, "from a pupil became the Principal of the Sanskrit College." The statue was "erected, with subscriptions raised by the public, as a token of their profound respect for his great virtues and a tribute to his eminent services to the country as scholar, author, educationist, reformer, and philanthropist."

The Pundit, who was born on the 26th September, 1820, and died on the 28th July, 1891, may be described without exaggeration as one of the most remarkable Bengalees of his generation. At the age of 21 he was in 1841 appointed Head Pundit of the College of Fort William, and in 1849 became Head Assistant. In the following year he was made a Professor at the Sanskrit College and became Principal in January, 1851. He was, in addition to his duties as Principal, appointed in 1855 a special Inspector of Schools, and helped in the establishment of a number of vernacular schools and also of girls' schools. But he came into conflict with the Director of Public Instruction in connexion with his efforts in the latter direction and threw up his appointment under Government in 1858. He continued, however, for some years after to be unofficially consulted by Government on educational matters: and had already in the Act of Incorporation of the Calcutta University in 1857, been named as one of its first Fellows. In 1877, he received a certificate of Honour at the Proclamation Durbar at Delhi, and in January 1880 was made a C.I.E. on the recommendation of Lord Lytton. While driving the late Miss Mary Carpenter from the Bally Station (near Calcutta) to the Utterpara Girls' School, he had in 1866, a serious fall from his carriage, from the effects of which he suffered up to the day of his death, a quarter of a century later. He was a Hindoo of the orthodox type, but he was deeply conscious at the same time of the need for improvement in the condition of the women of India. On their behalf he started both the widow marriage movement and the agitation against polygamy. The first received legislative sanction in 1856 by the Act which authorises the re-marriage of Hindoo widows: but the second ended in failure. He was never weary of advocating the cause of female education, supporting his arguments by quotations from the Shastras: and the foundation by him in 1864 of the Metropolitan Institution furnished the type and pattern for many similar schools for boys. His Sanskrit and Bengalee works possess a high educational value, and many of them still hold their position as standard authorities upon the subjects of which they treat. His death was largely mourned throughout Bengal, and the statue which is now engaging our attention, and which represents him seated in Oriental fashion and in a meditative attitude, is only one of several memorials which may be found in the important educational centres of the province.

RAI KRISTO DAS PAL, BAHADUR.—A little higher up the road, and at the junction made with College Street by Harrison Road, the great artery which runs from Howrah Bridge to Sealdah Railway Station, there stands Geflowski's full-sized statue in white marble of RAI KRISTO DAS PAL, Bahadur, C.I.E. It was unveiled in March, 1894, by Lord Elgin, the then Viceroy, and bears the following inscription upon its pedestal:—

"To the memory of the Hon'ble Rai Kristo Das Pal Bahadur, C.I.E. Born April, 1839. Died 24th July, 1884. As Secretary to the British Indian Association, as a Member of the Municipal Corporation, as a journalist and as a legislator, he brought to the service of his country a cultivated understanding, great talents, untiring industry and a lofty patriotism. This statue has been erected as a tribute to his memory by his grateful countrymen and many other admiring friends."

Rai Kristo Das Pal was eminently a man of the people: his father was of very small means, and his rise to influence and rank was entirely the result of his own merits and exertions. His connection with the British Indian Association, the great representative body of Bengal landholders, dated from December, 1858, when he quitted the office of translator to the Judge of the Twenty-four Perganas to act as Assistant to Baboo Hurrish Chunder Mukerjee, the then Secretary. In 1879, he was appointed Secretary, and continued to hold the post until his death. Such was the position he achieved for himself as spokesman of the landowning community, that in 1883, he was nominated as an Additional Member of the Viceroy's Council to represent the Bengal Zemindars in the discussions upon the Rent Bill which eventually became the Bengal Tenancy Act. He had already in 1875 been appointed to the Bengal Legislative Council and was three times re-appointed. As a journalist he was no less distinguished. Following Baboo Hurish Chandra Mookerjee in editorial charge of the *Hindoo Patriot*, he speedily brought that paper to a position of remarkable authority and weight. The power wielded by the so-called "Native Press" to-day is largely due to the sagacity and the force of character with which Rai Kristo Das Pal examined and criticized the public questions of his time. Sir Richard Temple, who had a high opinion of him, like every Lieutenant-Governor with whom he came in contact, described him as the best informed Indian he had ever met, with the exception of Sir Tanjore Madhava Rao. It is to be regretted that his statue should convey so inadequate an impression of his appearance and his personality: for as an orator and a publicist he was without a rival among his contemporaries in Bengal. A second memorial in the form of a portrait will be found in the Town Hall and another picture hangs in the Central Municipal Office.

RAJAH KALI KRISHNA DEB.—We must now continue our walk up College Street until we reach Beadon Street. Here we turn to the left, and proceed in a westerly direction as far as the pleasant open space, which goes by the name of Beadon Square, and stands at the junction of Beadon Street and Upper Chitpore Road. In the centre of this square is a handsome seated statue in marble of Rajah KALI KRISHNA DEB, Bahadur, of the Sobhabazar family.

Born in 1808, the Rajah was the second son of Rajah Raj Krishna Deb of Sobhabazar, and grandson of Maharajah Nubkissen, the famous Dewan of Lord Clive and successful rival of Nuncomar. After the death in 1867 of his relative, Raja Sir Radha Kanta Deb Bahadur, K.C.S.I., he assumed the position of leader of the orthodox Hindoo community in Bengal. He was a man of considerable literary talent, and his translations from the Sanskrit won for him gold medals from German, Austrian, French and Belgian Governments. He took a prominent part in all public movements and was a Justice of the Peace and a Fellow of the University. His death occurred in 1874 at Benares at the age of sixty-six. The statue which perpetuates his memory is very graceful in pose and attractive in execution. There is also a portrait in the Town Hall to testify to the regard and high esteem in which he was held by his contemporaries.

CHAPTER IV.

THE OLD FORT AND THE BLACK HOLE.

The idea of establishing a fortified fort somewhere near the mouth of the Hooghly, as the best means of protecting the English trade from the oppressive exactions of the Nabob of Bengal and his officials, seems to have been first suggested by William Hedges, who administered the Company's affairs in Bengal during the years 1682 to 1684. But the first step had still to be taken when Sir John Goldsborough came to visit Suttanuttee after Charnock's death in 1693 : and a spot was ordered by him to be enclosed with a mud wall, pending the necessary permission from the Nabob. This was not conceded until 1696, when Sir Charles Eyre was Agent, and then only indirectly. The Hindoo Rajahs on the westward of the river having rebelled against the Imperial authority, the Nabob begged the English, French, and Dutch to take steps to defend their interests. The invitation was quickly accepted, and preparations made for the construction of a fort. Two years later the English procured for the sum of sixteen thousand rupees, letters patent from Prince Azim-ush-shan, grandson of Aurungzeb, and now Nabob of Bengal, which enabled them to purchase from the holders the right to the rents of the three villages of Calcutta, Suttanuttee and Govindpore, adjacent to the factory. They had now the means to defray the charges of the small garrison required for their proposed fort, but the progress made in building was slow. Eventually on August 20th, 1700, the work was so far advanced as to be dignified with the name of the reigning king, and Fort William came into existence. There was little more, however, to meet the eye than a walled enclosure and a bastion. But in 1701 a second bastion was added, and in 1707, the two remaining bastions were added on the river-side, facing the older bastions on the east.

The spot chosen by Goldsborough was the highest piece of ground on the river-side. In order to picture it, we must remember that in those days the river flowed much further east than it does now, and that the present Strand Road was then deep under water. The actual site of the Fort is the plot now occupied by the General Post Office, the adjoining block of Government Offices, the Custom House and the East Indian Railway House. The warehouses built along the south side of the Fort skirted Koila Ghât Street. The north side was in Fairlie Place, and on the west the river lapped the walls. The east front looked out on Clive Street and Dalhousie Square, then known as the Lal Bagh or the Park. Immediately outside the Fort and before the east curtain-wall stood the Church of St. Anne consecrated on June 5th, 1709, and named after the patron saint of the Queen. It occupied the site of the modern Bengal Council Chamber and remained the church of the Settlement until 1756. In 1709 also, the old tank on the green in front of the Fort, was extended and deepened. It had formerly been within the enclosure of the old zemindar's cutcherry and still adorns the centre of Dalhousie Square. The year 1706 had already witnessed the destruction of the cutcherry, which had sheltered the Company's records since the days of Charnock, and the erection of a more imposing factory building.

The Fort was in shape an irregular tetragon. Its north side was 340 feet long: its south side 485: its east and west sides, each 710 feet. At the four corners were small square bastions, each mounting ten guns, and the main east gate, which projected, carried five guns. Curtain-walls about 4 feet thick and eighteen feet high connected the bastions. The wall on the river-side was of solid masonry, with embrasures for heavy cannon, and the space between this river-wall and the west curtain was closed at each end by small cross-walls with palisaded gates. Within, the fort was cut into two unequal sections by a block of low buildings running east and west, damp and unhealthy, and known as the Long Row, in which were housed the young gentlemen of the Company's Service. These were the Writers' Buildings of the first half of the eighteenth century. The northern or smaller section of the Fort contained the magazine and armoury, the dispensary and various shops and stores. It had one small river gate near which stood the flagstaff. The south section of the Fort had two gates, one leading to the river, the steps and the landing stage, the other opening out on the great avenue to the eastward, now variously called Dalhousie Square, North, Lall Bazar and Bow Bazar, leading to the "Boytaconnah tree" at Sealdah. The buildings on the south side were used for storing the Company's goods: the export and import warehouses built on the outside of the south curtain in 1741, following the line of Koila Ghât Street. West of the warehouses was the carpenter's yard.

In the middle of the south section of the Fort was the Governor's House, "the best and most regular Piece of Architecture" that was ever seen in the East by the much-travelled and observant Alexander Hamilton. This building formed three sides of a rectangle, the west and principal face being 245 feet long. In the centre of the western face was the great gate, and from it a colonnade ran down to the watergate and the landing stage. The large hall and the principal rooms of the factory lay on the first floor, which was approached by a grand staircase to the left of the great gate. The south-east wing contained the apartments of the Governor. A raised cloister ran round the three sides of the court enclosed within the building.

On either side of the east gate of the Fort and looking on to "Tank Square" there extended a double row of arches parallel to the east curtain-wall. The first row of the line of arches to the left served to contain a range of rooms built against the wall, the second row formed a verandah or piazza west of the rooms. Each of these arches measured 8 feet 9 inches. The first four between the gate and the south-east bastion were used as the court of guard, and were left open to the piazza in front of them. The next nine arches formed rooms, communicating with each other and employed as soldiers' barracks. They were separated from the piazza by a small dwarf wall or parapet built between the arches. The fourteenth and fifteenth arches adjoined the stairs leading to the bastion, and were completely walled in. This was the military prison or Black Hole, and here it was that the tragedy was enacted which has given a lurid prominence to the fateful year 1756.

Such then was the aspect of Old Fort William. For the visitor the best way to view the remains of the actual site is to turn down Koila Ghât Street and enter the Post Office compound through the old Post Office building and its new red brick extension. The sunken arches immediately in front, where the Post Office wagons are now kept, constitute all that survives of the Old Fort: they were once part of an arcade within the south curtain used for the import and export warehouses. The Postal employés have their tiffin-room above, and two arches at the east end have been closed in and made into a kitchen. The room thus formed is a good deal larger than the Black Hole, but it serves to give some idea of what it was like. Behind the old arcades ran the line of the south curtain wall. Here, as elsewhere, under the directions of Lord Curzon, the outline of the Old Fort has been (wherever practicable) marked off on brass lines sunk in the stone pavement, and the identity of the different features of interest indicated by inscribed tablets affixed to the adjoining walls. The first of the two tablets at this point bears the following inscription: "The brass lines in the stone on the adjacent ground mark the position and extent of the south curtain of Old Fort William." The second is thus engraved: "The two lines of twelve arches to the west of this tablet are all that now remains above ground of Old Fort William and originally formed a portion of the arcade within the south curtain. The Black Hole prison was a small room formed by bricking up two arches of a similar but smaller arcade within the east curtain, south of the east gate."

Passing on, to the right, up the compound of the Post Office, until the gate in Dalhousie Square is reached, the visitor walks along what was once the site of the parade-ground. On the right, in old days, were ranges of arches used as warehouses: and on the left was the parade-ground, partly paved with brick and partly turfed. At the Dalhousie Square gate is the actual site of the Black Hole to which we shall shortly return. The massive masonry gate which stood here until 1900 has been removed, so that the site of the prison may be easily visible, and the site itself has been covered with polished black marble and enclosed with a railing, an inscription on a black marble tablet being placed on the wall above in 1900 under the orders of Lord Curzon. Another tablet intending to guide visitors to the historic spot will be found at the corner of the Post Office by the gate on the side facing Dalhousie Square. Postponing further examination for the present, and passing through the gate into the Square, the visitor will see brass lines on the steps of the Post Office which mark the angle of the south-east bastion, the thickness of the wall being exactly indicated by the space between the lines. On the wall adjoining is a tablet which tells us that the extreme south-east point of the bastion was 95 feet away. Proceeding northward along the footpath through Charnock Place a tablet will meet the eye at the corner of the red-brick office of the Collector of Calcutta, opposite the marble replica of the Holwell

Monument. This marks the entrance of the east gate through which the bodies of those who perished in the Black Hole were brought and thrown into the ditch of the ravelin. Proceeding still northward and entering the compound of the Custom House, the visitor will see a line of outhouses on the right. A tablet will remind him that these represent roughly the line of the Long Row in which the writers of the Company lived, and which divided the Fort into two sections. Walking on through the compound, a tablet is seen which marks the position of the west curtain-wall, immediately behind which in old days was the wharf and the river-side. Retracing his steps, the visitor, if he turns to the left and pushes his way into the purlieus of the Custom House, will find the brass lines and the tablet indicating the whereabouts of the north wall of the factory, the principal building in the Old Fort. Leaving the compound of the Custom House and walking along Clive Street to the East Indian Railway House, a tablet will be found commemorating the position of part of the north-east bastion: and turning down Fairlie Place, another will be observed marking the position of the north-west bastion. Continuing a little further down Fairlie Place and proceeding till the quadrangle of the Railway House is reached, the visitor will perceive on the wall to his right one more tablet recording the site of the North River Gate through which Seraj-ud-Dowlah entered the Fort on the evening of June 20th, 1756. Behind this tablet to the south of the gate stood the great flagstaff.

Finally, if the visitor be desirous of still further extending his researches, he will discover in the Victoria Memorial Hall collection, now temporarily housed in the Indian Museum, an admirable model of the Fort and the Church of St. Anne, prepared under the supervision of Dr. C. R. Wilson, whose labours have thrown so much light upon the whereabouts and the surroundings of the Old Fort and whose premature death in 1904, has been an irreparable loss to the small band of students of the past history of the British Empire in India.

The entire circuit of the Old Fort has now been made: but we have yet to pay our pilgrimage to the site of the Black Hole itself, which we have only hurriedly examined in passing. The visitor will discover the guide-tablet almost behind the Holwell obelisk at the northern end of the eastern verandah of the General Post Office building, which will enable the spot to be readily ascertained. It bears the words "Behind the gateway immediately adjoining this spot is the site of the Black Hole prison of Old Fort William." Entering the iron gate accordingly, which lies to the right of the tablet, the visitor will come in full view of a railed enclosure, containing a polished black marble pavement o- slab, which covers the exact breadth of the prison, 14 feet 10 inches, but not its full length of 18 feet, as about one-third of the area at the north end is appropriated by the Custom-House building. Immediately above the slab, and upon the wall of this building, is a smaller slab, also of black marble, which bears the following inscription:—

"The marble pavement below this spot was placed here by Lord Curzon, Viceroy and Governor-General of India, in 1900, to mark the site of the prison in Old Fort

William, known as the Black Hole, in which 146 British inhabitants of Calcutta were confined on the night of the 20th June, 1756, and from which only 23 came out alive."

For many years the spot remained altogether forgotten. But in 1863, Mr. R. Roskell Bayne, in the course of preparing the foundations of the East India Railway Company's offices, came upon what he saw must be the remnants of the northern curtain and bastions of the Old Fort: and by careful measurements and further excavations, he was enabled to plot out not only the site of the Black Hole, but to verify the recorded descriptions of the Fort by contemporary writers. The small depth to which the foundations of the curtain walls were carried, astonished Mr. Bayne. When the ground was faulty, *sâl* timbers were freely used and built upon, but deep foundations appeared not to be thought of. The masonry, however, was of such strength that pickaxe and crowbar were of no avail, and blasting by gunpowder was resorted to. Mr. Bayne's researches were continued by Dr. Busteed with much care and labour and completed by Dr. C. R. Wilson in 1891, when a portion of the old Custom House was pulled down, and the ground opened up for laying the foundations of the new offices of the Calcutta Collectorate. During these latter investigations, the walls and lower dungeon of the Black Hole were found, and the site being now fixed without doubt, the opportunity was taken to mark the spot with a granite slab, which bore, however, no inscription and very properly has been removed to make way for Lord Curzon's commemorative tablet.

A reference to the last edition of Dr. Busteed's *Echoes from Old Calcutta* will disclose on page 28 a "conjectural view" of the Black Hole and adjacent chambers as seen from the parade-ground within the Fort. With its details in our mind, we may repeat briefly the description we have already given. There was a double row of arches running from the fortified gate in the eastern curtain wall (which fronted Dalhousie Square) to the south-east bastion. The two arches at the end, adjoining the steps which led up to the bastion, were bricked up and used as a military prison. The dimensions of the room are given by Orme as "not twenty feet square." Holwell calls it a cube of about 18 feet: but Secretary Cooke, another of the survivors, is more precise, and says it was about 18 feet long and 14 feet wide. On the east and south it was bounded by dead walls, on the north by a dividing wall reaching to the roof, in which was a door, and on the west, looking out on the parade ground, the outer arches had been blocked up, space being left only for two small windows strongly barred with iron. These windows were the only outlet for light and air, but the relief afforded was of the slightest. "Before the chamber," writes Orme, "was a verandah or open gallery of arched masonry, and intended to shelter the soldiers from the sun and rain: but being low, it almost totally obstructed the chambers behind." The windows faced this verandah, and the dark, dismal and stifling nature of the accommodation may be imagined, even when the chamber was put to its legitimate use as a punishment cell.

In 1803, when Lord Valentia made the grand tour, the

Black Hole prison was still standing. It was then part of a godown, and so filled with goods that entrance was impossible. Nine years later it was on the point of disappearance. A correspondent, *Asiaticus*, who must not be confused with the Captain Philip Dormer Stanhope who wrote under the same name in 1785, has left the following account of it in a letter to the *Asiatic Journal*: "The formidable Black Hole is now no more. Early in the year 1812 I visited it. It was situate in the Old Fort of Calcutta and was then on the eve of demolition. Since that time the Fort has come down, and on its site have been erected some extensive warehouses of the Company. I recollect joining one of the party in Calcutta for the purpose of paying a last visit to this melancholy spot. It consisted of three married ladies, two gentlemen, their husbands and myself. The ladies were successful, by noise and laughter, in dissipating gloomy recollection, but I had been better pleased had they suffered us to recall in some measure to our minds those events connected with the spot on which we stood. It presented on entering, the appearance of an oven: being long, dark and narrow. One window, if I recollect right, was the utmost, and this secured by bars. The escape of even the small number who survived the horrid fate of the rest is surprising, and can only be accounted for by the accident of their being near the window, and the night air, which in Bengal is commonly damp, allaying the fever which consumed the rest. Perhaps too the pungent effluvia of the dead bodies, which on all sides surrounded them, may have possessed on the atmosphere, in some slight degree, the effects of vinegar; thus converting what at the moment must have appeared the most dreadful of evils into a security for those who outlived the night."

The number of persons who became prisoners, on the Fort falling into the enemy's hands, on the evening of the 20th of June, 1756, was one hundred and forty-six. Some were English, some were "black Christians" or half-caste Portuguese: and there was hardly a condition in society unrepresented. They were all disarmed, and ordered to await the pleasure of Seraj-ud-Dowlah, who presently entered the Fort in his litter by the north river gate. Holwell had three interviews with him, the last being held in the great hall of the Governor's House. After much useless discussion the Nabob retired to rest, giving orders that the prisoners should be secured for the night, but that no harm should happen to them. What followed may best be told in Holwell's own words:—

"As soon as it was dark, we were all, without distinction, directed by the guard over us to collect ourselves into one body and sit down quietly, under the arched verandah, or piazza, to the west of the Black Hole prison and the barracks to the left of the Court of Guard; and just over against the windows of the Governor's easterly apartments. Besides the guard over us, another was placed at the foot of the stairs at the south end of this verandah, leading up to the south-east bastion to prevent any of us escaping that way. On the parade (where you will remember the two twenty-four pounders stood) were also drawn up about four or five hundred gun men with lighted matches. At this time the factory was in flames to the right and left of us; to the right the Armoury and

Laboratory; to the left the Carpenter's yard; though at this time we imagined it was the cotta warehouses. They ordered us all to rise up and go into the barracks to the left of the Court of Guard. The barracks have a large wooden platform for the soldiers to sleep on, and are open to the west by arches and a small parapet-wall, corresponding to the arches of the verandah without. In we went most readily and were pleasing ourselves with the prospect of passing a comfortable night on the platform, little dreaming of the infernal apartments in reserve for us, for we were no sooner all within the barracks than the guards advanced to the inner arches and parapet-wall, and with their muskets presented, ordered us to go into the room at the southernmost end of the barracks, commonly called the Black Hole prison, whilst others from the Court of Guard, with clubs and drawn scimitars, pressed upon those of us next to them. This stroke was so sudden, so unexpected, and the throng and pressure so great upon us next the door of the Black Hole prison, that there was no resisting it; but like one agitated wave impelling another, we were obliged to give way and enter. The rest followed like a torrent, few amongst us, the soldiers excepted, having the least idea of the dimensions of a place we had never seen: for if we had, we should at all events have rushed upon the guard, and been, as the lesser evil, by our own choice, cut to pieces. Figure to yourself, if possible, the situation of a hundred and forty-six wretches, exhausted by continual fatigue and action, thus crammed together in a cube of about eighteen feet, in a close sultry night, in Bengal, shut up to the eastward and southward (the only quarters from whence air could reach us) by dead walls and by a wall and a door to the north, open only to the westward by two windows strongly barred with iron, from which we could receive scarce any the least circulation of fresh air."

The monsoon, as a matter of fact, did not burst until the night of the following day, the 21st, when it rained in torrents. Those who know from bitter experience what a Calcutta night can be like during the last few days before the "breaking of the rains," must take into account also the heat and the smoke of the burning buildings around, if they desire to realize how utterly unbearable the temperature must have been. It will serve no useful purpose to recall in detail the horrors which marked the passing of the next ten hours. "Nothing in history or fiction can approach them:" and we may be content with borrowing Dr. Busteed's admirable summary of this portion of Holwell's narrative. On realizing the trap they were in, Holwell besought his fellow-captives to endeavour to keep calm as their only chance of escape from death. At first they listened to his entreaty, and nothing was heard but the cries and groans of the many wounded. Holwell had been one of the first thrust into prison, and had gained the window nearest the door, where he took with him two of the youngest wounded officers. From his position of advantage he tried to bribe an old jemadar of the guard to try and get the door opened or the prisoners divided: but it was of no avail. In a few moments all were streaming with perspiration and tormented with an intolerable thirst. All, save Holwell and two or three next to him, tore off their clothes. In order to procure some movement of air, an attempt was made to sit and rise alternately at word of command, but this proved fatal to many who (so tightly were they wedged) had not strength to regain their feet and were trampled to death. From time to time fruitless efforts were made to open the door. In about an hour all, except those at the windows, were becoming outrageous from thirst. In response to their cries for water, the old jemadar had some brought up in skins to the window nearest the door. Holwell and the two wounded lads took it in as fast as they could, in hats squeezed through the bars, but the little that wetted the lips of those who clutched for it merely intensified their agonies. More terrible to Holwell even than his own thirst were the entreaties of those at the back of the prison whom he could not reach, "calling on me by the tender consideration of friendship and affection, and who knew they were really dear to me." So uncontrollable was the desire for water that those who had posts of vantage at the other window, forsook them and fought for the smallest drop. For two hours the struggle was prolonged, to the enjoyment of the wretches without who doled out paltry supplies and held up lanterns to the bars to gloat over the Inferno within.

Holwell's strength now began to fail him. His immediate companions were dead at his feet, and "determined to give up everything I called to those nearest to me and begged, as the last instance of their regard, they would remove the pressure upon me and permit me to retire out of the window to die in quiet. They gave way, and with much difficulty I forced a passage into the centre where the throng was less by the many dead. I travelled over the dead to the further end of the platform. Death I expected as unavoidable, and only lamented its slow approach, though the moment I quitted the window my breathing grew short and painful." Soon the deprivation of air caused torturing pains in the chest, and in a few minutes he had "by an effort of double the strength I ever possessed," pushed his way to the opposite window to where he had formerly been. "I cried aloud for water for God's sake. I had been concluded dead, but as soon as they heard me among them, they had still the respect and tenderness for me to cry out 'give him water,' nor would one of them at the window attempt to touch it until I had drunk." But the relief obtained at the cost of such sacrifice was altogether insufficient. "I was observed by one of my miserable companions on the right of me in the expedient of allaying my thirst by sucking my shirt-sleeve. He took the hint and robbed me from time to time of a considerable part of my sleeve, though after I detected him, I had even the address to begin on that sleeve first, when I thought my reservoirs were sufficiently replenished, and our mouths and noses often met in the contest. This plunderer, I found afterwards, was a worthy young gentleman in the service, Mr. Lushington, one of the few who escaped from death and since paid me the compliment of assuring me he believed he owed his life to the many comfortable draughts he had from my sleeve."

By about half-past eleven the greater number of those still living were delirious. As a last effort to gain air, several who were behind leapt and scrambled on the backs and heads of those in the front rows and grasping the bars so held their position while life and strength lasted. So great was the throng and pressure, even when the floor was strewn with dead, that Holwell at his second post found himself with a heavy man on his back and head, a "Dutch Sergeant" on his left shoulder, and a topaz (native soldier) bearing on his right. Many died standing in the inner ranks: and presently only those were alive who by reason of their endurance or their place near the windows had been enabled to escape death. Holwell's personal recollection of his torture ceased at two o'clock. "I found a stupor coming on apace and laid myself down near the southernmost wall of the prison." When the day broke he was found lying under the dead upon the platform. Captain Mills (now captain of the Company's Yacht), who was in possession of a seat in the window, had the humanity to resign it, "although life was equally dear to every man and the stench arising from the dead bodies was grown intolerable:" and he slowly revived. At six o'clock the next morning, when the door of the prison was opened only twenty-three persons were found still alive. The bodies of the dead were promiscuously thrown into a ditch of an unfinished ravelin in front of the east gate, and covered with earth, and here it was that Holwell afterwards erected the obelisk to their memory which Lord Curzon has restored to Calcutta.

The majority of the survivors were not further molested. Some did not immediately leave Calcutta and found shelter in two ruined houses of the settlement where they were fed by Omichand: but on the 30th June a "drunken European sergeant killed a Moorman" and all the English were ordered out of the city. Others lost no time in making their way down to Fulta to swell the crowd of helpless men, women and children who were huddled together with Drake on board the ships and in wretched huts on shore. Holwell was reserved for a different fate. With three companions he was handed over to Meer Muddun, one of the nabob's generals, who sent them to Moorshidabad. The journey lasted over a fortnight. Nothing better than a leaky country-boat was provided for the prisoners. They lay without shelter of any kind, on bamboos, covered with boils and heavily ironed: their food and drink was rice and the water of the river "which you know," writes Holwell, "is neither very clear nor very palatable in the rains, but there was enough of it without scrambling." On arrival at Moorshidabad they were led in chains through the city: but this was the end of their troubles, for they were shortly afterwards released along with Watts and Collet who had been captured at Cossimbazar, and permitted to join the remnants of the English at Fulta.

Let us for a moment walk over to the obelisk in the Square behind us and read once again the names inscribed upon its tablets. Of many there is nothing to record beyond the tragic death which has procured them immortality. Others are not without their *vates sacer:* and a few stray notes may not be without interest regarding the more prominent of those who stand commemorated upon the site of their rude grave. Foremost among the ill-fated band of Englishmen was John Buchanan, Captain in the Hon'ble Company's Service, who held by the Fort when Minchin, the Commandant, deserted it, and who was the senior Military officer to perish in the Black Hole. From a petition, dated the 9th of June, 1758, and filed in the Calcutta Mayor's Court by Warren Hastings "of Cossimbazar, gentleman," respecting the administration of Buchanan's estate, an interesting discovery has been made by the Rev. H. B. Hyde, whose translation to the Archdeaconry of Madras has robbed Bengal of an indefatigable delver into her past and St. John's Church of a devoted pastor. It has now been established that Buchanan's widow, Mary, was none other than the first Mrs. Hastings, who died a year later at Cossimbazar, and whose tomb in the old Residency burying-ground was for years daubed with a brilliant blue under the orders of some unæsthetic individual in authority. She must have been among the ladies who were sent on board the ships when the assault on the Fort became imminent, and it is more than likely that Hastings, who made his own way down the Ganges to Fulta after his escape from Moorshidabad, met her, and, it may even be, married her, in that dismal refuge. Hitherto the lady has always been erroneously described as the widow of Captain Dugald Campbell, an officer who was accidentally shot at the capture of Budge-Budge, during the operations preceding the entry into Calcutta of Clive and Watson on the 2nd of January, 1757.

Of the eleven members of Council in the Bengal Presidency, Holwell was one of the very few in Calcutta who remained at his post. P. R. Pearkes, Fifth of Council and Accomptant, remained until the capture of the Fort, and escaped, according to Mills, in the confusion which ensued. Of the others, William Watts, Second of Council, and Mathew Collett, Seventh of Council, were at Moorshidabad, and Richard Becher, the kinsman of Thackeray's mother and Fourth of Council, was Chief of Dacca. The remaining four—Roger Drake, the Governor and Cash-keeper, Charles Manningham, Third and Export Warehouse-keeper, William Frankland, Sixth and Import Warehouse-keeper, and William Mackett, Ninth and Buxey, fled in company of Minchin, the Commandant, and left their comrades to their fate. Edward Eye, Tenth of Council and Store-keeper, and William Baillie, Eleventh of Council and Military Store-keeper, perished in the Black Hole. Of the manner of Eyre's death we have a graphic picture. Holwell had forced his way to the back of the chamber, while the frenzied struggle for water was at its height, in order that he might rest upon a stone-sill and die, when, he says, "my poor friend Mr. Edward Eyre came staggering over the dead to me, and with his usual coolness and good-nature, asked me how I did: but fell and expired before I had time to make a reply."

On the same north-western face of the monument stand recorded the names of other servants of the Company of every rank from the highest to the lowest. Gervas Bellamy, the senior chaplain, had been in India since 1726, and although in his sixty-sixth year, had fought like a lion during the siege. When Holwell for the second time gave up hope, he laid himself down, he tells us, by "the gallant old man who lay dead, with his son the Lieutenant, hand-in-hand, near the southernmost wall of the prison." Jenks and Revely were merchants: Coales, in the quaint language of the time, was "Register of Dusticks and Collector of Consulage;" in other words, was in charge of the Company's Customs. Law, Jebb and Carse were factors, and Valicourt, a junior merchant. Fourteen of the succeeding names are those of young writers, many of whom had not been above a year or two in the country. Clayton and Witherington, who with Buchanan complete the tale, were captains in the military service of the Company. On the south-western tablets are the names of their comrades—three Lieutenants and four Ensigns, two of the latter, no doubt, the lads that Holwell strove to preserve from death so long as his strength and theirs endured. With them, too, died the Sergeant-major Abraham and the Quartermaster Cartwright. In Jacob Bleau, whose name is inscribed along with theirs, we have perhaps lighted upon the "Dutch Sergeant" who sat on Holwell's shoulder when he was gasping for air at the second window. Colin Simson was one of the two engineers of the garrison: the other, O'Hara, escaped on board the ships, and so did the Adjutant, Alexander Grant, who is said to have fought at Culloden for Prince Charlie, but he lived to make amends by voting for immediate action before Plassey. Two other officers, Lieutenant Blagg and Ensign Piccard, would appear, according to Holwell's epitaph, to have been among the victims of the Black Hole. But research has established that they perished otherwise, and their names will be found on the tablet on the southern face of the monu-

29

ment. Blagg was cut to pieces on a bastion refusing to surrender to the last. In one of the sorties of which he was the leader, a young writer, Charles Smith, was killed by his side after despatching four or five of the "Moors." The other soldier, Piccard, who died of his wounds before the Fort was taken, was the hero of the gallant action at Perrin's Redoubt where he spiked four of the enemy's guns.

Thomas Leach, whose name is one of those on the south-western tablet, was another hero. He was the Company's smith and the parish clerk of St. Anne's. Holwell tells us he had made his escape after the surrender, but returned just before it was dark, to inform him he had provided a boat for his escape. But Holwell told him the step was one he could not prevail upon himself to take, as he would thereby very ill repay the attachment the gentlemen and the garrison had shown to him: whereupon the smith replied that he would not leave him and was resolved to share his fate. His fidelity cost him his life. Of humble origin, he well merits the tribute which Holwell pays "to the memory of one to whom I had in many instances been a friend, and who on this occasion demonstrated his sensibility of it in a degree worthy of a much higher rank." Another victim who claims attention in Holwell's narrative is Peter Carey, "an officer of one of the ships who had behaved with much bravery during the siege:" he was close behind Holwell when he forced his way to the second window and helped him to make his final retreat. "The poor wretch had been long raving for water and air: I told him I was determined to give up life, and recommended his gaining my station. On my quitting he made a fruitless attempt to get my place, but the Dutch sergeant who sat on my shoulder supplanted him. Poor Carey expressed his thankfulness, and said he would give up life too: but it was with the utmost labour we forced our way from the window. He laid himself down to die, and his death, I believe, was very sudden: for he was a short, full, sanguine man. His strength was great, and I imagine had he not retired with me, I should never have been able to force my way." His wife, "a fine woman, though country born," was in the prison with him and was the only woman that survived: and it would seem that other members of his family shared his fate.

That there were women and, it is to be feared, also children among the unfortunate prisoners, may be accepted without question: the difficulty arises when the determination of the number is attempted. Holwell speaks only of "one hundred and forty-six wretches exhausted by continual fatigue and action." But Secretary Cooke, who was also a survivor, has an allusion to one woman; and Captain Mills, another survivor, who wrote immediately after the event, gives the number of those confined as "144 men, women and children, of whom upwards of 120 were miserably smothered." Beyond such vague statements, however, there is nothing to guide the enquirer in these narratives: and other sources of information are equally meagre.

The name of one woman, Eleanor Weston, appears,

nevertheless, in the revised list of those who perished in the Black Hole which has been inscribed on the south-western face of the obelisk: and Maria Cornelius was certainly one of those killed during the siege of Calcutta, but it is a question whether in the Black Hole or not. Regarding the latter, whose name does not find inclusion among the tablets, nothing is known. For particulars regarding Eleanor Weston, we must turn to the wife of Peter Carey. This woman undoubtedly survived the horrors of the night. Holwell makes distinct mention of her: and Cooke's reference to one woman among those in the Black Hole is evidently to her. Tradition has it that she was carried off by the Nabob's people, but if so, she was speedily restored to liberty. Her name does not occur in the list of "European sufferers" to whom payments by way of compensation were made in 1759 and 1760: but she lived to see Wellesley ruling over India, if we are to credit the gentleman who visited her on August 13th, 1799, at her house in Calcutta, "situate in an angle at the head of the Portuguese Church Street," and recorded the fact on the fly-leaf of his copy of Holwell's Tracts, now in the possession of Mrs. Beveridge. The notes of this observer, a Mr. Thomas Boileau, who was an attorney of the Supreme Court and died early in the nineteenth century, are quoted by Dr. Busteed in his *Echoes from Old Calcutta* (third edition, page 36), and from them it will appear that Mrs. Carey "not only confirmed all which Mr. Holwell had said" on the subject of the tragedy, but added that, besides her husband, her mother, Mrs. Eleanor Weston (her name by second marriage), and her sister, aged ten years, had also perished therein, and that other women, the wives of soldiers, and children, had shared a like fate.

There is no mention of Mrs. Weston in Mr. S. C. Hill's List of inhabitants in the English settlements in Bengal in 1756: but it is clear that she has been included in the list upon the authority of the passage just cited. Mrs. Carey's age at the time of the interview is given as fifty-eight, upon her own statement, in which case she must have been about 15 in the year of the capture of Calcutta: and in a subsequent note on the same fly-leaf her death is said to have occurred on March 28th, 1801. Whether Mrs. Eleanor Weston was or was not a relative of Charles Weston, the friend of Holwell and benefactor of St. John's Church, must remain a matter of conjecture: but it is at all events deserving of record as a possibility.

Two other women, Ann Wood and a Mrs. Bowers, are said on doubtful authority to have survived the awful night. The name of the latter unquestionably appears in the "list of sufferers," as the recipient of several small sums. And in Hicky's *Gazette* there occurs during the year 1780 a paragraph relating to her: "Mrs. Bowers," it runs in Hicky's typical slipshod fashion, "was a young woman and inhabitant of Calcutta, when it was taken by the Moors in the year——where upwards of——British subjects were confined in the dungeon; she concealed herself until after night in one of the warehouses in the factory, from whence she made her escape on board a small vessel lying in the river opposite the old Fort."

Our information as to Mrs. Wood rests upon the statement made by Captain E. Buckle in his history of the Bengal Artillery. "The following," says Buckle, "was copied from an inscription on charcoal on the wall of a small mosque on the declivity of a hill about a mile from Chunar, and the same distance from the Ganges, in October, 1780. 'This is the place of confinement of Ann Wood, wife to Lieutenant John Wood, taken prisoner by Jaffer Beg, Commandant to Sir Roger Dowler [*sic*], taken out of the house at Calcutta where so many unhappy gentlemen suffered; the said Jaffar Beg obtained promotion of Segour Dowler [*sic*] for his long service, Foujdar of Chunar Gar. I, Alexander Campbell, was taken, along with the unfortunate lady, at eleven years old, by the same persons, who made me an eunuch; my only employment was to attend this lady, which I did in this place for four years. 1762, May 3rd, the said Jafar Beg sent to acquaint the lady that if she did not consent to live with him the 4th of the said month, she should be strangled, and by my hands; the 3rd, at midnight, we jumped out of this window and got to the river side, where I hired a boat for fifty gold rupees, to carry us safe to Chinsurah, where we arrived on the 11th. The first news we heard was that Lieutenant Wood died for grief; as soon as she heard this, she fell sick and died the 27th of the month. Mr. Drake behaved with the greatest imprudence, he did deserve to be shot! shot! shot! Alexander Campbell; I am now in Dowlah's service.'" Captain Buckle adds that Mrs. Wood's apartment, "which is all the house consists of, is 9 feet 5 inches by 8 feet 9 inches, and 7 feet 9 inches high; the window, 18 inches." Mr. Hill gives no corroboration of this pitiful little romance, but there is no doubt that there was an officer of the name of Wood in the Militia who delivered stores into the Fort before the siege and supplied cattle at Fulta.

Of the twenty-three survivors of the Black Hole little is known, with the exception of five or six. With Holwell's career, both prior and subsequent to the tragedy, most students of Indian history will be familiar. He was the son of a London timber merchant, whose family had been ruined in the Jacobite cause, and was born in Dublin in 1711. Like his historian, Dr. Busteed, he began life as a member of the great medical profession. When in his twenty-first year he came to Calcutta as surgeon's mate of an Indiaman. He remained eleven years at the Presidency, and in 1742 was formally appointed one of the surgeons on the establishment at Fort William. It is on record that he took an active part in the Municipal administration of the settlement, and was twice successively elected Mayor. Ill-health sent him home in 1749. During the voyage he drew up a scheme for reforming the "Zemandary of Bengal" which he submitted on arrival to the Directors, and which was received with such satisfaction that he returned to Calcutta as "youngest in Council" and zemindar, a post carrying with it the duties of Collector as well as of Judge. He lost no time in setting his house in order. The methods by which the Company's revenues were farmed by middlemen were completely altered, and the revenues of the zemindary were speedily doubled. At the time of Seraj-ud-Dowlah's attack on Calcutta, he had risen to be Eighth of Council. After the

Black Hole, he was sent in irons to Murshidabad with three companions, but was released and made his way to the ships at Fulta. In shattered health he proceeded home with despatches, and it was during the rapid voyage (as it was then considered) of five months that he wrote his well-known narrative of the tragedy in the form of a 32-page letter to "William Davis, Esqre., from on board the *Syren* sloop, this 28th day of February, 1757." It was translated into German in 1799, and a second English edition appeared in the shape of an appendix to his "India Tracts," when he had become a Fellow of the Royal Society.

He did not remain long in England. In consideration of his services the Directors by a large majority nominated him as the successor of Clive in the governorship: but he declined the honour and was then named Second in Council. But a fresh election to the "Chairs" took place before he started, and the new Board relegated him to the position of Ninth. Owing, however, to the departure of seniors, he found himself Fourth in Council on his arrival at Fort William: and in 1759, he became Second. It was not long before his military talents were once more called into requisition. In the same year (1759), when Calcutta was denuded of troops during the fighting with the Dutch, and the Militia were called out to defend the settlement, this command was entrusted by Clive to Holwell. Next year, the governorship devolved upon him after Clive's departure for Europe and until the orders of the Court were received. But he held the office for barely six months, for the Directors appointed Henry

Vansittart of the Madras Council to the post. Among the Orme manuscripts, says Dr. Busteed, there is a gossippy letter written from Calcutta to Drake in England, from which we learn how Holwell received the news of his supersession. "As soon as he heard of Mr. Vansittart's appointment, he seemed greatly shocked, but with his usual gaiety, and taking a pinch of snuff, said he was glad of it, for the fatigue of the chair was too much for him to be ablé to hold it three months longer." He determined, nevertheless, not to remain in India, and during the summer of the year 1760, he applied for leave to resign the service, giving as his reason "the many unmerited and consequently unjust marks of resentment which I have lately received from the present Court of Directors." His position had, in fact, become untenable. A year previously, Holwell had on December 29th, 1759, joined with Clive and the nine other Members of Council in signing an indignant protest to the Court against the insulting manner in which they had been addressed and accused of peculation. The original draft in Holwell's writing was, says Dr. Busteed, in the possession of his great-grandson. It opens by declaring that "the unprovoked and general asperity" of the Court's letter was such that they felt bound to expostulate with freedom" thereon. "Permit us to say," they continued, "that the diction is most unworthy yourselves and us, in whatever relation considered, either as masters to servants, or gentlemen to gentlemen." The answer to this outspoken epistle was not written until nearly twelve months had elapsed: when the Court ordered the summary dismissal of Holwell and three others. One is glad to think with

Dr. Busteed that Holwell anticipated the blow before it had time to fall upon him. He left India in September, 1760, before the fatal despatch had been penned, and died at Pinner near Harrow on the 15th November, 1798, at the age of 87. It would seem that he must have fallen upon evil days towards the end, for the tombstone in the Park Street burying-ground of Mr. Charles Weston, clerk at St. John's Church, winner at a lottery of Tiretta Bazar in Chitpore Road, and one of the jurors at Nuncomar's trial, records that "he manifested a grateful mind by cherishing in his old age his former employer and benefactor, the late Governor Holwell." Weston, who was an Eurasian, had been Holwell's medical apprentice, and like him had changed his pursuits: "what could I expect from following the medical profession when I saw a regular bred surgeon and so clever a man as Mr. Holwell charge no more than fifty rupees for three months' attendance and medicine." He was often heard to say that Seraj-ud-Dowlah's forbearance to Holwell and the latter's release from captivity were due to the intercession of the Nabob's ladies instigated by the natives of Calcutta who loved Holwell for his kind treatment of them during his tenure of office as Zemindar.

There hung until recently on one of the side landings of Government House a quaint portrait of Holwell, watching the progress of the brick and plaster obelisk which he erected at his own expense, in memory of his dead comrades. The artist's name is unknown, in spite of the statement made by Lady Dufferin in her Viceregal Life in India, and also by Mr. H. G. Keene in the Dictionary of

National Biography, that it is the work of Sir Joshua Reynolds. It was purchased in 1892, during the administration of Lord Lansdowne, through the negotiations of Dr. Busteed from a Canadian descendant of John Zephaniah: and has now been transferred to the Victoria Memorial Hall collection, which is temporarily housed in the Indian Museum.

Of Holwell's fellow-survivors, shorter notices must suffice.

Henry Lushington, the young writer of eighteen, who owed his escape from death to the "refreshing draughts" he drew from Holwell's shirt-sleeves, was one of those cruelly murdered with Ellis at Patna under the orders of the renegade Sumroo in 1763. An eulogistic inscription in Eastbourne Parish Church commemorates his many virtues and his brave death, but perverse posterity, we fear, remembers him rather as the writer of the *loll coggedge*, the famous duplicate treaty on red paper, at the foot of which Admiral Watson's name was forged, by order of Clive, for the deception of Omichund. Secretary Cooke, who made his way down to Fulta with Lushington and almost died in that camp of woe, survived to become a member of Council and to give evidence in 1772 before the Parliamentary Committee that gave Bengal Hastings as its first Governor-General. James Mills, the Captain of the *Diligence* snow, who gave up his place at the window to Holwell, and was fortunate enough to save his life in spite of his self-abnegation, lived on until the year 1811. When on leave in England a few years after the Black Hole, he married the celebrated actress, Mrs.

Vincent, whose impersonation of Polly Peachum in the Beggar's Opera had taken London by storm. She returned with him to India, but died in 1802 at Hampstead. In commenting upon the old sea-captain's death, which took place in the homely suburb of Camden Town, the *Gentleman's Magazine* called attention to the fact that he was not the last survivor of those who had witnessed the surrender of Calcutta, and claimed that distinction for his fellow-prisoner, John Burdett, "late of Ealing, now a resident at Totton, near Southampton." No record of Burdett's death has, we believe, been discovered, and in the absence of any evidence to the contrary, he may very well be the individual referred to in a letter which appeared in the London *Standard* of January 21st, 1889, and which is quoted by Dr. Busteed in the latest edition of his book. The assertion is there made that in the year 1840 there was living in the neighbourhood of Hastings in Sussex a man of about one hundred years old, "who had been one of those thrust into the Black Hole of Calcutta." Burdett arrived in India to take up his writership on the 4th August, 1755, and in the ordinary course of things could not have been more than sixteen years of age at the time. This would place the date of his birth in 1739, and there is no inherent improbability in setting him down as the centenarian in question. He was one of Clive's opponents in Council in 1765, and was dismissed the service in consequence and sent home. With Ensign Walcot and Richard Court, a senior merchant, he was Holwell's companion in the terrible journey to Moorshidabad, which they were forced to make as prisoners of the Nabob. Court was subsequently nominated to Council "for behaving very well," but was drowned in the Hooghly on the 7th May, 1758. Walcot, who helped Lushington when dawn broke to look for the corpse (as they supposed) of Holwell, went to Chandernagore on his release from Moorshidabad. Later, he appears to have served under Kilpatrick, who arrived from Madras almost immediately after Drake's flight from Calcutta and assumed command of the troops; but the privations he had undergone were too much for him, and he appears to have died at Fulta some time in the autumn of 1756.

The story of the Black Hole cannot be dismissed without a reference to the attempts which have been made of recent years to demonstrate that the entire incident is a figment of Holwell's brain. It may be that not one word on the subject of the tragedy is to be found in the contemporary Mahomedan writings or in the Hindoo traditions of the time. It may also be that the English at Fulta sank so low in their misery and their hunger that in the "complimentary letter" they addressed to Seraj-ud-Dowlah, they were able to content themselves with complaining a little of the hard usage of the English Honorable Company and had not a single reference to make to the massacre of their fellow-countrymen. Finally, it is certainly the fact that the letters of Clive to Seraj-ud-Dowlah before the battle of Plassey are silent on the matter of the Black Hole, although dwelling in detail on the injuries received by the English at the hands of the Nabob and formulating many charges against him. But it is not the case, as has been gravely asserted, that the first and last allusion ever made by Holwell himself to the event in which he played so prominent a part, is contained in the letter of the 28th day of February, 1757, written in the roundhouse of the ninety ton sloop which was conveying him home. There are no less than five contemporary sources of information, of which two have no connection with Holwell. Lists of persons killed in the fighting and in the Black Hole "overheated and for want of water," as well as those who took refuge at Fulta, were sent to England and published in the English and Scotch newspapers of the time. It is perfectly well-known that Orme, who was in 1756 a Member of Council at Fort St. George, and had been a writer in Calcutta prior to that date, wrote to many of the actors in the scenes he proposed to describe and obtained their written evidence while all the events were fresh in their memory. Among those who answered his queries were Secretary Cooke and Captain Mills, both, as we know, survivors of the tragedy. The latter's account, written on sixteen pages of a pocket book, is still to be seen in original among the 231 volumes of Orme's copperplate manuscripts in the India Office. Then we have the contemporary accounts by William Tooke and George Gray, two servants of the Company who were present in the Fort during the siege: and lastly, it has only to be remembered that Holwell refers to the tragedy in no less than seven letters, of which six were official, and that his first list of casualties was drawn up in August, 1756, only six weeks after the fatal night. The absurd supposition can be passed over that Holwell was allowed to erect a monument in commemoration of the victims of a tragedy which never took place: but in face of this evidence, it is imposing a hard task on posterity to invite them to declare that Orme and Mills and Tooke who corroborate him, have perjured themselves. Seraj-ud-Dowlah may not have been quite the monster he is painted by Macaulay and Malleson: but his responsibility for the "horrid act of violence" of the 20th June, 1756, is not to be brushed away in any offhand manner by the professional white-washers.

The remaining history of Old Fort William may be told in a few words. While in the possession of the Nabob, some of the inner buildings were demolished and a mosque erected, but after the recovery of Calcutta the place returned to its original use. In June, 1758, the Company's goods were all removed and the place was entirely given up to the Military for barracks. Towards the end of 1759, orders were given to build slight apartments on "the cotta godowns and the Long Row" for the reception of the officers of Colonel Coote's battalion, and in 1760, the space between the East gate and the Black Hole prison was made into a temporary church. Mrs. Kindersly's allusion in 1767 to "St. John's Chapel" being "some of the rooms" in the Old Fort, suggests that the old Court of Guard and adjacent barrack-room had received little more to adapt them to their sacred purposes than a western enclosing wall, and the high pitched roof shown in old drawings. Sophia Goldborne in "Hartly House," a collection of letters published in London in 1789, describes the chapel as "a ground-floor," and makes at the same time an allusion to a godown under it, which is perhaps the underground chamber discovered in the excavations of 1891. Such as it was, it remained the official church of the settlement until the completion of St. John's in 1787, and the chapel originally intended to be built within the new Fort was not provided until 1826. By the beginning of 1767, all the military were withdrawn from the place, in order that it might be converted into a Custom House, and various warehouses and other buildings were erected to adapt it to its new uses. Daniell's views still show a complete exterior in 1770: but from this time onwards its fortunes steadily declined. The river gradually receded, and the tide of life left it to flow in other channels. The old Custom House at the southern extremity of the Old Fort disappeared during the reforming administration of the Marquis of Hastings, and with it the last vestige of the historic walls which had for so many years reminded Calcutta of an older and humbler order of things. The foundation-stone of the New Custom House was laid on Friday, February 19th, 1819, with imposing Masonic ceremonies, and all Calcutta congratulated itself upon the vast improvement thus effected in the appearance of the city. Finally, in 1868 the opening of the General Post Office banished out of sight and mind for nearly thirty years all memories of the Old Fort and of the tragedy of suffering and humiliation which it was its fate to witness.

CHAPTER V.

ST. JOHN'S CHURCH.

THERE are few public buildings in Calcutta richer in their memories of bygone days than the old church of St. John, the "original parish church of Bengal." Visitors cannot fail to mark the demure old-world edifice which stands retired from the road at the corner of Council House Street and Hastings Street, and like some city church in modern London lives and broods upon its past glories. With the advent in 1815 of Dr. Middleton, the first Bishop of Calcutta, it became the cathedral of the settlement, and was not deposed from its pride of place till the consecration of St. Paul's by Bishop Wilson in October, 1847.

It was not of course the earliest church in Calcutta. That honour appertains to St. Anne's which stood at the corner of Dalhousie Square and Clive Street, on the spot now occupied by the octagonal chamber of the Bengal Legislative Council. "About fifty yards from Fort William," writes Captain Alexander Hamilton, "stands the church built by the pious charity of merchants residing there, and the Christian benevolence of sea-faring men, whose affairs call them to trade there." The steeple was very lofty, and it is related "how magnificent was the old church, to which the Governor on every Sunday walked in solemn procession, attended by all the civil servants and all the military on duty." But St. Anne's lost her tapering spire in the furious cyclone of 1737, and in 1757, it shared in the general destruction of Calcutta by the army of Seraj-ud-Dowlah.

The last chaplains who officiated in the Church of St. Anne were the Reverend Gervas Bellamy, senior chaplain, who perished in the Black Hole in the 30th year of his chaplaincy, and the Reverend Robert Mapletoft, of old High-Church Stock, who died among the fugitives at Fulta. The records of the church were destroyed during the "Troubles," but among his manifold labours on behalf of the church he loved so well, Mr. Hyde, now Archdeacon of Madras, and from 1888 to 1899, chaplain of St. John's, has had the whole of them transcribed from duplicates discovered by him at the India Office. The Parish Registers are now therefore complete from 1713 onwards. A list of the senior and junior chaplains of the parish, from John Evans of Jesus College, Oxford, and Bishop successively of Bangor and of Meath, who arrived in Bengal in 1678, to the present day is preserved in the Vestry-room of St. John's.

The place of St. Anne's was after a while taken by a Chapel built on the south of the Eastern gateway of the Old Fort and abutting on the site of the Black Hole. But for three years after the recovery of the factory, Protestant Calcutta worshipped in the Portuguese Church of our Lady of the Rosary at Moorghihatta. Various substitutes were proposed from time to time. The theatre which stood before the sack, at the corner of Mission Row and Lall Bazar, was one of these. "We are told," say the Court of Directors in their public letter of March 3rd, 1758, "that the building formerly made use of as a

Theatre may with a little expense be converted into a 'church' or public place of worship. As it was built by the voluntary contribution of the inhabitants at Calcutta, we think there can be no difficulty in getting it freely applied to the before-mentioned purpose, especially when we authorise you to fit it up decently at the Company's expense, as we hereby do." But the suggestion was not adopted: and no definite step was taken until an opportunity and a locality were alike supplied by the construction of the new Fort where the village of Govindpore once existed. On March 24th, 1760, the Council "taking into consideration the unwholesome dampness of the church now made use of, as well as the injustice of detaining it from the Portuguese," ordered a survey to be made of "the remains of the gateway in the Old Fort" and a report to be furnished as to "what it will cost to put it in tolerable repairs and make it fit for a chapel, till such time as the chapel designed in the Fort be erected." An entimate of Rs. 2,500 was supplied, and in the following July, the part of the building adjoining the battered eastern gateway of the Old Fort was converted into a chapel. It was built against the east curtain and immediately south of the gateway. Its southern end must have abutted on the Black Hole prison then used as a "store of merchandise." Sophia Goldborne in "Hartly House" describes it as a ground-floor, but there is a reference to a godown under it which is probably the underground chamber discovered in the excavations of 1891. Mrs. Kindersley's allusion in 1768 to St. John's Chapel being "some of the rooms" in the Old Fort suggests that the Old Court of Guard and adjacent barrackroom with their verandah had received little more than a western enclosing wall and a covering. This makeshift "chapel of the Old Fort," as it was called, served as the Presidency Church for twenty-seven years, the "chapel designed in the new Fort" not being provided until 1826. Its roof, which was of high pitch, an unusual architectural feature in Bengal at that time, is shown in two of Daniell's views taken about the year 1785. Like the edifice which succeeded it and served for so long as the Cathedral, it was dedicated to St. John the Baptist and both church and chapel were consecrated on his name day. Holwell was a mason of high rank, and at the time of the construction and the opening of the chapel, he was, pending the arrival of Vansittart, "President in the Bay and Governor and Commander-in-Chief for Fort William in Bengal for the United East India Company": and it was an old opinion that the Craft, who made liberal contributions towards the cost, were the suggestors of the name.

In 1770, there arrived in Calcutta, as chaplain, William Johnson. Fate has ordained that the fame of this worthy should survive as the fourth and last husband of the much married "Begum" Johnson who lies buried in the old churchyard: but justice demands his commemoration as the man to whom Calcutta really owes the church of St. John's.

Six years after his arrival, he petitioned the Council to provide a permanent building in lieu of the "only apology" for a place of worship which had excited the ire of Mrs. Kindersley. For seven long years the project was shelved by the Court of Directors: and it was not until

1782, that it finally took shape. No thought was entertained of building on the old site of St. Anne's. The spot must have been still traceable when Johnson first opened his attack, for the land was certainly lying unoccupied in 1779, and was actually treated by the Council as *coomar* or waste, and so the absolute property of the Company. But Johnson preferred no request for it: and on November 18th of that year, the whole was granted by a pottah to Mr. Thomas Lyons, and the present Writers Buildings were erected thereon. Another site, however, was speedily made available by the influence of Warren Hastings, who took the keenest interest in the scheme for a new church from its inception.

On April 3rd, 1782, the Maharajah Nubkissen conveyed to Hastings for the sum of sicca rupees 10,000 the "Old Powder Magazine Yard" which had been sold by the Company at private auction on January 11th, 1774. The land was offered by Hastings to the Building Committee, and a week before he resigned his office of Governor-General in 1785, he formally made it over to a perpetual succession of trustees, in trust for the purpose of building a church. According to the original notice of sale, the property was nearly a square of one hundred yards. It is represented to-day by the whole of the present St. John's compound east of the church together with the public footway beyond the compound wall. On the north, where the *Englishman* press now incessantly pulsates, was the house of the head surgeon of the Presidency Hospital, and "a house occupied by Captain Hog." On the south was a range of godowns, where a long line of gaunt two-storied buildings hides the view from Hastings Street. In the centre was the disused magazine, a massive circular brick erection of sixty feet diameter, and exactly where the new parsonage house now stands there was a tank of about one hundred feet square. On the west, was the old burying-ground, where lay the bones not only of Job Charnock, "always a faithful man to his Company" (as his masters gratefully wrote of him after his death), but of Admiral Watson, the liberator of Calcutta and capturer of Chandernagore, and of a host of unremembered worthies such as Sir John Goldsborough, the planner of Old Fort William, and Governor Robert Hedges, nephew of the author of the Diary, who, "after a sickness of nine days, departed this life at between six and seven o'clock on the evening of December 28th, 1717," and by his own wish lies in a nameless grave.

With a site thus secured, the appropriateness of which could not be gainsaid, Chaplain Johnson set to work with renewed energy to collect the funds. A great lottery was organised in 1784, which was the rage of the settlement for five months: and a sum of more than 30,000 rupees was realized. In the meantime, Lieutenant Agg, of the Bengal Engineers, who had offered his services as architect, had been busily at work, and on April 8th of the same year, the foundation-stone was ready to be laid. The Governor-General being away up-country, Mr. Edward Wheler, the Senior Member of Council, gave a public breakfast in the morning at the Old Court House, at which, says the *Gazette,* "were present the other members of Council and many of the principal inhabitants of Calcutta." A procession was then formed "to the ground upon which the new Church is to be built," and the stone was well and truly laid with full Masonic ceremonial. The engraved brass tablet affixed on the occasion testifies that the building was being raised "under the auspices of the Hon'ble Warren Hastings, Governour of India."

It was originally intended that the church should be thrown up to view by wide open spaces all around. To the east, as we have seen, lay the magazine-yard, and north and south, and extending some distance to the west was the old burying-ground filled with huge masonry monuments, some of which are shown in Daniell's picture taken within twelve months of the completion of the church. What is now "Garstin sahib-ka-barrick" on the north was then waste-ground over a filled up tank, for the Presidency General Hospital which stood on that site had been in 1768 removed to its present position in the outskirts of Bhowanipore. But extension in this direction was not proceeded with: and a similar fate overtook the endeavours of the building committee to obtain an outlook towards the river. The Government actually agreed to level the whole of its "Buxie kannah" buildings, where now stand Messrs. Ahmuty's premises and the Stationery Office on the opposite side of Church Lane, but they speedily retracted their consent, and the grant was cancelled on the 24th August, 1785.

Another scheme which was at one time in contemplation was the building of the steeple on the spot where the old gunpowder magazine had stood, but this would have brought the altar to the west instead of to the east end, and it must have been for this reason (according to Mr. Hyde) that the idea was abandoned, and the foundations of the edifice laid wholly (unless the eastern portico be excepted) within the limits of the old burying-ground, with the spire, as it now stands, at the west, and the magazine-yard as a frontage to the east.

On the 8th May, 1787, the new church being then nearly complete, a "general vestry" of the inhabitants of Calcutta was held to re-establish the parish organization. With the minutes of this meeting the existing series of modern vestry proceedings opens. The meeting was presided over by Lord Cornwallis, the Governor-General who had arrived in India the previous year, and there were ten gentlemen present besides the chaplains. Up to this time there had been one churchwarden for the parish which then comprised the whole Bengal Presidency and one sidesman. It was now resolved that there should be two churchwardens, as in an English parish, and two sidesmen, who were to qualify by taking oath in the Supreme Court: and these elected by the general vestry with the two chaplains henceforth constituted the "select vestry." In their hands were placed the administration of the funds and affairs of the church—an arrangement unique in Bengal—and they were also *ex-officio* Governors of the Free School, an institution originating out of a Charity Fund as old as the days of St. Anne's.

The work of construction occupied fully three years: and the ceremony of consecration was witnessed by Lord Cornwallis, who had brought out with him the necessary legal instruments under the seal of the Archbishop of

Canterbury. The day fixed for the solemnity was Sunday, the 24th of June, 1787, being the nativity of St. John the Baptist. The Governor-General attended, and with him the members of Council and the Judges of the Supreme Court, and "a very numerous and respectable company of ladies and gentlemen," as the official report tells us.

And so the church of St. John came into existence. As Sir John Shore has put it, "A pagan gave the ground: all characters subscribed: lotteries, confiscations, donations received contrary to law were employed in completing it. The Company contributed but little: no great proof they think the morals of their servants connected with religion." The church has externally undergone little alteration. In the Vestry is a copy of a drawing of the entire edifice taken in 1788 by Daniell, and another taken in 1795 from the same spot by William Baillie. These show the church to have been originally as at present, with the exception of the wide porticoes on the north and south which were erected in 1811, during the Governor-Generalship of Lord Minto, and the carriage porch at the west and the sacrarium at the east end, both of which were added within the present generation.

The chief entrance in olden days was in the middle of the eastern wall. If you were a person of fashion (says Mr. Hyde), yet did not choose to go to church in your yellow chariot, you would arrive in a neat sedan-chair gleaming with black lacquer. You brought at least seven servants with you, four chair bearers, two running footmen with spears and one *Kittesol* boy to hold a parasol over your head. If you had official rank your silver mace would occupy the services of at least another runner. Alighting at the great eastern staircase of Chunar stone, you ascended under the screen of your huge painted parasol to a tiled-paved terrace beneath the eastern portico. Here a sentry with a firelock guarded the entrance. Acknowledging his salute you found yourself in a wide narrow vestibule, and at the back of the shallow curved recess that enclosed the altar. (This vestibule was not abolished until 1811.) To the right and the left were staircases leading up to the doors of the galleries. Passing under one of these staircases into the interior, you saw that the altar was set in an apse and on a pavement of white Chinese marble. Above it hung Zoffany's picture of the Last Supper, and it was protected by a curved railing. The body of the church would be found paved with black or blue-grey marble and occupied by the pews of the humbler members of the congregation and persons of the lower official ranks. These pews probably all faced north and south on either side of a broad central aisle. The tall pulpit with the reading-desk stood in front of the western gallery, which was only just large enough to contain the organ and singers, and at the angles of this gallery were the pews of the chaplain's families and of the churchwardens and sidesmen. The handsome columns supporting the galleries and the roof were then of the plain Doric style, like those of the exterior. They were converted into the Corinthian in 1811.

On the north and south were also galleries which in those days were for the exclusive accommodation of the "quality." In the midst of the northern gallery was the bowed-out pew of the Governor-General and his Council, for the tradition that makes the south to be the side of dignity in the nave of a church has always been reversed at St. John's. Matching this pew in the southern gallery was the place of the Judges of the Supreme Court. On the executive side of the church the ladies were at first grouped by themselves, while the gentlemen sat behind the judiciary. But the ladies as a body took so violent a dislike to sitting with their faces towards the south—probably on account of the glare—that a notification in the *Gazette* of October 11th, 1787, required the gentlemen to change over with them. A local poet in the previous number of the *Gazette* indulges in the following effusion over the incident:

> " The Ladies on the Lord relied
> To dignify their forms divine
> But now forsaken by their pride,
> To Court the praying maidens join."

These northern and southern galleries will be looked for in vain by the visitor of to-day. During the quadrennial repairs in 1901, they were removed, the reason advanced being that it was otherwise impossible to give the congregation the full benefit of modern improvement in the way of electric lighting and electric fans. There are those who regard the alteration in the appearance of the church as worthy of commendation: but it may be questioned whether too great a heed has not been paid to the cry of modernization. In any case the disappearance has been involved of the great chandelier and brass sconces presented at the cost of Rs. 10,000 by Robert McClintock, one of the merchant princes of Calcutta, ruined by the financial *débacle* of 1836. In the steeple hung the bell, dated 1777, now cracked almost in half. This had probably been brought from the Chapel in the Old Fort. There was a clock also in the steeple, but it was lower in olden days than it is now. The tower is built of Chunar stone, and hence arises the local name of Pattharee Girja or Stone Church by which the edifice is still known.

The Vestry-room of St. John's is well worth a visit. The richly-chased communion plate was the gift of the East India Company, and has been in use for more than a century. Equally noteworthy from their antiquity are the churchwarden's staves, which have many a time been borne in front of the Governor-General when he worshipped in state: and were only employed upon such occasions. In the original register may be seen the entry made by Chaplain Johnson of the marriage on July 10th, 1777, of "Miss Varlé of Chandernagore and Mr. George Francis Grand, writer in the Hon'ble Company's service"—the beginning of the chequered life's history of the "Queen of Ganges, Queen of Seine" who fascinated Junius in Calcutta and reappeared in Paris as Talleyrand's Princess. Immediately below, by the strangest of coincidences, the union is recorded on August 8th, of Warren Hastings with "Anna-Maria Apollonia Chapusettin," his "dearest Marian," the beautiful Mrs. Imhoff. Both these weddings were performed at private residences, the latter, it may be, at Hastings' residence at the corner of Old Court House Street and Esplanade Row. There are two other entries in the register of which the visitor will be glad to secure a glimpse—those which record the marriages of William Makepeace Thackeray's parents and grandparents. "Sylhet" Thackeray who bore the same Christian names as his grandson, and who came out to India in 1766 in the same ship as Madam Grand's future husband, was married in St. John's Church on January 31st, 1776, to Miss Amelia Richmond Webb, a descendant of the General Webb of Wynendael fame, who is immortalized in *Esmond*. Their second son Richmond was the novelist's father, and was married in his turn, on the 13th October, 1810, to the daughter of John Harman Becher, a kinsman of the Richard Becher who shared with his wife the agonies of the flight to Fulta and was the colleague in Council of Clive and Holwell in the happier days which followed it. Five years later, Richmond Thackeray was borne to his last resting-place in the North Park Street burying-ground. Among other archives is still preserved a letter in the scholarly hand of Sir William Jones, setting out the reasons why he and his brother-justices of the Supreme Court declined to subscribe to the fund for the building of St. John's: and yet another in which may be read, in Hastings' own phrases, his modest acceptance of the compliment paid to him by inscribing his name on the first stone of the new church. On the walls of the Vestry-room are pictures of the church at various stages of its history, and portraits of chaplains, such as John Evans and Mapletoft and Johnson, and of benefactors such as Charles Weston, the friend and patron of Holwell, and Charles Sealy, first Registrar of the Supreme Court and ancestor of a Viceroy in the person of Lord Northbrook. To the fostering care of Mr. Hyde is due many of these adornments, and all who desire to know more about the Calcutta of periwigs and patches, of *hookah-burdars* and parasol bearers, of Holwell and Francis, are heartily recommended to purchase, firstly, a copy of Dr. Busteed's fascinating "Echoes from Old Calcutta," and secondly, a copy of Mr. Hyde's no less indispensable chronicles of the "Parish of Bengal." The illustrations with which Mr. Hyde's book is adorned are an all-powerful lure in themselves, for they reproduce all that is notable among the treasures with which the Vestry-room of his old church is enriched.

On either side of the western gallery of the church are pedestals, intended, as the inscriptions upon them assert, to serve as memorials of Lord Cornwallis and Lord Minto, the Governors-General, "under whose auspices," in 1787 and 1811, respectively, the old cathedral was "founded and consecrated" and "enlarged and improved." While, however, the pedestal on the north which bears the name of Lord Cornwallis is surmounted by his bust, the other is bare and unadorned. The explanation for the invidious contrast thus presented must be sought in the Vestry-records for the year 1897. The bust of Lord Minto which stood upon the pedestal to the south was overthrown during the earthquake of that year: and was so completely shattered that restoration was found to be impossible.

It is not the only monument that has vanished. Chantrey's fine statue of Bishop Heber on his knees, formerly stood in the Eastern portico (behind the spot where the altar has now been placed) and was a prominent object from without. But it was removed in 1847 along with the episcopal throne, to the new Cathedral, by Bishop Wilson.

Upon the western wall of the gallery hangs the celebrated painting of the Last Supper by Zoffany which once served as an altar-piece. The picture was presented to the Church by the artist on April 9th, 1787, and was in its place over the altar when the ceremony of consecration was performed in the following June. Since that day it has suffered many vicissitudes. A correspondent writing in 1888 to the *Statesman* under the designation of "A Quille Penne" is very vehement in his denunciation of the condition of neglect into which it had been allowed to fall and his disapproval of its present location. "To see the damage done and to observe the rapid progress in the shameful treatment which must end in the total ruin of an invaluable work of art, cannot but excite the indignation of the most indifferent visitant. The painting is so badly hung that it is only at certain hours, and when the church is fully lighted, one can examine the picture. However, at any time, it is possible to see only too well the tarnished broken wooden frame, denuded in many places of the gilding, the scratched dinted surface, the torn frayed canvas, and the large hole near the nose of Judas Iscariot." The disadvantages of the situation remain unchanged, although it may be conceded that the picture is more fortunate than when it lay in the large covered verandah now converted into an open portico for the convenience of carriage-seekers, where it was at first removed after its deposition from the place of honour over the altar. From thence it journeyed to the vestry, and finally to its present place over the gallery. But, as far as the condition of the painting is concerned, there is little cause of complaint to-day: for it appears to be in an excellent state of preservation.

All the figures in the picture are said to have been painted from life, part of the figure from one person and part from another: and there seems no reason to doubt the fact, for the faces are quite unidealized and some of them are commonplace to a degree. The identity of the originals is not easy to establish. The Apostles are asserted to be portraits of leading merchants of the city: and Father Parthenio, a Greek clergyman well-known at the time, is stated to have sat for the figure of the Saviour. The disciple John, who is leaning upon his shoulder, is declared to be Mr. Blacquire, for many years a police-magistrate. If this be the case, the selection must be adjudged to be an inappropriate one, for John Clark Marshman in his biography of Carey, the elder Marshman and Ward, describes Blacquire as "a Brahmanized European" notorious for his hostility to Christianity and his indifferent character. Around the identity of Judas Iscariot quite a miniature controversy has raged. It is remarkable that his is the most prominent figure in the middle ground, the other apostles and Christ occupying the background. The interest is clearly intended to centre on the betrayer, upon whose countenance the conflict of passion and the strife within him are markedly portrayed. There are some, notably a correspondent writing in the *Statesman* in 1888 under the name of "Gamin de Bon Accord," who award the distinction of supplying the original of Judas to "a certain English resident at the Court of Lucknow," who had made himself particularly disagreeable both to the Nawab and the painter and was made to figure not only as Judas in the Calcutta picture, but as a prominent figure in a lewd fresco, which was the work of Zoffany, and was defaced, along with others of a similar character, by order of Sir Robert Montgomery in 1858. The information so given is said to be taken from a book entitled "The Diary of an Englishman at the Court of Oudh," which came into the hands of the *Statesman's* correspondent during the course of a sea-voyage. And the diary is further quoted as stating that, although such pictures make one ashamed of his species, "still the person so gibbeted richly deserved the treatment, for like his prototype Judas Iscariot, he afterwards committed suicide." If this conjecture be correct, the portrait may be set down—with some measure of safety—as that of a certain Mr. Paull, a servant of the Company. He was promoted to be Resident at the Court of Oudh by the Marquess Wellesley, but repaid him with gross ingratitude. For on his return to England he became a member of Parliament and attacked the policy of Lord Wellesley with great severity. On the dissolution of Parliament, however, he lost his seat, and shortly afterwards committed suicide early in the present century. Others, again, find the original of Judas in Mr. Tulloh, a well-known Calcutta auctioneer of the period, and the story goes that the victim sought the protection of the law. But a careful search in the records of the Supreme Court for the years 1786 or 1787 or "within the next few years" has failed to bring to light the traces of any such suit between Tulloh and Zoffany. There was, it may be noted, nothing unusual in the conduct of Zoffany in thus using his pencil to gratify private dislike. At one time a member of the Royal Academy, he greatly scandalized English royalty by painting a picture in 1774 entitled the "Life School," in which he introduced a portrait of the Queen as she was when Princess of Mecklenburg and another of a supposed admirer of hers. The consequence of this outburst of malice, provoked, it was said, by some action of the Queen which offended him, was that Zoffany found it convenient to leave England. He came to India in 1784, and for fourteen years resided at Lucknow, where he became a conspicuous favourite with the Nawab. It is a mistake to describe him as Sir John, for he was never knighted. He died at Kew in 1810 at the age of 75.

There was nothing singular in this peculiarity on the part of Zoffany of introducing portraits of living personalities into his picture. Hogarth freely depicts well-known characters of his day in his Harlot's and Rake's Progresses: and it is an historical fact that Michael Angelo revenged himself in the same way on the Pope's master of ceremonies when painting the picture of Hell in the Pope's private chapel. One of the damned souls so closely resembled the master of the ceremonies that every one recognized the picture. Whereupon the aggrieved official complained to the Pope, and begged that the painter might be ordered to deface the portrait. But Pope Clement enjoyed the joke as much as the painter did, and asked the master of ceremonies in what department his likeness appeared. "In Hell" was the reply. "Why, then," rejoined the

Pope, "you know very well I and the Church have only power to deliver a soul from Purgatory, the picture must remain."

Zoffany, it is said, always charged his pictures at Rs. 1,000 per figure : and the value of his gift to St. John's Church may, therefore, be estimated at about Rs. 13,000. When he was leaving Calcutta, shortly after the completion of this picture, a proposition was made to present him with a ring of Rs. 5,000 in value, but the low state of the Vestry fund not admitting of this, a handsome and appropriate letter was submitted, as a "testimonial of the respect in which they (the Committee) held his abilities as an artist." Another Last Supper piece by Zoffany may be seen in East Brentford Church near London.

There are a number of interesting memorial tablets upon the walls of the church which will repay inspection. We may therefore now descend from the gallery and commence our circuit from the left hand or northern side of the main door which is situated immediately under the gallery.

We may first notice a marble tablet in memory of John Henry Barlow of the Bengal Civil Service, third son of Sir George Hilaro Barlow, Bart., G.C.B., Governor-General at Fort William from October, 1805, to July, 1807, and subsequently Governor at Fort St. George (on the recall of Lord William Bentinck from that post) from December, 1807 to August, 1813. He was born, December 7th, 1795, and died at Contai, Hidgelee, 11th September, 1841. "He served the State for a period of 27 years, his life exhibiting a rare harmony of the qualities of mind and heart that stamp their chief value on official private and Christian character." Barlow was a contemporary at Haileybury of Andrew Stirling, whose monument is hard by. He arrived in India in 1813, and was Salt Agent at Hidgelee at the time of his death.

Adjoining is a marble tablet bearing the name of Lieutenant-Colonel Henry Hawtrey, Commanding 3rd B. L. Cavalry, who died (at Ghazipore) 7th July, 1833, aged 49 years. It was erected as a mark of respect and esteem by the officers of his corps.

Just beyond Colonel Hawtrey's tablet is the north staircase leading to the gallery. We now turn to examine the more important tablets on the northern wall.

First comes a marble tablet, in commemoration of Richard Vaughan, Taxing Officer, Chief Clerk of the Insolvent Court, Keeper of the Records and Muniments and Receiver of the Supreme Court, who died at Calcutta, 31st January, 1843.

These appointments were united in one individual "under the new arrangement for the remuneration by salaries instead of fees, as proposed by the Judges in their letter of the 25th April, 1836, and approved by Government." Vaughan was the first incumbent.

The next recalls a sad memory of the Mutiny of 1857. It commemorates the fate of Henrietta, aged 30 years, wife of Captain R. P. Anderson, 25th Bengal N. I., and Hilda Mary, aged 7 months, daughter of Captain R. P. Anderson, who " died from sheer want of proper nutriment during the siege of Lucknow." Captain Anderson's small two-storeyed house, situated on rising ground, formed the south-eastern angle of the Residency position, and from it to Gubbins' house extended the south front. By the side of this little outpost ran the Cawnpore road, and the enemy being only a few yards away on the left and in front, an incessant fire was kept up night and day. "It was severely handled and almost destroyed by the enemy," writes Lady Inglis in her diary. "It was perhaps the most exposed post in the whole garrison and the only one called by the name of its own commander during the siege." The garrison consisted of Captain Anderson, a subaltern officer, nine privates, and a sergeant of Her Majesty's 32nd Foot and eight volunteers: among them, an Italian and a Frenchman and Mr. Capper of the Bengal Civil Service "who did regular duty as a common soldier and a precious, good and attentive one he was." They were kept constantly at work, and could afford no aid to their stricken families. "Five babes were buried last night," runs an entry in one of the daily records of the siege: and no less than 53 European or East Indian children died during those terrible eighty-seven days. Mrs. Anderson's death is noted by Lady Inglis as taking place on August 17th, ten days after her husband and his comrades had with the utmost difficulty repelled a mighty assault upon their frail defences.

To the right of this pathetic little monument is a marble tablet which challenges attention by reason of the circumstances of the death it records. It is erected in memory of George Cracroft Aubert, aged 25 years, "who on the evening of the 29th April, 1843, riding homeward from the residence of a friend, was overtaken by a sudden storm, and with the horse that bore him, was struck dead by lightning."

By its side is a marble tablet to the memory of Trevor John Chichele Plowden "an affectionate husband and father, an upright public servant, and virtuous citizen, who for thirty years worshipped God in this church: this simple memorial of love and respect is erected by his wife and children: born June 4th, 1784, died July 7th, 1836." He was a member of the Bengal Civil Service and "Salt Agent at the 24-Pergunnahs and Jessore" at the time of his death, which took place, according to Dodwell and Miles, on board the *Hibernia* on July 7th, 1836. In 1827, he served the office of Sheriff of Calcutta. The Plowdens have been closely associated with Upper India for more than a century. "Some people will tell you that, if there were but a single loaf of bread to be divided in India, it would be divided equally between the Plowdens, the Trevors, the Beadons, and the Rivett-Carnacs." The advent of the competition-wallah has in many an instance broken the hereditary link: but Trevor Plowden has been followed in the service by both son and grandson of the same name. Trevor John Chichele Plowden the second, was a member of the Bengal Civil Service from 1827 to 1860, and his son, the third of the line, served from 1868 to 1900, and after filling the office of Resident at Hyderabad for nine years and attaining to the dignity of a K.C.S.I., died in November, 1905.

Further on is a marble tablet adorned with a coat-of-arms and inscribed with the name of Walter Nisbet, Bengal Civil Service, died October 11th, 1833, aged 43 years: "Who, though dead, still liveth in the recollections of his sorrowing relations and of those numerous friends whose attachment he conciliated during twenty-three years residence in Calcutta." Nisbet was one of the first group of cadets, who passed out of Haileybury. He arrived in India in 1809, and when he died at Garden Reach in 1833, was holding the office of Export Warehouse-keeper.

The next is a handsome marble monument surmounted with military arms and trophies by W. Pistell. A soldier in uniform and a female figure in a posture of grief are represented upon either side of a funeral casket. Beneath is the following inscription:—

"This cenotaph was erected by the Neemutch Field Force in honour of their Commander, Lieut.-Col. John Ludlow, C.B. This distinguished officer entered the Bengal Army on the 16th February, 1795: and his career was marked by an ardent devotion to the duties of a soldier, a generous enthusiasm and unabating zeal which shed a lustre on the profession to which he belonged. By his heroic intrepidity in the arduous contest between the British troops and those of the Rajah of Nepaul in the years 1814 and 1818, he obtained the unqualified approbation of the Supreme Government of India and the Honours of the Bath from his Sovereign. His life fell a sacrifice to the energy of his spirit which led him into the field at the head of his division, while suffering under a painful and dangerous illness, under which he sank in camp at Baroda on the 22nd September, 1821, in the 44th year of his age."

The following occupy the space between the Ludlow cenotaph and the monument to Adam in the corner:

Cenotaph, with medallion portrait in memory of Lieut.-Col. John Weston, of the Bengal Military Establishment, who died July 31st 1819, (on board the *Eliza*) on his voyage from Prince of Wales Island to Calcutta. Erected by his uncle.

Marble Tablet: bearing the name of Andrew Stirling, second son of Admiral Stirling of Woburn Farm, in the county of Surrey, who died at this Presidency on the 23rd of May, 1830, in the 36th year of his age. Erected by his father.

Stirling was Persian Secretary to Government and Deputy Secretary in the Secret and Political Department under Lord William Bentinck. At Haileybury, during the years 1811 and 1812, he carried off almost every prize there was to win. He arrived in India in 1813, and his name is still recognized as that of an authority on the history of Orissa. He "died at Chowringhee," after an illness of ten days: and it is recorded in the *Bengal Obituary* that his remains were followed to the grave by a large concourse of mourners, European and Native: "among the latter were observed the whole of the distinguished native princes, nabobs, rajahs and others."

Another Mutiny memorial succeeds, commemorating James Erskine, mortally wounded at Lucknow during the Mutiny, aged 21 years. Erskine was a trooper in Captain Barrow's famous regiment of volunteer horse ("Barrow's devoted band," as Outram named them), which played so prominent a part in the campaign that began with Havelock's departure from Allahabad on July 6th, 1857, with a force of 1,964 men, all told, and ended on September 25th with the relief of the Residency. When Havelock reached Benares on June 18th, he found himself terribly hampered by the want of European cavalry and applied for permission to raise a troop out of the "officers of regiments which had mutinied or had been disbanded, of indigo-planters, of patrols, of burnt-out shop-keepers; in short, of all who are willing to join me." Lousada Barrow of the 5th Madras Light Cavalry (afterwards Commissioner of Lucknow in 1864, and Chief Commissioner of Oudh from January to April, 1871), undertook the task, and a force of about 18 officers and men left Allahabad with Havelock. On the road four more joined, and this was the total strength of the "regiment" during the whole of the engagements until the crossing of the Ganges for the first time on July 20th, when it was reinforced by some 40 men from different regiments: and later, when encamped at Mungulwar, some half dozen more officers joined them. But the nominal roll as prepared by Barrow, shows no more than 40 as a constant total in the later stages: 20 military men and 20 civilian volunteers. Small as their number was, they were the heroes of many a gallant exploit. At the battle which won back Cawnpore on July 16th, Barrow and his eighteen sabres charged a whole regiment of rebel cavalry and routed them, not desisting from the chase until six out of the brave handful of Englishmen were disabled. As they rode back, the soldiers greeted them with a cheer, and Havelock exclaimed "well done, gentlemen volunteers! I am proud to command you!" And when they found themselves beleaguered in the Residency along with the garrison they had come to rescue, they cheerfully assumed charge of Innes' Post "close to the church, one of the most exposed parts of the works." Erskine, however, was mortally wounded on September 25th, as the relieving force were fighting their way through the streets of Lucknow. "We advanced without interruption," writes a comrade in a Journal published in 1858 by the Baptist Mission Press at Calcutta, "until we arrived at the Char Bagh, a very large garden surrounded by a high loop-holed wall just on the outskirts of the city. As we rode along, our heads and shoulders appeared just above the wall, giving a very good mark for the enemy, who were there waiting for us. They opened fire, and, I am sorry to say, one of our young volunteers, by name Erskine, was shot in the side. He was one of three young fellows who came all the way from Calcutta to join us. Poor boy: well did he do his duty: he died 3 or 4 days before we got out of Lucknow" on November 17th.

We now arrive at the cenotaph of John Adam, Acting Governor-General of India from January to August, 1823. This stands at the north-east corner and is a fine work of art. On either side of the tablet bearing the inscription stands a female figure, the one on the right holding the *fasces*, and the other on the left, a plumb-rule, as emblems of civil authority, and justice.

A full account of Mr. Adam will be found in the chapter on Government House, where his picture hangs in the breakfast-room. It will be sufficient in this place to transcribe the inscription on the memorial tablet which is in itself a biography, noticing merely that he attained to the high office of member of the Supreme Council at 41 years of age: and acted as Governor-General after Lord Hastings' departure when he was 45. "To the memory of John Adam, eldest son of the Right Honourable William Adam, Lord Chief Commissioner of the Jury Court in Scotland. He arrived in Bengal, 1796, and passed through the highest offices in the service of the East India Company. Placed in the Supreme Council in 1819, he was again appointed to that station when the usual term of holding it had expired. From January to August, 1823, he acted as Governor of India. Bad health compelled him to embark for England in March, 1825, but he died (off Madagascar) on the 4th June, in the 47th year of his age, and his remains were committed to the ocean. His indefatigable zeal and exemplary integrity: the firmness of his conduct: his devoted views and the wisdom of his measures, have been recorded by the Supreme Council of Bengal and those who preside over the affairs of India in England. The modesty of his demeanour, his cultivated and intelligent conversation, the kindness of his nature and active benevolence will long be cherished in the hearts of those who dedicate this marble to his virtues."

In spite of this encomium, it is to be feared that Adam's rule of seven months is remembered, if at all, only for his deportation of James Silk Buckingham, the editor of the *Calcutta Journal,* during his administration of the office of Governor-General. The outcry was very great among the Europeans, and the leading part in the agitation was taken by Mr. John Palmer, the "Prince of Merchants," whose bust is in the Town Hall.

Adjoining and completely obscured by the organ is a marble slab, in memory of another acting Governor-General William Butterworth Bayley, of Hopehall near Eccles, Lancashire, and of the Bengal Civil Service, born 30th November, 1781, died 29th May, 1860.

"A typical Indian official of the Wellesley school." He was the uncle of Sir Edward Clive Bayley, Member of Council from 1874 to 1878, and father of Sir Steuart Colvin Bayley, Lieutenant-Governor of Bengal from 1887 to 1890. He arrived in India in 1799, and was appointed temporary member of the Supreme Council in February, 1822, but resigned in the following December. In November, 1825, he was again appointed and held the office until 1830. From March to July, 1828, he officiated as Governor-General during the interregnum between Lord Amherst's departure and Lord William Bentinck's arrival. He was elected a Director of the East India Company in 1833, and sat on the Board until 1858, filling the office of chairman in 1840.

We have now arrived at the east end of the church. Within the chancel and behind the altar-rails is a plain marble slab in the ground with this single inscription: "T. F. M., D. D., Obiit VIII Julii 1822." These words mark the last resting-place of Thomas Fanshaw Middleton, F. R. S., first Bishop of Calcutta. He was born in 1769, the only son of the Rector of Kedleston, in Derbyshire, and was educated at Christ's Hospital and Pembroke College, Cambridge. When he was, in May, 1814, consecrated Bishop of Calcutta in Lambeth Palace Chapel, he had been for two years Archdeacon of Huntingdon. On the afternoon of November 28th, 1814, he stepped on shore in the City of Palaces "without any éclat for fear of alarming the prejudices of the natives," to quote his own words. His first appearance in public was at the fête given at Government House on December 2nd, 1814, in honour of the general peace: but it was only his indisposition that prevented that distinction from accruing to the St. Andrew's Dinner of that year to which he was specially invited and at which one of the toasts was "the Bishop of Calcutta," followed by the appropriate tunes "Put the gown on the Bishop" and "My native land I've bid adieu." The church of St. John was constituted by him the Cathedral of the Diocese: and it continued as such until 1847, when Bishop Wilson removed the throne to St. Paul's. His nine years' episcopate was largely taken up with extended tours to Madras, Ceylon and Bombay, and even as far afield as Penang, which were all included in his Diocese. In Calcutta, his energy and powers of organization found ample scope, but the work in which he displayed the keenest interest was the formation of the Bishop's College, of which he laid the foundation stone at Seebpore in December, 1820. These buildings have recently passed into the possession of the Civil Engineering College, but their days are numbered, for that institution is under orders of removal to Ranchi. Venturing out one evening in the month of July, 1822, for a drive in an open carriage before the sun had gone down, he received a sunstroke from which he never recovered, and on the 8th of the month he died after five days' illness. His funeral did not take place till the 17th, and was an imposing public ceremony. Among the pall bearers were Mr. John Fendall, Mr. John Adam and Mr. Butterworth Bayley, Members of Council, Sir Francis Workman Macnaghten, the Chief Justice of the Supreme Court, and General Hardwicke. One who knew the Bishop has described him as being "above the ordinary stature of man, strongly framed, of a florid and commanding countenance, animated and energetic in manner." And Charles Lamb, who was his school-fellow at Christ's Hospital, gives us a vignette of him in his episcopal days. "M. is said to wear his mitre high in Idea, where the *regni novitas* (I dare say) sufficiently justifies the bearing." He was only 53 at the time of his death.

The stained glass window above the altar is a memorial of Henry Inglis of Cherrapoonjee, whose name is still well remembered in Assam as one of its industrial pioneers.

On the walls of the chancel surrounding the altar are the following Tablets:—

(1) John Mathias Turner, D.D., Lord Bishop of Calcutta, died 7th July, 1831, aged 45 years.

"A scholar, philanthropist and a man of God." He lies buried in the church, and to the west, by the side of two Chief Justices of the Supreme Court and Sir Benjamin Malkin.

(2) Right Revd. Daniel Corrie, LL.D., late Lord Bishop of Madras, and formerly Archdeacon of Calcutta:

"The friend and fellow labourer of Henry Martyn; the beloved Prelate," died 5th February, 1837, aged 59 years.

Dr. Corrie was the first of the chaplains on the Indian establishment to attain to an Indian Bishopric. His friendship with Henry Martyn commenced when they were undergraduates at Cambridge: and they sailed for India within a few months of each other: Martyn in the autumn of 1805, Corrie in the beginning of 1806. Their first home in Bengal was together. There was on the banks of the Hooghly near Serampore, until the river washed the ruins away a few years ago, a picturesque Hindoo Pagoda which went by the name of Aldeen. David Brown, another chaplain, under whose roof the young men were staying, had fitted it up as a study and chapel, and it became a favourite meeting place where Carey, Marshman, and Ward from the neighbouring mission at Serampore often met and foregathered with their brother clerics. Corrie and Martyn met at Cawnpore for the last time in 1810: and their paths thereafter diverged into widely different regions. In 1818, Corrie was transferred from Benares to be senior chaplain at the Presidency. Four years later, Bishop Middleton died: and was followed in less than five weeks by Loring the Archdeacon. Corrie became Ecclesiastical Commissioner of the diocese, and on Heber's arrival in October, 1823, was at once appointed to the Archdeaconry. The deaths of Heber in 1825, of James in 1828, and Turner in 1831, placed him successively in charge of the Indian Church: and on three of the occasions the duty devolved upon him of preaching the funeral sermon of the deceased prelate. It was fully expected on Bishop Turner's death that Corrie would be nominated for the Bishopric: but it was necessary that no time should be lost in filling up the appointment and Dr. Daniel Wilson was appointed. In 1834, the creation of the sees of Madras and Bombay gave the opportunity for his promotion: and he was nominated for the former. He was consecrated in England in June 1835, and arrived at Fort St. George in the following December. But his episcopate was destined to last only eighteen months: and he died as recorded in February, 1837, at Madras, where his name will be handed down to posterity in connection with Bishop Corrie's grammar school.

(3) Henry Lloyd Loring, D.D., First Archdeacon of Calcutta, died 4th September, 1822, aged 38 years.

Upon the extension in 1813 of the Charter of the East India Company for a further period of twenty years, the King was empowered to create a Bishop's see in Calcutta and an Archdeaconry in each of the three Presidencies, the salaries of the appointments to be borne by the Company. Loring was appointed first Archdeacon of Calcutta. He sailed for India with Bishop Middleton in 1814, and officiated with Corrie at his funeral service on July 17th, 1822. A few weeks later he fell a victim to cholera.

On the south of the chancel is one of the finest memorials in the church. It is a white marble cenotaph inscribed:—

"To the memory of Alexander Colvin. This tablet is inscribed by the merchants of Calcutta, who having for forty years witnessed in him an union of those talents and virtues which best adorn their profession and do most honour to a character in private life, thus record their affectionate esteem for him while living and their sorrow for his death. Born 3rd April, 1756, died 15th December, 1818."

This is an extremely handsome monument in white marble by Richard Westmacott. The figure of the Hindoo woman who sits to the right of the inscription is charming in its grace and simplicity. And praise almost as high must be accorded to the two female figures above, which are placed upon either side of a beehive, the symbol of industry. Alexander Colvin was the uncle of John Russell Colvin, Governor of the North-West from 1853 to 1857, who died in the Fort at Agra during the mutiny: and great-uncle, therefore, of Sir Auckland Colvin, Lieut.-Governor of the same provinces from 1887 to 1892, and of Sir Walter Colvin the well-known barrister of Allahabad. "In or about 1778," says Sir Auckland Colvin in his life of his father, "Alexander Colvin was the first of the family to risk his fortunes in India, tempted by what connexion, or led by what hopes, cannot now be known. There he established a house of business, known later as the house of Colvin, Ainslie and Cowie: and while Hastings was enlarging the limits of the Company's rule, Alexander Colvin attended to his ventures. His name not infrequently occurs in old *Calcutta Gazettes* and Records. He may have served on a jury before Sir Elijah Impey. He must have discussed over his tea and his bananas, the squabbles of the Governor and his councillors: and have presented his homage to the adored 'Marian.' The scandal of Madam Grand will have been to him a subject, first of discreet enquiring and later of pious reprobation. He preferred, we may be sure, as became a sober Scotch body, the joys of his home in Hastings Street to the masquerades at the Harmonic House." He was joined in business by his brother James, the father of John Russell, who had been a midshipman in his youth, but left the navy to set up his household gods in Calcutta. Returning early in 1789 to England to recover health, James Colvin found himself present at the taking of the Bastille. The House of Colvin Cowie & Co. continued to be the leading agency firm in Calcutta until the seventies: its place of business is still at No. 4, Hastings Street, where Alexander Colvin lived and where John Russell Colvin was born in 1807.

Immediately above the Colvin monument, at the eastern end of what was once the south gallery, may be discerned a memorial bearing the name of Charles Lionel Showers, Senior Captain of the 19th Regt., B. I. "who in the assaults of the fortified heights of Malown on the 25th April, 1815, led one of the principal columns to a separate attack, in the most gallant style and gloriously fell at its head just when in personal conflict he had with his own hand slain the chief of the enemy." He was aged 35. Two other officers of the same regiment are also commemorated. "On the same occasion in the gallant execution of his duty, fell Lieut. Humphery Bagot, of the same regiment, aetat. 25, and in the same campaign, equally honorable, fell Lieut. Edward Wilson Broughton of the same regiment, aetat. 26." The bas-relief below the inscription is a representation of the exploit which cost Showers and Bagot their lives: while at the top are the words "Pro Patria."

The capture of Malaun, on the Upper Sutlej, from the oldest of the Gurkha leaders, Amar Singh, was one of the most brilliant feats of the campaign by which Sir David Ochterlony retrieved the blunders which cost the valiant, but headstrong Gillespie his life before the hill-fort of Kalanga. After a brief but vain resistance, the Gurkha Government saved their capital from entry by Ochterlony's victorious troops by signing the treaty of Segowlie, which stripped them of nearly all their lowland possessions, turned Kumaon into an English province and placed an English Resident for the first time at the Court of Khatmandu. For his successful conduct of the war, Ochterlony received a baronetcy, and Lord Moira, the Governor-General, was created Marquess of Hastings. The 1st (Prince of Wales' Own) Goorkha Rifles preserves the recollection of this campaign in its second title of the "Malaun Regiment."

Proceeding forwards to the South-east Corner, we next see a marble tablet in memory of Lieut. Peter Lawtie, of the corps of Engineers in the army of Bengal, who died in Nepal in 1815, aged 23 years. This is also a handsome monument. A sepoy with his hands clasped is represented gazing into a coffin which is held open by an angel at whose feet an anchor is shown. The dress of the sepoy is noticeable. It appears to consist of an uniform coatee and bandolier, a necklace, slippers, and a pair of short, tight *jungias* or drawers which leave the legs and thighs entirely exposed. The monument, like the preceding one, was erected, as the inscription on it testifies, by Sir David Ochterlony and the officers under his command, in memory of one of their comrades of the first Nepal War.

Dr. William Twining, whose name now catches the eye, was a distinguished surgeon in Calcutta during the time of Lord William Bentinck, as the inscription upon his monument shows: "In grateful recognition of benefits derived from the successful application of professional ability and in testimony of respect and esteem for modest worth and active philanthropy. This tablet erected by his friends and patients is consecrated to the memory of William Twining, M.R.C.S., obiit August, 25th, 1835, aged 45." Twining enjoyed the distinction of having served as a young man in the capacity of Hospital Assistant under the Duke of Wellington throughout the whole course of the Peninsular War. In March, 1814, he was promoted to Staff Assistant Surgeon, and entered Paris with the allied army as a member of General Lord Hill's staff. He was also present at Waterloo. In 1821, he accompanied Sir Edward Paget to Ceylon as his personal surgeon: and two years later followed him to India, on his appointment to be Commander-in-Chief. In 1824, he exchanged from the King's to the Company's service and became an Assistant Surgeon on the Bengal Establishment. He remained for a short time on Sir Edward Paget's staff, and was then appointed first permanent Assistant Surgeon at the General Hospital—a post he held until his death. His private practice is said to have been enormous: people of all ranks, European and native, flocking to avail themselves of his skill. In 1833, he published an important book upon Cholera, having in the previous year brought out a work on the Diseases of Bengal, a copy of which is sculptured below his monument. His death was caused by the rupture of a blood vessel due to exertion in assisting to lift a gentleman who was violently thrown out of his carriage and was lying helpless with a fractured thigh. It is on record that he was a rigid water drinker: and that he regarded indulgence of the table of every kind as an unpardonable offence in a man who wished to preserve his health in a tropical climate.

The two next tablets are in memory of chaplains of the church:—(1) John Henry Taylor, B.A., died at sea 30th April, 1891, aged 44 years. Senior Chaplain of St. John's Church from December 1885 to April 1888. (2) Revd. Arthur Hamilton, B.C.L., son of Sir Francis Hamilton, Bart., born 2nd February, 1806, died at sea, 2nd April, 1858. Chaplain of St. John's Church, December 1850 to January 1858.

Adjoining is a black marble tablet: erected in memory of Lieut.-Col. J. Jervis, died at sea, 3rd September, 1849, aged 52 years.

Next in order may be noticed a long Latin epitaph in honour of Major Gavin Young, Judge-Advocate-General of the Bengal Army, "an accomplished scholar, an able writer, and a true Christian:" who died on March 6th, 1841, aged 56, and lies buried in the cemetery in Lower Circular Road.

Close by is a marble tablet in memory of James Barwell,

of the Bengal Civil Service, who died 16th April, 1833, aged 49 years. He was the son of Richard Barwell of Transtead Park, Sussex, better known to India as the colleague and faithful supporter of Warren Hastings against Francis and the "majority" in Council. For 16 years he filled the office of Sub-Treasurer of the Presidency. "The best qualities of head and heart combined alike to distinguish his public and private life."

A tablet of modern erection is the next: a marble slab, commemorating L. P. Delves Broughton, Administrator General of Bengal for more than thirty years, and officiating Judge of the High Court from 1878 to 1882. Born January 16th, 1836, he died in Calcutta, January 3rd, 1903.

We now come to one of the glories of the church: the cenotaph of Lieut.-Col. James Achilles Kirkpatrick "of the Hon. E. I. Company's Military Establishment of Fort St. George, who after filling the distinguished station of Resident at the Court of Hyderabad for upwards of nine years and successfully conducting during that period various important negotiations, died at Calcutta, 15th October, 1805, aged 41 years."

This must be accounted, together with the Colvin monument, to be one of the finest monuments in the church and commemorates a remarkable man. It is by James Bacon, junior, and is a beautiful piece of sculpture. Justice poising a plummet and Science armed with a telescope are the central figures, and are represented as seated upon a plinth which upholds a funeral urn. Justice clasps to her bosom a cameo portrait of Kirkpatrick. At the side of Science appears a full-wattled cock presumably the bird of

Aesculapius: her hand reposes upon a pillar sustaining a statuette of an emblematical personage notched all over with wounds. The urn bears the arms of the Kirkpatrick family between the masks of Vulcan and Mercury: the dripping dagger and the motto "I mak' sikker" recalling the historic message conveyed by Roger Kirkpatrick to Robert the Bruce after the murder of Red John Comyn in the church at Dumfries. Space is found in the lower panel for a representation of Mother Ganges, who rests her hand upon the armorial shield of the Company. Behind this medallion rises a caduceus entwined with branches of oak and holly. At the base of the whole composition is a trophy of flags and military weapons.

It would require a volume to relate the romantic incidents of the career of James Achilles Kirkpatrick, Resident at Hyderabad from 1798 to 1805. His courtship and marriage with Khair-un-nissa, the granddaughter of the Nizam's buxey or paymaster, recalls the legend of Lord Bateman, the noble lord of high degree who won the love of his Moorish captor's daughter. The story has been told by Sir Edward Strachey in Blackwood in 1893, and elaborated six years later by Mr. Julian Cotton of the Madras Civil Service in the pages of the *Calcutta Review*. The wooing was effected in truly Oriental fashion. Kirkpatrick was sitting alone in the Residency one evening, when an old lady was brought in a palanquin to the house and demanded an interview. To his astonishment she turned out to be one of those old women who play the part of matchmakers in eastern society. She told Kirkpatrick how the Begum had seen him through the purdah during an entertainment at her grandfather's house and had fallen desperately in love at first sight: and that she had come as an emissary to arrange this marriage. Kirkpatrick refused to listen to the old lady, who with much difuculty was persuaded to leave the Residency. But a few evenings later another palanquin was brought to the house, and from it stepped the young Begum, who threw herself at the feet of the astonished Resident, and declared that her affections had been irrevocably fixed on him for some time, that her fate was linked to his, and that she would be content to pass her days with him as the humblest of handmaids. The result of this extraordinary meeting was that the Resident sought the hand of the Begum Khair-un-nissa from the Nizam, who communicated the request to the young lady's father. After much demur the buxey gave his consent to the marriage, stipulating that the rite should be performed in accordance with the customs of the Muhammadan faith. As may be imagined, the outside world stared and scoffed and blamed and understood nothing. Lord Wellesley hearing that Major Kirkpatrick had turned Muhammadan, wrote, censuring the Resident's conduct, and for some time it looked as though Kirkpatrick would be recalled. In the end, however, the true story of the affair became known and Wellesley, not only withdrew his threats of removal, but forwarded very handsome expressions of the Governor-General's sense of Kirkpatrick's great public services and promised to recommend that the King should be asked to confer a baronetcy upon him. The marriage was celebrated in due course, and was an extremely happy union, as the gallant British officer was as devoted to his beautiful princess as she was to him. He built her a beautiful Palace in Hyderabad, called the Rangmahal, which was demolished by Sir George Yule when Resident in 1863-67, an act of vandalism for which it is hard to forgive him. All that remains as a memory of Khair-un-nissa is the beautiful Rangmahal Garden, the trees of which she planted. There were two children as the result of the union, a boy who died young, and a daughter, Catharine Aurora, the Kitty Kirkpatrick of Carlyle's Reminiscences and the Blumine of his Sartor Resartus, who married Captain James Winsloe Phillipps and died at Torquay in 1889 at the age of 87. Wellesley could be cool and calculating as well as insolent and overbearing, and his change of front towards Kirkpatrick's marriage demands little explanation. He was not completely appeased it is true: and his brother Arthur did not hesitate to express to him his very unfavourable opinion of what he called the pompous and overbearing behaviour of the Resident. But Kirkpatrick's services were too valuable to be dispensed with. Henceforth he was left in peace to live *con amore* the life of a Sultan at Hyderabad. The most important of his achievements were the six treaties concluded by him with the Nizam between 1798 and 1804, which provided for the protection of the State by the British; the establishment of a garrison of horse, foot, and artillery at Secunderabad, the cost of which, in perpetuity, was met by the cession of a large territory, now included under the Madras Presidency, and known as the Ceded Districts: the disbanding of Perron's and Raymond's French levies; the deportation of French officers from Hyderabad; and the making of commercial arrangements which limited the Nizam's power to levy duty on goods in transit through his State. Those were the days before "Citizen" Tippo was crushed, when Napoleon was the scourge of the civilized world, and Trafalgar had yet to be fought. Kirkpatrick, like his chief, loved Oriental magnificence and persuaded himself, as Wellesley did and others of a later day have done, that such magnificence gave real importance to Englishmen in the eyes of native courts and of the people of the country. So intense was the thoroughness with which he threw himself into his Asiatic surroundings that he altogether dropped his English name in his dealings with the court of the Nizam, and in the vernacular correspondence is known only as Hushmat Jung, the "Magnificent in Battle." Of this magnificence, as it was seen by Mountstuart Elphinstone and Edward Strachey (described by Kirkpatrick as 'two superior young men passing through Hyderabad on their way to Poona') we have a record in Elphinstone's diary of September, 1801. After a visit to Seringapatam, where their host, Arthur Wellesley "as usual 'rowed' Hushmat Jung," they proceeded to Hyderabad and stayed there three months. Here is Elphinstone's account of the European Nabob. "Major K. is a good-looking man: seems about thirty, is really about thirty-five. He wears mustachios: his hair is cropped very short and his fingers are dyed with henna. In other respects he is like an Englishman. He is very communicative and desirous to please: but he tells long stories about himself, and practises all the affectations of which the face and eyes are capable." One of his tales was that his hookahburdar, after cheating and robbing him proceeded to England and set up as the Prince of Sylhet, took in everybody, was waited upon by Pitt, dined with the Duke of York, and was introduced to the

King. On the following day at dinner, Kirkpatrick "talked with much pomp about the sources of springs, and with execrable taste about Homer," a sore point with Elphinstone who had the Iliad and Odyssey at his fingers' ends, and used to spend hours in a cave reading the classics which he carried about with him in camp upon a special camel. His description of a presentation at Court helps one to realize Captain Grindlay's water-coloured sketches of the ceremonial visits between the Resident and the Nizam. "Went to Durbar. Major Kirkpatrick goes in great state. He has several elephants, and a state planquin, led horses, flags, long poles with tassells, etc., and is attended by two companies of infantry and a troop of cavalry. Behind the Nizam sat the first man in the country, Shums-ul-Omra. There were many other people sitting and standing. Among the latter were several women. Female sentries, dressed something like Madras sepoys, were on guard before the doors, and about twenty or thirty women were drawn up before a guard room in sight." In October, 1804, Kirkpatrick was promoted to the rank of Lieut.-Colonel, and in September, 1805, he proceeded to Calcutta to confer with Lord Cornwallis who had returned to India as Governor-General for the second time. But Cornwallis was already dead at Ghazipore when he arrived: and he himselt had been seized with a dangerous illness on his journey, which terminated fatally on October 15th, at the house in Chowringhee of his kinsman, Charles Buller of the Bengal Civil Service, whose wife, Isabella, the daughter of Kirkpatrick's brother William, was the belle of Calcutta in her youth. There is unhappily no trace of the tomb in the North Park Street cemetery, where he was buried with full public honours, but, according to the *Bengal Obituary*, the inscription upon it was the same as that which appears upon the cenotaph before us, though the latter has an addition of a dozen lines of verse.

The next two monuments are from the chisel of Richard Westmacott, R.A., and are well worthy of study.

The first is a marble monument: in memory of George Cruttenden, late Major, Hon. E. I. Co., Bengal Army, died at Macao, 23rd March, 1822, aged 54 years. His "long term of military service," affirms the lengthy inscription, "fulfilled with every mark of good desert, was followed by an active part in civil life, pursued with equal talent and integrity." In the centre of the monument is a medallion portrait. To the left is a male figure of an Indian, and to the right a Hindoo woman seated and clasping an infant. Below are sculptured panels upon either side of the inscription, which appear to be intended to illustrate the benevolence of the deceased, who had retired from the army in 1809 to join the firm of Crutttenden Mackillop and Co., of Bankshall Street. The name of Cruttenden is a familiar one in the early history of Calcutta. Edward Holden Cruttenden was second in Council at Fort William in 1753, but was dismissed from the Company's service two years later becoming a "free merchant." He was present through the siege and with his wife and three children took refuge at Fulta. His house and spacious grounds which were situated immediately to the north of the Fort, played a prominent part both in the defence and attack, and are conspicuously marked in Will's map of Calcutta in 1756.

The second also in marble, was erected by public contribution to Michael Cheese, Surgeon on the Bengal Establishment and Garrison Surgeon of Fort William, who died on the 14th January, 1816, and lies buried in the North Park Street burying-ground. The bas-relief on the monument, as on the tomb in the cemetery, represents the story of the Good Samaritan.

Adjoining is a marble tablet, commemorating James Pattle of the Bengal Civil Service, who died 4th September, 1845, aged 69 years, and also Adeline, his wife, who died at sea, 11th November, 1845, aged 52 years.

Mr. Pattle entered the Civil Service in 1790, and at the time of his death at his house in Chowringhee, was Senior Member of the Board of Revenue and the oldest servant of the Company in active employ. In accordance with his wish he was not buried in Calcutta, but his remains were preserved in spirits and conveyed to England, where they were deposited in the family vault at Camberwell. Mrs. Pattle was the daughter of Chevalier Antoine de L'Etang, Knight of St. Louis, (1757—1840) who had been a page of Marie Antoinette, and going out to Pondicherry to escape *a lettre de cachet* remained in India until his death, which occurred at Ghazipore in 1840. Their daughters were popularly known in the Calcutta of the day as "the beautiful Miss Pattles," and were as accomplished as they were charming. Charles Hay Cameron, Law Member of Council from 1842 to 1848, married the best known of them: and an account of both husband and wife will be found in the chapter in the Town Hall, where Cameron's picture hangs in the main vestibule. Mrs. Cameron's four sisters married respectively, General Colin Mackenzie (a distinguished "political," and not to be confused with the Surveyor-General of India of the same name), Henry Thoby Prinsep the elder, whose bust may also be found in the Town Hall, Henry Vincent Bayley, Judge of the High Court from 1862 to 1873, and Earl Somers. But this by no means completes the enumeration. "You must know," writes Mr. Frederick Leveson-Gower, a visitor to Calcutta in 1850, "that, wherever you go in India, you meet with some member of the Pattle family. Every other man has married, and every other woman has been, a Miss Pattle."

The marble tablet, which comes next under review, bears the name of Sir Benjamin Heath Malkin, Judge of the Supreme Court at Fort William from October 6th, 1835, to October 21st, 1837, when he died. His intimacy with Macaulay, who was Law Member of Council, as is well known, from June 1834 to January, 1838, has procured for him the honour of posthumous commemoration from that eloquent pen. For the inscription upon the tablet before us, like that upon the statue of Lord William Bentinck, which stands before the Town Hall and the memorial in St. Paul's Cathedral to Vans Agnew and Anderson, is written by Macaulay. "A man eminently distinguished by his literary and scientific attainments, by his professional learning and ability, by the clearness and accuracy of his intellect, by diligence, by patience, by firmness, by love of youth, by public spirit, ardent and disinterested, yet always under the guidance of discretion, by rigid uprightness, by unostentatious piety, by the serenity of his temper, and by the benevolence of his heart. He was born on the 29th September, 1797, he died on the 21st of October, 1837." Such are the glowing words in which Macaulay sums up his friend's character. We may fittingly reserve our own tribute of respect until we stand beside his tomb in the churchyard. He lies almost facing the western portico by which we have entered the church, and by the side of Bishop Turner and Chief Justices Blosset and Puller. His funeral hatchment, along with those of the two Chief Justices, hangs opposite on the northern wall: while immediately above us, on the southern wall, are ranged the hatchments of the first four Bishops of Calcutta, Middleton (died 1822), Heber (died 1826), James (died 1828), and Turner (died 1831). Still closer to the west gallery is a marble tablet by a son to a father in memory of one of the many victims of the disastrous war with Affghanistan with which the name of Lord Auckland is so tragically associated. Lieut.-Colonel Thomas John Anquetil, the inscription records, of the "44th Regt., B. N. I., was massacred in the performance of his duty, during the insurrection at Jugdulluck in Affghanistan, at Cabul, while commanding Shah Soojah's force on the 12th January, 1842, aged 60 years." When Dost Mahomed, the Ameer of Kabul, received a Russian mission in 1838, Lord Auckland chose to regard this as an act of hostility and declared war. For a time all went well. Kandahar and Ghuznee were captured, and Kabul occupied. The Dost fled, and in 1839, the year of Ranjeet Singh's death, Shah Sujah was installed as Ameer in the Bala Hissar. A garrison of 10,000 British soldiers was left in possession of Kabul and the chief places in Affghanistan: and the organization of Shah Soojah's troops was entrusted to Brigadier Anquetil, a distinguished soldier in the Company's service, who had been Deputy Adjutant-General in India and latterly in command of the Oudh Contingent force. As far as opportunity and time admitted, he introduced much order and many improvements into the army scattered as it was through the country. Dost Mahomed surrendered in November, 1840, to Sir William Macnaghten, Lord Auckland's Chief Secretary, who had been made envoy at the Court of Kabul. But his withdrawal to India on a handsome pension marked the beginning of the storm. On the 2nd November, 1841, Macnaghten's colleague, Sir Alexander Burnes, was murdered in his house by a mob of Affghans. No effort was made to avenge his death: and events developed so rapidly that by the following month five thousand English soldiers and sepoys found themselves shut up in a weak cantonment, with supplies cut off and the sharp Affghan winter setting in. On December 11th, the word was given for the evacuation of all the English strong places in Affghanistan: but the promised supplies were not forthcoming. Macnaghten, who had just received intimation of his appointment as Governor of Bombay, was shot dead by the Dost's son on December 23rd. The panic was now complete, and on January 6th, 1842, Elphinstone marched out of the cantonments, leaving four officers as hostages, and all his treasure, stores and ordnance except six guns. During these disastrous events, Anquetil was second or third in command: but in the unhappy and fatal retreat, he succeeded to the chief command and "restored order where all was confusion." With the exception, however, of a hundred and twenty men, women and children, including Elphinstone himself and Lady Sale, whom Akbar, the son of the Dost, took prisoners on the way and a few score sepoys who afterwards straggled into Peshawar, none were to survive the horrors of that flight in mid-winter. Thousands perished in the Khurd Kabul pass alone. In the Jugdulluck pass, the slaughter was renewed, and here Anquetil himself fell. After that all was disorder, desperation and annihilation. On the 13th January, a solitary Englishman, Dr. Brydon, half dead from wounds and exhaustion, was seen guiding his jaded pony towards the gates of Jellalabad. He was the one survivor of the Englishmen who had escaped captivity only to perish on the road to safety, and by a strange fate it fell to his lot to pass unscathed through the terrible experience of the siege of the Lucknow Residency in 1857. It is interesting to note that as recently as March last (1905), the death was announced of Mrs. Walker, widow of Colonel Walker of the Bengal Horse Artillery, who was stated to have been the last survivor of the adult English prisoners of Akbar Khan in Affghanistan. Among those who were children at the time, Sir Arthur Trevor, late member of the Viceroy's Executive Council, and Major-General W. S. Trevor, V.C., a former Public Works Secretary to the Government of India, are still alive (1905). The latter was eleven years old at the time of the disaster, and the former, who was born at Jellalabad in April, 1841, an infant in arms.

Under the staircase on the south which leads to the gallery is a marble monument in memory of Sir Charles William

Blunt, Bart., who died at Pultah on 29th September, 1802, aged 72 years. Pultah, a few miles above Barrackpore, is now the headquarter of the Calcutta Waterworks. The baronetcy dates from 1720. Blunt did not come out to India until he was 53 years of age. Barwell is found recommending him to Hastings for a writership in 1783, as having run through his fortune and deserving patronage for the sake of his family of three sons and eight daughters. Hastings gave him the post of agent for the supply of army bullocks, and he obtained in addition a share in the Post-office. Both his ventures brought him wealth, and when he died, he is said to have been worth £100,000. A curious story is related of him that he built a mausoleum for the carcases of his dead race-horses, which was still to be seen at Pultah about the year 1845. On the 20th May, 1795, two of his daughters were married "from Lady Shore's garden house," Lydia to Sir Alexander Seton, Bart., of the Bengal Civil Service (who died in 1811), and Anna Maria to the Hon. Charles Andrew Bruce (who died in 1810), Governor of Prince of Wales Island and brother of the seventh Lord Elgin. Another daughter, Charlotte, married Hastings' stepson, Sir Charles Imhoff. She nursed Hastings in his last hours, and a letter of hers, "blistered with tears," conveyed the news of his death to his life-long friend David Anderson. Blunt's third son William, also a civilian (who died in Madras in 1860 at the age of 81 years), was one of the holders of the short-lived office of Governor of Agra. He was appointed on March 20th, 1835, in succession to Sir Charles Metcalfe, who never actually took over the appointment to which he had been gazetted in November, 1834: and he handed over charge on December 1st, 1835, to Mr. Alexander Ross. His brother, Sir Charles Richard Blunt, the fourth baronet (1775-1840), was also a Bengal Civilian, and subsequently M. P. for Lewes, and was one of the chief mourners at Warren Hastings' funeral in 1818. Another Sir Charles William Blunt (1810-1890), the sixth holder of the baronetcy, was an advocate of the Supreme Court in the thirties and forties; while his cousin, Sir William, the seventh and late baronet, was once more an Indian Civilian and served in Bengal from 1846 to 1875. Remarkable as this record is, there was nothing unusual in earlier days in the presence of men of hereditary title in the ranks of the Indian Civil Service. An old Bengal Civil List counts no less than nine baronets and eleven sons of peers in its ranks.

On the western wall under the gallery, and to the south of the main entrance are the following :—

(1) Black marble tablet: Col. W. C. Faithful, C.B., died at sea, 16th March, 1838, aged 55 years. After a service of 35 years in India.

(2) White marble tablet: Capt. John Martin, 41st Regt., N. I., drowned on board the ship *Protector* in a gale off the Sandheads on 19th October, 1838, aged 38 years.

(3) Black marble tablet: Lieut. and Adjutant Robert Harvey Turnbull, 24th Regt., B. N. I., killed in action with the Choars (at Bandee) on the 1st January, 1833, aged 25 years.

(4) Capt. and Brevet-Major John Griffin, 24th Regt., B. N. I., who fell in the action fought between the British and Seikhs at Ferozeshah on 21st December, 1845, aged 47 years.

(5) Marble tablet: George Palmer, died at Purnea, September 10th, 1840. "No man possessed a more kind or benevolent heart. In manners plain, in council wise, in judgment upright, in piety and charity unostentatious: in all the relations of husband, father, and friend, exemplary and beloved." The name of Palmer has vanished from the records of the English in India. But in the days of Hastings, William Palmer, his Private Secretary, wielded both authority and influence. He married a princess of Delhi, and his son, John Palmer, was the "Prince of Merchants." At Hyderabad another branch of the family, with the Rumbolds, reigned supreme during the twenties. Their power was deemed so dangerous, that Sir Charles Metcalfe was compelled to intervene between the impoverished Nizam and the firm, which stopped payment in consequence.

The north and south galleries, as we have already noticed, have been removed. In the northern gallery there was formerly placed a tablet to the memory of Capt. Robert Adair McNaughten, of the 61st Regt., N. I., who died on May 18th, 1845, aged 49. No trace of this monument can, however, be found. There is yet another tablet in the church, which we may note before leaving it. It runs: "In memory of George Edward Lynch Cotton, Bishop of Calcutta. Consecrated 1858. Drowned at Kushtia 1866." The deceased has, properly speaking, no claim to a memorial in St. John's as he never preached there. But it is only fitting that the memory of the lamented prelate, whose name survives as the founder of Bishop Cotton's Schools, at Bangalore and Simla should be commemorated in the parish church of Bengal as well as in the more modern Cathedral of St. Paul's where there is a mosaic to his memory.

We have now completed our circuit and are once more at the main entrance on the west: from which we may make our way into the churchyard.

CHAPTER VI.

ST. JOHN'S CHURCHYARD AND THE CHARNOCK MAUSOLEUM.

In St John's Churchyard, Calcutta possesses a relic of her past older by nearly eighty years than the Cathedral of Middleton and Heber which stands in her midst. From the time of Charnock until the opening in 1767 of the South Park Street Cemetery (now itself disused), it was the sole burying-place of the settlement. The Englishmen whose bones here mingle with the dust, took part in great events and little knowing left a rich inheritance to the nation. The graves of only a few remain to-day. The excavation of the foundations of the Church was the cause of the disappearance of many of the obelisks and pyramids which our forefathers in Calcutta loved to place over their dead and which form so prominent a feature of every view of the old Burying-place prior to 1780. Others were removed in 1802, when they are stated by *Asiaticus* to have fallen into such a condition of irreparable decay that it was deemed necessary to pull down most of them "in order to prevent any dangerous accidents which the tottering ruins threatened to such as approached them." The stone and marble tablets were then cleared from the rubbish and laid against the wall of the cemetery "where they now stand." On this passage, Mrs. Emma Roberts, writing in 1830 thus comments:—"This act of desecration, the work of the reverend gentleman at the head of clerical affairs (the Rev. David Brown) gave great umbrage to the Christian population of Calcutta, who became exceedingly incensed at the root-and-branch work considered expedient to level the churchyard and get rid of all its incumbrances." The inscribed slabs no longer incline against the churchyard wall, but imbedded in cement form a paved terrace round the foot of the Charnock Mausoleum, where the epitaphs in raised letters are as fresh to-day as when they were first cut. There is many a grave, nevertheless, which the visitor will wish had been suffered to remain undisturbed. One only need be singled out, for it will occur to the mind almost without suggestion. William Hamilton takes rank, next to Charnock, among those to whom the Calcutta of to-day would gladly pay its last tribute of respect. But he has shared the fate in death of the other good surgeon of the Company whose fame, even as his, is writ large in the early annals of the English in Bengal. Gabriel Boughton, who obtained for his countrymen the privilege of free trade, died at Rajmahal, whither he had gone to tend one of the ladies of Shah Sujah's seraglio: but neither tomb nor tombstone mark his resting-place in the cemetery of that ancient capital of the Prince Governors. So, too, not a vestige survives of the spot where rests the man who was content to demand as his fee from the Mogul the gift of the "three villages of Calcutta, Chuttanuthy and Govindpore in the pergannah of Ameirabad." We read that the tombstone was discovered in the preparing of the foundations of the steeple or western porch of the church. No thought was taken of the grave itself which the tombstone must have covered: but it was decided by the Vestry on the 7th

January, 1786, "in accordance with a wish expressed by the late Governor-General Hastings," to place the slab "in the centre niche of the entrance at the east end of the church, and that the inscription be beautified by gilding the letters." There is no indication of this resolution having been carried out. The site of the grave has been altogether forgotten: and the slab with its letters ungilded is now in the Charnock Mausoleum.

Still there is more than one quaint massive piece of masonry to remind us of the debt we owe to the past. We can pause and dream of the foundation of Calcutta before the very spot which shelters the honoured remains of Charnock, the Father of the City. The names of Admiral Watson and brave little "Billy" Speke carry us back to the days when Calcutta was in the hands of the "Moors," and English ships of war sailed up the Hooghly to bombard and capture Chandernagore. The tomb of Begum Johnson is an epitome of the history of the city from the days of Clive to those of Minto. What memoirs of Macaulay in Calcutta are not awakened by the grave of Sir Benjamin Malkin, one of that noble group of philanthropic and talented men in the thirties to whom modern India is indebted for the boon of English education.

As we pursue our meditative way among the scattered survivors of this once crowded city of the dead, we shall find ourselves at every turn haunted by the spirits of many an Anglo-Indian celebrity of bygone days whom the memory will not willingly let die.

Entering the churchyard by the gate in Church Lane,

four plain monuments within an enclosure meet the view to the west of the church. These cover the remains of two Chief Justices of the Supreme Court—Sir Richard Henry Blosset (1823), and Sir Christopher Puller (1824), of a puisne Judge of a later date, Sir Benjamin Heath Malkin (1837) and of a Bishop of Calcutta, Dr. James Mathias Turner (1831). It is a melancholy commentary on the short-lived character of an Indian reputation that Malkin and Puller are better known as part-authors of musty law-reports, and Blosset as the uncle of George Grote the historian of Greece, than as occupants of the Calcutta Bench.

SIR ROBERT HENRY BLOSSET was the son of the Rev. Dr. Henry Peckwell, an eminent preacher, and took the name of Blosset from his mother who belonged to a Huguenot family. His predecessor as Chief Justice of the Supreme Court, was Sir Edward Hyde East, whose statue stands on the staircase which forms the main entrance to the High Court from the Maidan. He was sworn in on December 23rd, 1822, and died on February 1st, 1823. It is related of him that he was almost as accomplished a linguist as Sir William Jones. He was a perfect master of French, Italian, German, Latin, Greek and Hebrew, and had some knowledge of Spanish. As regards the languages of India, he employed the long sea-voyage to Calcutta in acquiring them. "The interval, to most persons tedious and to some intolerable, was to him a refreshing season of enjoyment." By the time his ship cast anchor at Hooghly, he was so well versed in Hindoostanee as to be already teaching others on board, possessed in addition a competent knowledge of Persian and was making considerable advances in Sanskrit. The Grotes with whom Sir Henry Blosset was so closely connected, were represented in India from 1833 to 1868 by Arthur Grote, brother of the historian and nephew of the Chief Justice, who retired in the latter year as a member of the Board of Revenue and whose picture hangs in the rooms of the Royal Asiatic Society. His wife, Helen Anne Grote, died in 1838, at the age of 18, on board the *Megna* Pilot vessel off Kedgeree: and lies buried in the North Park Street Cemetery. Two other Grotes were in India about the same period, both sons of the same George Grote, " of Badgemore, in Oxfordshire, and Selina Mary Blosset, who was a woman of extraordinary beauty." One, Lieutenant Frederick Grote of the Bengal Artillery, was aide-de-camp to Lord Amherst, and died in Calcutta in 1828, aged 21. The other, Robert Grote, was a young civilian, and died at Jesspore near Moradabad in 1829, at the age of 20.

SIR CHRISTOPHER PULLER was the immediate successor of Sir Robert Henry Blosset: and his tenure of office was even briefer. He was sworn in as Chief Justice on April 18th, 1824, and died on May 26th, six weeks later. Those were not healthy days for Chief Justices in Calcutta. Sir Charles Edward Grey, who followed Sir Christopher Puller, was more fortunate and held the office for seven years: but Sir William Oldnall Russell, who came next, was sworn in on July 4th, 1832, and died on January 22nd of the ensuing year.

SIR BENJAMIN MALKIN was a contemporary in

India and intimate friend of Lord Macaulay, whose last tribute, as we have already seen, stands engraved upon a tablet within the church. There is an interesting reference in the *Competition-wallah* to Malkin and the society in Calcutta of which Macaulay was the pivot. Those were days when the education of the people of the country was the all-engrossing topic of conversation—was it to be Oriental or English? Those on the side of Macaulay pressed for the latter and won the day. "A noisy and enthusiastic breakfast party frequently met to discuss the subject which was next their hearts—men, such as Sir Edward Ryan, Charles Trevelyan, John Russell Colvin, Sir Benjamin Malkin, an able Judge and a ripe scholar," and Ross Mangles, afterwards Chairman of the Directors in 1857. "And there, too, was Macaulay, in high delight at finding himself in a country where so much was to be learned: keeping the company far on towards noon over the cold curries and empty tea-cups until the consciousness of accumulating boxes drove them one by one to their respective offices." Malkin's tenure of office was as short as the esteem in which he was held by his contemporaries was great. He was sworn in as a puisne Judge of the Supreme Court in succession to Sir John Franks, on October 6th, 1835, Sir Edward Ryan being then President of the Court, and Sir John Peter Grant, father of the Lieutenant-Governor, his brother puisne. His death took place almost exactly two years later, on October 21st, 1837, and his place was filled by Sir Henry Wilmot Seton, who followed Sir Edward Ryan as Chief Justice in 1843. He was a Fellow of Trinity College, Cambridge, and the son of a miscellaneous writer, who bore the same name as himself. A funeral hatchment accompanies the monument within the church.

BISHOP TURNER was the fourth Bishop of Calcutta, and in the shortness of his Indian career furnishes, like those who lie beside him, an object-lesson of the deadliness of the Calcutta climate in the twenties and thirties. "Experience," it was written in 1755, "teaches us to verify this general observation that men's lives advanced to or nigh the age of forty are very precarious in such a change of climate from their native country." The aphorism had lost none of its tragic application in the course of seventy years. Blosset was 47, Puller 50, Malkin 40, Dr. Turner 45: and Dr. John Thomas James, his predecessor in the see, 42, when they "fell a victim to the insalubrity of the climate," as the inscriptions of the period put it with melancholy repetition. Dr. James landed in Calcutta in January, 1827, and died on board the *Marquess of Huntley* in Saugor Roads in August, 1828. Dr. Turner's episcopate did not exceed a similar period, and of the total period of one year and seven months, eight only were spent in Calcutta. But during that brief space of time, he was able to leave his mark upon the city in more ways than one. The formation of the District Charitable Society, the establishment of the High School in Chowringhee (which has since 1863 entered upon a new existence in Darjeeling as St. Paul's School) the building of the church and the Free School Church at Howrah,—the promotion of Seaman's Chapel "near the Strand," and the foundation of the Infant School, are all due to his initiative and encouragement. Nor were the other Presidencies forgotten.

Madras, Bombay and Ceylon were each visited in turn: and the Bishop's premature death in Calcutta on July 7th, 1831, was held to be largely due to the privations and the fatigue of the overland journey undertaken by him from Madras to Bombay. It is a curious commentary on the times in which he lived that one of his first acts upon arrival in India was the promotion of an address to the Governor-General praying for the suspension on Sundays of "all business in the Government offices as could without embarrassment to the services, be dispensed with."

To the right of these monuments and to the north-west of the Church stands a lofty and graceful cenotaph set up on twelve Grecian pillars, which was erected some 90 years ago, at the joint expense of Mr. William Cooper, then a member of Council, and Mr. George Hatch, of the Board of Revenue, to commemorate the officers who fell at Rampore during the second Rohilla War on the 26th of October, 1794, after a gallant resistance. Inside there is a platform designed for some military trophy which was never erected. For many years also the monument bore no inscription of any kind, but the omission was repaired by Government in 1895, and the following now appears on its eastern face:—

"In memory
of
Colonel George Burrington.

Major Thomas Bolton.	Captain Norman MacLeod.
Captain John Mawbey.	Captain John Mordaunt.
Lieut. Andrew Cummings.	Lieut. William Hencksman.
Lieut. John Plumer.	Lieut. William Odell.

Lieut. Edmund Wells.	Lieut. Y. Q. M. Birch.
Lieut. Joseph Richardson.	Lieut. Edward Baker.

Lieut. Fireworker James Telfer.

and the European and native non-commissioned officers and privates who were killed in the second Rohilla War in October, 1794."

The village near which this action was fought was anciently known as Beetura but is now appropriately named Fatehganj west (the city of victory). On the right of the road from Rampore to Bareilly a large red sandstone obelisk with an epitaph similar to the one here marks the spot where these brave men lay down their lives. In memory of the victory the word 'Rohilcund' is borne among many other honourable distinctions on the colours of the Royal Munster Fusiliers, a regiment which is a reorganization of the old Bengal European Regiment.

Facing the Rohilla cenotaph on the west is the tomb which perpetuates the memory of a gallant little midshipman who fell at the siege of Chandernagore in 1757. The memorial slab which is fully sixteen feet high is both singularly and inaccurately worded. The following inscription is cut upon it in enormous letters :—

"Here lyes the body of William Speke, aged 18, son of Hy. Speke, Esq., Captain of His Majesty's Ship *Kent*. He lost his leg and life in that ship at the capture of Fort Orleans, the 24th of March, anno 1757."

As a matter of fact, Chandernagore was taken on March 23rd, and "Billy Speke," who, according to Ives, the Surgeon of the *Kent*, was only sixteen years old, died on the

13th April, or nearly a fortnight afterwards. During the bombardment, the *Kent,* which mounted seventy guns, lay so near the Fort she was attacking, that the musket balls fired from her tops by striking against the chunam walls of the Governor's house in the centre of the citadel were beaten as flat as half-crowns. The French, who stood to their pieces as long as they had any to fire, made a most determined resistance, and the English flagship suffered so severely that by the end of the day she had lost 37 killed and 74 wounded, and had only one commissioned officer uninjured. The same shot that gave young Speke his death-blow struck his father also. But the latter's wound was not mortal. The rest of the moving tale may be told in Ives' own words. It is impossible to read them without feeling all the grief of the kind-hearted doctor for the loss of the young shipmate for whom he sorrowed so affectionately. "On my attempting to enquire into the condition of his wound, he solicitously asked me if I had dressed his father, for he could not think of my touching him before his father's wound had been properly taken care of. I assured him that the Captain had already been properly attended to—'Then,' replied the generous youth, pointing to a fellow-sufferer, 'pray, Sir, look to and dress this poor man who is groaning so sadly beside me!' I told him that he had already been taken care of and begged of him with some importunity that I now might have liberty to examine his wound. He submitted to it and calmly observed, 'Sir, I fear you must amputate above the joint!' I replied, 'My dear, I must!' I then performed the operation above the joint of the knee: but during the whole time the intrepid youth never spoke a word or uttered a groan that could be heard at a yard distance. Both the father and son, the day after the action, were sent with the rest of the wounded back to Calcutta. The father was lodged at the house of William Mackett, Esq., his brother-in-law, and his son was with me at the hospital." Mackett's house is shown in Wills' map of Calcutta in 1753 as situated in Clive Street to the east, behind the premises now occupied by Messrs. Graham & Co. He was Ninth in Council at the time of the capture of the Fort by Seraj-ud-Dowlah, and was carried away, as Holwell records, to Fulta in the ships against his will. The hospital stood in 1757 to the north of St. John's Churchyard at the corner of Council House Street and Hare Street. "In the first eight or nine days, I gave the father great comfort, by carrying him joyful tidings of his boy: and in the same manner I gratified the son in regard to his father. But, alas, from that time all the good symptoms which had hitherto attended this unparalleled youth began to disappear! He had been delirious the evening preceding the day on which he died: and at two o'clock in the morning in the utmost distress of mind, he sent me an incoherent note written by himself in pencil, of which the following is an exact copy: 'If Mr. Ives will consider the disorder a son must be in, when he is told he is dying and is yet in doubt whether his father is not in as good a state of health. If Mr. Ives is not too busy to honour this chitt, which nothing but the greatest uneasiness could draw from me. The boy waits an answer.' Immediately on receipt of this note, I visited him, and he had still sense enough to know who I was. He then began with me. 'And is he dead?' 'Who, my dear?' 'My father, Sir.'

'No, my love; nor is he in any danger, I assure you: he is almost well.' 'Thank God! then why did they tell me so? I am now satisfied and ready to die.' At that time he had a locked jaw, and was in great distress, but I understood every word so inarticulately uttered: he begged my pardon, for having (as he obligingly and tenderly expressed himself) disturbed me at so early an hour, and before the day was ended, surrendered up a valuable life."

From this chronicle of tear-stained victory we pass on to the annals of a period when the city saved by the prowess of Billy and his shipmates had no existence. To the north of the tomb of the young hero is the Charnock Mausoleum, a massive structure octagonal in form, and with a double dome which lays claim to be the oldest piece of masonry in Calcutta. In each face is a low and narrow archway. It was so placed as to immediately front the original entrance to the burying-ground which opened north of it, where the houses now intervene between it and the modern Hare Street. It is likely that it contained, when first erected, two table monuments, side by side, whose covering slabs of black stone now fill up one of the western arches of the chamber. The date of its erection, says Archdeacon Hyde, who has discussed the question with much thoroughness, may fairly be assumed to be that of the cutting of the inscription in memory of Charnock which he puts at some date prior to 1696-97. He points out that the slab which bears Charnock's name contains also that of his eldest daughter Mary, the wife of Charles Eyre, and his successor in the office of Agent. She died on February 16th, 1696-97, three years after her father, and examination of the lettering makes it plain that the two inscriptions are not contemporaneous. Eyre took charge of the agency on January 23rd, 1693-94, and since the inscription slab was *in situ,* with its lower half vacant, when his wife died, the erection of the Mausoleum cannot be dated many months earlier or later than the year 1695.

There can be no doubt, that whoever else may afterwards have been interred within the great tomb, the body of Charnock must have occupied the central position and still rests there. Excavations made in 1892 as the result of the state of disrepair into which the Mausoleum had fallen, disclosed human remains in the centre of the floor, lying east by west: and had the work been persisted in, there is every likelihood the mortal part of the Father of Calcutta would have been discovered. There are four black stone slabs now within the tomb. The two in the centre commemorate Charnock and his daughters, Mary Eyre and Catherine White, whose husband Jonathan's stone lies among those which encircle the base of the Mausoleum outside. Flanking them on the right is a slab in memory of Mrs. Maria Eyles, and on the left is the well-known tablet which recalls the name of Surgeon William Hamilton. The inscriptions on the slabs are as follows:—

(1) D. O. M. Jobus Charnock Armiger Anglus et nuper in hoc regno Bengalensi dignissimus, Anglorum Agens mortalitatis suae exuvias sub hoc marmore deposuit, ut in spe beatae resurrectionis ad Christi judicis adventum obdormirent. Qui postquam in solo non suo peregrinatus esset diu, reversus est domum suae aeternitatis decimo die Januarii, 1692. Pariter jacet Maria, Jobi primogenita,

Caroli Eyre Anglorum hicce Praefecti conjux charissima quae obiit 19 die Februarii A. D. 1696-97.

(2) Hic jacet Catherina White, Domini Jonathanis White uxor dilectissima et τοῦ μακαρίτου Jobi Charnock filia natu minima quae primo in partu et aetatis flore annum agens unum de viginti, mortem obiit, heu! immaturam 21 Januarii, 1700. Siste parumper Christiane lector (vel quisquis es tandem) et mecum defle duram sexus muliebris sortem qui per elapsa tot annorum millia culpam primae Evae luit parentis et luet usque dum aeternum stabit. In dolore paries filios—Genesis III. 16.

JOB CHARNOCK came out to India in 1655 or 1656. Nothing is known regarding his birth, parentage or early life. He first appears in the records of the Company, as Junior Member of the Council of Cossimbazar: and in a nominal roll of that factory entered in the Court Books under date 12th—13th January, 1658, there may still be read the words: "Job Charnock, Fourth, salary £20." From Cossimbazar he was transferred to Patna as chief. In 1671, an order of the Court increased his salary to £40 a year: and in 1675, he was awarded an additional £20 a year "as a gratuity." Five years later, he was, in 1680, established as Chief of the Cossimbazar factory and "Second in the Council of the Bay," with the right of succession to Mathias Vincent who was then "Chief of the Bay" at Hooghly. Nevertheless he was twice superseded, once by Sir William Hedges and again by John Beard the elder. On August 25th, 1685, Beard died at Hooghly: but Charnock was at almost open war with Shaista Khan, the Nabob, and all communications with Cossimbazar factory were cut off. In April 1686, he gave his enemies the slip and reached Hooghly where he at once assumed the chief direction of the English affairs. Four years were to elapse before the foundation of Calcutta, but henceforth his history is that of the city of which he is the Father. Besides the two daughters buried by his side, he had a third, Elizabeth, the wife of William Bowridge, who survived in Calcutta until 1753.

Of Charnock's wife no grave or monument has survived: but the romance which tradition has thrown over the marriage is well-known. It will be found in its earliest form in the narrative of Capt. Alexander Hamilton: "The country about being overspread with Paganism, the custom of wives burning with their deceased husbands is also practised here. Before the Mogul's war, Mr. Chaunock went one time with his ordinary guard of soldiers to see a young widow act that tragical catastrophe, but he was so smitten with the widow's beauty that he sent his guards to take her by force from the executioners, and conducted her to his lodgings. They lived lovingly for many years and had several children. At length she died after he had settled in Calcutta, but instead of converting her to Christianity, she made him a proselyte to Paganism, and the only part of Christianity that was remarkable in him was burying her decently, and he built a tomb over her, where all his life after her death he kept the anniversary of her death by sacrificing a cock on her tomb after the Pagan manner. This was, and is, the common report, and I have been credibly informed, both by Christians and Pagans, who lived at Calcutta under his agency, that the story was really true matter of fact." Hamilton published his "New Account of the East Indies" in 1727, but his description of Calcutta must be dated some twenty years earlier. Sir Henry Yule rejects this story altogether, because the sacrifice of a cock is not Hindoo, but if it be that Charnock's marriage took place while he was attached to the factory at Patna, an explanation may be found in the fact that the rite forms part of the worship of the Panch Pir or Five Saints in Behar, a cult which though primarily confined to low class Muhammadans, is there adopted also by Hindoos. The probability is that Hamilton is merely repeating contemporary scandal with regard to the heathen sacrifice, and that the remainder is true. For the "poetic epitaph" connected with the name of Joseph Townsend, the "Pilot of the Ganges," whose tombstone is one of those placed around the Mausoleum, shows clearly that the tradition regarding the manner in which Charnock won his dusky bride had strong hold of the Calcutta of a succeeding generation. The verses are well worthy of quotation, by reason of their corroboration, whether by accident or design, of this portion of the story told by Hamilton:—

"I've slipped my cable, messmates, I am dropping down with the tide,
"I have my sailing orders, while ye at anchor ride:
"And never, on fair June morning, have I put out to sea,
"With clearer conscience or better hope or heart more light and free.

"Nay do not cry, my Katie, only a month afloat
"And then the ring and the parson, at Fairlight church, my doat,
"The flowerstrewn path—The Press Gang!—No, I shall never see
"Her little grave where the daisies wave in the breeze on Fairlight Lee.
"Shoulder to shoulder, Joe, my boy, into the crowd like a wedge!
"Out with your hangers, messmates, but do not strike with the edge!"
"Cries Charnock," scatter the faggots! Double that Brahmin in two!
"The tall pale widow is mine, Joe—the little brown girl's for you."
Young Joe (you're nearing sixty) why is your hide so dark?
My Katie was fair with soft blue eyes—who blackened yours?—Why, hark!
The morning gun! Ho, steady! The arquebuse to me,
I've sounded the Dutch Admiral's heart as my lead doth sound the sea.
Sounding, sounding the Ganges, floating down with the tide,
Moor me close by Charnock, next to my nut brown bride,
My blessing to Katie at Fairlight: Holwell, my thanks to you.
Steady, we steer for heaven, through scud-drifts cold and blue."

The third slab, which is of solid dark green granite all but black in appearance, commemorates a personality who ranks second only to Charnock in the chronicles of the English in Bengal. It bears the following inscription in high relief: "Under this stone lyes interred the body of William Hamilton, Surgeon, who departed this life the 4th December, 1717. His Memory ought to be dear to this Nation, for the Credit he gained ye English in Curing Ferruckseer, the present King of Indostan, of a Malignant Distemper, by which he made his own Name famous at the Court of that Great Monarch, and without doubt will perpetuate his Memory as well in Great Britain as all other Nations in Europe."

WILLIAM HAMILTON, a cadet of the noble family of the Hamiltons of Dalzell, came out to India in 1709 as Surgeon of the Frigate *Sherborne*, which "mustered" at Portsmouth on January 11th, 1790, (O.S.) the monthly pay of the Captain, Henry Cornwall, being entered in the ledger as £10, and the doctor's as £3-10-0. After a voyage to Bencoolen the ship proceeded to India and anchored off Fort William in October 1710. Disputes having broken out between captain and crew, the ship was despatched to Madras on January 19th, 1711. She arrived in February with only nineteen men and boys out of her full complement of fifty. On March 3rd, the numbers having been made up, the *Sherborne* was sent with reinforcements to Cuddalore and Fort St. David, where the English were engaged in hostilities with the Rajah of Gingee. While the ship was at Fort St. David, Hamilton left the crew and made his escape to Madras in a country-boat.

In the ledger of the *Sherborne,* the account of William Hamilton closes with the scornful word "run": but he continued his flight to Calcutta, and in December 1711, was taken on to the Company's establishment as second Surgeon in Calcutta. He was appointed to accompany Surman's Embassy to Delhi in January, 1714: and it was during his stay in the capital that he cured the Emperor Ferokh Shah in November, 1715. In consequence, so runs the tradition, the prayers of the English were granted. The purchases of the three villages of Govindpore, Suttanuttee and Calcutta, was confirmed: permission was given to acquire Zemindari rights over the neighbouring villages: and the privileges of free trade and a free use of the Mint were accorded.

The Embassy left Delhi on its return journey in July, 1717, and reached Calcutta on November 22nd. Hamilton died in Calcutta on the 4th December following. The Persian inscription which stands below the English one on his tomb, says that "having raised his name in the four quarters of the earth by the cure of the King of kings, the protection of the world, Muhammed Farrukhsiyar, the victorious, and with a thousand difficulties having obtained from the Court, the asylum of the world, permission to return to his country, he died as decreed by God." His will is still extant among the consultations. It was executed on October 27th, 1717, at "Surugegurra on board the boats going for Bengal" from Delhi, and he describes himself in it as "William Hamilton, Chyrurgien of Bengall in the East Indies." He bequeathed to Mr. John Surman "my large Diamond Ring that I had given to me by King Ferruckseer and likewise my culgie," and "to the Church of Bengall one thousand rupees."

Surgeon Hamilton's tablet is to the right of Charnock's. On the left, beyond that of Catherine White, is a slab, which, like that of Hamilton, has been transferred here from another portion of the old burying-ground. It bears the following inscription:—

"*Virtus post funera vivit.*—This monument was erected in memory of Maria Eyles, daughter of Sir John Wittewrong, Baronet: and relict of John Gumley, Esq., who died Chief of Dacca in January, 1742-3. After being again married a short time to Edward Eyles, Esq., of Council at Fort William, she concluded this life with a becoming resignation, the 21st August, 1748: being well esteemed and much regretted by those who were acquainted with her engaging qualifications and personal merit."

In the consultations for January, 1748, Edward Eyles appears as "of Council" at Cossimbazar. Later on in the year he was Zemindar at Calcutta. He must have left Calcutta or died before the "Troubles," for his name does not appear as a house-owner in Wills' map of 1753, or in Mr. Hill's list of Europeans and others in the English Factories in Bengal at the time of the siege of 1756. He must not be confounded with Holwell's "good friend" Mr. Edward Eyre, Tenth of Council and Storekeeper, who perished in the Black Hole and was brother to a "Dean of Wells and to Mr. Robert Eyre, formerly Chief of Patna."

Around the base of the Mausoleum are laid a number of tablets removed from the burying-ground, ranging in date from 1693 to 1767. Beginning at the northern entrance, the visitor will find the tombstones in the following order, proceeding from left to right:

1. Mrs. Martha Orme, widow of the "Reverend Robert Orme," died February 4th, 1735: aged 67: and Mrs. Louisa Teresa Meredith, their daughter, the wife of James Meredith, "inhabitant of this place," died September 12th, 1741, aged 27.

This is a long inscription in Latin. One wonders who the "Reverend Robert Orme" may have been. He finds no mention in Archdeacon Hyde's Parochial Annals of Bengal, and was not therefore one of the chaplains of the "parish of Bengal." The historian of British India (1728—1801), who bore the same name, was a Writer at Fort William in his earlier days: but his period of residence was from 1744 to 1752, in which latter year he was transferred to Fort St. George. He rose to be Fourth in Council of that Presidency, but did not return to Calcutta. James Meredith was an attorney. He appears constantly (says Dr. C. R. Wilson) in the proceedings of the Mayor's Court from 1734 onwards.

2. Mrs. Jane Smart, relict of Jonathan Smart (see No. 8), died September 10th, 1753, aged 50 years.

3. Mr. James Ross, of Calcutta, Merchant, died October 7th, 1751, aged 45. Below is a quotation from Horace (Odes 1, 4, 13) with an English rendering from "Francis' Translation" (the father of Sir Philip Francis.)

"With equal pace impartial fate
Knocks at the palace and the cottage gate:

Nor should our sum of life extend
Our growing hopes beyond their destin'd end."

Johannah Ross, who inscribed these verses "to the memory of her tender and dear husband," gave her name, according to Upjohn's map of 1794, to an old Ghat which stood close by her house in the Great Bazar.

4. Hester and John, infant son and daughter of William and Sarah Livesay (see No. 11) who died in August, 1716.

5. Elizabeth, late wife of Jonathan Cooper, and daughter of Captain Henry Burton (see No. 14), died March, 1719, aged 29.

Jonathan Cooper's will was proved (says Wilson) in the Mayor's Court on the 3rd September, 1719: but "as his wife died some months before him in the term of his voyage then bound to Goa," it was set aside. His goods were sold "at outcry" and the proceeds paid into the Company's cash.

6. Mary, wife of Richard Wallis, "departed her life" August 3rd, 1718, aged 31.

7. Anna Moore, died December 1st, 1740.

A most pathetic inscription in Latin prose: with an English verse translation below.

"Beauty doth lay interr'd beneath this stone,
And every virtue sweetly joined in one.
Blessed was the man possess'd of such a wife:
Most bless'd was I, while God preserved her life;
Think what I've lost, kind reader: tell me then
Who in the world is wretchedest of men."

Anna Moore was the wife of Thomas Joshua Moore, a senior merchant, who was acting as sub-accomptant at the time of her death. The lettering on this tablet, lying face upwards and exposed to the elements, is gradually becoming faint.

8. Jonathan Smart, senior (husband of No. 2), died September 4th, 1745, aged 48, and his son, Jonathan Smart, junior, died September 8th, 1747, aged 25.

9. Charlotte Becher, wife of Richard Becher. "Underneath this stone lyeth the remains of Charlotte Becher, the affectionate wife of Richard Becher, Esq., in the East India Company's service in Bengal. She died the 14th day of October in the year of our Lord 1759, in the 21st year of her age, after suffering with patience a long illness occasioned by grief for the death of an only daughter, who departed this life at Fulta the 20th day of November, 1756. This monument is erected to her memory by her afflicted husband."

Richard Becher was Fourth in Council and Chief at Dacca during the "Troubles". Here Mrs. Becher and her child were made prisioners, but through the good offices of Courtin, the French Chief, were released and permitted to join the forlorn colony at Fulta. In 1759 he was Third in Council under Clive and at the Presidency, for he was the senior of the "Quorum of Zemindars," the other two being Frankland and Holwell, who in May of that year drew up the famous Proceedings which regulated the wages of "the menial servants of the settlement." From September 1767 to May, 1768, he was Zemindar. It is related of him that he retired with a competence to England in 1774, but lost his savings through the failure of one to whom he had entrusted them, and was compelled to return to India. He was re-admitted as a writer in 1781, but died in Calcutta in great poverty on November 17th, 1782. The stone over his grave in the South Park Street Burial-ground records that it is "sacred to the memory of an honest man." The Parish Register notes his marriage to Miss Charlotte Golightly on November 29th, 1752, and on July 3rd, 1754, the christening of the little one Charlotte, who died during the sad days of waiting at Fulta for the avenging army of Clive and Watson. It is worthy of record that after Becher's return to Calcutta in 1781 no less than fifteen Bechers came to India in the course of fifty years. Among them was John Harman Becher, whose daughter Anne married Richard Thackeray in 1810, and on July 18th, 1811, became the mother of the novelist.

10. Captain Isaac D'Varenne, died October 24th, 1730, aged 37.

By his Will, dated the 17th October, 1730, he leaves the major part of his estate to his wife Elizabeth, "whom I do also appoint with Mr. William Weston of this town, inhabitant, executors." This William Weston, Registrar of the Mayor's Court, was the father of Charles Weston, the benefactor of Holwell in his old age and winner of the Tiretta Bazar in the lottery of 1791. Mrs. Elizabeth D'Varenne married in 1731, Mr. Solomon Margas, senior merchant, who died at Fulta in 1756.

11. William Livesay, "Merchant, after he had voyaged

in these parts many years, an eminent supercargoe, to the general satisfaction of his employers and the public good of trade, rests here (much lamented by those who knew him) with his wife Sarah and three children Hester, John, and William, who were all born and departed this life according to the following account . . . . . Mr. William Livesay, after sorrowing some time for his said family, departed this life November 16th, 1719, aged 40 years, 1 month, and 6 days." William Livesay's will was proved on November 21st, 1719. He desires "to be buried along with my wife and children, and that there may be a strong and handsome tomb built over us."—*Wilson.*

12. Mrs. Sarah Bourchier, died February 12th, 1738-39, aged 35 years. Richard Bourchier, who, according to *Asiaticus,* built the old Court House (which stood on the site of St. Andrew's Kirk) and gave it to Government to be used as a Charity School, was in 1733 Second of Council at Fort William and Master Attendant of the Port. From 1750 to 1760 he was Governor of Bombay, and it was under his advice that Clive and Watson decided, in February, 1756, to attack Geriah, the stronghold of the piratical prince, Tullagee Angria. He died penniless and insolvent in retirement.

13. Richard Cary, Merchant, died November 15th, 1708, aged 35 years.

The following pathetic extract from the Bengal Public Consultations of November 23rd, 1710, has reference to Richard Cary's widow *née* Jane Nicks, married at Madras April 23rd, 1702, and who after his death remarried also at Madras James Collinson on July 6th, 1710-11.

"Mrs. Cary, widow, having made application to us for relief, being very poor and needy, ordered the Minister and Church to pay her Rs. 30 monthly for her maintenance."

14. Captain Henry Burton, late Commander of the ship *Loyall Captain* from Fort St. George, died December 25th, 1693, aged 42 years.

The prefix *Loyall* seems to have been a favourite one. We read of the *Loyall Merchant* anchoring in Madras roads in 1668, and in the list of ships for the "Coast and Bay" for the season 1708-1709, are the *Loyall Bliss* of 350 tons and the *Loyall Cook* of 330 tons.

15. Captain Christopher Cradock, died July 30, 1714, aged 33 years.

16. "Joseph Townshend, Pilot of the Ganges, skilful and industrious, a kind father and useful friend: died 26th June, 1738, aged 85 years."

This stone slab was found on the 5th July, 1869, eighteen inches below the level of the Churchyard, over a brick-built grave. It commemorates the same "Pilot of the Ganges" whose name stands so closely linked with that of Charnock in the verses quoted on an earlier page. "Joseph," says Dr. Wilson, should be "Josia." He is constantly mentioned as "Josia" Townshend in the Consultation Books.

17. "Peter Markland, a factor in the Hon'ble Company's Service, who departed this life 1725. To his memory this tomb is erected by Captain Richard Gosfright, Commander of the *Fordwich*." He arrived at Calcutta in the *Fordwich* in August 1722, and died intestate.—*Wilson.*

In 1730, an English squadron, under Captain Gosfright of the *Fordwich*, was despatched up the Hooghly, with instructions to seize all vessels belonging to the " German Company at Bankebazar " and succeeded in capturing the *St. Theresa* without any opposition. But a large vessel managed to get away and anchor in a position commanded by the guns of the Bankebazar Fort, and as it was not deemed advisable to follow her, she contrived to escape and put out to sea. The German Company here referred to is the Ostend East India Company, which founded a settlement in 1724 on the left bank of the Hooghly, some fifteen miles northward of Calcutta. Bankebazar does not appear in the maps of the present day, but was on the east bank of the Hooghly where Garulia now stands, opposite Bhadreswar. It was so strongly fortified that the English and the Dutch combined together to induce Shujah-ood-deen the Nabob of Bengal (1725-1739), to despatch a force against it : and it was taken after a long and gallant resistance and the fortifications razed to the ground.

18. " In memoriam Jonathani White Angli et in rebus Anglorum administrandis in hoc Bengalae regno olim Secundi : qui anno suae peregrinationis trigessimo quarto abhinc in aeternas migravit domos vigesimo tertio die Januarii, anno domini 1703."

We have already made the acquaintance of Jonathan White, for he was the husband of Charnock's youngest daughter Catherine, who died in childbed in 1700, and lies buried by the side of her father and sister within the mausoleum.

In 1695, we come across Jonathan White for the first time, as Secretary to the Council in the Bay. When Bengal was constituted a separate Presidency in 1699, and Sir Charles Eyre constituted its first President, it was ordered that there were to be four members of Council: namely, John Beard, second and accountant, Nathaniel Halsey, third and warehouse-keeper, Jonathan White fourth and "purser marine," and Ralph Sheldon, fifth and receiver of revenues. In 1703, White had risen to be second in Council under the Presidency of John Beard, who died in 1705 at Fort St. George: the third was Ralph Sheldon, and the fourth was John Russell, afterwards Governor of Fort William from 1711 to 1713. White seems to have died without making a will, but in the old Company's diary for 1703-04, there is preserved the copy of a "paper wrote with his own hand, as very well known to us, but without date interlin'd nor firm'd or seal'd." It will be found reproduced at page 350 of the first volume of Dr. C. R. Wilson's *Early Annals of the English in Bengal,* and is full of a quaint interest of its own. "The Hon'ble John Beard, President, and Ralph Sheldon of Council for the Right Honourable Company's affairs in Bengall" are named as Executors. He gives "unto my servants Killeram, Annuntram Siddo, Chunee, Beatrice and Maria, my former slaves each twenty rupees" and wills and appoints "that my body be interr'd near my late wife in her father's toomb, and that a toombstone of about one yard square be engraved in the usuall manner and sett up in said toomb." The slab which bears his name is exactly like the one to the memory of his wife, which is within the Charnock mausoleum: but it has not been placed inside, and must have been one of those collected from the ruinous tombs in the churchyard in 1802.

He appears from the context of the "paper wrote with his own hand" to have married again: but he orders that the daughter Catherine, who cost his first wife her life, is to be sent to England for education "with good attendance and prôvisions for soe tender an infant the voyage."

19. "Here lyeth the Body of Charles Beard, Esq., who departed this life the 30th December, Anno 1747, aged 49 years. He was the son of John Beard, Esq., formerly President of this place."

There were two John Beards in succession at the head of the Company's affairs in Bengal. The first was, on the displacement in 1684 of Sir William Hedges, appointed Agent at Hooghly under Fort St. George: he died in 1685 and was succeeded by Charnock. The second became Agent at Calcutta in 1699, and was second President at Fort William from 1701 to 1704. He was superseded by the Rotation Government, and died at Madras in 1705, worn out by the constant bickerings between the Old and New Companies which were not composed finally until the appointment as President of Anthony Weltden in 1709. The widow of John Beard the second's son Charles, whose tombstone is here preserved, lived in Clive Street in a house on the site of what is now the Royal Exchange, an item of contemporary topography supplied by Wills' map of 1753. She was still alive in 1756 when Calcutta was captured, and was among those who took refuge at Fulta.

19*a*. *" Here lies interred the body of Mrs. Frances Rumbold, wife of Thomas Rumbold, Esq., who departed this life in childbed, August 22nd, 1764, aged 26. This monument is erected in memory of the many virtues she possessed, and which made her truly amiable in the several relations of a child, a wife, a parent, and a friend."

This lady, *née* Berriman, was the first wife of Sir Thomas Rumbold, Bart., Governor of Fort St. George from February, 1778 to April, 1780. She was married to him at Madras on June 22nd, 1756. The Rumbolds furnish an apt illustration of Kipling's saying that certain families find their way to India, generation after generation, as dolphins follow in line across the open sea. The scandal of the day declared Thomas Rumbold to have begun life as a boots at Arthur's, the fashionable gaming house in St. James's, or in the alternative as a tide-waiter at the London Docks. As a matter of fact, he was the youngest son of William Rumbold, of the Company's service and second at Tellicherry, who in his turn had been the son of another William Rumbold, also of the Company's service: and his uncle Henry was Secretary to the Council at Fort William and died in Bengal in 1743. He

* According to the *Bengal Obituary*, which was published in Calcutta in 1848 by Messrs. Holmes, and Co., the undertakers as "a record to perpetuate the memory of departed worth," Mrs. Frances Rumbold's tombstone is named as one of those existing in the churchyard. It is not to be found at the present day, and the manner of its disappearance is unknown: but it has been thought as well to include it in the list as given in these pages, on account of the undoubted historical interest which attaches to it. It is also recorded in Urquhart's Oriental Obituary (1809) Vol. II, p. 106.

entered the Company's service in 1752 as a writer, but before long exchanged the civil for the military profession. After serving with Stringer Lawrence in the operations round Trichinopoly in 1754, he accompanied Clive to Bengal in 1756 and received a Captain's commission for his gallantry at the siege of Calcutta. He was Clive's aide-de-camp at Plassey and was severely wounded. He now reverted to the Civil Service, and in 1760, was third at Chittagong. Subsequently he became chief at Patna, and from 1766 to 1769 was "of Council" at Fort William. He had now made his fortune and returned to England where in 1770 he took his seat in the House of Commons as member for New Shoreham. In 1777, he succeeded Pigot as Governor of Fort St. George: and landed in Madras in the following year. During his tenure of office, Pondicherry capitulated to Hector Munro, and both Governor and General were created baronets. After his final return to England he continued to sit in Parliament and play the part of a nabob till his death in November, 1791. He left his estates to his children by his second wife, who was the daughter of Edmond Law, Bishop of Carlisle: but by his first wife (whose epitaph we are here considering) he had two sons. The eldest who died in 1786, was aide-de-camp to Sir Hector Munro at the siege of Pondicherry and carried home the despatches and the colours of the fortress for presentation to the King. The second son and second baronet, Sir George Berriman Rumbold, whose birth cost his mother her life, was seized by order of Napoleon while Minister Resident at Hamburgh in 1804, and conveyed as a prisoner to the Temple in Paris. He died at Memel in 1807. Two of his sons came to India and joined the banking house of Palmer & Co., at Hyderabad, where they both lie buried. George died in 1820, and Sir William, the third Baronet, in 1833, the latter leaving five sons, each of whom succeeded in turn to the baronetcy which is now held by the youngest, Sir Horace Rumbold, the well-known Ex-Ambassador. Rumbold Kote in Chudderghat, still perpetuates the connection of the family with Hyderabad, but the link has been snapped which bound them to India for more than a century.

20. Mrs. Jane Douglas, died November 7th, 1755, and her daughter Helen aged 3, who predeceased her mother on June 22nd, 1755 : wife and child of Mr. Charles Douglas, third son of Sir William Douglas of Kelhead, Baronet.

21. Captain George Goring, third son of Sir Henry Goring, Baronet, died November 11th, 1750, aged 40 years.

He was the son of the fourth Baronet and describes himself as a "Mariner" in his will which is dated December 30th, 1738. His nephew, Sir Harry Goring, the sixth Baronet, married John Anna, the only daughter of John Forster, Governor of Fort William from 1746 to 1748.

22. "Here lyeth interred the Body of Margery Jones, daughter of George Croke, Merchant, formerly of Council of this place. She was marry'd in Fort St. George to Captain John Jones, the 23rd of October Anno 1711, who afterwards being appointed Master Attendant for this Settlement, she dyed here the 25th April, 1723, aged 30 years 1 day."

23. Mrs. Jane Martin, wife of Lieutenant-Colonel Fleming Martin, died September 15th, 1766, aged 35 years.

24 & 25. "In piam memoriam Margeritae Adams, Revdi Domni Benjamanis Adams Ecclesiae Xsti, in Bengala Pastoris dilectae olim conjugis obiit decimo 3 tio Calendarum Septembris anno Domini 1703."

"Mors Janua Vitae. Piorum nitamur exemplis, doctorumque sermonibus, Perangusta enim est via quae ad vitam ducit et pauci qui inveniunt. Mat. 7, 14."

These two small slabs originally formed the ends of a small masonry tomb. Adams was third in order of those who held the office of Chaplain "at the Bay of Bengal,"

He was elected in November, 1699, arrived on June 6th, 1700, and returned home in Michaelmas, 1706. He set afoot in 1704 a vigorous project for the building of a Presidency Church, but left Bengal before his exertions bore any fruit. Before sailing for England he made his will, sealing it with a signet in the Persian Character reading "Benjamin Adams, an Englishman."

26. "Samuel Jones, son of Captain Samuel Jones of London, who died Purser of the ship *Dutchess*, June 19th, 1704."

The *Dutchess* reached Calcutta in January 29th, 1704: and the consultation book speaks of "The Pacqt. of the *Dutchess* from the Honourable Managers of the United Trade being this day brought to us by Mr. Samuel Jones, purser of said ship."—*Wilson.*

27. "Radulphus Sheldon, Armiger et Illustris Sheldoniani stematis haud indigna Proles, mortalitatis suae exuvias in spe beatae resurrectionis sub hoc tumulo depoauit Aprilis 26, 1709. Aetat. 37."

He died at Hooghly and was buried in Calcutta on the following day.

A note in the *Bengal Obituary* seeks to connect Ralph Sheldon, as the inscription upon this tablet does, with Gilbert Sheldon who succeeded Juxon as Archbishop of Canterbury in 1663, and was as remarkable for his attachment to Charles the First as for the munificent support he accorded to the advancement of learning in the University of Oxford. It appears that the Archbishop had a brother Ralph, who was the representative of the family—an ancient one in Staffordshire—and the suggestion is that the Ralph Sheldon commemorated here was his son. But we are aware of no ground for the connection, and Dr. Wilson describes him as belonging to the Sheldons of Beoly in Worcestershire. In any event Ralph Sheldon challenges remembrance on his own account as the First Collector of Calcutta, having been so appointed to receive the revenues with the rank of Fifth of Council when Bengal was constituted a separate Presidency in 1699. He was subsequently one of the Chairmen in the Rotation Government, which was the outcome of the rivalry between the "Old London Company" and the "New English Company," and lasted from 1704 until 1709. A curious light is thrown upon the remoteness of India from England in those days by the concluding episode with which Sheldon's name is connected. When the Directors in November, 1709 resolved to replace the management of their affairs in the hands of a single President, Anthony Weltden was nominated by them to the post. Weltden arrived at Fort William towards the end of July, 1710, bringing with him a commission in which Sheldon, who had already been dead for over a year was named as Third of Council. On the 4th March, 1711 further promotion came to hand for the dead man. The *Success,* which had "mustered in the Downs" on July 22nd, 1710, arrived in the Hooghly on March 1st, 1711 and six days later "weighed again and about noon got up to Calcutta and anchored opposite the Fort," which she saluted with seven guns. She brought a packet revoking Weltden's commission and appointing by another commission, dated June 23rd, 1710, "the Hon'ble Ralph Sheldon, Esq., Governor of Fort William and President of Bengall." But the decrees of the India House could not reverse those of fate: and the place went to John Russel who stood named as Sheldon's Second of Council and deserves remembrance as Oliver Cromwell's grandson.

28. "Here lies interred the body of Elizabeth Mabbe, wife of Captain John Mabbe, Mariner, who departed this life the 19th of May, 1699, in ye 23rd year of her age."

29. Elizabeth, wife of William "Barrwel" died September 25th, 1731, aged 22. William Barwell was a factor from 1722, and was appointed President and Governor of Bengal in 1748, but was "dismissed by order of the Court" after fourteen months' service, as indeed was his successor Adam Dawson. He was father of the better-known Richard Barwell, who supported Hastings so consistently in Council, retired to England in 1780 with a fortune reputed to amount to eighty lakhs, became a member of Parliament and was the typical nabob of his day. He owned extensive property in Calcutta including the land upon which Writers' Build-

ings were erected by Thomas Lyons in 1776, and which he rented to the Company for Rs. 31,720 "current rupees" per annum. His house at Kidderpore is now the Military Orphan Asylum. When he died in England in 1804, he was 63 years old, and this would place his birth in the year 1741.

30. "Francis Ailey, Thomas Ailey, Richard Gourlay, obt. August 19th, September 5th and 14th, 1708. Francis aged 3 years, 3 months, Thomas 5 years, and Richard 18 months."

The tomb of these three children recalls the passage in Sir William Hunter's *Thackerays in India*: "The price of Britsh rule in India has always been paid in the lives of little children. To many of the early fathers of Calcutta, the curse on the rebuilder of Jericho came bitterly home: "He shall lay the foundation thereof in his first-born: and in his youngest son shall he set up the gates of it."

On the path skirting the walk of Church-Lane, and to the west of the Charnock Mausoleum are a row of massive masonry tombs. Taken in their order from the north-west corner of the Churchyard, they are the following:—

31. Mrs. Frances Johnson. This is of course, the famous "Begum" Johnson, remarkable for her longevity, her influence and popularity in Calcutta society and her four weddings. The inscription upon her tomb, which is built in the form of a Greek shrine, amply (although not always correctly) sets out her life's history. She was the second daughter of Edward Crook, Esq., of Herefordshire "Governor of Fort St. David on the Coast of Coromandel,"

and was born the 10th of April, 1725. Her father, prior to his retirement from India, was offered the Government of Fort St. George, but he declined the appointment on account of age and infirm health and returned to his native country where we read he was "received with high respect by the Court of Directors." On the 3rd November, 1744—not in the year 1738 as recorded by the epitaph, which would place her only in her thirteenth year—she married Parry Purple Templer, nephew to Thomas Braddyll, "then Governor of Calcutta" and holder of that office from 1738 to 1745. "By him she had two children who died infants." Her husband died in January, 1747-48, and in November of the same year, she married again. "Her second husband was James Altham of Calcutta, who died of the small-pox a few days after the marriage." His death in fact occurred within a fortnight, and he was buried on November 12th. "She next intermarried" on November 24th of the following year, 1749, "with William Watts, Esq., then Senior Member of the Supreme Council, by whom she had issue four children" of whom one William, died in infancy. In 1756, the year of the capture of Calcutta by Seraj-ud-Dowlah, Watts was chief at Cossimbazar. He was no courtier as John Law, the chief of the neighbouring French factory at Saidabad, was. Instead of cultivating the young Nabob's friendship, he was not only suspected of conniving at his supersession, but was unwise enough to return a bold and uncompromising reply to the demand made upon him to demolish his newly-built fortifications. An immediate advance on Cossimbazar resulted in the surrender of the English without the firing of a shot, and the dramatic suicide of John Elliot, the Lieutenant in command of the slender garrison. Watts, who was in the *killah* or palace at Moorshidabad at the time, and his wife and his three surviving children Amelia, Edward and Sophia were imprisoned in the city. The mother of Seraj-ud-Dowlah befriended them, however, and, it is said, took Mrs. Watts and her little ones into her zenana. After the lapse of thirty seven days, while the Nabob was pursuing his victorious career at Calcutta, she contrived to send them by river under escort to the French factory, where they were hospitably entertained by Law, the elder son (it may be noted) of the famous financier's brother.

The surrender of Fort William and the Black Hole tragedy completed the discomfiture of the English. On the Nawab's return to Moorshidabad, he was prevailed upon to permit Watts to join his family, and the French chief soon found himself sheltering not only the fugitives from Cossimbazar, but Holwell and his fellow-survivors. A few months later, the news of the doings of Clive and Watson changed Seraj-ud-Dowlah's hostility to indecision and alarm. Thinking Watts a weak simple person, he re-admitted him to his councils, with the result that the Englishman found it an easy task to hoodwink him during the intrigues which preceded Plassey. In 1760, Watts and his family returned to England, where he died. Of the three children, the epitaph gives the following account :—

"Amelia married the Right Honourable Charles Jenkinson, afterwards Earl of Liverpool, by whom she had issue one child, Robert Banks, now Earl of Liverpool" and Prime Minister of England from 1812 to 1827; "Edward, now of Hanslope Park in the county of Bucks; Sophia, late the wife, and now the widow of George Poyntz Ricketts, Esq., late Governor of Barbadoes." At the time of their captivity in Moorshidabad, these children were six years, four years and one year old, respectively. Mrs. Watts returned alone to Bengal in 1769 to administer her husband's estate. On the 1st June, 1774, she "intermarried with the Reverend William Johnson, then principle (*sic*) Chaplain of the Presidency of Fort William." She was now in her 50th year, and it may be guessed that her final matrimonal venture was not altogether a successful one. She refused to accompany her husband to England in 1788, and he had to console himself as best he could with the three-and-a-half lakhs of rupees he is said to have carried away by way of a competence. For the next quarter of a century she continued to reside in Calcutta, and her house was the rendezvous of the fashionable world of the settlement. Her fortune was ample, and her hospitality, as we are told, dignified and generous. She lived "to the northward of the Old Fort" where Governor Cruttenden's spacious mansion had stood before the siege and where a row of business offices now forms the northern side of Fairlie Place. She died on the 3rd of February, 1812, having nearly completed her 87th year—"the oldest British resident in Bengal, universally beloved, respected and revered." So concludes the epitaph. The old burying-ground, then closed for forty years, was re-opened in her honour. During the Government of Lord Wellesley she had been accorded the special privilege of selecting her last resting place northward of the monument erected over the grave of Admiral Watson at the north-west angle of the churchyard: and here she was interred. "The funeral" we read, "was attended by a numerous company, among whom were the Right Honourable the Governor-General (Lord Minto) in the state coach with six horses, and a detachment of the body guard: the Honourable Sir Henry Russell (Chief Justice of the Supreme Court and uncle of the ill-fated Rose Aylmer), the Honourable John Lumsden, Esq. (Member of Council), and other high officials of the settlement. "Her manners," we learn from the *Bengal Obituary*, "were cheerful, polished and highly pleasing. She abounded in anecdote: and possessing ease and affability of communication, her conversation was always interesting, without any tendency to fatigue the hearer. Her views of life were correct and the benevolence of her heart and the warmth of her affections continued unimpaired to the latest period of her life." We of a later generation can only fairly imagine the charm which intercourse must have possessed with one who had had sight of Seraj-ud-Dowlah and speech with Clive and Watson and who lived to see John Company dictating terms to Holkar and Scindia and the very Mahrattas whose onslaught on Calcutta she had once so much dreaded.

We next approach the tomb of one whose fate it was to die in the full tide of success, but whose name is imperishably written upon the annals of old Calcutta. We will let the simple yet eloquent inscription speak for itself:—

(2) "Here lies interred the Body of Charles Watson, Esq., Vice-Admiral of the White, Commander-in-Chief of His Majesty's Naval Forces in the East Indies, who departed this life the 16th day of August, 1757, in the 44th year of his age. Geriah taken February 13th, 1756: Cal-

cutta freed, January 11th, 1757: Chandernagore taken, March 23rd, 1757. Exegit monumentum ære perennius."

A few words may be added by way of supplement to the glorious list of achievements which are here recorded.

Charles Watson was the son of a prebendary of Westminster and was born in 1714. He entered the navy in 1728, as a Volunteer on board the *Romney*, and having high influence at the Admiralty, passed rapidly through the subordinate ranks.

On the 9th March, 1754, His Majesty's ship *Kent* of 70 guns commissioned by Captain Henry Speke and flying the flag of Rear-Admiral Charles Watson of the Blue, Commander-in-Chief in the East Indies, sailed from Plymouth with the *Tyger, Salisbury* and *Cumberland* and two other ships (which became almost immediately disabled), and a large body of troops including Adlercron's Regiment of Marines who were later to help Clive to win the battle of Plassey. The expedition was intended to support the Company's operations in the Indies against the French who were under Bussy and Lally cementing the foundations of empire laid by the genius of Dupleix. The log of the *Kent* may be seen at the Record office in Chancery Lane, and a journal of her voyage was published in 1773 by her Surgeon, Edward Ives. On the 11th November, 1755, the squadron anchored in Bombay harbour and there found Lieut.-Colonel Robert Clive who had lately landed on the island with three companies of the King's Artillery with the design of co-operating with the Mahrattas against the French in the Carnatic and the Deccan.

A truce had, however, been just concluded: and the opportunity was taken to rid the settlement of a neighbouring pest, the pirate Tullagee Angria: whose stronghold Geriah was captured on the 13th February, 1756. Angria's power was completely destroyed, and his entire fleet burnt. The treasure recovered amouted to nearly £150,000 and innumerable stores and cannon were taken. After refitting his ships, Watson sailed for Fort St. George with Clive on board, and reached Madras Roads at the same time as the news of the English disaster in Bengal. Watson (who had been promoted on June 4th to Vice-Admiral of the White) and his second in command, Pocock, were under orders to return home: but it was at once decided that the whole force at their disposal with Clive in command of the land troops, should proceed at once to the Hooghly. The voyage was beset with many hindrances and nearly two months elapsed before anchor was cast at Fulta. The recapture of Fort William, and the burning of Hooghly and Bandel followed in rapid succession. As the star of Calcutta rose, the English began to cast longing eyes on the Naboth's vineyard at Chandernagore which lay so temptingly within reach. The arrival from Europe of news that war had been declared against the French served as a pretext: and fortune further favoured the English with a demand from Seraj-ud-Dowlah (now thoroughly cowed) for assistance against a Pathan invasion of his territories. On the 3rd March, Clive's army left Fort William *en route* for Moorshidabad. Nine days later, Chandernagore was reached, and relying on Watson's promise of support so soon as the water in the Hooghly would allow of the passage of his ships, Clive sent the following day a summons to Renault, the French Governor, to surrender. The attack began two days later, and by the morning of the 16th, the English in spite of the determined resistance of the French, had driven their enemies into the citadel and occupied the surrounding houses which gave them the practical command of the Fort. Renault's only hope now lay in blocking the narrow passage formed by a sandbank in the river a short distance below the town, in order to arrest the progress of Watson's squadron. Four large ships and a hulk were sunk and a large chain and boom laid across: but the chain was at once cut by a party from the *Tyger*, and the French pilots and boatmen hurried away without staying to sink two other ships which would have completely effected their object. Their misfortunes were caused by the defection of the only artillery officer in the garrison: a Sub-Lieutenant by the name of Cossart de Terraneau, whom tradition connects with the betrayal of the river passage to the English Admiral. As a matter of fact, Watson solved the riddle in a perfectly natural manner, for the masts of the sunken ships were left standing so as to mark their position: and de Terraneau, so far from corroborating the story by committing suicide in despair and grief, lived on until 1765. By the 18th of March, the *Kent*, the *Salisbury* and the *Tyger* anchored out of the range of Fort d'Orleans half a mile below the narrow passage, and waited for the rising of the tide off the Prussian Octagon, so called because it was the headquarters of the commercial agent of an Embden company of merchants. Four days later, the water served the ships, and in the early morning of the 23rd, Clive's men stormed the battery covering the passage, while the fleet, guided by the lights placed the evening before on the masts of the sunken vessels, moved into position opposite the Fort and opened fire at six o'clock. By half-past ten all was over: and Renault hoisted the white flag and demanded a parlev. His own picture of the situation is as graphic as it is terse. The bastions were undermined, the guns dismounted, the garrison demoralized by the loss of all the gunners and nearly two hundred men to such an extent that "no one could show himself on the bastions demolished by the fire of more than 100 guns." Still though defeated, the French were not disgraced. Watson's passage of the river in the face of a destructive fire from the Fort was a feat remarkable in the naval history of the times: but it may be questioned whether it does not yield the palm to Renault's gallant eleven days' defence, without a military engineer, with only a few sailors from the French East Indiaman *Saint Contest* to work his guns, and with only 500 Europeans and 50 Topasses to oppose to Clive's disciplined sepoys and Englishmen. The English loss was the heavier of the two. Their casualties amounted to 206, as against 150 killed and wounded of the French, figures which are invested with a significance all their own when the numerical weakness of the forces engaged is borne in mind. Renault and his Council were kept close prisoners until the overthrow of Seraj-ud-Dowlah at Plassey; and the town after a pillage of four days, was razed to the ground as a "laudable national revenge" for the conduct of Lally who had destroyed the English factors' houses at Fort St. David and sold the materials. The work was carried out so effectually that "only a few indigent widows' huts" remained standing. The palmy days of this "large, rich and thriving colony were at an end and with her fall vanished into thin air all the dreamy ambitious projects of Dupleix."

The remaining months of Watson's life were spent at Fort William in a vain combat with the deadly climate of Calcutta. The mortality at the naval hospital was very great. Ives who was in charge of it, recorded the deaths of 180 men, exclusive of those slain in battle, between Christmas Day, 1756, and November 7th, 1757. Among them was the gallant Admiral himself who died on the 16th August. A monument by Scheemakers erected by the Company in the north transept of Westminster Abbey hard by the graves of Gladstone, Pitt, Fox, and Grattan, does honour to the memory of this great and noble man: and a baronetcy was conferred in 1760 upon his son Charles, a boy of nine years old. The more modest tribute of Calcutta must be sought here: yet what need had Watson of statue of marble or of bronze? *Exegit monumentum ære perennius.*

To the south of Admiral Watson's grave are two other tombs; possessing no historical interest in themselves, but meriting nevertheless a passing glance by reason of their massive construction and old-world appearance.

(3) Mrs. Elizabeth Reed, wife of John Reed, who departed this life the 16th September, 1767, in the 26th year of her age, and her infant son who died the 17th November, following, aged one month and 12 days. "One who adorned the admirable virtues of a dutiful child, a sincere and loving wife, a tender affectionate parent, a kind relation and true friend, a humane mistress and a real well-wisher to all her fellow-creatures."

Through some confusion, the child's birth stands recorded as having taken place later than the decease of its mother.

A John Reed was Chief at Chittagong from December, 1768 to October, 1769: (see Sir Henry Cotton's History of Chittagong.)

(4) "Here lyeth the Body of Mrs. Eleanor Winwood, late wife to Major Ralph Winwood, who departed this life on the 22nd day of September, 1766, aged 22 years. Requiescat in pace."

This is the only epitaph remaining in the churchyard which contains a prayer for the soul of the deceased. Turning round after inspecting it the visitor cannot fail to be struck with the delightful charm of the scene before him. The stone steeple of the venerable Church reveals its entire height, while between the trees, across a wide expanse of *maidan,* the elegant colonnades that surround the sacred edifice mingle with those of the Rohilla cenotaph into a picture of beauty which painters and photographers alike have hitherto neglected.

Lieut.-Colonel Ralph Winwood of the Company's service, whose widow Eleanor Venner is here commemorated married as his second wife, the widow of Chaplain Parry on the 2nd July, 1770. Parry, who held his office from 1763 to 1769, was incontinently dismissed, in a manner which reminds us of George the Third and the Royal Marriage Act, for solemnizing the marriage of a Member of Council without the permission of the President, who was then Lord Clive. He was restored after two years suspension during which time he not only performed his clerical funtions, but consoled himself with taking share in the much criticized salt, betel and tobacco monopoly, sanctioned by Clive as the authorized method by which the Company's servants might grow rich. If we are to believe the somewhat jaundiced *Considerations* of Mr. William Bolts, Parry's two-thirds share brought him in no less than £2,800 the first year and £2,200 the second. But his enjoyment of his fortune was very brief. He died on April 13th, 1769, and is buried in the South Park Street burial-ground which he lived just long enough to consecrate.

CHAPTER VII.

THE PARK STREET CEMETERIES.

(By Mr. Julian Cotton, i.c.s.)

It has often been a matter of wonder that Calcutta residents so seldom visit the cemeteries in Park Street where their predecessors have been laid to rest long years ago. From the days of Sophia Goldborne down to the more recent times of Hunter, Kipling and Busteed, these "great magazines of mortality" have been explored by authors who have made them famous. To the general public they are unaccountably little known. Burials are no longer allowed in them, except to the owners of family vaults, but as a record and a relic of the past these homes of the "old dead" have an interest which is practically inexhaustible.

A ramble among the tombs will teach the visitor more about the career of our ancestors in the Land of Regrets than many an hour spent over musty records. A description of these places, as they appeared in 1785, is thus given by Sophia Goldborne: "Alas! Arabella," she writes in sentimental strain, "the Bengal burying grounds (for there are two of them) bear a melancholy testimony to the truth of my observations on the short date of existence in this climate. Obelisks and pagodas are erected at great expense; and the whole spot is surrounded by as well-turned a walk as those you traverse in Kensington Gardens, ornamented by a double row of aromatic trees, which afford a solemn and beautiful shade; in a word, not old Windsor Churchyard with all its cypress and yews is in the smallest degree comparable to them; and I quitted them with unspeakable reluctance." The opposite point of view appears in a poem on Calcutta published in 1811 by an anonymous author. "I hate," he writes, "the grounds with pyramids oppressed, Where ashes moulder in sepulchral rest, Where long effusions of the labouring pen Weep o'er the virtues of the best of men, And fond affection rears the pond'rous stone, To worth and wisdom pluck'd at twenty-one."

Drive with us, gentle reader, to the further end of Park Street and judge for yourself. The first graveyard we reach between Park Street and McLeod Street is the French or Tiretta's Burial Ground: the key of which is with the durwan of South Park Street Cemetery. The history of the person after whom this God's acre is named is worth recalling. Edward Tiretta was an Italian from Treviso near Venice, and is identified by Busteed as one of the boon companions of Casanova. He had to fly his country for a political offence and drifted to Calcutta, where he held for many years the post of Superintendent of Streets and Buildings. So well did he prosper in that profession, that he acquired a bazaar in the Chitpore Road still known as Tiretta's Bazaar. Later on he became bankrupt and his bazaar was offered by his creditors as prize in a lottery and won by Mr. Charles Weston. It is now the market for bird and beast-fanciers. The oldest tomb in Tiretta's Burial Ground is that of his wife Angelica, daughter of the Count de Carrion, who died in 1796 at the age of 18. She was first buried in the Portuguese or Barretto's burial ground at Boitakhana, but two years afterwards the husband, "under circumstances too painful to relate," had her remains exhumed and transferred to this enclosure which he bought for the purpose, and then presented to "all the Catholic Europeans and their immediate descendants dying in this settlement." Madame Tiretta lies surrounded by a motley company of foreigners —Venetians, Corsicans, Bretons, Milanese, Genoese, and the natives of such remote places as Mauritius and the island of Elba. The second oldest tomb is that of Tiretta's friend, Mark Mutty the Venetian (1797). But the most strangely fortuned of all those who are buried here is the little known Vicomtesse Adeline de Facieu (died 1855). She was the widow of Jean de Facieu, a French nobleman and colonel of cuirassiers, who migrated to India with his family in 1830 and served Runjeet Singh and his successors as commandant of cavalry till his death in 1843. His son Marie Henri Joseph had an even more eventful career. After succeeding to his father's command, he left the Punjab in 1844 and served through the Indian Mutiny as a volunteer. He was then employed by Kings Mindoon Min and Theebaw of Upper Burma as a general of cavalry. When the country was annexed, he removed to Rangoon and died there a pensioner in 1893, a strange ending for one whose ancestors had been "écuyers et capitouls" of Toulouse.

Crossing McLeod Street and still keeping to the left, we reach the Mission Cemetery. Everyone must have noticed as an eyesore an immense light-blue tomb, conspicuous for its colour among its grey companions. This is the family vault of the Kiernanders, where sleeps by the side of his two wives the Rev. John Zechariah Kiernander, a Swede, and the first Protestant Missionary to Bengal. *Asiaticus* records that padre Kiernander had not been long in Calcutta when he lost his "lady," but "he had the fortitude not to give himself up to vain lamentations, for, a few months later, the remembrance of all former sorrows was obliterated in the silken embraces of opulent beauty." In other words, he took as a second wife a rich widow. But it should not be forgotten that he devoted much of his wealth to the cause of Christianity and built the Old or Mission Church at his own expense. He died at Calcutta on the 29th December, 1799, aged 88.

Just on the right as you enter the Cemetery from the road is a suggestive name, that of Richard Burney, for 18 years Headmaster of the Kidderpore Orphanage, who died at Rangoon in 1808 in his fortieth year. A son of Dr. Charles Burney by his wife Elizabeth Allen, he was a half-brother of the celebrated Madame D'Arblay, better known to fame as Fanny Burney, Johnson's "little character monger," the authoress of Evelina.

And now to cross the road and enter the South Park Street Cemetery, which is the most interesting of all these deserted graveyards. It was opened on August 25th, 1767, for the reception of the body of Mr. John Wood, a writer in the Custom House, whose tomb was subsequently levelled to make way for the western cross road. Numbers of tablets from monuments similarly removed have been collected and inserted in the walls of the little house at the entrance. Not the least noteworthy is one high up on the right hand to Samuel Oldham (1788), the undertaker, who first brought to Calcutta the Gour stone from which so many of these slabs were cut. His initials "S. O. fecit" are to be seen on many a Bengal tombstone, from Admiral Watson in St. John's Churchyard to James Skinner, the uncle of "Secunder Sahib," at Berhampore, in the Mofussil. Here in Calcutta, he rests so surrounded by examples of his handicraft, that his epitaph might well have been written "Si monumentum quaeris circumspice."

Straight in front of the visitor at the junction of the central main walk with the second pathway leading east is the best known tomb in all this Indian Père la Chaise—an unpretentious structure topped by a fluted pillar broken across. It commemorates Rose Aylmer, Landor's early love. Her brief epitaph concludes with an insipid quotation from Young's Night Thoughts. The verses it should bear, and which it is hoped a Viceroy may one day cause to be carved upon it, are Landor's haunting lines:

"Ah, what avails the sceptred race?
Ah, what the form divine?
What every virtue, every grace?
Rose Aylmer, all were thine.
Rose Aylmer, whom these wakeful eyes
May weep, but never see,
A night of memories and sighs
I consecrate to thee."

Rose Aylmer died in 1800 at the house of her aunt, Lady Russell, one of the many English girls who died untimely in the East when hill-stations and the Suez Canal had not been invented to afford rapid escape from the malarious plains of Bengal. Another instance was Miss Charlotte Loftie, who died in 1789, aged 18. Her death, too, was recorded in verse in the Calcutta newspapers of the time. But alas, the verse was borrowed from Matthew Prior, and Charlotte Loftie does not share the immortality of Rose Aylmer. Her sister married General John Garstin and "only grieved her husband when she died" (1811). Garstin commanded the Bengal Engineers, designed the Town Hall at Calcutta, and built the extraordinary Gola or granary still existing at Bankipore. He too was laid to rest here in 1820.

Next to Rose Aylmer is another grave associated with a poet greater than Landor, Lord Byron. The memorial is that of a young sailor, Captain William Mackay (great uncle of Charles Mackay, the author of "Cheer, Boys, Cheer"). "The marble (1804) records his manly fortitude, which his interesting narrative* of the shipwreck of the *Juno* will testify to future times." As Dr. Busteed has told us, it was this narrative falling into the hands of Byron as a schoolboy that furnished him with the incident of "the two fathers in the ghastly crew" which forms the most pathetic detail of the shipwreck of Don Juan.

Away to the west amongst a forest of obelisks and sarcophagi towers the whitewashed pyramid of Sir William Jones (1794) with this noble epitaph written by himself.

*The narrative will be found reprinted in Charles Mackay's "Thousand and One Gems of English Prose."

"Here was deposited the mortal part of a man who feared God, but not Death, who thought none below him but the base and unjust, none above him but the wise and virtuous." Near at hand lie some distinguished civilians; Augustus Clevland (1784), the boy Collector and hero of the wild folk in Rajmehal; Richard Becher (1782), Thackeray's maternal grandfather; and Edward Wheler (1784), Barwell's successor in Council, whose epitaph recites his whole pedigree.

The visitor should not miss at the end of the right hand walk the stately monument to Lucia, (1772) the young wife of Robert Palk, who as Judge of the Court of Cutcherry first committed Nuncomar for forgery. A visit to this tomb inspired the famous but altogether imaginative idyll to "Lucia" in the last chapter of Rudyard Kipling's "City of Dreadful Night."

"The tender pity she would oft betray,
Shall be with interest at her shrine returned,
Connubial love connubial tears repay,
And Lucia lov'd shall still be Lucia mourned."

Further on is the last resting-place of the East Indian poet Derozio, who was cut off in 1831 at the early age of two-and-twenty. Another Anglo-Indian lyrist lies buried in this Cemetery in the person of T. W. Smyth (1863), but his grave bears no inscription. Near the tapering pillar to Colonel Valentine Blacker, (1826) historian of the Mahratta war and the hero of Blacker's Gardens, Madras, is to be found the most remarkable piece of architecture that this necropolis affords. This is nothing more or less than a Hindoo temple erected over the remains of Major-General Charles Stuart, better known as "Hindoo Stuart" from his conformity to native customs and ideas. He built a temple at Saugor and when he went to Europe took his idols with him. In 1828, he died at his residence at Wood Street; and rests here surrounded by the emblems of that idolatry which in life he cherished and preferred. His peculiar choice of a memorial recalls the monumental freak of John Hessing (1803), Dutch Commandant in the service of Scindia, who rests in the Padretolla at Agra under a red sandstone model of the Taj, which cost a lac of rupees! His son Colonel George Hessing (1826) keeps Stuart company here.

Past two more streets of tombs rises against the southern wall a pillar to the memory of Thomas James Taylor (1839) "second son of Thomas Taylor, Esq., and of Lady Lucy, youngest daughter of Charles Earl of Stanhope and grand-daughter of the immortal Chatham." Originally a Madras Cavalry officer, Taylor became a member of the Calcutta firm of Livingstone, Seyers and Co. The most pathetic part of his burial here is that he was the Old Mortality of these Park Street burial grounds and wrote an article on them in Richardson's "Bengal Annual or Literary Keepsake" for 1836 which ends with the words "I have never entered that graveyard since." He re-entered it to be buried there only three years later.

Now let us turn back to the heart of the cemetery, where the dead lie thickest. The visitor cannot fail to be struck by an enormous pyramid, which occupies more space than any other monument on the ground and must be noticed by any one driving towards the cemetery who looks over the wall at the angle made by Park and Rawdon streets. Dr. Busteed assigns this nameless pile to Elizabeth Jane Barwell, the young bride of Richard Barwell, hero of the "more curricles" story. His "lady," a Miss Sanderson, was once the toast and pride of the settlement. Twelve paces to the north of her "is chested" Sir John Clavering (1777) Hasting's choleric antagonist in council. Close by sleep the mother and children of Sir Robert Chambers; and under a mound without name one of Nuncomar's Judges, Stephen Caesar Lemaistre. Death, too, clutched his brother puisne, Hyde (1796) who rests not far from Sir William Jones' obelisk. Colonel and Lady Anne Monson (1776) lie under two low brick arches without so much as a tablet to their memory. The searcher may identify them by the tomb exactly opposite on the other side of the path which is that of Mrs. Margaret Kinsey (1813).

Before leaving this group we may pause over other dead whom the world remembers, but whose graves are quite forgotten; Charles Weston (1809) the friend and associate of Holwell, one of the jury at the Nuncomar trial, a Eurasian of great wealth and boundless generosity, who delighted to distribute with his own hand at his residence in Chinsurah one hundred gold mohurs a month to the poor; Colonel Thomas Deane Pearse (1789), "Father of the Bengal Artillery" and known to fame as Hastings' second in his duel with Francis; Mary Bowers (1781), a survivor of the Black Hole, "fidgeted into her grave" according to Hickey from fear of losing a hard-earned fortune; Burrish Crisp (1811) one of the witnesses to

Richmond Thackeray's marriage; Colonel Lillyman of the Engineers (1774), who helped to build the present Fort William; and Sir John Royds (1817), the Judge who gave his name to Royd Street; Colonels Bruce (1796) and Edmonson (1789), veterans of the Rohilla campaigns, the latter with a fine Latin inscription; and a cracked slab to George Bogle (1781) "late Ambassador to Tibet" whose fame reached the ears of Doctor Johnson.

This is but a sprinkling of those whose bones lie strewn in South Park Street. Here are civilians young and old, some of them Baronets and not a few of them Honourables; Impeys and D'Oylys, Prinseps, and Vansittarts, Shakespears and Plowdens; military men of every rank from Philip D'Auvergne and Colin Mackenzie (great among antiquarians) down to young aides-de-camp like Grote (brother of the historian) and Doveton; physicans who begin with Tysoe Saul Hancock, the correspondent of Hastings, Chidley Coote, a nephew of the General, and Rowland Jackson, Mrs. Fay's attendant, and include more recent doyens of the medical tribe in Twining, who served at Waterloo, John Adam and Mountford Bramley; chaplains of the calibre of David Brown, Thomas Yate and Christman Diemer; three successive Master Attendants of the Port of Calcutta in the persons of Henry Wedderburn, Cudbert Thornhill and William Hope, the first two of whom survived the troubles under Surajah Dowlah; sea captains as courageous as Hunt and Frost and Poynting, "commander of the ship *Resolution* in the service of the United Company of Merchants of England trading to the East Indies, who most bravely defended the *Resolution* against thirty sail of the Maharatta fleet"; Francis Le Gallais, keeper of the Harmonic Tavern where old Calcutta gloried and drank deep; Syars Driver, architect of the Roman Catholic Cathedral, which he did not live to see, and Short the name-father of one of our streets; and last, but not least, innumerable Hooghly Pilots, a service older than the Covenanted Civil Service, whose family vaults recall the hereditary calling of these "Pilotts of the Bengall River." Nor in this catalogue of departed dust should be omitted such a nondescript as Captain J. W. Porte, late of the Mahratta Army, whose relict lived to draw her pension to the age of ninety.

Of the many dwellers in this city of the dead one has his memorial in Westminster Abbey. This is Captain Edward Cook, R. N., who in the year of Seringapatam fought one of the most brilliant frigate actions on record and died at Calcutta in the hour of his triumph. He was aged only 26, but such was his fame that he was accorded the honour of a public funeral. The inscription on his tomb in South Park Street runs: "Sacred to the memory of Edward Cooke (*sic*), Esq., Captain of H. M. Ship *La Sybille*, who received a mortal wound in a gallant action with the French frigate *La Forte*, which he captured in Balasore Roads, March 1st, 1799, and brought to this port, where he died 23rd May, 1799. Aged 26 years." The *Times* in a leading article on August 3rd, 1799, upon this memorable feat of arms expressly declares that "Captain E. Cook, who commanded the *Sybille* is a son of the famous navigator of that name, and the officer who undertook the hazardous negotiation between Lord Hood and the Magistrates of Toulon, previous to our taking possession of that town and harbour." The action occurred at night between 9 P.M., on the 28th February and 2-30 A.M. the next morning. The *Forte* was at the time the largest and most heavily armed frigate afloat being one-third larger than the *Sybille*. She was originally "laid down for a 74" and carried 50 guns, or six more than her adversary. There is a graphic description of the fight in the life of Captain R. W. Eastwick, who witnessed it as a prisoner on board the *Forte*. The French frigate had been playing havoc at the Sandheads with the British shipping and had just captured Eastwick's ship the *Endeavour* and seven others in the Bay, when the *Sybille* fell in with her and compelled her to strike her colours. The French fought to the bitter end, losing Admiral De Sercey (a pupil of Suffren's), the Captain, all three Lieutenants and 55 killed and 85 wounded out of a crew of 300. Finally, the senior surviving officer—a mere lad—begged Eastwick with tears in his eyes to hail the English ship and report that the Frenchman had struck. *La Forte* was then a dismantled hulk. On the *Sybille* there were only 15 casualties, the fire from the *Forte* having gone clear over the heads of her crew and never having been brought to bear properly on her deck. But among them were not only Cook, but Captain Davis, of the Scotch Brigade, A.D.C. to Lord Mornington (as he then was) who was serving on board as a volunteer. To commemorate Cook, the East India Company erected a striking monument in St. John the Evangelist's chapel in Westminster Abbey. It is the handiwork of Bacon junior and stands near the monuments of Sir John Franklin and General Wolfe. A basrelief represents the *Forte* and *Sybille* in close action and another depicts Captain Cook wounded and supported by a sailor. The inscription records that it was erected by the Company as a grateful testimony to the valour and eminent service of the deceased "who on the 1st of March, 1799, after a long and well contested engagement captured *La Forte,* a French frigate of very superior force, in the Bay of Bengal, an event not more splendid in its achievement than important in its results to the British trade in India."

The visitor with leisure will do well to devote a separate morning to the North Park Street Cemetery on the other side of the road. Though less ancient than its fellow, which is termed in old registers the "Great Burial Ground," it too has its quota of well-known names. As we survey its rows of blackened sepulchres, a monument on the right to Captain Nathaniel Bacon (1799) who died "sincerely regretted by all who had the pleasure of knowing him," dazzles us with all the glory of new whitewash. Elsewhere the tombs of men of real distinction have been allowed to decay till they dropped. In this way has disappeared the memorial of Colonel James Achilles Kirkpatrick (1805), Resident at Hyderabad a century ago. He was no less famous in the lists of love than of war, and his marriage reads like a tale from the Arabian Nights. A Begum of high degree fell in love with him at sight; and he married her after the most daring and unconventional of wooings. Such an oriental did Kirkpatrick become that he was known in the Nizam's Capital as Hushmat Jung or the "Magnificent in Battle" and a bazar opposite the Chudderghat Residency still goes by the name of

Hushmat Gunge. In the Rang Mahal or old Residency Zenana was born his daughter Katharine Aurora, the offspring of one romance and the heroine of another. She died at Torquay in 1889 and was not only the "Kitty Kirkpatrick" of Carlyle's Reminiscences but according to some the Blumine of his "Sartor Resartus."

Seven years after this dashing cavalier found his grave in Calcutta, there was borne to rest near him a Collector of the 24-Pergannas of the honoured name of Richmond Thackeray, memorable as the father of England's greatest novelist. His monument is little cared for: but the stumpy tree which obscured it was cut down some years ago at the instance of the present writer and the inscription newly picked out with black paint. The work now needs re-doing and should be the duty of the State. Let us glance at the tomb, which is near the western boundary wall and read Hunter's interesting volume on the "Thackerays in India" when we return home. Next to Collector Thackeray is the little grave of his "only daughter" Sarah, to which Hunter makes a veiled reference in his articles contributed to the *Englishman*, "as a pathetic feminine reminiscence of the dead man's youth," but omits in his book. "Sally" Thackeray, as she was generally called, was Thackeray's daughter by Charlotte Sophia Rudd. She was born 19th November 1804 (not 1806, as calculated on her tablet) and baptized 23rd September 1815, just ten days after her father's death. On 20th July 1820, under her second name of Sarah Radfield, she married Mr. James Blechynden, a civil architect and died a widow in 1841.

Wandering now to the north-west angle of this cemetery, we find a large neglected family vault with many tablets, one of which reads "John Palmer, *Friend of the Poor,* born 8th October, 1767, died 21st January, 1836, aged 69." This good old man was once Calcutta's richest merchant prince and senior partner in the great firm of Palmer & Co., whose fall in 1830 shook Calcutta society to its foundations, followed as it was by the collapse of six other houses of agency between 1830 and 1834 for a total of seventeen millions sterling. Palmer, whose bust may be seen in the Town Hall, lived in the large house in Lal Bazar, which was subsequently the old Police Office. His father who died a General at Berhampore in 1814, had been confidential Secretary or rather confidential minister to Warren Hastings and was Grand's proposed second in his duel with Francis.

Among a wilderness of graves beyond Palmer's, will be found lying on the ground a slab to Colonel George Alexander Dyce (1836) "many years in the service of the Begum Sombre" of Sirdhana, Meerut. His son, the Chevalier David Ochterlony Dyce-Sombre, married a Viscount's daughter and spent some of his days in a mad house.

It is a relief to note the tomb of William Waite (1805), the honest blacksmith of Clive Street, "who on every occasion chose rather to give up than exact a right by an appeal to the law." James Outtram's widow records on his monument (1821) "Thou wert a friend to all save thyself, the sole exception." And what can be more pathetic than the simplicity of "Poor Tom Page (1814): Ubi animus ex multis miseriis requievit."

A word must be said of the other forgotten sahibs who haunt these solitudes; "Guru" Jones (1821), lost heir to an Irish peerage, but better known as the architect of the Seebpore College and pioneer of the Bengal Coal industry: young Graham (1800) the boy civilian, killed on his sixteenth birthday when engaging a French privateer in the Ganges; the good surgeon Michael Cheese (1816) over whose sepulchre is sculptured the parable of the Good Samaritan; Doctor William Pitt Muston (1837) the hardly used inventor of a new army dooley; "Old Masters" of the civil service such as the philanthropist E. J. Shore (1837) a son of Lord Teignmouth; John Elliot (1818) Calcutta's municipal reformer; N. J. Halhed (1838), scholar, judge and linguist; Peter Speke (1811) "long a ruling voice in the Supreme Council." These mingle with soldiers and sailors, like Colonel George Ball (1811), "glorious from the campaigns of Lord Lake," and Ambrose Kepling (1801) "one of the oldest commanders out of this port." Everywhere too are little marble crosses to mark the resting place of the lost infants with which so many of the early families of Calcutta paid their debt to the East.

From North Park Street the visitor should pass on to the Lower Circular Road Cemetery. Crossing the boulevard which covers the site of the old Mahratta Ditch, he will find himself in a short space of time before the portals of another great Campo Santo, opened in 1840 for the remains of a little child: it has been ever since the repository of the Calcutta dead. Near the entrance is conspicuous the tomb with handsome bas-relief of Sir W.

H. Macnaghten, Bart., Envoy to the Court of Cabul and Governor elect of Bombay, who fell with "Secunder" Burnes in the Cabul massacre of December 1841, and whose remains were rescued and placed here by his widow sixteen months later. Almost opposite "the Great Elchee" is encased in wire netting the monument to Sir William Casement (1843), member of the Supreme Council, who has the honour of a bust in the Town Hall. In that death-dealing decade were buried here many illustrious men, the most forgotten of whom, perhaps, is David Drummond (1843), the teacher of Derozio, an eccentric Scotch dominie, who kept a school in Dhurrumtollah, near where Hart's livery stables now stand. Drummond was a poet himself, but his book of verses never saw the light. It was his dying wish that these poems—written in his native Doric—should be published in Scotland, but the ship that carried them was lost and thus perished (according to Thomas Edwards, the biographer of Derozio) "some of the first Scottish lyrics since the days of Burns and Tannahill." He sleeps off his sorrows beside other forgotten educationists, such as Jacques Isaac D'Anselm, Comte de Clavaillan (1846), first Head Master of the Calcutta Hindu College and Henry Blochmann (1878), Principal of the Madrasa, who lies at rest next his little son.

In 1841 was entombed here David Carmichael Smyth, B.C.S., whose brother, when a Captain of Bengal Engineers, married at Cawnpore in 1817 Anne Becher, the widow of Richmond Thackeray. The novelist's stepfather was afterwards Superintendent of Addiscombe, and lived to a patriarchal old age. Dying at Ayr in 1861, his epitaph was written by Mrs. Ritchie, and ends with the "Adsum" quotation from the Newcomes.

Here, too, is the grave of John Edwardes Lyall (1845), Advocate-General, who passed away at Barrackpore at the early age of 35. He was a contemporary of Gladstone at Oxford and President of the Union in 1831. His Indian law students have cherished his memory by a tablet in the Presidency College to "the zealous friend of the natives and the first gratuitous lecturer on Jurisprudence in this Hall." Nor is he the only legal light buried here. The law is also represented by James Colebrooke Sutherland (1844), Secretary to the Law Commission: by James Drinkwater Bethune (1851), founder and endower of the Society that bears his honoured name; by John Paxton Norman (1871), assassinated on the steps of the Town Hall when acting as Chief Justice; and by Henry Vincent Bayley (1873), the last of the "Old Brigade" of *quihyes* to smoke a hookah in the Bengal Club. Of civic dignitaries whose features live in canvas or marble in the Town Hall and Municipal Office, several have found sepulchre here; Becket Greenlaw (1844), whose tomb is on the left as you enter; Henry Mead, the brilliant editor, drowned in the Hooghly (1862); and John Blessington Roberts (1880) who rose from a police constable to be Presidency Magistrate. The Civil Service has given of its ablest in John Dent (1845), Provisional Member of Council, Madras; in Henry Whitelock Torrens (1852), a renowned orientalist; and coming to recent times, Colman Patrick Macaulay (1890), and Stephen Jacob (1898), the distinguished financier and aintly-minded Christian. An even more eminent name in inance is that of James Wilson (1860), Secretary to the Treasury under two Premiers, and specially sent to India o restore order in a financial crisis. Immediately behind iis grave is the resting place of two sons of Archbishop French. A later notability is Sir John Woodburn (1902) Lieutenant-Governor of Bengal. Nor are military men wanting in the record; Sir Alexander Mackenzie (1841), ' Knight Baronet " and Captain in a marching regiment; Major Gavin Young (1841), Judge Advocate-General; William L. Mackintosh (1844), A.D.-C., to Lord Hardinge, and Superintendent of the Mysore Princes; and Colonel Henry Forster, C.B., (1862), the Eurasian officer who was complimented in Parliament by the Duke of Wellington. Among humbler heroes there are not a few Americans, who as sea-captains or merchant venturers, met their death in the city by the Hooghly.

And if the Autobiography of the Dead in a Calcutta Cemetery were ever to be written, who better could do it than William Cotes Blacquiere, who landing in India in 1771 was buried here on August 15th, 1853 at the age of 94. Sixty years a Magistrate and a Mason, the friend of Sir William Jones and the St. John of Zoffany's altarpiece of our old Cathedral, his career is a true standpoint from which to view life and labour in India.

But the sun is now high in the heavens. Let us leave the dwellers in these sad settlements along Park Street and Circular Road to their daily spell of silence and repose. Another day we will wend to the old military cemetery at Bhowanipore (opened in 1782) and stand before the grave of Henry W. M. Thackeray, Surgeon of the Bengal Artillery (1813), whose tomb was "a tribute of gratitude from the pupil to the memory of his master." He sleeps there in strange company with Captain Donald Macintyre (1809 a native of Lochandside, Argyleshire, "and late of the Mahratta service"; with the child of Mrs. Esther Leach, a sergeant's wife, who was the greatest Calcutta actress of her day; with Eliza Bellamy, "who followed for 34 years the profession of midwife in India," and at the other end of the scale Doctor Henry Harpur Spry (1842), Fellow of the Royal Society. The poor dead Thackeray was a cousin of Richmond Thackeray, who headed his relative's *cortége* to the grave and was himself carried out for burial two years later.

Here at Bhowanipore will be found the dust of two great generals; Sir Thomas Valiant, K.C.B., K.H., (1784-1845), the hero of a hundred fights, who died in his bed while commanding the garrison at Fort William, and Sir William Lockhart, G.C.B., (1841-1900), leader of the Tirah expedition in 1897 and afterwards Commander-in-Chief in India. Less ambitious but equally glorious are the records written over the tombs of Major William Turner (1841) of the 50th Foot, who served for 34 years in Holland and in the Peninsular and lost an arm at the battle of Vittoria: and Captain William Armstrong (1841), of the 21st Royal North British Fusiliers, "who was the eldest of three brothers who entered her Majesty's service and died within three years of each other, the second in Canada, and the third in Western Australia."

It is not easy to exhaust the interest of these old Calcutta graveyards. They are something more than mere fields where the dead are stored away unknown. They are a touching and instructive history, written in family burial plots, in mounded graves, in sculptured and inscribed monuments. They tell us of the past, its individual lives, of its men and women, of its children, of its households. We find no such record elsewhere of the price paid for Calcutta by generations of bygone Englishmen, who lived and died at their work. To the reader who desires to study still further these mortuary memorials, there is a comprehensive Directory of the Dead to hand in the "Bengal Obituary" published in 1848 by a firm of Cossitollah undertakers. This volume preserves not only the epitaphs of the multitude that have disappeared, but summarises in thumb nail sketches the careers of the many notabilities whose deaths are monumentally recorded in the now closed-up graveyards of the past.

CHAPTER VIII.

ST. PAUL'S CATHEDRAL.

THE Bishopric of Calcutta was created in 1813, and the first four incumbents of the See—Middleton, Heber, James and Turner—were enthroned in the old Cathedral Church of St. John; which for 32 years remained the Cathedral of the Diocese. So long ago, however, as the year 1819, the idea of a new Cathedral Church was entertained, and a design and plan on a grand scale were prepared, but the project fell through. Twenty years after it was revived by Bishop Wilson, who succeeded Turner in 1833, and prosecuted by him with characteristic energy. He applied to Government for a site, and the moment the present one, which is exceptionally finely situated at the extreme south of the Maidan, was granted he took possession. A Committee was appointed, and on the 8th October, 1839, the foundation stone was laid.

The design and plans were prepared by Major (afterwards General) W. N. Forbes, of the Bengal Engineers, the architect of the Mint and carried out under his superintendence. The style of the building is "Indo-gothic," that is to say, spurious gothic adapted to the exigencies of the Indian climate. The extreme length of the building is 247 feet and its width 81 feet, and the transepts 114 feet. The height of the Tower and Spire from the ground is 201 feet, and the walls to the top of the battlements, 59 feet. The western vestibule which supplies the principal entrance is 36 ft. by 22 ft. 8 inches. The lantern beneath the Tower is 27 feet square, and opens by lofty arches to the transepts. The dimensions of the main body of the Cathedral are 127 feet by 61 feet, and it is spanned by an iron-trussed roof, adorned with gothic tracery. The chimes of the Clock which is the work of Vulliamy, are very melodious. The great bell bears the inscription—"Its sound is gone out into all lands." During the great earthquake of the 12th June 1897 the upper part of the steeple fell, but it has since been restored.

The Cathedral was consecrated by Bishop Wilson on the 8th of October, 1847. The expenditure on the building was about 5 lakhs of rupees. About seven and a half lakhs was raised, of which the Bishop gave two lakhs—one lakh for the building and one for the endowment. The East India Company appointed two additional chaplains, and contributed a lakh and a half towards the building. The subscription raised in India amounted to a lakh and a quarter: in England to £13,000, besides a grant from the Society for the Propagation of the Gospel of £5,000; one from the Society for the Promotion of Christian Knowledge of £5,000; and a gift from Mr. Thomas Nutt, of London, of £4,000. The Communion Plate was the gift of Her Majesty Queen Victoria.

The main entrance is by the west, and access is had by a lofty enclosed verandah or porch, 61 feet high by 21 in length. Over the porch is the Cathedral Library, containing a good collection of books in Divinity and general literature, the bulk of which was bequeathed by Bishop Wilson. All persons who can bring a letter of recommendation from a clergyman or other sponsor of position are freely admitted to the privilege of using the Library and books may be also taken out under certain conditions which are not very onerous. The Library contains a fine marble bust of Bishop Wilson and a valuable clock which is also his gift, and which was presented to him in June 1832, by his former parishioners of St. Mary's Islington.

Before we descend, we should not forget to examine the lower lights of the great west window of the Cathedral which are very fine and are not visible from below. The window, which was designed by Sir Edward Burne Jones, is a memorial to Lord Mayo, Viceroy of India from 1869 to 1872, who was assassinated at Port Blair in February of the latter year.

In the vestry, which is on the ground floor, will be found a large folio manuscript volume, entitled "History of the Erection of St. Paul's Cathedral Calcutta drawn up by the Rev. J. H. Pratt, Bishop's chaplain" which contains a plan of the Building at p. 265.

There are some fine monuments in the vestibule and in the north and south transepts; of which the principal will be indicated as we make our way round the building. In the vestibule, we may notice the following :—

Upon the western wall, and to the north of the entrance is a brass tablet in memory of Lieutenant William Charles Owen of the 3rd Hussars, and 3rd Queen's Own Bombay Light Cavalry, "who met a brave soldier's death when charging the enemy" at the disastrous battle of

Maiwand during the Afghan war of 1880. The epitaph continues with these remarkable words. "The holiest place on earth on which to live or die is not on encaustic soil or tessellated pavement, but at the post of duty."

To the left on the northern wall is a fine marble tablet erected by the Officers of the Corps of Bengal Engineers in 1862 in honour of their comrades who fell during the "Indian Revolt" of 1857 and 1858. The names are engraved on a panel of black marble in the centre, surrounded by sixteen medallion portraits and a panel below representing the gallant blowing up of the Kashmir gate at Delhi, by Lieutenants Duncan C. Home, V.C., and Philip Salkeld, V.C. The moat may be seen spanned by a few beams of wood. Against the door in the gate bags of powder have been heaped up, and an English engineer is crawling over the beams with a light in his hand. Two others are watching him from the moat below. To the left three men are carrying off a wounded comrade. While endeavouring to fire the charge, Salkeld was mortally wounded but he handed over the slow match to Corporal Burgess who performed the task just as he too fell mortally wounded. Among the other names commemorated may be noticed those of Captain C.W.W. Fulton, the life and soul of the beleagured garrison of the Residency, to whom was given by common consent of his comrades the proud title of "Defender of Lucknow," and Colonel Hugh Fraser, C.B., who acted as Chief Commissioner in the North Western Provinces upon the death of John Russell Colvin in September 1857 until Lord Canning's arrival in Upper India in February 1858.

Beyond in the north-eastern corner is a beautiful gothic mural monument, erected by the Government of India, which commemorates the tragic death of the Hon'ble John Paxton Norman, Officiating Chief Justice of Bengal, who was assassinated on the steps of the Town Hall on the 20th September, 1871, as he was on his way to take his seat in court. He was appointed one of the first barrister puisne Judges of the High Court at Fort William, upon its constitution in 1862: and acted as Chief Justice in 1864 during the absence of Sir Barnes Peacock on leave. His death took place while he was officiating for the second time and when he was on the point of retirement. He was a true friend to the people of India, and took a hearty interest and an active part in all measures for their advancement. "Above all men, it might be asserted of him that he had not an enemy."

The monument is surmounted by a cross, and flanked by two columns bearing figures of angels. Within the arch there is a division into three compartments. In the highest is seated Justice holding her scales, with a background of coloured tiles. The middle compartment is cut into two by a tree. On the right are two Muhammadan merchants and a camel, with a mosque in the background. On the left are a Hindoo father and mother, a cow, and two children, one in its mother's arms, and the other feeding the cow: behind them is a Hindoo temple. The lowest compartment contains the inscription.

To the right is a tablet in commemoration of a number of officers of the Artillery, Engineers and 11th, 29th and 43rd Native Infantry who fell in the Bhutan campaign of

1864, 1865, and 1866. It is surmounted by a shield and a medallion within which is a helmet. On one side of the shield is a cannon, on the other three cannon-balls, and from behind the shield and medallion issue four flags, two on each side. Above is a wreath. The names of fifteen officers appear on the tablet, no less than four of whom (Griffin, Garstin, Mayne and Cumine) were majors.

Crossing over to the southern side of the vestibule, we may observe in passing a mural tablet surmounted by a sword, and above it a medallion displaying in their correct colours the Bruce crest (a lion rampant) the Bruce motto "Fuimus" and the cross of the Order of the Bath. It was erected in memory of Lieutenant-Colonel Herbert Bruce, C.B., of the Bombay Staff Corps, "who after a distinguished service of twenty-four years in India, died at Suez on his voyage to England on the 24th February, 1866, aged 40 years." Close by is a tablet in commemoration of the Officers of the British India Company's service who perished by the loss of the steamer "Camorta" in a cyclone off the south coast of Burmah in May, 1902. Next to these are monuments to two distinguished Engineer Officers which deserve more detailed notice.

The first is a marble tablet in memory of Major General Daniel George Robinson, R.E., for twelve years Director-General of the Telegraphs of India, who also died at sea, homeward bound, on July 27th, 1878, aged 51 years. His bust by Geflowski, "subscribed for in affectionate remembrance by over 400 members of the Department," adorns the vestibule of the Central Telegraph Office in Dalhousie Square.

Adjoining is another marble tablet with two supporters, surmounted by a fine bust by Theed of Major-General William Nairn Forbes, of the Bengal Engineers, architect of the Cathedral and Mint, "and various other public buildings. He was born at Blackford in Aberdeenshire, April 3rd 1796 and died near Aden, on his way to England, May 1st, 1855." The monument is "erected by the affection of his friends and fellow-citizens." Forbes' connection with the Cathedral was merely that of architect. With the Mint he is linked by ties of the closest character. He not only designed and constructed that noble building and erected all the complicated machinery in it, but superintended the operations of the institution as Mint Master for upwards of twenty years. To mark their sense of his eminent services the East India Company placed a marble bust of Forbes by Foley in the Mint in 1858. The bust in the Cathedral was given by Bishop Wilson in the year preceding.

Passing eastward under the Tower Arch, we find upon the same side of the Church a marble monument in memory of seven officers of the 68th Native Infantry who "died during the Mutiny of the Native Troops and subsequent operations from 1857 to 1859. Some on the field of battle, some by the hands of their own followers, others from disease—all doing their duty." One of the names, that of Lieut. James Augustus Dorin, recalls memories of Joseph Alexander Dorin, who, with Barnes Peacock and John Peter Grant, shared as members of his Executive Council the anxieties of Lord Canning during these eventful years.

To the east is a fine marble monument by J. H. Foley, R.A., which commemorates William Ritchie, the playfellow and friend of William Makepeace Thackeray. On each side of the pedestal, supporting a bust of Ritchie, are full-length figures, the one on the right representing Law, and the other on the left Religion. At the base are Ritchie's arms and crest and the motto: "virtute acquiritur honos."

The inscription was written by Thackeray himself, and runs as follows:—

"A memorial of the affection of friends and fellow-citizens for William Ritchie of the Calcutta Bar and Inner Temple, Member of the Council of the Governor-General, Vice-Chancellor of the University, and twenty years a resident in Calcutta. To a clear intellect and sweet and generous temper England had added her highest education and God his grace. Public-spirited, wise, and beloved, his career was one of rare success, breeding no envy. His death was felt to be a calamity alike public and private and carried grief into many households, but left to all who mourn him the bright assurance of his rest in Christ. He died in Calcutta March 22nd, A.D. 1862, in his 46th year."

Ritchie was admitted as an advocate of the Supreme Court in March, 1813, and filled the office of Advocate-General from 1855 to 1861. In September of the latter year he was appointed a provisional member of the Supreme Council, and was confirmed as Law Member a month later. He died on March 22nd, 1862, and was succeeded by Sir Henry Sumner Maine. Ritchie's mother,

Charlotte, was the daughter of "Sylhet" Thackeray, the grandfather of the novelist and the founder of the family's connection with India. Readers of Thackeray will remember the passage in one of his *Roundabout Papers* where he pays a last tribute to Sir Richmond Shakespear, another cousin, who died in the very year in which Ritchie was appointed Law Member of Council. "In one of the stories by the present writer, a man is described tottering 'up the steps of the ghaut,' having just parted with his child, whom he is despatching to England from India. I wrote this, remembering in long, long distant days such a ghaut, a river-stair, at Calcutta: and a day when, down those steps, to a boat which was in waiting, came two children, whose mothers remained on the shore. One of those ladies was never to see her boy any more: and he, too, is just dead in India "of bronchitis, on the 29th October." We were first cousins: had been little friends and playmates from the time of our birth: and the first house in London to which I was taken was that of our aunt, the mother of His Honour the Member of Council. His Honour was even then a gentleman of the long robe, being, in truth, a baby in arms. We Indian children were consigned to a school of which our deluded parents had heard a favourable report, but which was governed by a horrible little tyrant, who made our young lives so miserable that I remember kneeling by my little bed of a night, and saying "Pray God, I may dream of my mother!" Thence we went to a public school: and my cousin to Addiscombe and to India......And Fort William guns are saluting in one man's honour, while the troops are firing the last volleys over the other's grave—over the grave of the brave, the gentle, the faithful, Christian soldier." Two of Mr. William Ritchie's sons have been closely connected with India. Mr. John Gerald Ritchie, served in the Bengal Civil Service from 1875 to 1900, and was Chairman of the Corporation of Calcutta from 1892 to 1895. Mr. Richmond Thackeray Ritchie, C.B., who is married to a daughter of the novelist, entered the India Office by open competition in 1877 and is now Secretary in the Political Department.

Almost facing Ritchie's tablet is a monument to the memory of James Bruce, eighth Earl of Elgin and Kincardine, K.T., Governor-General of India from March 12th, 1862, to the date of his death at Dharamsala on November 20th, 1863, at the age of 52. The monument was erected by Government in recognition of the many eminent services rendered to his country, as Plenipotentiary to China and Governor and Governor-General in succession of Jamaica, Canada, and India. It takes the form of a cenotaph with an inlaid brass cross, at the base of which is inscribed the Elgin motto "Fuimus." The cenotaph is surmounted by a large gothic canopy. Within this is a marble medallion portrait, which hardly does Lord Elgin justice, and below the head are four bronze panels, with the words "Jamaica," "Canada," "China," "India." The first represents a white man speaking to negroes. In the second are English settlers felling trees, while an Indian chief in a recumbent attitude and a squaw with an infant in her arms, observe their labours. In the third, Lord Elgin is addressing a mandarin, while a Chinaman unfolds the flag of China at their feet. The fourth represents a scene in an Indian camp, with a tent and elephant in the background, and a Parsi, a Sikh soldier and other Indians in front.

Thomas Bruce, the seventh Earl, who is best known to fame as the Ambassador to Turkey and collector of the Elgin marbles, was connected with India through his brother, the Hon'ble Charles Andrew Bruce (died 1810), Governor of Prince of Wales' Island, whose wife Anna Maria, daughter of Sir Charles Blunt, Bart., of the Bengal Civil Service, died at Hooghly "after one day's illness" on September 19th, 1790, and lies in the South Park Street Burying-ground. Victor Alexander Bruce, the ninth Earl, was Viceroy and Governor-General of India from 1894 to 1899.

Immediately beyond and opposite the memorial to the officers of the 68th Native Infantry, is the monument by J. H. Foley, R.A., of Sir Henry Montgomery Lawrence, K.C.B., "who fell in the memorable defence of Lucknow on the 4th July, 1857," a very graceful marble tablet supported by serpentine pillars, with white marble medallion portrait.

The inscription is worth reproduction: "In memory of the great and good Sir Henry Montgomery Lawrence, K.C.B.," it runs, "Christian, statesman, philanthropist and soldier: who, in the Punjab, Rajpootana, and Oudh, taught how kindly subject races should be ruled: who, first in India, founded hill asylums for British soldiers' children, and who fell in the memorable defence of Lucknow, 4th July, 1857, beloved and mourned by natives and Europeans. As the monument he would have most desired, the community of Calcutta and Bengal joined with that of Upper India in founding a "Henry Lawrence Memorial Asylum for soldiers' children" at Murree, in the hills of the Punjab: they also erect this tablet in the Cathedral to keep among them his memory and example." The circumstances of Lawrence's tragic end have obscured in the public mind the earlier chapters of his official career; but his name is still venerated in the Punjab, where he and his brother John were placed in joint charge by Lord Dalhousie after the downfall in 1849 of Ranjeet Singh's Kingdom. It was the view of the elder that the feudal nobility of the conquered province should be treated with consideration and kindness, and he regarded his policy, not only as just in itself, but as the best for securing friends to the new Government. The sympathy of John Lawrence with the cultivators ranged him upon the opposite side, and in the result both brothers tendered their resignation. That of Henry was accepted, and the younger was left to carry on the work of pacification according to his own lights. The outbreak of the Mutiny gave John Lawrence his opportunity, and he was hailed on every side as the saviour of India. But his magnificent successes were in reality the justification of Henry Lawrence's policy of wise conciliation. The chiefs, for whom he had interceded and sacrificed his post, and whose ancient rights were respected as the outcome of the struggle, cast in their lot with the English and enabled John Lawrence to send our troops out of the Punjab to Delhi. As Henry Lawrence lay dying in the Residency, we learn from Sir Joseph Fayrer, whose manuscript diary has lately been placed at the disposal of Mr. Forrest, that one of the subjects which seemed to be most present to the departing hero's mind was the causes of the revolt and of the troubles in which he and his garrison were involved. He talked frequently in an excited but impressive way, says, Sir Joseph, and spoke of the injudicious method in which the native landholders had been dealt with by the Government, and among other things he declared more than once with emphasis, " It was the John Lawrences, the Thomasons, the Edmonstones (and others) who brought India to this." We may condemn the judgment as unduly harsh: but Henry Lawrence is at any rate right in this, that if the English in India have ever again to fight for their supremacy, the friends of which they will most stand in need are the great landowning class.

Under the Tower there kneels in full canonicals Reginald Heber, Bishop of Calcutta from 1823 to 1826: a superb monument in white statuary marble, executed by Sir Francis Chantrey, R.A., in 1835. The base bears the one word, " Heber." Reginald Heber was third Bishop of Calcutta. There are two other statues to his memory, both from the chisel of Sir Francis Chantrey, the one in the south aisle of the choir of St. Paul's Cathedral, London (which is similar to the present), and the other in St. George's Cathedral, Madras, which represents him in the act of laying on of hands. Heber lies buried in St. John's Church Cemetery, Trichinopoly; his death on April 3rd, 1826, was occasioned, as is well known, by failure of the heart's action caused by plunging into a bath at the house of Mr. John Bird, the District Judge, when in an exhausted condition. He was related, through his wife, to Sir William Jones, who married Mr. Heber's aunt in the year

(1783) of the Bishop's birth, and himself died in Calcutta in 1794.

Turning to the right into the south transept, we may notice a white marble tablet on the eastern wall in memory of Sir Henry Miers Elliot, K.C.B., the "dulce decus" of the Bengal Civil Service, who died at Simon's Town on December 20th, 1853, aged 45 years. Elliot was born in 1808 and educated at Winchester. He was destined for New College: but the demand of the East India Company for civilians beyond the numbers regularly trained tempted him in 1826 to try for an appointment in their service, and he was first of "competition-wallahs" to pass an open examination for an immediate post in India. His Oriental languages as well as his classics proved so good, that he was actually placed by himself in an honorary class. His early service was spent in Northern India: but in 1847 he was appointed Secretary to the Governor-General in Council in the Foreign Department. In this capacity he accompanied Lord Hardinge to the Punjab and drew up an admirable memoir on its resources. As Foreign Secretary, he also visited the Western frontier with Dalhousie on the occasion of the Sikh War, and negotiated the treaty with the Sikh chiefs by which the settlement of the Punjab and Gujrat was secured. For these services he received a K.C.B. in 1849. Throughout his official career he devoted his leisure to study. In 1845 he published at Agra his supplement to the projected official "Glossary of Indian Judicial and Revenue Terms," which is described by Horace Hayman Wilson, as "replete with curious and valuable information, especially as regards the tribes and class of

Brahmins and Rajputs." A second edition appeared in 1860. His chief completed work, however, was the "Bibliographical Index to the Historians of Muhammadan India," in which he proposed to give an analysis of the contents and a criticism of the value of 231 Arabic and Persian historians of India. But he only lived to bring out the first volume in 1849. Failing health compelled him to seek a change of climate, and he died on his voyage home, after twenty-six years' continuous service in India. He left large manuscript collections behind, which were posthumously edited. The History of India, as told by its own historians, " published between 1866, and 1877, testifies to the width and value of his historical research, for it was he who amassed the ' materials for the eight volumes which now form his memorial for all time.' His learning in another direction was illustrated by the History and Folklore and Distribution of the Races of the North-Western Provinces," which found an editor in Mr. John Beames, B.C.S., in 1869.

Memories of a terrible catastrophe are recalled by an adjoining brass which bears the name of Colonel Frederick Sherwood Taylor, of the Royal Engineers, and Consulting Engineer for Railways to the Government of India, who was killed by the landslip at Naini Tal on September 18th, 1880. Rain had fallen in torrents on the 16th and continued during the 17th and 18th, by which time 33 inches had fallen in the twenty-four hours. At ten o'clock on the morning of Saturday, the 18th, a slight slip occurred behind the Victoria Hotel, which stood to the north of the northern corner of the lake, and buried several natives and one European child. The Assistant Commissioner, Mr. Leonard Taylor, with a number of police and labourers, and Captain Balderstone, at the head of a detachment of soldiers, were at work clearing away the débris and rendering assistance to the wounded, when at 1-30 P.M., the whole precipitous cliff overhanging the hotel fell with a tremendous roar, burying at once the hotel, the relief party, the Assembly rooms, library, orderly-room, road and garden. Almost every person in the building and grounds was entombed, and it was found utterly impossible to extricate any of them.

Opposite Sir Henry Elliot's tablet are two memorials of the Indian Mutiny. The first is a tablet inscribed with the names of a young Bengal civilian and his sister, the one 21 and the other 20 years old at the time of their tragic death. Sir Mountstuart Goodricke Jackson, Bart., was a godson of Mountstuart Elphinstone, whose aide-de-camp, as Governor of Bombay, his father Sir Keith Alexander Jackson, the second baronet, had been. He had only arrived in India the year before the Mutiny broke out, and in June 1857 was Assistant Commissioner of Seetapore, an important military station in Oudh, fifty-one miles from Lucknow. On the 3rd of that month, the three native regiments which formed the garrison rose in mutiny and murdered their officers. They next attacked the house of the Commissioner, George Jackson Christian, where the women and children had been collected. The position soon became untenable, and the handful of English were forced to fly. Christian and his wife and child were shot down, and so also were Henry Bensley Thornhill, another

Assistant Commissioner, and his wife. Jackson and his two sisters, Captain Patrick Orr, Lieutenant G. H. Burns, Sergeant-Major Morton and a few others, succeeded in escaping to the jungles near the Fort of the Mithowlee Rajah, who refused to receive them: and after remaining in hiding for several weeks and suffering the extremity of distress and privation, the few survivors were ultimately taken prisoners and sent to the Kaisar Bagh at Lucknow in two separate parties. Here they were murdered, Miss Amelia Georgina Jackson and those with her, on the 24th September, 1857, and Sir Mountstuart and his fellow captives a few weeks later, on the 16th November. A memorial known as the Orr Monument now marks the spot. Of the whole number, only three escaped, one child, who was smuggled into the Alum Bagh by a faithful servant, and two ladies, Mrs. Orr one of the refuges from Mohumdee near Shahjehanpore and the second Miss Jackson, who were rescued by Colin Campbell's relieving force in March, 1858. Miss Jackson subsequently married her cousin Elphinstone Jackson of the Bengal Civil Service, who was a Judge of the High Court at Fort William from 1863 to 1873, and died in the latter year. The family is unrepresented to-day in the Civil Service, but it was a typical one of its kind when Haileybury ruled the land. The first baronet, Sir John Jackson, was a Director of the East India Company from 1807 to 1820 and M. P. for Dover. Two of his sons were in the Bengal Civil Service: Welby Brown Jackson, Judge of the Sudder Adawlut, who served in India from 1821 to 1853, and died as recently as 1890. and Colville Coverley Jackson who accompanied Colin Campbell's force, and was present at the recapture of

Lucknow, but died at Benares in June 1858, from the effects of a fall from his horse. The son of Welby Jackson was Mr. Justice Elphinstone Jackson, while a daughter became the wife of Sir William Grey, Lieutenant-Governor of Bengal from 1867 to 1871. Sir Keith George Jackson, the present holder of the family baronetcy, is the brother of Sir Mountstuart, and was a boy of fifteen when the title passed to him.

Just above the Jackson memorial, is a marble tablet representing a sarcophagus with a wreathed sword upon it. The inscription records that it is "Sacred to the memory of Robert Welbank Macaulay, M.D., Surgeon on the Bengal establishment, who died on board the Hospital Ship *Mauritius* at Talien Whan, in the north of China, on the 15th July, 1860, when proceeding on service with the China expeditionary force, aged 37 years." It is erected "in affectionate remembrance of their former comrade by the officers of the 1st Regiment of Sikh Cavalry 'Probyn's Horse.'" The regiment derives its name from the fact that it was raised for service during the Mutiny by the present General Sir Dighton Probyn, V.C. The second mutiny tablet is also connected with the massacre at Seetapore. Captain George Thomas Gowan was Commandant of the 9th Regiment of Oudh Irregulars which formed part of the garrison of the station. He was the son, as the tablet records, of Major-General G. E. Gowan, of the Bengal Artillery, and was in the 35th year of his age, when he "fell, whilst endeavouring to recall the mutinous sepoys of his own corps to order and obedience." The officers both of the two Irregular Regiments and of the

41st Native Infantry had been warned by Mr. Christian, the Commissioner, that grave symptoms of disaffection had appeared among their own: but they clung to their belief in their loyalty and were shot down without opportunity for defence or escape. The wife of Captain Gowan, who is also commemorated on the tablet was a daughter of Major-General James Stuart of the Bengal Army. Both she and their infant son, were cruelly murdered as they were attempting to fly with the other women and children after the attack on the Commissioner's house.

Adjoining these two tablets and to the south of Sir M. Jackson's, is placed a marble tablet in memory of George Carnac Barnes, C.B., of the Bengal Civil Service, from 1837 to 1861, who died May 13th, 1861, aged 43.

During the Mutiny, George Carnac Barnes was Commissioner of the cis-Sutlej States, and did excellent service in collecting supplies for the Delhi force and in keeping the communications open with the aid of the loyal Sikh feudatories. "So splendidly was his work done that never was an attempt made to intercept the supplies of stores and ammunition." It is said that in one week he collected for transport purposes 2,000 camels, 2,000 men and 500 carts. To him and also to Mildmay Ricketts, the Deputy Commissioner of Loodhiana, was due the preservation of peace in the cis-Sutlej districts, a matter of vital importance. He ended his career as Foreign Secretary to the Government of Lord Canning. In the present generation, the family reputation in India has been worthily upheld by his nephew, Sir Hugh Shakespear Barnes, who after holding the office of Foreign Secretary in his turn, was Lieutenant-Governor of Burma from 1903 to 1905, and is now a member of the Secretary of State's Council.

As we make our way into the transept, we perceive in its eastern corner, Lady Canning's monument, removed from Barrackpore Park, where it was originally erected. It is an immense marble platform, ornamented with mosaic work, and surmounted by a cenotaph, with a beautiful carved headstone. It bears the following inscription :— "Honours and praises, written on a tomb, are at best a vain glory, but that her charity, humility, weakness, and watchful faith in her Saviour will, for that Saviour's sake, be accepted of God, and be to her a glory everlasting, is the firm trust of those who knew her best, and most dearly loved her in life, and who cherish the memory of her departed. Sacred to the memory of Charlotte Elizabeth, eldest daughter of Lord Stuart De Rothesay, born at Paris, 31st March, 1817 : died at Calcutta, 18th November, 1861 : wife of Charles John Viscount and Earl of Canning, first Viceroy of India. The above words were written 22nd November, 1861, by Earl Canning, who survived his wife but seven months. He left India on the 18th March, died in London on the 17th June, and was buried in Westminster Abbey on the 21st June, 1862." Lady Canning's death was caused by an attack of malarious fever, contracted in passing through the Terai on her return from a visit to Darjeeling. She lies buried in the Park at Barrackpore.

"At a lovely bend of the river—Lady Canning's favourite haunt—her body rests," writes Sir Henry Cunningham in his life of Lord Canning, "'Honours and praises,' so runs the epitaph which her husband's hand inscribed, 'written on a tomb, are at best, a vain glory;' vain, too, the regrets of the saddened hearts which mourned far and wide in India the loss of the beautiful and gifted woman who had with such fortitude and devotion shared the anxieties and lightened the labours of Lord Canning's troubled reign. Her serene courage in hours of danger and anxiety when the hearts of many were failing them for fear, her readiness to help in all beneficial projects, and her sympathy with human suffering, her nobility of character shining bright above catastrophe and vicissitude, made her death a public loss, a common sorrow, and made her memory now one that Englishmen treasure among the precious relics of their country's past."

Directly to the east of Lady Canning's tomb is a fine mural tablet executed by J. G. Lough, in 1846, in memory of Sir William Hay Macnaghten, Bart., Bengal Civil Service, who was assassinated at Kabul in 1841. On either side are full-length Indian figures, behind each of whom is seen a crouching lion. To the right is a Hindoo with the fingers of his left-hand on the lion's mane, on the other side is a Mussulman, with his right leg crossed in front of his left, and his right knee resting on the lion's head. Above the tablet is Macnaghten's coat of arms with his motto, "Hope in God." The whole is surmounted by a statue of Sir William Macnaghten in fine relief, seated in a chair and turned towards the right of the spectator. The briefest notice of the career of this distinguished servant of the Company must suffice. He was the second son of Sir Francis Workman Macnaghten, Puisne Judge of the Supreme Court from 1816 to 1825, whose portrait by Chinnery hangs in the present High Court. Arriving in India in 1809 at the age of sixteen as a Cavalry cadet on the Madras Establishment, he rapidly acquired a reputation as an Oriental linguist. After serving for some months as assistant to the Hon. Arthur Henry Cole, Resident at Mysore, he received in 1814 an appointment in the Bengal Civil Service. Here he continued his study of the Eastern languages with such ardour and success that he received at different times six degrees of honour and ten medals of merit, in addition to rewards and prizes of books for his proficiency. At the anniversary meeting of Lord Wellesley's College at Fort William in 1816, Lord Hastings in noticing his exertions observed that there was not a language taught in the College in which he had not earned the highest distinctions which the Government of the College could bestow. His first important post was that of Registrar of the Court of Sudder Dewany to which he was gazetted in September, 1822, and which he held for eight years and-a-half. Here his industry was as remarkable as it had been in his student days. In addition to his official duties, he published three volumes of decided cases, more than two-thirds of which he reported with his own hand, and brought out the two standard treatises on Hindu and Mohammadan law. In 1830 he was selected by Lord William Bentinck to accompany him as his Secretary throughout his tour in the Upper and Western Provinces and on his return to Calcutta in 1833 was entrusted with the charge of the Secret and Political Department of the Government of India. In October, 1837, he was attached once more as Secretary to the

Governor-General when Lord Auckland proceeded to the North West Provinces: and visited Simla in his suite. The next three years of his life were spent in diplomacy. He was deputed to Lahore to conclude the tripartite treaty arranged between Ranjeet Singh, the British Government and Shah Shujah, the puppet King whom Lord Auckland was determined to place on the throne of Dost Muhammad. Thence he accompanied Lord Auckland to the great gathering of the British troops at Ferozepore, and in his capacity as British Envoy set out with them to escort Shah Soojah to Kabul. The military chronicles of the time have told how Ghuznee was taken, how Dost Muhammad fled, and his family surrendered themselves as prisoners, and how Shah Sujah was installed in the Bala Hissar and a considerable portion of the army sent back to India. Macnaghten remained behind with Eliphinstone and his force, and in 1840 was honoured with a baronetcy. In June of the same year he was provisionally appointed a Member of the Supreme Council, and in September, 1841, he received intimation that the Court of Directors had nominated him to the Governorship of Bombay in succession to Sir John Rivett-Carnac. But he never assumed charge of either of these high offices, for he became the first victim of a rising which ended in the complete destruction of the British army of occupation. He had fixed the early part of November, 1841, for the departure from Kabul: when in a conference with Akbar Khan, the son of Dost Muhammad, he was shot dead on the 23rd December, 1841, with the pistols which he had presented to him a few days before. His remains were subsequently rescued from the pit into which they had been thrown and interred on

April 22nd, 1843, in the Circular Road Cemetery where the handsome tomb erected by his widow may be seen close to the main entrance. The inscription in the Cathedral reads as follows :—" To the memory of Sir William Hay Macnaghten, Baronet, of the Bengal Civil Service. His mind, liberally endowed by nature and enriched by education and research, was quickened into action by high and generous impulses, alike conducive to good and great results and to honourable distinction : thus, that character became developed, whose excellence, acknowledged without dissent, was regarded without envy from the modesty which embellished it. Entrusted during a long course of arduous service with confidential authority, he advanced the reputation he had early established : until, whilst Envoy at the Court of Cabul, honoured by his Sovereign : and on the eve of assuming the Government of Bombay, his bright career of earthly usefulness was arrested. Revolt had burst forth upon the land : and on the 23rd day of December, 1841, in the summer of his manhood and his fortunes, in the forty-eighth year of his age, he fell by the hand of an assassin. His public acts will be found recorded in the annals of his country : this memorial is the last tribute permitted to private friendship."

Above the Macnaughten monument hang the old colours of the 18th Bengal Infantry, which were placed here in 1886 on the presentation of new colours by the Marchioness of Dufferin and Ava : the regiment being then under command of Colonel A. C. Toker, C.B., as a tablet below the colours records.

To the right of the colours is a black marble tablet in a

recess of the northern wall in memory of Count Robert Adrian Stedman, C.B., Lieutenant-Colonel in the Bengal Light Cavalry who "died at sea on his way to England between Calcutta and Madras on board the steamer *Haddington* proceeding to England at 3 in the morning of April 12th, 1849, aged 59 years." "He served in the Bengal Light Cavalry 41 years and one month."

Colonel Stedman entered the Bengal Cavalry as a cadet in 1808. He was a Count of the Holy Roman Empire, and the son of Lieutenant-Colonel John Gabriel Stedman (1744-1797) author of the well known book on Surinam who married firstly Joanna, a native of Surinam and secondly Adriana Viertz Von Coelhorn, grand-daughter of the famous military engineer. Another son of John Gabriel Stedman, Captain John Cambridge Stedman of the 34th Regiment Chicacole Light Infantry, was killed on the 11th January, 1826, at the capture of the Setong stockade during the Burmese war which ended in the capture of Arracan, Pegu and Tenasserim. There is a monument by Clarke the "Birmingham Chantrey" in the Fort Church at Madras to his memory and those of his brother officers, killed and fatally wounded on the same occasion. The Stedmans are still represented in the male line by General Sir Edward Stedman, K.C.I.E., Military Secretary at the India Office, and in the female line by Sir Henry John Stedman Cotton, K.C.S.I. M.P., whose bust will be found in the Town Hall, and who is the grandson of "Surinam" Stedman's daughter.

Before leaving the transept we may note two of the tablets on the wall to the north of Lady Canning's tomb.

Almost immediately behind is a mural tablet in memory of Captain Ralph Dowson, 5th Bengal Native Infantry, who died at Bombay on the 26th February, 1851, aged 33 years. "He distinguished himself in Afghanistan, Mooltan, and Goojerat. His brother officers have erected this slab to commemorate the gallant deeds and private worth of a man who was an honour to the service and an ornament to his regiment."

In the extreme western corner and beyond the door is a marble tablet in memory of Henry Woodrow "formerly Fellow of Caius College, Cambridge, six years Principal of LaMartiniere, Calcutta, some time Secretary to the Council of Education, twenty years Inspector of Schools: and latterly Director of Public Instruction in Bengal. He was born at Norwich, 31st July 1823 and died suddenly at Darjeeling on the 11th October, 1876" at the age of 53. His bust stands in the vestibule of the Senate House under which head an account of his career will be found.

We may now return to the Heber statue and cross over to the north transept.

On the western wall of the passage leading to the transept is a large brass tablet which commemorates the Manipore tragedy of the 24th March, 1891, when the following English Officers were murdered:—Mr. James Wallace Quinton, C.S.I., Chief Commissioner of Assam, Col. Charles McDowal Skene, D.S.O., of the 42nd Gurkha Rifles, Mr. Frank St. Clair Grimwood of the Indian Civil Service, Political Agent at Manipore, Mr. William Cossins, also of the same service, Assistant Secretary to the Chief Commissioner, and Lieut. Walter Henry Simson, of the 43rd Gurkha Rifles. The tablet also bears the name of Lieut. Lionel Wilhelm Brackenbury who with others, native officers and soldiers of the 44th Gurkha Rifles, fell in action at Manipore on the same day: and of William Babington Melville, Superintendent of Telegraphs, and James O'Brien, a signaller in the same department, who were murdered at Myangkhong, on the Silchar-Manipore road, on March 26th, 1891. The tragedy was occasioned by the Government of India's despatch of Mr. Quinton to arrest in open Durbar the Senapati, or Commander-in-Chief of the Manipore "army," who had engineered a palace revolution. When the party reached Manipore they were besieged in the Residency and surrendering on terms, were beheaded in the Palace enclosure. For their complicity in the crime, the Rajah was deposed and the Senapati and his principal supporter the Tongal General hanged.

To the north of and next to the Manipore tablet is a marble slab in memory of Col. Robert Abercromby Yule, of the 9th Lancers, "a man greatly beloved, a modest and accomplished soldier, and as brave as ever drew a sword," killed at the head of his regiment on the evening of the 19th June, 1857 "in an encounter with the rebel force in rear of the camp at Delhi." The deceased was a man of letters as well as a soldier and wrote in 1856 a poem entitled "the Banyan Tree," quotations from which will be found in "Hobson Jobson." He was the brother of Sir George Udny Yule, K.C.S.I., C.B., (1813-1886) Commissioner of Bhagalpur during the Mutiny and afterwards Chief Commissioner of Oudh (1861) Member of the Supreme Council (1867-1868) and Resident at Hyderabad from 1863 to 1867. He was as famous as a shikari as he was distinguished as an administrator. It was during Sir George Yule's tenure of office at Hyderabad that James Achilles Kirkpatrick's famous Rung Mahal palace was pulled down. A third brother was the well known Sir Henry Yule of the Bengal Engineers (1820-1889) also a K.C.S.I., and a C.B., geographer and editor of Marco Polo's Travels and of the Diary of Sir William Hedges for the Hakluyt Society: who was from 1862 to 1869 a member of the Secretary of State's Council. The father of the Yules was William Yule (1764 to 1839) a Major in the Company's service, who was himself an orientalist of repute and whose valuable collection of Persian and Arabic manuscripts was presented by his sons to the British Museum. Robert Yule was the second son and was forty years old at the time of his gallant death. His epitaph here was written by his brother Henry.

On the wall opposite are marble tablets to Sir Richard de Latour St. George, Bart., a young subaltern in the Bengal Artillery who died at Landour at the age of 25 on the 14th October, 1861, and to Sir Robert Barlow, Bart., B.C.S., for more than sixteen years a Judge of the Sudder Court who died January 21st, 1857, aged 59 years. The latter is in the form of a marble cross. Sir Robert Barlow was the fourth son of Sir George Hilaro Barlow, Bart., Governor-General of India from October 1805 to July 1807, and subsequently after his supersession by Lord Minto, Governor of Madras from December, 1807 to August, 1813. He was created a baronet in 1803 and several of his descendants have been members of the Indian Civil

Service. The one here commemorated was the second baronet. The fourth and late baronet, Sir Richard Wellesley Barlow was his nephew and the grandson of General Sir William Nott. He served in the Madras Civil Service from 1855 to 1884.

Below the Barlow memorial is a tablet inscribed with the name of Cecil Mackintosh Stephenson, Agent of the East Indian Railway Company, who died at sea on the 21st November, 1875, aged 56 years. The tablet is declared to be "erected, as a mark of their sincere esteem and respect by more than five thousand officers and men of the East Indian Railway (and others desiring to join) who have also placed a similar tablet at the Railway terminus, Howrah, and instituted a scholarship in the diocesan school at Naini Tal for sons of the East Indian Railway servants."

Turning round the corner to the left, we find a tablet in memory of Thomas Reid Davidson, who coming out to India in 1819 as a writer on the Bengal establishment ended his official career as Resident at Nagpore, in the Central Provinces, where he died on August 30, 1851, at the age of 52 years. He was a member of the Board of Revenue at Calcutta from 1846 to 1848, in which year he was appointed to Nagpore.

To the east of the Davidson tablet we next come across the famous memorial to Patrick Alexander Vans Agnew, of the Bengal Civil Service and Lieut. William Anderson, of the First Bombay Fusiliers, who were murdered under the walls of Mooltan, on the 19th April, 1848, after being treacherously deserted. The inscription was composed by Lord Macaulay and runs as follows:—"Not near this stone, nor in any consecrated ground, but on the extreme frontier of the British Indian Empire, lie the remains of Patrick Alexander Vans Agnew of the Bengal Civil Service and William Anderson, Lieutenant, 1st Bombay Fusilier Regiment, Assistants to the Resident at Lahore: who being deputed by the Government to relieve at his own request Dewan Moolraj, Viceroy of Moultan, of the fortress and authority which he held, were attacked and wounded by the Garrison on the 19th April, 1848, and being treacherously deserted by the Sikh escort, were on the following day in flagrant breach of national faith and hospitality barbarously murdered in the Edgah under the walls of Moultan. Thus fell these two young public servants at the age of 25 and 28 years, full of high hopes, rare talents, and promise of future usefulness; even in their deaths doing their country honour: wounded and forsaken they could offer no resistance; but hand in hand calmly awaited the onset of their assailants; nobly they refused to yield, foretelling the day when thousands of Englishmen should come to avenge their death, and destroy Moolraj, his army and fortress. History records how the prediction was fulfilled. They were buried with military honours on the summit of the captured citadel, on the 26th January, 1849. The annexation of the Punjab to the British Empire was the result of the war, of which their assassination was the commencement. The Assistants to the Resident at Lahore have erected this monument to the memory of their friends."

The Punjab had seemingly been conquered by Hardinge as the price of the pitched battles of Ferozeshah, Aliwal and Sobraon, and Henry Lawrence installed at Lahore. But at the beginning of 1848 while Lawrence was away in England a new storm gathered. Mulraj, Governor of Multan, had agreed to resign his post: and Vans Agnew with Anderson and a small body of Sikh troops were ordered to install Khan Singh in his place. A little more than two years after Sobraon, Vans Agnew and Anderson were attacked and wounded as they were riding out of the Fort at Multan. They took shelter at the Idgah Mosque and sent word to the ex-Governor Moolraj. But the mob and the Sikh soldiers had passed beyond control, and as the day closed in the crowd began to swarm round the mosque. "A company of Moolraj's Muzhabees, or outcast Sikhs, led them on," writes Herbert Edwardes. "It was an appalling sight, and Sirdar Khan Singh begged of Vans Agnew to be allowed to wave a sheet and sue for mercy. Weak in body from loss of blood, Vans Agnew's heart failed him not. He replied: 'The time for mercy is gone: let none be asked for. They can kill us two if they like: but we are not the last of the English: thousands of Englishmen will come here when we are gone and annihilate Moolraj and his soldiers and his fort.' The crowd now rushed in with horrible shouts and surrounded the two officers. Anderson from the first had been too much wounded to move: and now Vans Agnew was sitting by his bedside holding his hand and talking in English. Doubtless they were bidding each other farewell for all time. Goodher Singh, a Muzhabee, so deformed and crippled with old wounds that he looked more like an imp than mortal man, stepped forth from the crowd with a drawn sword, and after insulting Vans Agnew with a few last indignities, struck him twice upon the neck, and with a third blow cut off his head. Some other wretch discharged a musket into the lifeless body. Then Anderson was hacked to death; and afterwards the two bodies were dragged outside, and slashed and insulted by the crowd, there left all night under the sky." It is touching to record the brave Vans Agnew's unshaken faith in his countrymen. Nine years later, the dying speech of Thomas Kirkman Lloyd, the gallant Magistrate of Humeerpore, who gave up his life rather than leave his post, was instinct with the same trust and the same spirit of prophecy: "Have the English not come yet?" were his last words as he stood awaiting his death at the hands of the mutineers. And in neither the one case nor the other was the trust misplaced or the prophecy unfulfilled. While Lord Gough, the Commander-in-Chief, and Dalhousie were deliberating on the advisability of a hot-weather campaign, Herbert Edwardes marched up from Bannu, with his own levies, and some troops under Colonel Van Cortlandt (who had exchanged Runjeet Singh's service for John Company's) and thrice defeated Mulraj, finally shutting him up in Multan.

The next act in the tragedy is illustrated by the adjoining tablet on the East wall. "Raised in friendship and regret by his schoolfellow the Earl of Dalhousie, Governor-General of India," it tells of the soldier's death of Major George Montizambert of the 10th Regiment of

Foot, on the 12th September, 1848, during the siege of Multan which followed, and which was ended by the storm of the city by General Whish on the 22nd January, 1849. Mulraj did not surrender, however, until his fortress was a mere wreck and two great breaches in the walls rendered further resistance hopeless. Montizambert fell in the terrible attack on the "Dharmsala," where his gallant regiment of Lincolnshire men penetrated into the enemy's enclosure by climbing the trees and dropping down into the thick of their foes. He rests under an obelisk fifty feet high in the citadel of Multan alongside Vans Agnew and Anderson.

The remainder of the story is soon told. "The Sikh nation," Dalhousie had said at a banquet given to him at Barrackpore, "has called for war, and on my word, Sirs they shall have it with a vengeance." He was true to his undertaking. The battles of Chillianwallah and Gujrat were followed by the surrender of the last of the Sikh leaders at Rawal Pindi and the annexation of the Punjab on the 29th March, 1849.

Just to the south of Major Montizambert's memorial and on the same eastern wall is a tablet in commemoration of the loss of the Pilot vessel "Coleroon" which perished with all hands on board, in a cyclone in the Bay of Bengal on the 5th and 6th November, 1891.

In the northern corner of the eastern wall is a memorial in honour of Colonel Richard Baird Smith, C.B., and A.D.C. to Queen Victoria, a mutiny hero, and in his later years Master of the Mint at Calcutta, who died at Madras at the age of 42 on December 13, 1861. It is a fine cenotaph, with an inlaid cross, surmounted by a gothic canopy, and containing a representation of the Resurrection in high relief. Baird Smith's wife was Florence de Quincey, the second daughter of the celebrated Thomas de Quincey. The inscription on the cenotaph is in the following terms:—

"In memory of Colónel Richard Baird Smith, of the Bengal Engineers, Master of the Calcutta Mint, Companion of the Bath, and Aide-de-camp to the Queen, whose career, crowded with brilliant service, was cut short at its brightest. Born at Lasswade, N.B., 31st December, 1818, he came to India in 1838. Already distinguished in the two Sikh wars, his conduct on the outbreak of revolt in 1857, showed what a clear apprehension, a brave heart, and a hopeful spirit, could effect with scanty means in crushing disorder. Called to Delhi as Chief Engineer, his bold and ready judgment, his weighty and tenacious counsels, played a foremost part in securing the success of the siege, and England's supremacy; and the gathered wisdom of many years spent in administering the irrigation of Upper India trained him for his crowning service in the survey of the great Famine of 1861, the provision of relief, and the suggestion of safeguard against such calamities. Broken by accumulated labours, he died at sea, December 1861, aged scarcely 43. At Madras, where his career began, his body awaits the resurrection unto life, whilst here the regard and admiration of British India erects this cenotaph in honour of his virtues and his public services."

There are a number of other tablets in the north transpet but attention need only be drawn to four. The first, which will be found on the northern wall to the east of the door, is a small brass tablet in memory of Lieut. Eric Henry Ernest Green, who was killed by a Muhammadan fanatic at Shabkadr on the 25th March, 1900. It is "erected by his old Headmaster" Dr. Welldon, Bishop of Calcutta from 1898 to 1902. The second, which is immediately below it, commemorates a Commissioner of Police of Calcutta, Mr. Arthur Henry James, who held the office from 1897 to 1901 and died at Bournemouth on the 18th November of the latter year. The third recalls a prominent resident of Calcutta for many years in the person of Mr. Frederick John Ferguson, Official Trustee of Bengal, who died on December 5, 1867, at the age of 52. And the last records the name of Capt. John Paton Davidson, of the Bengal Staff Corps, who at the age of 28 fell fighting in command of the Crag piquet in the Khyber Pass on the 13th November, 1863. The manner of his gallant death is now forgotten, but his fall was the precursor of the Black Mountain expedition of 1868 under General Wilde, which broke the power of the fanatical Wahabees on the north-western frontier.

Over the entrance door to the north transept is a stained glass window, placed, as a Latin inscription upon a brass tablet below it records, in memory of the Rev. T. H. Burn who died in 1863 "much lamented by George Lynch Cotton, sixth bishop of this see, to whom for seven years he was a faithful and useful helper." It was erected after the Bishop's death by his widow in accordance with his wish: "viri sui voluntatis haud immemor ponendam curavit."

In the western corner, and to the left of the spectator as he stands facing the door, is a tablet erected by his brother officers, as a tribute of their regard, to Second-Lieutenant Charles Leverton Donaldson, of the Bengal Engineers, "who fell in execution of his duty among the foremost during the operations before Rangoon on April 12th, 1852" aged 21 years. Owing to a succession of outrages committed on British subjects by the Burmese Governor of Rangoon, for which all reparation was refused, the government of India declared war in 1852 on Pagan Min, the King of Burma: and towards the close of the year, Lord Dalhousie proclaimed that the whole of the province of Pegu was annexed to the British Empire. It was in the course of these military operations that this young subaltern fell.

The other tablets in the north transept are not of sufficient historical or personal interest to detain us, and we may return once more to the Heber statue and make our way into the body of the Church.

Here in the entrance to the Church we shall find several memorials which call for examination.

Immediately to the left of the statue, and on the northern wall is a marble tablet in memory of Colonel A.B. Dickens, C.B., of the Bengal Staff Corps; Deputy Commissary-General, who died at Lucknow on October 18th, 1876, aged 52 years: "erected by his brother officers of the Commissariat Department, in which he served for upwards of a quarter of a century, as a mark of esteem and regard." Colonel Dickens served in the Mutiny as Deputy Assistant Commissary-General with Sir Colin Campbell's Field Force, and was present at the Relief of Lucknow, earning mention in despatches on two occassions.

Below we may notice in passing a brass which records that one of the mosaic panels in the reredos is placed in remembrance of Francis Lestock Beaufort, a well known member of the Civil Service whose portrait hangs in the Judge's Court at Alipore and who died in September 1879 at the age of 62.

Adjoining on the east and on the same wall is a handsome marble tablet with portrait medallion, which preserves the memory of Sir John Woodburn, K.C.S.I., Lieutenant-Governor of Bengal from 1898 to 1902, who died at Belvedere on November 21st of that year. An account of his career will be found in the chapter on the statues of Calcutta in connection with the statue by Mr. George Frampton, R.A., which will shortly be erected on the southern side of Dalhousie Square.

To the East again is a small tablet in memory of Lieutenant D'Arcy Wentworth Thuillier, Adjutant of the Viceroy's Bodyguard, who died at Dehra Doon on June 13th, 1881. He was a son of General Sir Henry Edward Landor Thuillier, C.S.I., Surveyor-General of India from 1861 to 1878, and brother of Colonel Sir Henry Ravenshaw Thuillier, K.C.I.E., who was also Surveyor-General of India from 1886 to 1895 and died in 1906 at the age of 93.

Immediately opposite the Woodburn memorial is a large brass tablet in commemoration of those members of

Lumsden's Horse who fell in South Africa during the Boer War 1900. It bears the following inscription:—

"This tablet has been placed in this Cathedral by Lord Curzon, Viceroy and Governor-General of India, Honorary Colonel of Lumsden's Horse, in honour of those members of the first corps of British Volunteers from India who have fought and died for the Empire. Lumsden's Horse, raised by Lieut.-Col. Dugald Mactavish Lumsden from British subjects of the Queen in India, left Calcutta 250 strong in February 1900 to take part in the South African War under the Command of Field Marshal Lord Roberts.

They lost by death in action.

Major Eden Currie Showers,	at Hontuck 30/4/00
Trooper Rt. James Clayton Daubeny	,, ,,
,, Henry Charles Lumsden	,, ,,
,, Robert Apton Case	,, ,,
,, Arthur Fred. Franks	,, ,,
,, Arthur King Meares	at Vet Run 6/5/00
Sergeant Walter Larkins Walker	at Roxburgh 26/12/00

By death from sickness

Trooper Montague Beadon Follett at Johannesburg 7/7/00

Lance Corporal John Martin Halliday Maclean at Pretoria 29/8/00

These sons of Britian in the East, Fought not for praise or fame, They died for England and the least Made greater her great name."

To the west of this memorial is a large marble monument surmounted by a helmet and a sword. Hanging over the edge of the tablet is a medal with a crown and under it the words "Meeanee, Hyderabad, 1845." Underneath is the coat of arms of Lieutenant-Colonel William Adam Anstruther Thomson, of the 9th Bengal Cavalry, in whose honour the tablet is erected by his widow. The inscription sets out that he died in Calcutta on August 3rd, 1865, aged 42 years. "He served throughout the Scinde compaign on the personal staff of Sir Charles Napier, after which he was two years Adjutant of the 15th Irregular Cavalry, Commandant of the Governor-General's Bodyguard for eleven years under Lord Dalhousie and Lord Canning, and Political Agent at Moorshedabad, which appointment he held at the time of his death."

Immediately beneath may be seen a brass which records the placing of a mosaic in the reredos in memory of Frederick Augustus Barnard Glover, of the Bengal Civil Service, who filled the office of Judge of the High Court at Calcutta from 1864 to 1876.

The eastern end of the Church has several features of interest to offer. The original East Window was the gift of the Dean and Chapter of Windsor. The subject was "the Crucifixion," after a design by Benjamin West, R.A. It was originally intended as a present from King George the Third to St. George's Chapel, Windsor, but from some cause unknown was never erected in the place designed. It cost £4,000. This window was destroyed by the great cyclone of 1864, and the present one was then erected by subscription from designs by Messrs. Clayton and Bell.

The window to the right of the great east window was erected in 1880 by the Government of India to the memory of the Right Reverend Robert Milman who succeeded Cotton as Bishop of Calcutta in 1867, and died at Rawalpindi in March, 1876. He was a worker of no common vigor and earnestness, and his death was caused by the great change of temperature and exposure to wet and fatigue which he underwent after leaving Calcutta on his last tour of visitation. The Bishopric of Lahore is the memorial of the European community to his labours and his devotion to the work of the Church in India. From 1872 to 1876 Dr. Edgar Jacob, the present Bishop of St. Albans, was his chaplain.

On the other side of the great east window is a white marble tablet to the memory of the Right Reverend Daniel Wilson, fifth Bishop of Calcutta (1832 to 1858), and first Metropolitan of India, who died in Calcutta on the 2nd January, 1858. Bishop Wilson's remains are buried beneath the altar of the Cathedral which is so deeply indebted to his munificence.

The Reredos is a recent erection of alabaster adorned with panel pictures in Florentine mosaic, and was designed by Sir Arthur Blomfield, A.R.A. The three central panels represent the Annunciation, the Adoration of the Magi and the Flight into Egypt, the remainder being devoted to illustrations of the life of St. Paul.

One of the panels of the Reredos contains a tablet in Mosaic work to the memory of George Edward Lynch Cotton, Bishop of Calcutta from 1858 to 1866, and second Metropolitan of India, who was accidentally drowned in the Ganges at Kooshtea, while on a visitation tour, October 6th, 1866.

Dr. Cotton was appointed to the see of Calcutta from the Head Mastership of Marlborough in succession to Dr. Wilson. He had been travelling for some time in Assam and elsewhere at the time of his death, and had nearly completed his tour. On the evening of the 6th October, he consecrated the cemetery at Kooshtea and despatched his chaplain to telegraph to Calcutta announcing his speedy return. There being then no railway, he walked down to the water's edge to re-embark on his steamer. It was dark as he ascended the gangway which had no handrail and he lost his footing and fell into the river, which was much swollen by the rains. So sudden and complete was his disappearance that although attempts were made at once to rescue him, no trace of his body or even of his hat could be found. The work which will always be most closely associated with Bishop Cotton's name is the establishment of the well-known schools at Simla and Bangalore for the education of Anglo-Indian children.

Other panels contain representations in mosaic of various episodes in the life of St. Paul. The following are the memorials to which reference is made in the series of six brass tablets which are placed in the nave.

The second panel on the southern or right-hand side of the altar, representing "St. Paul before Felix" is a memorial erected by his brother-judges in 1877 to Mr. Frederick Augustus Barnard Glover, Judge of the High Court from 1864 to 1876.

The third panel on the same side, representing "St. Paul's Shipwreck," is placed in memory of "Charles Goodwin Norman of this city, who died near Aden on the 25th January, 1878," aged 54: and is the tribute of his friends in Calcutta.

The sixth panel of mosaic, which represents the "death of St. Paul," is dedicated in memory of Alexander Aeneas Robertson, merchant of Calcutta, and was added in 1882.

Of the remaining panels, the one representing "St. Paul's Farewell to his disciples" was given in memory of Francis Lestock Beaufort of the Bengal Civil Service and his wife, by their children.

The panel representing "St. Paul Preaching in Prison" was erected in 1883 in memory of Johnstone Smith, for many years resident in Calcutta, by his friends.

The episcopal throne, which stands to the south of the altar, is a memorial to the Right Reverend Ralph Johnson, who succeeded Milman in 1876 as Bishop of Calcutta and Metropolitan of India, and held the see until his retirement in 1898. A fine portrait of Dr. Johnson by Mr. Harold Speed hangs in the Town Hall as another public tribute to the esteem and regard entertained for him by the members of the Indian Church.

The organ-loft on the opposite side, contains a remarkably fine organ of 41 stops, built by Joseph Willis and Sons, of London, which was opened on St. Paul's Day, January 23rd, 1881.

In addition to the seating accommodation in the centre,

there are raised lines of pews on either side. The carving is worth inspection. The seat reserved for His Excellency the Viceroy will be found at the head of the dais of pews on the southern side. The Lieutenant-Governor's pew is the first on the northern side of the body of the Church: and immediately behind are the seats of the Chief Justice of Bengal.

There are exits both to the north and the south of the altar and we may make our choice accordingly.

CHAPTER IX.

THE OLD MISSION CHURCH.

In the centre of Mission Row, once known as the Rope Walk and the scene of hard fighting during the "Troubles" of 1756, the visitor will come upon the Old Mission Church. Second only to the Armenian Church of St. Nazareth as the oldest place of Christian worship in Calcutta, she can carry back her memories to the days when Clive ruled as Governor over the re-conquered settlement and Hastings had no loftier task to engage him than the suppression of malpractices in the Company's piece-goods business at Fort St. George. It has been related elsewhere how the Presidency Church of St. Anne was one of the many buildings in Calcutta which met with destruction at the hands of Seraj-ud-Dowlah and his victorious troops, and how for nearly thirty years the Portuguese church in Moorghihatta and, at a later date, a makeshift chapel in the ruined Fort were deemed to suffice officially for the spiritual wants of the English inhabitants of Calcutta. But, while the Directors and the "Worshipful Sir and Sirs" of the Council at Fort William discussed and deliberated regarding the erection of a Protestant Church, a private individual took it upon himself to act. In September, 1758, there arrived in Calcutta on the invitation of Clive, a Swedish missionary whose name was destined to be imperishably connected with the history of the city. John Zechariah Kiernander was ordained to the ministry at Halle on the 29th November, 1739, at the age of twenty-eight, and attaching himself to the Danish Mission in South India, which had been founded by Ziegenbalg and Plütschau in 1706, he embarked for the East and landed at Cuddalore in 1740. Here he was at once placed by the British authorities at Fort St. David in possession of the Portuguese Church, from which the Catholic priests were incontinently banished: and for eight years he laboured with devotion and success, establishing schools, and preaching indefatigably both in Portuguese and in Tamil. In the midst of his good works, the settlement was attacked by the French, and on the 4th May, 1758, it was surrendered to Lally by Alexander Wynch, the English Governor. Though treated with every courtesy by the French Governor, who prevented the pillage of the Protestant Mission's property, Kiernander was compelled to take refuge at Tranquebar, the head quarters of the Danish Society of which he was still a member. But he had while at Cuddalore fallen in with the man who was to influence the whole of his later career. Upon the capitulation of Fort St. George to La Bourdonnais in 1746, Robert Clive fled from the town by night in the disguise of a Mussulman and made his way to Fort St. David, which became the seat of the Company's Government for the next six years.

The well-known incident in the life of Clive when he refused to pay money lost at the card-table to players who were proved to have cheated, took place at Fort St. David: and it was here also that he fought his famous duel with a military bully who had made himself the terror of the little garrison. Nor did his connection with the forgotten fortress cease with his removal to Bengal, for in the annual list of covenanted civil servants of the Company for the year 1757, there appears the name of Colonel Robert Clive as "Deputy Governor of Fort St. David, at present commander of the troops in Bengal." When Plassey had been fought and won, and the English re-established at Fort William, he bethought himself of his friend, and when Kiernander and his wife arrived in Calcutta, they were received with a hearty welcome. A free house was assigned to him, and here on the 4th November, 1758, a son was born to the missionary, to whom Clive and his wife, and William Watts the second of Council, and his wife (the famous Begum Johnson of a later day) stood sponsors. Soon after Kiernander's arrival he established a Mission School, and in 1763 we find him applying to Vansittart, the Governor, "for a convenient place for a Portuguese Protestant Church." His request was acceded to in the following order in Council of the 25th November, 1763: "Agreed the Secretary to acquaint him that we will give up the house, which was the Collector's Office, for the purpose of holding the charity school in, and as the apartments will sufficiently admit of it, that he has our permission to use it also as a church for his converts." Four years later, however, the house was required for official purposes, and Kiernander set to work to provide a church of his own. The structure was estimated to cost Rs. 20,000, but it actually needed nearly Rs. 68,000, to complete it, out of which Kiernander paid no less than Rs. 65,000. The Church, which may thus be said to have been erected at the cost of a single individual, was consecrated on the

23rd December, 1770, and named Beth-Tephillah or "the House of Prayer." The architect was Boutant de Mevell a Dane, who died during its construction: but the building was a very different one to the Old Mission Church of to-day. For it was for many years nothing better than a clumsy, unplastered brick edifice, of small dimensions, and hemmed in on every side by old houses. Within it was exceedingly uncouth, with a brick pulpit built against the wall, and its aisle of rough uncovered tiling. A few rude benches and pews of unpainted plank formed the general seats, with a small number of chairs without pews, for the gentry; and it was calculated to accommodate only about two hundred persons. It was indeed most comfortless, and it was pronounced by the then society of Calcutta utterly unsuitable for the reception of an European congregation. Yet it was strongly built of good masonry, and lofty, and appeared worthy of being made attractive to a larger assembly.

From the reddish tint of the bricks of which it was composed, it came to be known among the people of the country by the name of the *Lall Girja*, or Red Church and it is still so called by them, in spite of the fact that for nearly a century, the walls have been of a light stone colour.

Kiernander's first wife Wendela was the sister of Colonel Fischer of the Madras Army, and it was chiefly with her wealth that the church was constructed. At her death in 1761, he married a Mrs. Anna Woolley who is described by one of his biographers as "a young luxurious woman who cared little for the souls of the heathens," but we may take leave to accept the judgment with reserve, for when she died in June, 1773, her husband placed it upon record on her tombstone that she was one who "practised every virtue that adorns the character of a Christian," and she bequeathed her jewels for the benefit of Beth Tephillah. With the proceeds, which amounted to Rs. 6,000, Kiernander built a Mission School on his own ground, in the rear of the church, which was capable of holding 250 children. Subsequently a parsonage house was also erected adjoining the church.

In 1778 Kiernander's sight failed him and for three years he was totally blind from cataract, during which period his son Robert, the godson of Clive, had charge of his affairs and appears to have launched out in a number of extravagant speculations. We hear of a house of the Kiernanders in Camac Street which went by the name of Beth Saron, and a garden-house at Bhowanipore, which was called Saron Grove and which is occupied to-day by the London Missionary Society. Kiernander recovered his sight in 1781, but fresh troubles overtook him. He had imprudently signed bonds for his son, and although the aggregate amount of his liabilities was no more than his property would have realized if disposed of to advantage, the creditors grew alarmed and the Church with all its appurtenances was placed under the seal of the Sheriff. Kiernander betook himself to the Dutch Settlement of Chinsurah, where he was appointed chaplain on a salary of Rs. 50 a month: and his property was announced to be brought under the hammer. At this crisis, Charles Grant of Maldah, afterwards an East India Director, and the father of Lord Glenelg, stepped forward and restored the Old Mission Church to religious uses. He paid the sum at which it was appraised—ten thousand rupees—and on the last day of October, 1787, transferred to three trustees the church, schools and burying-ground in Park Street which had been purchased for the use of the congregation. When Chinsurah was captured by the English in 1795, Kiernander found himself once more a prisoner of war, but his captivity was purely nominal and he returned to Calcutta in the same year and took up his abode in the house of his son's widow. Here he died in 1799 at the patriarchial age of 88, and lies buried in the Mission burying-ground between his first and second wives in a massive family vault.

The successor of Kiernander as pastor of the Mission Church was David Brown, the garrison chaplain, and one of the trustees under the deed of Charles Grant, who "zealously and gratuitously discharged the duties of the office for twenty-one years." Encouraged and aided by the fine taste and scientific abilities of his respected friend, Mr. William Chambers, who was also his co-trustee, Mr. Brown was not long in making a beginning to enlarge and improve the building. It was also gradually fitted up in a manner suitable to the climate, abundantly lighted, and supplied with an excellent organ.

In a view of the "Great Tank," which is attributed to Daniell, and may be referred to the period between 1787 and 1790, the Church is shown to have assumed the appearance which it bears at the present day. As we have noticed in an earlier chapter, there was at the time a vacant plot of land on the south side of Tank Square, upon which building was restricted under the orders of the Company, and the noble proportions of the Church stand out prominently in the background of the picture.

In 1793 Brown was appointed to the junior chaplaincy at the Presidency Church of St. John, and in 1797 he succeeded to the senior chaplaincy. It became necessary consequently to appoint a permanent Chaplain to the Mission Church and this was done at the close of 1808.

When Mr. Brown was appointed to the Senior Chaplaincy, he also took a great interest in the enlargement and beautifying of the Presidency Church (St. John's), and during the time that Church was closed for these purposes the Governor-General and his suite, with the whole congregation, gladly availed themselves of the one kept open solely by Mr. Brown's fostering attentions.

On Sunday, the 23rd September, 1804, being the anniversary of the battle of Assaye, a sermon "suitable to the occasion" was preached by Brown before the Marquess Wellesley and his brother Major-General Arthur Wellesley at the Old Church. "And here," says the author of Memorial sketches of the Rev. David Brown, "BRITAIN'S WELLINGTON has suffered the graceful tear stealing from the heart, to adorn his manly cheek," on being reminded, from this pulpit, that it was *'God who covered his head in the day of battle.'*

The original Church, as Kiernander built it, appears to have been a plain, oblong building, extending from the present west porch to the beginning of the semi-circular chancel in the east.

In 1774 the school-house had already been erected. It will be found to-day in the lower flat of the parsonage. In 1791 the east chancel was added and the rooms above the school-house built. In 1809 the Church was enlarged, probably southwards. The Mission House was built in 1807, but as there seems to be mention made of a Mission House as already existing before 1785, it is not clear whether No. 9 or No. 10 Mission Row is intended. The upper flat was added in 1801.

The Church at one time had galleries. The present chancel was added quite recently in 1895. The steeple was a conspicuous ornament of the edifice until the year 1897, when it was so shaken by the earthquake that it was taken down and has never been rebuilt.

In 1870, during the episcopate of Bishop Milman, the Old Church, together with its Parsonages and other property, was made over to the Church Missionary Society on the condition that it should henceforth supply it with suitable Chaplains. Since that time the services of the church and the management of the affairs of its large parish have been under the direction of the Clergy of that Society.

The church contains a number of interesting memorials, of the more important of which a brief summary is subjoined :—

Beginning from the new chancel on the north, which was added in 1895, are tablets in the circular eastern end of the church bearing the following names:

(1) Mrs. Hannah Ellerton, died January 21st, 1858, aged 86 years. This is the lady who assured the Rev.

James Long that she had a vivid recollection of the duel between Hastings and Francis and could remember the day when there were only two houses in the "road to Chowringhy."

(2) The Rev. Henry Perrott Parker, M.A., of Trinity College Cambridge, formerly assistant minister of this church and corresponding Secretary in Calcutta of the Church Missionary Society. He was subsequently appointed to the Missionary see of Eastern Equatorial Africa, and died near the Victoria Nyanza in 1888 at the early age of 35 years. His successor in the office of Bishop was Hannyngton, whose tragic fate will be fresh in the minds of many.

(3) Dr. Daniel Corrie, first Archdeacon of Calcutta, and later first Bishop of Madras, was for some time also chaplain of the church: and his connection with it is commemorated by a black marble tablet, which records that he was the "friend and fellow-labourer of Henry Martyn." He died at Madras in February, 1837, in the second year of his episcopate and the 59th of his age.

(4) The memory of Dr. Daniel Wilson is perpetuated by a similar tablet immediately below that of Corrie.

(5) Adjoining is a stone monument in memory of Henry Davenport Shakespear, who was from 1835 to 1838 a member of the Supreme Council, and died in Calcutta while holding that office on March 20th of the last named year. He was a colleague of Macaulay, who resigned the appointment of Law Member just two months before Shakespear's death. The family was a well-known one

in bygone days in Calcutta and was closely connected with that of the Thackerays.

(6) We next come to a black marble tablet with these simple words: "to the poor the Gospel was preached in this Church by the Rev. David Brown twenty-five years. Ob. ap. Calcutta, 14th June, 1812" (at the house of John Herbert Harington in Chowringhee). Brown, who was a Yorkshireman by birth, first arrived in Calcutta in 1786, when he was placed in charge of the Free School: but to this was superadded almost immediately a brigade chaplaincy in the Fort and the incumbency of the Mission Church. The last he continued to hold even after his appointment to be Presidency Chaplain in 1794. His son, Charles Philip Brown (1798-1884) was in the Madras Civil Service from 1816 to 1854 and is still remembered in South India as a most wounderful Telugu Scholar.

(7) Below Brown's tablet is one which testifies that the Rt. Rev. Thomas Dealtry, second Bishop of Madras, "as senior minister of this church preached the gospel of Christ with earnest faithfulness for upwards of seventeen years." He was associated with the church from 1829 to 1847 and died at Madras in 1861 at the age of 61.

(8) On the opposite side of the altar is a black marble tablet in memory of the Ven. John Henry Pratt, M.A., F.R.S., Archdeacon of Calcutta, who died at Ghazipore in 1871. The Pratt Memorial School in Lower Circular Road bears witness to the esteem and regard in which he was held by his contemporaries.

(9) Below the Pratt tablet is another inscribed with

the honoured name of Henry Martyn, who landed at Fort William in May, 1806, at the age of 25, and after labouring unceasingly in the Mission field, died of the plague at Tocat in Armenia on October 16th, 1812, at the age of 32. "He was a burning and shining light." Says the inscription: and apart from his purely missionary efforts, "his own works," says the annalist in the Bengal Obituary, "praise him in the gates, far above human commendation." By his means, part of the Liturgy of the Church of England, the Parables, and the whole of the New Testament were translated into Hindustanee, and the Psalms and the New Testament were rendered into Persian. Sir J. F. Stephen has truly said of him that his was "the one heroic name which adorns the annals of the Church of England from the days of Elizabeth to our own." Among Macaulay's earliest compositions is the following epitaph on Martyn written in 1812 when in his thirteenth year.

"Here Martyn lies. In manhood's early bloom
The Christian hero finds a Pagan tomb.
Religion, sorrowing o'er her favourite son,
Points to the glorious trophies that he won.
Eternal trophies! not with carnage red,
Not stained with tears by hapless captives shed,
But trophies of the Cross! for that dear name,
Through every form of danger, death, and shame,
Onward he journeyed to a happier shore,
Where danger, death and shame assault no more."

(10) A little further to the right is a black tablet in memory of the Rev. Thomas Thomason, "erected by a grateful and affectionate people, in remembrance of his

long and faithful ministry." He died at Mauritius on his way to England on June 22nd, 1829, at the age of 55 years. His ministry commenced in 1808 with his arrival in Calcutta, and it is said that within six months he found it necessary to enlarge the church. When the Earl of Moira (Lord Hastings) assumed charge of the office of Governor-General in 1813, he made it a practice to attend the Mission Church: and Thomason was appointed to accompany him as Chaplain during his tour in the Upper Provinces.

(11) Immediately below the memorial to Thomason is one of the most interesting tablets in the church. It bears the following inscription: "In memory of Charles Grant, Esq., late a Director of the Hon'ble East India Company, and formerly a civil servant of this Presidency: who was distinguished by his unwearied zeal in promoting the cause of religion in India, of which this church, purchased at his expense, and preserved for the service of God, is a proof and a monument. He died in London October 31st, 1823, aged 78 years." At the time of his historic intervention, he was fourth Member of the Board of Trade, and lived, as we have already noted in its place, in the lane which bears his name in the first house on the right-hand side from Cossaitollah.

(12) Near at hand is a "marble dedicated by the Trustees of the Old Church to the memory of George Udny, Esq., late of the Hon'ble Company's Bengal Civil Service, and many years a member of this congregation." He was Member of Council from 1801 to 1807, when he resigned, and would appear to have lived on in Calcutta,

for it was here that he died on October 24th 1830, in the 70th year of his age.

(13) In the corner formed by the southern and eastern walls is a white marble tablet in memory of Stephen Jacob, C.S.I., for many years Comptroller-General of India Treasuries, and as such the signatory of the Government Currency Notes. He died December 11th 1898.

(14) On the opposite or western wall is a tablet inscribed with the name of Wale Byrne (1805-1855), a famous champion in the forties and fifties of the cause of the East Indian community. He was himself of mixed parentage.

(15) Immediately to the right of Wale Byrne's tablet is a black marble slab in memory of the Rev. Walter Hovenden, B.D., a former Chaplain and Secretary to the Bengal Military Orphan Institution. He died at the Sandheads on September 30th, 1832, at the age of 49. His career is a remarkable one from the fact that he served for many years in the Army and commanded the 38th Foot, at Madras. Ill-health compelled him to dispose of his commission, and for some years he lived in Ireland on an estate belonging to the family and served on the Commission of the Peace for the County. Late in life he entered himself at Peterhouse, Cambridge, and taking Holy Orders was appointed to Calcutta as Chaplain and Secretary to the well-known institution at Kidderpore. His degree of B.D. was conferred on him by the Archbishop of Canterbury.

(16) A last tablet commemorates an Arab lady of distinction who was converted to Christianity. "Waliun Nisa

Begum, a native of Jedda and daughter of a Haji, driven in early life to seek a peace which Mahomedanism could not afford, she found rest in Christ and was baptised in this Church, February 16th, 1871. After labouring in the cause of the Gospel in the Zenana Mission at Lucknow, she died at Mursidabad, December 8th, 1876."

ST. ANDREW'S CHURCH.

Called also "THE SCOTCH KIRK" and "LAT SAHIB KI GIRJA."

This is a handsome Grecian building in connection with the Church of Scotland. The native name no doubt owes its origin to the ceremonial when the foundation stone was laid, and to the connection of Lord Moira with the Church through his wife the Countess of Loudoun and Moira.

The Church stands on or near the site of the Old Court House, directly facing Old Court House Street. Occupying this prominent position, it forms, with its tall massive spire, one of the familiar features of the town. On the north and south there are elegant porticos, with lofty Doric pillars; and on the north there is also a spacious carriage entrance, added at considerable expense by the congregation, with the consent of Government, in 1838.

The Scotch congregation was formed in 1815 by the Rev. James Bryce (afterwards Dr. Bryce), a fine full length portrait of whom, by Sir John Watson Gordon, may be seen in the vestry. Service was conducted at first in the Asiatic Society's Hall, and afterwards in the Old College (formerly the Exchange). Government having given a grant of one lakh of Rupees, besides the site, valued at Rs. 30,000, the laying of the foundation stone was fixed for St. Andrew's Day, (30th November) 1815; when the Countess of Loudoun and Moira attended in state, and there was an imposing masonic, military, and civil display.

After the foundation stone had been laid, and other forms gone through, Dr. Bryce addressed the Countess of Loudoun and spoke of the hereditary attachment of the family which she represented to the principles of the Church of Scotland, and the support they had given to its ecclesiastical polity in days of difficulty and danger. "To this address the Countess made a short and appropriate reply, expressive of the pleasure she felt in being present at so interesting a ceremony, and assuring the Kirk Session that they might depend on Her Ladyship's attachment to the Church of her native country." The builders were Messrs. Burn, Currie and Co. It was opened for public worship on 8th March, 1818.

The Kirk Session having resolutely set themselves to complete the Church in a proper style, in the faith that the money required would be got somehow, laid the floor with marble, completed the spire, erected a railing, improved the approaches, &c., &c., so that the entire cost was nearly a lakh in addition to the Government contribution. Subscriptions were readily forthcoming to the extent of Rs. 36,000, but with reference to the balance the Session found themselves in such serious difficulties that they were driven to apply to Government for the whole or part of the proceeds of a Lottery, basing their application on the ground that the Church might be considered one of the improvements to which the Lotteries were devoted. Government, however, indicated in reply, that municipal improvements were the objects principally considered in the appropriation of the Lottery, and the Kirk Session were driven to issue debentures, bearing high rates of interest, secured on the revenues of the Church. The effect of this was that the debt continued gradually to increase, and the final liquidation, under certain stringent conditions, was arranged for by Government, first of all by an advance, in 1823, and finally by an absolute payment, in 1834, of Rs. 80,000.

An " Euharmonic Organ," much admired at the time, was placed in this Church, and this is probably the earliest instance of instrumental music having been successfully introduced into the service of the Church of Scotland. The original organ was replaced in 1858 by a much finer one, built by Messrs. Gray and Davison of London, at a cost of upwards of Rs. 10,000.

The Clock was placed in the Tower in 1835, Government having contributed Rs. 2,200, and the public Rs. 2,700.

The affairs of the Church are managed by the Kirk Session, consisting of a body of Elders, presided over by the Chaplain, or the Chaplains in turn, when there are two. This body, along with the corresponding bodies in Madras and Bombay, has the right of sending representatives to the General Assembly of the Church of Scotland which meets annually in Edinburgh, a privilege which the Imperial Parliament and the Church acting in concert have not conferred on any other branch of the Church of Scotland, except that in Holland.

An interesting tradition hangs about the spire. Bishop Middleton, the first Bishop of Calcutta, believed that the Church of England had a monopoly of spires, not only in England but everywhere in the British dominions, Scotland perhaps excepted. Dr. Bryce who had been his fellow passenger from England, and whom, according to Sir John William Kaye, he found to be even worse than his other main enemy the "prickly heat," was naturally of a different opinion, and on hearing that the Bishop had used his influence to prevent him from getting the sanction of Government to erect a spire, he declared that he would not only have a "steeple" higher than that of the Cathedral Church of St. John, but that he would place on the top of it a cock to crow over the Bishop, which came to pass accordingly. Government, it is alleged, as a salve to the Bishop's wound, directed that though the rest of the building might be repaired, this audacious bird should not have the benefit of the Public Works Department. In spite of this, or as cynical people might perhaps say *because of this,* the cock still continues to stand, and seems as capable as ever it was of crowing over any adversary.

The picture of Dr. Bryce hanging in the vestry came out in the unfortunate *Protector,* which was lost in the gale in October 1838 off the Sandheads, when only five of the crew were saved. Miss Eden in her "Letters Up the Country" has an interesting reference to this horrible disaster. The packing case containing Bryce's picture was one of the few things rescued from the wreck.

MONUMENTS, &c.—Besides the painting of Dr. Bryce (who was as redoubtable as a journalist as he was famous as a preacher), there is in the vestry a companion portrait of the Rev. Dr. Charles, who was the second to occupy the position of Senior Chaplain of the Church, also a portrait of the Rev. J. Macalister Thomson, 14 years the Chaplain of the Church. There are also various marble monuments, amongst which may be mentioned those erected to the memory of the Rev. Dr. Brown (Dr. Bryce's colleague) who died at Malacca in 1830; the Rev. D. Mieklejohn (Dr. Charles' successor in the Senior Chaplaincy), who died at Calcutta in 1850; the Rev. Dr. Ogilvie, of the General Assembly's Institution, who died at Penang in 1871; Mr. James Allan, of Dykes & Co., a very zealous Elder of the Church, and founder of the Vernacular School in Rawdon Street, now under the management of the Kirk Session; and the Rev. J. Macalister Thomson. The visitor will also notice the monument to a distinguished soldier Lieut-Col. William Mactier, C.B., of the Bengal Light Cavalry, who died at Jaunpore. on the 16th September, 1855, aged 62.

THE CATHEDRAL (MURGHIHATTA.)

(15, *Portuguese Church Lane.*)

WHEN Job Charnock settled in Calcutta in the year 1690, a few Portuguese followed him, and the English Government allotted them a piece of land on which the friars of the Order of St. Augustin erected a temporary chapel of mat and straw. In 1700 a brick chapel was erected at the cost of Mrs. Maria Tench, (whose father Edward appears in early Calcutta history as master of the Ketch *Samuel* in 1688) and enlarged in the year 1720, by the liberality of Mrs. Sebastian Shaw. The tombstones to the memory of these benefactresses are to be seen on either side of the high altar of the present Cathedral. This chapel suffered in the sack of Calcutta in 1756 and its records were destroyed: but together with the Armenian Church it escaped total destruction. On the recovery of Calcutta it was seized for the use of the English settlers but was restored to the Portuguese in 1760. "Taking into consideration the unwholesomeness and dampness of the Church now made use of as well as the injustice of detaining it from the Portuguese," runs the entry in the Proceedings of the Council for March 24th, 1760, "ordered the surveyor to examine the remains of the gateway in the Old Fort and report what it will cost to put it in tolerable repair and make it fit for a chapel." In the year 1796, the Portuguese determined to throw down their old church, and build a more spacious one in the modern style. The first stone of the new church was laid on the 12th March, 1797, and on the 27th November, 1799, it was consecrated and dedicated to *The Virgin Mary of Rosary*. The building cost 90,000 rupees, 30,000 of which was raised from the revenues of the church, the remainder from public subscription, all deficiencies being made up by Joseph and Louis Barretto—two opulent brothers, then the heads of the Portuguese community in Calcutta and members of a family which has given two governors and a Patriarch to Portuguese India. The architect was Mr. Thomas Syars Driver who died on the 6th December, 1797, before its completion.

The old Archiepiscopal Palace adjoins the Cathedral which is chiefly used on grand occasions, for the solemn and imposing ceremonies of the Roman Catholic church. On such days the spacious building is too small for the faithful.

In the Cathedral lie buried the following Vicars-General of Bengal,—Dr. John Louis Taberd, Bishop of Isauropolis (died 1840), William Kelly who died in 1842 at Hussenabad in the Sunderbunds, William Kennedy (died 1846), Dr. Rabascall (died 1846), Ignatius Storck, O.S.B. (died 1855), Patrick Joseph Carew, Archbishop of Odessa (died 1855) to whom Calcutta is indebted for St. Xavier's College, Augustus Van Heule (died 1865).

Beneath the altar is also interred Archbishop Paul Goethals (1833-1901) the first Archbishop of Calcutta, a most distinguished prelate and a devoted friend to India. His Library which should be better known than it is, was bequeathed by him to the See. It is a perfect storehouse of information upon every subject connected with India and many of its volumes are to be found nowhere else in Calcutta.

In the Cathedral compound lie buried Count John Lackersteen (1804-1869), one of the greatest benefactors of the church; and the wife and daughter of Cudbert Thornhill. The monuments within date back as far as 1712. The old Armenian families of Shahriman, Hazarmall and Agavally are severally represented and there is a curious epitaph to a certain Leo which runs: "Hic Armenus Leo nomine dictus, at quem mors ipsa facta Leo Nazareth patri meo Persaeque patriae tollere non parcit, jaceo appositus ad patres."

FREE CHURCH.

(Wellesley Square.)

On news reaching Calcutta of the disruption that had taken place in the Church of Scotland, those who sympathised with the Evangelical party formed themselves into a congregation, and met for the first time as a separate body, for divine service on the 13th August, 1843, in the Freemasons' Hall, Bentinck Street. Dr. Duff, supported by all other missionaries hitherto in connection with the Church of Scotland, officiated on the occasion. The Rev. John Macdonald, one of the missionaries, consented to act as their minister, until one should be got from home. At the same time it was resolved to erect a permanent place of worship, a Committee was appointed, and a subscription was opened for this purpose. While the Committee was in search of a temporary place, the Directors of the Parental Academic Institution, now the Doveton College, kindly offered the use of their Hall for that purpose. The Congregation accordingly met for divine worship in it until the new Church was opened in August 1848.

In December 1843, the present site, comprising 2 beeghas 2½ cottahs, was bought at a cost of Rs. 8,850. In May 1844, a plan prepared by Captain Henry Goodwyn, of the Engineers, was adopted. The cost, exclusive of fittings, was estimated at Rs. 30,000. In January 1846, the building was fast approaching completion, the internal finishing alone remaining to be done, when, on the night of the 15th, the roof fell in, the brick pillars on each side of the centre aisle, which supported it having given way. The whole building, save the spire, was found in so unsatisfactory a condition, that the walls had to be taken down, and the foundations to be piled and relaid. A new plan was agreed upon, and the aisle pillars dispensed with. The contract for rebuilding it at Rs. 30,000, exclusive of subsequent additions, was put into the hands of professional builders. Some of the members of the congregation on this occasion came forward with wonderful liberality. In addition to previous subscriptions, Mr. Abraham F. Hawkins, C.S., Judge of the Sudder Adawlut gave Rs. 10,000 and lent other Rs. 15,000, at 5 per cent; Dr. Nicolson gave Rs. 5,000; and several others Rs. 2,500 each, and these were afterwards supplemented, until the whole cost, amounting to Rs. 1,15,558, was subscribed, with the exception of Rs. 5,000, received from the Colonial Committee in Edinburgh.

When finished, it looked, as it does still, the neatest Ecclesiastical building in Calcutta.

The Congregation, though small, has been remarkably liberal. From 1843 to 1890 they subscribed for congregational, missionary, and miscellaneous purposes, Rupees 13,57,907

THE BAPTIST CHAPEL.

(*Lall Bazar.*)

This Chapel was opened for worship on the 1st of January, 1809. It was erected from funds collected and subscribed principally by the three celebrated Missionaries of Serampore—Carey, Marshman, and Ward,—who were the first Pastors of the Church, formed in connexion with it.

THE BAPTIST CHAPEL.

(*Circular Road.*)

This Chapel, was erected in 1819 by the efforts of the Missionaries of the Society who first settled in Calcutta, and who were formerly known as "the Junior Brethren," and included in their number Eustace Carey, a nephew of the celebrated Dr. Carey. It contains tablets to the Revs. John Chamberlain (1821), John Lawson (1825), James Penney (1839), W. H. Pearce (1840), William Yates (1845) and John Wenger (1880).

ST. THOMAS' CHURCH

(*Free School Street*)

Commonly called the Free School Church, is a neat edifice attached to the Free School. It was erected chiefly through the instrumentality of Bishop Turner, the School funds subscribing upwards of half a lakh of Rupees towards the work. It is the property of the Governors of the Free School.

The foundation stone was laid by Lady William Bentinck on the 13th April, 1830, and on the 2nd February, 1833, it was consecrated by Bishop Wilson. The church contains a memorial to Miss Mary Bird (1834), sister of R. M. Bird, C.S., Judge of Gorakhpore. She devoted herself especially to the Christian women of Calcutta, who speak Hindustani, 'for whom she wrote or translated a number of Hindustani manuals.

ST. PETER'S CHURCH.

(*Fort William.*)

The Fort Church was completed in 1835. It is a handsome edifice, in the gothic style of architecture, very neatly fitted up. There is a fine east window, a carved reredos, and an oriel window over the west entrance, filled with stained glass, also a handsome marble pulpit and reading-desk.

The Church is expressly designed for the accommodation of the European Troops, but there are also sittings for the public. There is a good organ and choir.

The earliest monuments are to the memory of those officers of the Tenth Foot and of the 21st Royal Scots Fusiliers, who died while stationed at Fort William in the early forties. There are also memorials to the officers and men of the illfated Bengal regiments (5th Native Cavalry and 5th Native Infantry) "who fell in gallant but hopeless conflict in the disastrous retreat from Cabul between the 6th and 13th January 1842." A tablet "erected by the Commander-in-Chief and Officers of Her Majesty's Army in India" commemorates Col. W. H. Dennie, C.B., a romantically chivalrous soldier, who was killed before Jellalabad 7th April 1842. He predicted the disaster to Eliphinstone's army, even to the receipt of tidings by a solitary survivor.

THE ARMENIAN CHURCH OF SAINT NAZARETH.

This will be found at the corner of Khengraputty (the quarter of the brush-sellers) and Armenian Street. It is most conveniently approached from Old China Bazar Street and may be easily distinguished by its dome. The Church enjoys the distinction of being the oldest place of Christian worship in Calcutta, and dates from the year 1724.

The Armenians have been settlers in India from the earliest times. In 1562, during the reign of Akbar, they erected a church at Agra, and the inscriptions in the Old Cemetery in that town sufficiently indicate that they were an important as well as a flourishing community. To Calcutta they appear to have found their way prior to the advent of Job Charnock, as there is an old tombstone in the Armenian language in the burying-ground adjoining the Church, which records the fact that "Rezabeebeh, the wife of the late charitable Sookeas, departed this world to life eternal on the 21st day of Nakha in the year 15" of the new era of Julpha, which corresponds with the 11th of July 1630, A.D. When Job Charnock established himself at Suttanuttee in 1690 the Armenians at Chinsurah, were specially invited to come to the new settlement at Calcutta, and several must have availed themselves of the invitation, as it is on record that in 1690 a small chapel of timber was erected for their use by the Hon'ble East India Company, in accordance with the terms of an agreement dated 22nd, June 1688, which ran as follows:—

"Whenever forty or more of the Armenian nation shall become inhabitants of any garrison cities, or towns, belonging to the Company in the East Indies, the said Armenians shall not only enjoy the free use and exercise of their religion, but there shall also be allotted to them a parcel of ground to erect a church thereon for worship and service of God in their own way. And that we also will, at our own charge, cause a convenient church to be built of timber, which afterwards the said Armenians may alter and build with stone or other solid materials to their own good liking. And the said Governor and Company will also allow fifty pounds per annum, during the space of seven years, for the maintenance of such priest or minister as they shall choose to officiate therein. Given under the Company's larger seal, June 22nd, 1688."

This chapel stood about 100 yards to the south of the present church of St. Nazareth, and the site of the present church was then used by the Armenians as a burying-ground.

In consequence of the increase in the Armenian community this chapel became too small, and the present church was erected in 1724 by voluntary subscriptions raised amongst the flourishing community under the auspices of Aga Nazar. In commemoration of the great zeal manifested by him in this matter, the church was called St. Nazareth. The architect was a man named Gavona (Leon) an Armenian, who was brought out from Persia in consequence of the total absence of skilful architects in Calcutta in those days. The steeple was added in 1734 by Aga Manuel the son of Aga Hazarmall, who lies buried under the steeple, and the inscription on whose tombstone is very pathetic. "In this tomb," it runs, "there lies interred the body of an innocent martyr, who while sleeping soundly in his bed in the small hours of morning was murdered in cold blood by the enemy unawares and without any just cause whatsoever" on the 30th May, 1757: "Oh! ye who may come to this my tomb, have pity upon me." The church was repaired and embellished in 1763 at the expense of the famous Aga Petrus Aratoon, who died in 1778 and was buried inside the Church. In 1790 it was again considerably improved by the late Aga Catchick Arrakiel, an eminent Armenian merchant of Calcutta, who presented the clock, erected houses for the clergy and built the surrounding walls. Aga Catchick Arrakiel died on the 25th July, 1790, and was likewise buried inside the church. There is inside the church a black mural tablet to his memory, erected by the grateful Armenian community of Calcutta.

The tombstones in the churchyard are many of them of ancient date. The inscriptions are mostly in the Armenian language, the earliest English epitaph being that of Mrs. Bartis Weskin who died on November 18th, 1781. One slab bearing military emblems is to the memory of Aga Emin (died 1809), a celebrated soldier, who attracted the notice of Sir William Jones. Among other eminent Armenians who are buried here may be mentioned the father of Aga Manuel, Aga Hazarmall Satoor (died 1734), who left money for the express purpose of adding a steeple to the church; "Mahtesey" Petrose Woksan (died 1760), the word "Mahtesey" denoting "pilgrim," and applied to one who has gone on pilgrimage to the Holy Sepulchre at Jerusalem; Gregory the Archimandrite who died at Calcutta in 1781 while collecting contributions for the see of Etchmiazin in Armenia; Archbishop Philippus of Etchmiazin who died in Calcutta in 1813 while similarly engaged; a second Gregory the Archimandrite who also died in 1831 while upon the same deputation; Massy Babu John or Abdel Massy Martyrose (died 1802) who bequeathed an annual grant of Rs. 4,200 to the District Charitable Society; Gregory Apcar (died 1847) and Arratoon Apcar (died 1863) members of the well-known commercial house of Apcar & Co., and Peter Jacob Paul (died 1862) and his distinguished son Sir Gregory Charles Paul, K.C.I.E., (died 1900), who for twenty-five years held the office of Advocate-General of Bengal.

THE GREEK CHURCH,

Stands in Amratollah Street, access to which is easily had from Canning Street. It was erected in the year 1780, and dedicated to the Transfiguration of our blessed Redeemer on Mount Tabor. It owes its foundation to Hadjee Alexias Argyree, the first eminent Greek who settled in Calcutta. In the year 1770 Argyree sailed as Interpreter with Captain Cudbert Thornhill (after Master Attendant at Fort William), in the ship *Alexander* from Calcutta, bound for Mocha and Jedda. They met with a severe gale and the vessel was dismasted. At the moment of extreme danger, when all expected that the vessel would founder, Argyree made a solemn vow to heaven that if they survived the peril he would found a Church in Calcutta for its Greek inhabitants. The ship weathered the storm, and arrived without further mishap at Mocha, and on his return to Calcutta, Argyree obtained permission from the Government to establish a Greek Church. A small house near the Portuguese Church was purchased for divine service. But death put a period to the further pious intentions of Argyree, and it was not until three years after his death at Dacca in August, 1777 that the foundation of the present Church was laid in June, 1780. The purchase of the ground and the erection of the building cost 30,000 rupees, towards which the estate of Argyree and his family contributed a considerable sum, the remainder being made up by voluntary contributions, Warren Hastings heading the subscription list with 2,000 rupees. The first minister of the church was Father Parthenio, a native of Corfu, who settled in Bengal in 1775 and who is said to have sat for the figure of our Lord in Zoffany's "Last Supper."

The edifice was consecrated on the 6th of August, 1781. In the Church is a sanctorum. The thurifer and chandeliers are of silver and made after the Turkish fashion. The Greek society in Calcutta it may be noted, is called "The Orthodox Brotherhood of Greeks in Calcutta," and comprises many wealthy and influential members of the mercantile community.

The most interesting monuments are those to Alexander Argyree of Philippopolis (1777), the founder of the church and to Demetrius Galanos, an Athenian, who died in 1833. The Persian chronogram on his cenotaph runs: "Afsos! Falatún i zaman raft;" "Alas! The Plato of the age has gone." Galanos died aged 72 at Benares where there is another monument to him; as well as one which runs. "The stranger Demetrius Galanos the Athenian to the stranger Peter Federof the Russian."

THE PARSEE AGIAREE, OR FIRE TEMPLE.

Situate in No. 26, Ezra Street, was built by the late Mr. Rustomjee Cowasjee, the well-known merchant and one of the largest ship-owners of Calcutta, and was consecrated on the 16th September, 1839. The Rustomjee family have been domiciled in Calcutta for over a century and its members have always occupied a leading position in the city. The present head of the family is Mr. Rustomjee H. M. Rustomjee, the grandson of Mr. Manackjee Rustomjee, who died on the 22nd December, 1891, and son of the late Mr. Heerjeebhoy Manackjee Rustomjee, C.I.E., whose death occurred in the year 1904. On a marble slab at the entrance to the Temple is the following inscription:—

"In the name of the Holy Hormuzed, this Fire Temple

was built at Calcutta by Rustomjee Cowasjee Banajee, Esq., and was consecrated according to the rites of the Masdiasna Religion for the service of God and the observance of Sacred Rites of the Zoroastrian Religion in the 3rd year of the reign of Her Majesty Queen Victoria on the 17th day Shurosh of the 1st month Furvurdeen Kudmee in the year of Yezdezerd 1209 and of Zoroaster 2229 (corresponding with Monday, the 16th September of the Christian year 1839)."

THE PARSEE TOWER OF SILENCE,

Situate in Balliaghatta Road, was erected by the late Nowrojee Sorobjee Bengalee, and was consecrated on the 28th January, 1822. He was a Parsee merchant in Calcutta, and the grand-father of the late Mr. Sorabjee Shapoorjee Bengalee, C.I.E., well-known as a member of the Bombay Legislative Council during the eighties.

HEBREW SYNAGOGUES.

NEVESHALAON.

(No. 9, Old China Bazaar Lane.)

THE NEW SYNAGOGUE.

(THE "SHIELD OF DAVID.")

Canning Street.

The New Synagogue, erected by Mr. E. D. J. Ezra, in memory of his late father, so well known to several generations of Anglo Indians as "Daoud Ezra," was opened in September, 1884. The building taken externally, presents a fine yet unpretending frontage, and if it were not for the spire, its use would be difficult to divine. Inside, however, the effect is that of one of the handsomest and best arranged places of public worship in Calcutta. Examined in detail, one is struck by the taste and richness of the ornamentation, and yet the effect is that of an extreme, and, if we may so speak, solemn simplicity. The building which is in the Italian Renaissance style, measures 140 feet in length by 82 feet in width over all. Entering the building through a very handsome portico at the east end, the main portion is found to consist of a nave and two aisles with an apse at termination, octangular in plan to the west, beyond which is a chamber following the same lines in which are kept the Books of the Law. The nave is 92 feet long, and 33 feet wide, and is 52 feet high from floor to ceiling. The aisles are each 75 feet long by 15 feet broad, and are 34 feet high from floor to ceiling; but they have intermediate floorings, 16 feet above the ground floor, forming galleries for the ladies of the congregation. There is also a gallery on the same level across the east end of the nave, above which is a fine rose window, 13 feet in diameter, glazed with coloured glass. On either side of the portico are entrances to staircases leading to the galleries; these can also be used as exits from the nave in case of necessity. The one to the south-east is in the basement of the clock tower, above which rises the elegant spire which reaches to the height of 140 feet from the ground. The clock has four dials, and chimes the hours and quarters on a peal of five bells. The edifice contains an inscription to " Elias David Joseph Ezra, the Father of the Jewish community who to orthodox principles united a heart susceptible of all that is good. This magnificent synagogue, Maghan David, was built at his sole expense on a site belonging to the old synagogue Neveh Shalom. He was born 20th February, 1830, and died 3rd February 1880."

CHAPTER X.

GOVERNMENT HOUSE.

THE present official residence of the Viceroy, during the four or five winter months of his stay in Calcutta, is situated in a fine enclosure of some six acres, on the north of the Esplanade and standing back from the Maidan, over which it enjoys a clear view of two miles to the south. There are entrances six in all upon all four sides. Particularly noticeable on the east and west are the four fine gate-ways, surmounted by the figure of a lion, with sphinxes upon the lower arches.

The main attraction of Government house undoubtedly lies in its collection of portraits of the various occupants of the high office of Governor-General of India. The collection was begun towards the close of the eighteenth century by the acquisition of the pictures of Lord Clive and Warren Hastings. But the real founders of it are Lord Dalhousie and Lord Northbrook. In a minute dated the 15th February, 1856, Lord Dalhousie called the attention of the Court of Directors in characteristic fashion to the poor array of portraits in the Council-Chamber and "the stately apartments of the palace which Lord Wellesley built for the Government of India:" and recommended that steps should be taken to procure a likeness of at least each one of the line of Governor-Generals. "Those who are to be seen," he continued, "appear to have been unequally and strangely selected: Warren

Hastings is there, and my Lord Wellesley and the Marquis Cornwallis: but far the greater number are absent. Half an acre is covered by a likeness of Mr. John Adam: but Lord Hastings is thrust away over a doorway in kit-cat, and not a square inch of canvas has been allotted to Sir Charles Metcalfe or to Lord William Bentinck."

The question was taken up by the India House, and several copies of pictures were made and sent out, but sixteen years later, there were still serious deficiencies in the Collection. The Government of India were addressed on the subject during the temporary Viceroyalty of Lord Napier of Merchistoun upon the assassination of Lord Mayo: but when Lord Northbrook assumed office in 1874, he found that nothing had been done and personally interested himself in the matter, with the result that the series was made complete. Under present arrangements, the supply of pictures of outgoing Viceroys is in the hands of the Home Department of the Government of India, which periodically invites the attention of the Secretary of State to the subject. The collection does not include those who have temporarily held office for short periods as Governor-General except Lord Metcalfe and Mr. John Adam: and the only absentee among the permanent incumbents is Sir George Barlow, who was confirmed in July 1806 after acting since October 1805, but was relieved by Lord Minto in July, 1807, and transferred to Madras. A catalogue of the pictures was compiled in 1897 under orders of Lord Elgin, the then Viceroy, by Col. A. G. Durand: but the work is not accessible to the public: and as it is inaccurate in several particulars, a full description of the pictures derived from this and other sources, is given in the course of the ensuing pages.

THE VARIOUS GOVERNMENT HOUSES.

The first Government House in Calcutta stood within the precincts of old Fort William, and was evidently an imposing building, for it was honoured with the praise of Captain Alexander Hamilton, who saw it as early as 1717. After the capture of the settlement by Seraj-ud-dowlah and its recovery by Clive and Watson in 1757, the house in the Fort was discarded, and an official residence erected for the President, on the riverbank south of the old Fort. In August, 1767, it was found to be in a ruinous condition, and a new site was selected not far from the spot where the modern building stands. In Wood's map of 1784, the situation of Government House is shown (as now) between Court-house-street and Council-house-street, but the enclosure did not extend as far west as it now does. At the south-east corner of Council-house-street stood the Council-Chamber, over against the building then called the Accountant-General's office and now designated the Treasury. In other words, both Government House and the Council-House stood on the ground now forming the Government House enclosure, the Council-House being to the west of Government House. There was an older Council-House still, which was condemned in 1764 as ill-adapted for the "privacy which is often requisite." "Tradition," says Dr. Busteed, "I do not know with what truth, places this, south of the Exchange, on a site afterwards occupied by the Private Secretary to the Viceroy." It would be in this older Council house that the historic incident occurred in June, 1763, when Mr. Stanlake Batson struck Hastings in the face during a Council meeting.

The only Governor-Generals who occupied this third Government House, which went by the name of Buckingham House, were Hastings, Sir John Macpherson, Lord Cornwallis, and Sir John Shore. But Hastings' residence in it was extremely intermittent. For three years after his marriage in 1777 to the Baroness Imhoff, he appears to have lived in the house she had formerly occupied (now the offices of Messrs. Burn and Co., in Hastings Street) and to have used Government House only for official purposes. At a later date, he preferred to pass his time at his country-house in Alipore and came into Calcutta only to transact public business. His private office is said to have been situated in the house now occupied by Messrs. Scott Thomson and Co., the Chemists, which stands at the corner of Court-house Street, facing the Government House enclosures and his initials were to be found, until recently, scratched upon a pane of glass in one of the windows of the house.

This disinclination of Hastings to live in Government House is easy of explanation. It was neither imposing nor capacious. Grandpré who visited Calcutta in 1790, in the days of Cornwallis, commented in most disparaging terms on the quality of the accommodation provided for the Governor-General.

"He lives in a house on the Esplanade opposite the citadel. Many private individuals in the Town have houses as good. The house of the Governor of Pondicherry is much more magnificent." Public receptions were as a rule held, either in the Court-House, where St. Andrew's Church now stands, or at the Play house, which was in Clive Street immediately behind Writers' Buildings on the site of Messrs. Finlay Muir and Co.'s offices. When Lord Wellesley, then Lord Mornington, arrived in Calcutta in 1798, the practice was still in use. We read in the *Gazette* for December 13 of that year "The Right Hon'ble the Governor-General having appointed Monday, the 17th instant, for the celebration of His Majesty's birthday, there will be a Ball and Supper at the Theatre on the occasion, at which His Lordship desires the favour of the company of all the Gentlemen belonging to the Civil and Military Service of His Majesty and of the Hon'ble the East India Company."

But these makeshift arrangements were not to the taste of the new Governor-General. His soul rebelled against the paltry dimensions and the mean appearance of the official residence which had served his predecessors: and he did not rest until he had obtained the sanction of the Court of Directors to the construction of a worthier dwelling-place for the head of their Government in India. The execution of his grandiose conception was entrusted to Captain Charles Wyatt, of the Corps of Engineers, and the first brick was laid with appropriate solemnity on the 5th February, 1799. The cost of erection was about thirteen lakhs of rupees: the land is said to have cost Rs. 80,000, and the furniture half a lakh. The general architectural design of the building partakes of the ordinary character of the time, technically classified as the Queen Anne and Georgian Pediment and Portico Style. The tradition which declares Government House, Calcutta, to be a reproduction of Kedleston Hall, Lord Scarsdale's seat in Derbyshire, is based upon the circumstance that the latter is a fine example of the style to which the former belongs. The resemblance does not as a matter of fact extend beyond the plan, and even in this respect, the similarity is confined to the main feature of a central building, connected by galleries with four distinct wings. In internal arrangements in the several elevations and in the roof, the two edifices are completely distinct. Taken as a whole Government House is a noble building, but its want of height is a serious fault. While the building was in progress, the Governor-General lived in the present Fort in a house now known as the Outram Soldiers' Institute.

The "great apartments of the new Government House" were opened for the first time on the 4th May, 1802, "being the anniversary of the fall of Seringapatam": and henceforth it has been the scene of all the historic ceremonies of state that have taken place in Calcutta.

THE PRESENT BUILDING.

The building consists of a central block, containing the Marble Hall or Durbar chamber and the Ball-rooms, and four wings, which may be considered as distinct houses, and are connected with the main portion by means of galleries. Each of these wings is so constructed that, from whatever side the wind may blow, a through current of air can be obtained through every room. The Council-chamber occupies the first floor of the north-east wing. The south-west wing is devoted to the Viceroy's establishment: here is his private room, and those of his Private Secretary and Aide-de-camp. On the floor immediately below is the Private Secretary's office, and rooms for the staff of clerks whose services are in perpetual requisition to deal with the mountains of papers which daily come before the Viceroy. In the south-east wing is the private drawing-room of Her Excellency. The north-west wing, as well as the upper stories of the other wings, are reserved for the private accommodation of the house-party. The ground-floor is almost entirely taken up by the offices of the Aides-de-camp and others belonging to the Viceregal household. The grand entrance lies on the north side and is approached by a handsome and spacious flight of steps, leading to a noble portico on the first floor. Upon these steps custom has ordered that Calcutta society shall assemble to greet arriving Viceroys: but it is seldom used except upon such occasions of state, the ordinary entrance being beneath the stairs. We may however imagine ourselves in the position of a state guest and enter by the portico: when we shall find ourselves at once in the great marble banqueting hall, composed in reality of three separate chambers, which we propose to name in the order in which we encounter them. The walls and pillars of the rooms are of plain white chunam highly polished, and the coffered ceilings which are tastefully decorated in gold and colors, are after the designs of Mr. H. M. Locke, formerly Principal of the School of Art.

THE BREAKFAST-ROOM.

The northernmost room is known as the Breakfast-room. At the eastern end stood until very recently an admirably executed white marble statue by James Bacon junior of the *Marquis Wellesley* erected, as its inscription records, by the public subscription of the inhabitants of Calcutta. It has now been transferred to the Victoria Memorial Hall collection at the Indian Museum.

Upon the walls are a number of interesting portraits:

(1) James Andrew Brown Ramsay, tenth earl and first *Marquess of Dalhousie,* Governor-General of India from 1848 to 1856: died in 1860 aged 48.

He is represented seated in a plain black suit and wears the green ribbon and star of the Thistle.

The artist was Sir John Watson Gordon, P.R.S.A., and the year of the painting 1857. His statue by Sir John Steel, R.S.A., which originally stood opposite that of Lord Wellesley, was placed in the seventies in the Dalhousie Institute, where it now is. It is intended to remove it to the Victoria Memorial Hall when that building has been completed.

(2) Edward Law, second Baron and first *Earl of Ellenborough,* Governor-General of India from 1842-44: born 1790, and died as recently as 1871.

The picture is signed J. Hayes, London, and is a full-length life-size portrait.

The erratic and theatrical rule of this Governor-General will be always memorable for its dramatic termination. He was abruptly recalled by the Court of Directors, in spite of the strenuous opposition of the Board of Control. Nor was the step without justification. He set out for Calcutta resolved on a policy which at a farewell dinner given to him at the India House he summarized in the words "to restore peace to Asia." But the whole of his term of office was occupied with wars, one of vengeance and two of annexation and aggression. The war of vengeance followed the massacre at Kabul in 1842 and the sieges of Ghaznee and Jelalabad: and after its successful termination he indulged in grandiose displays and bombastic harangues, which were universally ridiculed in the absence of special correspondents to "write them up" as essential accompaniments to the good Government of an oriental race. His next step was to annex Scinde and to invade Gwalior. But the patience of the Directors was exhausted, in spite of the victories of Napier at Meeanee and of Gough at Maharajpore and Punniar. They had no control over his policy: his despatches were haughty and disrespectful: and with the civilians from whom the Court derived its information, he was most unpopular. The Governor-General was ordered to make over charge of his Office to Mr. William Wilberforce Bird, the senior member of Council, and he sailed for England on June 15th, 1844.

But his connection with India was not over. He had already three times filled the office of President of the Board of Control, firstly, under the Duke of Wellington from 1828 to 1830, when he had boldly advocated the transfer of the Indian Government to the Crown, again during the Hundred Days of Sir Robert Peel in 1834-35, and lastly for a few weeks in 1841 when Peel formed his second ministry. He returned to the post under Lord Derby in 1858, but had held it barely three months, when he earned fresh notoriety for himself by his censure of Lord Canning for the proclamation by which after the fall of Lucknow, he announced the confiscation of the soil of Oudh. Public feeling set in strongly against him, and he was compelled to resign. Henceforward he took no official part in public affairs. He held, until his death in 1871, the sinecure place of chief clerk of the pleas in the Queen's Bench, said to be worth £ 7000 a year, and given him by his father who was Chief Justice of the King's Bench from 1802 to 1818.

(3) Sir Charles Theophilus Metcalfe, first *Lord Metcalfe:* acting Governor-General from March 1835 to March 1836, and subsequently Governor of Jamaica and Governor-General of Canada.

This picture also bears the name of "Hayes of Berner's Street" but as a matter of fact is a copy of the picture by F. R. Say which hangs in the rooms of the Oriental Club in Hanover-Square, London. It was copied together with the picture of Lord Hastings, which is in the Throne-room, in 1857 at the request of the Secretary to the East India Company. There is another copy of Say's portrait of Metcalfe by Charles Pote, an Eurasian artist, in the Town Hall.

(4) Sir John Shore, first *Lord Teignmouth*, Governor-General of India from 1793 to 1798: born 1751, raised to the peerage in October 1797, and died in 1834.

Shore began his official career as a convinced follower of Francis, but personal intercourse with Hastings made them friends for life. Like Cornwallis, he was a strong advocate of economy, and prided himself on being attended by only one-fourth the number of aides-de-camp to which Hastings had been accustomed. As a statesman, he displayed a lack of firmness which provokes a good deal of comment from Hastings' Calcutta correspondents. "We are timid, where we ought to be bold, and daring, even to temerity, in occasions that require lenity and conciliation," says Turner of Shore. "He has a miserable constitution and suffers himself to be depressed by constant regrets of his absent family," writes Colonel Palmer, the father of the "Prince of Merchants." "A good man————but as cold as a Grey Hound's Nose," is Toone's verdict.

This picture is another of those signed by Hayes and like the others is probably a copy. Its subject arrived in Bengal as a writer in May 1769: and took a prominent part in the compilation of the code of laws for Bengal which was published in 1793. He became Governor-General in that year on the departure of Lord Cornwallis and held office until Lord Wellesley's arrival in 1798. "Pacific habits and skill in revenue were Sir John Shore's distinguishing qualifications." His second son, Frederick John Shore, was also an eminent member of the Civil

Service. He died in Calcutta in 1837 in his 39th year and lies buried in the North Park-Street Cemetery.

THE DINING-ROOM.

Passing through the Breakfast-Room, we come to the Dining-Room. Two rows of dazzling white columns divide this noble chamber into a central apartment and two aisles. Along the eastern and western walls are ranged the well-known busts of the Twelve Cæsars, captured, according to tradition, from a French Ship, together with the portraits of Louis XV. and his Queen which hang elsewhere on the south-eastern staircase. The extremely handsome chandeliers which adorn this and some of the other principal apartments are also usually referred to the same origin. According to Lord Valentia, however, it would appear that most of the girandoles and mirrors in Government House were bought at the sale of the effects of Claude Martin which was held at Lucknow on October 15th, 1801, after the General's death. And in the first volume of Walter Hamilton's "Description of Hindustan" (published in 1820) a similar reference may be found.

At the end of the Vista, adding a perfect finish to the general effect, is the Throne-Room, opening on to a fine semicircular verandah overlooking the south and so named from its containing the Throne of Tippoo Sultan—a gilt chair with low back, low sloping arms, and red cushions.

THE THRONE-ROOM.

In the Throne-Room, the place of honour is occupied by

portraits of King George the Third and Queen Charlotte. Both are the work of Allan Ramsay, assisted by Reinagle and were originally painted for the coronation of the King and Queen on September 22nd, 1761. They became the "ambassadorial type" and were copied for all foreign Courts and representatives of the Sovereign.

Next to Queen Charlotte hangs (5) the posthumous portrait of *Mr. John Adam*—acting Governor-General of Fort William in Bengal from January to August 1823, between the departure of the Marquess of Hastings (Lord Moira) and the arrival of Lord Amherst. This is one of the gems of the collection—a very powerfully-painted picture by Sir Thomas Lawrence and a fine specimen of his style. Adam was the eldest son of the Right Hon. William Adam. Chief Commissioner of the Jury Court for Civil Causes in Scotland, and a daughter of the tenth Baron Elphinstone. Having at the age of 15 obtained a Bengal writership through his uncle, the Hon. William Fullerton Elphinstone, he sailed for India with his cousin Mountstuart Elphinstone, and arrived at Calcutta in February 1796. In 1817 he was made provisional Member of Council at the Presidency, and in 1819 was confirmed in the appointment. Ill-health compelled him to resign the service in 1825 and he sailed for Europe: but died off Madagascar on the 4th June at the age of only 46. His tenure of office was chiefly memorable for his deportation of James Silk Buckingham, the editor of the *Calcutta Journal,* for his outspoken comments upon official acts and persons—a startling reminder that it was not until 1835 that the Press in India obtained its freedom.

(6) Francis Rawdon Hastings, Second Earl of Moira and First *Marquess of Hastings,* K.G., G.C.B., Governor-General of Fort William in Bengal and Commander-in-Chief from 1813 to 1823.

He is wearing the ribbon and Star of the Garter and the badge of the Bath round his neck. It is a full-length portrait; and was copied in 1857 by J. Hayes from the picture by Samuel Lane, which was presented to the Oriental Club in London by Sir Charles Forbes, Bart., in May, 1836. Lane, who was born in 1780 and died in 1836, deserves to be singled out for notice in passing, from the fact that he was deaf and almost dumb from childhood. He was a pupil of Farington and also of Sir Thomas Lawrence, and had a large practice on account of the recognized fidelity of his likenesses. Lord Hastings, who was so created in December, 1816, survived his return from India three years and died in 1826 at Malta, where he was the Governor, at the age of 72. He was one of those who enjoyed the personal friendship of "the first gentleman in Europe."

(7) *William Pitt Amherst, Second Baron Amherst of Montreal, and first Earl Amherst of Arracan.*—Governor-General of Fort William in Bengal from 1823 to 1828: born, 1773, died 1857. This is a copy by George F. Clarke of a picture by Sir Thomas Lawrence, and was procured at the instance of Lord Northbrook in 1875. It is the only memorial of Lord Amherst in Calcutta, although a street in the northern quarter of the town perpetuates his name. He was the nephew of Jeffery Lord Amherst, who commanded the forces in North America from 1758 to 1764, and was

afterwards Commander-in-Chief in England from 1793 to 1795: and his succession to his uncle's barony in 1797 was under special remainder. In 1816 he was despatched on the well-known mission to China, when he refused to make the kow-tow. The earlier years of his government of India were taken up with the first Burmese war, which cost 20,000 lives and nearly fourteen millions sterling, but added to the British Empire Assam, Arracan and Tenasserim, provinces which have proved well worth the conquering. In 1826 he was created Earl Amherst of Arracan in commemoration of his achievement. With his name must also be associated the inauguration in the same year of Simla as the summer sanitarium of the Governor-General. After his return to England, he lived in retirement. His eldest son, Jeffery, died at Barrackpore in 1826.

There formerly hung in the Throne-Room and immediately outside it on the south-east staircase, two other pictures, both by Robert Home, the one of Lord Wellesley, and the other an extremely interesting one of the Duke of Wellington, painted in 1804 and purchased by Government from the painter for Rs. 2,000 in the following year. These have now, under orders of Lord Curzon, been transferred to the collection ultimately destined for the Victoria Memorial Hall, which is now temporarily housed in the Indian Museum. The gaps created by their departure have been most appropriately filled by a portrait of His Majesty King Edward the Seventh:

At the door of the Throne-Room on the south-east staircase, are a number of portraits:

(1) H. R. H. Prince Albert Victor, *Duke of Clarence and Avondale:* born 1864, died 1892.

This was painted by A. Soord in 1894, and is a duplicate of the one presented to H. R. H. the Duke of York on his marriage.

(2) *Lady William Bentinck*—A good picture, probably by Hayes.

Lady Mary Acheson, second daughter of Arthur Acheson, first Earl of Gosford, married in 1803 Lord William Bentinck. She accompanied him both to Madras and Calcutta and survived his death in 1839.

Other pictures represent Shere Ali, Ameer of Kabul from 1863 to 1879 (an equestrian portrait) Maharajah Jaswant Singh, Chief of Bhurtpore from 1853 to 1893, the present Nizam of Hyderabad as a child, Fath Ali, Shah of Persia from 1798 to 1834, Maharajah Mohender Singh, ruler of Patiala from 1862 to 1872, and Saadat Ali Khan, Nawab of Oudh from 1798 to 1814 (the last-named probably by Home.)

Attention may also be drawn to a portrait of *Lord Beaconsfield,* painted by E. N. Downard and presented by the Earl of Lytton.

On the same south-east staircase is a remarkable picture on twilled canvas by George Wilson, a Scotch artist, who made a large fortune in India and died in Edinburgh in 1797. It represents Mahammad Ali, Nawab of the Carnatic from 1754 to 1805, and known also as Wala Jah the

Nabob of Arcot. A similar picture to this, but with a different background, is in the Royal Collection at Hampton Court Palace.

A special interest attaches to the two large pictures of Louis the Fifteenth, King of France, and Queen Marie Leczinska, which are also hung on the south-eastern staircase. Both are the work of Carl Vân Loo and are said to have been captured by an English man-of-war from a French ship on its way to the Mauritius. There is an exactly similar picture of the Queen, also by Van Loo, in the Louvre, and dated 1747, when she would have been 44 years of age.

THE BALL-ROOMS.

Above the Marble Hall are the Ball-rooms, which occupy the whole of the second floor of the main building. The floors are of polished teak, and the rooms correspond in arrangement to the apartments below. Over the Throne-Room is the public drawing-room: in the centre is a large ball-room, divided by a double row of pillars; and on the north is a smaller ball-room.

We may now descend to the first floor by the staircase in the north-east wing.

Here are the portraits of—

(1) Edward Robert Bulwer-Lytton, second baron and first *Earl of Lytton,* Viceroy and Governor-General of India from 1876 to 1880: died in 1891, aged 60.

This is a copy of a portrait by Sir John Millais, Bart., R.A., and was sent out in 1877 during Lord Ripon's Viceroyalty.

Lord Lytton, who was himself a poet and scholar, succeeded his father, the novelist and politician, in the peerage in 1873: and was advanced to an earldom in 1880 on the conclusion of his tenure of office as Viceroy. He was Minister at Lisbon from 1874 to 1876: and after his return to Europe was ambassador at Paris from 1887 until his death in 1891. His administration of India was made eventful by the terrible famine in Southern India, the Second Afghan War (which made the reputation of Lord Roberts) and the Queen's assumption of the title of Empress at a great Durbar at Delhi in 1877.

(2) Thomas George Baring, *Earl of Northbrook*, Viceroy and Governor-General of India from 1872 to 1875.

Painted by W. W. Ouless, R.A., in 1883. The portrait has been engraved and published by Messrs. Graves of London. It represents Lord Northbrook seated in an easy-chair, dressed in his Peer's robes. A statue was erected by public subscription in commemoration of his administration and stands to the south of the High Court.

THE COUNCIL CHAMBER CORRIDOR.

In the curved corridor on the left, leading to the Council-Chamber are the following portraits:—

(1) *Lord William Henry Cavendish Bentinck*, Governor-General of Fort William in Bengal from 1828 to 1834,

and first Governor-General of India from 1834 to 1835. He was born in 1774 and died in 1839. His statue by Sir Richard Westmacott, R.A., stands opposite the Town Hall.

This picture was procured by Lord Northbrook through Lady Ossington, Lord William Bentinck's niece, in 1875. It is a copy of the picture belonging to the Duke of Portland at Welbeck, and was described by Lady Ossington as "an exact copy of the original which was done, I believe, in Paris in 1839, the year of his death, and the likeness is very good."

(2) George Eden, second Baron and first *Earl of Auckland*, Governor-General of India, 1836-1842. He survived his return from India for seven years and died in 1849 at the age of 65. His statue stands opposite the Eden Gardens.

The picture was painted by A. Stuart Wortley in 1878 "from two likenesses in the possession of His Lordship's family." Another portrait of Lord Auckland is in Government House, but it is "very poorly painted," and when Lord Napier of Merchistoun was acting as Viceroy in May 1872, on the murder of Lord Mayo, the attention of the Secretary of State was called to the circumstance and a request made that a better picture might be procured. Mr. Stuart Wortley's painting was eventually the result, but it needed a second despatch from Lord Northbrook five years later to obtain it.

(3) George Frederick Samuel Robinson, first *Marquess of Ripon*, Viceroy and Governor-General of India from

1880 to 1884. Painted by Sir Edward J. Poynter, now President of the Royal Academy.

Lord Ripon succeeded to the heritage of the Second Afghan War, but his tenure of office was emphatically a peaceful one. It was marked by what is known as the Ilbert Bill Agitation, the extension of local self-government, and the restoration of the state of Mysore to its hereditary Hindoo dynasty. Lord Ripon's popularity with the people of the country has never been equalled by any other Viceroy: and his departure from India in 1884 was accompanied by the most remarkable demonstrations of esteem and admiration.

Before his assumption of the Viceroyalty, he had filled a number of important offices at home. From 1863 to 1866 he was Secretary of State for War, and from 1868 to 1873 Lord President of the Council. He presided over the famous Alabama Commission and received a marquessate in recognition of his services. Since his return to England, he has been First Lord of the Admiralty (in Mr. Gladstone's short government of 1886), and from 1892 to 1895 was Secretary of State for the Colonies. He occupies at the present moment (1906) the office of Lord Privy Seal in Sir Henry Campbell-Bannerman's Ministry. Although in his seventy-ninth year, his interest in Indian questions and his influence upon English politics continue unimpaired.

(4) Frederick Hamilton Temple Blackwood, first *Marquess of Dufferin and Ava,* Viceroy and Governor-General of India from 1884 to 1888: died in 1903, aged 75.

A copy by Miss Hawkins from the painting by Frank Holl, R.A., which has been engraved by Wehrschmidt. A statue of Lord Dufferin erected by public subscription, stands at the head of the Red Road.

(5) Charles John Canning, second Viscount and first *Earl Canning:* Governor-General of India from 1856 to 1858, and first Viceroy and Governor-General of India from 1859 to 1862: created an Earl on May 21st, 1859: born 1812, died 1862. The picture which is weakly painted is the work of C. A. Mornewick, better known as a marine painter, and was procured by Lord Northbrook in 1875.

(6) *Sir John Lawrence,* Bart., Viceroy and Governor-General of India from 1864 to 1869: created Baron Lawrence in 1869, on his retirement: born 1811, died 1879.

Painted by Val. C. Prinsep, R.A., and procured through the Secretary of State during Lord Northbrook's Viceroyalty in 1875.

(7) Richard Southwell Bourke, *Earl of Mayo*: Viceroy and Governor-General of India from 1869 to 1872: assassinated at Port Blair in the Andamans in 1872 in his 51st year. This picture, which is by Mr. George F. Clarke, and was painted in 1875, is not a success. But the artist had nothing to work upon except photographs, and several artists of note who were approached declined to attempt the work on account of the difficulty of producing a satisfactory likeness.

Hanging also in this corridor are the two latest additions to the Gallery.

(8) Henry Charles Keith Petty-Fitzmaurice, fifth *Marquess of Lansdowne,* Viceroy and Governor-General from 1888 to 1894: Painted by Frank Holl, R.A., but left unfinished at his death and completed by Mr. Hugh G. Riviere. His statue by the late Mr. Harry Bates, R.A., confronts that of Lord Roberts on the Maidan, in the centre of the Red Road.

(9) Victor Alexander Bruce, ninth *Earl of Elgin* and Kincardine, Viceroy and Governor-General of India from 1894 to 1899.

Painted by Sir George Reid, P.R.S.A., and a fine portrait.

Lord Elgin's Viceroyalty was marked by a succession of untoward events; the disastrous earthquake of 1897, which destroyed Shillong and devastated Assam and Eastern Bengal: the great famine of the following year and the outbreak of plague in Bombay in 1896: the rising in Chitral and the series of frontier expeditions to which it gave birth: and the murders of Mr. Ayerst and Lieutenant Rand in Poona. Among purely domestic proceedings may be named the abolition of the Presidential army-system, the creation of Legislative Councils for the Punjab and Burma, the formation of the latter province into a Lieutenant-Governorship, the re-imposition of the Cotton and other Customs duties, the celebration of the late Queen-Empress' Diamond Jubilee, and the passing of the much-discussed and much-debated Sedition Bill. Lord Elgin who is now in his 57th year, had had little or no experience of public affairs before his assumption of the Viceroyalty in succession to Lord Lansdowne: but since his return to

England he has presided over the South African War Commission and the equally important Scotch Churches Commission and he is now (1906) Colonial Secretary and a member of the Cabinet. He was created a Knight of the Garter in 1899. It would be impossible to describe him as a popular Viceroy, and indeed he made no efforts to secure such a reputation. A portrait by a private admirer has been presented to the inhabitants of Calcutta and hangs in the Town Hall.

THE COUNCIL-CHAMBER.

In the Council-Chamber are the following portraits :—

(1) *Sir Henry Hardinge,* G.C.B., Governor-General of India from 1844 to 1848 : created Viscount Hardinge of Lahore and of King's Newton in the County of Derby on May 2nd, 1846.

Painted by George F. Clarke after Sir Francis Grant, P.R.A.

This picture was procured by Lord Northbrook through the Secretary of State in 1875.

(2) James Bruce, eighth *Earl of Elgin* and twelfth Earl of Kincardine, Viceroy and Governor-General of India from 1862 to 1863 : born 1811 : died 1863.

This is also a painting by George F. Clarke after Sir F. Grant, P.R.A.

He is represented in diplomatic uniform with the Stars of the Thistle and Bath, the China War Medal, and the ribbon of the Bath across his breast.

The picture is a copy of a full-length portrait in the possession of the Fife County Council and was procured in 1875 during Lord Northbrook's Viceroyalty.

Before coming to India, Lord Elgin had filled the offices of Governor of Jamaica and Governor-General of Canada and had twice conducted missions to China in the capacity of Plenipotentiary. He was the son of the famous collector of the Elgin marbles, and from 1859 to 1862, he filled the office of Postmaster General in Lord Palmerston's first administration. His tenure of the office of Viceroy of India was of the shortest possible duration. He died at Dharmsala in November, 1863, in the midst of an exploring journey he had undertaken from Simla through the mountain tracts of the Punjab.

(3) Richard Colley Wellesley, second *Earl of Mornington,* and first *Marquess Wellesley,* K.G., K.P., Governor-General of Fort William in Bengal from 1798 to 1805.

This picture, which is both full-length and life-size, is probably by Home, and is poorly painted, the figure having a stunted appearance. As in the other picture also by Home, which formerly hung in the Throne-room, and has now been added to the Victoria Memorial Hall collection, he is represented as wearing two Stars, one of them being the Star of the Order of St. Patrick and the other the Star and Jewel of Tippoo Sultan, originally tendered to him by the victorious Mysore Army and subsequently presented to him by the Court of Directors. The latter Star was first worn by him on May 4th, 1802, the anniversary of the fall of Seringapatam, when "the great apartments of the new Government House were opened for the first time." Below the frame on either side are fashioned in gilt wood tigers' head and the representation of a tigerskin festooned between them, presumably a reference to the death of Tippoo Sultan, the Tiger of Mysore. Supported on this is an elliptical wooden panel painted in gold and monochrome, and depicting, as far as can be judged, the installer of Krishnaraja Wadiar, in whose person the Hindoo dynasty of Mysore was restored in 1799.

It is apparently a sketch for a larger picture. The artist is unknown. Other portraits of Lord Wellesley are to be found in the Council-Room at the India Office (also by Home, but belonging to a different period) in the entrance to the Hall of Christ Church, Oxford, and in one of the corridors of Windsor Castle. The last-named was exhibited by Sir Thomas Lawrence at the Royal Academy in 1813.

(4) *Robert Lord Clive,* Baron of Plassey: Governor of Bengal from 1758 to 1760, and again from 1765 to 1767: born 1725, died 1774.

A half-length figure, the size of life, boldly painted by Dance with very forcible shadows.

A picture, similar in size—but differing in attitude and in background, is in the possession of the Earl of Powis. In it an engagement of troops occupies the background and a cloud of smoke issues from behind the figure towards the right. In the present one the background consists of rich trees, surrounding a piece of water with a distant view of mountains beyond. This picture has been engraved by Bartolozzi, and also, on a small scale by Edwards, as a frontispiece to Malcolm's life of Clive, published in 1836.

(5) *Warren Hastings,* the first Governor-General of Fort William in Bengal from 1774 to 1785.

This is a copy of the famous picture referred to both by Macaulay and by Lord Mahon in his History of England (Vol. VII of the Third edition of 1804).

The motto "Mens æqua in arduis," which according to both was below the picture is now above it.

The original of the picture which is by A. W. Devis, and authenticated as such in a large mezzo-tint Engraving executed in 1784 by Henry Hudson, was sent home in 1885 to be cleaned and was by order of the Secretary of State deposited in the National Portrait Gallery where it now is. The present copy by Miss J. Hawkins was sent out in 1887. It is interesting to notice the marble bust inscribed on the pedestal "Clive" which stands within a circular niche behind the figure in the picture.

By order of the Secretary of State, copies of Mr. C. J. Tomkins' engraving of the picture were distributed in 1894 to the official residences of each Governor and Lieutenant-Governor in India.

(6) Charles, second Earl and first *Marquess Cornwallis,* K. G., Governor-General of Fort William in Bengal and Commander-in-Chief from 1780 to 1783 and again in 1805: died at Ghazipur on October 5th, 1805, aged 67.

This is a fine picture. A dark curtain or tent extends across the top of the canvas and hangs down behind the full length standing figure of the Governor-General. To the right the curtain is raised showing in brilliant sunshine across the plain a view of Seringapatam. Groups of Indians and native troops (the old Madras Sepoy) and British soldiers occupy the middle ground: beyond are rocks in which tent ropes are fixed. In the further distance troops are in motion and elephants carrying howdahs.

The picture was painted by A. W. Devis and purchased on the occasion of Lord Cornwallis' departure for England in 1793, by public subscription for twenty thousand Sicca rupees, which at the then rate of exchange, amounts to £2,166.

There is another portrait of Lord Cornwallis by J. S. Copley in the Guild Hall of the City of London, and there are Statues of him in the Calcutta Town Hall and also at Madras (in the Fort) and at Bombay (in the Elphinstone Circle).

(7) Gilbert Elliot *Lord Minto,* Governor-General of Fort William in Bengal from 1807 to 1813: created Earl of Minto on his return from India: died in the following year at the age of 63.

Painted by George Chinnery, who resided in Calcutta from 1802 until 1822, and died at Macao about the middle of the century, having spent nearly fifty years of his life in India and China.

Lord Minto as Sir Gilbert Elliot, was one of the Managers for the House of Commons at the impeachment of Warren Hastings, and in 1783 he was designated as one of the "Seven Kings" or Parliamentary Directors to be appointed under the provisions of Fox's abortive India Bill. From 1794 to 1796 he was Viceroy of Corsica, and in 1797 he was created a peer. It was he who when moving for the impeachment of Sir Elijah Impey in 1788, gave the imaginative account of Nuncomar's execution which was so skilfully followed and improved upon by Macaulay. His son Alexander Elliot, a young writer who died in India at an early age in 1778, and was an intimate friend of both Hastings and Impey, had in 1775 acted as interpreter at Nuncomar's trial, being "eminently skilled in the Persian and Hindoostanee language:" When thirteen years later it fell to the lot of the father to play so prominent a part against the son's friend, he felt the position keenly, for in a letter written to his wife in 1788, he says: "I never saw Hastings until to-day and had not formed anything like a just idea of him. He looks as if he could not live a week. I always feel uncomfortable in the reflection of his connections with Alick, and I cannot say I was insensible to the idea of seeing him to-day." Prior to his appointment to the Governorship of India, he had filled the offices of Viceroy of Corsica, during the short British occupation of the Island, and President of the Board of Control. When he landed in India in 1807, fifty years exactly had elapsed since the British merchants of Calcutta had become sovereigns of Bengal: and one of his aides-de-camp who visited the battle-field of Plassey in 1808, was conducted over the ground by one who had been an eye-witness of that memorable victory. His administration was distinguished by the capture of the Isle of Bourbon and Mauritius from the French in 1810 and of Java from the Dutch in 1810: and these achievements are commemorated by Chinnery in the picture before us. It was he also who despatched Metcalfe to Runjeet Singh's Court at Lahore, Malcolm to Teheran, and Mountstuart Elphinstone to Kabul, with the object of establishing friendly relations with the several powers which held the keys of the North-Western frontier. He died in England in June, 1814, only a few weeks after his return from India.

There is no record of the manner in which this portrait of Lord Minto by Chinnery found its way into the collection: but it may be identified with the portrait brought out to Java in May, 1813, by His Majesty's frigate *Hussar* the vessel which conveyed Lord Minto to England later in the year. The description of the Java picture, as given in the *Calcutta Gazette* of October 17th, 1818, tallies exactly with that of the Government House picture: and there was moreover no reason why a portrait of the English conqueror of Java should have remained at Batavia after the restoration of the island to the Dutch and the withdrawal of Sir Stamford Raffles, the English Governor and the army of occupation.

Lord Minto was extremely popular in Calcutta during the six years of his residence: and it is singular that there should be no public memorial of his administration. There is, it is true, a statue in a niche of the great courtyard of the India Office, and this painting at Government House.

But neither in the Town Hall, which was completed during his term of office, nor in St. John's Church which was enlarged and improved "under his auspices," are his social and political achievements commemorated. Yet there were certainly at least two other portraits of Lord Minto in Calcutta at one time.

In 1887 some interesting information was placed on record by Colonel R. Home, then in the Public Works Department of the Government of India, regarding the pictures attributed to his grandfather. In his note, he speaks of four at Government House of which two are of Lord Wellesley and one of the Duke of Wellington, of these one of Lord Wellesley hangs hard by, and the others have been transferred to the Victoria Memorial Hall Collection. The fourth (he asserts) is of the Earl of Minto painted in 1812: and it is stated that it is in the Calcutta Town Hall. No such picture can, however, be identified in that collection: and it must be supposed that Col. Home referred to the picture which is certainly the work of Home in the collection of the Royal Asiatic Society. Another portrait was also painted of him by Chinnery: but it has equally disappeared. On Lord Minto's departure from Calcutta in December 1813, he was entertained by the "settlement" at a ball at Moore's Assembly Rooms. Seven hundred cards of invitation were sent out: and the journals of the period record as an incident of the evening that "Mr. Chinnery's admirable portrait of his Lordship in a sitting posture was placed in the hall and received the admiration of all, for the grandeur of conception and great power of execution which it displayed." What has happened to this picture? The context points to its having been obtained by public subscription: and it is not likely that it was presented to the retiring Governor-General, for in that case the circumstance must have found mention in the report of the proceedings. In the ordinary course it would have been placed in some public room in Calcutta: but where? It will be noticed that the posture in this second picture of Chinnery is different from that of the Government House painting: so that it was clearly a separate work of the artist. The mystery remains unsolved: and in view of the circumstance which has once more associated the name of Minto with India, it will be seen that a special interest attaches to it.

THE SECRETARY'S ROOM.

In the Secretary's Room, south of the Council-Chamber are two pictures. The first is a representation of the lying-in-state of Lord Mayo in the Marble Hall of Government House, painted by a Local artist, the late Mr. Alexander E. Caddy. The second is a portrait of Sir Charles Wood, Bart., President of the Board of Control from 1852 to 1855, and Secretary of State for India from 1859 to 1866. He was created *Viscount Halifax* in 1866 and died in 1885, in his eighty-sixth year.

The picture is a copy by A. Mornewick after George Richmond, R.A., and was presented by Lord Northbrook.

SOUTH-EAST & SOUTH-WEST CORRIDORS.

In the Corridor of the South-East wing on the second

floor and in the corridor of the South-West wing on the first floor, are a series of portraits of the members of the Mysore family, mostly painted at Seringapatam or at Vellore in 1801 by T. Hickey, an artist who resided in the Madras Presidency and painted a number of pictures connected with the downfall of Tippoo. The most notable among these is the representation of Prince Gholam Muhammad, K.C.S.I., the eighth son of Tippoo, who visited England in 1854: and was the builder of the handsome mosque which stands at the corner of Bentinck Street and Dhurumtollah. These Mysore pictures were formerly in Government House, Barrackpore, and were transferred here under the orders of Lord Dufferin.

In the private drawing-room of Her Excellency is a picture of her late Majesty, painted by Angeli in the later years of her life. This is a facsimile of the one displayed at the Proclamation Durbar at Delhi in 1877.

NORTH-WEST CORRIDOR.

In the corridor of the North-West wing on the first floor are three pictures, the most interesting being a view of the Taj Mahal at Agra by William Hodges, R.A., who travelled in India from 1777 to 1784; and whose collection of Indian views, aqua-tinted by himself, is well-known.

Another interesting picture in the same wing is the portrait of Akbar Shah, Emperor of Delhi from 1806 to 1837, and successor of Shah Alum, the blind old Sovereign whom Lord Lake restored to his puppet throne after the battles of Aligarh and Laswarree. The painting was formerly in the palace of the late ex-King of Oudh who died at Garden Reach in 1887: and was purchased in 1890. A reproduction in chromo-lithography of a similiar portrait will be found in Sir William Sleeman's Rambles and Recollections of an Indian Official, published in 1844.

GROUND FLOOR.

On the ground floor at the foot of the North-East staircase is a portrait of Sheikh Karim Buksh "burra Khansammah" or head Butler at Government House from 1848 to 1877. His term of service which commenced with Lord Dalhousie and ended with Lord Lytton extended over the administrations of seven Viceroys.

In the dining-room on the ground floor is a half length full sized portrait of Maharajah Beer Chunder Deb Barman, the late ruler of Hill Tipperah, which is interesting from the circumstance that it is painted by himself. There is a second portrait of him, painted by his son the Burra Thakoor, in the Corridor on the Ground Floor of the south-east wing. Both the paintings were presented during the Viceroyalty of Lord Dufferin.

In the grounds are several objects of historical interest. On the South side is a fine brass 32-pounder, taken from the Sikhs at Aliwal and bearing an inscription in Gurmukhi—on either side is a brass howitzer, curiously ornamented with tiger's heads and claws, taken at Seringapatam.

There is also another remarkable trophy on the North

side in the shape of a large iron gun with a carriage representing a dragon taken from the Chinese, and erected by Lord Ellenborough in commemoration of the peace signed under the walls of Nanking in 1842.

Two other large brass guns may be seen; the one inscribed "Meeanee, 17th February," and "Hyderabad 20th of March, 1843" perpetuates the victories of Sir Charles Napier and the annexation of Scinde. The other on the north-west bears the legend "Ghuznee, 6th September, Cabul, 16th September 1842," and commemorates the prowess of Pollock and Nott in the second Afghan war. This was originally a Dutch gun and bears the inscription "Assuerus Koster me fecit, Amstelredam 1630," with the representation of a ship in full sail and the Dutch Company's monogram V.O.C.

The exterior of the House has been lavishly ornamented with pinnacles during the Viceroyalty of Lord Curzon, but the result has not been (in the opinion of many) to add to the beauty or the dignity of the edifice. The royal arms surmount each of the wings, two of the representations facing north, and the remaining two south. These stand boldly out against the sky and are conspicuous objeots from a distance. The thick grove of trees which surrounds the Government House enclosure is an addition of comparatively recent years. The ground is shown completely bare in pictures of the early portion of the nineteenth century.

CHAPTER XI.

THE HIGH COURT.

A LITTLE to the west of the Town Hall, and almost at the junction of Esplanade west with the Strand Road, stands the High Court, an imposing building in the gothic style of architecture. The foundations were laid in March, 1864, and the work of construction completed in May, 1872. To the late Mr. Walter Granville, the Government Architect, must be accorded the credit of the design which in its general idea would appear to have been inspired by the Town Hall at Ypres. The building occupies the site of the old Supreme Court which stood upon the western portion only, and of three private residences, regarding which a word or two may be said. To the east of the Supreme Court, which was erected between 1780 and 1784, and of which it was said that there was not in the whole town a meaner building externally, there ran a narrow gully, and to the east of that again was the house of Longueville Clarke, whose name has already passed into the category of forgotten things, although he died as recently as 1863. But he deserves commemoration as a famous advocate of the thirties and forties and one of the leading figures in the public and social life of the Calcutta of his day. We have already encountered him in these pages as the father of the Calcutta Ice House, and he was also the founder of the Bar Library in June, 1825, and one of the most prominent movers in the establishment of the Metcalfe Hall in 1838. Next to his house, and at the corner of the Esplanade and Old Post Office Street, lived in the fifties Mr. William Macpherson, Master of the Supreme Court and brother of that distinguished lawyer, Sir Arthur George Macpherson, who was a Judge of the High Court from 1864 to 1877. Behind him, in Old Post Office Street itself, and still on land now covered by the High Court, was the residence of Sir James William Colvile, whose connection with the Supreme Court was threefold, for he was Advocate-General in 1846, puisne Judge from 1848 to 1855, and successor of Sir Lawrence Peel as Chief Justice in the last named year. The Supreme Court, it must be added in defence of that institution, was more imposing inside than out. On the upper floor was the Grand Jury Room, where that dignified body met to throw out the indictments presented to them or to return a true bill. Downstairs was the Court-room, where their Lordships sat to determine the quarrels of those that dwelt within the limits of the Mahratta Ditch. And in one of the many rooms in the building were the chambers of Sir William Jones, who succeeded Le Maistre as a Judge of the Court in 1783 and died in Calcutta in April, 1794. It is said to have been his habit to walk to the "New Court House" every morning from the quiet bungalow at Garden Reach, where he spent his evenings with pundits and moonshees and corresponded with Johnson and Burke. At Bhowanipore, in the building to the south of the race-course, which is now used as the Military Hospital, was located the Company's appellate tribunal both civil and criminal, with jurisdiction over the rest of the Presidency and known as the Sudder Adawlut.

A word or two regarding these vanished Courts may not be without interest. The Supreme Court was erected by the celebrated Charter of the 26th March, 1774, and consisted of a Chief Justice and three puisne Judges, subsequently in practice reduced to two. It was a Court of Chancery and a Court of King's Bench in one, and possessed in addition exclusive criminal jurisdiction within the "town of Calcutta" as well as a certain general jurisdiction through the Presidency of Fort William, which might be founded on the personal status of the defendant or conceded by agreement of parties. The leading purpose for which the Court was instituted was, "to protect the natives from oppression, and to give India the benefits of English law:" in other words, that a ready-made substantive body of law, in the main coincident with the principles of English Common Law and Equity, should be introduced into the new settlement of Calcutta, and be carried into effect by a professionally trained Court of co-ordinate rank with the Superior Courts of Westminster Hall, and that through the authority and power of this court, independent of the local Government, all Englishmen throughout the country, whether official or other, should be rendered responsible for their relations and behaviour to the native population according to those principles.

On the whole, in spite of certain early extravagancies the Court discharged its very difficult and exalted duty with good temper and success. The list of its Judges from Sir Elijah Impey to Sir Barnes Peacock, contains names which stand distinguished on the roll of the English Bar; and it is hardly too much to say that the Supreme

Court so taught the people of Bengal to understand the reign of law that the lesson will never again be unlearned.

The Company's Courts at the Presidency were established in 1772, when the East India Company undertook the administration of civil and criminal justice throughout Bengal, Behar, and Orissa, on a plan drawn up by Mr. Hastings and four Members of the Council. They were two in number. The Sudder Nizamut Adawlut was the appellate court of criminal jurisdiction, while the principal court of civil justice was the Sudder Dewani Adawlut. The latter originally sat under the superintendence of three or more Members of the Council, to hear appeals from the Provincial Courts in causes exceeding five hundred rupees.

In 1780, the avocations of the Governor-General and the Members of the Council having prevented their sitting in the Court of Sudder Dewani Adawlut, Sir Elijah Impey was induced, in addition to the Chief Justiceship of the Supreme Court, to allow himself to be made sole Judge of the Sudder Dewani Adawlut. Macaulay has chosen to describe this transaction in his most vitriolic language. "The Chief Justice was rich, quiet and infamous. His conduct was of a piece with almost every part of it that comes under the notice of history. No other such Judge has dishonoured the English ermine, since Jeffreys drank himself to death in the Tower." But there was nothing in the incident to warrant either vehemence or vituperation: and Impey's "interference" was wholly beneficial. He at once framed rules for the regulation and guidance of all the subordinate local Courts and for directing their practice; and it may be said that these still constitute the ground-work of the Mofussil system of administration of justice. Two years afterwards, the superintendence of this Court was, on a resolution of the Home Legislature, re-assumed by the Governor-General and Council. In 1801, it was enacted that the Court of Sudder Dewani Adawlut should consist of three Judges, namely, a Chief Judge, to be selected from the members of the Supreme Council, and two Puisne Judges, to be selected from the covenanted civil servants of the Company. And in 1805 it was found inconvenient that even the office of Chief Judge should be held by a member of the Supreme Council, and the Governor-General in Council was directed to select that officer from among the civil covenanted servants of the Company, not being members of the Supreme Council. This arrangement was afterwards again changed, and again once more re-established. And at the time of the union of the two Courts in 1862, the Sudder Dewani Adawlut consisted of four Judges in all, an equal number presiding over the Sudder Nizamut Adawlut.

At the outset, in 1772, the work of the Mofussil Courts was necessarily somewhat crude. The administration of justice under the new system seems, however, to have rapidly improved and there can be no doubt it was more satisfactory to the people than that under the native rule. Gradually, too, the education and example afforded by the Supreme Court had their effect. By degrees the method and practice developed under the superintendence and direction of the Sudder Adawlut assimilated itself, though imperfectly, to the European model; and after more than sixty years' experience it was judged best to revert to the system which had commended itself to Hastings, and to replace the double machinery under which justice was administered by one comprehensive organization, controlled by an English barrister and largely composed of professional ingredients.

The High Court of Judicature at Fort William in Bengal, to give it its full title, was accordingly constituted by Letters Patent on the 14th May, 1862, by virtue of the powers conferred by a statute of the preceding year (24 & 25 Victoria, cap. 104). The first Chief Justice, Sir Barnes Peacock, and twelve puisne Judges were named in the Letters Patent. At the same time the Supreme Court, and the Sudder Nizamut Adawlut and Sudder Dewani Adawlut were abolished. Of the New High Court Judges, eight were the existing judges of the Company's courts, and of the remaining four, two, Sir Charles Jackson and Sir Mordaunt Wells, were members of the Supreme Court, and Mr. John Paxton Norman and Mr. Walter Morgan (afterwards Chief Justice of Madras) were elevated from the Bar.

Upon the newly-created High Court were conferred all the powers and authorities of the abolished Courts: and by fresh Letters Patent on the 28th December, 1865, further provision was made regarding the jurisdiction of the Court.

The Court at the present time is constituted of a Chief Justice and fourteen Puisne Judges, the full number authorized by the Letters Patent being fifteen. Of these the Chief Justice and six Judges are Barristers, three being members of the local Bar and three appointed from England. Five of the remainder are members of the Covenanted Civil Service, and three are native gentlemen (Hindus) who were leading Vakeels of the Court. They are all equal in regard to judicial authority and duty; but the Chief Justice is head of the Court, and has the control of the establishment in its various branches. The Puisne Judges rank after him according to the order of their respective appointments. The present Chief Justice is Sir Francis William Maclean, K. C. I. E., who was appointed in 1896. His Lordship sat in Parliament from 1885 to 1891 as member for the Woodstock division of Oxfordshire and from 1891 to 1896 held the office of Master in Lunacy in England.

The general jurisdiction of the Court extends over Bengal proper, Behar, Orissa, Chota Nagpore and Assam, thus covering an area of about 200,000 square miles (*i.e.*, an area approximately four times that of England and Wales), with a population of some 80 millions of people.

This jurisdiction is largely administrative as well as judicial, because in the absence of a Governmental Department of justice, much of the management of the Local Courts is entrusted to the High Court.

For administrative work, the court acts by committees: and the supervision of the subordinate civil judiciary is usually entrusted to one of the civilian judges who presides over what is known as the English Department.

The judicial work divides itself broadly into two classes,

original and appellate. The original is that which comes before the Court as a Court of first Instance, and may be said to be limited territorially to the Town of Calcutta, thereby preserving a distinction which dates from the institution of the Mayor's Court in 1726. The appellate consists of all matters, very heterogeneous in kind, criminal and civil, which are brought before the Court by way of appeal or for revision, from the District and other subordinate Courts, and includes appeals from the original jurisdiction.

For the disposal of the judicial work, original and appellate, the Court sub-divides itself into specified Benches of one, two, or more Judges in each, according to the character of the work which the Bench is intended to take. But the decision of a Bench which is constituted of but one Judge (as is usually the case for original work) is not necessarily the final decision of the Court and an appeal from it lies to a larger Bench of two or more Judges.

The present High Court Building accommodates both the appellate courts and the Court of First Instance or original jurisdiction. Its main facade is on the south and looks upon the Esplanade and the Maidan. A grand colonnade runs along the lower storey: the capitals of the pillars are of Caen stone, admirably sculptured, and each one of a different design. In the centre of the facade is a massive tower 180 feet high, from which a view may be obtained of Calcutta and the surrounding country, which well rewards the labour of the climb. Underneath the tower is the principal entrance, through which we pass into a magnificent quadrangle enclosing a shady garden and a fountain. The principal staircase will be found in the tower. It is of fine proportions and the statue of Sir Edward Hyde East (which has already come under our notice in the chapter on the statues of Calcutta) occupies a prominent place at the head of the first flight of steps. To the east of the quadrangle, in Old Post Office Street, is the carriage entrance for the public: while there are private entrances for the Judges on the west and the east. A new block is in course of construction on the north, which it is intended to devote to a new Sessions Court and a Jury Room—the latter a convenience represented by the merest makeshift in the present building. On the ground floor of the existing structure are various offices including the court of the Master and Official Referee and a barred room on the south in which prisoners awaiting their trial at the Sessions are detained. On the first floor are the Courts (on the south), the Judges' private rooms (on the north), the Judges' Library (on the west), the Bar Library (on the east), the Pleaders' and the Attorneys' Libraries (in the north-east corner) and the offices of the Registrars on the Appellate and Original sides, the former on the west and the latter next to the Bar Library. On the upper floor are various offices including those of the Clerk of the Crown, the Court Receiver and the Legal Remembrancer, the barristers' luncheon-room, and the Advocate-General's chambers.

The Courts are eight in number. Seven of them are on the southern side of the quadrangle and the eighth which is occupied by the Criminal Appellate Bench, is on the north, in close proximity to the Judges' rooms. The

Sessions Court which is also used as a Civil Court of first instance is at the south-eastern corner. Facing the Bench will be noticed the dock, the platform of which slides back in order to admit the prisoner who is brought up through a species of trap-door from the detention-room below.

At stated times in the year, Criminal Sessions are held, over which one of the Judges presides in his scarlet robes. Many of the customs of the days of the old Supreme Court are kept up. The Judge marches in solemn procession to take his seat preceded by the Sheriff of Calcutta and the Deputy-Sheriff and attendants carrying the mace and sword, the anchor of Vice-Admiralty and other insignia of office and accompanied by javelin-men. The proceedings are opened every day by the following proclamation, repeated three times in a loud voice by the marshal of the Court: "Oyez! Oyez! Oyez! All persons that have any thing to do before my Lord the King's Justice of Oyer and Terminer and general gaol delivery and at these Admiralty Sessions draw near and give your attendance. Oyez! Oyez! Oyez!"

On the eastern wall of the Sessions Court hangs a portrait of Sir Henry Russell, Bart., fourth Chief Justice of the Supreme Court, robed in red. It was painted by Chinnery in 1812. Sir Henry Russell succeeded Sir William Dunkin (who died in Calcutta) as a puisne Judge of the court in 1797. He was promoted to the office of Chief Justice in 1806, on the retirement of Sir John Anstruther, and reigned until 1813, when he was followed by Sir Edward Hyde East. It is to be feared that Sir Henry Russell's eminence as a Judge stands in danger of eclipse by his relationship to Rose Aylmer whose fame is "carved as it were in ivory or in gems" in Landor's touching elegy. The well-known entry in the *Calcutta Gazette* for the first week of March, 1800, has been often quoted, but it will bear one more repetition. "On Sunday last, at the house of her uncle, Sir Henry Russell, in the bloom of youth and possession of every accomplishment that could gladden or embellish life, deplored by her relatives and regretted by a society of which she was the brightest ornament, the Hon'ble Miss Aylmer." The tapering column may still be seen which marks her last resting-place in the old burying-ground in Park Street, and the reader will find that it has received its due meed of commemoration when he comes to visit that "desert of death" with its pitiful memories and its record of tenderness and greatness and grief. Sir Henry Russell's relationship with Rose Whitworth Aylmer was through his first wife. The fourth Lord Aylmer and he were married to sisters of Earl Whitworth, the British Ambassador at Paris, who was publicly insulted by Napoleon after the peace of Amiens. The Chief Justice's house in Calcutta was in the street which now bears his name, and tradition places it on the spot now occupied by Nos. 12 and 13, where Sir Barnes Peacock and John Paxton Norman lived after him. He named his youngest daughter Rose Aylmer in memory of his niece, and notwithstanding vague suggestions which are seemingly to the contrary in Landor's poem "Abertawy" there can be no doubt he was much attached to her. Three of his six sons entered the Company's service. Henry (1783-1852), who succeeded his father in 1836 in the baronetcy which was conferred upon him in 1812, was

Resident at Hyderabad in 1810, and earned from Wellesley the compliment of description as "the most promising young man he knew." The others were Charles, who entered Parliament as member for Reading after leaving India and died in 1856, and Francis Whitworth, who became Salt Agent at Chittagong and died there in 1852 in the 44th year of his service. The baronetcy is still enjoyed by the family. The third baronet was one of the first recipients of the Victoria Cross for gallantry, in the Crimea, and the fourth who died as recently as 1898, and was the Chief Justice's grandson, revived the legal traditions of the family by attaining to a County Court Judgeship which he held from 1874 to 1885.

Passing along the public corridor which runs from end to end of the southern side of the quadrangle on the first floor, we shall find in the court immediately to the west of the great staircase, a full-length portrait of the Honourable Shambhoonath Pundit, a Kashmiri Brahmin by caste, and Judge of the High Court from 1863 to 1867. He was the first Indian to administer Justice upon the Bench of the High Court, his predecessor Baboo Rama Persad Roy, a son of the famous Rajah Ram Mohan Roy, having died before he could take his seat. There is no direction, perhaps, in which the changes wrought in India during the reign of Queen Victoria have manifested themselves more significantly than in this. Sixty years ago, the presence of Judges of Indian birth upon the Bench would have been scorned as an impossibility. To-day no High Court is regarded as complete unless it counts a Hindoo and Muhammadan lawyer among its members: and Sir Romesh

Chunder Mitter's tenure of office of acting Chief Justice in 1882 has amply demonstrated their fitness to occupy even the chair of Impey and Ryan and Peacock. Nor could there be a better testimony to the manner in which Indian Judges have discharged the trust reposed in them than the honoured remembrance in which the names are held of Dwarka Nath Mitter, in Calcutta, Ranade, Tyabji and Telang in Bombay, Mahmood in Allahabad, and Muttuswamy Aiyar in Madras: while among those retired Judges who are yet living Sir Gooroo Dass Banerjee and Mr. Ameer Ali are regarded as the leading authorities upon Hindoo and Muhammadan law.

At the end of the corridor is the Chief Justice's Court which corresponds in dimensions to the Sessions Court at the opposite extremity. The walls are panelled, and the Royal arms above the Chief Justice's chair impart an air of dignity which will strike the visitor as somewhat lacking in the other Courts.

On the western wall, facing the Bench, are three fine portraits. On the left is that of Sir John Anstruther, Bart., who followed Sir Robert Chambers as Chief Justice of the Supreme Court in 1798 and more fortunate than some of his successors, held the office for nearly eight years. The Grand Jury on the 5th December, 1805, presented Sir John Anstruther with an address, thanking him for his services in the administration of justice, and asking permission to place his portrait in the Town Hall "when that building was completed." The petition describes Calcutta as "one of the wealthiest and most populous cities in the world." Sir John Anstruther retired from the Bench in February, 1806, and was succeeded by Sir Henry Russell. He died in 1811. In 1798 he was created a baronet of Great Britain, and in 1808 succeeded his brother as fourth holder of the baronetcy of Nova Scotia already enjoyed by the family. In the centre hangs a portrait by Chinnery of Sir Francis Workman Macnaghten, Bart., puisne Judge of the Supreme Court from March 1816 to March 1825: and the father of Sir William Hay Macnaghten, who was assassinated at Cabul in 1841 on the eve of his departure to take up the governorship of Bombay. Sir Francis Macnaghten's whole legal career was passed in India. He was enrolled as an advocate of the Supreme Court at Fort William in 1791, and subsequently became Advocate-General. In 1807 he was appointed to be a puisne Judge in Madras, and nine years later was transferred to Calcutta on the retirement of Sir William Burroughs. He acted as Chief Justice in 1823 on the death of Sir Henry Blosset, and again in 1824 after that of Sir Christopher Puller, two victims of the climate whose combined tenure of office did not exceed four months. His popularity in Calcutta was very great, and when he resigned his seat on the Bench in 1825, and sailed for England, "he was accompanied to Chandpal Ghat by Sir Anthony Buller (the junior puisne Judge), the barristers, attorneys and officers of the Court, and a large concourse of the community, and certainly a more honourable tribute could not possibly be paid to anyone." He was created a baronet in 1836, having four years previously succeeded to the family estate and the chieftainship of clan Macnaghten. He died in 1843: and the legal talent of himself and of his distinguished son, who was as learned as a lawyer as he was famous as a diplomatist, has displayed itself in the present generation in the person of his grandson Lord Macnaghten, who has since 1877 filled the high office of Lord of Appeal in Ordinary in England. The family is an ancient one. Sir Alexander fell at Flodden in 1513, and John Macnaghten joined his forces to that of Claverhouse and helped him to win the battle of Killiecrankie in 1689.

The third of the pictures in the Chief Justice's Court is of Sir Richard Garth, Chief Justice of Bengal from 1875 to 1886, a remarkably fine picture painted in 1887 by the Hon. John Collier, and a worthy memorial of one who earned universal respect and esteem by the manner in which he upheld the highest and best traditions of judicial dignity and independence. He survived his retirement by many years and died in London in March 1902.

In the Judges' Library, which lies to the north of the Chief Justice's Court, there are a number of equally interesting portraits. The room is not open to the public, but an application in writing to the Registrar of the Appellate Side, whose office adjoins, should procure admittance without difficulty for visitors who are provided with a letter of introduction. The Library is a chamber of noble proportions, but the light is not good and it cannot be said that the pictures are seen to their best advantage.

In the room of the Registrar, there hangs on the southern wall a portrait by the late Mr. C. W. Furse, A.R.A., of Sir William Comer Petheram, Chief Justice from 1886 to 1896. It must be adjudged to be an extremely disappointing specimen of that artist's work: the black robes create a sombre impression which finds no relief in the dark background or in the painting of the face. Sir Comer Petheram was from 1884 to 1886 Chief Justice at Allahabad, before his transfer to Fort William on the retirement of Sir Richard Garth.

Upon the wall opposite hang two paintings which create a very different impression. The one on the right hand of the entrance to the Judges' Library represents Mr. Charles Binny Trevor, Judge of the Sudder Dewani Adawlut from 1856 to 1862, and a puisne Judge of the High Court from 1862 to 1867. He was one of the Judges named in the Charter by which the High Court at Fort William was constituted in 1862. In the Great Rent Case—which was heard by the whole Bench of fifteen Judges—he boldly differed from the Chief Justice and carried the day. As the poet has it—

"Then first his judgment Trevorus
Read out in language clear
And such a silence then was kept
A pin's drop you might hear.
At length when all grew weary
And sleep proclaimed her reign,
Great Trevorus thought 'twas time enough
To close the lengthen'd strain.
And this is how the learned Judge
The Rent Case did decide:
He settled that a tenant
Who twelve years should abide
Upon his landlord's property
Should have an owner's right

> To share the rent, and landlord
> Should get it as he might."

His retirement took place in 1867, after thirty-five years service: and he died in England in 1899.

On the left hand side of the door is a fine portrait of John Russell Colvin. His tomb stands in the Agra Fort in conspicuous solitude before the deserted audience-chamber of Akbar: and posterity remembers him as the Lieutenant-Governor of the North-Western Provinces in the Mutiny year, whose fate it was to die in his beleaguered capital just five days before the last great assault which planted the British flag once more upon the walls of Delhi. But he was no less famous in his day as a lawyer and a judge, as the following brief record of his career will amply demonstrate. The son of James Colvin of the famous Calcutta house of Colvin, Ainslie and Cowie and the nephew of Alexander Colvin, whose marble monument by Westmacott in St. John's church testifies to the esteem in which his brother merchants held him, John Russell Colvin was born in the business house in Hastings Street in 1807. He passed out of Haileybury in 1825 at the head of his term and arrived in Calcutta in March of the following year. Passing rapidly through the college at Fort William, where he distinguished himself at Persian, he obtained his first appointment at the close of 1826, as assistant to Sir William Macnaghten (of Kabul fame) who was then Registrar of the Sudder Adawlut. He was set in due course to acquire administrative experience in Cuttack and later at Hyderabad: and in 1830 found himself again in Calcutta where he filled various secretariat offices. In

March 1836, he was selected by Lord Auckland on his arrival in India to be his Private Secretary and returning with his chief to England in 1842 he remained there until 1845 when he left it for the last time. His next post was of a diplomatic character, Sir Henry Hardinge sending nim to relieve Henry Lawrence as Resident in Nepal. After a year he was appointed to succeed Sir Henry (then Captain) Durand as Commissioner of the Tenasserim Provinces in Lower Burma. At the beginning of 1849 he was recalled to Calcutta by Lord Dalhousie to take his seat on the Bench of the Sudder Dewani Adawlut. "The Bengal public," writes Sir Auckland Colvin in his biography of his father, "were somewhat astounded at the appointment. The objections were many. With some he had no experience. With others he had no temper. Again he had no knowledge of legal matters." He speedily falsified the predictions of one and all. It was true enough that he brought with him to the Bench little experience of law beyond what he had gained in rough and ready fashion at Moulmein. But it was not long before he established a commanding position for himself in the court. Before he left it in 1853 to go to Agra as Lieutenant-Governor, he had become *facile princeps*: so much so, that, as Sir Charles Trevelyan put it in the memoir of his friend which he contributed to *The Times* "it was commonly said that the pleaders had to be sometimes reminded that they ought to address the Court and not Mr. Colvin." The value of a Judge's work is to be found in his judgments rather than in any record of administration. But Colvin did not content himself with laying down sound principles of law. "The Sudder Court when he joined it had a questionable reputation. Barristers who ventured across the Maidan from the Supreme Court came back with strange tales of the quality of justice administered at Bhowanipore: of antiquated procedure: of misuse of evidence: of arguments misapplied." Colvin laboured successfully not only to raise the Court to the level which a Court of Appeal should occupy, but to improve the quality of all courts subordinate to it. He especially aimed at raising the character of the native bar: and when a meeting was called in Calcutta in 1857 to do honour to his memory, the leader in the movement was Rama Persad Roy, the most eminent of the pleaders of his day, whom death alone robbed of the honour of being the first High Court Judge of Indian nationality. "The three years Colvin passed on the Calcutta Bench were," says his son, "possibly the happiest in his life. He was among valued friends. His health in the moist Calcutta climate gave him none of that anxiety which many feel. In Hastings' House at Alipore he extended to all his acquintances a wide and warm hospitality. His reading had made him an excellent companion: and he delighted in converse with the best and ablest of those about him." He had been admitted in his younger days to the intimacy of Macaulay: and he is one of those honoured by mention in Macaulay's letters to his sister among "the little circle of people whose friendship I value and in whose conversation I take pleasure." In 1853 he was called once more to high administrative office by the death at Bareilly of James Thomason, the Lieutenant-Governor of the North Western Provinces: and the last four years of his life were passed away from Calcutta.

He died at Agra on the 9th September, 1857, worn out and assailed by the shafts of hostile criticism. "If I have erred in any steps, hard has been my position," he wrote to Ross Mangles, the Chairman of the Court of Directors, a few months before his death, "and you will bear lightly on my memory."

Entering the Judges' Library, we shall best begin our survey of the portraits by proceeding at once to the southern end of the room. Here our attention is at once drawn to the half-length portrait of Sir Robert Chambers which hangs on the door. The picture is probably by A. W. Devis (1763-1827) whose name is misspelt as "Davis" on the frame, although Dr. Busteed who has reproduced it in his *Echoes from Old Calcutta* ascribes it with some hesitation to Home. There can however be no doubt regarding the beauty and artistic value of the painting which represents Chambers in his scarlet robes, seated and with his face resting on his hand. It is perhaps hardly necessary to recall that Chambers was one of the original judges of the Supreme Court appointed by the Charter of 1774. Like his colleagues, Impey and Hyde, he arrived in India married and was accompanied also by his mother who died in Calcutta in 1782. He was, says Dr. Busteed, the only one of the first four judges who can be said to have had an English reputation before coming to India. The brothers Scott, who achieved peerages as the Earl of Eldon and Lord Stowell, were his schoolmasters at Newcastle-on-Tyne, where he was born: and at the time of his elevation to the Bench, he was Vinerian Professor of Law at Oxford, where he was a member of University College.

He had also the distinction of friendship with Dr. Johnson, and belonged to the famous Literary Club, where he foregathered with Burke and Goldsmith and Sir Joshua. There are frequent references to Chambers in Boswell, and when he sailed for India, he took with him to Calcutta a letter of introduction from Johnson to Warren Hastings, which may be seen among the select manuscripts in the British Museum, and which speaks clearly enough of the estimation in which he was held by "the old philosopher." Chambers succeeded Impey as Chief Justice, but although the latter left India in November, 1783, he did not take his seat as such until September, 1791, when, it is said, a salute was fired from Fort William. He held the office until August, 1798, when he was offered a peerage, but preferred a pension of £ 2,000 a year. His death took place near Paris in 1803 at the age of 66, and his body was brought to England and buried in the Temple Church, where a monument by Nollekens was erected to his memory. Lady Chambers, who remained with him throughout his twenty five years' residence in India, survived until 1839, when she died at the age of 81. Their daughter, married in 1799 Colonel John Macdonald, son of the famous Flora Macdonald. Chambers lost several children in Calcutta, as the inscription testifies upon the family tomb in the South Park Street burying ground: and their eldest son Thomas Fitzmaurice Chambers, was lost at the age of six in the wreck of the "Grosvenor" on the coast of Africa in August, 1782. In the same tomb was buried in 1793 Mr. William Chambers "Prothonotary and Persian Interpreter to the Supreme Court," who would seem to have been a relative.

To the right of Chambers, is a full-length portrait, with hand outstretched and in full judicial panoply of Sir Elijah Impey, Chief Justice of the Supreme Court (need it be said?) from October 1771 to November, 1783. The name of the artist as painted upon the descriptive label is "Zoffany, 1782" but, as Dr. Busteed has pointed out, the date is clearly wrong, for Zoffany did not leave England until 1783. It is possible of course that he arrived in Calcutta in time for Impey to sit to him, for the Chief Justice did not sail for Europe until December of that year. There is another portrait of Impey by Zoffany in the National Portrait Gallery in London, which represents him seated and in the ordinary dress of the period. A third painting by Tilly Kettle which depicts him in his robes of office, formerly hung in the Chief Justice's Court and has been lent by the present Chief Justice and Judges to the Victoria Memorial Hall collection now temporarily housed in the Indian Museum. Both are of a later date to Kettle's picture, for Zoffany did not arrive in India until the close of the year 1783. The career of Impey has been so mercilessly treated by Macaulay that it may seem to many to be as futile a task to clear his memory as to exonerate Seraj-ud-Doulah from the charge of complicity in the Black Hole tragedy. But he was in reality neither venal nor vicious, and deserves to be commemorated as a great Judge. He was a distinguished graduate of Trinity College Cambridge and after his call to the Bar by the Honourable Society of Lincoln's Inn, was second only to Dunning on the western Circuit. At the time of Nuncomar's trial in 1775, he was forty three years of age : and though older than any of the Colleagues who left England with him, he was able to withstand the climate of Calcutta for nine years. The occasion for his return from India, as is well known, was a recall to answer certain charges before Parliament: but the motion for impeachment was lost. He died in 1809 at Newick Park in Sussex and lies buried at Hammersmith. "I have a note" says Dr. Busteed in his *Echoes from Old Calcutta,* "that it never fell to Impey's lot to pass another capital sentence" after his condemnation of Nuncomar, but he adds that he is unable to quote any authority for this. There are several members of Impey's family buried in Calcutta. Two of them were in the Company's service: Hastings "a factor" who died in Calcutta in February 1805 at the age of 24, and Edward, whose daughter Adeline (died 184?, aged 20) rests in the Circular Road cemetery, and whose son, Colonel Eugene Clutterbuck Impey, C.I.E., served through the Mutiny, and was Lord Lawrence's military secretary during the years 1863 and 1864. Another Impey of the same Christian name as the Chief Justice, died in Calcutta in 1821, "zealous and skilful in his profession," the nature of which is not stated upon his tombstone: and it is only during the past year that another Impey (Mr. W. H. L. Impey, C.S.I.,) died at Naini Tal while holding the High Office of Chief Secretary to the Government of the United Provinces.

On the opposite or right hand side of Chambers hangs an equally fine portrait of Sir Lawrence Peel, painted by Sir Francis Grant, P.R.A. Sir Lawrence Peel, who was first cousin to the Prime Minister, was born in 1799. His connection with India dates from March, 1841, when he joined the Calcutta Bar upon appointment as Advocate-General. Upon Sir Henry Wilmot Seton's promotion in 1843 to the office of Chief Justice, he took his place as a puisne Judge, and five years later succeeded him in the headship of the Court. During the years 1854 and 1855 he acted as Vice President of the Supreme Legislative Council. His popularity in Calcutta was very great, and liberality unbounded. It is said that he gave away in public charity the whole of the official income of £8000 a year which he drew as Chief Justice. Upon his retirement from India in 1855, he was appointed a member of the Judicial Committee of the Privy Council, and held the office for many years. He died unmarried in 1884 at "Garden Reach" Ventnor, a name eloquent of past associations which he did not permit to be dimmed by the lapse of years.

As we turn to leave the library by the door on the north by which we have entered it from the Registrar's room, we shall notice three more pictures. On the left of the doorway is the portrait of Sir William Burroughs, Bart., puisne Judge of the Supreme Court from November, 1806, to December, 1815, painted in 1818 by Sir Thomas Lawrence, P.R.A. Sir William Burroughs like Sir Francis Macnaghten, was one of those Judges of the Supreme Court who rose to the Bench from the local Bar. He was enrolled as an advocate of the Supreme Court at Fort William on November 10th, 1789, and shortly afterwards was appointed Advocate-General, and thereafter puisne Judge in succession to Sir Henry Russell. His daughter Louisa was married in the year of his elevation to the Bench to

Sir Thomas Strange, who from 1798 to 1801 was Recorder of Madras and "President of the Court of Mayor and Aldermen," and became first Chief Justice of Madras in the latter year, holding the office until 1817. Sir William Burroughs was at the time in Madras, but did not wait for the wedding which took place from Government House, the bride being given away by Lord William Bentinck. Burroughs was created a baronet in 1829 but his only son died in 1814 of wounds received before Bayonne, and the title became extinct at his death in 1829.

Next to Sir William Burroughs' picture and over the entrance is a portrait of John Herbert Harrington, Judge of the Sudder Adawlut from 1801 to 1807, and Chief Judge from 1811 to 1814 and again from 1824 to 1825. This is in some respects one of the most remarkable pictures in the room. It represents the distinguished Orientalist seated at a table and turning half round to consult with a moonshee at his side. Like the picture of Colvin in the adjoining room, it is painted with a brightness and freshness of colouring which is full of attraction. Harrington arrived in India as a writer in 1780. In 1793 we come across him as reporter and three years later as Registrar to the Sudder Court. He was appointed fourth member of the Board of Revenue in 1798, but returned to the Sudder Dewani and Nizamat Adawlut as Judge in 1801. Eleven years later he became Chief Judge and continued in that office until 1819 when he took furlough to England. He was absent for two years and on his return in October 1821 was provisionally appointed a member of the Supreme Council. In December 1822 he was confirmed in the appointment but resigned it in August 1823 in order to proceed up-country as senior member of the Board of Revenue "in the Northern Provinces" and Agent to the Governor-General at Delhi. In 1824, however, he reverted to his former post of Chief Judge of the Sudder Court: and in April 1825 he was reappointed a member of the Supreme Council, and President of the Board of Trade, and continued to hold that office until his retirement in 1827. He was for some years honorary "professor of the Laws and Regulations of the British Government in India" at Lord Wellesley's College of Fort William, and was also President of the Council of the College. As an authority upon the Indian system of jurisprudence of his day he stood without a rival. The three volumes in which (from 1805 to 1817) he collected his "Elementary Analysis of the Laws and Regulations enacted by the Governor-General in Council at Fort William in Bengal for the Civil Government of the British territories under the Presidency," are a standing monument to his learning. He was also President of the Asiatic Society in 1824, and stands honourably commemorated as the Editor of the Persian and Arabic works of Sadi (Calcutta 1791 to 1793). Calcutta has perpetuated his memory by the street off Chowringhee which bears his name. He died in London in 1828, barely a year after his retirement from India. His signature appears in the memorable "Rule" of John Adam's short administration, whereby on the 14th March, 1823, it was sought to restrict the liberty of the Press. The preamble of the document sets forth its justification by reciting that "matters tending to bring the government of this country into hatred and contempt and to disturb the peace, harmony and good order of society have of late been frequently printed and circulated in the newspapers." Arguments couched in almost identical words have done duty more than once in succeeding years when constituted authority has been too sensitive to appreciate the fact that the virulence of public criticism is not necessarily in inverse ratio to the importance of the grievance against which it is directed.

To the right of the doorway, and flanking the portrait of Sir William Burroughs, is the picture by Sir Martin Archer Shee, P.R.A., of Sir Edward Ryan, one of the most distinguished Chief Justices of the many who have presided over the Supreme Court. He was appointed a puisne Judge in May 1827 at the age of 34, in succession to Sir Anthony Buller. In December 1833 he became Chief Justice on the death of Sir William Oldnal Russell, whose tenure of office lasted only from July 1832 until January of the following year, and with whom he had in 1825 published a volume of reports of Crown cases reserved, when they had been fellow-advocates in Westminster Hall. Upon his retirement in 1843, he was sworn on the Privy Council and sat as a member of the Judicial Committee until 1862. But his judicial duties formed only part of the work to which he devoted the latter years of his life. On the constitution in 1855 of the Board of Civil Service Commissioners he was nominated as one of the unpaid members of that body: and in April 1862 he became first salaried commissioner. During his presidency the scope of the commission was enlarged year by year. The test examination for nominees for Civil appointments in the Home Service was succeeded by limited competition in 1860 and then followed by open competition under the order in Council of 1870. From 1858 onwards the control of the examinations for the Indian Civil Service was also in his hands. He filled the office of Vice Chancellor of the London University from 1871 until his death in 1874 at the age of 81.

There are frequent references to Sir Edward Ryan in the writings which treat of Calcutta in the twenties and the thirties. He was one of Macaulay's intimates and numbered like Charles Hay Cameron, William Macnaghten and John Macpherson Macleod among those who "in my opinion are the flower of Calcutta society and I often ask some of them to a quiet dinner." All the weight of his influence was thrown on the side of Macaulay in his battle on behalf of English education: and the Law Commission, of which Cameron and Macleod were the Members, owed much to the learning and experience which he was always ready to place at their disposal. Victor Jacquement stayed with the Ryans at Garden Reach when he visited Calcutta in 1829 and has left an account of his association with them. "Notwithstanding his Judgeship." he writes "Sir Edward is a great lover of science:" but the Frenchman did not quite relish Lady Ryan's ideas of the manner in which Sunday should be spent. "In the country," he continues, "where I have been living six months with Sir Edward Ryan, one of the Judges, I was next door, or rather next garden, neighbour to the Chief Justice (Sir Charles Edward Grey). Well, he was the first to inform me that Lady Ryan was "very strict," and that notwithstanding the good humour and want of strictness of the Knight himself, I might find Sunday a very dull day with them. He therefore invited me to take refuge with him on that day, at least to dine, take a walk and play a game of chess in the evening, while his wife gave us music. You may image, my dear friend, that I learnt many things during those charming evenings from a man who has for the last eight years held a judicial situation in India either at Madras or in Bengal." It is to be feared that Sir Charles Grey who died as recently as 1865, has been completely forgotten: but he was puisne Judge at Madras from 1818 to 1825, and Chief Justice of Bengal from 1825 to 1832, and achieved the unusual honour for a lawyer of appointment after retirement as Governor of Jamaica, where he succeeded the eighth Lord Elgin in 1847 and reigned until 1853.

Making our way to the opposite end of the quadrangle, we shall find in the outer room of the Bar Library (to which alone the public are admitted) the portraits of Sir Gregory Charles Paul, K.C.I.E., and of Mr. Manomohan Ghose. The latter's public services have been also honoured by a portrait in the Town Hall, and an account of his career will be found in the chapters which deal with that building. Sir Charles Paul, who was admitted as an advocate of the Supreme Court in November, 1853, achieved the unique distinction of filling the office of Advocate-General for no less than thirty years. In 1870-1871 he officiated as a Judge of the High Court and it fell to his lot to try and sentence to death the murderer of Chief Justice Norman. But he declined a permanent appointment on the Bench and on the retirement of the Advocate-General, Mr. T. H. Cowie, in 1872, he was selected as his successor, and held the appointment until within a few months of his death in December, 1900. He was the first member of the Armenian community to rise to the official headship of the Bar, and the position was won by him entirely by his individual merit and ability.

The inner room of the Bar Library is strictly reserved for the use of advocates of the Court: and not even members of the sister branch of the profession are admitted. But, if the visitor is so fortunate as to possess a barrister acquaintance, he should endeavour to get a sight of the manuscript Notes of cases, in the handwriting of Mr. Justice Hyde, which are preserved within. There are no less than fourteen volumes of them, but the first of the series should be particularly asked for. On one page was to be seen—until some Philistine destroyed it a year or two ago—the note in Hyde's own writing of the first sitting in October, 1774, of His Majesty's Supreme Court at Fort William at the Old Court House. A little later the following may yet be read: "Memoranda, 1775, July, 24th. Signed the Kalendar containing the order for the execution of Nuncomar. He was Hanged. I think the day was Saturday, August 12th, but I am not sure." On another page of the same volume is a transcript of the evidence given by the Governor-General and Barwell in the historic trial itself. And if we emulate Dr. Busteed and take up the later volumes, we shall catch many a glimpse of life in old Calcutta. In an entry of October 22nd, 1779, "the first day of the fourth term in the 19th and 20th year of the reign of His Majesty King George the Third," we read

"Mem: Sir E. Impey, Chief Justice, was absent by reason of illness. He has a swelling of the double chin. Sir Robert Chambers was also absent by reason of illness. Yesterday the fever began with him. I (John Hyde) have had the fever and am not yet perfectly free from the consequences: for I have a slight degree of pain and weakness in my left foot and a slight degree of dizziness in my head." But, illness or no illness, the dignity of the Court was never forgotten. Three days later the proceedings of the day are prefaced with the announcement that "I came to court in my Scarlet Robe to-day, because it is the day of the King's accession and is therefore treated by the Courts of Law in England as a gala day, to appear in their finest cloaths, and I think it proper, most particularly in this place, that all manners of tokens of respect to His Majesty should be shown, and especially by those who have the honour of holding offices under His Majesty's authority on his appointment. All signs of loyalty to the King of England are too much neglected in this country. I believe they did not even fire a salute at the Fort, which is a shameful neglect, if it is not worse—a designed disrespect." The words of Impey to Thurlow are an entertaining pendant to this outpouring of loyal sentiment. "Hyde is an honest man but a great coxcomb. His tongue cannot be kept still and he has more parade and pomp than I have yet seen in the East."

The Judges have presented to the Victoria Memorial Hall collection the entire court record of the "King versus Nuncomar": and it may be hoped that the Bar Library will at no distant date follow the example of their Lord-

ships, by the presentation of these volumes. For practical purposes, they are useless, for there are fair copies of the "notes of cases" in the Library: and as a matter of fact no learned counsel dreams of consulting them now-a-days. But although their law may be musty and out of date, and although many of the pages are in tatters, the value and interest of these records, from an antiquarian point of view, are undeniable.

The Attorney's Library, contains a small portrait of Chief Justice Norman, who was assassinated in 1871 by a Muhammadan fanatic as he was ascending the steps of the Town Hall, where the sittings of the original side of the Court were being held during the construction of the present building. There is an elaborate monument to his memory in the Cathedral. He was one of the four barrister judges named in the Letters Patent of 1862, and at the time of his death was acting as Chief Justice pending the arrival of Sir Richard Couch who had been appointed to succeed Sir Barnes Peacock. In English legal circles his fame survives as part-editor of Hurlstone and Norman's "Exchequer Reports."

In the Library of the Pleaders or Vakeels, are the following portraits of distinguished members of that body, but none of them, it is be feared, are entitled to be classed among works of art, (1) the Hon'ble Dwarka Nath Mitter, Judge of the High Court from 1867 until his death in 1874: (2) Sir Romesh Chunder Mitter, Judge of the High Court from 1874 to 1890, and acting Chief Justice in 1882, who died in 1899: (3) Sir Gooroo Dass Banerjee, Judge of the High Court from 1888 to 1904, and still a prominent member of orthodox Hindoo Society in Calcutta: (4) Mr. R. E. Twidale, a much respected pleader of Indo-Anglian parentage who died in August 1893: (5) Baboo Kalee Mohan Dass, (1860 to 1887): (6) Baboo Hem Chunder Banerjee, distinguished not only by reason of his long and successful tenure of the office of Senior Government Pleader, but also as a poet: in his later years he was afflicted with blindness and compelled to live in retirement: (7) Dr. Troyluckho Nath Mitter, one of the earliest to obtain the Doctorate in Law from the Calcutta University, who died April 18th, 1895.

CHAPTER XII.

THE TOWN HALL.

ON the Esplanade, to the west of Government House, and standing between the Treasury Buildings and the High Court, is the Town Hall, erected by the inhabitants at a cost of seven lakhs of rupees.

The place of the Old Court House in Dalhousie-Square, after its demolition in 1792, was not immediately taken by any public building in which Calcutta could meet and make merry. For several years the gap was supplied by such forgotten places of entertainment as "Wright's New Tavern" near St. John's church, "Moore's Assembly Rooms" in Dacre's Lane, the "Exchange and Public Rooms" in Lyon's Range, and the "Harmonic Tavern" in Lall Bazar which was capable of "accommodating five or six hundred persons with ease" and which entered upon a new lease of life in 1803 under the management of one Mr. Robert Beard. But on February 21st, 1804, the inhabitants of Calcutta formally decided in public meeting to erect a Town Hall "for the convenience of the Settlement and for the reception of the statues of the Marquess Wellesley and the Marquess Cornwallis." A lottery for five lakhs of rupees was announced in 1805 "under the sanction and patronage of His Excellency the Most Noble the Governor-General in Council." Ten per cent of the proceeds and the surplus were to be applied to the cost of building the Town Hall, which seems, however, to have taken an unusually long time to complete. An inscription in English and Urdu on either side of the southern facade records the fact that "during the administration of Lord Wellesley this edifice was designed, and completed under the Government of Lord Minto in the year of Christ 1813," the architect being "John Garstin, Colonel of Engineers." It is a fine building, in the Doric style of architecture, with a magnificent flight of steps leading to a grand portico on the south. Here stands Sir Richard Westmacott's beautiful statue of Warren Hastings, which with that of Lord Cornwallis within has already received notice in the chapter on the statues of Calcutta.

The carriage entrance is to the north under a lofty covered portico. The building consists of two storeys, and is used for public meetings, dinners, concerts, and balls. These ordinarily take place on the upper floor, which is boarded with teak and is 30 feet in height.

The great saloon, which runs from end to end of the upper floor of the building, is 172 feet in length by 65 feet in width, and is divided into a centre room and two aisles by a double row of pillars. At the western end is a music gallery, and at the eastern a raised platform.

On the south-front are two corner-rooms 43 feet by 21 feet, and a central one 82 feet by 30 feet, the last named being situated immediately over the portico. These rooms are utilized as card and supper-rooms, on the occasion of any public celebration in the Town Hall. In the centre room were held for many years the meetings of the Corporation of Calcutta, until the opening in the year 1905 of the Municipal Council Chamber in the new offices in Corporation Street.

The great room on the lower floor is paved with marble and has a height of 23 feet. It is very rarely used, and is heavily shored by wooden and iron props, which materially interfere with its seating capacity. At the western end is Bacon's fine statue of Lord Cornwallis, but Wellesley's statue (which is in Government House) seems never to have been placed here. The smaller rooms on the south are devoted to Municipal purposes. The western room is occupied by the Court of the Municipal Magistrate, who determines cases under the Calcutta Municipal Act, and the eastern room accommodates his establishment of clerks and copyists.

The most convenient method of visiting the Town Hall and inspecting its excellent collection of portraits and statuary, is to approach by the great carriage entrance on the North.

In the lower vestibule, flanking Geflowski's seated statue of Maharajah Roma Nath Tagore and facing the visitor as he enters are the busts of Mr. John Palmer and of Mr. Charles Beckett Greenlaw. At the foot of the left staircase is the bust of Baboo Ram Gopal Ghose, and at the foot of the right staircase that of Baboo Peary Chand Mitra.

Maharajah Roma Nath Tagore, C.S.I., was born on October 26th, 1801, and died on June 10th, 1877. He was the younger brother of Dwarka Nath Tagore, whose portrait will be found in the great hall upstairs, and the cousin of Prosunno Coomar Tagore, C.S.I., the great benefactor of the Calcutta University, whose bust is also on the floor above. As a member of the Bengal Legislative Council, to which he was appointed in 1866, he so stoutly advocated the rights of the agricultural community that he was named the "Ryots' Friend." In municipal matters he played a prominent part: and it was chiefly through his exertions that the Hindu burning-ghât at Nimtollah was retained upon its present site. He was nominated to a seat in the Viceroy's Council in 1873 and created a Raja. In the following year he was made a Companion of the Star of India by Lord Northbrook in recognition of the services rendered by him in connection with the famine: and on the occasion of the visit of King Edward to Calcutta, while Prince of Wales, he acted as President of the Committee of Reception. At the Proclamation Durbar of 1877, he was advanced by Lord Lytton to the dignity of Maharajah. Although not as wealthy as other members of his distinguished family, his whole career was one of public usefulness and benevolence. Finance and Political Economy were his favourite studies, while in religion he was a devoted adherent of the theistic tenets with which the name of Rajah Ram Mohan is so closely connected.

Mr. John Palmer, whose bust by Sir Francis Chantrey is a beautiful piece of work, was the second son of Lieutenant-General William Palmer, the celebrated private secretary and confidential minister of Warren Hastings, who subsequently became Resident in turn at the Courts of Poona, Hyderabad and Delhi, and died in 1814 while a General on the staff at Berhampore. The son, who was born on October 8th, 1767, served for a time in the Navy and was a midshipman with Sir Edward Hughes' squadron in the East Indies during its engagements with the fleet of the Bailli Suffren. After the peace of Paris in

1783, he came to Calcutta and entered the firm of Burgh Barber & Co. On the death of Mr. Barber, he became under his will a partner in the business and also the owner of the palatial house in Lall Bazar, with which his name remains so closely associated as the dispenser of magnificent hospitality, and which he afterwards sold to the Government for the purpose to which it is now put of a police office and court. Later he entered into partnership with Mr. Henry St. George Tucker, afterwards (in 1843) Chairman of the Court of Directors: and the house of Palmer & Co., rose to a pitch of almost unparalleled prosperity. The Marquis of Hastings, Governor-General from 1813 to 1823, was a close friend of Palmer and always alluded to him as the Prince of Merchants—a title which he richly deserved, according to contemporary opinion, on account both of his unrestrained individual liberality and the scale upon which his commercial transactions were conducted. But the short tablet—"John Palmer, the Friend of the Poor"—which marks his grave in the North Park Street burial-ground, affords an even more expressive indication of his character. He endeared himself to the people of the country by his kindness of manner and his uprightness of dealing, and time was when his name stood good for a crore of rupees in the market. In 1830, however, the great house failed in the most disastrous fashion and drew down with it most of the old established agencies in the city. The scenes that ensued were remarkable. So unshaken was the public confidence in him in spite of the general panic, that many leading natives came forward with offers of substantial assistance: and the creditors of the firm unanimously placed Mr. Palmer's name at the head of the list of assignees. The Chief Justice, Sir Charles Edward Grey, when the list was presented to him, regretted that a legal objection existed to such nomination : but he seized the occasion to pay a tribute to Mr. Palmer's character and to express a deep sympathy in his misfortunes. Mr. Palmer survived the crash for six years, which he spent in re-establishing his business : and it is on record that he devoted the profits he made to the support and assistance of those who had been ruined by the downfall of the late firm. When he died on the 22nd January, 1836, his remains were followed to the grave by a more numerous concourse than had perhaps ever attended any funeral in Calcutta : and the inscription upon the bust in the Town Hall, which is the outcome of a public subscription, bears eloquent testimony to the estimation in which he was universally held. His daughter married Mr. William Taylor, whose removal by Sir Frederick Halliday from the Commissionership of Patna furnishes one of the most discussed controversies to which the Indian Mutiny gave rise. As a public man, Mr. Palmer was claimed by the *Englishman* of his day to have been the Father of the Free Press of India. When Mr. Adam, after Lord Hastings' departure, deported James Silk Buckingham of the *Calcutta Journal*, he took an active part in the agitation which restored the Press to the liberty it finally obtained under Lord Metcalfe. The *Englishman*, summing up his character on the day after his death, described him as " a man, whose heart prosperity could never harden, nor adversity subdue, which melted like wax before the fire at the misfortunes of others, but was as adamant in endurance of his own."

The bust of Mr. GREENLAW which is by Weekes, bears the following inscription: "Charles Beckett Greenlaw, Esquire, Secretary to the Marine Board. This bust has been erected by the community of British India, in token of the devoted enthusiasm and untiring energy with which, for twenty years, against the most disheartening difficulties, he ably, zealously and perseveringly advocated the cause of steam communication and finally secured its establishment, 1843." Mr. Greenlaw died on June 15th, 1844, shortly after entering upon his sixty-first year, and lies buried in the new cemetery in Circular Road.

The bust of Baboo PEARY CHAND MITRA commemorates a man remarkable in many respects. A pupil of Derozio at the old Hindoo College, he preferred commerce to Government service. He was, however, for a long time Secretary to the Public Library, and was the author of several novels in Bengalee, of which the best known is "Alarer Gharer Dulal" or the Spoiled Child. It has been translated into English and also dramatized, and is full of humour and literary power. His life of David Hare in English and Bengalee was likewise much praised at the time: and his affection for the memory of the watchmaker-philanthropist found vent also in his foundation of the Hare Anniversary, which was celebrated every year, on the 1st of June, the day of his death, for forty years. He was first Secretary to the British Indian Society and to the Bethune Society, and one of the original members of the British Indian Association, and the first Secretary of the Society for the Prevention of Cruelty to Animals. In 1868 he was appointed a member of the Bengal Legislative Council and helped largely in passing the Act which led to the establishment of the last named society. As a Justice of the Peace and Honorary Magistrate and a member of the Corporation under the Act of 1863, he took an active part in local public movements. In later years he became first a spiritualist and then a theosophist. He died in November, 1883 at the age of 69.

The bust of Baboo RAM GOPAL GHOSE bears no inscription. He also was one of the poet Derozio's pupils, and at an early age renounced Hinduism, adopting English food and mode of living. He betook himself to commerce to which he owed the introduction to David Hare, and after gaining experience as a banian and later as a partner in an European firm, he started business upon his own account under the style of R. C. Ghose & Co., and became both rich and successful. In his political and social views he was most enlightened. It was chiefly owing to his encouragement and support that Dr. Goodeve was enabled to arrange for the sending to England of four students of the Medical College. The liberality of his views was also illustrated by his setting the example of sending his daughter to the Female School established by the then Law Member, Mr. Drinkwater Bethune: and when the East Indian Railway was first projected, he was one of the first to recognize its feasibility and its great possibilities. He was above all, however, distinguished for his eloquence as a speaker: and *The Times* praised his speech on the renewal of the Charter Act of 1853 as a "masterpiece of oratory." From Government he received the honour of nomination to a seat in the Bengal Council which he filled from 1862 to 1864 : and so great was his success in his commercial career that the local administration offered him the second Judgeship of the Presidency Small Cause Court, an offer he wisely declined, feeling no doubt that it was too much to expect of a man to make good boots because he had given satisfaction as a tailor. He was a leading member of the British Association from its establishment in 1851, and was the first Bengalee to systematically advocate and pursue public agitation for the redress of grievances. His death occurred in January, 1868, at the age of 51.

Proceeding upstairs by the right-hand staircase, we find ourselves confronted by a large picture of an individual of obviously high rank, although undistinguished by the riband or star of any order, dressed in a scarlet uniform coat with epaulettes, white breeches, and top boots. His right hand holds a roll of paper which rests upon a table : and the background is formed by a heavy curtain which is partially lifted on the left hand side of the canvas and discloses a balcony and a pillar beyond which may be discerned what is evidently a view of the Maidan and Fort William. The label upon the picture describes it as a portrait of Lieutenant-Colonel Colin Mackenzie, Surveyor-General at Madras from 1807 to 1819, Commanding Royal Engineer at the reduction of Java in 1811, and Surveyor-General of India from 1819 to 1821, who died in Calcutta on the 8th May, 1821, at the age of 68. The identification is not so glaringly inappropriate as that which formerly professed to discover the original in Lord Clive: but there is reason to doubt its accuracy. Others have sought to connect it with Major-General John Garstin, of the "Corps of Engineers," the architect of the Town Hall, who died in Calcutta on February 16th, 1820, and lies buried in the old south Park Street Cemetery. In both cases however, there is nothing but the merest of guess work to go upon: and still less probable is the suggestion which is indirectly made in the latest edition of Murray's handbook that Lord Gough, the victor of Chillianwallah and Goojerat, and Commander-in-Chief in India from 1843 to 1849, is the individual represented. The temptation is great to identify the picture with the full-length portrait painted by Robert Home in 1812, of Lord Minto, Governor-General of India from 1807 to 1813 and declared by Colonel R. Home of the Public Works Department, to be in the Town Hall, at Calcutta, in the course of a minute recorded by him in 1887 on the subject of the paintings attributed to his distinguished grandfather. There is undoubtedly a portrait of Lord Minto by Home in the Asiatic Society's collection, but it is a half-length. In this picture and also in Chinnery's acknowledged portrait of the Governor-General at Government House, the closely-cropped white hair and white whiskers are as prominent as they are in the painting of the unknown before us. But the similarity fails as regards the features, and the military uniform raises another difficulty, inasmuch as the first Earl of Minto was not a soldier. Upon the question of the painter, it is possible to speak with greater certainty. The composition is almost exactly that of Home's portrait of Lord Cornwallis, which hangs in Government House, Madras: the flagstaff in the latter giving the perpendicular which in the Town Hall picture is done by the pillar.

In the painting also by Home of General Sir William Medows, which is in the same collection, the horizon-line is marked by a light in identical fashion with the two others. The brush-work is likewise the same in all cases: and there can be little doubt that Home is the artist of this, as he undoubtedly is, of the other canvases. Home returned from Lucknow to Calcutta in 1797 and died here in 1834. It is conceivable that upon the completion of the Town Hall in 1813, he was invited to paint the portrait of Garstin the architect: and that this is the result. But the suggestion as far as the present writer is aware, can be based upon nothing more than conjecture in spite of its plausibility.

The space now occupied by this picture was formerly filled by a magnificent equestrian portrait of Gerard Viscount Lake, Baron of Delhi and Laswarree, Commander-in-Chief in India from 1800 to 1807. Along with the marble bust of the Duke of Wellington, which stood on the pedestal now supporting the bust of Sir Proby Cautley, it has been removed, with the permission of the Corporation, to the Victoria Memorial Hall collection now temporarily housed in the Indian Museum.

Having now mounted to the upper floor we will commence our survey of the pictures by the one in the furthermost left-hand corner, nearest to the one we have ventured to identify with Major-General Garstin. It is Muir White's portrait of Rai Kristo Das Pal, Bahadur, C.I.E., the famous orator and journalist whose statue stands at the junction of College Street and Harrison Road, and whose career will be found described elsewhere.

WILLIAM WILBERFORCE BIRD.—Next to him on the right hangs a fine full-length portrait by F. R. Say of Mr. WILLIAM WILBERFORCE BIRD, of the Bengal Civil Service, who sat as an Ordinary Member of the Supreme Executive Council, with only short intermissions, from March, 1838 to September, 1848. He acted as President of the Council and Deputy Governor of Bengal in 1842, while Lord Ellenborough was gratifying his taste for pageantry at Ferozepore: and carried out the humane designs of Lord Auckland by signing the Act which formally abolished slavery in India. When Lord Ellenborough was recalled by the Board of Directors he officiated as Governor-General, pending the arrival in July 1844 of that erratic statesman's successor and brother-in-law Sir Henry Hardinge. The Chairman of the Court responsible for this much-criticized step was Mr. John Cotton, formerly of the Madras Civil Service, who had in 1833 married the daughter of Mr. Bird as his second wife. Mr. Bird died in London on the 1st June, 1857.

The two large pictures of QUEEN VICTORIA and the PRINCE CONSORT by Winterhalter which are next in order, were presented to the Town of Calcutta in 1842 by Dwarka Nath Tagore on the occasion of his visit to London.

SIR HENRY COTTON.—Midway between these two pictures there was placed in the spring of 1904 the marble bust by Mr. H. H. Armstead, R.A., of Sir HENRY JOHN STEDMAN COTTON, K.C.S.I., Chief Secretary to the Government of Bengal from 1891 to 1896, and from 1896 to 1902 Chief Commissioner of Assam. Sir Henry Cotton who was born in 1845, is a member of an old Anglo-Indian family and the grandson of Mr. John Cotton whose name has just been mentioned in connection with Mr. William Wilberforce Bird. For more than a century and a half the interests of his family had been wrapped up in India and no less than five generations of his family have continuously served the Government, whether of John Company or of the Queen. His own association with the administration of Bengal was of the most intimate character. He was Under Secretary to Government under Sir George Campbell, Junior Secretary under Sir Richard Temple and Sir Ashley Eden, and Secretary to the Board of Revenue under Sir Rivers Thompson. By Sir Steuart Bayley he was made Secretary to Government, and his tenure of office as Chief Secretary continued through the Lieutenant Governorship of Sir Charles Elliot to that of Sir Alexander Mackenzie. From first to last, therefore, his direct connection with the Government of Bengal covered a period of nearly thirty years: and during the whole of that time his interest in the civic life of Calcutta was of the closest and keenest description. For many years he served as a member of the Corporation, and acted as its Chairman in 1887 during the absence on leave of Sir Henry Harrison. Two years previously his advocacy of the cause of the ratepayers in connection with a commission of enquiry appointed by Sir Rivers Thompson, was recognized by an offer to place his bust in the Town Hall: but the honour was respectfully declined and the present memorial was erected after his retirement, twenty years later. The inscription upon the pedestal commemorates Sir Henry Cotton as a "true Friend to

India and her people," and it would be hard to name another official so universally and completely popular with the Indian community. At the recent General Election Sir Henry was returned to Parliament in the Liberal interest as member for East Nottingham and acts as Chairman of the Indian Parliamentary Party in the House of Commons. A replica of the bust by the same sculptor has been placed in the Town Hall at Gowhatty as the result of a public subscription among the inhabitants of Assam.

LORD METCALFE.—Beyond the picture of the Prince Consort hangs that of LORD METCALFE, "the Liberator of the Indian Press." Charles Theophilus Metcalfe was the second son of Sir Thomas Metcalfe, Bart., who "having served in a military capacity in the East Indies," as Sir Bernard Burke has it, filled the office of a Director of the East India Company from 1787 to 1812, and was created a Baronet on December 21st, 1802. He was born at Calcutta in 1785, and at the age of 15 obtained a writership on the Bengal Establishment. In 1804 he performed his first piece of important public service as political assistant with the head-quarters of Lord Lake's army. This was followed three years later by his despatch on a special mission to the Court of Runjeet Singh at Lahore. He then acted as deputy secretary to Lord Minto when that Governor-General visited Madras, and in 1811 he became Resident at Delhi. Lord Moira, better known perhaps by his later title of Marquess of Hastings, appointed him his private secretary in 1817, but in the following year he was posted to Hyderabad as Resident at the Court of the Nizam. On the death in 1822 of his elder brother Theophilus, who was in the Company's China service and was president of the select committee at Canton, he succeeded to the baronetcy. Five years later (1827) he became a member of the Supreme Council at Calcutta, which then consisted of the Governor-General, the Commander-in-Chief, and two members of the Civil Service. By a special resolution of the Court of Directors his tenure of office was in 1831 extended from five to seven years. In November 1834 he was appointed to the newly-created provincial government of Agra, but was compelled to remain in Calcutta as acting Governor-General in consequence first of Lord William Bentinck's absence and then of his resignation. He acted in that office until the arrival of Lord Auckland in 1836. The interregnum was lengthened by the fact that Sir Robert Peel had first appointed Lord Heytesbury, but the occurrence of a ministerial crisis led to the cancellation of the appointment and the substitution of Lord Auckland by the Whigs. The Directors were in favour of Metcalfe's nomination: but the passing by him of the Act of September 15th, 1835, which removed the vexations restrictions on the liberty of the Indian Press, altered their views regarding him, and when the Governorship of Madras fell vacant in 1837, he was overlooked and the post given to Lord Elphinstone, the nephew of his friend and contemporary Mountstuart Elphinstone. Metcalfe accordingly retired from the service on New Year's day 1838, without proceeding up country to take over charge at Agra. In July 1839 he was appointed Governor of Jamaica and achieved great popularity by the reconciliation he was able to effect between the proprietors and the emancipated negroes. He remained in the Island until July 1842, and from January 1843 to December 1845 he filled the office of Governor-General of Canada. In the beginning of the last-named year he was advanced to the peerage as Baron Metcalfe of Fern Hill in the county of Berkshire, but he never took his seat in the House of Lords. His health was beginning to fail and he resigned his Governor-Generalship and returned to England, where he died at Malshanger, near Basingstoke. He left no heirs, but the baronetcy descended to his brother and is still enjoyed by the family. The inscription which perpetuates his memory in Winkfield Parish Church was written by Macaulay.

Metcalfe's popularity in India was very great. He was universally recognised as an able and sagacious administrator of unimpeachable integrity and untiring industry; and his participation in the "Liberation of the Indian Press" won for him the esteem of Anglo-Indians as well as of the people of the country. The Metcalfe Hall, at the corner of Hare Street and the Strand Road, was erected in his honour, all the different public subscriptions being combined for the purpose. His bust by E. H. Baily, R.A. which stood until recently in the vestibule of the Hall, has now been transferred to the Victoria Memorial Hall collection at the Indian Museum. A statue by the same sculptor may be seen in the Central Park at Kingston in Jamaica. There are portraits of him, besides the present one, at Eton (by J. J. Masperier), in the Oriental Club, London (by F. R. Say), and in the Kingston Town Hall. The Town Hall portrait is a copy of the one by F. R. Say in the Oriental Club in London, and is by Charles Pote, a local artist of mixed Anglo-Indian parentage. A second copy of the picture, by Hayes, is at Government House in the breakfast room on the first floor.

KESHUB CHUNDER SEN.—Next to Lord Metcalfe is a large full-length portrait (painted by Muir White in 1886) of KESHUB CHUNDER SEN, the great Hindu religious reformer. He was born in 1838, and in 1857 joined the Adi Brahmo Somaj under the late Maharshi Debendra Nath Tagore. In 1865 he withdrew from the society owing to differences of opinion, Debendra Nath adhering to a more conservative policy in matters of ceremonial and customs, and Keshub advocating a rupture with the past in such important questions as widow remarriage and inter-caste matrimonial connections. In 1866 he started the Brahmo Somaj. In February 1870 he went to England and had an audience of the Queen. It was chiefly through his exertions that the Civil Marriage Act became law in 1872. It prohibits bigamy and permits remarriage of widows, and legalizes intermarriage when both parties have made a declaration that they were not Hindus, Mahomedans, Jains, Christians, Buddhists or Parsis. In 1878 Keshub married his daughter to the Maharajah of Cooch Behar according to Hindu rites: and this was followed by the defection of a section of his followers, who formed the Sadsaran Brahmo Somaj. Keshub's addresses, whether delivered in Bengalee or in English, were remarkably impressive: but he never attained to the rank or the influence of a powerful Hindu reformer such as Chaitanya. He died after a lingering illness on January 8th, 1878, at the age of only forty.

HENRY THOBY PRINSEP.—Immediately below the picture

of Baboo Keshub Chunder Sen, and in the upper corner of the left-hand staircase, is a marble bust of HENRY THOBY PRINSEP, the elder, the Mæcenas of Sanskrit and Persian learning of his day, and the unavailing opponent of Macaulay in his efforts to establish English as the medium of education in India. At the commencement of the year 1835, the operations of the Committee of Public Instruction, of which Macaulay was President, were brought to a standstill by a decided difference of opinion. Half the members were in favour of Arabic, Persian and Sanskrit learning : the other half in favour of English and the Vernacular. The battle was fought over a sum of ten thousand pounds set apart by Parliament for the promotion of literature and science and "the encouragement of the learned natives of India." On the "Anglican" side Macaulay was supported by his brother-in-law Sir Charles Trevelyan, then a rising Bengal civilian, Dr. Alexander Duff, whose portrait hangs elsewhere in the Hall, John Russell Colvin, who was to meet his death in the beleaguered Fort at Agra during the Mutiny, Richard Mertins Bird, the "father" of the revenue settlement of the North Western Provinces, and Holt MacKenzie, who was afterwards sworn of the Privy Council on appointment to the Secretaryship to the Board of Control. The leaders of the Orientalists were Horace Hayman Wilson, Longueville Clarke, the well-known barrister, and the two Prinseps, Henry Thoby and James, the latter Assay Master at the Mint and eponymous hero of Prinsep's Ghât. Some idea of the strong feeling excited may be formed from the fact that Clarke actually challenged Dr. Duff to a duel. An elaborate minute was presented to the Council by Macaulay which may be found in the pages of his nephew's "Competition-Wallah," and on March 7th, 1835, a decree was promulgated by Lord William Bentinck of which the concluding sentence was as follows: "His Lordship in Council directs that all the funds which these reforms leave at the disposal of the Committee shall be henceforth employed in the imparting to the native population a knowledge of English literature and science, through the medium of the English language." Henry Thoby Prinsep was at the time General Secretary to Government. He had arrived in India in 1808 and been appointed to that office in 1827 during Lord Amherst's administration. In 1840 he was appointed a member of the Supreme Executive Council, and three years later he left India. From 1850 to 1858 he was a Director of the Hon'ble East India Company, and after the transfer of the administration to the Crown sat for fourteen years as a member of the Council of the Secretary of State for India. He died in 1878 at the age of eighty-six. His younger son Valentine, the well-known Royal Academician, came to India to paint the Proclamation Durbar of 1877, and died in 1904. His elder son, Henry Thoby Prinsep the second, and "last of the Haileybury men," filled the office of Judge of the High Court at Calcutta from 1878 to 1904, and was created a Knight in 1894, and a K.C.I.E. on retirement ten years later. He was for twenty-six years Provincial Grand Master of Bengal in Freemasonry, and his portrait hangs in the Masonic Hall in Park Street.

Sir William Nott.—Over the centre of the staircase on the left and facing the upper lobby is a large full-length portrait of Major-General Sir William Nott, G.C.B., Commander of the Army of Kandahar and capturer of Ghuznee in the Afghan War of 1842. Nott, who was born in 1782, was the second son of a Herefordshire yeoman and inn-keeper. A Bengal Cadetship was obtained for him, and he embarked for India in 1800. He first saw active service in a small expedition despatched against the tribes on the west coast of Sumatra under Captain Hayes of the Bombay Marine in 1803. He did not again serve in the field until 1838, when on the outbreak of the first Afghan War in 1838 he was placed at the head of the 42nd Native Infantry and immediately after promoted to Major-General and appointed to command the 2nd Brigade of the 1st Division of the Army of the Indus. He was left behind at Quetta, while the army under Sir John Keane went forward to Kabul to place Shah Sujah on the throne. Later he was placed in charge at Kandahar, and here the news reached him of the murder of Barnes and Macnaghten and the retreat and annihilation of Elphinstone's force. But he bravely held his ground, and repeatedly marched out and beat the enemy wherever he could. Sir George Pollock forced the Khyber and relieved Sale at Jellalabad: and a few months later Nott once more led his sepoys out of Kandahar, stormed Ghuznee on the 30th August, and joined Pollock at Kabul. Lady Sale and her fellow-captives were rescued by Sir Richmond Shakespear (the playfellow of Thackeray's youth), the great Bazar of Kabul was blown up in expiation of Macnaghten's murder, and Nott and Pollock returned to India to receive a Knighthood and a handsome pension from the Court of Directors. Nott visited England in 1844, but his health was completely broken, and he died at Caermarthen on January 1st 1845. A son of his, Charles Augustus Nott, who was an Advocate of the Supreme Court, lies buried in the Circular Road Cemetery, and two infant sons in the South Park Street Burial-Ground. His wife, who died suddenly at Delhi in 1838, was a daughter of Mr. Henry Swinhoe, a leading attorney and member of a family still well known in Calcutta. There are a number of public memorials of Sir William Nott. A full-length portrait by Brigstock, a Welsh artist, hangs in the Town Hall at Caermarthen: and a statue of him stands in the market-place of the same town. The Oriental Club in London also possesses a picture of him. And yet this painting in the Calcutta Town Hall was, until two or three years ago, absurdly labelled with the name of "Lord Wellesley."

Returning to the upper lobby, we find a number of busts and pictures confronting us as we seek to enter the great hall. Beginning from the left, the first is the portrait of Nawab Bahadur ABDUL LUTEEF, C.I.E., founder of the Mahomedan Literary Society of Calcutta, and one of the most enlightened and progressive Mahomedans of his time (1828-1893). He was a distinguished executive servant of Government and Member of the Bengal Legislative Council from 1862 to 1875.

SIR WILLIAM CASEMENT:—On the left hand side of the entrance is a Marble bust of Major-General SIR WILLIAM CASEMENT, K.C.B., of the Bengal Army, Military Member of the Supreme Council from 1839 to 1844, who died of cholera at Cossipore at the age of 64 on April 16th of the last named year. The inscription over his tomb in the

Circular Road Burial-ground records that "after 47 years and 6 months of distinguished service, partly in the field, partly as Secretary to the Government in the Military Department and finally as a Member of Council, when about to proceed to his native country crowned with well-merited honours and distinctions, he was swayed by a sense of duty to accede to the pressing instance of the Governor-General in Council to defer his departure from India : a step which exposed him to the attack of the fatal malady which terminated his valuable life." He served throughout Lord Lake's campaigns of 1803 and 1804 and also in the Nepaul war of 1815. His tenure of the office of Secretary in the Military Department began in 1818 and lasted twenty years.

Sir Henry Norman :—Upon the wall above is a portrait (painted in the seventies) of Field-Marshal Sir Henry Wyle Norman, G.C.B., G.C.M.G. It is sixty-two years ago—1844—since Sir Henry Norman obtained his first appointment into the Bengal Infantry and served through the Sikh War of 1848-49, and was in many actions on the Peshawar frontier as principal staff officer. During the Indian Mutiny he was Assistant Adjutant-General and acting Adjutant-General, and was present at the siege and capture of Delhi and the relief and capture of Lucknow. He was subsequently Assistant Military Secretary to the Duke of Cambridge, and returned to India as Military Secretary to the Government of India. From 1870 to 1877 he was Military Member of the Supreme Council, and sat in the Council of the Secretary of State for India from 1878 to 1883. In 1883 he was appointed Governor of Jamaica, and in 1888 proceeded in the same capacity to Queensland, where he remained until 1893. While at Brisbane he was offered the Viceroyalty of India by Mr. Gladstone in succession to Lord Lansdowne, whose term of office was expiring in January, 1894: and telegraphed his acceptance, only to withdraw it almost immediately. On his return to England he presided over the West India Royal Commission in 1897, and was also a member of the Royal Commission on the war in South Africa. He was appointed Governor of Chelsea Hospital in 1901, and Field-Marshal in 1902. In India he will always be remembered as the founder of the Indian Staff Corps. He died in 1905, in his eightieth year.

Below the portrait of Sir Henry Norman stands the white marble bust of the Hon'ble Baboo PROSUNNO COOMAR TAGORE, C.S.I., the munificent founder of the Tagore Law Professorship in the University of Calcutta. A fine seated statue of him has been placed in the vestibule of the Senate House, under which head a short biographical account of him will be found in the chapter on the statues of Calcutta.

CHARLES HAY CAMERON:—Next on the wall hangs a fine portrait (painted in 1849) of CHARLES HAY CAMERON, member of the Indian Law Commission from 1835 to 1843, and Law Member of the Supreme Council from 1842 to 1848. The inscription on Lord Holland's statue in the grounds of his house in Kensington affirms his claim to the remembrance of posterity to lie in his boast that he was "nephew of Fox and friend of Grey." So of the career of Mr. Cameron there could be no better epitome than the legend "disciple of Bentham and friend of Macaulay:" for his whole public life is deeply tinged by his association with these two great masters, the one of thought and the other of action. He was born in 1795, and was the son of Charles Cameron, Governor of the Bahama Islands, by Lady Margaret Hay, daughter of the fourteenth Earl of Erroll. His great-grandfather, Dr. Archibald Cameron, was the younger brother of Donald Cameron, "gentle Lochiel," who played so prominent a part in the rising of the clans in 1745, and was himself one of the chief among those who helped to conceal Bonnie Prince Charlie in the Highlands. His execution in 1753 provoked much animadversion and a bitter comment upon the action of George II from Dr. Johnson. Mr. C. H. Cameron was called to the bar at Lincoln's Inn in 1820, and enjoyed the distinction of being a disciple, and ultimately perhaps the last surviving disciple of Jeremy Bentham. When the Act of 1833 added a fourth member to the Supreme Council in India (which until then had been the Council of Bengal) and established a Law Commission, of which one member was to be appointed from England, Macaulay was selected for the former and Cameron for the latter post. On Macaulay's resignation of the office of Law Member in January 1838, Cameron was provisionally appointed. He received the permanent appointment in 1842 on the retirement of Mr. Andrew Amos, and held it until March 1848, when he was succeeded by Mr. John Elliott Drinkwater Bethune, whose efforts on behalf of female education in India are commemorated by the Bethune College. Mr. Cameron took an important part in the work of codification begun by Macaulay, and was his chief adviser and co-operator in the preparation of the Indian Penal Code, which displays abundant signs of Bentham's inspiration. His interest in the introduction of English education among the natives of India was great: and during the whole of his stay in the country he was a member of the Board of Education and succeeded Macaulay as its President. On his departure the grateful feelings of the educated native community found expression in a public meeting, at which he was formally thanked and asked to sit for the portrait which hangs before us. After his return to England he lived in retirement, but in 1853 he published an "Address to Parliament on the duties of Great Britain to India in respect of the education of natives and their official employment," in which he advocated a more liberal treatment of the Hindoo population. He was a man of cultured intellect and intimate with the most distinguished men of his day, especially Browning, Tennyson, and Sir Henry Taylor, who were frequent visitors at his house at Freshwater in the Isle of Wight. In later life he wore a long flowing white beard of patriarchal dimensions which entirely altered his appearance from what it had been in India. He died in 1880 at the great age of 85: surviving by one year his wife, whom he had married in India in 1838. Mrs. Julia Margaret Cameron was the third daughter of Mr. James Pattle the "Father" of the Bengal Civil Service at the time of his death in Calcutta in 1845: and in later life in England she became famous as an exponent of artistic photography. Among her sitters were Tennyson, Browning, Garibaldi, Herr Joachim and Sir John Herschel, the astronomer, who had been her friend from girlhood, and whose son William, now a retired Bengal Civilian and the present baronet, was the inventor of the system of identification by thumb-marks.

RAJAH SIR RADHAKANTA DEB :—Immediately below the portrait of Mr. C. H. Cameron is a fine marble bust of Rajah SIR RADHAKANTA DEB Bahadur, K.C.S.I., one of the most eminent of the many eminent men produced by the famous Sobhabazar Raj family. He was born in Calcutta in 1784, and was the son of Rajah Gopee Mohun Deb, who in his turn was the adopted son of the celebrated Maharajah Nubkissen, Clive's Persian Secretary. He died at Brindaban in 1887, having devoted the whole of his life to the cultivation of literature, the spread of English education, and the revival of Sanskrit learning. He was a zealous coadjutor of David Hare in establishing village schools, and was the first modern Hindoo who advocated female education. In religion he was the most orthodox of Hindoos, and his rigid conservatism would not permit him to support Lord William Bentinck's legislation for the abolition of *suttee,* the suppression of polygamy, and the conferring of the right of inheritance in cases of intestacy upon Native-Christian converts. In all these movements he led the orthodox community and protested actively but ineffectually, against their inclusion in the Statute Book. The independent and uncompromising attitude he assumed in connection with these questions did not however operate as a bar to the favour and confidence of Government. He presided over the British Indian Association from 1857 to his death, was created a Rajah Bahadur on July 10th, 1837, and on the extension of the Order of the Star of India in 1866 was the only Bengalee gentleman honoured with the title and decoration of K.C.S.I. In the portrait which hangs close by above the bust of Sir Proby Cautley, he is represented as holding in his hand his famous Sanskrit Dictionary, *Sabdak al padrum*, which will always remain as a monument of his profound scholarship: and which gained for him not only honorary titles and diplomas from the learned societies of Europe, but the special distinction of a gold medal from Her Majesty the late Queen Victoria.

SIR PROBY CAUTLEY :—In the westernmost corner of the vestibule, and below the portrait of Rajah Sir Radhakanta Deb, there has been placed upon a massive granite pedestal a marble bust of Colonel SIR PROBY THOMAS CAUTLEY, K.C.B., Bengal Artillery. It bears the following inscription upon its base: "To commemorate the completion of a great public work, to preserve the features of its author in the land enriched by his labours, this bust was erected by men of various races united in admiration of the genius which conceived, and the skill which executed the Ganges Canal. MDCCCLIV." Sir Proby Cautley, the projector and constructor of the Ganges Canal, and member of the Council of the Secretary of State for India from 1858 to 1868, was the son of a Suffolk clergyman and was born in 1802. At the age of sixteen he joined the Bengal Artillery, and shortly after was appointed by Lord Amherst assistant to Captain, afterwards Colonel, Robert Smith, who was then employed in reconstructing the Doab Canal. In December, 1825, he was recalled to military duty and joined in the siege of Bhurtpore under Lord Combermere. At the conclusion of the campaign, he rejoined his work on the canal, which was opened in 1830: and in the following year he succeeded to the charge of the canal, which he held until 1843. The great work of his life, the Ganges Canal, which is here commemorated, and which was the subject of a famous controversy with Sir Arthur Cotton of rival engineering fame, was under consideration for many years before it was actually taken in hand. It was first recommended by him at a very early period of his service: but it was not until 1837-38 that the severe famine led to the re-examination of the project: and in 1840 he submitted a report to Lord Auckland, which was sanctioned by Government. The actual construction of the work was not, however,commenced until 1843, and its progress was much retarded by the opposition of Lord Ellenborough. In 1845, Cautley was compelled by ill-health to take leave to Europe, and during his absence his place was filled by Major, afterwards Sir, William Baker. On his return to India in 1848, he was appointed Director of Canals in the North West Provinces. Under the active encouragement of Lord Dalhousie and of the Lieutenant-Governor, Mr. James Thomason, the canal made rapid progress, and was opened on the 8th of April, 1854. In the following month Cautley left India, receiving on the occasion of his embarkation the honour of a salute from the guns of Fort William. On reaching England he was created a Knight Commander of the Order of the Bath, and in 1858 he was selected to fill one of the seats on the newly-constituted Council of India, which he retained until 1868. He died at Sydenham on the 25th of January, 1871. In addition to his achievements as an Engineer, Sir Proby Cautley rendered distinguished service, in conjunction with Dr. Hugh

Falconer, by his geological and palæontological explorations in the Sewalliks: and their joint discoveries obtained for them in 1837 the award by the Geological Society of the Wollaston Medal in duplicate. Both Cautley and Falconer (1808-1865) were prominent members of the Asiatic Society of Bengal during their residence in Bengal: and a marble bust by Butler of the latter and a plaster cast of the bust in the Town Hall of the former stand in the Society's rooms.

We have now completed our survey of the pictures and busts in the lobby. Passing into the great saloon, we may turn at once to the right and proceed to the western end of the room.

SIR HENRY HARRISON.—The first of the pictures upon the northern wall is that of Sir HENRY LELAND HARRISON, of the Bengal Civil Service, Chairman of the Corporation of Calcutta from 1881 to 1890, who died of cholera at Chittagong in the year 1892 at the age of 55. It can hardly be said that the painting adequately commemorates the man or the many important services rendered by him to the town of Calcutta. As an undergraduate Sir Henry Harrison filled the office of President of the Oxford Union Society in 1860: as a District Officer in Bengal his reputation stood second to none: and as Chairman of the Corporation he not only gained the confidence of the popular representatives of the city, but advanced numerous important sanitary and other reforms which completely altered the aspect of Calcutta. The great central road which connects Howrah Bridge with Sealdah Railway Station is perhaps the most striking of his municipal achievements, and is properly honoured with his name. On his retirement from the office of Chairman he was appointed a member of the Board of Revenue, and was holding this appointment at the time of his sudden death. He was knighted in 1887 on the occasion of the Jubilee of Queen Victoria: and was from 1886 to 1892 a leading member of the Bengal Legislative Council.

A marble bust of Sir Henry Harrison which was the outcome of a spontaneous subscription by the members of the Corporation and the officials and subordinates of the Municipality, formerly stood in the lower corner of the left hand staircase, leading to the vestibule we have just quitted. It was unveiled on May 31st, 1893, by Sir Henry Cotton, then Chief Secretary to the Government of Bengal, and is in every way a worthier memorial than this portrait of one of the greatest and most successful chairmen who have presided over the municipality of the capital city of the Empire. During the course of the present year (1905) it was removed, in accordance with a resolution of the Corporation, to the entrance lobby of the Municipal Council Chamber in the new offices in Corporation Street together with the bust of Mr. William Mearns Souttar, Chairman of the Corporation from 1878 to 1881, and the portraits of Mr. John Blessington Roberts, Chairman of the Justices from 1862 to 1871, Mr. Harry Lee, Chairman of the Corporation from 1890 to 1895, and Mr. Robert Turnbull, C.I.E., Secretary to the Corporation from 1857 to 1888, all of which had formed until that time part of the Town Hall collection.

BISHOP WILSON.—Next to the picture of Sir Henry

Harison hangs an extremely fine portrait by Marshall Claxton of Dr. Daniel Wilson, Bishop of Calcutta from 1832 to 1858, and first Metropolitian of India. This painting is said to have suffered shipwreck on its voyage out to India, and it would seem that some damage must have been sustained, for a " restorer " has found occasion to write " repinxit Kroomholtz " in a corner of the canvas. In spite of these vicissitudes, the picture challenges attention as a remarkable piece of work, the painting of the clever intellectual face being especially good. The length of his episcopy, his great age (he was in his eighty-first year when he died) and his striking personality combined to render Bishop Wilson's tenure of the see of Calcutta at once memorable and remarkable. He was the son of a silk manufacturer in Spitalfields, where he was born in 1778. At first apprenticed to business, he resolved in his eighteenth year upon taking Holy Orders, and in 1798 entered St. Edmund Hall, Oxford. He won the University Prize for English Essay, the subject being " Common Sense," in 1803, the same year in which the Newdigate Prize was awarded to Heber for his celebrated poem on " Palestine." From 1804 to 1812 he remained at Oxford as tutor at St. Edmund Hall, and then came to London. In 1823 he was appointed vicar of Islington, and was still holding that office when in March, 1832, the bishopric of Calcutta was offered to him. The tragic death of Heber in 1826, and the abruptness with which the climate of Bengal had closed the short episcopates of James and Turner, Heber's immediate successors, operated to bring about the refusal of the See by several men of eminence to whom it was offered in turn. " If no one can be found, I am ready to go," wrote Wilson, when the subject was first mentioned to him: and he held the mitre accepted under such adverse conditions for twenty-six years, although he was in his 55th year when he arrived at Calcutta in November, 1832. He entered at once upon his duties with a zeal and energy that never relaxed. His tours through India and Ceylon were long and repeated, and extended as far as Singapore, Moulmein, Borneo, and Malaca. It is to him that Calcutta owes her Cathedral upon the Maidan. He laid the foundation-stone on October 8th, 1839, and consecrated it upon the same day of the year 1847. His liberality was on a princely scale. Out of the total sum of seven and a half lakhs absorbed by the building of the Cathedral he subscribed nearly one-third: and the Cathedral Library, where his bust appropriately stands to commemorate his generosity, found its nucleus in his bequest of the whole of his books. The formation in 1834 of the Sees of Madras and Bombay and the removal in 1849 of the Bishop's Palace from Russell Street to its present site in Chowringhee, may also be cited among the events of his episcopate. At the end of 1856, he fractured his thigh by a fall, from the shock of which he rallied but never completely recovered: and on January 2nd, 1858, he died and lies buried in the vault at the east end of the Cathedral, which is his chief monument. He had always resolved to end his days in India: and during the whole of his residence in the East he took only one holiday to England—from May, 1845, to December, 1846—and then under the compulsion of his medical advisers. His punctuality and business habits remained to the last. Lord Dalhousie spoke of him to Lord Canning as "the best man of business he had to deal with in India." Numerous anecdotes survive to bear testimony to the originality of his character. He allowed himself a directness of personal remark which those who did not know him were often tempted to regard as rudeness, and he was a man of peculiar mannerism which verged upon eccentricity. But he fully established his claim to be regarded as a great Bishop: and it speaks much for the position he achieved that his memory stands out clear and distinct among the holders of the See of Calcutta, in spite of the fact that he was followed by prelates of the calibre of Cotton and Milman.

SIR RIVERS THOMPSON.—The next portrait is that of a Lieutenant-Governor of Bengal, whose tenure of office was full of storm and stress. SIR AUGUSTUS RIVERS THOMPSON, K.C.S.I., C.I.E., was the son of a North-West civilian who filled for many years the office of Judge of the Sudder Court at Agra and died at that station in 1849. His great-grandfather George Nisbet Thompson was even better known in the Anglo-Indian official world. Originally admitted as an advocate of the Supreme Court in 1779, he became Private Secretary to Warren Hastings and ranked as one of the great proconsul's intimates. Rivers Thompson himself was educated at Eton where he distinguished himself by both playing in the cricket eleven (beating Harrow and Winchester) and rowing in the eight (defeating Westminster) in 1847. From Eton he proceeded to Haileybury after his nomination to a Bengal writership, and he arrived at Calcutta in December, 1850. After filling a medley of judicial and executive appointments (according to the fashion of those times) he became Secretary to the Government of Bengal in 1869. He refused a seat in the High Court in 1875, and was sent instead to officiate as Chief Commissioner of British Burma. Two years later (1877) he was confirmed in the appointment, but a year later he was made a member of the Supreme Executive Council: and after holding that office exactly three years, he succeeded Sir Ashley Eden as Lieutenant-Governor of Bengal in 1882. His administration was completely overshadowed by the agitation in connection with what has come (very incorrectly) to be known as the Ilbert Bill. The origin of that measure was a note submitted in March, 1832, by Sir Ashley Eden, when Lieutenant-Governor, to the Government of India, and Mr. Ilbert had not even taken his seat in Council at the time and knew nothing of the matter until the various Local Governments had sent in their replies. Sir Rivers Thompson's attitude upon the subject was a strong one of opposition from the outset, and it is characteristic of the large-mindedness of Lord Ripon that he should have nominated as Sir Ashley Eden's successor in office a colleague whose aims were so completely and so candidly in opposition to his own upon a question he had so much at heart. There can be no doubt indeed that the virtual surrender of the Government of India to Anglo-Indian feelings was mainly due to Sir Rivers Thompson's hostility to the proposal. Another important controversy in which Sir Rivers Thompson found himself engaged, was centred around the Bengal Tenancy Act: and the manner in which he asserted his opinions in this connection, no less than in connection with the Ilbert Bill, did not enhance his popularity with the Indian community. But his services were greatly appreciated by the Anglo-Indian population, and it is due to their initiative that Mr. James Archer, A.R.S.A., was commissioned in 1887 to paint the portrait which now hangs upon the walls of the Town Hall. His retirement from the Lieutenant-Governorship in March, 1887, at the conclusion of his term of office, was followed by a complete breakdown in health: and he led the life of an invalid in Europe until his death at Gibraltar in November, 1890.

The next two pictures are of particular interest, for they are unique of their kind. The wives of Viceroys have often as difficult and laborious a part to play as their husbands: but custom has decreed that their services shall pass without public commemoration. Lady William Bentinck, whose portrait hangs in Government House, was for many years the solitary exception to the rule: but the spell may now be deemed to be broken. The stately full-length portraits of Lady Lansdowne and Lady Dufferin by Mr. J. J. Shannon, A.R.A., which here hang side by side are both of them the product of public subscription among the inhabitants of Calcutta and are specimens of the painter's art which any town might be proud to possess.

The Marchioness of Lansdowne, whose picture is on our left, is the daughter of the first Duke of Abercorn. She was married in 1869 to the fifth Marquess of Lansdowne and accompanied him both to Canada and India. Since the year 1895 her *salon* at Lansdowne House has been one of the most important and magnificent of the centres of political life in London.

Harriot Marchioness of Dufferin and Ava, unhappily

since 1902 a widow, is the daughter of Mr. Archibald Rowan Hamilton and was married in 1862 to Lord Dufferin, then a simple baron. Like Lady Lansdowne, she has presided over society both at Ottawa and at Simla: but this has been only a small portion of her official career. For she has been Ambassadress at no less than four Continental capitals in turn: at St. Petersburg from 1879 to 1881, at Constantinople from 1881 to 1882, at Rome from 1888 to 1891, and finally at Paris from 1891 to 1896. Her books, "My Canadian Journal" and "Our Viceregal Life in India" bear ample testimony to her literary ability, her powers of observation, and her wit: and the Fund for supplying medical aid to the women of India, is a standing monument of her humanity and her skill in organization.

SIR WILLIAM GREY.—To the right of Lady Dufferin, we shall find the portrait of the fourth Lieutenant-Governor of Bengal. SIR WILLIAM GREY, K.C.S.I., was the fourth son of the Hon'ble and Right Reverend Edward Grey, Bishop of Hereford and grandson of the first Earl Grey. He was born in 1818 and after a short residence at Christ Church, was appointed by his cousin Lord Howick, afterwards the third Earl Grey, to a clerkship in the war office. While serving there he was nominated to a writership in the Bengal Civil Service which had been placed at the disposal of his uncle, the second Earl Grey, the Premier of the first Reform, by Sir Robert Campbell, Director of the East India Company from 1817 to 1852. He arrived at Calcutta in December, 1840. From 1845 to 1847 he was Private Secretary to Sir Thomas Herbert Maddock,

Deputy Governor of Bengal: and in April, 1851, was at the special request of the Directors appointed Secretary to the Bank of Bengal. When Bengal was constituted into a Lieutenant-Governorship in 1854, he became one of the Secretaries to the Local Government, under Sir Frederick Halliday. In 1859 he was taken up into the Government of India and appointed Secretary in the Home Department. Three years later he became a Member of the Supreme Executive Council: and held the post until in 1867 he was nominated to succeed Sir Cecil Beadon as Lieutenant-Governor of Bengal. It is noteworthy that during his tenure of office as Member of Council, there was considerable difference of opinion, notably in connection with the treatment of the Oudh taluqdars, between him and Lord Lawrence, who was nevertheless magnanimous enough not to oppose his translation to the executive charge of the Lower Provinces. The régime of Sir William Grey was not distinguished by any event of such magnitude as those, which in the shape of the Mutiny, the indigo troubles and the Orissa famine had marked the rule of his three predecessors. But the zemindars will always cherish his memory with respect by reason of his strenuous opposition to an education cess: and with his term of office must also be connected the appointment of Sir William Hunter to compile the gazetteer of Bengal and the terrible devastation caused by the cyclone of 1867. Sir William Grey resigned the Lieutenant-Governorship in March, 1871, having been in the previous February installed a Knight Commander of the Order of the Star of India. In 1871, Grey was appointed to succeed Sir John Peter Grant as Governor of Jamaica: but the climate was uncongenial to him, and in 1877 he returned to England where he died in the following year. The portrait which hangs in the Town Hall is the outcome of a public meeting held on the 11th February, 1871; and its presence here is indicative of the esteem in which he was held by the educated Indian community. He has been described as a Bengal Whig of the better kind, with a view of administration resting on a tolerance of opinions and even prejudices, and a great kindness to natives in India: and it was by reason of his gentleness and forbearance, his considerateness, his justice and his conscientiousness that he found his way to the hearts of the people.

Mr. MANACKJEE RUSTOMJEE, whose portrait by Puckle Roper, hangs next in order, was one of the foremost Parsee merchants of his day in Calcutta. He was the grandson of Mr. Cowasjee Banajee, the head of the once famous Calcutta house of Rustomjee Cowasjee and Co., and was born in Bombay in 1815. The firm was actively and extensively engaged in the China trade and owned a fleet of no less than thirty opium clippers, of which the reputation was such that fifteen of them were chartered by the British Government during the China War of 1839. In early life, Mr. Manackjee Rustomjee was for some years in China, but in 1837 he came to Calcutta and was admitted a partner in his grandfather's and father's firm. Having taken a leading part in the organization of the Union Bank, he became, unfortunately, very seriously affected by its failure in 1849: and, the system of companies with limited liabilities being then unknown to the law, he was compelled to surrender his entire property to his creditors.

Although he continued in business, he was unable to regain the commanding position in the mercantile world which he had enjoyed until this disastrous event: but he never lost the confidence and respect of his fellow-citizens which he had already won, and until the day of his death in 1891, he was regarded as one of the foremost and most public-spirited members of the Indian community in Calcutta. In 1870 he was appointed Persian Consul, and in 1874 Sir Richard Couch, the then Chief Justice, conferred upon him the high distinction of selecting him as the first Indian to fill the distinguished office of Sheriff of Calcutta. For many years he was also a local Honorary Magistrate and Justice of the Peace and was on more than one occasion nominated by Government as a Commissioner of the Municipality. In unveiling on the 1st February, 1898, the portrait which hangs before us and which was the outcome of the public subscription of all classes of the community, Sir Alexander Mackenzie, the Lieutenant-Governor of Bengal, summarized his career in the following appreciative words:—"There was no man in all Calcutta more respected and esteemed by every section of the community, European and Native. In all his public offices, he did his duty in a quiet, unobtrusive, unostentatious way, and never dreamt of making office serve him. In this way he won for himself a reputation and position which was in its way unique. To men of the present generation he was a living link with the past. He had seen fifteen Governor-Generals come and go and known them all, and his memory had stored up a wealth of experience such as no other man in Calcutta could pretend to. This experience and hoarded wisdom he devoted to the cause of peace and goodwill, and he inherited in the love and respect of every class of the community that blessing which is the sure reward of the peace-maker under whatever religious persuasion he may be found." He was worthily succeeded in the position of public usefulness which he had created for himself by his son Mr. Heerjeebhoy Manackjee Rustomjee, C.I.E., who succeeded him as consul for Persia and in 1902 filled in his turn the office of Sheriff of Calcutta. The sudden death of this distinguished Parsee citizen of Calcutta in the early portion of 1902 has created a gap which has been sadly felt not only in the public life of the city but also in the world of Freemasonry, in which for nearly a quarter of a century he occupied a position as prominent as it was useful.

The portrait by Archer of Mr. ROBERT TURNBULL, C.I.E., Secretary to the Corporation of Calcutta from 1857 to 1880, which was next in order, has been lately removed to the new Municipal Office in Corporation Street. In its place has been hung Mr. Edward Ward's picture of Mr. FREDERICK JOHN MARSDEN, Chief Presidency Magistrate of Calcutta from 1877 to 1894. There is no denying the merit of the painting both as a likeness and as a work of art: but the general result is nevertheless unfortunate and will strike the visitor as somewhat unpleasing. The picture was formerly in the centre room in the south.

SIR CHARLES STEVENS.—Continuing our tour of the great saloon, we next come upon the full length portrait of Sir CHARLES CECIL STEVENS, K.C.S.I., presented to the city of Calcutta by the Zemindari Panchayet, an association of landowners. Sir Charles Stevens is an Australian by birth. He entered the Indian Civil Service in 1860, taking the third place: and afterwards served as Divisional Commissioner in Chota Nagpur, Bhagalpore, and Patna; and was in 1891 appointed to the Board of Revenue. In 1897 he acted as Lieutenant-Governor of Bengal for six months during the absence on sick leave of Sir Alexander Mackenzie. He retired a year later after serving three terms of office as Additional Member of the Viceroy's Council: and in 1888 was advanced to the dignity of K.C.S.I. While in India he was noted for his love of music and horticulture, and was President of the Agri-Horticultural Society of Calcutta.

The Rev. C. H. A. Dall, whose picture hangs in the corner, was an eminent Unitarian Minister in Calcutta.

Investiture of the Duke of Edinburgh.—The epithet of artistic can scarcely be applied with justice to Muir White's large picture above the platform at the eastern end of the great saloon. It represents the Durbar held at Calcutta on December 30th 1869, on the occasion of the investiture of the Duke of Edinburgh with the insignia of a Knight Grand Commander of the Order of the Star of India: and is a blaze of colour, not always of the most harmonious character. But it is full of interesting likenesses of Indian celebrities of a bygone generation. On the dais is Lord Mayo, in the Robes of Grand Master of the Order: and to the right distinguished by the broad green riband of the Thistle, is the Governor of Madras, Lord Napier of Merchistoun, who was two years later to have the melancholy duty of acting as Viceroy after Lord Mayo's assassination at Port Blair. Among the ladies in the background are Lady Mayo and Lady Napier of Merchistoun, and present also behind a purdah is the Begum of Bhopal, according to the official record of the ceremony. Prince Alfred stands in the foreground, and immediately behind him, in the white mantle of the Secretary of the Order, is Sir Charles Aitchison, then Foreign Secretary and afterwards from 1882 to 1887 Lieutenant-Governor of the Punjab. The eight banners suspended above are those of the Knight Grand Commanders of the Order present. These may easily be distinguished by their mantles, but seven only of them are discernible. On the left hand of the spectator are three. Commencing from the foreground, they may be identified as follows: Sir W. R. Seymour Vesey Fitzgerald, Governor of Bombay, with whom the Duke is about to shake hands, Rajah Rundheer Singh of Kapurthala, and Maharajah Jyajee Rao Scindia of Gwalior, whose scarlet Mahratta head-dress forms a conspicuous feature of the back-ground. On the right hand, taken in the same order, are the Maharana of Dholepore, the junior G.C.S.I., at the time, Sir William Rose Mansfield, Commander-in-Chief in India, and afterwards Lord Sandhurst, Maharajah Rughoo Raj Singh of Rewah, a gigantic figure, and Maharajah Ram Singh of Jeypore. Among the K.C.S.I.'s may be noticed on the left, Sir Richard Temple, then Finance Member of Council, Sir Henry Marion Durand, also a Member of Council, and the Maharajah of Vizianagram, whose memory lives as that of a generous patron of chess and a large-minded philanthropist. Behind them stands Mr. James Fitz James Stephen, who had only been a few days in office as Law Member of Council. On the opposite side may be observed in the fore-ground in a dark uniform Mr. Abdallah David Sassoon, C.S.I., the Bombay merchant-prince, who was in 1890 created a baronet under the style of Sir Albert Sassoon. To his right emerge the head and shoulders of the second Sir Jamsetjee Jeejeebhoy. Other prominent figures in the picture are Major-General Sir Neville Chamberlain, K.C.S.I., Dr. Joseph Fayrer, C.S.I., both on the Prince's staff, Colonel Richard Strachey, C.S.I., Public Works Secretary, Major Owen Tudor Burne, the Viceroy's Private Secretary, Colonel Henry Norman, Secretary in the Military Department, Mr. George Noble Taylor, Member of Council, his colleague, Lieutenant-Colonel R. H. Meade, C.S.I., then Governor-General's Agent in Central India, Sir John Strachey, Sir William Grey, Lieutenant-Governor of Bengal (the two last not yet entitled to wear the K.C.S.I.), and Major-General Albert Fytche, C.S.I., then Chief Commissioner of British Burma. The absence of Bengalee members of the Order of the Star of India is noticeable. When it was constituted in 1861, it was ordered to consist of the Sovereign, a Grand Master and 25 ordinary Knights, together with extra Honorary Knights. Lord Canning was appointed to be first Grand Master but none of the 25 Knights were connected with Bengal. In 1866 it was enlarged and ordered to consist of 3 classes, 25 G.C.S.I.'s, 50 K.C.S.I.'s and 100 C.S.I.'s. There are now (1905) 35 G.C.S.I.'s, 85 K.C.S.I.'s and 167 C.S.I.'s.

Mr. James Gibbs, C.S.I., C.I.E., whose portrait occupies the eastern-corner of the wall on the south, entered the Bombay Civil Service in the year 1846. He was a son of

Michael Gibbs, Lord Mayor of London in 1845, who lives in the earlier volumes of *Punch* as the object of much good-humoured banter. In May 1880, a few weeks before Lord Ripon's assumption of the Viceroyalty, he was appointed to succeed Sir Alexander Arbuthnot as an ordinary member of the Supreme Council and retained the office for the full period of five years, retiring in May, 18[illegible]. His previous services had been altogether on the Bombay side where he had filled the appointments of Judge of the High Court and Member of Council, the latter from 18[illegible] to 1879. He died in 1886 in England.

The painting which hangs next represents the Reverend KRISHNA MOHAN BANERJEE, one of the most distinguished adherents which the small native Christian community of Bengal has yet possessed. Born in 1813, he was converted to Christianity by Dr. Duff, whose portrait hangs close at hand and was a pupil of Derozio, the gifted young Eurasian poet who died at the age of 22. He did much useful work as a municipal commissioner and as a Fellow of the University and for many years was Pastor of Christ Church in Cornwallis Square. The decoration of C.I.E., which he received from Government, the degree of Doctor of Laws with which the University of Calcutta honoured him and the honorary chaplaincy conferred upon him by the Bishop of Calcutta are eloquent proofs of the value of his public services and of the esteem in which he was held. It is said that he knew eleven languages, and all of them well. He died in 1885 at the age of 72.

The portrait immediately to the west is that of RAJAH KALI KRISHNA DEB, "Knight of the Goorkha Star, grandson of Maharajah Nubkissen, leader of the orthodox Hindoo community, and Sanskrit scholar." He stands also commemorated by a statue in Beadon Square, and a summary of his career will be found in the chapter on the statues of Calcutta.

SIR HENRY RICKETTS.—The most notable of the recent additions to the Town Hall collection of pictures adjoins in the shape of a fine full-length portrait of the late Sir HENRY RICKETTS, K.C.S.I. The painting, which is the property of the British Indian Association, hung until recently in the Association's rooms, but it has rightly been adjudged worthy of a more public situation and has been handed over to the custody of the Corporation. The career of Sir Henry Ricketts belongs, it is true, to the past, but there were few officials more honoured and respected in his day. Arriving in India in 1821, when Lord Hastings was Governor-General, he served for twelve years in Orissa and was Commissioner of the Cuttack Division from 1835 to 1839. A tablet in the old cemetery at Balasore records that he "never forgot Balasore nor the Ooryahs." In 1841 he was appointed Commissioner of Chittagong, and his name is still gratefully remembered in the division, where (writes Sir Henry Cotton, who was one of his successors) his seven years' settlement operations form the greatest triumph of mofussil administration ever known in Lower Bengal. He joined the Board of Revenue in Calcutta in 1848, and in 1854 was nominated by Lord Dalhousie to the Supreme Council. During the eventful period of Lord Canning's administration and throughout the Mutiny he continued as a member of that body. Having previously refused the Chief Commissionership of the Central Provinces, he was in 1860 offered the Lieutenant-Governorship of the North-West Provinces, but he declined the post also on the ground (now-a-days, it is to be feared, rarely advanced when high office is under consideration) that his failing health would not permit him to do justice to its responsibilities. Retiring from the service in the same year, he lived on in honoured retirement until 1886, when he died at Surbiton at the age of 83. He was one of the best of the old school of Anglo-Indian officials, and as a settlement and revenue authority held the foremost rank among his contemporaries.

Bishop Johnson.—We now arrive at Mr. Harold Speed's admirable portrait of the Most Rev. Edward Ralph Johnson, Bishop of Calcutta and Metropolitan of India from 1876 to 1898. The Bishop is depicted seated on his episcopal throne and the pose is very striking and characteristic. In a corner of the canvas may be seen the coat of arms of Dr. Johnson, impaling those of the See. If Bishop Wilson enjoys the distinction of the longest episcopate among those who have held the metropolitan See, Dr. Johnson, who is only four years behind him in that respect, may claim to be the only Bishop of Calcutta who has not left his bones in India. Middleton, the first Bishop, lies buried in St. John's Church and Heber, his successor, at Trichinopoly: James and Turner fell victims to the climate in quick succession: Wilson fulfilled his wish and ended his days at Calcutta: Cotton, who wore the mitre from 1858 to 1866, was drowned at Kooshtea: and Milman, Dr. Johnson's immediate predecessor, died in

1876 at Rawalpindi. Before coming to India, Dr. Johnson was from 1866 to 1876 rector of Northenden and during the last five years of that period Archdeacon of Chester. His twenty-two years' residence in Calcutta was marked by much energy and vitality. The memorial of Milman in India is the Bishopric of Lahore, endowed by public subscription after his death. That of Dr. Johnson is the establishment and organisation of no less than five new Sees—Lucknow, Tinnevelly, Nagpore, Travancore and Cochin, and Chota Nagpore—all of which except that of Nagpore, were in full working order before his retirement. His successor was Dr. Welldon, Head Master of Harrow, who held the office, however, for only four years and was compelled by reason of health to resign in 1902.

Major-General Sir HENRY MARION DURAND, K.C.S.I., C.B., whose picture hangs next, was from July 25th 1865 to June 1st, 1870, an ordinary Member of the Supreme Council. In the latter year he was appointed on the recommendation of Lord Mayo to succeed Sir Donald McLeod as Lieutenant-Governor of the Punjab. But his tenure of the office was of the briefest possible character. On January 1st, 1871, he was making his entry upon an elephant into the town of Tonk, near the Mahsud border, when the howdah in which he was sitting came in sudden and violent contact with a low archway under which he was passing, and he was flung to the ground with such force as to cause fatal injuries to the spine. "What a little thing! It will be a warning," were almost his last words. He lies buried in the Churchyard at Dera Ismail Khan, now the headquarters of a district in the North West

Frontier Province. His connection with Bengal was throughout his career of the slightest possible character, and the presence of his portrait in the Calcutta Town Hall can only be accounted for by the sympathy occasioned by the tragic circumstances of his death. Entering the Bengal Engineers in 1828, he made his first voyage to India in the following year with Dr. Duff, whose portrait is not far off: and was appointed to irrigation work in Upper India where he served under Proby Cautley. In 1838 he accompanied Sir John Keane's "Army of the Indus" to Kabul by way of Kandahar, and earned the title of the "hero of the gate of Ghuznee," by blowing open the great gate of that fortress with his own hand. "Captain Thomson, of the Bengal Engineers, directed the movements of the explosion party; and with him were his two subalterns, Durand and Macleod, and Captain Peat of the Bombay Corps. Lieutenant Durand, was obliged to scrape the hose with his finger ends, finding that the powder failed to ignite on the first application of the port-fire." Returning to India from Kabul, he went on leave to England, but came out once more as Private Secretary to Lord Ellenborough (Governor-General from 1842 to 1844), and was present at the battle of Maharajpore. In September, 1844, he succeeded the gallant Major Broadfoot (who fell at Ferozeshah) as Commissioner of the Tenasserim provinces, and took up the difficult question of the revenue assessments. He was removed from his office in 1846 by Sir Herbert Maddock, the President in Council, and obtained no redress in England. During the Sikh War of 1848, he fought both at Chillianwallah and Gujrat, and became political agent successively at

Gwalior and at Baroda. In 1856 he reverted to his own line as Inspecting Engineer of the Presidency Circle, but was restored by Lord Canning to political employ and appointed Agent to the Governor-General in Central India. In the Mutiny he was compelled by Holkar's troops to evacuate the Residency at Indore, but fought several actions and re-conquered Western Malwa. He was deputed to England to represent the views of the Government of India on the re-construction of the native army, and was nominated in 1859 by Sir Charles Wood to a seat in the newly-formed Secretary of States Council. But he returned to India two years later on the invitation of Lord Canning, as Foreign Secretary. He became an ordinary member of Council in 1865 in succession to Sir Robert Napier (Lord Napier of Magdala) and was created a K.C.S.I. in 1867. The final stage in his career was reached in 1870, when, as narrated above, he was appointed to be Lieutenant-Governor of the Punjab. Of his sons, the eldest, Sir Edward Law Durand, served as Resident in Nepaul in 1888 and was created a baronet in 1892: the second, Sir Henry Mortimer Durand, now Ambassador at Washington, was a member of the Bengal Civil Service, from 1873 to 1898 and Foreign Secretary to the Government of India from 1884 to 1894: and the third, Colonel Algernon Durand, now a member of the Corps of Gentlemen-at-Arms, was Military Secretary to Lord Elgin while Viceroy of India from 1894 to 1899.

DWARKANATH TAGORE.—The next picture is a portrait by F. R. Say of DWARKA NATH TAGORE "merchant, philanthrophist and reformer." Upon the back of the canvas there appears an advertisement, bearing date 1843, of a firm of artist's colourmen, which is of interest, not only by reason of its special reference to the painting, but also as an illustration of the perils of prophecy. It is addressed "To Artists" and runs as follows: "The notice of those painters and amateurs who have not yet had an opportunity of inspecting a picture painted exclusively with silica colours and glass medium is respectfully directed to No. 288 in the present exhibition of the Royal Academy. The subjoined are extracts from the *Art Union* of June 1843 relative to this picture, No. 288, "the Hindu gentleman Dwarkanath Tagore," F. R. Say, painted by subscription for the Town Hall, Calcutta. "An admirable subject for a pictorial portrait. This celebrated person is painted in the full costume of the Hindu of condition: he is turbaned and shawled: and so successfully has the artist met the spirit of his subject that he has not only left his work a meritorious portrait but a valuable picture. The colouring is wonderfully brilliant. In this respect, indeed, it is beyond all question the most remarkable work in the exhibition. It is only just to state that this picture is painted with the medium and colours prepared by Mr. Miller of 56, Long Acre, London, and for which he has more than once challenged a trial in the advertising columns of the *Art Union*. Few who look upon this work will hesitate to believe that its peculiar brilliancy is derived from some unusual means: what those means really are, it is the duty of every artist to enquire and ascertain." Viewed in its present condition the picture may be allowed to merit some portion at least of the encomium of the *Art Union's* critic. But when the restoration of the Town Hall portraits was entrusted in 1901 by the Corporation to Mr. Alexander Scott, this canvas was found to be one of the worst in the collection. The paint had been all mixed up with the varnish and the most careful handling was required. In the result the face and the handsome Cashmere shawl were restored to their normal colour, and the hookah and other accessories in the background once more brought into the prominence they are intended to occupy. "It is only necessary" wrote Mr. Scott in an interesting note drawn up by him, "to compare this picture with the portrait in oils of William Wilberforce Bird which hangs in the vestibule, to be supplied not only with a forcible illustration of the superiority of oil painting over all other methods, but also with a warning to painters not to make important pictures the subject of experiment with new nostrums." Dwarkanath Tagore, who was born in Calcutta in 1794 was the nephew and adopted son of Rammoney Tagore. He acquired the elements of English at Mr. Sherbourne's school in the Chitpore Road, but the greater part of his education was gained from intercourse with friends, of whom Ram Mohan Roy must be reckoned among those who influenced his mind most largely. At an early age he lost his adoptive father from whom he inherited a number of estates: but he was not content to live upon his patrimony and commenced practice as a legal and commercial agent. His abilities attracted the notice of Government: and he was in succession appointed to be Dewan to the Salt Agent and Collector of the 24 Parganas and Dewan to the Board of Customs, Salt and Opium. At the beginning of his public life he co-operated with Ram Mohan Roy in supporting the abolition of *Suttee,* which was effected by Lord William Bentinck in 1829. In the following year he helped to found the Union Bank and was elected Treasurer and a Director. He resigned his appointment under Government in 1834, and almost immediately afterwards started the firm of Carr Tagore & Co., in connection with which he worked coal mines at Raneegunge, a sugar factory at Ramnuggur, filatures at Kamarkali, and Indigo factories at Sealdah and in other parts of Bengal. During the next ten years of his life Dwarkanath played a considerable part in almost all the public movements of the day. He was the first native Indian appointed to be a Justice of the Peace, and his position in Indian society was one of the greatest influence and importance. The reorganization of the Hindoo School, the establishment of the Medical College, and of the Fever Hospital, the agitation for the freedom of the Press, the foundation of the British Indian Association, the development of steam communication between England and India, were all in turn indebted to him for support. The royal splendour of his hospitality earned for him the name of "Prince Tagore." He delighted to entertain distinguished and talented men of every description at his beautiful house at Belgachia, which had once been the favourite haunt of Lord Auckland, and was afterwards sold to the Paikpara Rajah by Dwarkanath's son, Maharshi Debendra Nath, on the failure of the Union Bank which impoverished him. It was here that the present King Emperor was entertained in 1875 by the Indian aristocracy of Calcutta on the occasion of his visit to the city. In January 1842, Dwarkanath started on a voyage to Europe. He was everywhere received with much distinction, and had interviews with the Queen and Prince Consort, Louis Philippe and most of the celebrities of the day. His portrait was painted by Count D'Orsay, the "Prince of Dandies," and he may be easily recognized under a thin disguise in one of Thackeray's novels. He returned to India at the end of the year and in commemoration of his visit presented the Town of Calcutta with the picture of the late Queen and Prince Consort which hang in the vestibule. In March 1845 he started upon his second and last visit to the west. Before his departure he offered to take with him any two Medical College students who might be willing to go and to pay for all the expenses of their education in England. Dr. Goodeve one of the Professors of the College offered to pay the expenses of a third and raised an additional sum by private subscription to enable him to add a fourth: and in the end Dwarkanath had four students entrusted to his charge. After more than a year spent in visiting France, England and Ireland he died of fever in London on August 1st, 1846, and lies buried in Kensal Green cemetery. His abilities and his public services, had already received recognition during his lifetime. The picture which hangs before us and was painted while he was in England on his first visit, is the fruit of public subscription. And a marble bust, erected in his honour by his "fellow-citizens of Calcutta" in January 1842 stands in the vestibule of the Metcalfe Hall. It is half obscured by bookshelves and packing cases as a result of the transfer of the Imperial Library to the Hall: but it is to be hoped that it has not been forgotten, and that it is intended in course of time to transfer it to the Victoria Memorial Hall.

There is nothing which need detain us long over the picture of the EARL OF ELGIN, Viceroy of India from 1894 to 1899. It is the gift of Rajah Shib Chunder Banerjee of Bhagalpore, and represents Lord Elgin in the robes of Grand Master of the Order of the Indian Empire. An account of his Viceroyalty will be found in the chapter on Government House where his portrait by Sir George Reid, P.R.S.A., hangs in the corridor leading to the Council Chamber.

DR. DUFF.—The inscription upon Norman Macbeth's large full length portrait of Dr. Duff which hangs next, appropriately commemorates him both as "missionary and educationist." Born in Scotland in 1806, the Rev. ALEXANDER DUFF was for thirty years one of the most prominent figures in the educational world of Calcutta. Having been appointed in 1829 to the important office of first Missionary to India from the established Church of Scotland, he sailed for Portsmouth in October of that year in the "Lady Holland" East Indiaman. His voyage was an eventful one: for the ship was wrecked near Capetown and again off Saugor Island, and the passengers and crew barely escaped with their lives. He arrived in Calcutta in May, 1830, and on the 13th July, opened in the house now numbered 51, Upper Chitpore Road and then known as Feringhi Komul Bose's house, the institution which now bears his name and is located in Nimtollah Street. It has long been the largest in India: but it started upon its prosperous career with five boys, ignorant of the veriest elements of education and incapable even of paying a fee. During the early period of Macaulay's connection with Calcutta, which lasted from 1834 to 1838, Duff was able to render him valuable assistance in the furthering of the cause of English education among the people of India, and served, as has been related elsewhere, as a Member of the famous Committee of Public Instruction. In 1836 Duff visted England and in the following year received the degree of D.D. He did not return to India until 1839. When the disruption in the Church of Scotland took place in 1843, he associated himself with the Free Church and with unremitting energy secured the continuance under their new auspices of the educational and religious institutions with which he was connected. On the occasion of a second visit to Scotland in 1850, he was chosen Moderator of the General Assembly of the Free Church: and filled the office during the year 1851. In 1853 he was examined before a Committee of the House of Lords on Indian affairs, and contributed valuable materials for Sir Charles Wood's famous Education Despatch of 1854. He took a principal part in the establishment of the Calcutta Review and for several years was its editor. In July 1863 he finally quitted India and died on February 12th, 1878, at the age of 72.

MANOMOHAN GHOSE.—The last portrait on the southern wall of the great saloon is that of Manomohan Ghose, one of the greatest and most successful criminal advocates on the rolls of the High Court at Calcutta and a recognized leader of the Indian reform party during the eighties and the nineties. He was born in 1844 and died suddenly at Krishnaghur in 1896. In 1862 he left for England with Mr. Satyendra Nath Tagore to compete for the Indian Civil

Service. They were the first two youths of Indian nationality to undertake the journey for that purpose. Mr. Tagore was successful, but Mr. Ghose was not and he returned to India as a member of the English Bar. He was the second native Indian barrister to be admitted as an advocate of the High Court. The first was Ganendro Mohun Tagore, the Christian son of Baboo Prosunno Coomar Tagore, C.S.I., who was admitted in March, 1860: but as a matter of fact, he never practised. The second was Manomohan Ghose admitted in May, 1868. The third was the late Mr. W. C. Bannerjee, admitted in March, 1870. Mr. Ghose paid more than one subsequent visit to England on political missions. In 1885 he addressed many meetings during the general election of that year, and at Birmingham he had the honour of speaking under the presidency of Mr. John Bright. He was a zealous supporter of the Indian National Congress, and when that body held its sixth session in Calcutta in 1880, he acted as President of the Reception Committee. In the practice of his profession, he was the kindest-hearted of men: and many an innocent person accused of a capital offence owes his life to his exertions, offered without fee or reward.

In the centre of the three smaller rooms, which lie to the south, there hang a couple of pictures. The one on the south wall is a portrait of Rai Hurro Chunder Ghose Bahadur, Judge of the Calcutta Small Cause Court from 1854 to 1868. A marble bust, which renders more adequate justice to this distinguished Bengalee, stands in the main entrance to the Small Cause Court buildings, where it was unveiled on the 8th March, 1876, by Sir Arthur Macpherson, then a Judge of the High Court. Before his appointment as Small Cause Court Judge, Hurro Chunder Ghose was for twenty years a member of the subordinate Civil Judiciary in Bengal and in 1852 was gazetted as Junior Police Magistrate of Calcutta on the unanimous recommendation of the Judges of the Sudder Dewani Adawlut. Two years later he was transferred to the Small Cause Court where he remained until his death in 1868 at the age of 60. In his youth he was a favourite pupil, as the Rev. K. M. Banerjee had been, of David Hare and Derozio: but unlike others, he maintained his Hinduism. He enjoyed the confidence of Lord William Bentinck and Lords Auckland and Dalhousie and was in the words of Chief Justice Norman who presided at the memorial meeting held in his honour at the Town Hall on the 4th January, 1869, "the very model of what a native gentleman should be."

The inscription upon the second portrait in this room records that it represents Mr. F. J. Johnstone, M.I.C.E., Chief Engineer and Secretary to the Government of Bengal in the Public Works Department from 1891 to 1896. He was created a C.I.E., upon retirement from Government service in the last named year. It appears from the concluding portion of the inscription to have been presented to Mr. Johnstone "by a number of his subordinates and workers in token of their esteem and admiration of his qualities as head of the Public Works Department," and it is not known how it found its way to the Town Hall.

CHAPTER XIII.

THE METCALFE HALL AND IMPERIAL LIBRARY.

ONE of the most interesting additions to Calcutta during recent years is undoubtedly the Imperial Library, which occupies the building known as the Metcalfe Hall, at the junction of the Strand Road with Hare Street. The history of the Hall itself may first be told. It was erected as its name imports, to perpetuate the memory of Lord Metcalfe, who officiated as Governor-General of India from March 1835 to March 1836, during the interval between the departure of Lord William Bentinck and the arrival of Lord Auckland, and more particularly to signalize the last great act of his public life in India, the emancipation of the press. A manuscript narrative is in existence which describes in the words of Mr. Longueville Clarke, a distinguished advocate of the time and one of the chief promoters of the movement, the various stages which culminated in the erection of the Hall: and a short extract from it will not be without an interest of its own. "On the 18th February, 1838," writes Mr. Clarke, "at a public meeting in the Town Hall it was proposed by Mr. James Pattle and seconded by Dr. John Grant, that a subscription should be opened to erect a statue to Sir Charles Metcalfe, and present him with a service of plate. I met this with the following proposition, which was seconded by Dr. J. R. Martin, and unanimously carried out. "That by combining together the different public subscriptions which are now raising to offer testimonials to Sir Charles Metcalfe, it would enable the whole Indian community to express in a more distinguished manner their appreciation of the character of that eminent man." I then suggested the erection of a public building to be called the Metcalfe Hall, the ground floor to be devoted to the museum and committee-rooms of the Agricultural and Horticultural Society, and the second floor to the Public Library, both these institutions having long been the peculiar object of the solicitude and bounty of Sir Charles Metcalfe. This was also unanimously carried and it led to the appointment of a joint Committee. Sir Edward Ryan was appointed President, and I acted as Honorary Secretary."

The appropriateness of the selection at the time could not be gainsaid. The Public Library had no better habitation for several years than the lower rooms of the house of a Dr. Strong in Esplanade Row. Here it remained until July 1841, when it was removed to the Fort William College building in Lyon's Range, which accommodated it until its final removal to the Metcalfe Hall in June, 1844. The Agri-Horticultural Society was equally destitute of a building adapted for the purposes of official meetings or for the display of their curious models of agricultural implements, seeds and specimens of produce. A contribution of "Company's rupees" 10,000 from the Society's funds opened the subscription list: individual members added another Rs. 3,000: the Public Library gave about Rs. 6,000: and a sum of about Rs. 70,000 was ultimately collected. The Government gave the site upon which the Hall now stands, and which in 1840 was occupied by "a building rapidly falling into decay which has been temporarily appropriated to the 'Sailor's Home.'" A plot of ground "at the south-east corner of the enclosure of Tank Square" was asked for on behalf of the subscribers, but the request was refused, as Lord Auckland was "of opinion that those spaces of the town which are appropriated to light and ventilation ought not to be given up for purposes of building." The foundation stone of the Hall was laid with masonic honours on December 19th, 1840, by Dr. James Grant, Grand Master of Bengal, assisted by Dr. James Burnes, Grand Master of Western India and 350 Master Masons. "The ceremony was performed in the presence of the Governor-General, and all the members of Council, the Miss Edens, and more than 200 ladies and a countless number of spectators." Three of the members of Council present, it may be added, have achieved the honour of a public memorial in the Town Hall: William Wilberforce Bird, who acted as Governor-General in 1844, Henry Thoby Prinsep, the elder, and Major-General Sir William Casement. Of the other names mentioned in Longueville Clarke's narrative, James Pattle, Member of the Board of Revenue, stands commemorated by a tablet in St. John's Church: Dr. J. R. Martin subsequently became Sir Ronald and Dr. James Burnes was brother of Sir Alexander ("Secunder") Burnes, who was assassinated at Kabul in 1842.

The work of construction was completed in 1844. The order of architecture is taken from the portico of the Temple of the Winds at Athens, and the design was chosen by Mr. C. K. Robison, the architect, for its lightness and durability. A broad flight of steps leads to the portico or colonnade on the west or river front, and there is a covered colonnade entrance to the east, with another similar flight of steps which lead up to the entrance hall. The building is raised on a solid but ornamental basement, ten feet in height, and columns, thirty in number and thirty-six feet in height, rise from this basement and support the general entablature of the building, giving it externally much the appearance of a Greek temple of one lofty storey. The columns and colonnade nearly surround the whole building. It was intended to carry them entirely round, but the scheme could not be put into execution from want of funds. Internally there are two stories, which for many years were occupied in the manner suggested by Longueville Clarke when the project for the building was originally adopted. But the Public Library languished under lax management and inadequate support. the offices of the Agri-Horticultural Society failed to attract public interest, and the building itself was suffered to fall into disrepair.

The idea of creating in Calcutta an Imperial Library which should be worthy of the name, owes its inception to Lord Curzon. It was formally opened by the late Viceroy on the afternoon of the 30th January, 1903. In the course of his speech His Excellency drew an entertaining picture of the atmosphere of confusion and collapse in which the Metcalfe Hall had been living for years, and which he was attempting to dissipate. "When I came to Calcutta four years ago," he said, "one of my first undertakings was to visit the Government Offices and public buildings of this City, in order to see what they were like, and how the work was conducted inside them. I heard that there was a Public Library and that it was located in a building known as the Metcalfe Hall. So one afternoon I paid this place a visit. I found that the lower storey was occupied by an institution known as the Agri-Horticultural Society, which had collected there a number of glass bottles and jars on shelves containing seeds and specimens, and some rusty implements and ploughs. I daresay they were very useful in their own way and place. But it seemed to me that they were singularly out of place in the Metcalfe Hall, while I heard that their somewhat dismal appearances found its reflex in the financial position of the Society which was also in a state of what is sometimes described as genteel decay. Then I walked upstairs to this floor which belonged to the Calcutta Public Library, and I found the shelves in these rooms—not, I may say, the present shelves, which are entirely new—filled with books, the majority of which had parted company with their bindings, while the room in which we are now met was occupied by a few readers of newspapers and light fiction, whose tenancy of the library was freely disputed by the pigeons who were flying about the inside of the room, and evidently treated it as their permanent habitation. Both of these experiences had rather a disquieting effect upon me. Then about the same time I visited the Home Department, and I found stacked there in a crowded and unsuitable building the large library of books belonging to the Government of India and known as the Imperial Library, practically accessible to none but officials, useless for purposes of study or reference, and unknown to the public at large. Putting together these various experiences, it seemed to me an obvious duty to work for some sort of amalgamation, and thereby to give to Calcutta what the chief City of a great Province with a million people, itself also the capital of the British Empire in India, ought most certainly to possess, namely, a Library worthy of the name. It also seemed to me that this building erected in memory of a distinguished British statesman, and situated in the heart of the business quarter of the town, and in close proximity to the public offices, was the very place for such an institution, and that it was a pity to see it given up to pigeons, plants and ploughs. I therefore approached the Council of the Agri-Horticultural Society and the shareholders of the Public Library, to ascertain whether they would be willing to part with their interests, such as they were, in the building, and to allow Government to resume full possession. After prolonged negotiation, this was satisfactorily arranged. The rights of both parties were acquired by purchase by the Government of India, and an Act was subsequently passed to validate the transfer: the Metcalfe Hall was taken over, a Librarian was procured from England, and arrangements for the constitution of the new Library were seriously taken in hand. The building has been entirely renovated and refurnished, the collection of books from the Government Library has been brought over, and placed in its new habitation, and the enormous number of books in the old Public Library has been examined, weeded out, and re-arranged. The total number of books in the Library is now a little short of 100,000. The Government of India has created a staff and provided an annual sum for their payment, for the upkeep of the building, and the purchase of new books: and now, after two years of incessant work, we are introducing our child, I hope a robust as well as a learned child, to the Calcutta public and inviting them to take notice of her and patronise her now that she has made her bow to the world."

Let us now accept the invitation extended by Lord Curzon and enter the Hall by its principal entrance on the east. Ascending a flight of steps under the covered colonnade, we shall find ourselves in a vestibule which leads into a main hall sixty-three feet by thirty feet. A fine bust in white marble of Lord Metcalfe by E. H. Baily, R.A., formerly stood in the vestibule, but it has been removed to the Indian Museum and placed in the collection destined for the Victoria Memorial Hall. A similar honour for some unaccountable reason has been denied to the equally handsome bust by Weeks of Dwarkanath Tagore, the enlightened Hindoo reformer, which has been permitted to remain neglected amid a wilderness of blue-books and administration reports. For the whole of the lower floor, which is both dark and obscure, has been utilized exclusively for purposes of storage. All the books not in ordinary demand are kept here, and there is room for adding to their number for some years to come.

The upper floor is reached by a handsome stair, and is devoted to the current uses of the Library. As we go upstairs, we must not overlook the interesting series of views of old Calcutta which hang on the walls. Arriving at the last step, we may make our way into the ante-room of the Library. Here, after the fashion of the British Museum and the Bodleian Library we shall be called upon to deliver up our sticks and umbrellas: and when this rite has been performed, we may profitably spend a few minutes in the examination of the historical objects and documents which are shown in the glass-cases on our right. Facing the entrance is the private room of the Librarian, Mr. J. Macfarlane, who had gained much experience as an Assistant Librarian in the British Museum, and is the author of a valuable work on "Library Administration," and of a monograph on Verard, a Paris Printer of the 15th Century.

A corridor to the left separates the office of the staff and the attendants, which lies to the north, from the Private Reading Room reserved for students who wish to study and write in comparative solitude. At the end of the corridor lies the Public Reading Room which occupies the whole of the river front of the building. Two replicas in black marble of the bust of Lord Metcalfe, which once stood below, as we have recorded, are placed, one in the private, and the other in the public, reading-room. All these rooms in the upper floor are of much the same dimensions as those in the lower storey, when allowance for the subdivisions has been made: but they are thrown more open by means of arches, and the roof is twenty-six instead of twenty-two feet high, admitting of galleries with side lights above. Electric lights and fans have been added since the conversion of the building from its former uses, and the Reading-Rooms now bear a cheerful and well-ordered aspect, which must come as an agreeable surprise to the habitués of the old Calcutta Public Library with its air of general disorder and its dingy appointments.

The conditions under which literary research and study were perforce carried on before the establishment of the Imperial Library can be faintly realized by supplementing by a few concrete examples the words of Lord Curzon which we have just been quoting. A certain Mr. Andrews, who had a circulating Library in Calcutta in 1780, complains in an advertisement, of the loss he has sustained "owing to gentlemen going away, and in their hurry not recollecting their being subscribers to the Library, or having any books belonging thereto." He adds that "books are kept too long, and in many cases cut, or leaves are torn out." We fancy if the truth were known that the experience of the Calcutta Public Library during its life of sixty-five years, would not be found to differ greatly from that of Mr. Andrews. It is heart-rending to take up copies of the original first edition of "Waverley" or "David Copperfield" or "Pride and Prejudice," and to find page after page disfigured by an unsightly stamp which gives the book the appearance of a branded sheep or waler horse. But even such heroic precautions would seem to have been futile. While the British Museum copy of Hicky's Gazette, the earliest newspaper in India, is page-perfect though incomplete, its fellow in Calcutta, which was once the property of the Public Library, has been in places mutilated, and the unique page containing the account of the duel between Hastings and Francis has been cut out by some literary miscreant. The Government Departments had no better part to play.

When the Imperial Parliament took over the business of governing India from John Company in 1858, Sir George Birdwood tells us that one of the first acts of the new masters of the Indian House was to order a general sweep to be made of the old records that from 1726 had been preserved there with scrupulous solicitude. No less than three hundred tons of priceless manuscripts and volumes were sold to a firm of paper makers to be boiled, bleached and bashed into low class paper pulp. In India similar and even greater follies have been consistently perpetrated. As early as 1756, we read in a despatch from the Court of Directors that a leaf torn out of the original diary of Surman's embassy to the great Mogul in 1717 "was picked up in a public necessary house which the Writers make use of, and is now in our hands." The briefest enquiry will show that more than one volume of the secret correspondence of Clive and Watson is missing from the series of Government records in Calcutta, and the whereabouts are totally unknown of the original deeds of St. John's church which in the time of Lord Cornwallis, were certainly in the possession of Government. Even more glaring perhaps than the sins of commission have been those of omission. Much of Sir Thomas Munro's original correspondence lay long unheeded in the dingy cupboards of a mofussil collector's office in the Madras Presidency. So too at Chittagong, there were to be seen twenty years ago quite a number of official documents, a few entirely in the handwriting of Warren Hastings, and all bearing his signature and those of Francis, Barwell, Clavering and Monson. It is impossible to say what has been their fate: but it is more than probable that an iconoclastic record-keeper can account for the disappearance of many that the white ants have spared. And there are illustrations as melancholy to be found among the records in Calcutta itself. It is positively distressing to send for the files of *The Times* or of the local newspapers in the endeavour to elucidate some knotty point in the history of the city. The Government officials in whose custody they formerly reposed, have neither troubled to keep them up-to-date nor scrupled to use the scissors when some particularly interesting paragraph chanced to meet their eye.

Such is the inheritance into which the present Librarian and the Superintendent of the Reading Rooms were inducted three years ago. And if we have detailed the enormities of the past, it has been mainly to point the contrast with the present. It may be safely declared that under the skilled supervision of Mr. Macfarlane and the watchful eye of Mr. Madge, the opportunities of the literary felon and the official vandal are irretrievably gone. In spite of the ravages of years, there are still many treasures to be jealously guarded. The Library of the Home Department, which was formed in 1891 by the combination of various departmental libraries, has contributed many important and interesting books. The Calcutta Public Library was inaugurated by the gift of four thousand volumes from the Library of Lord Wellesley's short-lived Fort William College, and contained in addition large quantities of books and pamphlets on Indian subjects, many of which, especially those printed in India, are rare and obtainable with difficulty elsewhere. Some ten thousand of its books, mostly novels, have been distributed among twenty-five selected institutions and libraries in Calcutta, but every volume of permanent interest and real value has been retained. As a result, the Imperial Library is well furnished with most of the important books in English dealing with India. Additions are being regularly and systematically made, and not only English works, but books on India in French and German and other European languages will be found upon the shelves. The Library also possesses a good collection of volumes upon general subjects, especially History and Travel, and a collection is now in the course of formation of all the best books in Urdu, Persian, Arabic, Bengali, and Hindi, from all parts of India. Arrangements are also being made for the supply of all official publications relating to Native States.

When the Library was first opened the Government of Bengal consented to make over any books which had been received in the Bengal Library, and which might be required for the use of the Imperial Library. Accordingly, about three hundred works, including periodicals, were selected by the Librarian, and received from the Bengal Library. The publications of each year sent to the Government of Bengal, in accordance with the Registration Act of 1867, are now drawn, as far as required, from the Bengal Library, and in 1904 the number of books so obtained was 725 volumes, or parts of volumes, in English, Bengali, and Sanskrit.

In November, 1903, the Asiatic Society of Bengal gave permission for books to be taken from their Library for perusal at the Imperial Library, and books may also be borrowed from the Library of the Board of Examiners.

The resources of the Imperial Library are thereby greatly increased, but the results appear to have been somewh disappointing, so far, for the Librarian records in his report for 1904, that during that year only twenty books were borrowed from the Asiatic Society, and thirty-eight from the Board of Examiners during the last nine months of the year. Still, as catalogues of these Libraries are to be found, among others, on the desks in the Readin Room, the number of requisitions should expand, as th advantages of the many standard works available to th public are more fully appreciated. The catalogues of th Library itself are being systematically and exhaustiv prepared under the direction of Mr. Macfarlane, the fru of whose long experience, gained as an Assistant Libr rian in the British Museum, are visible upon almost eve page. Several have been already completed, such as th Author Catalogue, the Reading Room Catalogue a Index, the Monthly Lists of Accessions, the Card Ca logue—which comprises all additions to the Author Ca logue arranged in a single alphabet, and is contained cabinets which stand in the reading room. A subje index is in the press, and should prove the most usef and most generally consulted, of all the catalogues, wh completed. With all these catalogues available, there no difficulty in obtaining any information required. Eve book is classified, and can be found without delay. I matters requiring exceptional acquaintance with the re sources of the Library, the assistance of the Librarian most willingly given: while Mr. E. W. Madge, the kind Superintendent of Reading Rooms, is always on the sp and ready to place at the disposal of the researcher h veritably encyclopædic knowledge of Anglo-Indian books and book-lore.

"The general idea of the Library is that it should contain all the books that have been written about India in popular tongues, with such additions as are required to make it a good all round Library of standard works of reference." The principles laid down in these words by Lord Curzon in his inaugural speech are being steadily acted upon in the matters of additions to the Library. In the year 1904 over fifteen hundred volumes were added by purchase, and some three hundred English books were presented by various donors. Among the latter were a number of illustrated books from Lord Curzon and the Rajah of Hill Tipperah. These have been placed in the Public Reading Room in special cases suitably inscribed, and the visitor should not neglect the opportunity of examining them. In the vernacular department, a valuable collection of printed books and manuscripts, in Arabic, Persian and Urdu, have been received from the Zemindar of Bohar and set apart in a special room to which the name of the Bohar Library has been given. A manuscript catalogue has been made of these books, and is available for consultation. The number of official publications acknowledged during the course of a year is also very large. Upwards of 3,000 publications of the Government of India and Local Governments, issued in 1904, were received in the Library, together with 2,588 issued in previous years, and supplied in answer to applications; and no less than 1,086 British Parliamentary Blue Books were received during the year.

With regard to loans, no book that is on the shelves in the reading room is lent out to the public, but most of the other books, and also a collection of duplicates—of which a portion are duplicates of books in the reading room—are available for lending-out purposes. Manuscripts, especially of valuable books, are not as a rule lent, and when books are lent, security equal to the value of the books is required, except in the case of the proprietors of the old Calcutta Public Library. Books are lent all over India in accordance with the above-mentioned terms.

On a separate stand, near the Superintendent's table, will be found all the latest books bearing on India, and the latest Government of India Reports. New books are placed on this stand as received, and kept there for a week or two before being relegated to their proper sections.

It is satisfactory to note that the public have not been slow to avail themselves of the privileges conferred by the Imperial Library. In 1903, during the eleven months it was open, 15,093 readers made use of the reading room; in 1904 the number increased to 24,297, and in 1905 to 30,269 making an average of 100 readers on ordinary week days. During the current year (1906) there has, so far, been a corresponding increase and the number of readers will no doubt continue to show an upward tendency as the manifold advantages of the Library and its admirable arrangements become more widely known.

NOTE.—Since Chapter XIV has been in type, a decision is announced to have been arrived at regarding the dispersal of the collection of pictures, books, MSS. old armour, etc., which is eventually to be placed in the Victoria Memorial Hall at Calcutta, if it is ever built, and which has been temporarily housed in the Indian Museum. The collection has been on view for some three years and has been added to from time to time since Lord Curzon presided at the opening ceremony. But the trustees of the Memorial, recognising the risks that are likely to be run by leaving rare and valuable articles exposed for an indefinite time, have just decided to place them in safe keeping. A carefully prepared list has been made out showing every separate exhibit and with whom it is to be placed. The very large pictures will remain in the Museum, others will go to Government House, Belvedere, the Town Hall and the Commander-in-Chief's quarters in Fort William. Many of the articles lent by Indian Chiefs and gentlemen or by public bodies will be returned to them. The list will state how everything has been disposed of and thus when the time comes the collection can be gathered together again. This is the only course that could be followed in the circumstances, especially as doubts have arisen as to the practicability of building the Memorial Hall on the site selected on the Maidan.

CHAPTER XIV

THE VICTORIA MEMORIAL HALL COLLECTION.

PENDING the building of the Victoria Memorial Hall, four galleries on the upper floor of the Indian Museum have been put at the disposal of the Trustees, for the housing and exhibition of the collection of objects connected with the history of British India, which is now in process of being brought together for the Memorial Galleries. This collection, which has already attained considerable proportions, comprises portraits and busts of famous men, original treaties and other documents, old prints of Indian scenery, personal relics of Her late Majesty Queen Victoria, illuminated manuscripts, coins, medals, arms, and a number of most interesting historical objects.

The Exhibition remains open annually from December to May, the respective dates of re-opening and closing being duly announced in the local papers. The public are admitted daily from 10 A.M., to 5 P.M., except on Thursdays, when the Museum is closed till noon; and on Fridays, when it is closed all day.

On the upper landing at the head of the grand staircase are grouped the statues and busts which have been already acquired for the collection. In the centre is a marble statue, by Marshall Wood, of the late QUEEN-EMPRESS, representing her in the days of her youth. Upon the face of the pedestal is a bas-relief depicting the Imperial Assemblage at Delhi of 1877. The inscription records that the statue was presented to "the Indian people" by Mahtab Chand Bahadur, Maharaja Dhiraj of Burdwan, "in commemoration of Her Majesty's gracious assumption of the Imperial title on January 1st, 1877." A second inscription informs us that "the pedestal commemorating the same auspicious event" was presented by Aftab Chand Mahatab Bahadur, the succeeding Maharaja Dhiraj of Burdwan.

LORD WELLESLEY.—A full-sized marble statue of the MARQUESS WELLESLEY, (1760-1842) by John Bacon, junior, stands upon a white marble pedestal to the right of the Queen's effigy. It is simple in pose, but full of dignity and command. The following is the inscription upon the pedestal: "Marquess Wellesley, Governor-General of India from 1798 to 1805. Erected by the British inhabitants of Bengal in testimony of their high sense of the wisdom, energy and rectitude of his administration."

Richard Colley Wellesley, first Marquess Wellesley, was the eldest son of the Earl of Mornington, whom he succeeded in that title, and elder brother (as is well known) of the great Duke of Wellington. A friend and follower of Pitt, a trained statesman from his youth up, a ripe scholar, and for four years a leading member of the Board of Control, his appointment to the Governor-Generalship of India at the age of thirty-eight seemed the most appropriate and wisest of selections. But when he landed at Calcutta in May, 1798, few could have prophesied the great change that would be wrought by him over the face of India. From the first he laid it down as his guiding principle that the English must be the paramount power in the Peninsula. The trader was to give way to the administrator, the humble suppliant at the feet of the "conqueror of the universe" to the sovereign dictator and overlord. If the English are to-day the undisputed masters of a country whose people more than double Gibbon's estimate of 120 millions for all the races and nations who obeyed Imperial Rome, it is nothing but the development and fulfilment of the policy of imperialism initiated and fostered by Wellesley. The English had been in India for a century and a half when he arrived in the country, but their progress had been insignificant. At the end of his seven years' government all Hindustan lay at the feet of a company of English traders who, sixty years before, had been ignominiously chased from their factories in Bengal. Wellesley was able to carry out almost every part of his magnificent impatient scheme: but he had meanwhile exhausted the patience of the Court of Directors in London. These worthies could not brook the idea of ruling India from a palace. Their notions were those of the counting house and of the retail dealer in muslins and indigo. "The glorious little man" was recalled in disgrace: a series of attacks in Parliament and vote of censure from the Company whose dominions he had trebled were the only rewards of his statesmanship and courage. It was not until thirty years later that the outrageous verdict of 1807 was cancelled by the voting of a statue and a grant of £20,000 to the man to whom England owes the Imperial India of to-day. His statue adorns not only the vestibule of the India Office, but, until a few short months ago, was honoured fittingly enough with a place in the Government House in Calcutta which he built, and which is the best of monuments to the great proconsul, who, finding British prestige in India at its lowest point, raised it to its highest and left his countrymen supreme in Hindustan.

LORD DALHOUSIE.—To the left of Queen Victoria stands the full length marble statue by Sir John Steel, R.S.A., of the Marquess of Dalhousie, (1812-1860) Governor-General of India from 1848 to 1856. It was erected in his honour by public subscription and stood originally in the Throne-room at Government House opposite that of Lord Wellesley whence it was transferred to the Dalhousie Institute on the opening of that building "as a monumental edifice to contain within its walls statues and busts of great men." It has now been handed over to the Trustees of the Victoria Memorial Hall, together with the busts of Mutiny heroes by which it was surrounded.

James Andrew Broun Ramsay, tenth Earl and first Marquess of Dalhousie, was born in 1812. His father George, the ninth Earl, was from 1819 to 1828 Governor-in-Chief of Canada, and from 1829 to 1832 Commander-in-Chief in India. At Christ Church he was a contemporary of Lord Canning and the eighth Lord Elgin, who both followed him as Governor-General of India. In 1832 he became heir to the title by the death of his brother Lord Ramsay, and in 1838 he succeeded his father as tenth Earl. His only important public office in England was that of President of the Board of Trade to which Sir Robert Peel appointed him in 1843. When Peel retired from office in 1846, Lord John Russell offered him the Governor-Generalship of India, where his father-in-law, the Marquess of

Tweeddale, was already at the head of the Government of Madras. He survived his return from India by four years and died at Dalhousie Castle in 1860: his wife had predeceased him in 1853, her death occurring on her way home, within sight of the English shores.

It is not easy to give within a brief compass the chronicle of Dalhousie's eventful tenure of the office of Governor-General. The final subjugation of the Punjab in 1849, the addition, three years later, of the whole of the Irrawaddy from Rangoon to Prome to the British Dominions, and the annexation in 1856 of the territories of the Nawab Vizier of Oudh, constitute the achievements with which he completed the fabric of British rule in India. His application of the doctrine of "lapse" to the succession in native states has met with much adverse criticism: and his policy with regard to Oudh cannot be absolved from its share of responsibility for the Sepoy Mutiny. But with his name is also inseparably linked the whole history of British progress in India during the last century. It has been truly said that from the planting of trees in dry places to the building of railroads—from reforms in jail discipline to the diffusion of aids to knowledge among the people—nothing seemed too small or too great for the man who, at the age of thirty-six, found himself ruler of Hindustan. In every department of the State he wrought some change for the better. To him India is indebted for her penny-post, her telegraphs, her railways, her public works department, the thousand and one channels by which her internal development has manifested itself. The Civil Service of India was thrown open to public competition, and a heavy burden taken off the shoulders of th Governor-General, by the appointment of a Lieutenan Governor of Bengal. The author of this great work die a victim like Cornwallis and Canning and many another t his devotion to India's needs: but it will be long befor his name and his labours are forgotten.

Around the statue of the Queen have been placed in semi-circle the following busts, which we shall enumera in order, commencing from the corner of the grand sta case on the north :—

1. EDWARD FREDERICK VENABLES (1818–1858): marble bust by Sir John Steel, R.S.A., presented by th Council of the Dalhousie Institute, where it origina stood. Venables, a gallant indigo-planter, raised an organised a small body of horse during the Mutiny t keep order in the district of Azimgarh in the United Pr vinces. He was instrumental in rescuing many Europ eans from confinement, and took an active part with h levy in the campaign of the Goorkha contingent fro Nepal against the rebels in Oudh in July and Septemb 1857. It was said of him that at the battle of Azimga on September 20th, 1857, he "was always where fightin was hardest: he was first up at the first gun taken, an killed three men with his own hand." He was wounde during the pursuit of Coer Singh, the rebel leader in Behar and died April 19th, 1858.

2. JAMES PRINSEP, F.R.S. (1799-1840): a marble bus executed by H. Weekes in 1843: presented by the Asiat Society, of which he was the Secretary (in succession t

Horace Hayman Wilson) from 1833 to 1838. An account of his career will be found in the chapter on the Statues and Monuments of the City, in connection with Prinsep's Ghat, which was "erected in his honour by his fellow-citizens." He died in London in 1840. His services to the Asiatic Society were of unparalleled importance, and his administration of its affairs the most brilliant and successful in its annals. Besides contributing largely to numismatics and to science, he won for himself an imperishable name as the discoverer and first decipherer of the ancient alphabets of India.

3. CHARLES THEOPHILUS, LORD METCALFE (1785-1846): the "Liberator of the Indian Press." Acting Governor-General of India from 1835 to 1836: Governor of Jamaica from 1839 to 1842: and Governor-General of Canada from 1843 to 1845. A marble bust by E. H. Baily, R.A. It formerly stood in the vestibule of the Metcalfe Hall, and at the conversion of that building into the Imperial Library passed into the possession of the Government of India by whom it has been presented to the Victoria Memorial Hall.

4. CHARLES, MARQUESS CORNWALLIS (1738-1805): Governor-General of India from 1785 to 1793, and again for a short period in 1805: a marble bust executed by James Bacon in 1799: presented by Mr. C. W. McMinn of the Indian Civil Service (retired).

5. MAJOR JAMES RENNELL, F.R.S. (1742-1830): Surveyor-General of Bengal from 1764-1777: a bronze bust presented in 1903 by his grandson Sir James Rennell Rodd,

K.C.M.G., now Minister at Stockholm. "Among his eager fortune-seeking countrymen of the last century in Bengal, Rennell stands forth as an unique figure—a calm, distinguished man of science." Entering the navy at the age of fourteen, he joined the East India Company's fleet in 1763, and in the following year received an Ensign's commission in the Bengal Engineers from Governor Vansittart, and was appointed Surveyor of the "Company's dominions" in Bengal. "In that position he remained, without seeking promotion or concerning himself in money-making, throughout his thirteen years of Indian service. Indifferent to the vanities of social life, he kept a staff of draftsmen in Calcutta but buried himself in the recesses of Eastern Bengal to be near the centre of his work. Year by year he studied the great river-systems in which he discovered the key to the geography of the country. On his labours our knowledge rests. After his return to England in 1777, they won for him the highest rank among men of science. Still refusing offers of advancement, he quietly went on with his work until extreme old age, content to be "the leading geographer in England, if not in Europe, for a period of fifty years." He died at the age of eighty-seven and lies buried in Westminster Abbey. On October 15th, 1772, he married from Mr. Cartier's house at Dacca Jane Thackeray, the sister of "Sylhet" Thackeray and great aunt therefore of the author of "Vanity Fair." Among the autographs in the collection within may be seen a letter from Captain James Rennell, dated Fort William, 25th September, 1774, asking the Council to recommend him for a pension to the Court of Directors, so that he may be able to retire.

6. Sir William Wilson Hunter, K.C.S.I., Historian of India (1840-1900): a bronze bust by W. Hamo Thorneycroft, R.A., and the replica of the one which stands in the Indian Institute at Oxford: presented by the Hunter Memorial Fund. The career of Hunter has so recently closed that the main achievements of his life of astonishing literary activity will be fresh in the public mind. His unfinished History of India constitutes perhaps his most enduring monument: but few have done more than he to bring home the realities and the romance of the "India of the Queen" to stay-at-home Englishmen. He was the nephew of James Wilson (1805-1860), who went out to Calcutta in 1859 as the first of the Viceroy's Financial Members of Council at the urgent request of Lord Palmerston, who saw in him the only man who could restore equilibrium to the Indian Exchequer after the Mutiny of 1857. Wilson's statue by Sir John Steel (a fine work of art) is among these in the Dalhousie Institute which have been handed over to the Victoria Memorial Hall. But for some obscure reason it has been left in solitude in the Institute building. It is to be hoped that when the Memorial Hall has been completed room will be made in the Temple of Fame for a man of whom it may truthfully be said that he died doing his duty.

7. The Duke of Wellington (1769-1852): a marble bust presented by the Rajah of Hill Tipperah.

8. Major-General Claude Martin (1735-1800): founder of the Martinière at Lucknow, Calcutta and Lyons: a marble bust.

9. Major-General Sir JAMES OUTRAM: marble bust by J. H. Foley, R.A.

10. Major-General Sir HENRY HAVELOCK (1795-1857): marble bust by Noble.

11. Brigadier-General JAMES GEORGE SMITH NEILL, C.B. (1810-1857): marble bust by Noble.

12. Brigadier-General JOHN NICHOLSON, C.B. (1821-1857): marble bust by J. H. Foley, R.A.

These four memorials of Mutiny heroes are presented by the Council of the Dalhousie Institute in which building they formerly stood.

13. The DUKE OF WELLINGTON (1769-1852): another marble bust executed in 1814 by P. Turnerelli: lent by the Corporation of Calcutta. It was formerly placed on the upper landing of the Town Hall.

Entering the rooms, we may begin our circuit of the first or Central Gallery by turning to the left: when we shall find the following pictures on the walls:—

(1) Sir WILLIAM JONES (1746-1794): Puisne Judge of the Supreme Court from 1783 to 1794, founder and first President of the Asiatic Society in 1784: painted during his boyhood by Sir Joshua Reynolds, P.R.A. Jones is represented as a youthful student, with dark eyes and short brown hair, dressed in a red blouse and sitting at a window reading. This, like the succeeding one, is presented by the Asiatic Society.

(2) Adjoining is another picture of SIR WILLIAM JONES by Robert Home, who, when presenting it to the Asiatic

Society on October 13th, 1813, speaks of it as "composed from the very slender materials which are left to the public." Jones was born in 1746 and lost his father, the mathematician and friend of Newton, when he was only three years old. He was educated at Harrow and University College, Oxford, where he improved his knowledge of Hebrew, gained some acquaintance with Chinese, mastered Arabic, and became a fluent scholar in German, Spanish and Portuguese. His aptitude in learning languages was extraordinary, and Sir John Shore has recorded that "many of the most learned Asiatics had the candour to avow that his knowledge of Arabic and Persian was as accurate and extensive as their own." There is a good story told of Jones in connection with his wonderful linguistic gifts. When journeying through France in 1782 he was introduced to King Louis the Sixteenth, and on being asked several questions regarding the provinces he had visited, astonished the King by replying in the particular dialect of each province referred to. When he had left, Louis remarked: "This is a most extraordinary man. He understands the language of my people better than I do myself." "He is a more extraordinary man than your Majesty imagines," rejoined one of the courtiers, "for he understands almost every language in the world, but his own." "Mon Dieu!" exclaimed the King, "then of what country is he?" "He is a Welshman, please your Majesty," was the reply. And if it be true that Jones never gave himself the pains to acquire Welsh, it was solely because he could gain little or no knowledge from it. He was called to the Bar in 1774 and tried in vain to induce the electors of Cambridge to return him to Parliament. His liberal opinions and his detestation of the American War and the Slave trade prevented his election, but he met with better success at Westminster Hall. In 1783 he was appointed a Puisne Judge of the Supreme Court at Calcutta, filling the vacancy caused long since by the death of Le Maistre in 1777. Early in the same year he married a daughter of Dr. Shipley, Bishop of St. Asaph, and thereby became uncle by marriage of Bishop Heber.

Upon arrival in Calcutta in the month of October, 1783, he took up his residence at Garden Reach in a bungalow almost opposite the buildings of what was once the Bishop's College at Seebpore. He performed his judicial functions with much ability, but his main pursuits were literary and juristical. His new environment suited him exactly as affording a wide field for the prosecution of his Oriental studies, and Warren Hastings and he found many interests in common. Together they founded the "Bengal Asiatic Society" in January 1784: and his eleven anniversary discourses to the Society as its first President and his contributions to the Society's researches made an era in the study of the Indian languages, literature and philosophy. He was the first English scholar to master Sanskrit, and as a jurist set himself to prepare a complete digest of Hindoo and Muhammadan law, which, however, he did not live to complete. He suffered much from the climate, and when Hastings saw him at Bhagalpur in December, 1784, he was a "perfect skeleton." And on his return to Calcutta after two months on the river he records that he could only preserve his health "by a resolution of never seeing the sun or suffering him to see me." His exertions finally overtaxed his strength, and he died at his house in Garden Reach on April 27th, 1793, at the age of 47 years. Jones was a man of most regular habits: and the manner in which he distributed his time is thus described by a contemporary writer: "He rose at daybreak and studied till breakfast time: after which during terms he attended his duty in the Supreme Court, making a regular habit of walking from his house at the bottom of Garden Reach to the Court House on the Esplanade, from whence he returned home at three o'clock and studied till four: he then went to dinner where he generally had a select party of friends assembled whom he entertained with the utmost gaiety till seven: when he returned to his literary labours and did not again quit till midnight. This was his constant habit from which he seldom or never deviated."

Below the portraits of Sir William Jones is a glass case containing most interesting documents addressed to the Chiefs of Chittagong and Midnapur by Carter, Hastings, Verelst and Vansittart. Hanging above is a painting by Ravi Varma, the well-known Travancore artist, of Rajah SIR TANJORE MADHAVA RAO, K.C.S.I., (1828-1891), Dewan in turn of Travancore, Indore and Baroda. He twice declined a seat in the Viceroy's Legislative Council.

(3) On the east is a portrait of RICHARD COLLEY WELLESLEY, Earl of Mornington, and first Marquess Wellesley (1760-1842). This picture, possibly by Robert Home, is not quite so large as the other portrait also said

to be the work of Home which hangs in the Council-Chamber at Government House.

(4) The next portrait is that of the MARQUESS OF HASTINGS, (1754-1826): Governor-General of India from 1813 to 1823. The picture comes from the Government House collection and is the "Kitcat picture" which Lord Dalhousie found "thrust away over a doorway." The painter's name is unknown. The portrait has been supposed by some to represent Sir Eyre Coote and the authorship assigned to Chinnery. When it was sent to England in 1890 to be cleaned, Sir George Scharf, Director of the National Gallery found at the back, a piece of paper inscribed "most probably Sir Eyre Coote." But there can be little doubt that the person portrayed is the Earl of Moira who was created Marquess of Hastings on December 7th, 1816, during his tenure of the office of Governor-General.

(5) On the north wall has been placed a full-length portrait of SIR ELIJAH IMPEY in flowing wig and scarlet robes. The picture has been lent by the Chief Justice and Judges of the High Court. It was painted in 1776 by Tilly Kettle, who appears to have arrived in Calcutta some four years earlier with a reputation earned by his skilful restoration of the large ceiling picture in the Sheldonian Theatre at Oxford, which had originally been the work of Robert Streater in the days of Charles the Second. This portrait of Impey may be accepted as a faithful likeness, for it was engraved for the memoir in which his son strove to set him right in the eyes of posterity, and it is no doubt the one for which the free merchants, free mariners, and

other inhabitants of Calcutta "begged the Chief Justice to sit" in the extremely flattering address they offered to him at the end of 1775, after the condemnation of Nuncomar. The picture, according to the prayer made by the presenters of the address, was intended for the adornment of the "Town Hall," by which was meant the Old Court House in the north-east corner of Tank Square; and on the demolition of that building it was no doubt transferred to the grand jury room in the new Court House on the Esplanade and has so passed into the custody of their lordships of the High Court. The portrait of Impey by Zoffany which hangs in the Judge's Library at the High Court is of a later date than Kettle's and must have been painted just before Impey left India in December 1783. Displayed below the picture is the original indictment against Nuncomar, in Persian and English, and by its side the fatal Jewel-bond and the other exhibits, also presented by the Chief Justices and Judges of the High Court.

On the other side of the door leading to the "Royal gallery" on the south is Mr. R. D. Mackenzie's large painting of the state entry of Lord Curzon and the Duke of Connaught into Delhi on the occasion of the Coronation Durbar on December 30th, 1902.

(6) The next picture is the magnificent equestrian portrait, lent by the Corporation of Calcutta, of Gerard Viscount Lake, Baron of Delhi and Laswarree (1744-1808) Commander-in-Chief in India from 1800 to 1807.

This picture of Lord Lake which formerly hung in the Town Hall, is among the finest works of art in Calcutta:

but the climate had worked such havoc with it that when it was restored in 1901 by the skilful hands of Mr. Alexander Scott, the most extraordinary transformation was the result. Lord Lake's horse which appeared of a dull and dirty brown colour was discovered to be a handsome white charger: a second horseman on a black was revealed in the right-hand corner of the picture, immediately behind the Commander-in-Chief and evidently representing his nephew and favourite aide-de-camp: and an animated background was also disclosed, depicting a military review and painted with the utmost detail.

The military career of Lake commenced in the year 17[illegible] when he was at the age of fourteen appointed an ensign in the first regiment of Foot-guards, now known as the Grenadier Guards. He served with the second battalion in the campaigns in Germany in 1760-62, and as a lieutenant-colonel went out with drafts to America in 1781, when he made the campaign in North Carolina under Lord Cornwallis, and took part in the sortie under Colonel Robert Abercromby from the British lines at York Town. Upon the surrender of Cornwallis, five days later he remained a prisoner on parole until the end of the war. On the formation of a separate household for the Prince of Wales, the future Regent, he was appointed his equerry: and was according to Wraxall a "pleasing exception" to the Prince's list of undesirable companions. From 17[illegible] to 1802 he sat in Parliament as member for Aylesbury: but in 1793, he commanded a brigade in the Low Countries and was present at the siege of Valenciennes, and the action at Lincelles which is inscribed on the colours of the three regiments of Guards. In December, 1796, he took over the command in Ulster, and, succeeding Sir Ralph Abercromby a few years later as Commander-in-Chief in Ireland, found himself confronted with the task of quelling the rebellion which stands so closely associated with the name of Lord Edward Fitzgerald. His most important service in this connection was the rout of the rebel forces entrenched on Vinegar Hill, overlooking the town of Enniscorthy in Wexford county, on the 21st June, 1798. "The carnage was dreadful," he wrote to Castlereagh, "the rascals made a tolerable fight of it." The arrival of Cornwallis at Dublin relieved him of the command-in-chief but as senior military officer he received on September 8th, 1788, the surrender of the French General Humbert at Ballinamuck near Cloone. After sitting in the Irish Parliament as Government member for Armagh in order to vote for the union, he returned to London and in October 1800, was appointed Commander-in-Chief in India, taking over charge of the office from Sir Alured Clarke at Fort William on January 31st, 1801. Two years later, Wellesley's plans for breaking up the great Mahratta confederacy were matured, and Lake was directed to commence operations against the powers of Berar and Gwalior, whose chief, Scindia, had in his service numerous battalions officered by Perron and other Frenchmen. Lake replied with a series of decisive blows which amply merited Wellesley's eloquent tribute to his "matchless energy, ability and valour." On the 7th August 1803 he marched from Cawnpore and in a little over two months, with a force at no time exceeding 8,000 combatants, he destroyed 31 of Scindia's European-trained battalions, stormed the strong fortress of Allyghur, took Agra after an eight days' siege, captured 426 pieces of cannon, and with the help of Arthur Wellesley, defeated the enemy in the five pitched battles of Allyghur, Delhi, Laswarree, Assaye and Argaum, the second being one of the most decisive ever fought in India. He entered the Imperial City as a conqueror and was received by the blind Shah Alum, once the opponent of Clive, but for long years the puppet of the Mahrattas, who "seated in rags under a tattered canopy, the sole remnant of his former state and surrounded by every external token of misery," conferred upon him the titles of Saviour of the State and Invincible in War. Lake's brilliant series of successes were followed up by the total defeat of Holkar near Furruckabad in November, 1804, and the capture of the fortress of Deeg on Christmas day. Bhurtpore alone resisted his army but the Rajah offered terms of peace which were accepted. Cornwallis' arrival in India in 1805 was the signal for Lake's supersession as Commander-in-Chief: but the Governor-General died almost at once at Ghazipore and it was Lake who made peace at Umritsar in December, 1805, and he was in February 1806 formally re-appointed to the Supreme Command. His work in India, however, was done, and he embarked for England from Calcutta in February, 1807, "receiving such an ovation from Europeans and natives as had never been accorded to any public servant before." He had already in September 1804 been raised to the peerage as Lord Lake, Baron of Delhi and Laswaree and of Aston Clinton, and on his arrival in England was advanced to a Viscounty. He did not long survive his return and died of a chill at his town residence in Lower Brook Street on February 20th, 1808. He lies buried at Aston Clinton in Buckinghamshire. "Lake was never so great as on the battle-field," writes Colonel Malleson in his Decisive Battles of India, "he could think more clearly amidst the rain of bullets than in the calm of his own tent. In this respect he resembled Clive. It was this quality which enabled him to dare almost the impossible. That which in others would have been rash was in Lake prudent daring."

We must now cross the room, passing on our way a series of cases containing coins, medals, seals, historic treaties (lent by the Nawab Bahadur of Moorshedabad, the lineal descendant of Meer Jaffer) and a complete set of the autographs of the Governor-General of India and the members of the Supreme Executive Council from Warren Hastings to Lord Ampthill who officiated for Lord Curzon during the summer of 1904. In the corner opposite Lord Lake's picture have been placed a cluster of portraits. Beginning from the window they are Baboo KESHUB CHUNDER SEN, (1838-1884) founder of the Brahmo Somaj: an oil-painting presented by his son-in-law, His Highness the Maharajah of Cooch Behar. JOHN CLARK MARSHMAN, C.S.I., of Serampore (1794-1877): founder of the *Friend of India*, 1821: author of the History of India and History of Bengal. He was the father-in-law of Sir Henry Havelock and son of Joshua Marshman, the companion of Carey and Ward. This picture is presented by his son, Mr. Reginald S. Marshman. Major-General SIR JOHN MALCOLM, G.C.B. (1769-1833), Governor of Bombay from 1827 to 1830. He arrived in Madras as a cadet at the age of 15. He was of such diminutive appearance that one of the Directors at the India House asked him half in jest, " What would you do if you were to meet Hyder Ali?" "Do," he replied, " why, sir, I would out with my sword and cut off his head." This show of pluck was deemed sufficient, and he was passed in spite of his youth. He was one of sixteen children, and it is a remarkable occurrence that he and two of his brothers, both admirals, Pulteney and Charles, were honoured on one and the same occasion with the dignity of Commander of the Bath. Malcolm's tenure of the Governorship of Bombay is memorable by reason of his historic conflict with the Bombay Supreme Court; which finally found itself reduced to one puisne judge in the person of Sir John Peter Grant, and was eventually compelled to yield.

Above Malcolm hangs a copy, presented by subscription, of Sir George Reid's portrait of SIR HENRY BARTLE EDWARD FRERE, Bart. (1875-1884), of the Bombay Civil Service, successively Commissioner in Sind, Member of the Supreme Council, Governor of Bombay (from 1862 to 1867), Member of the Council of India, and High Commissioner in South Africa. His statue stands on the Thames Embankment in London.

Adjoining the portraits of these Bombay celebrities has been appropriately placed a painting of SIVAJEE, (1627-1680) the great Mahratta chieftain. Sivajee's son, Shembhujee, was captured, blinded and executed by Aurangzebe: and his grandson Shahu was brought up by one of the daughters of that Emperor and proved a very unworthy successor. He abandoned all power to his minister,

Balajee, who became first Peshwa, and sank to the rank of Raja of Satara. This house came to an end in 1848, but the family is still represented, although not in direct descent, by the Rajah of Kolhapore. To the right and occupying almost the whole of the northern wall of this room is Vassili Verestchagin's magnificent painting of the present King-Emperor's State entry into Jeypore in February, 1876. The picture was painted from life by the famous Russian artist while travelling in India in 1875-76, and found its way to the United States. The present Maharajah of Jeypore, hearing of its existence in America, requested the assistance of Lord Curzon in enabling him to purchase it for the Victoria Memorial Hall: and the transaction was effected through the good offices of Colonel John Hay, then Secretary of State at Washington.

Immediately below this picture is the black stone throne or musnud of the Nawab Nazims of Bengal, Behar and Orissa—six feet in diameter and eighteen inches high, with four thick pedestals, the whole hewn out of one block. On one of the sixteen facets into which the rim is cut is an inscription in Persian to the effect that "this auspicious throne was made at Monghyr in Behar by the humblest of slaves, Khajah Nazar of Bokhara, on the 27th Shaban, 1052 of the Hegira," 1641, A.D. It belongs in its origin to the reign of Sultan Shujah, second son of Jehan and Subahdar of Bengal from 1639 to 1647 :and must originally have been kept at Rajmehal or Akbarnagar, as the Mahomedans called it, and afterwards taken first to Dacca and then to Moorshedabad by Moorshed Kuli Khan in 1704. Clive placed Meer Jaffer on this throne after the battle of Plassey in 1757 and saluted him as Nawab Nazim and Subadar of Bengal, Behar and Orissa: and himself took his seat upon it, side by side with Nawab Nazim Sujjum-ud-dowlah when the Company took over the Dewans of Bengal, Behar and Orissa. Drops of reddish liquid are said to issue from certain parts of the stone, which when dried leaves stains. This is due no doubt to the presence of iron, but the popular tradition regards them as tears of sorrow over the downfall of the Nizamat and transfer of the sovereignty of Bengal to the victors of Plassey. It has been absurdly said by a recent Bengalee historian of Moorshedabad that the stone will "shed" no more "tears" since Lord Curzon sat upon it in 1902. The throne has been presented to the Victoria Memorial Hall collection by His Highness the Nawab Bahadur of Moorshedabad, Ameer-ul-Omrah, G.C.I.E., the lineal descendant of Meer Jaffer.

To right and left of the Musnad are two brass cannons. The inscription upon the one to the right, which is the gift of the Nawab Bahadur of Moorshedabad records that it was cast by Kisordas Karmakar, a blacksmith. It belonged to Maharajah Kissen Chand Roy of Nuddea, who played an important part in the revolution which ended in the battle of Plassey. The other is an old Muhamadan gun captured from Aurunzeb's general Meer Jumla by the Assamese in 1662. From Assam it was carried away to Burma, and was taken by the English in 1824 during the first Burmese War and placed in the old Fort at Cuttack. On the completion of the light house at False Point in 1838, it seems to have been removed there and buried in the ground near the light house to hold the flag staff. It was subsequently brought to Calcutta by Captain E. W. Petley, the Port Officer, and presented by him to the Asiatic Society. The inscription upon it states that "this weapon was obtained by Maharajah Svargadev Jayadhavaja Sinha, having vanquished the Musalmans at Gauhati in the Saka year 1584."

Crossing over to the other side of the northern door of the room we find the following portraits. On the other side of doorway is the famous picture of WARREN HASTINGS by A. W. Devis, which formerly hung in the Council-Chamber at Government House and bore the legend *mens aequa in arduis,* to which Macaulay makes reference in the famous passage in his essays. The picture was sent home to be cleaned during the Viceroyalty of Lord Dufferin, when it was deposited under orders of the Secretary of State in the National Portrait Gallery in London and a copy returned to Calcutta which is now to be seen in the Council Chamber and to which the historic legend has been affixed. The original finds itself once more in Calcutta, owing to the courtesy of the Trustees of the National Portrait Gallery.

In the early stages of its career, this portrait by Devis was handed on from one to another of Hastings' friends like a charm, though opinion varied as to its merits as a picture. "After all," says William Larkins, the name-father of Larkins' Lane for whom it was painted, "I can assure you every other part but the face is a mere daub. Yet such as it is, with the Ring now on my little Finger it shall go with the Estate to be purchased as a lasting Monument of your kindness to me, to my Boy, your Namesake and Godson, who regularly salaams to it every Morning after he is dressed, for we both sleep in the same Room with your Resemblance. As for myself you are at my Right Hand upwards of 10 out of each 24 Hours, as that is now the Portion of my life devoted to the Desk." This dearly beloved son, who was "very proud of calling himself Hastings Behaudur," and "often points up to your picture saying Jeetee Ro," died in 1788. Matrimonial troubles had destroyed in poor Larkins the hope of founding a family, and when he quitted India in 1793, he left the portrait with Chapman. Chapman, leaving Calcutta in 1794 for the salt agency of Conti, entrusts to Turner "that excellent portrait done by Devis which many of your Friends agree in thinking by far the best they have seen. It is at present in the Hands of Hudson, a Mezzotinto Scraper, who as far as he had advanced in the Work promises to make from it a most excellent engraving." Turner hung it in the upper hall of the Alipore house, but restored it to Chapman when he was leaving India. At Hay's suggestion, Chapman offered it to the Indian Government, and writes in 1796, "The Picture which I got from Larkins, now fronts that of the Marquis (Cornwallis) in the Government House." Sir John D'Oyly may intend to refer to it when he writes in 1805, "I saw your picture (an abominable one it is true by Zophanee) in a conspicuous place in the Council Chamber," but if this is so, his position as an intimate of Hastings declares him guilty of a very gross misdescription, when he ascribes the authorship to Zoffany.

Below the picture stand an ivory chair and a small table of the same material, which form part of a historic set of furniture. They were a present from Munny Begum, the widow of Meer Jaffer and "Mother of the Company" to Mrs. Warren Hastings, and for many years they were at Daylesford, the English home of Hastings. Their present possessor is the Maharajah of Durbhanga, by whom these pieces have been lent. "The Begum sent me more than one message expressive of her disappointment at my passing the city (Moorshedabad) as she had prepared an elegant display of your couches and chairs for my entertainment," writes Hastings to his wife from Calcutta on November 14th, 1784, "these are since arrived, with a letter for you, recommended most earnestly to my care. There are two couches, eight chairs, and two footstools, all of the former patterns, most delicately formed, and more to my taste than the others: not designed for fat folks nor romps: nor proper for you, my elegant Marian, to use in the presence of your husband." "The Begum" writes Hastings again to his wife on November 20th, 1784, "has sent me two couches, six chairs, and two footstools, of the former patterns. They are highly finished, and I have them all separately and strongly packed: but have not determined on their conveyance. She has added two chairs of buffalo horn, which I like better than the Ivory. They are modest, light and elegant, and as elastic as a Bow. These were all prepared for display in the expectation of my stopping to visit her: and great was her disappointment at my passing. However, they were immediately sent after me with a Letter for you, which I was charged with repeated injunctions to convey carefully and speedily to you."

In the north-east corner is the well-known portrait, by Tilly Kettle, of WARREN HASTINGS, from the collection of the Asiatic Society of Bengal. He is represented sitting at ease in a chair, with face turned a little to the left of the spectator. The dress is of the simplest kind— a fawn-coloured coat, waistcoat, and breeches, a white cravat, white stockings, and black shoes with plain gold buckles. In the distance to the right of the spectator is seen a landscape with a river flowing between high wooded banks.

Below the picture is shown, appropriately enough, the petition filed by Warren Hastings "of Cossimbazar, gentleman" in the old Mayor's Court on the 9th June, 1758, respecting the administration of the estate of Captain John Buchanan, one of the victims of the Black Hole tragedy, whose widow he had married, most probably during the dismal days at Fulta. The petition is accompanied by two other documents: the earlier is an inventory with an account of the proceeds of the property down to March 30th, 1756, and is signed by J. Z. Holwell, as "attorney of Mr. Hastings." The second is a similar and final account, brought down to January 31st, 1763, and is signed by Hastings himself. It had hitherto been supposed that the first Mrs. Hastings was the widow of Captain Dugald Campbell, an officer who was accidentally shot at the capture of Budge-Budge during the operations preceding the entry into Calcutta of the avenging army of Clive and Watson on the 2nd of January, 1757. The statement is repeated by all Hastings's biographers, from Gleig to Sir Alfred Lyall and the writer in the Dictionary of National Biography, and it is to Archdeacon Hyde that the credit is due of establishing, in the course of a paper read by him in 1899 before the Asiatic Society, the correct identity of the lady. In the old Residency burying-ground at Cossimbazar is an epitaph to the memory of Mrs. Mary Hastings and her infant daughter Elizabeth. The date of the former's decease, says Archdeacon Hyde in his paper, is given as July 11th, 1759, but her age was either not accurately known to Hastings, who, according to the epitaph, erected the monument, or else was half obliterated from the stone when the Bengal Government restored the whole in the year 1863, for it reads merely "in the 2 year of her age." Hastings was at the time in the ninth year of his service "making bargains for stuffs with native brokers" as a member of the English factory at Cossimbazar. His wife seems to have died when he was away from her, for in one of his letters of the period he speaks of "that damned trip to Rajemall (which I shall curse whilst I live)."

We next come to a portrait of Major-General the Honourable SIR ARTHUR WELLESLEY, K.B., (1769-1852) created Viscount Wellington of Talavera in 1809, and Duke of Wellington in 1814. There are several repetitions of this interesting portrait, which was painted on twilled canvas by Robert Home in 1804 and was purchased by Government from the painter for Rs. 2,000 in 1805. It formerly hung in the Throne-room at Government House. One of these replicas may be seen in a corridor of Buckingham Palace. It was engraved in mezzotint on a large scale by Charles Turner in 1806. The Duke is represented in uniform standing bareheaded and wearing the Star of the Bath. Behind him to the left is a tent: and to the right are mountains across a distant plain. Tents flying the Union Jack occupy the middle distance, and nearer in front are soldiers exercising at a large gun.

Next the main-entrance are three pictures.

The first is an oil-painting of SIR JAMES FITZ JAMES STEPHEN, K.C.S.I. (1829-1894), Law Member of Council from 1869 to 1872, and a Judge of Her Majesty's High Court of Judicature in England from 1879 to 1891. It is the gift of his son, the Hon. Mr. Justice H. L. Stephen of the Calcutta High Court. In a line with it is an oil-painting of SIR DAVID OCHTERLONY, Bart. (1758-1825), the hero of the Nepal War, whose memory is preserved in Calcutta by the Ochterlony Monument. The picture is presented by his nephew Sir David Ferguson Ochterlony, the present Baronet. Above them both hangs a portrait of SIR SYED AHMED KHAN, Khan Bahadur, K.C.S.I. (1817-1898), founder in 1875 of the well-known Anglo-Oriental College at Aligarh for the education of Mohamedans of the upper class.

The Trustees have several other paintings in other collection of historical portraits, but for the present they cannot be hung for want of room. These include—a portrait of Koonwar Ranaji Maharajah SIR JUNG BAHADUR, G.C.S.I. (1816-1877): Prime Minister of Nepal from 1846 to 1877: an oil-painting from the Government House collection. It was exhibited in the Royal Academy of 1868. A portrait by Robert Home of JAMES CUNNINGHAM GRANT DUFF (1789-1858), Resident at Satara from 1818 to 1822, and author of the history of the Mahrattas. The painting is one of those presented to the Asiatic Society in 1834 by Brigadier and Colonel Home. Grant Duff was a close friend of Mountstuart Elphinstone, who became godfather to his son, the late Sir Mountstuart Elphinstone Grant Duff, who was Governor of Madras from 1881 to 1886, and who died in January, 1906. For five years James Grant maintained himself as Resident at Satara, in the centre of the warlike Mahratta confederacy with only one European companion and a company of infantry; and the arrangements he prescribed both for the management of the Durbar and for the management of the revenue, remained as he left them for many years. He was compelled by ill-health to leave India in 1822: and succeeding about 1825 to the estate of Eden and taking the additional name of Duff, he occupied himself with completing his History of the Mahrattas which was published in 1826.

A portrait by Robert Home of Shah Ghazi-ud-din Hyder, King of Oudh from 1814 to 1827. He is dressed in a canary-yellow chapkan: and strings of pearls and other precious stones encircle his neck and bluish-yellow turban. Ghazi-ud-din Hyder was the first "King of Oudh," so-called. He was the builder of the Kaisar Bagh Tomb, the Shah Najaf, and the Khurshad Manzil, all familiar names in connection with the operations around Lucknow in 1857. His two immediate predecessors were Asaf-ud-Dowlah (1775-1797), the patron of Home and Claude Martin, who removed the capital from Fyzabad to Lucknow, and Saadat Ali Khan (1798-1814) who at the time of his accession was a refugee in British territory and obtained his throne only by the Governor-General's deposition of Wazir Ali, the murderer of Resident Cherry at Benares in 1798. Of Ghazi-ud-din Hyder, Lord Hastings writes in 1814: "His countenance is mild and good, though not betokening energy. The fashion in which he wears his beard, very grey, though he is scarcely forty, is singular. It is just in the state that the beard of one of us in the habit of shaving, would exhibit, if untouched for a week. And this is the case with his upper lip, as well as with the rest." Heber, who visited Lucknow in October, 1824, records in his diary: "I sat for my portrait to Mr. Home four times. He has made several portraits of the King, redolent of youth and radiant with diamonds. He is a good artist indeed for the King of Oudh to have got hold of. He is a quiet gentlemanly old man, brother of the celebrated surgeon in London, and came out to practise as a portrait painter in Madras during Lord Cornwallis' first administration." Home had left Lucknow in 1797 on the death of Asaf-ud-dowlah, but returned in 1808 on the invitation of Saadat Ali, who engaged him on a salary of Rs. 5,000 a year with permission to employ his leisure in private practice. He returned to Calcutta in 1797 and died there about 1834. We may now cross the room once more and make our way into the Royal Gallery, which lies to the south.

Ranged along the eastern wall of this room are a series of oil-paintings. Those numbered 1, 2, 3 and 5 in the list below are the personal gift of His Majesty King Edward the Seventh, and depict some of the chief scenes in the life of the late Queen-Empress. Picture No. 4 has been transferred from the northern ball-room at Government

House, and picture No. 6 was purchased by the Trustees to complete the series :

(1) Her Majesty Queen Victoria receiving the Sacrament at Her Coronation in Westminster Abbey, 10th June, 1837. (After C. H. Leslie, R.A.)

(2) Marriage of Her Majesty Queen Victoria and Prince Albert, in the Chapel Royal, St. James', 10th February, 1841. (After Sir George Hayter).

(3) Christening of His Royal Highness the Prince of Wales (the present King Edward VII.) in St. George's Chapel, Windsor Castle, 28th January, 1842. (After Sir George Hayter).

(4) Portrait of Her Majesty the Queen-Empress Victoria, in full royal robes, crowned and seated on the throne, painted by Sir George Hayter in 1862.

(5) Marriage of Their Royal Highnesses the Prince and Princess of Wales, in St. George's Chapel, Windsor Castle, 10th March, 1863. (After W. P. Frith, R.A.)

(6) First Jubilee Service of Her Majesty Queen Victoria, in Westminster Abbey, 21st June, 1887. (By John O'Connor).

(7) Second Jubilee Service of Her Majesty Queen Victoria at St. Paul's Cathedral, 22nd June, 1897. (After John Charlton).

These pictures will ultimately be placed in the vestibule of the Central Hall of the Memorial Hall, which will be called the Queen's Vestibule, and will be set apart for memorials personal to herself.

At the end of the room and in the centre is a small painting by Sydney P. Hall representing the Investiture of His Highness the Maharajah of Jodhpore with the G.C.S.I., by His Majesty King Edward the Seventh (when Prince of Wales) at a Durbar held on the Maidan at Calcutta on January 1st, 1876. It has been transferred here from the south-east wing on the first floor of Government House. The principal figures in the picture are Lord Northbrook, Sir Dighton Probyn, Lord Cromer (then Major Baring), the Maharajahs of Kashmir, Jeypore, Rewah and Travancore, the Maharajahs Scindia of Gwalior and Holkar of Indore, Sir Salar Jung, Lord Napier of Magdala, Sir Bartle Frere, Sir Charles Aitchison, and Sir Joseph Fayrer.

Upon either side hang full length portraits of King Edward the Seventh and Queen Alexandra, painted in 1863 by Chevalier T. Jensen. These are the gift of Maharajah Surjya Kant Acharjya of Mymensingh. Placed below them are bronze busts of the King and Queen.

Below Mr. Sydney Hall's pictures, and flanked by the bronze busts of the present King and Queen are the writing table and chair, which were in constant use at Windsor Castle by Queen Victoria for her daily correspondence. For many years the writing table contained her private letters and papers. These interesting memorials are the gift of the King-Emperor.

Underneath the picture of the King and Queen are glass cases containing historic letters by Hodson of Hodson's Horse, Malcolm, Sir Thomas Munro, Henry Lawrence, Eyre Coote, Pigot and Macartney and a most interesting document: the *bundobasti* addressed by Hastings to Rajah Gooroo Das, son of Maharajah Nuncomar and lent by the present representative of the family Baboo Debendranath Roy of Kunjaghata near Cossimbazar.

On the west wall are hung the tabard of the Herald at the Delhi Durbar of 1903, and the banderoles of the trumpets and drums together with photographs of the Durbar and original sketches of scenes at the Durbar by Mortimer Menpes. Here too are the following curious oriental miniatures :—

1. Asaf Jah, (Chin-Kilich Khan) Subadar of the Deccan from 1713 and founder in 1740 of the dynasty of the Nizams of Hyderabad. He died in 1748 at the age of 104 and, like Aurangzeb, lies buried at Roza near the caves of Elora.

2. Shah Jehan, (1628-1658): father of Aurungzeb.

3. Amir Chand of Jaipur, (drawn by Gobind Ram Patel).

4. Maharajah Siwai Jai Singh of Jaipur, (1699-1743): founder of the present dynasty of the State in 1728.

5. Guru Govind Singh, (1661-1708): the tenth Sikh Guru and remodeller of the Sikh Government.

6. Nur Mahal Begum or Nur Jehan, the famous Empress, wife of Jehangir.

7. Major-General Claude Martin, (1735-1800).

8. Sultan Farruck Siyar, (1713-1719): the Ferruckseer of Surman's Embassy and of the famous inscription in St. John's Churchyard in memory of Surgeon William Hamilton.

9. Aurungzebe Alamgir, (1659-1707), with his sons

Muhammad Sultan and Sultan Akbar; presented by Dr. Denison Ross.

10. Muhammud Sultan, (1719-1748).

11. A group of Miniatures of Moghul Emperors.

12. Five portraits of Moghul Emperors.

Arranged in a glass case along the western wall are letters from Lake, and other historical personages: and two documents of exceptional interest presented by Lord Curzon: the last letter written by Queen Victoria to India dated 14th December, 1900, and conveying to the "Vice Roy" her appreciation of the sympathy expressed by the people of India at the death in South Africa of Prince Christian Victor: and the signed message sent by King Edward the Seventh to be read by Lord Curzon as Viceroy at the Delhi Coronation Durbar on January, 1903.

Below the portrait of the Duke of Wellington are more documents bearing the signatures of Hastings, Francis, Ochterlony, and Jonathan Duncan, Governor of Bombay from 1795 to 1801.

Down the centre of the room is arranged an extremely valuable collection of arms lent by the chief feudatory princes and nobles of the Empire, which will well repay a close examination. Among the donors are the Nizam, the Maharajah of Mysore, the Begum of Bhopal, the Maharani of Udaipur, the Maharajahs of Patiala, Jeypore, Jodhpore, Ulwar, Rewah, Bikanir, the Maharao Rajah of Bundi, the Nawabs of Tonk and Bahawalpore, the Maharao of Kotah, the Rajahs of Jhind, Rutlam and Hill Tipperah, the Maharawal of Jeysulmere, the Raj Rana of Jhallawar, the Nawab Bahadur of Moorshedabad, the

Nawab of Banganapalle and the Maharajah of Sonbarsa. Upon the occasion of the Prince of Wales's visit in January, 1906, it was observed that there was no part of the Memorial Hall collection which appeared to afford him greater interest and pleasure than this.

We now return to the first room and cross over into the third room which lies to its north. Along the western wall are cases containing various objects of interest, chiefly presented by the Nawab Bahadur of Moorshidabad. Among them may be specially noticed some magnificiently illuminated Korans and an embroidered *Kanat* or screen, which surrounded the camp of the invading Mahrattas, and was looted by Ali Verdi Khan about the year 1746. The Maharatta Ditch which once encircled Calcutta remained for half a century to keep in remembrance the invasions of Bengal by the Mahratta hordes.

The following is a list of the engravings on the screens down the middle of the room, beginning with the right hand side of the southern screen :—

1. Robert Cornelis Napier, first Lord Napier of Magdala, (1810-1890): Commander-in-Chief in India, 1870-1876.

2. Sir Charles James Napier, (1782-1863): conqueror of Scinde (*peccavi*), Commander-in-Chief in India, 1849-1850.

3. Lieut.-Col. Arthur Wellesley, (1769-1852).

4. The same.

5. General Sir William Nott, (1782-1845).

6. Sir Henry Havelock, (1795-1857).

7. Stringer Lawrence, (1697-1775): the "father of the Indian Army."

8. Hugh, first Baron Gough of Ching Kiangfoo in China and Maharajpore and Sutlej in the East Indies: and Viscount Gough of Gujarat and Limerick, (1779-1869): Commander-in-Chief in India, 1843-1849.

9. The same.

10. Brigadier General Sir John Eardley Wilmot Inglis, (1814-1862): the Defender of Lucknow.

11. Sir Robert Henry Sale: (1782-1845) "Fighting Bob" Sale of Jellalabad: killed at the battle of Moodkee.

12. Major-General John Jacob, (1812-1858): of Jacob's Horse and Jacobabad.

13. Admiral Sir Richard King, Bart. (1730-1806), Vice-Admiral of the Red and C. in C. at the Nore: served on Admiral Watson's flagship in the East Indies in 1754-57: commanded the landing party at the capture of Fort William and Hooghly in January, 1757: and took home Watson's despatches to the Admiralty.

14. Lieut.-General Sir George Nugent, Bart. (1757-1849): Commander-in-Chief in India, 1811-1813.

15. Sir David Ochterlony, (1758-1825).

16. Sir James Hope Grant, (1808-1875): Commander-in-Chief at Madras 1861-1865.

17. Brigadier-General John Nicholson, (1821-1857).

18. Sir John Malcolm, (1769-1833): from the statue in Westminster Abbey.

19. General Sir George Hewitt, Bart., (1750-1840): Commander-in-Chief in India, 1807-1811.

20. General Sir George Pollock, (1786-1872): relieved Sale at Jellalabad in 1842: Military Member of Council 1844-1847.

.ue

engravings of Warren Hastings, ...em obtained from Miss Marian Winter, and including one of the bust in the Hastings Temple at Melchet Park, Wiltshire, erected by Major John Osborne in 1800.

On the Eastern wall of the rooms are rare guns, musical instruments, models and trophies, connected with memorable events in the history of India.

In the Northern corner of the room, at the entrance to the fourth and last gallery, is the original of the famous Allahabad treaty of 1765, by which the Dewany was granted to the Company. It contains the signatures of Shah Alum, who had come from Delhi, and of Clive and Carnac who had come from Moorshedabad with authority from the Nawab Nazim Nazim-ud-Dowlah.

The most prominent object in the fourth gallery, (which lies to the north of the third) is the well-known painting from the Government House collection in which John Zephaniah Holwell is represented superintending the building of the obelisk erected by him in memory of his fellow-sufferers who perished in the Black Hole. The monument was removed in 1821, but has since been replaced by a facsimile on the former site at the N.-W., corner of Dalhousie Square. The picture formerly hung in Government House on the north-eastern staircase between the first and second floors, and was through the exertions of Dr. Busteed purchased by direction of Lord Lansdowne in 1892, from the widow of one of the Governor's descendants in nada. A grandson of Holwell, Sir Richard James Holwell Birch (1803-1875) distinguished himself in the Sikh wars of 1845 and 1848: and was Secretary to the Government of India in the Military Department from 1852 to 1861: holding that office during the Mutiny year. In this gallery has also been placed a small picture representing the departure on February 25th, 1792, of the sons of Tippoo Sultan from their Father. It formerly hung on the south-east staircase of Government House. The authorship is ascribed by some to A. W. Devis, by others to Robert Home.

In this gallery there may also be seen most interesting models of Old Fort William (scale 10ft. = 1 inch), the Black Hole (scale 6 ft. = 1 inch) and the Battle-field of Plassey. On the walls are a series of engravings of old Calcutta by Lambert and Scott (1736), the brothers Daniel (1796), Salt (1809), Fraser (1824-25); and various plans of old Fort William and Maps of Calcutta; also engravings of historical pictures, such as Singleton's "Assault of Seringapatam and last effort of Tippoo," Sir David Wilkie's "Discovery of the Body of Tippoo by Sir David Baird" and others. In the centre of the room on a revolving stand is a series of photographs of Governors-General from Warren Hastings to Lord Curzon. One vacant space only has been left.

The Oriental Manuscripts which have been brought together, make a display such as can be surpassed in no European Library. Their number is small, but every one is a gem. Especially interesting is a complete Koran in the handwriting of the Emperor Aurangzeb.

21. Sir William Peel, V.C., K.C.B., (1824-1858).

22. Mr. John Adam: Acting Governor-General: January August 1823.

23. George, first Earl Macartney, (1737-1806): Governor of Madras, 1781-1785.

24. Joseph Hume, M.P., (1777-1855).

25. Admiral Charles Watson, (1713-1757): "Calcutta freed, January, 11th, 1757: Chandernagore taken March 23rd, 1757."

26. Anne, Countess of Mornington, mother of the Marquess Wellesley and the Duke of Wellington, whose busts are in the picture. Engraved by Thomas Hodgetts in December 1837, from the painting by Lady Burghersh.

27. Edward Geoffrey Stanley, 14th Earl of Derby, (1826-1893) Prime Minister in 1852, 1858, and 1866: and Secretary of State for India as Lord Derby 1858-59. Author of the Queen's Proclamation of 1858.

28. Colonel Colin Mackenzie, (1753-1821) Surveyor-General of Madras, 1810, and of India 1816, with his Brahmin Surveyors.

29. Edmund Burke, (1729-1797).

30. Major-General Claude Martin, (1735-1800)

31. Henry Dundas, first Viscount Melville (1742-1811): Member of the Board of Control in 1784 and President from 1793 to 1801.

32. Sir John Macpherson, Bart., (1745-1821): Governor-General of India from 1785 to 1786. (After George Richmond).

33. Sir Henry Montgomery Lawrence, K.C.B., (1806-1857).

34. Sir Colin Campbell, Lord Clyde, (1792-1863): Commander-in-Chief in India, 1857-1860.

35. The same.

On the opposite or left hand side of screens, beginning at the northern end :—

36. Mountstuart Elphinstone, (1779-1859): Governor of Bombay, 1819-1827.

37. John Laird Lawrence, first Lord Lawrence.

38. Charlotte Elizabeth, Countess Canning, (1817-1861): died and lies buried in Barrackpore Park.

39. The same.

40. Charles John, first Earl Canning, (1812-1862): Governor-General of India, 1856: first Viceroy 1858-62.

41. The same.

42. Henry Hardinge, first Viscount Hardinge of Lahore, (1785-1856): Governor-General of India, 1844-1848.

43. The same.

44. Lord Melville, (see No. 31).

45. William Butterworth Bayley, (1782-1860): Acting Governor-General, 1828.

46. Marquess of Hastings, (1754-1826): Governor-General of India, 1813-1823.

47. Lord William Bentinck, (1774-1839): Governor-General of India, 1828 to 1835.

48. Lord Hastings (as Earl of Moira.)

49. Lord Wellesley: a set of four.

50. Sir John Shore, Bart., created Lord Teignmouth in 1798, (1751-1834): Governor General of India, 1793-1798.

51. Lord Cornwallis, (1738-1805).

52. The same: an engraving of the statue in the Calcutta Town Hall.

53. A Series of twelve engravings of Warren Hastings, most of them obtained from Miss Marian Winter, and including one of the bust in the Hastings Temple at Melchet Park, Wiltshire, erected by Major John Osborne in 1800.

On the Eastern wall of the rooms are rare guns, musical instruments, models and trophies, connected with memorable events in the history of India.

In the Northern corner of the room, at the entrance to the fourth and last gallery, is the original of the famous Allahabad treaty of 1765, by which the Dewany was granted to the Company. It contains the signatures of Shah Alum, who had come from Delhi, and of Clive and Carnac who had come from Moorshedabad with authority from the Nawab Nazim Nazim-ud-Dowlah.

The most prominent object in the fourth gallery, (which lies to the north of the third) is the well-known painting from the Government House collection in which John Zephaniah Holwell is represented superintending the building of the obelisk erected by him in memory of his fellow-sufferers who perished in the Black Hole. The monument was removed in 1821, but has since been replaced by a facsimile on the former site at the N.-W., corner of Dalhousie Square. The picture formerly hung in Government House on the north-eastern staircase between the first and second floors, and was through the exertions of Dr. Busteed purchased by direction of Lord Lansdowne in 1892, from the widow of one of the Governor's descendants in

Canada. A grandson of Holwell, Sir Richard James Holwell Birch (1803-1875) distinguished himself in the Sikh wars of 1845 and 1848: and was Secretary to the Government of India in the Military Department from 1852 to 1861: holding that office during the Mutiny year. In this gallery has also been placed a small picture representing the departure on February 25th, 1792, of the sons of Tippoo Sultan from their Father. It formerly hung on the south-east staircase of Government House. The authorship is ascribed by some to A. W. Devis, by others to Robert Home.

In this gallery there may also be seen most interesting models of Old Fort William (scale 10ft. = 1 inch), the Black Hole (scale 6 ft. = 1 inch) and the Battle-field of Plassey. On the walls are a series of engravings of old Calcutta by Lambert and Scott (1736), the brothers Daniel (1796), Salt (1809), Fraser (1824-25); and various plans of old Fort William and Maps of Calcutta; also engravings of historical pictures, such as Singleton's "Assault of Seringapatam and last effort of Tippoo," Sir David Wilkie's "Discovery of the Body of Tippoo by Sir David Baird" and others. In the centre of the room on a revolving stand is a series of photographs of Governors-General from Warren Hastings to Lord Curzon. One vacant space only has been left.

The Oriental Manuscripts which have been brought together, make a display such as can be surpassed in no European Library. Their number is small, but every one is a gem. Especially interesting is a complete Koran in the handwriting of the Emperor Aurangzeb.

CENTRAL GALLERY.

EAST WALL.

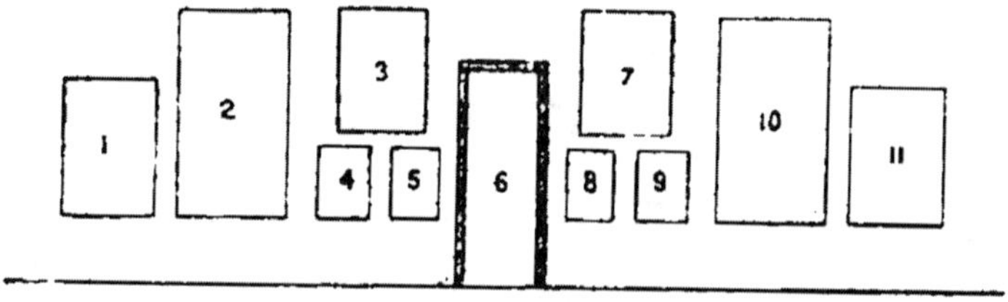

(1) Warren Hastings, (Kettle); (2) Duke of Wellington; (3) Sir Syed Ahmed; (4) Sir J. Fitz James Stephen; (5) Sir D. Ochterlony; (6) Door; (7) Sir Madhava Rao; (8—9) Sir W. Jones; (10) Marquis Wellesley; (11) Marquis of Hastings.

SOUTH WALL.

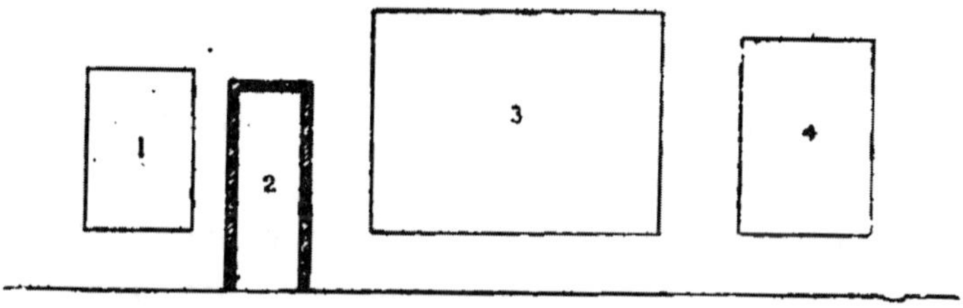

(1) Sir Elijah Impey; (2) Door; (3) State Entry into Delhi, (Mackenzie); (4) Lord Lake.

NORTH WALL.

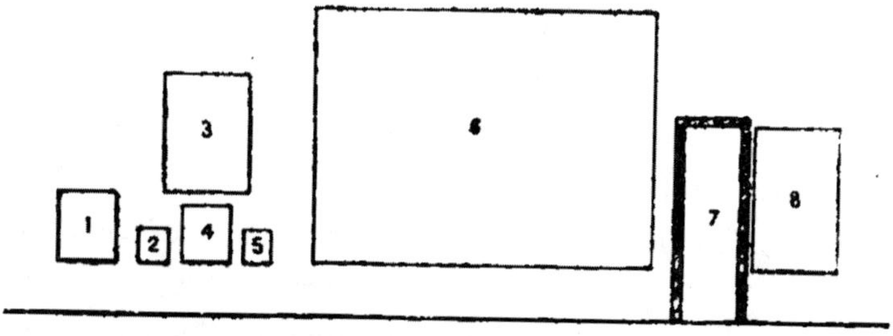

(1) Keshub Chunder Sen; (2) J. C. Marshman; (3) Sir Bartle Frere; (4) Sir J. Malcolm; (5) Sivaji; (6) Verestchagin Picture; (7) Door; (8) Warren Hastings, (Devis).

CHAPTER XV.

THE FORT WILLIAM OF TO-DAY.

THE history of Old Fort William has furnished the theme for many a student and enquirer: but its modern namesake has met with little favour as a subject for investigation. Until recently there was little published information obtainable upon the subject. But in 1902 there were published for private circulation some interesting and instructive notes by Major Churchill of the Royal Garrison Artillery: and two years later the late Dr. C. R. Wilson contributed in July, 1904, an article on the same subject to the *Calcutta Review*. There is, however, little to be said of the modern Fort William from a historical point of view. It has stood no siege, no gun has ever been fired against an enemy from its ramparts, and its baptism of fire is yet to come. And it must be confessed that the story of its building which has hitherto almost entirely occupied the attention of its chroniclers, makes neither pleasant nor edifying reading. Its lines were laid by Clive in August, 1757, upon his return to Calcutta after setting Meer Jaffer on the throne of Bengal. In the previous May a scheme had been brought forward by Captain Robert Barker, afterwards Commander-in-Chief, for the placing of the New Fort in the very centre of the Settlement. He examined the ground eastward of the old factory, and reported that "with a little expense" a proper spot might be cleared to the distance of about six hundred yards sufficient for a fort and an esplanade. Two months later, Captain John

Brohier, who was in the same year to level the houses and fortifications of Chandernagore with the ground, came forward with another proposal to build a hexagonal citadel to the south of the "old Dock," which stood somewhere about Bankshall Street. Three of the sides were to flank the river, and extensive works were to be carried round the town to a point above the Portuguese and Armenian Churches. On this line the houses were to be demolished for the space of at least five hundred yards, and the owners were to be provided for in the "Park," which was to be laid out in streets. The suggestion was considered by the Committee of Fortifications, and Clive arrived from Moorshedabad just in time to prevent the carrying into effect of the orders, which were actually given, to pull down all the buildings south of the Dock and of the Park. Clive's conception of a suitable site was of a different kind. On the riverside to the south of the settlement was the village of Gobindpore, founded two centuries earlier by the Setts and Bysacks, the Hindoo Fathers of Calcutta: and surrounding it was a thick tiger jungle which could be easily cut down. The whole colony, with their tutelary deity Gobindjee and its historic shrine, migrated to the north of Calcutta, and liberal compensation in money and in grants of lands was made to them for their dispossession. But the difficulties of the English had only just begun. When Brohier commenced work at the end of October, 1757, he could not get the labourers he required. Orders forbidding the employment of labour by private persons were repeated more than once but produced no effect. In 1762 the Engineer renewed his complaint of being in constant want of workmen, and was empowered by Government to seize all the bricklayers in Calcutta; but coercion continued of no avail. Four years later, the Engineer reported that of a thousand bricklayers in the Company's service all but twenty-three had been "seduced by private persons who gave greater wages." Finally, in 1768 the Council ordered that no person whatever residing within the Company's limits or under their protection should commence new buildings of any kind in or about Calcutta until they should think proper to revoke such order, and that all workmen not registered as engaged upon buildings already in hand should be seized for the public service. These orders were re-issued in January 1770 and proclaimed by beat of drum: and by the month of June the number of workmen employed on the Fort was returned at 10,000. But by March of the following year, the Engineer again complains that not more than three or four thousand men had been granted to him for the past seven months. The cunettes and ditches and the great sluice cannot be finished before the rainy season, he declares, unless another five thousand men are provided, and yet "if these works are retarded, the health of the garrison must suffer." The supply of material was as painful a source of difficulty and trouble as the supply of labour. The contractors took their time, and when they failed in their contracts, the Government had no hold over them if they resided outside the Mahratta Ditch. The only course was to apply to the Resident of Moorshedabad and direct him to use his influence with the Nawab Nazim to recover the penalty.

The Fort William was finally completed about the year

1773, at a cost of two millions sterling: at least five lakhs of this amount was spent in piles to ward off encroachment by the river which, as it happens, has receded in exactly the opposite direction. A contemporary account as given of the Fort in its earlier days has survived. "We are invited to dine in the New Fort," says Miss Sophia Goldborne in 1780, "at the Commanding Officer's, the Fort Major, whose house is situated within its circumference: and it is deemed one of the finest forts in the world, has a chain across the river, to secure the harbour from invasion, covers nearly five miles of ground, and has all the bustling charms of a garrison." A later description has been left for us by Mrs. Fay. "The town of Calcutta reaches along the eastern bank of the Hooghly: as you come up past Fort William and the Esplanade, it has a beautiful appearance. Esplanade Row, as it is called, which fronts the Fort, seems to be composed of palaces; the whole range, except what is taken up by the Government and Council Houses, is occupied by the principal gentlemen in the settlement, no person being allowed to reside in Fort William but such as are attached to the Army. Our Fort is also so well kept and everything in such excellent order, that it is quite a curiosity to see it, all the slopes, banks and ramparts are covered with the richest verdure, which completes the enchantment of the scene." Mrs. Fay's original letters from India were not published until 1817, but they relate to her residence in Calcutta in 1780 and the succeeding years: and the picture she draws in the words just quoted must be referred to that period. At an earlier date it would seem that it was proposed to allow private individuals to build residences in the

Fort: for we find the Dutch Admiral Stavorinus, who visited Calcutta about 1770, writing that "permission has likewise been given to every inhabitant of Calcutta to build, if he chooses it, a house in the Fort, provided it be equally bombproof: but in the year 1770 no one had yet felt any inclination to avail himself of this privilege."

There are seven gates to the Fort: the *Calcutta Gate,* leading to the Eden Gardens: the *Plassey Gate* to the south of Government House, called *Lall Darwaza* in the vernacular, possibly because it leads to the Lall Diggee in "Tank Square" and to Lall Bazar: the *Chowringhee or Royal Gate,* which faces Chowringhee; the *Treasury Gate,* above which is the official residence in Calcutta of the Commander-in-Chief in India, known in the vernacular as the *Pias darwaza* or Thirsty Gate, from the proximity of the old drinking tanks and reservoirs: the *Hospital Gate,* which faces the Racecourse: *St. George's Gate,* which derives its vernacular name of *Cooly Darwaza,* from the fact that it gives access on the south to the suburb of Hastings or Cooly Bazar: and the *Water Gate* or *Pani Darwaza,* facing the river bank near the Gwalior Monument. The various bastions have also names allotted to them. In 1766 they were known as the King's, Queen's, Prince of Wales' and Duke of Cumberland's Bastions, and the demibastions were distinguished as the Duke of York's and the King of Prussia's.

The Fort mounts about 600 guns of various calibres. The Garrison consists of one European regiment and one regiment of Native Infantry, together with one Battery of Garrison Artillery. The Fort is said to be capable of containing 10,000 men. Within the last few years, the most exposed portions of the Fort have been protected by guns of heavy calibre, and among them, some of 10 tons have been mounted on the battlements.

The Glacis and Esplanade is regarded as an appanage of the Fort, and is under the control of Government. It includes the space bounded by the Esplanade Row on the north, Chowringhee Road on the west, the River on the east, and Tolly's Nullah on the south.

In form Fort William is an irregular octagon, with five sides towards the land, and three towards the river. It is surrounded by a dry ditch which, however, can be filled with water by a sluice from the river. The whole of the defences are faced and palisaded with great care, and are kept in admirable condition. The works however are very little raised above the surrounding country, and do not present an imposing appearance externally. The Commander-in-Chief resides over the Treasury Gate: and each of the other gates has likewise a house over it used as the residences of the Brigadier commanding the Presidency District and the Chief Staff Officers of the Garrison. Within are fine ranges of Barracks for the accommodation of European and Native Troops, the Arsenal, Store-rooms, Magazines; also extensive Parade Grounds. Entering from the Chowringhee Gate, you pass through what was (before the Cyclone of 1864) a noble avenue of trees leading to the Outram Institute. This building, in spite of its present use as a soldiers' institute and garrison school, still goes by the name of Government House. It bears a tablet which explains the cause: for it bears the following inscription: "This house was built for the Governor-General and was sometimes occupied by him. Bishop Heber was accommodated in it by Lord Amherst when he first arrived in India in October, 1823." It has been asserted that the house was never as a fact occupied by a Governor-General. But the *Calcutta Gazette* of September 15th, 1779, records that when Lord Wellesley returned to Fort William from Madras in that year, he proceeded to the gates of the Fort and thence to the Government House "upon arrival in the Fort." Similarly, when the "new Government House" was ready for occupation in April 1802, we learn from the *Gazette* that Wellesley made his entry into it in state by way of Old Court House Street. "the troops being drawn up in a street, through which His Lordship passed, from the present Government House." And as early as 1786, on the occasion of Lord Cornwallis' arrival in Calcutta, we are told that he was met at the water side by a party of the Bodyguard and that he walked thence to the Fort, where his reception was public. The commission investing him with the powers of Governor-General and Commander-in-Chief was then read and he retired to breakfast, presumably at the Government House in the Fort. And even after the new Government House was occupied, it continued to be used for the accommodation of distinguished persons. When Lord William Bentinck visited Calcutta in the summer of 1805 in the capacity of Governor of Fort St. George, the official account of his reception in the Government *Gazette*, of July 4th, of that year distinctly states that His Lordship "arrived in the Hooghly River on the 27th June 1805, on board His Majesty's ship "Rattle Snake," Captain Lye.

His Lordship immediately proceeded to Fort William and was met by the Military Secretary and aide-de-camp to the Governor-General and the Town Major, who had been sent in the Government vessels to conduct his Lordship to Fort William." At six o'clock in the evening His Lordship "attended by the state boats and the band of the Governor-General landed at the Water Gate of Fort William and was received by the Commanding Officer, the Garrison Staff and several officers of the Governor-General's staff. His Lordship was then conducted through a street of troops to the Government House in the Fort which had been prepared for his reception." From these illustrations it is clear that the Government House in the Fort was in regular occupation and that at one time the Governor-General himself resided there. The custom in fact would appear to have been for the incoming Governor-General to make his official arrival in Fort William, and as he was officially Governor-General of Fort William in Bengal, such an arrangement was entirely natural and appropriate.

The Government House in Fort William is thus described by Heber, who was accommodated there on his arrival in Calcutta in 1823. "The house consisted of a lofty and well proportioned hall, 40 feet by 25 feet, a drawing room of the same length, and six or seven rooms all on the same floor, one of which served as a Chapel, the lower story being chiefly occupied as offices or lobbies. All these rooms were lofty, with many doors and windows on every side, the floors of plaster covered with mats, the ceilings of bricks, plastered also, flat, and supported by massive beams, which were visible from the rooms below, but being painted neatly had not at all a bad effect. Punkas, large frames of wood covered with white cotton, and looking not unlike enormous fire-boards, hung from the ceiling of the principal apartments : to which cords were fastened, which were drawn backwards and forwards by one or more servants, so as to agitate and cool the air very agreeably. The walls were white and unadorned except with a number of glass lamps filled with cocoanut oil, and the furniture, though sufficient for the climate, was scanty in comparison with that of an English house. The beds instead of curtains had mosquito nets : they were raised high from the ground and very hard, admirably adapted for a hot climate." This description will enable us to understand why Wellesley speedily tired of his temporary quarters and took possession of the house at Barrackpore which until then had belonged to the Commander-in-Chief. Upon the deposition in February, 1856 of Wajid Ali Shah, the last King of Oudh, he was brought down to Calcutta and lodged in this building in the Fort. He occupied it for three years before he went to the Palace in Garden Reach. Since then, it has been a garrison or Regimental Institute, being called the "Outram Institute."

Of the existing barracks, the oldest are the North and South Barracks and the Royal Barracks. The last named was completed in 1764, but the work of construction was apparently of a defective character, for a quarter of a century later it is announced in the *Calcutta Gazette* that "the foundation of the Royal Barracks in Fort William do not answer the expectation conceived respecting them, but on the contrary, they appear not sufficiently firm to support the weight of such a heavy structure." The North and South Barracks are of shortly later date, and were originally used as officers' quarters. In *Hicky's Gazette* of Saturday February 18th, 1780, there may be seen an advertisement of the offer of a reward of 100 sicca rupees for the recovery of certain articles stolen from the officers residing in the North and South Barracks.

The present Granary Barrack was from 1871 until a few years ago the military prison, but the tablet on the walls of the building affords clear indication of the purpose for which it was originally intended. The inscription on the black stone slab which is 3 feet long by 20 inches high runs: "This building contains 51,258 maunds of rice and 20,023½ maunds of paddy which were deposited by order of the Governor-General and Council, under the inspection and charge of John Belli, Agent for Providing Victualling Stores to this Garrison, in the months of March, April and May, 1782." The original building is 90½ feet broad by 127 feet long and about 25 feet high. It is built of brick in lime, and the external walls are 5 feet 3 inches thick. After the construction of the military prison it was found necessary to strengthen the bay at the south-west and to build up a cross wall to support the arch. There are eight bays of twelve spans and each cross wall has four arched openings of 12 feet span. The fifteenth charge against Warren Hastings at his impeachment was: "That he appointed his Private Secretary John Belli, Esquire, to be Agent for the Supply of Stores and Provisions for the

Garrison of Fort William in Bengal with a commission of thirty per cent."* A reference to Gleig's memoir shows that the erection of the granary and the provision of this enormous store of grain was part of a scheme devised by Hastings to avert a repetition of the great famine of 1770, which was said to have carried off no less than 76,000 persons in the streets of Calcutta in the course of three months. A chain of granaries was proposed on the banks of the two great rivers, to be built of solid masonry, and filled in time of plenty for use in years of scarcity. Writing to a friend in England on October 15th, 1783, Hastings says: "I have begun such a provision in the Fort, where we have bottled up 70,000 maunds and I do not intend to uncork it till it has stood twenty years." At Bankipore is a similar golah or granary, with walls 12 feet thick and pierced by four doors, one on each side. It is famous for the wonderful echo, the slightest movement or sound being repeated a hundred fold: but it has never been put to any practical purpose. The doors in fact open inwards, rendering its use an impossibility and it stands as a monument of a colossal mistake. The inscription upon it records that it was erected by Captain John Garstin, the architect of the Calcutta Town Hall "in part of a general plan ordered by the Governor-General in Council, 20th of January, 1784, for the perpetual prevention of famine in these provinces."

Of the low building in the St. George's Ravelin just beyond the second gateway, now used by the band of the

* The voting upon this charge was—Not guilty 23, guilty 3.

native regiment, Major Churchill says in his Notes that it was used as a place of confinement for the French prisoners captured during the war of the closing years of the eighteenth and opening years of the nineteenth century. That there was such a prison is clear: the *Calcutta Gazette* of January 7th, 1808, records that "in the course of Monday night, eighteen of the French prisoners of war, confined in Fort William, continued to make their escape by cutting a hole through the building in which they were confined. They are supposed to have gone down the river towards Kedgeree in the hope of seizing a pilot schooner or some other small vessel in which they may endeavour to get to sea. There is, however, much probability that their design will be frustrated, from the promptitude and alacrity with which they have been pursued. The opening through which the French prisoners escaped was so small that they must have forced their way through it with the utmost difficulty. The sentinels were at their post, but from the darkness of the night and the silence with which the escape was effected, no alarm or suspicion occurred until the following morning."

While in the Fort the visitor will do well to direct his steps towards the Water-Gate, near which is the arsenal. There can be little doubt that the arsenal is rightly conjectured to stand on the site of the old Artillery Barracks and gun-sheds. It is one of the sights of Calcutta and is well worth the bestowal of a spare hour: but it is necessary to procure a pass from the ordnance officer in charge, if admittance is desired. The building contains many interesting and instructive relics and trophies in the shape of colours taken from the enemy and others worn out by service in scenes of duty and of glory. The Armoury is a magnificent room, built under the orders of Warren Hastings, Governor-General of India, in 1777. Over the entrance is the following inscription: "Anno Domini 1777. These arms were arranged by order and under the auspices of the Honourable Warren Hastings, Esquire. Governor-General."

In the Pattern Room will be found samples of almost every shot and shell invented, and the deadliness of the shrapnell and the penetrating power of the palliser "chilled" can be leisurely examined. The old chain shot and many other early ideas in the missiles of war are represented. Our allies in Afghanistan have evidently progressed in the manufacture of ammunition, for in this section will be seen some very well made case shot and shell for *rifled* guns, also Cabul arms, consisting of carbines, long knives, swords, &c., brought to Calcutta by the Boundary Commission. The apparatus for firing rockets, blue lights, and also samples of hand grenades (for throwing over the walls of forts) and other offensive combustibles arrest attention, while the machine for testing cracks and other damages in large guns, the mountain battery equipments for camels and elephants, and an ingenious reversible bit for artillery horses deserve more than passing notice. Arranged on the walls are complete sets of tools issued to the army, comprising those for carpenters, blacksmiths, farriers, masons, etc. The sets of Afghan harness, brought over by Sir West Ridgeway, will be inspected with interest as shewing what the people are capable of. Here also will be seen a magazine rifle of newest pattern, and in close proximity a Brown Bess as used in the Crimean war; a Remington rifle from Egypt, and a musket with flints and bayonet, said to have been picked up on the field of Waterloo, in fact nearly all small arms from that date, including a Sharp's carbine, with winding tape and detonators, and early breech loaders. These form a very interesting group. Several trophies are exhibited, but mostly they have been fixed so high that the dates and mottoes on the *guidons* or bannerets are scarcely readable. There are some "Jehad" flags with crescent design taken from the Mahomedan regiments during the mutiny, and hanging close by, which will surely interest every European who gazes on them, the small flags of the Calcutta Volunteer Cavalry Guard of 1857. There are also old flags of the 7th B. C. (1805), 14th B. L. C. (1797) and the 62nd B. I., all silent evidences of good work done by those regiments in past years.

In the Main Armoury the visitor will be struck with the completeness of the arrangements and the thorough order and condition of the many thousands of weapons, ready for issue, he sees racked around him. An opportunity is given of studying the rapid strides made with regard to the manufacture of arms of all kinds. The swivel guns for forts, the successive Enfield, Snider, Martini-Henry and Magazine rifles, Pistols, Carbines (all designs and ages), together with swords for camp followers and a peculiarly useful sword for Pioneers, which forms at once an efficient and offensive weapon, being both sword and saw, are all displayed as it were in chronological order. In the centre of the room there is a capital specimen of a three pounder brass gun turned out in the Cossipore Gun Factory in 1845, and it bears comparison with others (among them a Whitworth) which have been imported from the old country. Here may be seen some quaint looking old sword-bayonets for rifles. They are over 2½ feet in length, and were in common use in 1857-8. The three edged sword with brass guard of Paris make (date not legible) forms an interesting curio.

On view also is a collection of guns captured by the British forces. These include Persian brass guns (179- taken in the Persian War; Spanish guns bearing the date 1721, with the Crown and name of Philip V. embossed upon them: these guns (some taken in Goa) are highly finished specimens and most elaborately ornamented with various designs. There are also guns from Kandahar and Thibet, and some taken at the siege of Seringapatam, dated 1790. There are numbers of old guns of various calibres lying about the court-yard, many of them having done the State good service in the days of the E. I. Company. On the ground floor attention will be drawn to the Park Artillery, which comprises a splendid stock of the newer classes of ordnance now in use, *viz.*, the Hotchkiss, Nordenfeldt, Gatling and Maxim guns.

The autograph book of the armoury is well worth inspection. Many distinguished visitors have been requested to inscribe their names and weights in the book, amongst other the late Duke of Edinburgh. Many Rajahs and Maharajahs have been weighed in the arsenal weighing chair and have left their names and weights on record. In 1786 the Fort was inspected by the Nawab Nazim of Bengal, Behar and Orissa, the titular sovereign of the province, in company with Lord Cornwallis, the Governor-General. One of the places he visited was the arsenal: and we learn from the *Gazette* of the day also that "the great guns were exercised and several shells thrown at which His Excellency and the Nawab expressed much satisfaction."

The Bazar, says Major Churchill, is one of the oldest existing buildings in the Fort, and was erected about the year 1787. From the Government *Gazette* of August 30th of that year, we learn that "the plan of a new pucka bazar in Fort William, as intended by Sir John Macpherson" (Hastings' successor as Governor-General,) "and laid out by the Chief Engineer, is now completed, with many extensive improvements, under the eye of the Commandant, whose cares seem to extend to the repair and correction of every abuse within the garrison. The new shops in this Bazar are all registered and the tariff of rates is precisely fixed and under such nice checks as to prevent every imposition of the natives: none are retained in it without a special license of the Commandant, and previously subscribing to all the rules and restrictions within which he has thought proper to confine their conduct." The old bazar, according to the same contemporary chronicler, had presented a very different appearance. It was "composed of an irregular and confused heap of straw huts, and not only collected filth and threatened contagion, but proved in fact an asylum for every thief that escaped the hands of justice in Calcutta. Robberies were daily committed without the possibility of detection, and the servants of officers corrupted and reduced either by example or the early opportunities offered them of disposing of the property of their masters: while a dark arcanum of roguery was to be met with in every corner of the bazar, and an alchymist ready who could without any decomposition of its parts convert by a few strokes of the hammer a silver spoon into a pair of bracelets in a trice."

Adjoining the Outram Institute is the Fort Church, dedicated to St. Peter. The original garrison church (according to Major Churchill) was built about the year 1785, and in design was intended (it is said) to resemble the Chapel of Trinity Hall, Cambridge. However this may be, there was evidently no Fort Church in 1798, for in that year the Military Department published a notification in the *Gazette* inviting plans and tenders for the construction of a chapel in the Fort. Nothing further appears to have been done in the matter for twenty years: but on Thursday, July 25th, 1822, the foundation-stone of St. Peter's Church, Fort William, was laid with full masonic ceremonial. The ceremony of consecration was not performed until 1828: although the building had been in use for at least three years previously. It contains a number of interesting monuments: almost every campaign of recent years being represented. The Afghan War of 1841-42 and the fatal retreat from Cabul contributes four tablets. Colonel Anquetil, Commander of Shah Sujah's force, who was massacred at Jugdulluck, is commemorated by another tablet in St. John's Church. Colonel W. A. Dennie, C.B., of the 13th Light Infantry, ("Fighting Bob" Sale's regiment) who fell before Jellalabad while leading a column upon the Afghan force under Akbar Khan, is a second hero of the same period. The personal narrative of his campaigns, published after his death by W. A. Steele, must be read by those who wish to appreciate the true merits of this impetuously brave and fiery soldier. The tablet here erected to his memory by the Commander-in-Chief (Sir Jasper Nicolls) and officers of Her Majesty's army in India, recapitulates a brilliant series of gallant services in the field. "Colonel Dennie served under Lord Lake in 1805 and 1806. During the Burmese war he twice distinguished himself. At Ghuznee on the 23rd July, 1839, he led successfully the attack at Bamean: on the 18th September 1840, he defeated Dost Mahomed in the Khoord Cabul Pass: on the 12th October, 1841, after Major-General Sir R. Sale was wounded, he directed the movements in a spirited manner. At Tazeen and Jugdulluck on the 22nd and 29th October, 1841, and between Gundamuck and Jellalabad on the 12th November, 1841, he sustained his military reputation. At Jellalabad on the 1st December, 1841, and 11th March, 1842, he led two successful sorties." His name heads the memorial erected in Canterbury Cathedral to the officers and men of his Regiment by their surviving brothers in arms.

Two tablets commemorate the rank and file of the 5th Native Infantry, who fell in Afghanistan in the years 1841-1842, and ten English Officers of the 10th Bengal Light Cavalry, who "with almost the entire of the 3rd, 4th, 5th and 6th troops of the corps, fell in gallant but hopeless conflict in the disastrous retreat from Cabul between the 6th and 13th of January, 1842." The remainder of the inscription upon the tablet is well worthy of quotation by reason of its simple eloquence and its pathos: "The lamented brave, whose death it records, though greatly outnumbered by a most treacherous foe in snowy wastes and rugged defiles for several days and nights together, without the shelter even of a tent, and suffering from the extremes of cold, hunger and thirst, in the depth of an Afghan winter, sold their lives dearly as became British soldiers."

The battles of Maharajpore (1843), Moodkee (1845), and Ferozeshahur (1845), have each their memorials in the shape of tablets to the fallen. The 67th Native Infantry commemorate the loss of three officers who died during the Burmah Campaign of 1853, and the 35th Royal Sussex Regiment have a similar monument in remembrance of the comrades killed in the operations in the Arrah District against the Mutineers in 1858.

The Government of India stand represented by a tablet in memory of Rear-Admiral John Horsford Cockburn, Commander-in-Chief of Her Majesty's Naval Forces in the East Indies, who died at Government House on the 10th February, 1872, aged 55.

A gallant episode of the Afghan War of 1879 is commemorated by a tablet which bears the name of Lieutenant Oswald Eric Stuart Forbes of the 3rd King's Own Hussars, "who, preferring active service to accompanying his regiment to England, joined the 14th Bengal Lancers at Cabul, and shortly after met a soldier's death in the Horse Artillery and Cavalry action of 11th December,

1879, at Kill Kazi near Cabul, in which two squadrons of the 9th Lancers and one squadron of the 14th Bengal Lancers, 214 Lancers in all, under General Massy, charged about 10,000 Afghans under Mahomed Jan, in the endeavour to check their determined advance and cover the retreat of the four guns of F. Battery, Royal Horse Artillery, under escort to join General Macpherson's column on the Arghandy Road." He was a little over 29 years old at the time of his death. More recent campaigns are recalled by other tablets, but we must leave the visitor to make his own acquaintance with them. The selection we have given has (it may be hoped) convinced him that the Fort Church is by no means to be omitted from the list of historic churches and chapels in Calcutta or from the category of places of interest in the Fort William of to-day.

CHAPTER XVI.

BELVEDERE AND ALIPORE.

THE official residence of the Lieutenant-Governor of Bengal goes by the name of Belvedere. It will be found in the pleasant suburb of Alipore, at the foot of the road leading from the Zeerut Bridge, and can easily be recognized from the figure of the Bengal tiger which since the last few months surmounts the central gateway.

The locality of Alipore itself is traditionally asserted to owe its name to Meer Jaffer Ali Khan, who took up his residence there upon his deposition by Vansittart in 1760 from the musnud at Moorshidabad upon which " the Nabob firm in war, Lord Clive the hero " had placed him after Plassey. There is a distinctly Mohamedan ring about the word which offers support to the tradition: and it is a fact that names such as Begumbari and Sahibabagan survive in the neighbourhood. The site of the Nabob's house has been placed by some where Belvedere now stands. By others a spot has been selected close to the modern Court of the Judge of the Twenty-Four Pergunnahs: and the presence of tombs of Mahomedan origin in the garden of the house at the southern corner of Alipore Lane and Alipore Road lends colour to the conjecture. It is further asserted that when Meer Jaffer was restored to the throne in 1763, he made over his entire property at Alipore to Warren Hastings as a gift " as a return possibly for kindness and attention received." Whether this be actually the case or not, Hastings was certainly an important land-owner in the suburb, and as early as June, 1763, we find an entry in the proceedings of the Council at Fort William which records that "Mr. Hastings requests permission of the Board to build a bridge over the Collighaut Nullah to his Garden House": and it is "agreed that his requests be complied with." The "Collighaut Nullah" is of course the Tolly's Nullah of to-day, which encircles Alipore on the north and east: and it is clear that Hastings lost no time in entering into the enjoyment of his newly-acquired property, which included the villages of Gopalnagore (lying to the east of the modern Belvedere) and Zeerut, lying to its north. We shall presently find that no account of Alipore can be written without an attempt to solve the many mysteries which owe their origin to his connection with it: and at the outset it will be as well to bear in mind the principal spots in the locality with which his name is associated. We must begin with Belvedere itself and include in our survey the Collector of Alipore's official residence, the Calcutta house of the Maharajah of Cooch Behar which goes by the name of Woodlands, the State Guest-house which is known as Hastings House, the gardens of the Agri-Horticultural Society, the block of houses which lie between it and Judge's Court Road, and finally the observatory enclosure which hides itself behind the Zoological Gardens.

Having thus mapped out our task, we will begin its accomplishment with the mansion of the Lieutenant-Governor himself.

There are many allusions to Belvedere as a place of residence near Calcutta, in writings of the eighteenth century. In February, 1762, the Court of Directors disallowed a proposal to purchase Mr. Frankland's house "for the refreshment of the Governor when the multiplicity of business will permit him to leave the town." But the prohibition seems later on to be relaxed. Stavorinus, a Dutch Admiral who visited Calcutta in 1769, writes that a newly-arrived Director of the Dutch East India Company at Hooghly was invited on his way up the river to dine by Mr. Verelst, then Governor of Bengal, at "his country-seat about two hours walk from Calcutta." And when in February, 1770, Stavorinus went with the Dutch Council to congratulate Mr. Cartier on his accession to the Governorship, he writes that "at six o'clock in the evening Mr. Cartier came to fetch the Director and his company to take a ride to his country seat Belvedere, about two Dutch miles from Calcutta, where we were entertained with an excellent concert performed by amateurs and an elegant supper." Five years later Warren Hastings, who had then become Governor-General of Bengal, writes of Belvedere, as the place where he saw Kamaluddin, who was afterwards one of the principal witnesses at Nuncomar's trial.

In November of the same year (1775), we find him inviting Sir Elijah Impey to stay with him at his "Country House" but this need not necessarily have been Belvedere, or indeed at Alipore at all, for we know of his having another residence at Rishera near Serampore, where a tablet has been erected at the instance of Lord Curzon to commemorate the fact. Mrs. Fay, the wife of a Calcutta Barrister, who was one of the first to try the overland route, and was made prisoner at Calicut by Hyder Ali, writes explicitly enough however in her "Original letters from India" of a visit paid by her to Mrs. Hastings in May 1780 at Belvedere House, "about, I believe, five miles from Calcutta, which is a great distance at this season." She describes the house as "a perfect *bijou*, most superbly fitted up with all that unbounded affluence can display: but still deficient in that simple elegance which the wealthy so seldom attain, from the circumstance of not being obliged to search for effect without much cost, which those but moderately rich find to be indispensable. The grounds are said to be very tastefully laid out." And Macrabie, that equally indefatigable chronicler of contemporary gossip, tells us that he was among those invited to a concert-party given by the Governor-General in February, 1776, at "Belvedere his garden." Is the Belvedere of these allusions the mansion which goes now-a-days by that name? According to one account, "Hastings lodged the Baron and Baroness Imhoff in a small dwelling, part of the walls of which still exist in Belvedere House. He lived near, and cultivated the intimacy. Hastings used to cross the plain in a palkee, and the nullah in a dinghee." It is added that he never himself lived on the site of what is now Belvedere. But the Rev. James Long, in his article on "Calcutta in the Olden Time" in the *Calcutta Review* for December, 1852, describes Belvedere "facing Alipur Bridge" as "once the favourite residence of Warren Hastings, but latterly he erected another house further south, and he is said to have hunted tigers in its neighbourhood." That Hastings had several houses in the locality is evident from a passage in one of his letters to his wife, in which he differentiates between them in the clearest possible manner. "I passed the three days of the week at Alipoor," he writes on January 21st, 1784, "and shall continue to be there for the entertainment of my present guests, as long as they stay with me, on Saturdays and Sundays. When they leave me, I bid adieu to Alipoor for ever, and I have actually advised the sale of it in three lots, the old house and garden forming one, the new house and outhouses the second, and the paddock the third." Advertisements relating to the sale of Alipore and also of his Rishera property are to be found in the *India Gazette* for January 24th, March 6th, and April 19th, 1784. But Alipore was still on the hands of Hastings, when he came to leave India in February, 1785. "I am now writing at Alipoor," he tells his wife in a letter of November 24th, 1784, "for it has been put up to sale and bought in again. I have sold Rishera for double the sum that was paid for it. This is a riddle and I leave it to your sagacity to unravel it." After Hastings had sailed, however, the sale was again announced to take place on May 10th, 1785, as Dr. Busteed has ascertained from an examination of the file of the *Calcutta Gazette* for that year in the British Museum: and "Mr. William Jackson the lawyer" bought the old house for 27,500 rupees, Nesbitt Thompson and Samuel Turner, Hastings' Secretary and Aide-de-Camp, combined to buy the new house for Rs. 27,000, and Mr. Honycombe or Honeycombe, an attorney and Secretary to the Justices, bought the paddock "containing 52 biggahs of ground surrounded with railed fence" for Rs. 7,500, leaving "near 70 biggahs of land between the paddock and Belvedere." The paddock is none other than the well known Penn estate long used for the cultivation of arrowroot, and is unrecognizable to-day under a load of bricks and mortar, for it is covered with the dwelling-houses of a large European colony. But the identification of the "Old House" and the "New House" is not so easy. Dr. Busteed finds the counterpart of the "Old House" in Belvedere: and thinks that Hastings may have retained Belvedere for his large social receptions only and lived in the smaller or "New House" when ruralizing at Alipore. But Belvedere, as a matter of fact, was not in the possession of Hastings at the time of the letters to his wife, which have been quoted and which were written in 1784. Existing documents show that in 1778 Hastings leased the villages of Gopalnagore (which lay to the east of Belvedere) and Zeerut, with Belvedere House itself, to Major Tolly, the maker of Tolly's Nullah, for a period of twelve years, with option of renewal for another twelve years: and Mr. Buckland in his History of Bengal under the Lieutenant-Governors, makes mention of an outright sale of Belvedere by Hastings to Tolly in February, 1780, transactions, it may be added, which hardly support the theory advanced in some quarters that Belvedere fulfilled the purpose now allotted to Barrackpore of providing a country residence for the head of the Government. Where then were the "Old" and "New" Houses of Hastings' letters? The subject has presented much difficulty to enquirers: and the present writer is far from claiming to have succeeded where others have been puzzled and disappointed. But from a careful examination of an interesting map of Alipore, drawn in 1780, which has come under his notice he conceives that the situation of these and other historical spots in Alipore may be traced. Two bridges are shown crossing the nullah, and correspond to the Zeerut Bridge of modern times and the bridge towards the east which links the Alipore Jail and the Collector's House with the Bhowanipore Road. From the Zeerut Bridge an avenue of trees gives access to Belvedere House: and the road which runs to the west of the Belvedere grounds and which is the Alipore Road of to-day, connects with this avenue. But there is another prolongation of it as shown in the map which is represented to-day by the road running through the observatory enclosure behind the Zoological Gardens. The tank which adds so largely to the beauty of the Zoo is distinctly given at the north-easterly extremity of this road. To the east of Belvedere is the building we know as the Collector's House, approached from the second bridge by another avenue. This is the house, occupied as we shall shortly learn, by Philip Francis, and it is conjectured by Dr. Chambers to have been the garden-house which Hastings obtained permission in 1763 to render accessible by the Bridge. On the western side of Belvedere a house can be clearly recognized on the site of Woodlands: it stands within a spacious compound which extends as far as Alipore Lane on the south and covers the whole of the present Native Infantry lines. It is submitted that it is identifiable with Hastings' "Old House" which was purchased by Jackson in 1785. On the north of this house and within the compound are two smaller buildings, tenanted in 1780 by Lieutenant Foley of the commissariat and Dr. Clement Francis, the Governor-General's body-surgeon. The northern boundary of the compound marches with the grounds of Barwell's mansion, (Kidderpore House) which then took in on the east the plots now appropriated by the sepoy hospital and the observatory. Immediately behind Belvedere on the south are the seventy biggahs not included in the sale of Hastings' property. A portion falls within the Belvedere boundaries, as they now exist, and the remainder is represented by the Agri-Horticultural Society's gardens. Here was the site of the house built by Julius Imhoff, the younger of the stepsons of Hastings, who made him a gift of the land. He was married to a Mohammedan lady, and the grave of his mother-in-law, the Begum, was alongside the house and was (Dr. Chambers assures the writer) to be seen as lately as 1896-1898 with a large Bougainvilla creeper growing over it. This was the only house owned by Julius Imhoff (who died in 1799) and is the one mentioned by him in his will as "my grounds situated behind that House or Mansion commonly known by the name of Belvedere House and at present occupied by William Augustus Brooke." Proceeding southward we find the paddock opposite the junction of Alipore Road and Alipore Lane: and, running to the east, is a road which corresponds to the modern Judge's Court Road and is an approach to a cluster of three houses, situated upon the spot now covered by the Judge's Court and Hastings House.

The opening out of Judge's Court Road and the transformation of the immediate neighbourhood into a fashionable European suburb have strangely disguised the landmarks of the locality. But if we turn to the announcement of sale after Hastings' departure "by Messrs. Williams and Lee at the Old Court House on the 10th May next" which Dr. Busteed has already found for us in the file of the *Calcutta Gazette* for 1785, reconstruction becomes comparatively easy. Lot 1 is "the house opposite the paddock gate consisting of a Hall, a large verandah to the southward, and six rooms:" and included therewith are "two small bungalows, a large tank of excellent water, and above 63 biggahs of land, partly lawn, but chiefly garden ground in high cultivation, and well stocked with a great variety of fruit trees." The second Lot is described as "an upper-roomed house consisting of a hall and two rooms on each floor, a handsome stone staircase and a back staircase all finished with Madras chunam:" and "a lower-roomed house containing a large hall and four good bed-chambers: a complete bathing-house containing two rooms finished with Madras chunam: a convenient bungalow containing two rooms and a verandah all round, a large range of pucka buildings containing stabling for 14 horses and four coach houses: other stables also thatched for 12 horses and 6 carriages and 46 biggahs of ground." Lot 3 is "the paddock containing 52 biggas of ground surrounded with railed fence." Now in the map of 1780, there are three houses distinctly shown. The first stands at the south-eastern corner of the paddock, and if the modern Judge's Court Road follows the alignment of the old continuation of Alipore Lane, its site was on the north-eastern portion of the compound of Hastings House as it is now demarcated. Its foundations are stated by Dr. Chambers to have been visible in 1897. There is another house behind it, slightly to the south-west, which from its situation may very reasonably be identified with Hastings House, and the subject of Lot 2: while its companion the "lower-roomed house," as indicated on the map, stands to the west of both the others, and has been swallowed up by the Judge's Court compound. The "large tank of excellent water" has survived, however, and may still be seen within the cutcherry precincts.

Having now completed our attempt at identification of the present with the past, we may return to the history of Belvedere, which we have left in the possession of Tolly. The Major did not long remain in India to enjoy his purchase. He became Lieutenant-Colonel in 1782 and resigned the service in January, 1784, just about a year before Hastings. Early in the same year he sailed for England in the "Dutton" and died before reaching St. Helena. From there the news of his death must have been despatched to Calcutta: for on October 28th, 1784, the following advertisement appears in a Calcutta paper: "To be let or sold, Belvedere House: apply to the Bank of Bengal." The house seems, however, to have remained in the hands of Tolly's representatives. It was announced in 1798 that the property was about to be cut up into building lots: but the next definitive stage in the history of Belvedere is not reached until February, 1802, when it is advertised for sale by public auction in the *Calcutta Gazette* by order of "Richard Johnson Esqre., attorney to the Administratrix of the late Colonel William Tolly." It is the first lot and is described as "that large commodious, and well-known house called Belvedere House, with 72 biggahs 8 cottahs 4 chittacks of land, more or less thereto belonging, at present occupied by and subject to a lease granted to William Augustus Brooke, Esqre.,* at the yearly rent of £350, payable at the house of Messrs. William Paxton & Co., of London (the house and premises to be kept in good repair at Mr. Brooke's expense) determinable on the 1st of August, 1802." The purchaser was a Mr. Nicholas Nugent of Calcutta, acting apparently on behalf of Mr. Thomas Scott. The house now passed through various hands, but the next notable tenant was General Sir Edward Paget, Commander-in-Chief in India from 1822 to 1825. He writes to his wife Lady Harriet Paget, that the "house is most cheerful, clean and gentlemanlike and I would not change it for the Government House." In September 1838 the house had passed into the possession of Mr. Charles Robert Prinsep, brother of Henry Thoby Prinsep the elder and James Prinsep, and a well known advocate of the Supreme Court, who was Advocate-General of Bengal from 1846 to 1849 and again

---

* Brooke was a civil servant and at the time of Hastings' departure from India in 1785 was chief of the Patna factory—a post which together with his first appointment to India, he owed to Wheler, the Member of Council who laid the foundation stone of St. John's Church in 1784 and died the same year. Brooke was longer lived. Heber mentions that he was entertained at Benares in 1824 by Mr. William Augustus Brooke who had been 56 years in India and was the oldest of the Company's resident servants, and as a matter of fact he survived until 1833 when he died at Benares at the age of 81, holding the office of Senior Judge of the Court of Appeal and Agent to the Governor-General at Benares. He was in Calcutta in 1794, and was "Principal in office" to Julius Imhoff who held the appointment at the time of Registrar to the Court of Appeal at the Presidency.

from 1852 to 1855. The Prinsep family bought the house from Mr. James Mackillop in June 1841 and sold it to the East India Company in 1854. Henceforward it becomes the official residence of the Lieutenant-Governors of Bengal. At first it was proposed to demand a monthly rent of Rs. 500, but the Court of Directors subsequently acceded to Lord Dalhousie's request and withdrew the impost.

The house has been enlarged and improved upon from time to time by successive Lieutenant-Governors. Its architecture is of a free Italian renaissance style developed or an ordinary Anglo-Indian building. Sir Richard Temple (Lieutenant-Governor from 1874 to 1877) thus describes its surroundings: "The official mansion is named Belvedere and well it deserves the name, being situated in a richly-wooded suburb where the bamboos grow in fine profusion and throw up their tall stems tapering to the most delicate sprigs and gracefully bending so as to overarch the roads and lanes. There too the plantain puts forth its great leaves several feet long, in form like a scimitar, and with a sheen on the surface resembling satin. In the middle of a park studded with groups of trees, stands Belvedere House. Its terrace overlooks a rich expanse of verdure, its flight of steps are environed by flowing creepers, its grounds covered with lotus and water-lilies, its garden encircled with various trees, the banyan, the almond, the bamboo, the cotton-tree and even by some specimens of the peerless "Amherstia." The building as it now stands would be hardly recognisable by its first official occupant, Sir Frederick Halliday. The construction of a verandah on the east side and the re-construction of a more commodious west wing were carried out in 1868-70 by Sir William Grey. Sir Ashley Eden (1877-1882) added the whole of the centre main facade with the steps, on the north side, and fitted the centre ball-room with a wooden floor. In Sir Steuart Bayley's time (1887-1890) the wooden glazed supper-room was made on the north side of the house. Under Sir Charles Elliott (1890-95) the rooms on the upper storey of the west wing were built, and an archway substituted for the door leading into the drawing-room from the main staircase. The tenure of office of Sir Alexander Mackenzie (1895-98) saw the introduction of electric lighting into the building.

There have been a number of Royal guests entertained at Belvedere: the Duke of Edinburgh by Sir William Grey in the cold weather of 1869-70, the King-Emperor, then Prince of Wales, by Sir Richard Temple in December, 1875, the Duke of Clarence by Sir Steuart Bayley in January, 1890: and the present Czar of Russia (Nicholas the Second), then Cesarewitch, by Sir Charles Elliott in January, 1891. And to these must now be added the names of the present Prince and Princess of Wales, the honour of entertaining whom on behalf of the community has fallen to Sir Andrew Fraser. The building contains full length portraits in oil of the late Queen Victoria, in her coronation robes, and of King Edward the Seventh, which hang in the great ball-room or Durbar-Hall, a chamber 114 feet long, and capable of being divided off into drawing-room and dining-room as occasion requires. Two fine oil paintings by Daniell, may also be noticed on the walls of the drawing-room. The one represents Old Court House Street, as seen in 1780 from the spot where St. Andrews Kirk now stands, and where the Court House then was: the other depicts a scene on the Hooghly with the present Fort William in the distance, and a handsome bungalow of the genuine old fashioned type in the foreground. At the western or dining-room end of the hall are hung portraits of Sir Charles Elliott (1891-95) and Lady Elliott, presented by the Mahomedan Literary Society of Calcutta. Other Lieutenant-Governors whose portraits are preserved on the landing at the top of the stairs are Sir John Peter Grant (1859-62) Sir Cecil Beadon (1862-67) and Sir William Grey (1867-71). In the dining room are also excellent engravings of the portraits in Government House of Holwell and Warren Hastings, and another of Bishop Wilson. The small drawing-room on the north contains portraits of Sir James Bourdillon, officiating Lieutenant-Governor from November 1902 to November 1903, and subsequently Resident in Mysore, and Lady Bourdillon. At the back of the building are the gardens and lawn-tennis grounds, and a fine ornamental jheel crossed by an iron bridge.

In Upjohn's Map of 1793 the house and grounds of Belvedere are very plainly shown. The house, as there depicted stands about 500 yards south of the Alipore Bridge over Tolly's Nullah, now called the Zeerut Bridge and reconstructed in 1854 and again (with complete disregard for the picturesque) in 1904. As given in the map, the shape of the house corresponds with its appearance at the present day: and there is the same main entrance drive from the west, and the wide circular expanse of lawn in front of the building. The boundary on the west, as to-day, is the Alipore Road. On the north runs an unfinished road—the encircling Belvedere Road of modern times—and there is a wicket-gate at the point where it now meets the Bhowanipore road just by the bridge over Tolly's Nullah. The bridge shown in the map of 1780 appears no longer but the identification is easily made. The unfinished road was the carriage-drive to the "Lodge" of Philip Francis and the wicket-gate the entrance to his domain. In spite of its modest name, the "Lodge" boasted of larger grounds even than those of Belvedere: the property included the site of the present Alipore Jail and Reformatory and its boundary on the north and east was Tolly's Nullah. According to Macrabie, his brother-in-law and Secretary, Francis purchased a lodge in the neighbourhood of Calcutta, consisting of "a spacious hall and four chambers and standing in the midst of twenty acres of ground, pleasant to the last degree." The purchase was made in 177[illegible] and six months before Francis left India, he sold the house and grounds in April 1780 to his friend Livius. The house is concealed to-day by the high unsightly walls of the Jail but if the visitor will make his way towards the bridge over Tolly's Nullah from the Belvedere Road, he will notice a road on his right and to the north of the Jail, which an inscription in bold letters informs him is designated "Thackeray Road." At the end of this road is the "Lodge," utilized now-a-days and for nearly a century past as the official residence of the Collector and Magistrate of the Twenty-Four Pergunnahs. A wing and an upper storey have been added, but otherwise it is the same house—the *villa inter paludes* where Francis held his weekly symposia. It was occupied in that capacity in 1812 by Richmond Thackeray, the father of the novelist: and hence the name of the road we have just traversed. There can be no doubt that the author of *Vanity Fair* passed several of the early days of his boyhood in this house at Alipore: but he was not born here. For on July 18th, 1811, the date of his birth, his father was living in Calcutta itself and holding the office of Secretary to the Board of Revenue, to which he had been appointed in 1807, at the age of 25 and after nine years' service: and the birthplace, it is believed, must be sought in the house in Free School Street which is now the Armenian College. Five months later, however, Richmond Thackeray became Collector at Alipore: and here he lived with his wife and little son, until on September 13th, 1815, he died, aged thirty-two years, ten months and twenty-three days, as the inscription tells us upon his tombstone in the North Park Street burying-ground. His name still survives in local official history by reason of his settlement of the suburban hamlets. The mother of William Makepeace Thackeray belonged to the family of Richard Becher, the colleague of Holwell in Council at Fort William and an "honest man" who died like his friend in poverty. Mrs. Thackeray was only twenty-three when she was left a widow, and shortly after married Captain Carmichael Smyth, afterwards Superintendent of the Company's Military College at Addiscombe. Her boy was sent to England in 1817, in company with his cousin Richmond Shakespear, who was afterwards to be the chivalrous rescuer of the captive English ladies and children at Kabul in 1842: but he never forgot his mother, and the home of his babyhood was long present in his memory. "He drew me your house in Calcutta," wrote his grandmother Becher to Mrs. Thackeray soon after his boy reached England, "not omitting the monkey looking out of the window and black Betty at the top drying the towels." She lived to see him famous and his name a household word among English folk: and lived also to see him in his grave. On the first anniversary of his death she followed him to her own last resting place. Although he never himself returned to India, Thackeray's pages are instinct with many an Anglo-Indian touch. Who is there that is not familiar with the picture in one of his "Roundabout Papers" of the parting on the ghat or river side stair of the two children from their sad-eyed mothers who remained on shore? Nor is this the only record that his pen has left of the loneliness and pathos of this ever-present tragedy of the Englishman's life in India. "Strong men alone on their knees," he tells us, "with streaming eyes and broken accents, implore heaven for those little ones who were prattling at their sides but a few hours since. Long after they are gone, careless and happy, recollections of the sweet past rise up and smite those that remain: the flowers they had planted in their little gardens, the toys they played with, the little vacant cribs they slept in as fathers' eyes looked blessings down upon them." It is well that those of our race whose lot it is to earn their bread amid the pleasant surroundings of an English home should learn something of the price of Empire that is paid by their countrymen across the seas: and who shall be found better fitted to teach the lesson than the creator of Jos Sedley and Captain Dobbin, of dear old

Colonel Newcome and incomparable Goliah O'Grady Gahagan? As we linger at the entrance to the Collector's House at Alipore and read the tablets which bear silent testimony to the old associations of the historic spot, how large a portion of the history of our rule in India stands epitomized before our eyes! The tablet upon our left tells us that "in this house resided Sir Philip Francis, Member of Warren Hastings' Council from 1774 to 1780 A.D." And the second: "William Makepeace Thackeray, the novelist, also lived here during his infancy, from 1812 to 1815 A.D." One wonders how often succeeding generations of Collectors have suffered their thoughts to stray back to the days when the fierce Francis battled for the supremacy which he won and lost, and the little Thackeray played hide and seek with his ayah and his bearer along the cool and sheltered garden-walks.

The Collector's house is not the only spot in Alipore with which the name of Francis is closely linked. The story of the famous duel with Hastings which signalized the early morning hours of the 7th August, 1780, has been set out in detail by Colonel Thomas Deane Pearse, the Governor-General's second, in a letter written in the following October to Lawrence Sulivan, the Chairman of the Court of Directors: and so effective is the style and the manner of the description that not only the scene but the features of the locality are vividly recalled as we read. The time chosen for the encounter was half-past five. On both sides the assistants were old fire-eaters. Pearse, the commandant of artillery, was a veteran with a record behind him of honourable service at Guadeloupe, Havannah and

Belleisle, and was, a year or two later, to gather fresh laurels in Eyre Coote's Carnatic campaign against Hyder Ali. He died a few miles up the river Hooghly where he had gone for change of air, in June, 1789, and his grave is among those in the North Park Street cemetery. Although he was only forty-seven at the time of his death, his epitaph records that "for the last three years of his life he was senior officer of the Bengal Army." Lord Cornwallis was present at the funeral, or, as the local chronicler of the day puts it, "His Lordship attended and drop't a tear, with the crowd."* The second of Francis was Colonel Henry Watson, the chief Engineer of the Presidency, "a contentious man, strongly opposed to Hastings" but entitled nevertheless to special remembrance at the hands of Calcutta as the pioneer of ship-building at Calcutta, the architect of Fort William in its final stages, and the maker of the Red Road and Old Court House Street and the surrounding Esplanade.

The original place of appointment, Pearse tells us, "was very improper for the business: it was the road leading to Alipore at the crossing of it through a double row of trees that formerly had been a walk of Belvedere garden on the western side of the house." The road is of course the modern Alipore Road, which still skirts the western wall of Belvedere: and a few trees may yet be

* In her admirable edition of Warren Hastings' letters to his wife, "Sydney Grier" notes that like so many of his contemporaries, Pearse married an Indian lady: and she adds on the authority of Colonel Hugh Pearse (the biographer of the Hearseys) that a son of his, named Mohammed, was educated at Harrow, but disappeared from view after leaving the school.

een on the small strip of greensward on the opposite ide. According to Dr. Busteed who has been over the ground with much care, the rendezvous was at the spot ıow marked by the second gate on that side leading in to he grounds. This is not in accordance with the tradiioṅ preserved by Mr. Long, which pointed out as the site wo trees "nearly opposite Alipore" which went by he name of the "Trees of Destruction" and were ' notorious for the duels fought under their shade." But hese trees were on the Calcutta side of Tolly's Nullah. Sophia Goldborne in *Hartley House* locates them "on the ace ground, at a distance from the immediate track of the oursers you will perceive :" and Dr. Busteed's topography nay be accepted without hesitation as the more reliable. Francis, we learn further from Pearse, proposed to turn ıside from the road into "the walk," seemingly a disused overgrown avenue of trees, close on their left, and straggling across the road. "But Mr. Hastings disapproved of he place, because it was full of weeds and dark : the road itelf was next mentioned, but was thought by everybody too ublic, as it was near riding-time, and people might want to ıass that way : it was therefore agreed to walk towards Mr. Barwell's house on an old road that separated his ground rom Belvedere, and, before he had gone far, a retired dry spot was chosen as a proper place." Barwell's house is still a landmark of Alipore under the name of Kidderpore House : and we have already ascertained the position of his "Old Road" in our examination of the map of 1780. The party would seem to have proceeded along this road n a northerly direction and turned aside to the left, almost ıt once into the grounds of Barwell's house. "Unless records or trustworthy tradition point to another locality. Dr. Busteed is inclined to think that the compound of N- 5, Alipore Road (the house at the junction with Alipo- Lane which goes by the name of Dilkhusha) holds nea- its northern boundary the site of the memorable duel. B- we may take leave to doubt whether the location is not to far to the south, and whether the spot is not rather whe- the sepoy hospital now stands to the north of Woodlands As soon as the suitable place was selected, the pistols we- loaded: and Colonel Pearse finding the gentlemen w- "both unacquainted with the modes usually observed these occasions," took the liberty to tell them that if th- would fix their distance, it was the business of the second- to measure it. Watson recommended fourteen pace- Hastings who was evidently in a fighting mood, "observ- that it was a great distance for pistols:" but as no actu- objection was made by him, Watson measured and Pear- counted. Francis got into position twice, and then d- covered that his powder was damp. Hastings "ca- down from his present" to give his rival time to rectify h- priming, and Pearse supplied him with a fresh charge fro- a cartridge. "Again the gentlemen took their stand both presented together, and Mr. Francis fired. M- Hastings did the same at the distance of time equal to t- counting of one, two, three distinctly, but not greater. Francis' bullet whizzed by the Governor-General's ear, b- that fired by Hastings "took place," entering the si- just below the right shoulder, and lodging in the oppos- side under the left. "Mr. Francis staggered and in a- tempting to sit down, he fell and said he was a dead ma- Mr. Hastings immediately went up to him as did Colo-

Watson, but I ran to call the servants." On Pearse's return ("I was absent about two minutes," he writes) he found Hastings standing by Francis, and Watson "gone to fetch a cot or palanquin from Belvedere to carry him to town." A sheet was brought and wrapped round the wound by Hastings and his second. "We had the satisfaction to find it was not in a vital part and Mr. Francis agreed with me in opinion as soon as it was mentioned." Previously, however "while Mr. Francis was lying on the ground, he told Mr. Hastings, in consequence of something which he said, that he best knew how it affected his affairs and that he had better take care of himself to which Mr. Hastings answered that he hoped and believed the wound was not mortal, but that if any unfortunate accident should happen, it was his intention immediately to surrender himself to the Sheriff." Upon the arrival of Watson with a cot, the wounded man was placed upon it. Pearse had "offered to attend him to town in my carriage, and Mr. Hastings urged him to go, as my carriage was remarkably easy." Francis agreed and "therefore, when the cot came, we proceeded towards the chariot, but were stopped by a deep, broad ditch, over which we could not carry the cot: for this reason Mr. Francis was conveyed to Belvedere." Dr. Busteed's gloss upon these details is full of interest. "The duellists," he writes, "on first arriving, drove up to the place of appointment. Why then not take the cot back into the main road to the "chariot" by the way along which Colonel Pearse had gone and returned so quickly? The supposition that occurs to me is this: they probably thought it prudent to carry the wounded man as little in the carriage as they could, as the cot must have been easier for him: they therefore directed the carriage to go on towards the Alipore (Zeerut) Bridge, meaning to take a short and diagonal cut across country with the cot and pick up the carriage at the Belvedere side of the bridge: so they proceeded through the low marshy ground in the direction of the present Hermitage compound and the Zoological gardens, till they were pulled up by a deep water course, a very likely thing to meet in the height of the rainy season. There they had to retrace their steps, and finally emerge by the cross-roads into the main road, where they had first assembled. Francis was probably in much pain and weakness by this time, and was counselled to give up the idea of going into town, but to make for the nearest port, Belvedere."

If we bear in mind that by "main road" Dr. Busteed is referring to the Alipore Road and the entrance-avenue leading to Belvedere from the Zeerut Bridge, we shall see how completely the picture accords with the details given in the map of 1780. The "crossroad" is of course the prolongation of the Alipore Road towards the north-west which we have already noticed to be represented by the road through the observatory compound. As regards the place to which Francis was conveyed, Hastings writing his well-known account of the duel to his wife on the "Thursday morning" upon which it took place, corroborates Pearse. "He is at Belvedere and Drs. Campbell and Francis," the one the Surgeon-General at the Presidency, and the other Hastings' own surgeon, "are gone to attend him there." But Francis' own account of the matter is discrepant, and at first sight introduces an element of confusion. An entry in his journal, quoted by Dr. Busteed, records that "after the first confusion had subsided, and after I had suffered great inconvenience from being carried to a wrong place, I was at last conveyed to Major Foley's house on a bed." Dr. Busteed conjectures that Foley as printed in Francis' memoirs is an error for "Tolly" the maker of Tolly's Nullah in whose possession Belvedere then was. The duel took place six months after the transaction of February, 1780, so that the Belvedere of Pearse and the "Tolly's house" of Francis are reconciled without difficulty. But a reference to the map of 1780 which has already been brought into requisition, will remind us of the two small houses located in the northern portion of what is now the Woodlands compound. They are immediately to the south of the spot we have ventured to name as the scene of the encounter: and one was tenanted by Clement Francis, the Governor-General's doctor, and the other by Lieutenant Foley, of the commissariat. It is quite conceivable that Francis was right and that he was first taken to Foley's and then to Belvedere. Still, what was "the wrong place" to which Francis says he was originally carried? Clearly, as Dr. Busteed conjectures, the spot where the "deep broad ditch" obstructed further passage and compelled a return to the cross-road. One wonders why his own "Lodge" was overlooked: but it was probably because of the distance, for the grounds of Belvedere and the "Lodge" would have to be crossed, and it is evident from his own account that the journey he had already taken caused him much bodily discomfort. He notes in his journal that on the very day of the duel (August 17th) "Mr. Hastings sends to know when he may visit me." On the 18th he records that "in these two days the pain I have suffered was very considerable"; the next day, there is this entry: "desire Colonel Watson to tell Mr. Hastings as civilly as possible that I am forced to decline his visit:" and on the 24th he is sufficiently recovered to "return to Calcutta." This last entry, observes Dr. Busteed, sufficiently disproves the old story so often told in Calcutta that Mrs. Ellerton, the mother-in-law of Bishop Corrie, remembered seeing Francis in a palanquin crossing over the bridge at Tolly's Nullah "all bloody from the duel." She may have seen him at the Belvedere side, but there would have been very little blood to see, as the sheet bound round him would have effectually concealed any bleeding from a bullet-wound. There is something very characteristic about Hastings' conduct during this "silly affair," as he describes it in a letter to Pearse's correspondent and his own friend, Lawrence Sulivan. In that letter, it is true, he affects to treat the matter lightly. "I have been ashamed" he writes "that I have been an actor in it, and I declare to you upon my honour that such was my sense of it at the time, that I was much disturbed by an old woman whose curiosity prompted her to stand by as spectatress of a scene so little comprehended by the natives of this part of the world, and attracted others of the same stamp from the adjacent villages to partake in the entertainment." But if he was "disturbed," he did not show it. "Mr. Hastings," we are told by Pearse, "seemed to be in a state of such perfect tranquillity that a spectator would not have supposed that he was about an action out of the common course of things." Towards his opponent he was scrupulously fair and held his fire until he was ready: but his remark about the fourteen paces, his objection to the spot first selected as it "was full of weeds and dark," and his deliberation in discharging his pistol, clearly show that however much he was "ashamed" of the part he was playing, he was determined to do execution.

To the south of Belvedere are the gardens of the Agri-Horticultural Society. At the entrance there has been placed a fine bust by J. C. Lough of Dr. William Carey, the famous Serampore missionary (1761-1834) by whom the Society was founded in 1820. The bust formerly stood in the vestibule of the Metcalfe Hall, but on the removal of the Society's headquarters from the ground-floor of the Hall in 1903 it was transferred to its present position. The Society possesses in addition portraits in oils of Sir Edward Ryan, Sir Lawrence Peel, and Messrs. A. Grote and J. A. Crawford, all former Presidents of the Society. There is also a small but unique portrait in chalk of Colonel Robert Kyd, the projector and founder of the Royal Botanic Garden, who died in 1793. It is in an excellent state of preservation though upwards of 100 years old. Unhappily, there is not at the disposal of the Society any suitable room in which these interesting pictures can be displayed: and as matters now stand they are not available for public inspection. It is perhaps not too much to hope that arrangements may be possible for the depositing of the collection in the Town Hall or the Victoria Memorial Hall on loan. The Society's gardens, like so many other spots in Alipore, are closely associated with the name of Warren Hastings. They occupy part of the "seventy biggahs of land between the paddock and Belvedere" of which mention has been made in a preceding page, and which were not included in the sale of the Alipore property effected after Hastings' departure from Calcutta. No attempt was made to dispose of this plot and it was given by Hastings to his stepson, Julius Imhoff when the latter settled in India. Mrs. Hastings had, as is well known, two sons by her first husband. The elder Sir Charles Imhoff, inherited Daylesford after his mother's death in 1837, and died as recently as 1853. He received a commission in the British army after serving for some years in one of the Prince of Waldeck's Regiments, and was allowed, with three other Englishmen, to accept the insignia and title of a Knight of the foreign order of St. Joachim. In 1796 he married Charlotte Blunt, the daughter of the "bankrupt baronet," Sir Charles Blunt, who had come out to India at the age of 53 to make a second fortune and died worth £100,000 at Pulta, near Barrackpore, in 1802. The younger brother, Julius, kept up the family connection both with Alipore and with the service of John Company: and an interesting account of his career may be found in an appendix to Sydney Grier's admirable edition of Hastings' letters to his wife. "In the grounds between Hastings' House and the Judge's Court is to be found the vault in which Julius Imhoff and his three children, William, Charles and John, lie buried." Julius Imhoff was like his brother Sir Charles, educated at Westminster, and went out to India in 1788. He was confirmed by the Court of Directors two years later in the nomination as writer which Hastings had given him, and in 1792 was appointed second assistant to the Collector at Moorshidabad. He returned to Calcutta in 1793 as registrar to the Court of Appeal: and it must have been about this time that he built his house at Alipore on the seventy biggahs, apparently as a speculation, in the hope that it might serve "for the use of the Court of Appeal." In his will he describes it as "my house and grounds situated behind that house or mansion commonly known by the name of Belvedere House, and at present occupied by William Augustus Brooke," who was its tenant in 1802, as we have already learnt. In 1797, he was made Collector of Midnapore and died in 1799. Among the Hastings papers in the British Museum are several letters from him to his step-father, breathing the utmost respect and affection towards him and his mother, and his will, which bears no date. Of his three sons, Charles, when a boy of five, was drowned with his nurse in 1802 in a well in the grounds of the Alipore house: and the other two were as boys in the charge of John Palmer, the Prince of Merchants. They were apparently natural children and of mixed blood: and in 1824 or 1825 they obtained Letters Patent legitimating them. John, who is described by Palmer as very dark in complexion, was brought up in Calcutta and lived there for many years. He met his death by murder in the house at Alipore. William, "who has a fine countenance, mild, open, intelligent, and bears a strong resemblance to his poor father," spent his youth at Daylesford with Hastings and his grandmother, and became a great favourite "but developed unsatisfactory traits of character as he grew older." His descent excluded him from the Company's service, and John Palmer was asked to settle him "in the indigo line" a scheme which does not seem to have been attended with much success. "He proved idle and fickle and was frequently out of employment": and he died before the arrival of the Letters Patent.

In 1803 Julius Imhoff's house was let or sold by his executors to Charles D'Oyly, the son of Hastings' faithful friend, Sir John Hadley D'Oyly,* who mentions his pleasure in the grounds which Hastings had laid out. Heber, who stayed with him at Bankipore, speaks of Charles D'Oyly, who succeeded his father in the baronetcy in 1818 as "the best gentleman-artist I ever saw." He had the advantage in 1808, of continuous instruction from "a very able artist of the name of Chinnery," and he appears in the Hastings correspondence as the sender of various specimens of his skill, notably a picture of "the large bannian tree at Alipoor, an old acquaintance of yours." The present baronet Sir Warren Hastings D'Oyly, an old Bengal civilian, is the grandson not only of Sir Charles, but of John Fendall, Member of Council from 1820 to 1825. In April, 1841, the house was sold to the Nawab Nazim of Moorshidabad, and is described in the deed of sale as having been formerly occupied by Sir Charles Theophilus Metcalfe, afterwards officiating Governor-General and "Liberator of the Indian Press." Metcalfe was from 1827 to 1834 in Council, and we have the following allusion to his life in Calcutta in his biography by Sir John William Kaye.

* Sir John D'Oyly (1754-1818) was member for Ipswich during the trial of Hastings. His wife Diana Rochfort, was a niece of Robert Rochfort, 1st Earl of Belvedere She died at Cheltenham in 1803 when Sir John returned to India. Have we in her title a clue to the name of the Lieutenant-Governor's residence?

"During the first years of his residence at the Presidency, he occupied a house on the banks of the river at Garden Reach. He subsequently removed to Alipore, a more inland suburb. Throughout all this period he enlivened Calcutta with magnificent hospitality. His house at Alipore was surrounded by spacious park-like grounds, and at early morning he might sometimes be seen riding in top-boots, an article of equipment in which he always rejoiced, on a plump white horse with a groom upon either side of him." In January, 1864, the property was sold by the Nawab Nazim to Sir Cecil Beadon, who had the house dismantled, and in 1867 and 1868 sold portions of it to the Secretary of State. Of this some was added to the grounds of Belvedere, and the remainder has now passed into possession of the Agri-Horticultural Society.

The road which lies immediately to the south of the gardens was at one time called Love Lane (says Mr. Buckland in his "Bengal under the Lieutenant-Governors") at the special request of a Collector of the Twenty-Four Pergunnahs who had wooed and won his wife there, but the name has vanished, and the whole of the road encircling the gardens and Belvedere itself is styled Belvedere Road.

Continuing down the Alipore Road towards the south, we find ourselves at its junction with Alipore Lane on the West, and Judge's Court Road on the East. If we walk down the latter road and leave the Judge's Court on our right, we shall come upon the enclosure which hides from view the Hastings' House of which we have been hearing so much in our excursions upon Belvedere. Of the actual connection of this house with Warren Hastings, there can be no doubt. It is indicated as we have seen in the map of 1780, which we have been consulting, and the date of its construction is ordinarily set down as 1776. Macrabie, the brother-in-law and Secretary of Francis, writes in February, 1776, "Colonel Monson dined with us in the country: after dinner we walked over to the Governor's new built house. 'Tis a pretty toy but very small, tho' airy and lofty. Those milk-white buildings with smooth shiny surface utterly blind one." The context shows that Macrabie cannot be speaking of Belvedere, for as we have seen, that was in no sense a "new-built house" at the time. His reference must be to Hastings' House: and it is more than likely that it is the "perfect bijou" of Mrs. Fay's description. That lady made her visit very shortly after her arrival in Calcutta in 1780, as she herself states, and the confusion was natural. In any case, it is the property which forms the subject of Lot 2 in the sale advertisement of 1785. Miss Kathleen Blechynden in the chatty book upon Old Calcutta which she has lately published, quotes within inverted commas the following extract, the source of which she does not indicate. It is not contained in Dr. Busteed's article on "Old Alipore Houses" in the Englishman for May 27th, 1892, to which reference has just been made, but it is obviously the work of a careful observer on the spot, and cannot be omitted from any discussion of the subject. "The description of the upper-roomed house in Lot 2 corresponds with the centre portion of Hastings' House, which is all that existed in Hastings' time—the little house which seemed to Mrs. Fay a "perfect bijou." The stone staircase still stands, but can hardly be called handsome, being narrow, winding and steep. The back staircase is also in good preservation; it is built into an odd corner-cupboardlike wooden shaft within a bathroom and is lighted by a small-barred window which opens into the room. The Madras chunam of the advertisement is lost under successive coats of whitewash. The hall and two rooms on each floor form the original house, the central block, while the wings are distinctly of a later date, as is evidenced by the style of the beams and burghas, and by the stucco work. The entire building is raised four feet from the ground, but only the wings are flued—another mark of the later period, and finally the walls of the wings do not "bond" into those of the central block. This is very apparent on the southern front of the building." The house has been since the year 1901 employed as a State Guest House of the Government of India. It was purchased in that year by Lord Curzon for that purpose, and the grounds have not only been laid out, but a second bungalow has been added. Its connection with Hastings and its present use have been duly commemorated: and a tablet records that "This house known as Hastings' House, originally the country seat of Warren Hastings, first Governor-General of Fort William in Bengal, 1774-1785, was bought as a State Guest House by Lord Curzon, Viceroy and Governor-General of India in 1901." Both the inscription, however, and the description we have just quoted must be taken on trust, for the public are not admitted within the precincts. Still the visitor must not leave the neighbourhood without paying a pilgrimage to the spot and gazing at the historic house from the entrance-gate. For Calcutta tradition connects Hastings' House with a famous ghost story. It is said that the great Governor-General drives up the avenue every evening in a coach and four and upon alighting walks through the house in evident search of something by which he lays considerable store. A curious corroboration of the story is furnished by a letter from Hastings to his great friend and late Private Secretary, Nesbitt Thompson, in Calcutta, which is dated the 21st July, 1785, and is referred to in the volume of Gleig's biography. "It pains me," he writes "to recur to the subject of my bureau. I have not as yet received any intelligence from you or Larkins about it. You cannot conceive my anxiety about it." *The contents of the bureau were evidently highly prized by Hastings, for on September 6th, 1787, the following advertisement regarding it appears in the *Calcutta Gazette*:—"Whereas an old Black Wood Bureau, the property of Warren Hastings, Esqre., containing, amongst other things, two small miniature pictures and some private papers, was about the time of his departure from Bengal, either stolen from his house on the Esplanade, or by mistake sold at the aucion of his effects: This is to give notice that Mr. Larkins and Mr. Thompson will pay the sum of two thousand sicca rupees to any person who shall give them such information as shall enable them to recover the contents of the bureau.

---

* George Nesbitt Thompson was great-grandfather of Sir Augustus Rivers Thompson, Lieutenant-Governor of Bengal from 1882-1887. The name of William Larkins is perpetuated in Calcutta by a lane which runs from Old Court House Street to Wellesley Place.

The loss seems never to have been made good: and it is impossible not to trace some connection between it and the ghostly visits so constantly paid by Hastings to his old haunts at Alipore. Some time in the early part of 1876, certain papers of his were discovered, however, in the archives of the India office. Can these have been a portion of the mysterious contents of the missing bureau?

As we walk back to Alipore Road up the Judge's Court Road, we may occupy ourselves with memories of another old-world romance which stands closely associated with Alipore.

The famous Madam Grand lived with her newly-married husband at a "red garden-house a short distance from the town," which tradition places in the modern Alipore-lane: and it was hither that Grand hurried on the night of December the 8th in 1778 when news was brought to him at Barwell's supper-table that "Mr. Francis was caught in my house and secured by my jemadar." Grand had left the bungalow, "the happiest man as he thought himself" to sup with Barwell, who was in the habit of entertaining his men friends every fortnight at Le Gallais' Tavern "in town." Scarcely had he sat down when a messenger brought the news that Councillor Francis "who lives behind the playhouse" had been surprised in his wife's room. He rushed from the table and called upon Hastings' Military Secretary, Major William Palmer (the father of John Palmer, the "Prince of Merchants") to request the use of his sword and his aid as a friend. The Major accompanied him to his house at Alipore where they found Mr. Shee held down on a chair in a lower apartment, begging the servants for release, with Mr. Shore (afterwards Lord Teignmouth and Governor-General) and Mr. Archdekin joining in the entreaty. The jemadar declared that he had seized Mr. Francis "to meet the vengeance of his master" as he came out of Madam's apartment: but that Shee and the other gentleman had upon a loud whistle from Francis scaled the wall and rushed in, with the result that the chief culprit had escaped during the scuffle which had ensued. Shore, however, accounted more honourably for his presence in such a midnight scene by saying that he and Archdekin were in the house opposite which belonged to Mr. Ducarel, when Shee appealed to them to come in and prevent their friend Mr. Francis from being murdered. Grand ordered the release of the intruders and without seeing his wife returned to Major Palmer's where "seated on a chair, borne down with the deepest grief" he "anxiously awaited the morning." The night over, he wrote to the "undoer of my happiness" to demand satisfaction. "The reply was laconic and easy: it was couched on these terms, that conscious of having done me no injury, and knowing that I laboured under a complete mistake, he begged leave to decline the proposed invitation, and that he had the honour to remain my most obedient, etc., etc."

Baffled in his attempt to take Francis' blood, Grand was more successful in securing satisfaction of a more substantial nature. An action in the supreme court followed, and was tried by three Judges, Impey, Hyde and Chambers. Judgment was delivered against Francis, the court holding that although no guilt had been substantiated, the wrong done to Grand by injuring his wife's reputation should be liberally compensated. The sum of Rs. 50,000 was accordingly agreed upon as the measure of damages: and while the Chief Justice was delivering judgment for that amount, Hyde in his zeal for the cause of morality and much to the amusement of the bystanders, interposed with an eager "siccas siccas, brother Impey"—the current rupee being then worth eleven per cent less than the sicca. Thus was created the animosity which afterwards led to the impeachment of Impey, writes John Nicholls, a Member of Parliament who knew the Chief Justice and Hyde before they went to India and left his Recollections on record. The original receipt for the historic "siccas" still exists, and may be inspected by those who will along with the yellowing records of the case among the High Court archives.

Regarding Madam Grand herself, a word or two cannot be denied. To be the *belle* of Chandernagore as a child, and the bride of a Bengal civilian before the age of fifteen, to be only twelve months later the heroine of a *cause célèbre* with a member of Council to whom fame persistently assigns the authorship of the letters of Junius, and then after a lapse of years to reappear in Paris as the wife of Talleyrand—these are vicissitudes enough to awaken the curiosity of the most matter of fact.

"There can be hardly any story more full of human interest than the romance which turned Catharine Noel Werlée, the daughter of the port officer at Chandernagore, into the Princesse de Benevento." The whole subject has been treated in the most fascinating form not only by Dr. Busteed but by Mr. Julian Cotton of the Madras Civil Service, in the pages of *Macmillan's Magazine* for September, 1900, and much of what follows will be borrowed from their words. It must be said at the outset, in defence of the lady, that Francis always laid stress on her steady implacability to his advances: and maintained to the last that although a lover he had not been a successful one. This was, moreover, the view taken by one of the judges at the trial: and it is impossible to believe that Chambers meant otherwise than honestly when he wrote that he had never heard of an adverse judgment being given on such insufficient evidence. The supposition also that Francis could have been escorted to a meeting of the sort by a retinue of the best known men in Calcutta, is barely credible. Madam Grand must have been more sinned against than sinning to have received in her riverside retreat at Hooghly the visits of Wheler, a member of Council and of Lady Chambers, the essence of respectability, who never took any step without first consulting her husband and who astonished Calcutta society by declining all invitations while he was ill and staying at home to nurse him. "The much tempted child wife" says Mr Cotton "is surely entitled to our sympathy and commiseration." According to the evidence at the trial, Grand went out every Tuesday evening and left his wife alone to read or play with her ayah. The reader will be inclined to agree with the Frenchman who wrote. "Toute la science du bonheur est renfermée dans un seul mot, et ce mot est occupation. La vie la plus occupée est la moins malheureuse."

If we are to believe Grand's account, he never set eyes on his wife again. Immediately after the trial, "he was advised by those friends who deeply felt for him, to change the air," and he exchanged appointments with the Head Commercial Assistant to the factory at Patna. While in Behar, he seems to have spent some of Francis' siccas in founding an indigo enterprise: but he did not neglect the interests of the Company. A number of letters written by him on revenue matters between 1783 and 1787 were (says Dr. Busteed on the authority of Sir Henry Cotton) thought worthy of republication by Sir George Campbell in a volume relating to certain periods of famine in India. His indigo concerns brought him into trouble at a later date and he was removed from the service. But he did not leave India until 1798. Among his fellow passengers was a Mahomedan of distinction, Mirza Aboo Talib Khan who has left a diverting pen picture of him: "A Mr. Grand was in the next cabin, a very passionate and delicate gentleman." A storm overtaking them, "Mr. Grand who was of an enormous size and whose cabin was separated from mine only by a canvas partition, fell with all his might upon my breast and hurt me excessively: what rendered this circumstance the more provoking was that if by any accident the smallest noise was made in my apartment he would call out with all that overbearing insolence which characterizes the vulgar part of the English in their conduct of orientals, 'what are you about? you won't let me get a wink of sleep,' and such other rude expressions." He failed to get redress from the Directors and in June 1802 we find him in Paris, where his former wife from whom he had been divorced four years previously, was moving in the first circles of fashionable society and inhabiting the splendid chateau of Neuilly. How had she come there?

There is a provoking gap in her career which forbids a satisfactory reply. Dr. Busteed has investigated the question of the date of Madam Grand's departure from India with his usual diligence and painstaking accuracy, and there can be no doubt, as he says, that the following paragraph in Hicky's *Bengal Gazette* for December, 2nd, 1780, refers to the fact :—" Samuel Tolfry Esqr.," (one of Francis' attorneys in the trial) " has embarked for Europe with a fortune of three lacks of rupees: he intends proceeding from Celon (*sic*) or Coringa in the Dutch ship that carries home Mrs. G.......d." Francis himself did not accompany her. He left India, according to one of Hastings' letters, on December 3rd, 1780, having first " engaged a passage in a Dutch ship which he has left for one in the Fox," and the very last entry in Francis' diary is of similar import: " 7th November. Discover at last that it is impossible to go in the Dutch ship, so resolve to take my passage in the Fox, Captain Blackburn." But was there " un autre protecteur qui l'emmena en Europe," as a French writer, following Lord Mahon, would have us believe? The individual named by them is William Mackintosh, son of the inventor of the waterproof, who was in India for a few months in 1779 and wrote an account of his "impressions:" but he left the country in February of the following year and cannot be the man. A new claimant has lately started up, however, in the person of Thomas Lewin, of the Madras Civil Service, a " brilliant man and a fine seductive gentleman." In a book published in 1905 and entitled " Famous Women of Wit and Beauty " it is stated that Lewin was a fellow-voyager from India with Madam Grand, that he lived for some years with her in Paris, and that when he left her and returned to England, he settled an annuity upon her. The author, Mr. John Fyvie, does not name the source from which he derives his information: and Dr. Busteed, by whom the present writer is favoured with these details, adds that he has failed to discover in the India Office any list of the passengers by the Dutch ship in which Madam Grand sailed. The story is not, however, without its interest: for sixteen years had yet to elapse before she fell in with Talleyrand: and little or nothing is known of the manner in which her life was spent during this period. But if we are to believe Lady Francis' memoirs of her husband, she refused assistance from her former lover and went to reside in France under the charge of two ladies, relatives upon her father's side, upon whom she became mainly dependent for her support. Whether Talleyrand met Madam Grand in England, where he sought refuge in the early days of the Revolution, or in New York, as others allege, it is circumstantially mentioned (says Dr. Busteed) by Michaud in the "Biographic Universelle" that she came to Paris with him from Hamburg in the opening months of 1796, and that Talleyrand shortly had the vexation to see his travelling companion arrested and sent to prison "comme conspiratrice." To obtain her release he wrote the characteristic letter to Barras, the Director, which Dr. Busteed sets out in full in his "Echoes from Old Calcutta," and which may also be found in the Memoirs of Barras as published in 1896.

The appeal to Barras' knowledge of "veritables Indiennes" was not made without intention. In his early days Barras was a cadet in the Regiment de Pondichéry: and was taken prisoner in 1778 by Sir Hector Munro at the capture of Pondicherry. It is on record in the capitulation that at the particular request of General de Bellecombe, the French governor, Barras' regiment was permitted to retain its colours. He was at the time a *chasseur*, ranking below a sub-lieutenant and of the grade of élèves officers: and his name may be seen in the muster-roll of prisoners under that designation. After the fall of the town he became a prisoner on parole in Madras and Poonamalle, which he spells Pont Damalé in his memoirs. The law of the 3rd Ventôse of the year III destined him to return to India with two other "commissaires," Le Tonneur de la Manche and Armand de la Meuse: but the party never started. On the 23rd Thermidor of the year II Barras had been named commandant General of the armies of Paris, and since 1795 he was wielding still greater power as one of the revolutionary Directors. He found himself able to befriend Madam Grand as successfully as he protected Joseph Beauharnais. Thereafter until the year 1802, she did the honours of Talleyrand's table and salon: but without the right to bear his name. The ex-Bishop of Autun had been in 1790 laid under a ban of excommunication by Pius the Sixth, which was not removed until 1801. But when he received the papal sanction to return to secular life, the story goes that Bonaparte, being scandalized at the fact that his demi-official receptions as Foreign Minister were held by Madam Grand, "ordered" a marriage. The ceremony was performed on September, 10th, 1802, before the Mayor of the tenth arrondissement of Paris: and the obliging Grand, who had already consented to a divorce, was provided by the Frenchified States of the Batavian Republic with an appointment at the Cape of Good Hope as Privy Councillor. Here he published his memoirs in 1814, and here we gain a passing glimpse of him in the diary of Sir James Mackintosh who met him at Capetown on his way home from Bombay. He remarried and died at the Cape on January 17th, 1820. His wife's second matrimonial venture was hardly more fortunate than her first. After their marriage the Talleyrands lived at Neuilly and were visited there by Sir Elijah Impey immediately after the peace of Amiens. But the couple separated soon after the battle of Waterloo, and Madame la Princesse visited England for a second time. When in London, she approached the Duke of Wellington to effect a reconciliation: but apparently without success, for it is known that she returned to France and lived apart from Talleyrand with an establishment of her own at the villa Beau Sejour at Autouil.

Francis' description of his Indian flame is all that the heart could desire. "Mrs. Grand," he says "was the most beautiful woman in Calcutta. She was tall, elegantly formed, the stature of a nymph, a complexion of unrivalled beauty and auburn hair of the most luxuriant profusion: fine blue eyes, with black lashes and eyebrows gave her countenance the most piquant singularity." Even when at the age of 36 she reappeared by the banks of the Seine, her loveliness created quite a sensation. Madame de Remusat records, "I have heard it said that she was one of the most charming women of her time. She was tall, and her figure had all the suppleness and grace so common to women born in the east. Her complexion w dazzling, her eyes of the brightest blue and her sligh turned up nose gave her, singularly enough, a look Talleyrand himself. Her fair golden hair was of pr verbial beauty." To the last she retained her wonder complexion and hair, and the deepening of the soft lines her face, although it may have altered, did not in any w detract from the physical charms which had in the days her youth fascinated Junius in Calcutta. As recently December 10th, 1835, she died in Paris at No. 80 Rue Lille: and was buried in Mont Parnasse cemetery. is sad to think that the tomb has been utterly neglected and that the pious traveller who makes his pilgrimage this Campo Santo to-day, is shown a moss-grown bed of nettles and weeds as the sepulchre of the most histori beauty that India has ever produced." And if this disq sition has been a long one herein must be found its jus fication.

CHAPTER XVII.

SOME CALCUTTA INSTITUTIONS.

THE ROYAL EXCHANGE AND BENGAL CHAMBER OF COMMERCE.

AT the corner of Clive Street and New China Bazar Street may be found the Royal Exchange and the Bengal Chamber of Commerce in a large imposing building once occupied by the Oriental Bank. The earliest Chamber of Commerce in the city was known as the Calcutta Chamber of Commerce and was founded in the year 1834, or two years before similar institutions came into existence in Bombay and Madras. There are unfortunately no records of the proceedings of the old Calcutta Chamber of Commerce available; all that is known about it is that, when it was originally instituted in 1834, it consisted of 79 members. So far as can be ascertained, its office was located in the buildings of the Bonded Warehouse, where the Bengal Chamber of Commerce also found a home, until it entered into the possession of its present building in 1893. Some light is thrown upon the formation of the Calcutta Chamber of Commerce by an old letter dated 19th December, 1833, which is still preserved in the office of the Bengal Chamber of Commerce. This letter, which is signed by three firms, *viz.*, Bagshaw and Co., Turner, Stopford and Co., and Cockerell and Co., was apparently circulated to all the principal mercantile firms of Calcutta in order to obtain their views on the compilation of a half-yearly statement of stocks of imports, and on the fly-leaf appear the signatures of presumably all the leading importing firms at the time in Calcutta, to the number of 25, the only one of which existing at the present date under the same name is the firm of Messrs. Gillanders, Arbuthnot and Co. It is interesting to notice that the firms in question consented to combine for the object indicated in the letter, only on condition that Mr. James Napier Lyall, one of the founders of the well-known firm of Messrs. Mackenzie, Lyall and Co., then carrying on business under the same name, and still existing among us, should be the confidential recipient of the various particulars from each firm and the compiler of the statement. Mr. Lyall was apparently an absolutely disinterested person unconnected with the import trade. A not unnatural inference to be drawn from this letter is that the merchants of Calcutta began to feel about this time the necessity of combination, and of the formation of a central body for mutual benefit, and that this feeling resulted in the formation of the Calcutta Chamber of Commerce in 1834.

The Calcutta Chamber came to an end early in 1853; and in November of that year the first half-yearly report of the Bengal Chamber was issued. Eighty-six Calcutta members and eighteen mofussil members joined the new institution. The number of firms and individuals at present on the roll is 156; but in addition we have no less than thirteen Associations, all of whom recognise the Chamber as their parent body.

Some twenty years later the question of establishing a Commercial Exchange in Calcutta was brought forward, and at a General Meeting of the Chamber, held on the 30th November, 1857, the scheme was inaugurated. The movement was so well received that 138 subscribers were registered, including parties not members of the Chamber, and a Special Meeting was held on the 25th of May, 1858 for the enrolment of the members, when the Managing Committee was elected to frame the necessary rules and regulations. The Exchange was opened on the 1st of June, 1858, and in the Report of the Committee of the Chamber, submitted at a General Meeting on the 4th September in that year, it was stated to be well supported. As it was managed by a distinct Committee, no further mention is made of it in the subsequent Reports of the Chamber; but at a meeting of the subscribers, held on the 29th of June, 1867, it was carried unanimously that the name of the Exchange be altered to the Brokers' Exchange. The scheme for a Mercantile Exchange remained practically in abeyance until revived in 1881, and was discussed, without result, at various times subsequently, until it took a practical shape in 1893, when Sir James L. Mackay was President, and resulted in the establishment of the present Royal Exchange, so designated by special permission of Her late Majesty the Queen, which was obtained through the good offices of the then Viceroy, the Marquis of Lansdowne. In order to carry through this important scheme the Chamber was incorporated under Section 26 of the Indian Companies Act, 1882, and purchased, by the issue of a Debenture Loan the premises of the Oriental Bank Corporation, which are now known as the Royal

Exchange Building. The opening was inaugurated in January, 1894, by a banquet to the Marquis of Lansdowne, the retiring Viceroy. The Chamber occupies the upper floor of the building, the lower floor being devoted to the purpose of the Royal Exchange, which has since proved an institution of great value to the mercantile community of Calcutta, and possesses some 600 members.

An important Department in connection with the Chamber is the Licensed Measurers' Department, which, under the control of a special Committee, undertakes the measurement and weighment of all the export cargo in the port, and the certificates of which are accepted in all quarters of the globe. This department provides employment at the present moment for a staff of about seventy Europeans and Eurasians, and at the rate the work is expanding, it is probable that before many years are over the staff will number at least one hundred.

Tradition marks out the building at present occupied by the Bengal Chamber of Commerce as having once been the residence of Sir Philip Francis and in still earlier days of Clive. An interesting relic of the Mutiny is still preserved in the Chamber in the shape of what is known as the Mutiny Gate, which was placed on the upper staircase in the troubled times of 1857 by the Manager of the Oriental Bank Corporation, which then occupied the building, as a possible safeguard against any attack which might be made on the Bank. Calcutta, however, as is well known, escaped the trouble which descended on so many other cities, and it is not recorded that the gate had ever to be closed. It remains, however, as a reminder of the great struggle in which the fate and future of India were hanging in the balance.

THE DALHOUSIE INSTITUTE

Is situated within Dalhousie Square, on the south side. Externally it has no pretensions to architectural beauty, but it contains a handsome hall, 90 feet by 45 feet, the walls of which are lined with marble, with a semi-circular roof, richly decorated. It also contains a library, reading-rooms and a billiard room. It was erected "as a monumental edifice, to contain within its walls statues and busts of great men." The Dalhousie Testimonial Fund, the Havelock, Neill and Nicholson Fund, and the Venables' Fund (raised to commemorate the heroic deeds of these distinguished men in the Mutiny of 1857) supplemented by public subscriptions to the extent of 30,000 rupees, were appropriated to its erection. The foundation was laid on the 4th March, 1865, with full Masonic honours, in the presence of Sir Cecil Beadon, Lieutenant-Governor of Bengal and a large assemblage.

The Hall is available for Lectures, Concerts, and other entertainments. The entrance portico was erected in or about 1824 (the Institute building having been tacked on to it) and contains a fine statue of the MARQUIS OF HASTINGS, by Flaxman, bearing the following inscription: "In honour of the Most Noble the Marquis of Hastings, K.G., Governor-General of British India from the year of our Lord 1813 to 1823. Erected by the British Inhabitants of Calcutta." And also a handsome mural tablet in brass, erected to the memory of Mr. John

HASTINGS, by Flaxman, bearing the following inscription: "In honour of the Most Noble the Marquis of Hastings, K.G., Governor-General of British India from the year of our Lord 1813 to 1823. Erected by the British Inhabitants of Calcutta." And also a handsome mural tablet in brass, erected to the memory of Mr. John

Remfry, the first Honorary Secretary of the Institute, to whose efforts the citizens of Calcutta are mainly indebted for the foundation of the Institute.

THE POST OFFICE.

This handsome structure is situated on the west side of Dalhousie Square, at the corner of Koila Ghat Street,—being a portion of the site of the old Fort of Calcutta. The removal of the old foundations was a work of great difficulty owing to the extreme hardness of the masonry, which, in many cases, could only be removed by blasting. The building was erected from designs by Mr. Walter B Granville, architect to the Government of India. It was opened to the public in the year 1868. It consists of two lofty storeys, the east and south fronts being faced with handsome Corinthian columns, flanked by massive piers, in which are the staircases. The south-east angle of the building is semi-circular, also faced with Corinthian columns, leading to a lofty circular hall, in which are the public letter boxes. This is surmounted by a lofty lantern crowned by a dome, which forms one of the most conspicuous landmarks of Calcutta. There is also a large clock with three illuminated dials. The building is approached by handsome flights of steps.

THE TELEGRAPH OFFICE

Will be found at the corner of Dalhousie Square, South, and Old Court House Street, East. The original design was made in 1868, and the ground cleared in 1870, but the building was not commenced till 1873. The style of architecture is one admirably suited to the requirements of the climate, somewhat resembling its neighbour—the Currency Office—but differing in its external decorations. The building stands upon a plinth, 4 feet 6 inches high, and consists of a main block facing Dalhousie Square, with a Tower at the east, and three wings—the east wing facing Old Court House Street, the other two forming a centre and west wing. The total height of the building is 66 feet above the plinth, and of the tower, which resembles an Italian campanile, 120 feet. The principal or northern front faces Dalhousie Square. The central entrance is of handsome design. The columns are well proportioned; the balconies and cornices bold and rich in decoration, and the general effect is exceedingly good. The Tower is carried up as a part of the main building as far as the roof, strengthened, however, at its four corners, by buttresses, which are continued to the top, although not originally intended to reach beyond the balcony level. The public entrance is in the centre of the north front The "establishment' entrance is by a broad flight of steps in Old Court House Street.

In the public lobby there stands at the entrance a handsome bust by Geflowski, erected in 1879 by the members of the Telegraph Department in honour of Major-General Daniel George Robinson, R.E., who was for twelve years (from 1866 to 1878) Director-General of Indian Telegraphs, and who died in 1891 at the age of 65. On the wall on the right hand as the public vestibule is entered is a tablet erected in memory of Mr. W. B. Melville, Superintendent of Telegraphs for the Assam Division, and signaller James O'Brien, who were murdered in March, 1891, at Myankhong during the rising in Manipore which resulted in the death of Mr. Quinton, the Chief Commissioner of the province, and a number of other British officers.

THE IMPERIAL SECRETARIAT BUILDING

Is situated on the west of Government House, and covers the site once occupied by Spence's Hotel, and Loudon Buildings. In the southern end is the Pay Office, while the north wing contains the Home Department, office of Surgeon-General and General Superintendent of Thuggee and Dacoity Department. The east wing has the Revenue and Agricultural and Forest Departments, office for Registration of Inventions and Designs, office of the Countess of Dufferin's Fund, and Imperial Record Department. In connection with the Patent Office a museum of models has been commenced, but it will be many years before the collection is much worth inspection. The present collection of models consists of sugarcane mills, railway sleepers, water lifts, punkah pulling machines, kilns, etc., etc.

Adjoining this block in Hastings Street is the extensive range occupied by the Government of India Printing Office.

THE CURRENCY OFFICE.

On the east side of Dalhousie Square, is a lofty building in the Italian style of architecture. The ground floor is the Office of Issue and Exchange of Government Paper Currency, and is worthy of a visit. The entrance has a very handsome gate, in three parts, of a very florid design in wrought iron. The central hall is of very grand proportions, and is lighted by sky lights surmounting three large domes. Here are the exchange counters for notes, gold, silver, and small change. To the left as you walk up the hall is a noble array of huge iron safes full of new note forms representing the value of many millions. The bulk of the silver is kept in strong vaults in Fort William, but a working reserve is kept in the Currency Office, in a vault of massive masonry lined throughout, roof, walls, and floor, with iron; an iron door six inches in thickness closes this room, which is further protected by a second iron door, and last of all by a massive iron grating.

The rooms above are very massively and handsomely finished, and are floored throughout with Italian marble, even to the third storey. Here is the residence of the Assistant Commissioner in charge of the Currency Office. The building was originally erected for the Agra and Masterman's Bank, and on the collapse of that institution (soon after its completion) it was sold to Government, who were at that time in quest of a suitable building for the Currency Department.

HIS MAJESTY'S MINT, CALCUTTA.

The Mint (native name, *Tuksal*) is situated on the Strand Road, about 200 yards north of Howrah Bridge.

The Mint Buildings occupy a large space of ground

on the east of the Road and on the opposite side the Mechanical Engineers' Quarters, the Warder's Quarters and those of the Inspector of Police are situated, and here also are the Stores Godowns, and a large water tank for the Engines of the Copper Mint.

There are really two Mints, the Silver and the Copper Mints, the former being much the larger and finer building. It was designed and constructed by Major W. N. Forbes, R.E., and took six years to build: it was erected on alluvial soil reclaimed from the river, the foundations being laid at an average depth of 25 feet below the level of Clive Street, so that there is as much brickwork below as above the surface. The architecture is Grecian Doric and the central portico facing the Strand was a copy in half size of the Temple of Minerva at Athens. This Mint was opened in 1831. In the Bullion room is a fine marble bust (on a pedestal) of Major-General Forbes, who constructed the Mint and presided over it for many years. The water tank for the Engines of the Silver Mint is at the south side of the main building, and beyond it are the Quarters for the Civil Guard, the Police attached to the Mint and the Military Guard House.

The Copper Mint, opened in 1865, consists of a very large block of buildings, to the north-east of the Silver Mint. The Mint Master's Office and the Accountants' Office, the Record Room and Library and the Mint Master's residence occupy a block in front of the Copper Mint, and opposite to this is the Assay Office and Laboratory. In the céntre of the Silver Mint is a quadrangle where the Bullion vaults are located, and between the

Silver and Copper Mints is an extensive workshop including a Brass and Iron Foundry, Carpenters' shops and Blacksmith's shop.

Persons wishing to view the Mint should apply to the Master of the Mint. The words "Application for Pass" should be written on the corner of the envelope. Parties of not more than 5 persons are allowed to go over, and 10 of these passes are granted. Special Passes are, however, frequently granted by the Mint Master as the applications by natives from the Mofussil are so numerous that the whole number allowed for are always applied for. The best time to see the Mint is between the hours of 11 A.M. and 1 P.M., in order to be present at the pouring of the molten Silver. Visitors should go to the Warder's Lodge to present their passes and get permission to enter the Mint.

FREEMASONS' HALL.

Since the year 1904 the headquarters of Freemasonry in Bengal have been installed at 54 Park Street. Its earliest place of meeting was the Old Court House, which stood at the north-east corner of Dalhousie Square until 1792, when it was finally demolished. Some five or six years before that event, however, the Craft removed to a building in Lall Bazar, just opposite the Police Office of to-day, and adjoining the once-famous Harmonic Tavern. In 1840, this house was given up, and for the next sixty-four years the premises at present numbered 55 in Bentinck Street were utilized as a Freemasons' Hall. The transfer to Park Street was not effected without a wrench, for the Old "Jadoo Ghur" in Cossaitollah had not lived its life in vain, and its Lodge-room and Banqueting Hall were eloquent of bygone days, when Sandeman and Blessington Roberts and Pitt Kennedy ruled the Province in turn from the District Grand Master's chair. But the change of habitation had become inevitable, and there can be no question that it has been altogether for the better. Freemasonry in Bengal boasts a record as ancient as it is honourable. Its earliest District Grand Master, George Pomfret, assumed office in 1728: and Lodge "Star in the East" its premier Lodge of England, is the oldest of any Lodge outside the United Kingdom on that roll, and dates from the year 1740. Roger Drake, the Governor, who ran away and lived to fight another day, was District Grand Master when the "Troubles" of 1756 overtook the settlement: and when the provincial Grand Lodge of Bengal was revived in 1759, after the recapture of Calcutta by Clive and Watson, the chair was filled in turn by William Mackett, uncle of the gallant little middy Billy Speke, whose tomb still stands in St. John's Churchyard, and by Culling Smith, afterwards a baronet and progenitor of Mr. H. C. E. Childers, Chancellor of the Exchequer from 1883 to 1885. Holwell was also a high office-bearer, and when during his short administration as Governor at Fort William the foundation-stone was laid on June 24th, 1760, of the makeshift Chapel of St. John on the site of the Black Hole, the ceremony was performed with full masonic solemnities. In 1790, Charles Stuart, Member of Council during the whole of Cornwallis' first Government, was District Grand Master: and in 1813 and 1817 the office was held by two other Members of Council, Archibald

Seton, and James Stuart. The Patrons of the Craft have been three in number—Lord Hastings, Lord Dalhousie and Lord Mayo—and the first named enjoys in addition the distinction of having been the first and only "Grand Master of All India." The Banqueting Hall contains a number of interesting portraits of Masonic celebrities, of which the following is a list:

1. His Majesty King Edward the Seventh: Grand Master of England from 1874 to 1901.

2. The Most Honourable the Marquess of Hastings, K.G., Governor-General of India from 1813 to 1823: Patron and Acting Grand Master for All India, 1813.

3. Major-General James Ramsay: District Grand Master of Bengal from 1854 to 1862.

4. Hugh David Sandeman, Esq., Accountant-General of Bengal, and member of the Bengal Civil Service from 1844 to 1874: District Grand Master of Bengal from 1862 to 1875.

5. John Blessington Roberts, Presidency Magistrate and Chairman of the Justices of the Peace from 1862 to 1871, and subsequently Superintendent of Stamps and Stationery: District Grand Master of Bengal from 1875 to 1877. This remarkable man commenced his career as a police constable and from 1848 to 1850 he filled the office of Grand Tyler in the same Grand Lodge over which he presided a quarter of a century later. He died in Calcutta on May 12th, 1880.

6. Sir Henry Thoby Prinsep, K.C.I.E., Judge of the

High Court at Fort William from 1878 to 1904: District Grand Master (in succession to Mr. John Pitt Kennedy, the distinguished advocate of the High Court) from 1878 to 1896 and again (on the death of Major-General Sir Arthur Godolphin Yeatman-Biggs, K.C.B.) from 1898 to 1904. Entering the Bengal Civil Service in 1855, before the days of competitive examination, he was when he retired forty-nine years later not only the Father of the Service but the last of the Haileybury men in harness in India. A bust of his father Henry Thoby Prinsep the elder, Member of the East India Company, will be found in the Town Hall.

7. John Jacob Louis Hoff, Esq., Grand Secretary of Bengal from 1844 to 1856: Deputy District Grand Master of Bengal from 1856 to 1862: appointed to the rank of Past Grand Junior Warden of England in 1853.

8. Henry Hover Locke, Esq., Director of the Government School of Art: Deputy District Grand Master in 1871.

9. Heerjeebhoy Manackjee Rustomjee, Esq., C.I.E.; District Grand Secretary of Bengal from 1880 to 1904: appointed to the rank of Past Grand Deacon of England in 1902.

10. Thomas Jones, Esq.: Deputy District Grand Master of Bengal in 1884 and again in 1891: appointed to the rank of Past Grand Deacon of England in 1897.

11. William Henry Fitze, Esq.: Deputy District Grand Master of Bengal from 1885 to 1887 and again from 1900

to 1902: appointed to the rank of Past Grand Deacon of England.

12. His Highness the Maharajah Sir Nripendra Narain Bhup Bahadur of Cooch Behar, K.C.I.E., C.B., Deputy District Grand Master of Bengal in 1890-91: appointed in 1887 to the rank of Past Senior Grand Warden of England.

13. Prosunno Coomar Dutt, Esq., the first Hindoo initiated into Freemasonry: Deputy District Grand Master of Bengal in 1895-96.

The District Grand Lodge holds its communications every Quarter in the Masonic Hall, 54 Park Street, where the office of the D. G. Secretary is located.

There are at the present time (1905) twenty Lodges meeting regularly in Calcutta and its suburbs under the English constitution. A list is subjoined. The meetings are held at the Freemasons' Hall in Park Street, unless otherwise stated:

"Star in the East," No. 67, A.D. 1740, 2nd and 4th Fridays of each month.

"Industry and Perseverance," No. 109, A.D. 1761, 1st and 3rd Fridays.

"True Friendship," No. 218, A.D. 1772, 2nd and 4th Tuesdays.

"Humility with Fortitude," No. 229, A.D. 1774, 1st and 3rd Mondays.

"Marine," No. 232, A.D. 1776, 2nd and 4th Mondays.

"Anchor and Hope," No. 234, A.D. 1776, 1st and 3rd Tuesdays.

"Courage with Humanity," No. 392, A.D. 1821, 2nd and 4th Thursdays.

"St. John," No. 488, A.D. 1842, Plassey Gate, Fort William, 2nd and 4th Fridays.

"Temperance and Benevolence," No. 1160, A.D. 1867, 1st and 3rd Wednesdays.

"Sandeman," No. 1374, A.D. 1871, Dum-Dum, 2nd Friday of every month.

"Prinsep," No. 2037, A.D. 1884, 25, Telkul Ghat Road, Howrah, 1st and 3rd Wednesdays.

"Thomas Jones," No. 2441, A.D. 1892, 39 Free School Street, 2nd Friday and last Saturday.

"Ubique," No. 2476, A.D. 1893, Barrackpore, 2nd and 4th of every month.

"Yeatman-Biggs," No. 2672, A.D. 1897, 1st Tuesday of every month.

"Defence," No. 2839, A.D. 1900, 2nd and 4th Thursdays.

"Federation," No. 2871, A.D. 1901, St. Stephen's School, Hastings, 3rd Saturday.

"Calcutta," No. 3054, A.D. 1904, 39 Free School Street, 2nd Tuesday.

"East India Arms," (Installed Masters) No. 3080, A.D. 1903, 1st Friday.

"Calcutta Emulation Lodge of Improvement": meeting under sanction of Lodge True Friendship, No. 218, once a month.

The following Lodges under the Scotch constitution also meet in Calcutta at 39 Free School Street.

"St. David in the East," No. 371, A.D. 1855, Calcutta, 1st and 3rd Wednesdays.

"St. Thomas in the East," No. 404, A.D. 1860, Calcutta, 1st and 3rd Wednesdays.

"Endeavour," No. 474, A.D. 1867, 2nd and last Mondays.

"Albyn," No. 813, A.D. 1894, 1st Tuesday.

THE ASIATIC SOCIETY.

The Asiatic Society of Bengal, one of the oldest Institutions of its kind, was founded by Sir William Jones, then Chief Justice of Bengal, on the 15th January, 1784. Warren Hastings, the then Governor, became its first patron. "The bounds of its investigations," says the illustrious founder in his first discourse, "will be the geographical limits of Asia, and within these limits its inquiries will be extended to whatever is performed by man or produced by nature."

The monthly meetings of the society are held on the first Wednesday of every month, at 9 o'clock P.M., at No. 57, Park Street, when antiquarian and scientific papers are read and discussed. There are about three hundred paying members. The entrance fee is Rs. 32, and Town members pay Rs. 40, and Mofussil members Rs. 32 per annum, for which they receive the publications of the Society and have the use of the large library. The business of the Society is administered by a council chosen annually. The meeting house is the property of the Society. Several additions were made to the original building in 1836 and 1850, to accommodate the increasing library and collections.

Since the foundation of the Society, its literary activity has been uninterrupted. The first publication had the title of "Asiatic Researches." They extend over twenty quarto volumes, issued between 1799 and 1839. In 1829, Captain James D. Herbert commenced to issue, in connection with the Society, a monthly publication, called "Gleanings in Science." He issued three volumes, the last one (vol III of 1831) being completed by Mr. James Prinsep, as Captain Herbert left for Lucknow to join his appointment as astronomer to the King of Oudh. In the beginning of 1832, Mr. James Prinsep changed the title of the "Gleanings" to "Journal of the Asiatic Society of Bengal," and continued to be the editor till 1838. The first seven volumes, from 1832 to 1838, contain his numerous essays on Indian Antiquities and Paleography, and his famous readings of the Asoka inscriptions. On his departure, the Journal became the property of the Society, and from 1839, when the "Asiatic Researches" ceased, bulky annual volumes have been printed. Since 1865, the Proceedings of the Society have been issued separately, whilst the Journal has since then been annually issued in two parts, each consisting of four quarterly numbers, the first part being devoted to Literature, Philology and Antiquities, and the second to Natural History and Science. The Journal and Proceedings contain annually from 800 to 1,000 pages.

Another department which has greatly added to the renown of this old Society is the "Bibliotheca Indica." In 1838, the Honorable Court of Directors gave the Society a monthly grant of Rs. 500, for the printing of Oriental works, and since that time the Society has issued, under the above title, over five hundred fasciculi of numerous Sanskrit, Arabic, Persian, Pali and Hindi works, both in original and in translation, among them a fine collection of Indian historians. This monthly grant was continued, and in 1858 the Imperial Government increased it by Rs. 250 per mensem for the same purpose. In 1870 the Imperial Government sanctioned Rs. 3,200 per annum for the classification, copying and purchase of Sanskrit Manuscripts in Bengal.

The Museum of the Society, up to 1866, contained a large collection of Zoological and Ethnological specimens, besides many Archæological reliefs and statues of great value, nearly all of which were presents made to the Society by its members. The Society being unable to provide space and funds for the maintenance of its ever-increasing collections, offered, in 1865, the Museum to Government, on condition that the Society was to receive *in perpetuo* free quarters in the new Imperial Museum, in Chowringhee, the building of which was about to be commenced. Government accepted this, and the transfer of the Society's Museum, under that condition, was legalised by Act XVII of 1866. The Society has, however, retained its rich collection of coins, copper *sanads,* portraits and pictures, busts, and its large library.

The Library contains above fifteen thousand volumes; among them more than five thousand Sanskrit, Arabic, Persian and Hindustani Manuscripts. There is also a fine collection of Burmese and Nepalese Manuscripts. The greater portion of the Manuscripts belonged formerly to the old College of Fort William. The bulk of the Arabic and Persian Manuscripts formed part of Tippu Sultan's library, and had been transferred from Seringapatam to the College of Fort William (1804). When the college was reduced, the Honorable Court of Directors presented the greater part of the library to the Society. Among the Manuscripts there are many masterpieces of caligraphy and oriental painting.

The collection of portraits, busts and paintings is well worth a visit. The most curious picture is that of a European in Indian costume with a native wife and two children. This has not been identified, but it is believed by Mr. J. J. Cotton to represent General DeBoigne, with his native wife Noor Begum and their son and daughter. Many of the more important and interesting paintings have been lent to the Trustees of the Victoria Memorial Hall and are temporarily on view at the Indian Museum.

The rooms of the Society are daily open to members from 10 to 5 o'clock, Sundays and holidays excepted. Strangers may visit the library and inspect the coins on application to the Honorary Secretaries.

THE BENGAL CLUB.

The Bengal Club is to be found at No. 33 Chowringhee, the former Calcutta residence of Lord Macaulay. It was instituted in the beginning of the year 1827, having as its first President the Honorable the Viscount Combermere, Commander-in Chief. There is no limit to the number of members. The management of the Club is vested in a President, Vice President, and seven other Members of Committee, who are elected annually. The number of members at present on the books of the Club exceeds 650. Members are admitted by ballot. All gentlemen received in general society in Calcutta are eligible. The Viceroy; the Commander-in-Chief in India; the Lieutenant-Governors of Bengal, the United Provinces, and the Punjab; Members of Supreme Executive Council, and the Lord Bishop of Calcutta, are entitled to privileges of members, without ballot, on payment of fees as permanent Members. There are three classes of permanent Members—Resident, Non-Resident, and Absent. The accommodation of the Club at present consists of five large houses—the Club Houses, No. 33, Chowringhee Road, a large house in the same compound, devoted to bed-rooms for members, the houses No. 1, Park Street, and No. 1, Russell Street, divided into chambers for members permanently residing, and the large house, No. 2, Russell Street, also divided into chambers. The club is a very pleasant resort; and the reading-room is kept well supplied with the best periodicals, etc., from every part of the world. The Bengal Club reciprocates with the Bombay (Byculla) Club, the Madras Club and the Hong-Kong and Shanghai Clubs, in admitting the members of those clubs, if visiting Calcutta, to all the privileges of Honorary Membership for the time being.

The Club House has been much altered since the days when Macaulay lived there and held his symposia in its rooms. Macaulay was not the only member of his family with Indian associations. His uncle General Colin Macaulay had been Resident in Travancore and died when Macaulay was in India, leaving him a legacy of £10,000.

In the early stages of its career, the Club was housed first in Old Court House Street, on the eastern side of Dalhousie Square, in the premises now occupied by Messrs. Newman and Co., the booksellers, and subsequently in Elysium Row. The subjoined cutting from the Bengal Hurkaru of some eighty years ago refers to the latter period: "The number of members on the 1st of March was about 210, of whom upwards of one-half are resident in Calcutta. The large club-house in Esplanade Row, which is at present occupied, contains, besides the public rooms on the two first floors, eight spacious and very airy and comfortable sleeping apartments completely furnished for Mofussil members visiting Calcutta. These were all lately occupied. The charge for them is only four rupees weekly. There is a house establishment of servants, so that an individual requires few private domestics. Breakfast, tiffin, and dinner are provided at the following rates for those who reside at the club, as well as all other members who choose to attend, *viz.*, breakfast, one rupee, tiffin, one rupee and eight annas, dinner, three rupees, wine, etc., being charged separately, about one and a half to three rupees a night, Sherry, French Claret, Port wine, and

Beer, being at the house. Diners alone are charged in common, all others are paid for by those only who drink them, any member can order his own dinner alone, when of course he is at liberty to call for such wines, etc., as he pleases, paying accordingly. For the accommodation of members who frequent the club to read the papers or periodical publications, or to play billiards, white wine and brandy and water are charged by the glass."

In the dining-room of the Club House are two very indifferent paintings which are said to represent Lord Nelson and the Duke of Wellington, and a fine full-length portrait of General Viscount Combermere, who filled in 1826 the office of first President of the Club. The portraits of two other Presidents hang in the reading-room. On the east wall is a striking likeness by Mr. A. S. Cope, A.R.A., of Sir William Macpherson, of the Indian Civil Service, Judge of the High Court from 1885 to 1900, in which year he retired. He enjoys with Sir Henry Thoby Prinsep the distinction of being the "last of the Haileybury men," and was President of the Club from 1886 to 1888 and again from 1890 to 1895. Opposite him is a portrait of Mr. Charles Martin, President in 1871 and 1872.

THE UNITED SERVICE CLUB

Is situated at No. 29, Chowringhee, and 1, Kyd Street. It was founded as the Bengal Military Club in 1845. On the 15th March, 1853, its designation was changed to the Bengal United Service Club. The number of Members is unlimited, and consists of Commissioned Officers and

Chaplains in His Majesty's Military and Naval services, and of Members of His Majesty's Indian Civil Service; also of such Barrister-Judges of the High Court as may have received permanent appointments from the Home Government. The Members are elected by ballot. The Governor-General, Commander-in-Chief and all ordinary Members of the Executive Council of the Government of India, may be admitted without ballot; also the Chief Justice of the Calcutta High Court. The concerns of the Club are managed by a Committee, consisting of a President and 12 Members stationed at the Presidency. The entrance fee of each member is fixed at Rs. 150, and in addition, a fee of 15 rupees as a donation to the Library Fund, and a similar sum as donation to the Billiard Fund. The subscription of each member is fixed at 18 rupees per annum, payable in advance, and 10 rupees per mensem in addition for each member resident in Calcutta; while the absentee subscription is Rs. 18 yearly. A limited number of rooms are alloted to resident members for permanent occupation, and there is also provision to the extent of the means of accommodation for temporary residents. The Club has recently been turned into a limited Liability Company and its main building occupies excellent new premises. The number of members is over 600.

THE NEW CLUB

Has its premises in Park Street in a house once used as a Seminary by Mr. William Meadows Farrell, and afterwards occupied by the Surveyor-General's office. The establishment of this Club in 1884 supplied a much needed want among a certain class of the community, and the present flourishing state of its finances evidences wise control on the part of the managing and sub-committees. The Club occupies fine commodious premises at No. 46, Park Street, and so great has been the demand for residential quarters, that the leasing of an adjacent house is under consideration. The Library is a feature of the Club which has been carefully and judiciously tended and a selection of new books is periodically made. The amusements consist of Lawn Tennis, Billiards, Smoking Concerts, House Dinners, Dances, etc., all of which are well patronised and generally approved of. The subscriptions are reasonable, and special rules exist for the election of casual and temporary members.

THE "SATURDAY CLUB."

Club House—No. 7, Wood Street.

This Club was established in August, 1878. The amusements most popular with members are Dancing, Concerts and Amateur Theatricals, and some excellent entertainments have been given from time to time in the Club Rooms. There is an excellent supply of newspapers and periodicals. Lawn Tennis forms a special feature, and there are several well-kept courts. The Committee have power to admit as Temporary members, persons proposed and seconded and temporarily residing in Calcutta. All ladies and gentlemen received in general society in Calcutta are eligible for admission as members of the Club.

CALCUTTA GOLF CLUB.

This popular Club was founded in 1829. The links are

extensive, and much has been done to improve the *maidan* over which the "Golfers" have to travel in a game. There is also a piece of turf used by the members for Bowls. The Club is the possessor of a handsome pavilion, which, however, according to Fort regulations, is deemed a portable building only, and as such, subject to removal at short notice. During the year several valuable prizes are competed for, the most important being the Club Gold Medal; Cashmere Silver Cup; Blackheath Gold Medal; Madras Silver Medal; Bombay Silver Medal; St. Andrew's Silver Challenge Tankard; Silver Challenge Cup.

In May 1891, a Ladies' Golf Club was founded and a course was laid out for them, on the opposite side of the casuarina avenue.

THE INDIAN MUSEUM.

At the junction of Chowringhee and Sudder Street, and adjoining the new building of the United Service Club on the south, is the massive stone edifice devoted to the purposes of the Indian Museum. It was erected from the designs of Mr. Walter B. Granville, the late Government Architect, and was opened to the public in the year 1875. The frontage towards Chowringhee extends over an area of 300 feet, while the depth facing Sudder Street occupies 270 feet. The façade has two stories of great height, in the Italian style of architecture, the two projecting wings and the central portico having elegant Corinthian columns. A broad flight of steps leads to a lobby, which opens on

PLAN OF THE INDIAN MUSEUM.

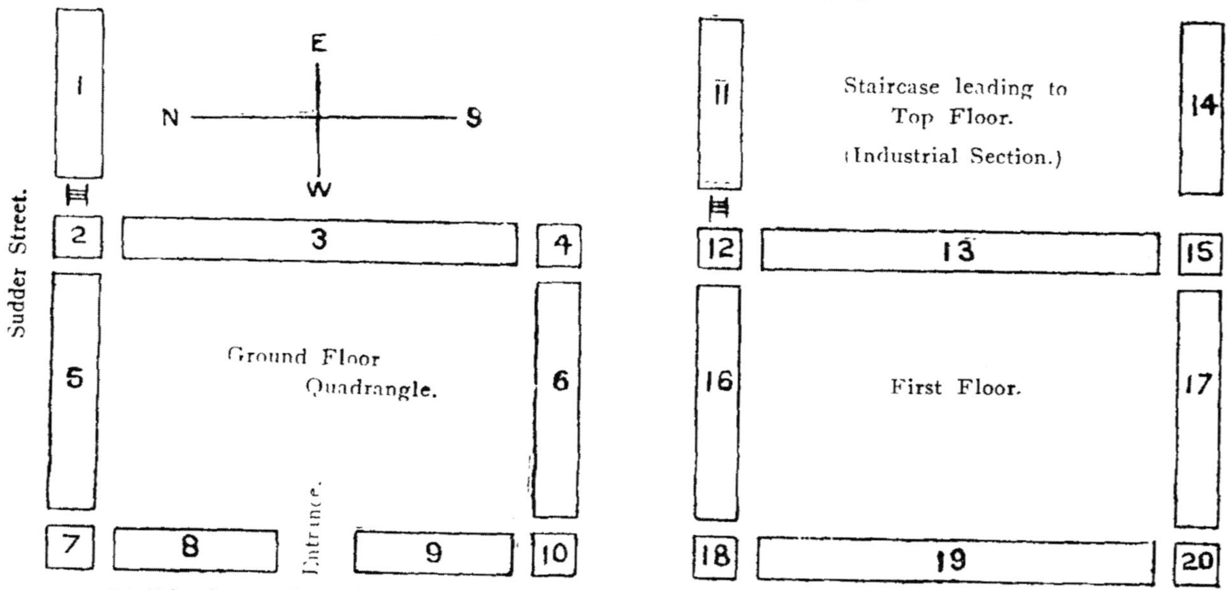

(1) Ethnology; (2—3) Invertebrates; (4) Archaeology; (5) Mineralogy; (6) Archaeology; (7) Geology; (8) Palaeontology; (9) Bharhut Stupa, (10) Graeco Buddhistic; (11) Art and Art-ware; (12—13) Mammals; (14) Commercial Products; (15) Birds; (16) Palaeontology; (17) Reptiles, Birds; (18—19—20) Victoria Memorial Hall Collection.

either side into a room eighty feet by thirty. Three series of arches lead to a double staircase of very fine proportions ascending to the right and left, and beyond the foot of the stair-case the lobby opens on to a grass-laid quadrangle 180 feet by 105 feet, surrounded by a selection of tropical plants; around this the inner sides of the building form a piazza or arcade. The piers of the arches are decorated on the side facing the quadrangle with engaged columns in the Roman Doric style on the ground floor, and in the Roman Ionic on the first floor.

The large hall at the head of the stair-case, over the portico is 59 feet long by 50 feet wide, and 50 feet high with a fine panelled ceiling, as at present. At each of the four corners of the building is a pavilion, 44 feet by 40 feet, in two stories; another storey exists on each of the two front corners, and in the original plans this was surmounted by a high-pitched mansard roof, as was also the room over the central portico. The upper exhibition galleries are lighted by arched sky-lights on two sides which leave the whole wall space available, and diffuse a soft and equal light through the room.

The Museum is open to the public daily, Sunday inclusive, excepting on Thursday and Friday in each week, on which days it is closed, except to students. From the 1st to the 15th May, and from the 1st to the 15th November in each year, the Museum is closed for cleaning and repairs. On closed days travellers can usually obtain admission to the galleries by applying to one of the officers. The hours during which the Museum is open to visitors are from 10 A.M. to 5 P.M. from the 1st February to 1st

November, and from 10 A.M. to 4 P.M. from the 16th November to the 31st January.

The nucleus of the Imperial Museum was formed by the Asiatic Society of Bengal, established so far back as 1774. In the year 1866, an Act was passed by the Governor-General of India in Council providing for the establishment of a Public Museum in Calcutta, "to be devoted in part to collections illustrative of Indian Archæology and of the several branches of Natural History, and in part to the preservation and exhibition of other objects of interest, whether historical or physical, in part to the records and offices of the Geological Survey of India, and in part to the fit accommodation of the Asiatic Society of Bengal, and to the reception of their Library, Manuscripts, Maps, Coins, Busts, Pictures, Engravings and other property." The Act provided for the erection of a building for this purpose, to be completed within five years from the date of the passing of the Act; and constituted a body of Trustees. It also provided that all expenses and salaries connected with the Indian Museum should be defrayed by the Government of India.

The provision in the Act for the accommodation of the Asiatic Society in the new building has not been carried out. In 1876, when the extent of the collections had been more maturely considered, along with some changes which it was found desirable to make in the constitution of the governing body, the Government arranged with the Asiatic Society that, for a pecuniary consideration, they should relinquish their claim to accommodation in the new building. A new Act was accordingly passed and received the formal assent of the Governor-General on the 17th December, 1876.

The Economic and Art Section owe their origin to Sir George Campbell. In 1874 that Lieutenant-Governor established a Museum in Hastings Street, not to bring together as he expressed it "things ornamental or curious, still less specimens of fine Art, but specimens of the ordinary products of Bengal, of its agriculture, its minerals, its manufactures, and its forests and wastes." For some years it had but a languishing existence: and in order to arouse public interest in it the collection was in 1883 transferred as an annexe to the Calcutta International Exhibition, which was held in what was then an open space in Sudder Street behind the main Museum building. At the close of the Exhibition it was augmented by a large series of Indian Products collected by the Government of India for the Exhibition; an extensive collection of the Art Manufactures of India purchased by the Bengal Government; the collection of models and Ethnological objects formed for the Exhibition, and other specimens presented by private Exhibitors. These collections were placed in charge of the Committee of the old Economic Museum under the new name of the "Bengal Economic and Art Museum." By Act IV of 1887 they were handed over on 1st April, 1887, to the Trustees of the Imperial Museum; the Bengal Government, however, continuing to supply the funds for their maintenance, and retaining a reversionary property in them, should the Trust, for any reason, be hereafter terminated.

The governing body of the Museum at present consists

of 21 Trustees, namely, the Accountant-General for the time being *ex-officio,* five Trustees appointed by the Government of India, five by the Government of Bengal, five by the Asiatic Society, and five more elected by the sixteen so appointed. The present Board includes the Heads of the Imperial and Provincial Scientific Departments; the Chief and the Revenue Secretaries, and the Directors of Public Instruction and of Agriculture of Bengal, and two other official members; a leading member of the English commercial community in Calcutta; and two influential representatives of Hindoo, and one of Mahommedan Calcutta society.

Visitors to the Museum will find it the more convenient plan to make the entire circuit of the ground floor, and then proceeding up the main staircase make the circuit of the upper floor.

Entering by the main entrance on the west, the Archæological galleries lie immediately on the right or south. These are four in number, and occupy the whole of the south-western and southern sides of the ground floor. On the east are the Invertebrates: in the north-east corner the Insects, and on the north the galleries devoted to Mineralogy and Geology. In the north-eastern corner is the first Palaeontological gallery. On the upper floor, the remainder of the Palaeontological Section is on the north, the Mammals occupy the Eastern Gallery, and the Reptiles and Birds are on the south. The whole of the Western side over the main entrance and the Archælogical collection below, has been temporarily appropriated by the

Victoria Memorial Hall Collection, which deserves a separate and entirely special visit.

THE SCHOOL OF ART.

(28, *Chowringhee.*)

Adjoining the Indian Museum will be found the Calcutta School of Art and Government Art Gallery. The Calcutta School of Industrial Art was founded in 1854 by an Association of gentlemen under the name of "The Society for the promotion of Industrial Art," which originated at a meeting held at the house of Mr. Hodgson Pratt in the early part of that year. The object of the Society was stated to be to form schools for East Indian and Native Students for instruction in: (*a*)—Elementary Drawing. Drawing from Models, and Natural Objects, and Architectural Drawing: (*b*)—Etching and Engraving in Wood, Metal and Stone: (*c*)—Modelling, including Pottery.

The School was placed under the charge of Mons. Rigaud, a French plaster-cast maker, and for some time the internal decoration of buildings in plaster formed the chief occupation of the pupils. A specimen of their work may be seen in the Bengal Legislative Council-room. Early in 1860 Mr. Garrick was appointed master, and a teacher of Wood Engraving was also employed. In 1864 the charge of the School was assumed by the Bengal Government. Mr. H. H. Locke, a gentleman experienced in Art as a profession, and in the management of Art Schools in England, was appointed Principal, and a systematic course of instruction in what may be termed the practical branches of the Fine Arts was inaugurated. The curriculum of the School now comprises: Freehand Drawing, Geometrical Drawing, Painting in Oil, Water Colours and Tempera, Practical Design, Architectural Drawing, Mechanical Drawing, Engineering Drawing, Modelling Wood, Engraving and Lithography. There are now more than 200 Students on the rolls, and the number is steadily increasing.

The recent exhibitions held under the auspices of the Calcutta Art Society, have afforded an opportunity to the public of seeing the excellent quality of works now being done in the Schools. The remarkable talent displayed in Portraiture and Still-life, the exactness and precision of the Pen drawing, and the vigour of the Modelling, will come as a surprise to many. Apart from the works of Art exhibited, the Technical Classes of Lithography and Wood Engraving are still doing excellent work. Well-known works done in the past, as the illustrations to Sir Joseph Fayrer's Thanatophidia and Babu Rajendralal Mitra's works on the Antiquities of Orissa, may be mentioned. Among the more recent ones which have been received with marked approval and may also be mentioned, are the illustrations to the Botanical Works of Sir G. King, F.R.S., and Dr. Prain, and numerous works commissioned by the Government of India. A great number of Models of Agricultural Scenes in Bengal were executed for the Imperial Institute. The figures were mostly of small size, but full of character. There were also a few life-size figures, modelled from nature, which may rank among the best specimens of modern native art.

Mr. W. H. Jobbins was appointed as a successor to the late Mr. H. H. Locke in 1887, and was himself succeeded by Mr. E. B. Havell in 1896. The teacher of Drawing is Signor Ghilardi.

The Government Art Gallery which is attached to the school and is open to the public contains a fine collection of Indian Art, including many remarkable examples of the Indian School of painting from the Mogul period down to the present day. These show that painting as a fine Art has reached a much higher state of development in India than is generally supposed. In the classes for practical design special attention is paid to stencilling, lacquer work, and to fresco decoration by the old Indian process as practised from the earliest times in the decoration of Indian buildings.

THE MUNICIPAL OFFICE.

The offices of the Corporation of Calcutta are situated in Corporation Street and occupy a large open space between that important thoroughfare and the Municipal Market. They are accessible not only from Corporation Street but from Chowringhee by a short strip of road, which has been recently widened and distinguished by the name of Chowringhee Place, and which runs immediately north of the Grand Hotel. The building as it now stands is in the form of a quadrangle. On the north, and opening out upon Corporation Street, are the old Municipal Offices which did duty for many years but were wholly insufficient for the accommodation of the many branches of the municipal administration of Calcutta. They have been handed over to the Corporation Press: and its stucco frontage presents an unfortunate contrast to the red brick of the remaining three sides of square which are supplied by the new offices. These have been constructed in accordance with the designs of Mr. Banks Gwyther F.R.I.B.A., and were completed in 1905. The eastern and western wings, which are connected with the old block by means of covered passages, are two-storied and contain the several offices of the executive and clerical staff of the Corporation. The south block is carried to a higher level, and the main feature is the Central Tower, which is raised to a height of 105 feet over the vestibule or the principal entrance to the Building, facing the New Market. To the right of the tower is the new Council Chamber and to the left are three Committee rooms, with residential quarters for the Secretary to the Corporation upon the floor above. Both the Council Chamber and the Committee rooms are approached by a vestibule and staircase. All the office rooms are provided with deep verandahs on the west side, while the Council Chamber and other rooms in the central block have verandahs on the North and South faces. The building is therefore not only well ventilated, but the corridors formed by the verandahs and passages afford easy communication between the several offices situated in the old and new buildings. Work is now being carried on on the land and roads round about the new buildings, and when this is completed, and the projected market square laid out on the south, with its lawn and gravel walks, the new Municipal Offices should present an appearance worthy of the city. It is intended to place in the centre of the square a Boer gun presented by the Government of India to the citizens of Calcutta as a memorial of the part played by India in the South Africa Campaign of 1899 and 1900.

The Council Chamber, which is well worth a visit, is most conveniently approached from the south by the vestibule beneath the tower. Ascending by a broad flight of stairs at the northern end of the vestibule, we find ourselves in a spacious lobby. To our left is the Council Chamber: on the right is a room for the use of the Commissioners, and beyond this are the Committee-rooms. The lobby is adorned with the busts and portraits of municipal worthies of the past, which formed until recently part of the Town Hall collection, and were removed here during the current year in accordance with a resolution of the Corporation. The busts at present are two in number, and both are the tribute of members and officers of the Corporation. The first is the marble bust of Sir HENRY LELAND HARRISON, KT., whose portrait and career have already claimed attention in the chapter on the Town Hall. The Chairmanship of the Corporation is ordinarily filled by a member of the Civil Service for two or three years at a time, and usually as a stepping stone to still higher promotion. Sir Henry Harrison held it uninterruptedly from 1881 to 1890 and enjoys the unique distinction of a nine years' tenure of the post. He was knighted in 1887 on the occasion of the Jubilee of Queen Victoria, and died suddenly of cholera at Chittagong in 1892. His chairmanship is rendered memorable by such important municipal events as the doubling of the water-supply of the city, the amalgamation of the suburban municipalities with the present Corporation and the opening of the great central road from Howrah Bridge to Sealdah which bears his name.

The second bust, which is also marble, is that of Mr. WILLIAM MEARNS SOUTTAR, of the Bengal Civil Service, Chairman of the Corporation from 1878 until his death in 1881. His brother Mr. Robinson Souttar (M.P. for Dumfriesshire from 1895 to 1900), was the contractor for the Tramway system in Calcutta upon its original introduction in 1880.

The portraits may be most conveniently dealt with in chronological order.

MR. JOHN BLESSINGTON ROBERTS, whose carefully trimmed whiskers of the Dundreary type conjure up memories of a long forgotten fashion, was Chairman of the Justices of the Peace from 1862 to 1871, in days when that body constituted the sole municipal authority for Calcutta. It is to the Justices that the city owes its water supply, its drainage system, its new municipal market, which bears however the name of Roberts' successor, Sir Stuart Hogg, and the lighting of its streets. Each achievement represents in itself a striking victory over prejudices and difficulties of every conceivable character, which only those who are familiar with the incidents of life in an Eastern city can adequately appreciate. Towards the close of his tenure of office, the relations of Roberts with the Justices became somewhat strained: and he retired from the office of Chairman to that of Superintendent of Stamps and Stationery. He died in 1880 at the age of sixty-one.

If Blessington Roberts is justly to be set down among

the four or five chiefs of genuine eminence, which the Corporation of Calcutta has been privileged to possess, an even higher rank must be accorded to Mr. ROBERT TURNBULL, C.I.E., for his municipal record is without a parallel. Commencing his career in 1857 as Secretary to the three Municipal Commissioners appointed by an act of the previous year "for the conservancy and improvement of Calcutta," he served the Justices in the same capacity from the moment of their assumption of civic authority in 1863 until their deprivation of it in 1876. And when a remodelled and representative Corporation came into existence at the bidding of Sir Richard Temple in that year, he continued to act as the right hand man of that new and untried body until the year 1888 when the suburbs were amalgamated with the city and a further extension of powers of self-government conferred upon them. So great was the esteem in which Mr. Turnbull was held by the Commissioners that upon his retirement in 1888, he was voted a special pension equal in amount to the salary he was drawing. He survived the severance of his connection with the Corporation for fourteen years and died in Calcutta in 1902 universally respected and regretted. The portrait, which commemorates his public services and his private virtues, is the outcome of a public subscription and was painted by Mr. James Archer, R.S.A., during Mr. Turnbull's lifetime.

Mr. HARRY LEE, I.C.S., whose name is preserved in the suburbs by a road which is rapidly rising in favour with the English inhabitants of the city, was Chairman of the Corporation from April 16th, 1890, to March 31st, 1895.

and served as a Member of the Bengal Legislative Council from 1892 to 1894. Few Chairmen have been so widely popular or so genuinely esteemed as Mr. Lee: and the premature termination of his career by cancer in 1895 was regarded upon all hands as a serious blow to the city. He was as energetic and vigorous in execution as he was courteous and engaging in manner: and he was a special friend to the student community of Calcutta, who have perpetuated his memory and his many kindnesses to them by the institution of the Lee Challenge Shield for Football, an appropriate memorial for one who was in his day an English "International."

Rai Kristodas Pal Bahadur, C.I.E., for many years took a prominent part in municipal affairs as a Justice of the Peace and later as Municipal Commissioner. His political services are commemorated by a statue which stands at the junction of Harrison Road and College Street, and a full account of his career will be found in the chapter which deals with the Statues of Calcutta. He died in 1884 at the age of 46: leaving a son Baboo Radha Charan Pal, who has worthily followed in his father's footsteps as an energetic and independent representative of the rate-payers on the Corporation.

We may now turn our attention to the Council Chamber, the entrance to which lies on our left. It was formally opened on the 17th June, 1905, by Mr. R. T. Greer, the late Chairman of the Corporation, prior to his departure on sick leave: and the Municipal Commissioners are to be congratulated upon having said a final farewell to the dingy room on the upper floor of the Town Hall in which they were for so many years compelled to hold their meetings. The chamber is lofty, well lighted, and fully equipped with electric lights and fans. A gallery at either end and the Chairman's dais relieve the monotony of the bare walls, and there is an air of dignity, as well as of comfort, about the appointments which is distinctly appropriate. Each of the fifty Commissioners is provided with a seat and a desk. These are arranged in horseshoe fashion, and all face towards a common centre, the Chair, which is placed on a raised platform directly beneath the eastern balcony, which was originally intended for the Reporters' Gallery. The chairs are upholstered in green morocco leather, and the arms of the Corporation are emblazoned in gold upon the back of each. Both seats and desks are placed on platforms which rise gradually towards the back, and an ample gangway runs between the separate blocks. On either side of the Chairman and also upon the dais but on a slightly lower level are the seats of the Vice-Chairman and the Deputy Chairman. Directly below the dais are the chairs of the Secretary and the official Reporter. The Chairman's dais is handsomely panelled, and the chair is heavily carved, with morocco leather seat and back, and surmounted by a gold panel and the Arms of the Corporation. In the centre of the hall there is an elaborately-carved table, and on the western wall there hangs an elaborate parchment document by which the college of Heralds have been pleased to grant arms to the Corporation.

The most serious defect, which the Council Chamber has yet been found to possess, has relation to the acoustic properties of the room. So bad in fact are they that the representatives of the Press have been compelled to desert the reporters' gallery over the Chairman's dais and claim accommodation on the floor of the House. It must also be acknowledged that the public gallery at the western end is hardly as suitably furnished and arranged as the necessities of the case would seem to require. But in other respects the Chamber is well able to meet criticism: and may even make so bold as to challenge favourable comparison with the halls of many another municipal body in the cities of the west.

The Corporation of Calcutta deals with an average annual income of some 67½ lakhs which at the current value of the rupee, may be set down in sterling as £450,000. As constituted by the latest legislative changes initiated by Sir Alexander Mackenzie and carried to completion by Sir John Woodburn, it came into existence on the 1st April, 1900, and is governed by the provisions of Bengal Act III of 1899. Abandoning the policy followed in the previous Acts, of vesting the entire Municipal Government of the city in the Commissioners, with permission to the Chairman to exercise such powers as were not expressly reserved to the Commissioners in Meeting, and subject to such conditions as the Commissioners might lay down, the new Act created three co-ordinate Municipal authorities, *i.e.*, the Corporation, the General Committee, and the Chairman, and distributed between them the functions considered by the framers of the Act most appropriate to each. The entire executive power is vested in the Chairman, to be exercised independently, or subject to the approval or sanction of the Corporation or of the General Committee wherever this is expressly so directed. Associated with the chairman, who is appointed by the local government and who is a member of the Indian Civil Service are a Vice-Chairman and a Deputy-Chairman. The former is elected by the Corporation and has been invested with the chief financial control. The latter is appointed by Government and is ordinarily a junior member of the Civil Service, but his principal duty, nevertheless, is the supervision of the revenue-collection and of the Building and Conservancy Department. To the Corporation, which is elected triennially, is reserved the right of fixing the rates of taxation and all those general functions which can be efficiently performed by a large body, "provision being made at the same time to prevent their deliberations impeding the transaction of business." The General Committee stands between the deliberative and the executive authority, and deals with those matters which are declared to be by their nature ill-adapted for discussion by the Corporation, and yet are too important to be left to the disposal of the Chairman alone. The total number of Commissioners has been reduced from 75 to 50, of whom 25 are elected by the ratepayers of the 25 wards who formerly returned double that number, and the rest appointed by Government, the Bengal Chamber of Commerce, the Commissioners for the Port of Calcutta, and the Calcutta Trades Association, in the proportion of 15, 4, 2, and 4 respectively. The General Committee consists of 12 Commissioners, one third of whom are elected by the Ward Commissioners, an equal number by the nominated Commissioners, and the remainder by Government. Provision has thus been made for the adequate representation of those commercial interests which have created modern Calcutta, but which, when left to the chances of election in the past, alleged themselves to be hopelessly outnumbered.

THE MUNICIPAL MARKET.

The Calcutta Municipal Market stands to the south of the Municipal Office. The establishment of a Market for the sale of all kinds of food for European consumption, was for years under consideration; but it was not until 1866, that it was resolved to construct one on a large and complete scale, and the old bazar called Fenwick's bazar, with the filthy lanes and bustee surrounding, was taken up for the purpose. The market was opened in 1874. It is an extensive building, forming three sides of a quadrangle. The principal entrance is in Lindsay Street, to which it presents a frontage of about 300 feet. The land and market building cost about Rs. 6,65,000. The market suffered severely at the outset of its career from the competition of the Dhurrumtollah Bazar, which was established in 1794 and stood at the corner of Dhurrumtollah and Chowringhee: and its fortunes did not prosper until the Justices subsequently bought the bazar for seven lakhs. The whole of this money was raised by Government loan, the interest of which is far more than met by the rents of the stalls and shops in the market.

A large number of improvements in the market have lately been effected: and it is in contemplation to erect an extension of the building on the land to the east. The management of the Market is excellent: and it is quite one of the noteworthy institutions of the city. To Mr. W. M. Jones, the late Superintendent, who died after a long tenure of office in 1906, is due much of the credit for its successful progress. The visitor will find that there is hardly anything he requires which he cannot obtain. The old idea of a Food Market has expanded into a scheme of the most comprehensive character: and while the meat is relegated to the East, and the vegetables to the West, the centre, with its wide corridor and comfortable shops, is given over to the vendors of every sort of miscellaneous goods. Mr. Rudyard Kipling in the last chapter of his Calcutta sketches published under the title of "The city of Dreadful Night" has given a lively description of the market and its frequenters.

THE UNIVERSITY SENATE HOUSE

Is situated in College Street. The building, which was opened in 1873, is a massive structure fronted by a spacious and lofty portico, supported by Ionic columns, beneath which a flight of stone-steps leads up to the main building. At the top of these steps stands a fine full-length statue in white marble of the late Hon'ble Prosunno Kumar Tagore, C.S.I., (1803-68) founder of the Tagore Law Professorship. The ceiling of the central hall rests upon Corinthian pillars. This fine hall is about 60 feet in breadth, and its length is more than 200 feet. It is flanked on either side by extensive corridors, 20 feet wide. One of two side rooms contains the University Library, which consists of a valuable collection of books, comprising

English works of reference, the chief authorities on Indian antiquities, and fairly complete sets of the Sanskrit, Arabic, Latin, French, and German classics.

Within the Senate House itself are a number of busts in honour of educational celebrities. These are placed in the entrance-hall.

(1) HENRY WOODROW, M.A., formerly Fellow of Caius College, Cambridge: for six years Principal of La Martinière, then for upwards of 20 years Inspector of Schools, and for the latter part of his service in the Education Department, Director of Public Instruction in Bengal. He was born at Norwich in 1823 and died at Darjeeling in October, 1876. The inscription sets out that "this bust is erected in affectionate remembrance, by desire of his native friends from funds chiefly contributed by them, to perpetuate his memory, and in recognition of his worth and his devotion to the cause of education in India." There is another bust in his honour at Caius College, Cambridge. He was educated as a boy at Rugby and was one of the six who took supper with Dr. Arnold on the evening before his sudden death. Many incidents of Woodrow's school-life are preserved in "Tom Brown's School Days" and are recognizable by Rugbeians of his day: but the author has assigned them to different characters. In November, 1840, he accepted the post of Principal of La Martinière and in 1854 was appointed Secretary to the Council of Education. He was transferred to Eastern Bengal in the following year as its first Inspector of Schools. He officiated as Head of the Department from September 1875 to January 1876, and, on the death of

Mr. Atkinson, was permanently appointed. With his pupils he enjoyed great popularity, and the *Calcutta Review* on receiving news of his sudden death spoke of him as the "Nestor of Education in Bengal." Macaulay's great education minute of February 2nd, 1835, was disinterred by Woodrow from the mass of official records in which it lay forgotten and was first published by him in May 1862.

(2) JAMES SUTCLIFFE, M.A., for upwards of 21 years Principal of the Presidency College, for 12 years Registrar of the University and for the last two years of his life Director of Public Instruction in Bengal. He was born in 1824 and died on July 29th, 1878. The inscription records that "this bust was erected by pupils and friends in India who retain a grateful recollection of his unvarying diligence and kindness."

(3) SIR CECIL BEADON, K.C.S.I., Fellow of the University of Calcutta, Lieutenant-Governor of Bengal from April, 1862, to April, 1867. Born 22nd December, 1813, died 18th July, 1880.

(4) CHARLES HENRY TAWNEY, C.I.E., M.A., formerly Fellow of Trinity College, Cambridge, and bracketed Senior Classic in 1860. He joined the Indian Educational Department in 1864, served for many years as Professor and Principal of the Presidency College, Calcutta, officiated three times as Director of Public Instruction in Bengal and was for eight years Registrar of the University of Calcutta. On retirement in 1895, he was appointed Librarian at the India office and held that post until 1903. He enjoys a high reputation as a Sanskrit Scholar. The inscription records that the bust was erected in January,

1895, "by his pupils and friends in India, who retain a grateful recollection of his unvarying kindness and a profound respect for the wide range of his learning and for his special erudition in the classical literature alike of Europe and of India."

(5) RAJA RAJENDRA LALA MITRA, C.I.E., Doctor of Laws: born 1824, died 1891. A distinguished Bengalee author and linguist. At the age of 22 he was appointed Assistant Secretary to the Asiatic Society of Bengal and held the office for ten years, during which he diligently studied Sanskrit and its allied languages. Sir Richard Temple described him as the most effectively learned Hindu of his day both as regards English and oriental classics. His knowledge of Sanskrit, Bengalee, Persian, Hindi, Urdu, and Uriya was profound, and he was acquainted in addition with Greek, Latin, French and German. His works upon Budh Gaya, the Antiquities of Orissa, and the Indo-Aryans are monuments of extensive and patient research and of deep and varied erudition. He filled the office in 1885 of President of the Asiatic Society of Bengal and was also President of the British Indian Association, President of the Central Text book Committee and a Municipal Commissioner for the Town of Calcutta. No Bengalee of his time is more fitly honoured by a memorial within the walls of the Senate House.

The following oil-paintings also adorn the Senate House; (1) of Rai Madhub Chunder Roy Bahadur, B.A., B.C.E., M.I.C.E., born 1st April, 1841, died 21st September, 1902, (by R. P. Banerjee); (2) of Dr. Trailokya Nath Mittra, M.A., D.L.; (3) of Her Majesty Queen Victoria, with the following inscription: "In commemoration of the victory achieved by the invincible British Army under the commandership of Lord Roberts, the object of the blessings of Raja Natta Narayan, the embodiment of Heroism in war. This portrait of Empress Victoria is presented to the University of Calcutta as a humble offering of veneration and loyalty by Sourindra Mohun Tagore, Mus. Doc., Calcutta, June, 1900."; (4) of the Rev. K. M. Banerjee, D.L., C.I.E., born 1813, died 1885; (5) of Rai Bunkim Chunder Chatterjee Bahadur, the famous Bengalee novelist, born 1838, died 1894.

LA MARTINIERE COLLEGE

Corner of Lower Circular Road and Loudon Street.

La Martinière of Calcutta, together with similar Institutions at Lucknow and Lyons, was founded by General Claude Martin. He was originally a common soldier in the French Army, and fought under Count Lally. He afterwards entered the service of the East India Company, and rose to the rank of Major-General. He amassed a princely fortune, and died at Lucknow on the 13th September, 1800. In his will he stated his property to be £ 477,101 12*s*. 10*d*.

General Martin bequeathed Rs. 2,00,000 to be devoted to the establishment of a School for the Christian inhabitants of Calcutta; and a further sum of Rs. 1,50,000 was bequeathed "to add to the permanency of the school." With great wisdom he refrained from burdening his educational bequests with any conditions except one, *viz.*, that the children, boys and girls, should be "taught the English language and religion." For thirty-five years however the benevolent purposes of the will were thwarted by the inability of the Supreme Court, as official guardian of all charitable bequests, to decide as to the proper course to be pursued and partly by "a rapid and melancholy succession of deaths among the Judges." La Martinière was finally opened on the 1st March, 1836, and the first Head Master of the Boys' School was Canon Christopher, afterwards a well-known figure in Oxford. By that time the bequest with interest had reached a total of nearly ten lacs of rupees. The capital now in the hands of the Accountant-General amounts to seventeen lacs.

The building completed in 1835 at a cost of £23,000 is of two storeys, and is surmounted by a large dome, which is employed as a library. In the centre of the building is the chapel, and on either side are ample accommodations for teachers and children. There are two porticoes, south and north, communicating with the chapel. Adjoining is a large and perfectly plain structure for the girls' department. The locality in which La Martinière is situated is known in Hindustani as *Panch Kottie*, on account of the five sister houses to the north of the school. Three out of these five houses are owned by the Institution. The area of the compound of the Boys' School is 7 acres 3 roods; and that of the Girls' School, 4 acres 1 rood. There are 77 boys and 40 girls on the foundation, who are maintained, educated, and put out in life. In addition to these foundationers, boys and girls are admitted both as Boarders and as Day Scholars on the payment of a monthly fee. The anniversary of General Martin's death is, in terms of his will, observed with peculiar honors. An appropriate sermon is preached to the children, and two silver medals for good conduct are presented to the best behaved boy and girl; all then adjourn to the dining room, where they partake of a sumptuous dinner and drink a toast in silence to the memory of the founder. The Annual Examinations and the Distribution of Prizes take place just before the Christmas holidays, when two Gold Medals are presented to the boy and girl who stand highest in their respective schools. Both the Boy's and the Girls' Departments of the Institution are affiliated to the Calcutta University up to the B.A. Standard, and are at present under very able and successful Educationists as Heads.

The following inscription inscribed on two tablets in English and Bengali characters is placed in the grand entrance of La Martinière: "This school, named La Martinière, was established and is supported by means of property bequeathed for that purpose by Claude Martin, a native of France, and a Major-General in the service of the Honourable East India Company. He was born in the city of Lyons on the 5th day of January, in the year of our Lord 1735, and died at Lucknow, in the Kingdom of Oude, on the 13th day of September in the year of our Lord 1800. This building was completed on the 31st December, 1835. Designed by J. H. Rattray, Esq., erected by J. P. Parker." Another tablet in St. John's Church testifies that "the sum of Rs. 50,000 sicca rupees is a gift granted by Major-General Claude Martin to the poor of

Calcutta, the interest of which is to be daily distributed in perpetuity." At Chandernagore, in the Church of St. Louis, is a third inscription; "la somme de cinquante mille roupies a été léguée par le Majeur-Général Claude Martin, nè à Lyons, afin que les intérêts en provenant soient distribués journellement aux pauvres de Chandernagore à perpetuité."

ST. XAVIER'S COLLEGE,

(10 *and* 11, *Park Street.*)

Was instituted by the Fathers of the Society of Jesus, who, in 1834, were sent by the Pope to support the cause of religion in Calcutta. It owed its first establishment to the pious generosity of two rich residents, one of whom vacated, and gave up his own house for the purpose, and the other furnished the College throughout, and bestowed a liberal pension for its support during the first few months of its existence.

In the year 1846, the fine building at present occupied by the College, and originally built for the Sans Souci Theatre, in Park Street, was for sale, and was purchased by the Right Rev. Dr. Carew for the sum of Rs. 40,000. It was at first called St. John's College. On the arrival of the Belgian Jesuits, in 1859, it was placed under their efficient management. The building has been improved and extended from time to time, and the house, No. 11, Park Street, has been added to the accommodation. The Institution has now on its rolls 500 scholars, including a large number of boarders. The College was affiliated to the University of Calcutta in January 1862. The discipline and training, mental and moral, pursued in the College, are well known and appreciated. Besides the Meteorological Observatory erected in the College premises, the Rev. Fr. Lafont, C.I.E., who for eight years filled the office of Rector, has exerted himself in establishing the first Spectroscopic Observatory in India, at a cost of Rs. 20,000, the Government of Bengal aiding with a handsome donation of Rs. 7,000.

DOVETON COLLEGE,

(41, *Free School Street.*)

This Institution was established on the 1st March, 1823, by John William Ricketts, "the Champion of the East Indian Community." The main objects in view were to effect an improvement in the defective system of education which then existed; and to provide for the Christian youths of Calcutta the benefit of a good education at a cheaper cost than it could then be obtained. The management was vested in a committee composed of parents and guardians and subscribers to the funds; and for years a large proportion of the Christian population owed their education to "The Parental." In 1854, a legacy of Rs. 2,30,000 was bequeathed to the Institution by Captain John Doveton, and a College Department (named after the generous legator) was added and affiliated to the Calcutta University. An Infant and Juvenile Department, and a School for Young Ladies were also formed in connection with it. The educational staff is strengthened, as necessity arises, by professors and masters from Great Britain. In addition to a number of Government scholarships annually awarded to the students of the College, who pass high in the University Examinations, there is a Lawrence deSouza Scholarship for English Literature, of the value of Rs. 50 per mensem, tenable for one year, and also an Arson Scholarship of the value of Rs. 13 per mensem, also tenable for one year. The College Department likewise receives a grant-in-aid from the local Government.

THE BETHUNE NATIVE FEMALE SCHOOL.

This school in Cornwallis Square was established by the late Hon'ble J. E. D. Bethune, for the education of the daughters of Native Gentlemen, and was the first of the kind in Calcutta. The foundation stone of the handsome building which it occupies was laid with great state, in November 1850, by the Hon'ble Sir John Littler, then Deputy Governor of Bengal. The buildings are spacious and admirably adapted for the purpose for which they were designed, and there is a fine residence for the Head Mistress. The pious memory of the founder is perpetuated both by a bust and an oil painting. John Elliot Drinkwater Bethune was counsel to the Home office in England for many years and was appointed Law Member of the Supreme Council in Calcutta in April 1848. Besides his ordinary official duties he undertook the presidency of the Council of Education: and took a keen interest in educational questions generally. He died in Calcutta in August, 1851.

THE BISHOP'S COLLEGE

Was established under the auspices of the Society for the Propagation of the Gospel at the urgent request of Bishop Middleton, by whom the foundation stone was laid on December 15th, 1820. It was founded for the purpose of (1), instructing native and other youths in the doctrine and discipline of Christ's Church, with a view to their becoming Preachers, Catechists or School Masters; (2), extending the benefits of education generally; (3), translating the Scriptures, Liturgy, and other religious works; and (4), forming a residence for European Missionaries on their arrival in India. Its first Principal was the Rev. William Hodges Mill, D.D., (1792-1853) who subsequently became Regius Professor of Hebrew at Cambridge, and was one of the founders of Tractarianism. There is a portrait of him in Bishop's College and a fine marble bust by Chantrey in the Asiatic Society's rooms. In 1830 the statutes were modified so as to allow of the admission of lay or general students not intended for clerical or educational work. The College possesses one fellowship and 21 scholarships. The holders of scholarships have rooms, boarding, and tuition free of charge.

The College was originally located in the buildings now occupied by the Seebpore Government Engineering College. In 1879, these buildings were sold to the Government, and the College was removed temporarily to the house No. 33, Circular Road, and subsequently the buildings and grounds of 224, Lower Circular Road, were purchased for them by the Society for the Propagation of the Gospel. There are now about 25 students in the College.

most of whom are natives of India and preparing for some form of Mission work. There are also two boarding Schools for Native Christian boys attached to the College, the High School numbering about 35, and the Central School, nearly 100. The last has an Industrial Department attached to it, which consists of a carpenter's shop and a printing press. The College, with its schools, forms the largest institution of the kind for the education of Native Christians in Calcutta.

THE PRESIDENCY HOSPITAL.

The premises now denominated the General Hospital, are in the Lower Circular Road and are situated to the south of the Presidency Jail. They were, in their original state, occupied as a private garden house when they were purchased by Government in 1768. They have been from time to time enlarged, and now afford ample accommodation in separate buildings, for patients and for the Medical Officers and establishment attached to the Institution. The situation of the Hospital is airy and healthy. It is open to Europeans of all classes. The charges are Rs. 5 per diem for a double room, and 3 and 2 respectively for a single room, according to accommodation in the private wards. These fees include food, medical attendance and nursing. There are 121 free beds for men, 18 for women, and 12 for children. There is also separate accommodation for infectious diseases.

THE MILITARY (OR STATION) HOSPITAL.

(*South of the Race Course.*)

This fine building, formerly occupied by the Sudder

Court, and which was originally erected for a Hospital, is now devoted to its legitimate purpose.

THE MAYO NATIVE HOSPITAL.

(Strand Road, North.)

So long ago as the year 1793, a Hospital was established by Sir John Shore, who was then ruling as Governor, in the Fouzdaree House, Chitpore Road, for the relief of "the native inhabitants of Calcutta generally, and more particularly for the labouring part of them." Its promoter was the Rev. John Owen, Junior Chaplain of St. John's. Subscriptions to the amount of 54,000 rupees were raised, and a monthly allowance of 600 rupees was granted by Government. In 1796, the Hospital was removed to "the open and airy road of Durrumtollah," in which thoroughfare there were only then three or four houses. In 1810, further contributions were given, and the Government allowance was increased to 1,000 rupees per mensem; this was subsequently increased to 2,000 rupees. The Institution pursued an uninterrupted career of usefulness until the year 1871, when a proposal was made to remove it to a more salubrious situation on the banks of the river, above the mint. The question was warmly discussed, but ultimately the proposal was carried. A portion of the Dhurrumtollah property was sold for 79,000 rupees. The Gurunhatta Dispensary, attached to the Hospital, fetched Rs. 18,000; Rs. 78,990 were raised by subscription; Rs. 10,000 were left by Mr. L. A. deSouza for building purposes, and the surplus of the Mayo Memorial Fund, Rs. 50,000, was transferred to the Hospital, so that without touching the funded property of the Hospital, amounting to about 3 lakhs of rupees, the Governors were able to meet the expenses connected with a new building. The new Hospital was designed by Mr. A. T. Osmond; Messrs. Mackintosh, Burn & Co., were the contractors; and the cost of erection, including the third storey more recently built, was Rs. 2,43,471. The deSouza Fund was not touched. His legacy of Rs. 10,000 continues to the present day, yielding Rs. 400 annually. The foundation stone was laid by Lord Northbrook, the then Viceroy, on the 3rd February, 1873, and the building was opened on the 5th September, 1874.

The building has three stories and gives accommodation for about 120 patients, with out-patients' rooms and quarters for the Resident Medical officer.

A portion of the old Hospital premises in Dhurrumtollah was retained for an out-door dispensary. There are three other dispensaries attached to the Hospital in Park Street, 57, Ripon Street, Chitpore Road, and in Sukea's Lane.

Opposite the Hospital, on the river Bank, is the Burning Ghat in which all Hindus who die in the Town are cremated.

THE MEDICAL COLLEGE HOSPITAL.

(College Street.)

This splendid building was erected from funds obtained from the Old and New Fever Hospitals, balance of the

Funds of the Lottery Committee, and a donation of Rs. 50,000 from Rajah Pertab Chunder Singh. The building was designed and erected by Messrs. Burn & Co., of this city. The foundation stone was laid on the 30th September, 1848, by the Marquis of Dalhousie with Masonic ceremonies, and the building was opened for the reception of the sick on the 1st December, 1852. The style of architecture is the Corinthian, and it is capable of accommodating over 300 sick people. It is a lofty structure and contains a handsome Operating Theatre.

The present Hospital has been found for some years to be too small for the number of patients seeking admission, and a new Hospital has been constructed to the south-west for obstetric cases and diseases of women and children, the present Hospital being reserved for surgical and medical cases only. The new Hospital is a three-storied building, consisting of a central block for the wards, and four wings, one at each corner, connected with the main building by short passages. This, the Eden Hospital, is now probably one of the most perfect Hospitals in the world, it having been designed according to the latest and most approved rules of sanitary science. The subsidiary buildings include two large blocks for the residence of the Hospital Nurses.

A new Eye Infirmary has since been erected to the north-east of the Hospital, and has been named after the native gentleman, Shamachurn Law, who gave the funds for its erection. This Hospital will accommodate 50 patients, besides containing two rooms for paying patients. A ward for the treatment of Jews, directly north of the main

Hospital building, was erected in 1887 at the sole expense of Mrs. Ezra, widow of the well-known Jewish Merchant of Calcutta. It can accommodate 20 patients, each being provided with a separate room and bath-room. Each of these separate hospitals constitute wards of the Medical College Hospital, and all are administered by a common head, *viz.*, the Principal of the Medical College.

ZOOLOGICAL GARDENS.

To those who can remember the dirty and rather dismal-looking approach to Belvedere, the improved and satisfactory condition of the neighbourhood, at the present, must afford a very striking contrast. Both east and west of the road-way leading from the Zeerut bridge were untidy, crowded, unsavoury bustees. To-day we shall find on the site of the old bustees the Calcutta "Zoo." A very large share of credit for the establishment of this pleasant resort is due to Sir Richard Temple, who was Lieutenant-Governor of Bengal from 1874 to 1877, but long before the scheme assumed any proper shape, Dr. Fayrer, C.S.I., in 1867, and again in 1873 Mr. L. Schwendler (known as the "Father of the Zoo,") had brought forward and strongly urged the necessity and utility of a Zoological Garden, and the Asiatic and Agri-Horticultural Societies were entirely in favour of such schemes: however, they had to be abandoned for want of a suitable site. In the year 1875 the Government of Bengal took up the matter in real earnest, and a large piece of land was granted, and the maintenance and management of the gardens secured. The public also helped very materially towards this object, and liberally contributed to the capital required for laying out the grounds and for the erection of buildings. The scheme flourished, and the Committee appointed by Government to carry out the preliminaries having entered *con amore* into the work, things were sufficiently advanced in the year following to admit of a complete prospectus being issued, setting forth the objects, the means of obtaining them, and the general rules of management.

The visit to Calcutta of His Majesty King Edward the Seventh, then Prince of Wales, was seized upon as an auspicious occasion. On the 1st January, 1876, the gardens were inaugurated by His Royal Highness, and in May of the same year they were opened to the public. Within three or four years the "Zoo" had already taken rank as one of the most popular institutions in Calcutta and in the "Exhibition Year" a total of 188,532 visitors was registered. The present perfect state of the gardens speaks volumes itself, and be it ever remembered to the credit of the *first* Committee of Management, and all those who have followed, but one desire has been cherished, namely, to carry out in its entirety the original programme, an excellent and complete one, and this has been done, and well done. In the grounds is a grey granite monument with the following inscription: "This obelisk was erected by public subscription to the memory of Carl Louis Schwendler, who died 6th January, 1882, and by whose energy and enterprise this Zoological Garden was established in 1876." It bears a medallion portrait of the "Father of the Zoo."

THE BOTANIC GARDEN.

(Seebpore.)

The Royal Botanic Garden (founded in 1786 by the East India Company, by the advice of Colonel Kyd, of the Bengal Engineers, who became its first Superintendent), is situated in the suburb of Howrah on the opposite side of the river from Calcutta and immediately below the Government Engineering College. The upper entrance gate of the garden is about 3½ miles below the Hooghly Bridge, and is easily reached by a good road which passes through Howrah and the village of Seebpore. The garden can also be conveniently reached by the river either by taking boat at Calcutta, or by driving down to the Nemuck Mahal Ghat on the Calcutta side, and there hiring a boat and crossing to the garden which is just opposite. In either case the best landing place is at the landing stage, which is about the middle of the garden.

The extent of the garden is 272 acres, and it has a river frontage of exactly a mile. Originally intended for visitors on foot only, the garden has, by the liberality of Government, been recently supplied with excellent driving roads, so that the whole of the grounds may now be gone over without leaving one's carriage.

No account of the Botanic garden can be complete without a reference to its founder. Colonel Robert Kyd was Military Secretary to Government when he first formulated in 1786 his proposal to establish a Botanic Garden, and his scheme proving acceptable to the Board of Directors, a piece of ground was selected for the garden and he was appointed Honorary Superintendent, a post which he held till his death on the 26th May 1793. The site of the Botanic Garden was chosen because of its nearness to Colonel Kyd's own garden at Shalimar, where, in the fashion of his day, he had a country house, a quaint description of which is quoted by Sir George King from a contemporary MS. which states that it was built by Colonel Kyd himself.

Colonel Kyd appears to have spent a good deal of his time at his garden-house, and to have been much attached to the place; for, in his will, from which extracts are given by Sir George King, he speaks of his collections of botanical drawings, of the plants in the environs, of the birds indigenous to the tract, and of the fish found in the Hooghly; the arrangement of all of which, he pathetically says, he had reserved for a future day. He speaks, also, of the little vessel, in which he, doubtless, took many trips on the river, probably using it regularly to go up to Calcutta. There are directions, too, for the upkeep of his garden, until his relative and heir, Major Alexander Kyd, should return to India, and careful provision for the future of those members of the establishment who were dependent upon him—notably two native boys who appear to have been slaves, alienated from friends and country, one a convert to Christianity. Above all, Colonel Kyd desired that he should be buried in his garden; and the sentence in which he directs that his last remains should be committed to the ground in his own garden, on the west side of the pukka-walled tank near to which an alligator pear tree now stands, shows how his last thought clung to the spot where, we cannot doubt, he had found many days of quiet happiness. Colonel Kyd's wish to be buried at Shalimar was disregarded. It was probably felt that it would be improper to allow so distinguished and honoured a servant of the Company to be laid in unconsecrated ground, and so his remains were interred in the South Park Street burial-ground. It was perhaps in deference to his known feelings on the subject that no tablet was placed over his tomb, so that, although the handsome, and to Calcutta residents, familiar monument in the Botanical Garden still bears testimony to his services, his actual grave remains obscure and unknown.

The land selected for the Botanic Garden ran along the river bank, the upper part being occupied by a few native huts, whose owners, having no other title than possession, were compensated and removed. The upper end of the garden was separated from Colonel Kyd's own grounds at Shalimar only by a ditch crossed by a masonry bridge, over which ran a metalled road. This portion of the ground was laid out as a teak plantation, but the trees not making a good growth for timber, the land was, thirty-four years later, in 1820, made over by Government as the site for Bishop's College. The lower end of the garden was the land, which had been occupied by the old native fort of Thanna, or Muckwah Thanna, which stood just about where the Superintendent's house now stands, and was a Mahomedan outpost built to protect the trade of the river. Mention of it is frequent in the old records of Calcutta. This portion of the garden, Sir George King tells us, was intersected by a small creek, which ran inland towards the great banian tree, which even in those early days had attained a considerable size. Ten years before Colonel Kyd proposed the foundation of a botanic garden, he had, while on a visit to the "eastern frontier" (the borders of Assam), found a variety of cinnamon growing wild and had brought back young plants of the species, which were "deposited in the Governor-General's garden." A year or two later some other specimens were obtained from the Bhutan mountains, and about the same time Captain Price, then in command of the Bengal Squadron, employed in the blockade and reduction of Pondicherry, brought some plants of the true cinnamon tree from Colombo. All these young trees were planted in the Governor-General's garden, and it was their successful transplantation to Bengal upon which Colonel Kyd laid stress as proving the practicability and unselfishness of his scheme, and which was, doubtless the consideration which induced his Honourable Masters to so readily accede to his wishes. In Ceylon, (at that period in the occupation of the Dutch) the cinnamon trade was so profitable as to arouse the jealousy of the East India Company, who must, therefore. have been agreeably surprised to find that the tree would flourish equally well in Bengal.

The Governor-General, Warren Hastings, in whose garden these cinnamon trees were planted, had left India before Colonel Kyd's scheme was matured in 1786, and it was Sir John Macpherson, the acting Governor-General who forwarded the proposal to the Board, and wrote in support of it in a letter in which he said: "The late Governor-General was a great encourager of the introduction of new articles of commerce and foreign productions into these Provinces, and I regretted very much that the state of the Company's finances prevented our purchase for them of his garden in which those plants were reared." These gardens were situated at Alipore and formed a portion of the large block of land which was Hastings' property.

The Botanical Gardens were established in 1786 and Colonel Kyd was appointed to the post of Honorary Superintendent, continuing in that office till the day of his death in 1793. He never lived in the garden himself, but preferred to reside at Shalimar. His successor, Dr. Roxburgh, built the present Superintendent's house in 1795, and in the same year a beautiful marble urn, sculptured by Banks, was erected to Colonel Kyd's memory in the garden. The monument was originally placed within a small "temple" or canopy of masonry, which protected it from the wearing effects of the elements. This building was taken down in recent years, and the monument itself now shows to advantage, a conspicuous object through the long vistas of fine trees which make the Botanical Gardens of to-day different indeed from what they were when their founder looked his last on them one hundred years ago.

Entering by the Howrah gate (at the north-west corner of the garden) the visitor is confronted by three noble trees—a Banyan in the centre, with a Peepul on either side. To the right of the entrance passes off a long avenue of Palmyra palms; to the left runs an avenue of various trees, while in the middle, and in a line with the gate, runs a broad road which the visitor is recommended to follow. This road, after a little, passes between two ornamental sheets of water, and then through a group of Casuarina trees, up the stems of many of which are trained specimens of various species of the climbing palms commonly known as rattans or canes. Emerging from this grove, the road enters the *Palmetum,* a large piece of ground chiefly devoted to the display of members of the noble family of palms.

In the *Palmetum* there is a striking avenue of a curious Cuban palm with a columnar white stem (*Ooredoxa regia*). The *Palmetum* is separated from the remainder of the garden by a canal which is crossed by three bridges. Having crossed the canal, the Flower Garden lies to the right. Here are arranged many beds of palms and of succulent and flowering plants. The latter are particularly brilliant during the earlier months of the year. Dotted about in this neighbourhood are the various conservatories devoted to the cultivation of delicate species and of plants not indigenous to India. Notable among these is the orchid house, which, during the hot season especially, presents a gorgeous display of orchids in bloom; at other seasons the visitor is more struck by the curious forms of stem and leaf displayed by these interesting plants than by their flowers. Opposite the orchid house stands a monument to the founder of the garden (Colonel Kyd), and running straight from it to the river entrance ghât is a broad walk flanked on either side by a line of Cuba Palms which has a singularly impressive effect. Leaving this walk on the left, and passing onward from Kyd's monument, is a road which the visitor should follow. By going along it a few hundred yards, a broad straight road is met with on the right which leads to the great Banyan tree. This wonderful tree is only about a century and a quarter old. Nevertheless it covers a space of ground 900 feet in circumference. Its trunk girths 51 feet, and from its branches 282 ærial roots descend to the ground. Passing from the Banyan tree in the direction of the river, is all that was spared by the cyclones of 1864 and 1867 of a noble avenue of Mahogany trees which were planted about the end of last century by Dr. Walter Roxburgh, the second Superintendent of the garden. In the opposite direction from the Mahogany avenue runs a broad road, on the left of which (going from the great Banyan) stands a monument to the celebrated botanist just mentioned, with the following beautiful inscription from the pen of Bishop Heber: "Quisquis ades, si locus suavitate mentem permulcet aut pie sentias de deo, habendus in honore tui ROXBURGHIUS, horum hortorum olim praefectus, vir scientiae botanices laude florens idemque amœnitatum agrestium summus artifex; conservat cinerem patria hic viget ingenium; tu fave of perfruere. Posuere superstites amici MDCCCXXII."

A little way beyond Roxburgh's monument, the road bends to the right through a double row of Deodars—trees regarded as sacred in Bengal. and often planted near Hindoo temples. Where the row of Deodars ends, there is a magnificent specimen of the *Terminalia Catappa* (often named Country Almond). Running at right angles to the Deodar avenue is a still more beautiful avenue of the graceful *Albizzia paludosa* alternated with the gorgeous flowered Brownea. Turning sharp to the right and walking along the southern half of this mixed avenue, the visitor is conducted to the Palm Conservatory, an enormous octagonal structure, with a central dome. The frame-work of this house is of iron, and its sides and roof are covered by wire netting, upon which is attached a thin thatch of grass. The interior of this conservatory is laid out in rockeries, between which are numerous winding paths. The plants being all in the ground, the stiffness and formality inseparable from large collections of plants in pots and tubs is entirely avoided, and the general effect is excellent. The house is a large one, each of its eight sides measuring 85 feet, its diameter being 210 feet, and the height of the dome 50 feet. The collection of plants is large and varied, and few conservatories in Europe can compare with it for beauty and effectiveness. Emerging from the palm house and proceeding along the road running westward, the banks of a lake are reached, on which there is a small collection of water fowl. On the left of the head of this lake stands a conservatory intermediate in height between the palm and orchid houses. This circuit will have brought the visitor back to the orchid house mentioned in a previous paragraph. Numerous other circuits may be made in these large grounds, each emulating the other in interest and in pretty landscape effects. To a lover of the beautiful. half or even a whole day is none too long to devote to exploring them.

The gardens abound with olants of interest too

numerous for mention here. The visitor in leaving should drive along the avenue which skirts the river (of which many fine views are obtained) and he should pass out by the Engineering College gate on the river bank at the south-west corner of the garden. These gardens have a European reputation; and among their Superintendents in past times are to be noted Roxburgh, Wallich, Griffith, Falconer, Thomson, Jack, and Anderson, all men of high botanical fame and whose published works are well-known to Botanists. A scientific publication under the title of "Annals of the Calcutta Botanic Garden" is issued under the editorship of the present Superintendent. There is a magnificent Herbarium in a large building in the south-east corner of the grounds; but this of course is of interest only to the skilled Botanist.

Amongst the benefits conferred on India by these gardens are the introduction of the Tea industry into Assam, and the acclimatization in British Sikkim of the quinine yielding Cinchonas. The gardens are open gratuitously every day from sunrise to sunset.

CHAPTER XVIII.

SOME TEMPLES & SHRINES.

HINDU TEMPLES.

THERE are not many Hindu temples in Calcutta which need detain the sightseer. But there are notable exceptions to the rule. The shrine of the goddess Kali (who may be regarded as the patron saint of the city) is at Kalighat, on the banks of the Nullah or canal which leaves the Hooghly at Hastings Bridge. Thither on certain days thousands of Hindus flock to make their poojah to the goddess. But all daily worship is performed in the house, or on the river bank, at bathing time. The houses of most rich Hindus have a "Thakoor-baree" or house for the god attached, in which poojah is performed by the family priest, but there is, so far as we are aware, only one Hindu temple worth naming in the city itself. This is called "Muddim Mohunjee." It is a public place of worship for the orthodox Hindu, and is situate at Bagh-bazar. It is calculated that many thousands of devotees visit this Temple daily; and on occasions such as "Junmoostoomee, Ras-jattra and Rath," both males and females attend in very large numbers to offer poojah to the god and goddess. There are also the ruins of the famous Five Jewel temple to be seen in the Chitpore

Road, which was built about the year 1730 by Gobindram Mitter, the "Black zemindar" of the days of Holwell. Its cupola was for many years the most conspicuous object in the city, over which it towered as the dome of St. Paul's does over the city of London. About 1820 it fell with a crash and has never since been rebuilt.

KALIGHAT.—The present temple of the goddess Kali at Kalighat is said to be nearly a mile or more to the south-west of the older temple, which stood in the sixteenth century at Bhowanipore.

It is situated on the bank of the old bed of the Ganges, at a distance of about three miles from Fort William, and is a massive masonry structure built with small bricks. Its height is about 90 feet, and it stands on a square base each side of which is about 75 feet. There is a long aisle on its south side, and raised platforms all round. A doorway occupies the centre of both the south and east sides of the main building. The present temple is of recent date, having been built by the Sabarna zemindars of Barisa in or about 1809. But it was, in fact, a renovation of an old temple, the existence of which can be traced back to the middle of the sixteenth century. There is an extensive Nat Mandir in front (south) of the temple. There are several other smaller temples of minor importance near the Kali temple. One of them, namely, that of Syamraya (Krishna) may be mentioned, as it is said to have been built early in the seventeenth century. The face of the idol of Kali is triangular shaped, and made of very fine black marble, resting on a huge square-shaped block of red granite, which forms the trunk. The hands, tongue, eyebrows, etc., of the idol are made of gold. The legend connected with the place is as follows.

Siva, one of the Hindu trinity, was not invited to a feast arranged for by his father-in-law Daksha. Sati, Siva's wife, however, persuaded her husband to allow her to visit her father on the occasion. But on arrival at her father's house she was so mortified at hearing her father speak ill of her husband that she immediately fell down dead. Furious at the news, Siva became mad with grief and "drunk with loss," and at once going over to the house of Daksha, he took up the corpse of his wife and placing it on his shoulders began making a tour round the world. He became so furious that all the other gods apprehended that unless he were pacified, the destruction of the world would be inevitable. But so long as the dead body of his wife was on his shoulders there was no possibility of soothing his anger. Vishnu therefore flung his disk (sudarsana chakra) at the body of Sati, and broke it into 51 pieces, which fell in a scattered shower to earth. Every spot where a fragment fell became from that moment a holy spot, full of the divine spirit of Sati. The names of these 51 places are described in a Sanscrit poem called "Pithamala" or "the Garland of Sanctuaries." Calcutta is one of them: for the little toe of the right foot of Sati is said to have fallen upon its site.

The Puranas state that the places sanctified by the fall of the fragments of the body of Sati, were recognised as Pithasthans, where the spirit of Sati, which is no other than divine energy, is worshipped along with a Bhairava or Siva in the shape of a Linga. The Linga Puran says that there are two kinds of lingas, natural and artificial. The pieces of stone that are found on the banks of the Narmada are natural ones and are called Vana Lingas; and those made out of gold, silver, copper, mercury, stone, clay, etc., are artificial ones. The Lingam representing the Bhairava Nakulesvar of Kalighat is said to be natural and self-begotten and occupies a site to the north-east of the shrine of Kali. For a long time Nakulesvar had no temple, though his consort, Kali, was honoured with a magnificent shrine surrounded by splendid buildings. A little thatched hut was the only thing consecrated to Nakulesvar, who had to wait till 1854, when a Punjabi merchant, named Tara Singh, erected the present stone temple. The temple is of square form measuring about 25 feet on each side, and, unlike others in Bengal, contains no wall, but has strong stone pillars over which stands an arched roof.

The large number of pilgrims that visit the temple of the goddess Kali invariably make it a point to bestow offerings on the Bhairava Nakulesvar. Ganges water or milk mixed with bhang, contained in little earthen jugs, to be had of the vendors in front of the temple, for one pice each, is poured over Nakulesvar by the devotees with a view to propitiate the god. A large gathering from Calcutta and suburban towns and villages is to be seen on the Sivaratra festival, when great enthusiasm is manifested in honour of the sanctity of the place and the efficacy of the worship of Siva. Nil Shashthi, the day preceding the Charak festival, is the occasion of attracting a concourse of people, including a large number of Hindu ladies, desirous of worshipping the Bhairava Nakulesvar. The profits arising from the offerings of the pilgrims are appropriated by the Haldars, the priests in charge of the temples of Kali and Nakulesvar. The predominant feature of the temple of Nakulesvar is the presence of a few Sanyasis, Hindu monks, who devote attention to the elucidation of the intricacies of Hindu philosophy and the injunctions of the Sastras.

At Meherpore, 1½ miles from the Alipore Collectorate, is a temple of Radhanath. This is reported to be an ancient Navaratna temple of good architecture. It was founded by one Ramnath Mundle more than a hundred years ago and was consecrated by him to the worship of Radhanath. The temple is reported to stand with its surrounding walls on an area of about 6 biggahs of land and was once very picturesque. It is now in a ruinous state.

A temple of Kali may also be found at No. 244, Bow Bazar Street, Calcutta. In a little building this Kali stands on a white figure representing a dead male. Contiguous to this building there is a little temple of Siva, which is said to be older than that of Kali. The Kali was established by one Srimanta Dom, of very low caste, who himself used to perform the duties of the priest to this goddess for a period of not less than 70 years up to the time of his death. The Dom used to treat the people of this quarter suffering from small-pox, and for this reason an idol of Sitala is kept adjacent to that of Kali. In this way the Dom became popular among the Eurasian residents of this quarter, who used to send offerings to this Kali, being thankful for cure from this particular disease. Hence the goddess has earned the name of Firinghi Kali.

TEMPLE OF SIDDHESVARI (Upper Chitpore Road, Calcutta).—It is said that after the Kali of Kalighat had attained renown far and wide, and a few years before the coming of the idol Madanmohan of Vishnapur to Calcutta, this Siddhesvari was established by a pious mendicant, who himself used to discharge the duties of priest. The late Abhaya Charan Mitra, one of the worshippers of this goddess, contributed much to meet the expenses of this temple. The old image of this goddess made of stone has been preserved in the temple as a relic, and the present image is made of clay about 7 feet high, standing on a figure representing a dead male. The goddess is standing in the posture of Kali in Siddhesvari form. It is said that formerly the river Hooghly flowed by this temple. The present building is of recent date. At the present day, of all the Kalis at Calcutta, Anandamayi of Nimtala Ghat Street, and Siddhesvari of Bagh-bazar are the only two which are daily attended by the greatest number of worshippers. There are two Siva lingas, one on each side of this Kali.

TEMPLES OF SIVA (Kenderdine's Lane, Calcutta).—One temple has nine pinnacles and each of the other two five. The temples are neatly constructed with bricks of old fashion, five or six inches in length. The late Trilokram Pakrasi, who was the Dewan of the Fort of Calcutta in his day, got these temples built for him and established one Siva in each of them. Their date of construction corresponds with that of the new Fort of Calcutta, and it is said that the materials used in them are of the same quality as those of the new Fort. The Sivas are about 5 feet in length and are well polished. They are rare specimens of their kind.

TEMPLE OF ANANDAMAYI (Nimtala Ghat, Calcutta).—It is said that more than a century ago this goddess was established by a Mohanta who had a chela (disciple) named Jagannatha, a dealer in straw. The Mohanta at the time of his death made over the goddess to the aforesaid Jagannath. A few years later Jagannath, on account of his straitened circumstances, sold this deity, together with the piece of land adjacent, to the late Narayan Misra, who was a pious man and conducted the worship of the goddess in a satisfactory manner. On the death of Narayan Misra his adopted son, Haradeva Misra, defrayed the expense of the worship. On the death of Haradeva Misra, his nephew, the late Zemindar, Babu Madhab Chandra Banerjee of Nimtala Street, inherited this property and became the proprietor of this temple. Madhab Babu was succeeded by the late Babu Sibkrishna Banerjee, who again was succeeded by his adopted son, Babu Nani Lal Banerjee, who is the present proprietor of this temple. The image of Kali is made of black stone standing on a white figure representing a dead male. It is about two feet high, and is considered by the worshippers of Kali as the pattern of its kind. The feet are a foot-and-a-half below the level of the road, and the whole figure is so firmly stuck to the ground that it has baffled several attempts of the devotees to raise it on a higher level. Although the present Nimtala bathing ghat and burning-place are at a considerable distance from this temple, the old ghat close to the temple can be seen even at the present day. That the place where the temple is standing is the old burying-place can be inferred from the fact that it is called Sasmana Kali. Of all the Kalis at Calcutta, Anandamayi is attended daily by a vast concourse of votaries, who present their offerings to the goddess.

TEMPLE OF SIDDHESVARI (Thanthania, Cornwallis Street, Calcutta).—This image was established by a Brahmachari named Udayanarayana, who continued to discharge the duties of priest to this goddess up to the time of his death. After his death, a Brahman of the Haldar class began to act as a priest of this deity. During his priesthood, in the Bengali year 1210, the late Babu Sankar Chandra Ghosh of Thanthania erected the present temple of the deity. On a tablet on the wall in the eastern side of the temple, the following inscription is seen: "Kali dwells in the heart of Sankara." Here the word Sankara is used in a double sense alluding to the name of Babu Sankara Ghose as well as to Sankara, meaning Siva. On another tablet on the wall on the western side of the temple is this inscription: "the temple of Mother Siddhesvari, established by the late magnanimous Sankar Ghosh, in the Bengali year 1210." From this it is evident that the temple was constructed 93 years ago, and the Kali appears to be some years older than the temple. Her image is of clay, and she is represented standing on the prostrate figure of a dead male.

THE NIMTALA BURNING GHAT.

The word Nimtala means the shade of the Nim tree. This is the chief place in Calcutta for the disposal of the Hindoo dead. This burning ghat, as it is popularly called, is not exactly the old site, but it is, as it must be and has always been, immediately on the river. The town having steadily encroached on the Hooghly, the ghat has many a time shifted its situation. The present structure is the construction of the Port Commissioners, who have, at no small cost, improved the river bank.

The old ghat could scarcely be approached. The Hindoos bitterly complained of the inconvenience experienced by them in the performance of their sad duty at the ghat. But those days are gone by and the present ghat has ceased to be the dreadful place associated in the Hindoo mind with *sashan*.

The process of cremation is cheap and simple. A pyre of wood is erected. The corpse is washed and robed in new clothes, a few *mantras* are uttered by the son or nearest relative, the corpse is then laid on the pyre and fire applied to it, when it is reduced to ashes in two or three hours. The whole ordinarily costs only Rs. 3-7 for adults, and Rs. 1-11-8 for minors under 10 years, according to the tariff fixed by the Municipal Commissioners. Paupers are burnt at the other Ghat: adults for Rs. 1-8 and minors for annas 13-6 only, and absolute paupers for nothing, the charge being borne by the Municipality.

MOHAMMADAN MOSQUES.

MOSQUES IN DHURRUMTOLLAH.—The finest mosque in

Calcutta is that at the corner of Dhurrumtollah Street, erected and endowed in 1842 by the late Prince Gholam Mahomed (son of Tippoo Sultan). It forms a conspicuous object from the north end of Chowringhee Road. At noon and at sunset hundreds of Mohammadans may be seen kneeling in the verandah. It bears the following inscription: "This Musjid was erected during the Government of Lord Auckland, G.C.B., by the Prince Gholam Mahomed, son of the late Tippoo Sultan, in gratitude to God and in commemoration of the Honorable Court of Directors granting him the arrears of his stipend in 1840." Above the middle arch, upon a tablet over the door of the entrance to the Musjid, is the following inscription:—

"The son of Sultan Tippoo, deceased,
Muhammad by name and praised indeed,
Not Muhammad himself, but his servant from the heart,
A follower of his religion, with sincerity and purity,
Built this pure dwelling-place
For praise, and prayer, and thanksgiving and blessing.
In its use like the Qibla and Islam (the Kaaba of Mecca);
In its glory like the Masjidi Aqsa (the temple of
Jerusalem.)
The Angel Gabriel said as a date for that building,
By way of its completion and as a blessing:
May God keep thee safe as the temple of Jerusalem.
By the blessing of the Apostles of Truth, and his family."

HAFIZ HATIM'S MOSQUE in Colootollah.—Erected in 1270 H., 1853 A.D. It bears the inscription:—

"Since the erection of this musjid was laudable,
Built as it was in an attractive style and lofty structure,

Ali bored the pearl of its date 'without difficulty.'
May God reward thee with good in both worlds."

The letters of the last line form 1270 after casting out two letters as directed in the previous line by a play in the original on the words, "without difficulty."

MOSQUE OF KITABUDDIN SARKAR, Calcutta (Sealdah).—No inscription. Built 67 years ago by Kitabuddin Sarkar. This mosque is a brick building in bad repair. It consists of two stories, the lower being a masjid and passage to the upper story, in which there is a smaller masjid and rooms for the Mujawir and other attendants.

The Mujawir in 1895 was Shaikh Hafizullah, a man of great sanctity, who is credited with miraculous powers. Many educated Muslims are his disciples. He is a venerable old man of some 65 years of age, and has been Mujawir at this masjid some 40 years.

Kitabuddin, who founded the mosque, was a prosperous merchant. He died soon after the mosque was completed. His son who succeeded him was a drunkard and spendthrift. No funds have been available for the support of the mosque for many years. It has no endowment. The current expenses are met by Shaik Hafizullah and his disciples.

MOSQUE AND TOMB OF BHONSRI SHAH, Calcutta (Chitpur.)—The masjid is nearer to Calcutta than the shrine on the north bank of the canal. The shrine is on the left-hand side going from Calcutta. It is approached from the bridge by a stair. It is frequented by both Mahomedans and Hindoos, and is reputed to have healing powers.

MANIK PIR'S TOMB, Calcutta (Upper Circular Road).—This shrine is situated near the junction of the Upper Circular Road with Manicktolla Street, approached by a narrow passage. There is no inscription on it, and all the information to be gained is that the shrine was that of Pir Syud Husam-ud-din Shah, known as Manik Pir, who came to Calcutta from Upper India. The Mujawir, who gave this information, stated that the shrine was fully a hundred years old, but could give no definite idea of the date.

JUMA PIR'S TOMB (Clive Street, Bara Bazar, Calcutta).—The place on which this shrine now stands was the shop of Kasinath, a *mudi* and an illiterate up-country man. The legend connected with it is as follows:—

"Kasinath was in the habit of going daily by boat to Hooghly and Bansberriah to buy goods. One day when he was returning, he saw a man standing by the riverside calling out to the different boatmen to ferry him across the river. Kasinath thereupon hailed him and offered to convey him across. He accepted the offer, and when they arrived he alighted from the boat and sat down to rest in Kasinath's shop, where he remained till the day of his death, Kasinath serving him all the time. Kasinath was advised by his guest, whose name was Jumma Shah, in or about the year 1805, to apply for one of the financial posts, which at that time, under the administration of Lord Cornwallis, the Governor-General, were being filled by native officials, which he did, and although he was uneducated, not even knowing how to read or write, yet by the favour and blessing of the saint he succeeded in gaining one of these appointments, and was posted as Diwan of the State and became known as Diwan Kasinath. His devotion to the saint Jumma Shah was so profound that he built the shrine at his own expense in the year 1808 A.D., or thereabouts; but being a Hindu by caste thought it improper to serve a Musalman saint; accordingly he sought for a devout Musalman to serve the saint and attend the shrine, and found one Guman Shah, elder brother of Jutti Shah, whom he engaged for this duty. On Jumma Shah's death he was succeeded by his younger brother, Jutti Shah. Maulavi Siraj-ul-Haqq, at that time the Qazi-ul-Quzzat of the late Sadr Diwani Adalat, advised Jutti Shah, and helped him with funds to build an Imambara in Machua Bazar Street of the town (Mirzapore), where it is now in existence in a dilapidated condition."

RAJAB ALI'S TOMB.—On the west side of Hastings near the Public Works Department godowns, is Rajab Ali's shrine. It is said to be about 100 years old. Rajab Ali was a native officer in the Governor-General's bodyguard who deserted and became a faquir. The date of his death, according to Dr. Ranking, the late Secretary to the Board of Examiners, was about 1790 A.D.

WAZIR ALI'S TOMB (Kasia Bagan Burial-ground, near the Bamun Bustee Police Thana, on the east side of the Circular Road).—Wazir Ali was the adopted son of Asuf-ud-Doulah, Nawab of Oude, who figures with Colonel Mordaunt and Claud Martine, in Zoffany's famous picture of "Colonel Mordaunt's Cock-match" painted in 1786. On Asuf-ud-Doulah's death in 1797, he was placed on the throne, but his foolish intrigues being reported to the Governor-General, he was deposed, and the late Nawab's son, Saadut Ali, raised to the throne. Wazir Ali was granted an annual pension of two lacs and ordered to repair from Lucknow to Benares, where Mr. George Frederick Cherry, the Resident, was to make arrangements for his proceeding to his ultimate destination. He was invited to Mr. Cherry's house to breakfast on January 14th, 1799, and came attended by a large "swarry" or armed retinue. He had plotted a general massacre but succeeded only in killing Mr. Cherry, Captain Edward S. Conway and Mr. Robert Graham. His men then made their way to the house of Mr. Davis, the Judge, who held them at bay with a hogspear on the winding staircase leading to his roof. Mr. Davis' story of his defence was published by him in a (now rare) little book bearing on the cover a representation of his historic spear. Wazir Ali was captured in Berar and confined in Fort William in a sort of iron cage, where he died of water in the chest in May 1817, at the age of 36, after a solitary confinement of 17 years and some months. The expenses of his funeral cost 70 rupees, and that of his marriage in 1794 thirty lacs! The inscription on his tomb, which is not far from the grave of one of Tippoo Sultan's sons, is as follows: "Truly the day of separation has rent my heart; may God rend the heart of the day of separation. Everything on earth is perishable, but the countenance of the great and glorious God remaineth for ever. O God, pardon and cover our transgressions; thou only art great and glorious and beneficent. When the Vizier of Hindustan, Wazir Ali Asuf Jah, quitted this place of vanity for the mansions of Paradise, I dived into the ocean of thought, in order that I might obtain the pearl containing the date of his removal, when suddenly my ears were assailed with the cry of 'Waee Dureegha' or 'Wo! wo!' from the race of the genii, the human race, and from the feathered tribes."

THE JAIN TEMPLE OF RAI BUDDREE DAS BAHADUR.

Every visitor interested in temples should make a point of seeing the Jain Temple at Maniktola, off Upper Circular Road, in the north of the town. It was founded in 1867 by Rai Buddree Das Bahadur, Mookim and Court Jeweller to the Government of India, and the pillar of the Jain community in Calcutta. The Jains, who are the Quakers of India, are non-conformists to the Brahmanical system of Hinduism. They are mostly traders; and though few in numbers, have attained great importance owing to their wealth. Like the magnificent series of temples and shrines on Mount Abu, the Maniktola temple is one of the many notable manifestations of the wealth and influence of their community. The temple is dedicated to Sital Nathji, tenth in order of the twenty-four Jain *trithankaras* or prophets.

From Rai Buddree Das Bahadur's Temple Street the traveller enters the temple through a superb archway. The view that meets his eyes is beautiful in the extreme. At the end of the fairy-like grounds rises the temple, built in the Jain style of Northern India. It is approached by broad marble steps, and flanked on three sides by a picturesque verandah. The walls are bright with mosaic, and the aisles within are a profusion of decoration from floor to ceiling. The glass and stone work is as artistic as the mosaic in pietra dura. In the centre of the sanctuary stands a hundred-branched chandelier. Around and outside the temple is a charming garden, laid out in walks, parterres and fountains, with statuary and pavilions. In one corner is a sheet of ornamental water, stocked with fish, which come to the surface when called. Elsewhere will be found guest houses and reception rooms. The visitor should not fail to ask for the drawing-room, which is most tastefully furnished and decorated. This combination of temple and garden is the work of a real artist, and both were designed by Rai Buddree Das Bahadur himself. They are open daily to the public from sunrise till evening. A special visit can be arranged by moonlight.

CHAPTER XIX.

UP AND DOWN THE RIVER.

(BY MR. JULIAN COTTON, I.C.S.)

No visit to Calcutta is complete without an excursion on the river.

In former times every Englishman arrived in Calcutta by the Hooghly. Nowadays, alas, our first view of the capital of India is gained from the train and not from the steamer. But the great river is always what it was, an unchanging landmark in the midst of all the change and chance that has transformed Calcutta from a fortified factory into a business metropolis. On its tide still float the country boats that greeted the eyes of Charnock. Its banks are lined with temples and ghats, many of them centuries old, overgrown with myth and fable. And though the Indiaman and the tea-clipper have given way to the liner and the "tramp," they are still navigated through the silt and the sand by the same race of Hooghly pilots that took the earliest factors "up the Barr of Ganges." The visitor, who looks out across the Maidan on to the masts and funnels that lie three and four deep in the river hardly realises the triumphs of engineering that have kept open the Port of Calcutta for ships of the largest tonnage. Let him stand of a morning on the Hooghly Bridge and watch the lines of tea flats and jute barges and the vessels flying the flag of nearly every nation in the world to be convinced that through this uncertain highway flows half the commerce of India.

But the river has other uses. Long before hill stations were thought of, Europeans regularly betook themselves up the Hooghly to escape the trials of a hot weather in their Chowringhee palaces. Governors-General started for their tours up-country by water, travelling in the grandest of state barges, with a flotilla of lesser boats bearing their suite and attendants. The Viceroy still has his villa at Barrackpore for week-end visits during the brief winter season that he spends at Calcutta; but the river-side retreats of the "old nabobians," as Hickey used to call them, are things of the past, and the tourist is more likely to be tempted to catch the mail to Darjeeling than to devote a day in a steamer between Garden Reach and Chinsurah. To-day, however, he must explore the river with us, for we have booked him a passage in the steamer which leaves Hatkola Ghat for Hooghly at 7-30 in the morning.

Turning the elbow of land which projects above the Royal Engineering College (late Bishop's College) we obtain a splendid view of the city and port with its massive buildings and forest of masts. Nothing makes Calcutta seem more un-Indian than the smoking chimney-stacks of Howrah, which recall so vividly the Southwark bank of the Thames. As we go northward towards Goosery the noble riverside bears more and more the impress of industrial activity. Prosaic cotton and jute factories jostle cheek by jowl with old-world temples and pagodas. Bally, some miles further on, is a study in contrasts. Most orthodox of holy places, it has come to be the home of most unorthodox Paper and Bone Mills. Tradition has it that it was to Bally that the Brahmins, who stood round

Nuncomar's scaffold, ran in horror to purify themselves in the river with cries of "Ah baup-aree" when they saw the Rajah really "turned off." At the adjoining hamlet of Utterpara, modern education has worked wonders, under the fostering care of the late Babu Joy Kissen Mookerjee (1808-1888); and the Library, College and Lecture Rooms founded by this philanthropic zemindar, are as energetically maintained by his son Raja Peary Mohun Mookerjee, C.S.I.

Barnagore immediately opposite, carries our minds back to the Dutch mynheers who had a "house and garden" here in the brave days of old. Streynsham Master who visited them in 1676 speaks of their "Hogg factory, where I am informed they kill about 3,000 hoggs in a year and salt them for their shipping." The village itself had "a famously infamous" reputation, and the admixture of races produced an Europeanized class of women known as the "Mosses," who have their modern counterpart in the white Tiyyas of Malabar. To-day Barnagore is a respectable Municipality and the seat of extensive mills for the manufacture of gunny-bags. A little way above are the temples of Dakhineswar or Dukshinsore where the Nabobs of Chitpore once hunted tigers. Passing Konnagar on the right bank, we arrive at Rishera, one of the many retreats up the river sacred to the memory of Warren Hastings. Close to Messrs. Birkmyre's Jute Mills is Rishera House, a fine old mansion, approached by an avenue of ancient mangoe trees, some of which are said to have been planted by the fair Marian herself.

Sooksagur, another riverside village, where Hastings

had a bungalow, was submerged in the sixties. From Croft, Hastings' friend, who made it a sugar factory, the place passed to Joseph Barretto, who lived there like a prince, and built a Roman Catholic Chapel for the use of his family. His successor, Laruletta, a Spaniard, converted the chapel into a residence for mahouts and fighting cocks; while things were at this pass, both villa and village were swallowed up by the river.

Opposite Rishera, Agarpara with its Church and neat Christian girls' school bears tribute to the pious labours of a famous lady missionary, Miss Wilson. We next perceive Khurdah, which is celebrated for its Rass Temple, built by the Gossains, and highter up is an imposing cluster of Siva Temples, the gift of the Biswas family. Tittaghur, a mile beyond, was a century ago the site of a busy dockyard where in 1801 was launched the "Countess of Sutherland" of 1,445 tons burthen. And now we get into view of Barrackpore, or, as the natives call it, Chanak. The theory that the name is derived from Charnock, who founded a small bazaar here, is quite untenable, for Chanak is a common Bengali appellation for a village and appears as Tchanuk in an old Dutch Map of India, drawn early in the seventeenth century, long before Job Charnock became a known man. Troops were first stationed here in 1772, and from that time forward it has acquired the name of Barrackpore, a hideous compound of an English word and a Sanscrit termination. As early as the days of Macpherson and Cornwallis, it was the country seat of the Governor-General. Sir John Shore, gave up the bungalow to the Commander-in-Chief, but

Lord Wellesley took it back. "I have been very well," he writes in June, 1801, "since Henry's arrival, residing almost entirely at Barrackpore, which, in my usual spirit of tyranny, I have filched from the Commander-in-Chief." In 1804, the cottage, for it was nothing more, was reported to be unsafe, and Lord Wellesley had it pulled down and replaced by a large bungalow, to be used as a temporary residence, while a great new palace costing 34 lacs was building on the spot, marked down as "green-house" in the plan of the period. The Court of Directors, however, nipped this magnificent idea in the bud, and the work was suspended, after the basement storey had been completed. The materials collected were all auctioned, but the shell of the building stood for several years, and evoked the following lament from Mrs. Maria Graham, (afterwards Lady Calcott and the authoress of Little Arthur's History of England) who saw it in 1810: "We landed at the Palace, begun by the Marquis Wellesley, but discontinued by the frugality of the East Indian Company; its unfinished arches showed in the moonlight like an ancient ruin and completed the beauty of the scene." Of the temporary bungalow adjoining, as it appeared in 1803, there is a vignette at the head of the first chapter in Lord Valentia's Travels. A decade later, Lord Minto was its enthusiastic occupant. "Barrackpore," he writes, "is really delicious and takes the sting out of India. The projected palace would have been magnificent, I have no doubt, but in perfect contradiction with every purpose of the place. It would have been to come from Calcutta to Calcutta again: and you must have had the same multitude of troublesome attendants, and have lived the same full-dress intolerable life at your country house as in town." Here he gave a grand ball and supper on January 12th, 1812, the anniversary of his wedding day "as appearing to myself more worthy of celebration than any other feast in the calendar especially," (and this is a delightful touch to any lover of the classics), "as it is also the birthday of Cicero, a gentleman, who attended us faithfully through the whole (Java) campaign. Seven hundred sat down to supper, and you see how I must oppress the province to support such extravagance."

Heber stayed at Barrackpore for two days in October, 1828, as the guest of Lord Amherst. He had his first experience of an elephant ride in the Park, and records in his Journal that the word bungalow is a corruption of Bengali! But the most vivacious visitor that the place had in those early days was the naturalist Jacquemont, who also took his first ride here on a "moving mountain," and enjoyed himself thoroughly in these sylvan surroundings. "Sometimes after lunch, which at two o'clock brought together all the inmates, and where I refrained from appearing very often from want of virtue to resist the *pâté de foie gras*, I used to go with Lady William Bentinck to her drawing-room, where the afternoon slipped away very pleasantly talking of the antipodes, rain and fine weather. In the evening after dinner, we had sometimes a little music, *en petite comité*. I used to monopolise Lord William at the end of the sofa at the further corner of the room; he talked to me of India, and I talked to him of the United States; then, at half-past ten, the signal for departure, I retired taking the arm of the friend, who among so many kind acquaintances I had already gained—I mean Colonel Hezeta. Often before entering the bungalow, which we inhabited together, we used to stroll till midnight through the immense walks of the beautiful park of Barrackpore."

This park of 250 acres, beautifully wooded and artistically laid out, is the feature of Barrackpore. Government House occupies an admirable situation, commanding a prospect of more than six miles down the river, "whose breadth here is sufficient for grandeur and not too much for beauty." In the grounds was formerly a menagerie of strange animals, but the collection was broken up about the time the Calcutta Zoo was being organised. The principal objects of interest in the Park are Lady Canning's tomb, and a Memorial Hall erected by Lord Minto in 1813 "to the memory of the brave." It contains tablets commemorating the officers who fell at the conquest of the Isle of France (Mauritius) in 1810 and of Java in 1811. This Valhalla has a most extraordinary echo. In 1843 inscriptions were added by Lord Ellenborough, to the officers who fell at Maharajpore and Punniar.

The parade ground of Barrackpore has been the scene of two mutinies of native troops,—in 1824, when the 47th B.N.I. refused to serve "across the black water" in the first Burmese War, and again in 1857 (the first act of the great Mutiny) when Mogul Pandy, after defying a score of English officers, was arrested by "the Chief," Lieut.-General Sir John Hearsey, K.C.B. In the station cemetery is the last resting-place of Hearsey's third son, a subaltern of Hussars, who was drowned here six years later; and among its other melancholy monuments is the tomb of Lord Amherst's son, Jeffrey, cut off at the age of 24 when Military Secretary to his father. Another inmate of these graveyards is Sergeant Hartigan, V.C., author of a once well-known book of military reminiscences.

Three miles from Barrackpore are the Pulta water-works, which supply Calcutta with drinking water. The splendid pumping machinery, the extensive settling tanks and the filtering beds are well worth inspection. Hard by is the village of Monirampore, memorable for its associations with a great Anglo-Indian family. Here lived James Prinsep, the famous father of six famous sons. He came out as a cadet in 1771, but never joined the army, becoming at once "an interloper." For ten years he was contractor for the chintz investments of the Company and set up an establishment for its manufacture at Monirampore. He also has the distinction of introducing the indigo manufacture into Bengal at Nilganj near Baraset. Latterly he turned his fertile mind to coinage, set up a mint at Pultah and contracted with Government for the first copper coinage ever struck in Bengal. In 1784 he was "bought out" by Government for an amount two-thirds short of what he had expended. In another house at Monirampore lived General Bennett Marley, the Nestor of the Indian Army, who landed in the country in 1771 and died here in 1842, at the age of 88. What "Tales of a Grandfather" could not this old veteran have recorded!

Opposite Barrackpore is the old Danish settlement of Serampore, which, according to one Governor-General, served the purpose of giving Barrackpore the pleasing view of a distant steeple. The visitor who lands at the ghat facing the church will be more than rewarded if he ventures on a little exploration. Once powerful Fredericsnagore (as the Danes called it after Frederick the Fifth of Denmark) has settled down to the prosaic existence of an industrial township: but in spite of steam cranes and mill engines, the place is rich in memories of the past. In 1799 the three Baptist missionaries, Carey, Marshman and Ward, settled here and set up their printing press, where they printed the Testament, not only in Bengali but even in Chinese, Prinsep lending workmen from Monirampore to engrave the wooden blocks for the Chinese characters. Thirty translations of the Scriptures, the first Bengali newspaper, and the *Friend of India* (progenitor of the Calcutta "Statesman") were here published; and it is wonderful to think that of the triumvirate of men, who accomplished this work, Carey had been a cobbler, Ward an apprentice to a painter, and Marshman a shop-boy.

With the permission of the Principal, we will now proceed to the College, an immense white edifice, which dates from 1821. The Library on the upper floor contains a valuable collection of books, and Dr. Carey's chair, crutches, and the old pulpit in which, as the saying went, Carey used to preach with simplicity, Mack with authority, and Marshman with length. Among the portraits is one of Carey with his moonshee, said to be by Zoffany, and another of Ward by Penny. Here too is the famous picture long pronounced to be that of Madame Grand by Zoffany. The tradition has been killed by Dr. Busteed, who was long a sturdy believer in it. His pamphlet "The Serampore portrait, is it Madame Grand?" conclusively proves the lady of the picture to be Princess Louisa Augusta of Augustenburg, sister of Frederick VI. of Denmark, who gave a charter to the College, and whose mother was the ill-fated Queen Caroline Matilda, daughter of Frederick Prince of Wales, and a sister of our George III. Princess Louisa was born in 1771 and married the handsome Prince in ruffles and a green riband who hangs near her on the wall. But the legend which has been an article of faith with every Serampore sightseer dies hard; and there can be little doubt that the Mission did once possess a portrait of the future Princess Talleyrand, though whither it has gone no one can tell. Kaye's article on Francis in the second volume of the *Calcutta Review* for December, 1844, (the volume is in a shelf in the Library not far from the portrait) speaks in so many words of "her portrait by Zoffani, now adorning the walls of Mr. Marshman's residence at Serampore," and Marshman himself, most accurate of men, corroborates the statement when commenting upon Kaye's article in his *Friend of India*. Miss Eden hands back the tradition further than Kaye. Writing from Barrackpore under date 19th April, 1837, she says: "I have such an interesting portrait to copy just now, a picture by Zoffany of Madame Talleyrand, when she was in this country as Mrs. Grand. It is so pretty. Captain C— borrowed it of the owner to have a copy made of it for himself, and as there are hardly any artists, and none good in Calcutta, I am copying it for him."

The last of the Danes has long passed away from Serampore, and the only souvenir of their rule is the monogram of Frederick VI which still lingers over the Jail, the Church and the Court House. The Church, originally Lutheran, was opened for service by Dr. Carey in 1805, and contains a memorial to him and his associates. In the cemetery are tombs of the factors of the Danske Asiatiske Compagnie, and there is one to a "Skibscapitain" in their service. An English sea-captain who is buried in the Mission graveyard in the person of Commander Mearing is worthy of remembrance, for he left half a lac in public charities.

Dr. Carey's old house is now sixty feet in the river, which has here cut away much of the bank. The Botanic Garden, established by him in 1800, contained in its palmy days, some 3,000 specimens of plants and covered six acres of ground. It is now jungle and the India Jute Mill covers part of the site. It is curious to note that the two great Botanists, Wallich and Voigt, were Danish subjects and both Surgeons at Serampore. Nathaniel Wallich was originally a Jew, named Nathan Wolff. His wife died at Serampore in the year of her marriage, aged 14. Voigt married Rachel Marshman, daughter of the famous missionary. Another daughter became Lady Havelock, wife of the hero of Lucknow, who was not only married but baptized here.

Time was when Serampore was most popular with Calcutta residents as a holiday resort, and generations of the "ladies and gentlemen of Fort William" patronised Parr's "Denmark Tavern" afterwards taken over by John Nicholl, "late of the Harmonic" and formerly steward to Sir Elijah Impey. The Danish settlement was also the Alsatia of Calcutta, and afforded refuge to any adventurer who found it prudent to escape from the metropolis.

A short walk will bring the visitor to the famous Aldeen House, and Martyn's Pagoda. The Pagoda was for many years used as the temple of Radhabullub, but abandoned as such when the river approached too near to allow Brahmans to receive gifts with a free conscience. The idol, composed according to tradition of the stone doorstep of the Viceroy's house at Gour, was removed with great pomp to a new temple, after it had paid a visit to Clive's Moonshee, the wealthy Raja Nubkissen in Calcutta, who tried hard to purchase it outright. The Pagoda and Park adjoining were then purchased by the Rev. David Brown, Provost of the College of Fort William, and Aldeen House was fitted up as his favourite residence. Hither came Henry Martyn in 1806, when waiting for a chaplain's appointment up-country, and in order to give him as much retirement as he wished, the Pagoda was prepared for his habitation. Under its vaulted shrine, room was found for an organ, and Martyn rejoiced "that the place where once devils were worshipped, has now become Christ's oratory." After Brown's death, it passed into other hands and in the forties was converted into a rum distillery, the bottles bearing the well-known "Pagoda" Brand. The pilgrimages of many Europeans to the spot, and, above all, the visit of Lord Lawrence, led the Hindoo family who now own it, to leave it as a simple ruin. It was lately restored by Lord Curzon and marked with a tablet. It stands opposite the second settling tank of the

Howrah water works, and Aldeen House is still used as a residence by the engineers.

After Serampore the next spot that will engage our attention is Chandernagore. It is the sole survivor of the foreign settlements on the Hooghly, and the trip up the river is well worth taking if only to see this little piece of France in India. The hero of Chandernagore is Dupleix. His bust (by Fagel of Paris) adorns the public gardens, and both the college and the pretty promenade on the river bank bear his name. His fortunes were indeed inseparably bound up with those of the city of "sandal wood." When he came to it as Intendant or Governor in 1731, the place was forlorn and languishing. During his ten years' stewardship, its trade grew to such an extent as to quite outstrip that of *messieurs les anglois* at Calcutta. The "red mullets," as he called his ships, were known as far afield as Mocha, Bussora, Jeddo, and China, and his emissaries even made attempts to tap distant Tibet. Such was the resurrection of Chandernagore, that when he left it in 1741 to be Governor of Pondicherry, it was the most flourishing settlement in Bengal with 2,000 brick houses and a population which a decade later had risen to 103,000. The present church covers the site of the older Eglise de St. Louis, where he married his wife Jeanne, the famous Joanna Begum, from whom he learnt the tongues and the talents of Oriental diplomacy. The visitor can still turn up the old registers, and find for himself the original *acte de marriage*. If he looks over the church he will notice in the porch a tablet commemorating Claude Martin's legacy of 50,000 Rupees to the poor of the town, and the second street of Chandernagore perpetuates the name of its benefactor. A less known soldier of fortune is called to mind by a pavement grave in the same church cloister to the memory of Jean Henri Piron who succeeded Raymond in the command of the Nizam's French contingent. Born at Huningue (in Alsace) in 1763 he died in 1807 at Gyretty in a country house known as the "Jardin de l'amitié." Gyretty to-day is but a heap of crumbling stones lost in jungle. The traveller who braves the discomforts of a drive to the ruins is reminded of Salar Jung's journey to the battle-field of Marathon—"ten hours in the dust to see a mound of mud." But time was when this was the finest building of its kind in India, and when its noble staircase and spacious saloon with ceiling and cornice "painted by the hand of a master," were thought to rival the splendour of the public rooms at Versailles. The palmy days of Gyretty House coincided with the Governorship of Monsieur Chevalier, (1769 to 1787) "qui soutenait contre Warren Hastings l'omnipotent proconsul anglais *une lutte de plume* véritablement héroique." In this house, 120 years ago, were assembled all the beauty and fashion of Chinsurah, Chandernagore, Serampore and Calcutta. On such occasions the avenue was blocked by hundreds of the gayest equipages. Warren Hastings and Francis and Clavering were always glad to lay aside for a few hours the quarrels of the portfolio and speed in their green painted budgerows up the river to pay a visit to the glorious villa of their Parisian neighbour.

Here it was that one of John Company's servants fell in love with a maiden of Chandernagore, who was destined to bear the palm for beauty not only by the Ganges but by the Seine. As Dupleix is the hero of Chandernagore so Catherine Noel Werleé is its heroine. Here in 1777, she was married at the uncanonical hour of 1 A.M. to Mr. George François Grand, an English Civilian of Swiss extraction. Her father, Pierre Werleé, whose signature often figures in the old baptismal books of the parish, was a sea-faring Breton who came to India in his youth. Before he was twenty he was *pilotin du Gange,* a post of even more importance then with the French than with the English. He rapidly rose to be master pilot and died here in 1786 at the age of 65, Capitaine du Port and Chevalier of the Order of St. Louis. Hickey immortalises him in an occasional note that "Verlet, the French pilot still remains quiet at his station at Balasore." He was twice married, firstly, at Chandernagore in 1744 to Marguerite de Silva, who left him a widower, and secondly, in 1758, when Lieutenant du Port at Pondicherry, to Laurence Alleigne, whose father was master armourer of the French Company. Their daughter, the fair Catherine, "cette rare et nonchalante beauté indienne," was born in 1762. Tranquebar of the Danes, is traditionally credited with being her birthplace: but here, at Chandernagore, were spent her early years and girlhood. The rambler among the tombs in the old French cemetery may still light upon the little mortuary chapel of her family inscribed with the name "Werleé."

It is difficult, especially in these days of the *entente cordiale* to regret that the relations of private friendship which existed between so many individuals of both nations could not avert the stern necessity of the bombardment and capture of Chandernagore by Clive and Watson in 1757. The story of the gallant defence of Fort Orleans has been told by Ives, Surgeon to Admiral Watson's flagship, who was himself an actor in the scenes he describes. The fortifications and public works were irretrievably demolished a few months later and Chandernagore has lived ever since on her past reputation. For a time Chevalier made her a name for hospitality and "luttes de plume": but in 1778 the place was again occupied by the English without resistance, Pierre Werleé's name appearing among those who signed the capitulation. In 1783, it was again restored to the French. During the period of English possession (as Hickey announces with much contempt) the office of Judge of Chinsurah and Chandernagore was given as a sinecure to Sir Robert Chambers, Judge of the Supreme Court. The old place was destined only once more to make a stir in history, and that was during the mimic counterpart of the French revolution in 1792, when the mob, headed by a bankrupt lawyer pursued Governor Montigny to Gyretty and brought him back to Chandernagore in triumph. Fearing that the parallel to Louis XVI might be completed by his decapitation, the Governor appealed to the English, who soon put down the disturbance and on the news of the declaration of war between France and England resumed possession of the town in June, 1793, which they did not relinquish till December 1816.

An amiable administrateur and twenty-five çipayes are now the only remnants of French power in Bengal. Chandernagore still has passing attractions for the week-end visitor, and the Hotel de France (formerly the "Thistle") is generally full for the 14th of July. It is said that the streets were never so crowded with cheap trippers as on the occasion of a public execution by guillotine, now happily a thing of the past.

The old Dutch settlement of Chinsurah is within three miles of Chandernagore. It was exchanged in 1824 for Sumatra (then known as Bencoolen), and the Fort and Government House were soon after demolished to make room for English barracks Of the glories of the Dutch occupation we have a lively picture in the pages of Stavorinus (1769) and of Laurent Garçin, F.R.S., a Swiss Surgeon in the Dutch service (1727), who declares that there were nowhere such fine houses in India. It is sad to compare these accounts with Mrs. Fenton's description of the place as it stood in 1827, when first turned into a depôt for British sepoys. This lady, who was the wife of a Company's officer, speaks of the old Dutch quarter as already "a city of silence and decay." Early in the seventies the troops were removed and the old barracks are now a cutcherry. All that remains of Fort Gustavus is a slab lying in the Commissioner's house inscribed with the familiar monogram V.O.C., and the anno domini 1687. An earlier date stone of 1656, which Stavorinus saw over the land gate, has disappeared. The visitor who looks into the quaint old church will be interested in the lozenge-shaped hatchments, which hang on the walls almost too high to be easily read. They are fourteen in number, seven on either side. Several of them commemorate Governors; Francois de Hase (1676), Nicholas Bankes (1683), Martin Huysman

(1685), Pieter van Dishoek (1701), George Louis Vernet (1777), and Pieter Brueys (1793), once Grand Master of the Masonic Lodge "Concordia." Governor Vernet, who was kinsman to the famous French painter of that name, had been in his youth page to Louis XV and deserves to be remembered for his kindness to the English refugees in 1756, when Second of the Dutch Factory at Calcapore. The Chinsurah church was built by him in 1767 "ad maiorem Dei gloriam," as is inscribed on a medallion over the east door; and in the vestry is an old stone taken from the fallen clock tower "gebowd door J. A. Schiterman Raad Extraordinar van Nederlands India an Directeur diser Bengaalse Directie 1744."

An older church at Chinsurah is that of the Armenians founded in 1695 by the brothers Margar, whose father Coja Johannes was from Julfa "in the country of Shosh." His epitaph describes him as "a considerable merchant honoured with the favours of Kings and Viceroys: he had travelled north, east, south and west, and rests here in a foreign land seeking his home." A great Armenian pilgrimage takes place every year to this sanctuary on the Saint's day of St. John the Baptist to whom the edifice is dedicated.

The old Dutch and Armenian cemeteries may claim a passing notice. In the former are buried two married daughters of Charles Weston, who lived at Chinsurah in the 1780's, and on the first of each month was wont to distribute the equivalent of a hundred pounds to the poor. Many of the tombs are those of Dutch officials, and one to Gregory Herklots, Fiscal of Chinsurah, who resided there 63 years and died in 1852 aged 84, (leaving 81 descendants !) speaks well for the salubrity of the place.

To the south of Vernet's Church is Hooghly College, located in a fine building, which originally belonged to the French General Perron of Mahratta fame. Among the early principals of the College were James Sutherland, of the "Bengal Harkaru," Captain D. L. Richardson, well known in the annals of Calcutta literature, and James Esdaile, the mesmerist.

Hooghly, a mile or two beyond Chinsurah, is famous for its Mosque. The actual builder of the Imambarah, as it is called, was Karamat Ali, the friend and companion of Bokhara Connolly: but both the Imambarah and the Muhamadan seminary attached owe their splendour to Haji Muhammad Muhsin, who dying at Hooghly in the Mukbara garden in 1812, bequeathed a vast fortune for their up-keep. As in the case of La Martinière the legacy was in litigation for years, and by 1836, when the matter was finally settled, the accumulations had reached an immense figure. The grand quadrangle is well worth seeing, and the walls of the hall and portico are curiously ornamented with verses from the Koran in gigantic characters.

Immediately above Hooghly is Bandel, now a locality devoid of European residents. Time was when it was the Baiae of Calcutta, and no place could vie with it in popularity. Our forefathers knew by heart the rhymes from the Poet's corner of an old *Calcutta Gasette*, ending, "Each other place is hot as hell, When breezes fan you at Bandel, Had I ten houses, all I'd sell, And live entirely at

Bandel." One may pace the riverside in vain now-a-days to find any trace of the ruins of its delectable mansions, lawns and deer-parks. Even the site of Hooghly House is in question, where Mrs. Hastings spent so much time with the Mottes, and where she received her husband's letter about the duel. Some put it at Gholghat; others say it was near the Portuguese church, which is now the great sight of modern Bandel. This, the oldest Christian place of worship in Bengal, if not in India, was founded in 1599, the year in which Queen Elizabeth sanctioned the establishment of the East India Company. It was burnt in the sack of Hooghly by the Moors in 1632, but the keystone, with the date 1599, was preserved and built into the gate of the new church erected by John Gomes de Soto in 1661. It is dedicated to Nossa Senhora di Rosario and contains a monastery once occupied by Augustinian friars, the last of whom died in 1869. The parish priest, who is under the jurisdiction of the Bishop of Mylapore in Madras, still goes by the name of Prior, but his powers are sadly shorn from the days when his predecessors ruled like petty governors, collecting rent and administering justice of their own. Some 380 biggahs of land, out of the 777 granted rent-free by Shah Jehan, are still enjoyed and yield a rental of Rs. 1,240. In the grounds of the Church stands the mast of a ship, said to be an ex-voto from a sea-captain whose vessel had escaped the perils of the "Bay" in 1665. There are tombs within to Elizabeth ex-Sylva (a quaint Latin rendering of the Portuguese de Silva), who died from the effects of the siege of Calcutta, in 1756; of Constantia Weston, second wife of Charles Weston, who lived through these same "troubles;" and of a lady centenarian named Bourrilhon, who died in 1887. Every November the church is thronged with pilgrims during the Novena of Notre Dame de Bon Voyage.

Bandel will terminate our itinerary up the river, much as Brundusium did that of Horace. How our forefathers enjoyed such an excursion seventy years ago may be read in the delightful poem of "Mr. Simms" by Henry Meredith Parker, of the Bengal Civil Service;

"And every Doorga Poojah would good Mr. Simms explore,
The famous river Hoogly up as high as Barrackpore,
And visit the menagerie, and in his pleasant way,
Declare that all the bears were bores.—Alas, and well-a-day!

Then if the weather it was fine, to Chinsura he'd go,
With his nieces three in a pinnace, and a smart young man or so,
In bright blue coats and waistcoats, which were sparkling as the day,
And curly hair, and white kid gloves, a lover like array;

And at Chinsura, they walked about and then they went to tea,
With the antient merchant Van der Zank, and the widow Van der Zee,
They were old friends of Mr. Simms, and parting he would say,
"Perchance we ne'er may meet again."—Alas, and well-a-day!"

Those wishing for a pleasant trip down the Hooghly in

the opposite direction may avail themselves of the opportunities offered by the Calcutta Steam Navigation Company, whose steamers ply daily from Armenian Ghat to Ullubaria, where commences the High Level canal to Midnapore. On our way we pass the ruins of the King of Oudh's palace, now a flourishing brick-works, and the mills and factories of Budge-Budge. Much water has passed under the Howrah Bridge, since the Fort was captured from Suraj-ud-Doulah by Clive and Watson. Miles away flows on the river past Fulta, which sheltered our refugees, and Diamond Harbour, long the anchorage-ground above which East Indiamen would not ascend, to Saugor Island and the Sandheads, from the sighting of which Bengal civilians used to date their appointments. The "pilot sahibs" cruising here in their brig know every inch of the eastern channel and can tell fearsome tales of the wreck of the Anglia and of the dreaded James and Mary shoal at the junction of the Hooghly and Roopnarayan rivers, where many a fine ship has met disaster.

Our task is now over, and we bid our readers "au revoir."

APPENDIX.

SOME BOOKS ABOUT CALCUTTA.

I.

[*This list is not an exhaustive one. Plans and books of views are shown separately.*]

Asiaticus (Philip Dormer Stanhope). Genuine Memoirs of Asiaticus (1780).

Atkinson (James). The City of Palaces, and other poems (1824).

Balaram Mullick. Home Life in Bengal: an account of the every-day life of a Hindu home at the present day (1885).

Bazlul Karim. Short account of Martyn's pagoda and Al-deen House at Serampore (1896).

Bevy (The) of Calcutta Beauties. A collection of poems (1785).

Beveridge (H.) Illustrated History of India. (Engraving of Holwell's obelisk) (1858-62).

Beveridge (H., Jun.) Trial of Maharaja Nanda Kumar (1886).

Binaya Krishna Deb (Raja). Early growth and History of Calcutta (1905).

Bengal Annual or Literary Keepsake. Edited by D. L. Richardson (1832).

Black and Co. Illustrated Hand-Book of Calcutta (1864).

Blanshard, (Sidney Laman). The Ganges and Seine: scenes on the banks of both (1862).

Blechynden (Kathleen). Calcutta Past and Present (1905).

Blochmann (H.) A paper on Old Calcutta (1864).

Bolts (William). Considerations on Indian Affairs (1772).

Brief History of the Cyclone at Calcutta and Vicinity, 5th October, 1864. (Calcutta, 1865.)

Buckland (C. E.) Bengal under the Lieutenant-Governors (1901).

Busteed (H. E.) Echoes from Old Calcutta (1899). *Illustrated.*

Caine (W. S.) Picturesque India (1898). *Illustrated.*

"Calcutta Gazette." Selections from, for the years 1784-1828, 5 vols. (1864-69.)

Calcutta; a Poem, 1811. (Reviewed with copious extracts in Asiatic Journal, 1828).

Calcutta Review. Articles on "Calcutta in the olden time." Vols. 18 (1852) and 25 (1855). By J. C. Marshman.

Calcutta University Magazine, 1895-6: Articles by B. N. Chunder.

Carey (W. H.) The Good Old Days of Hon. John Company (1882).

Chowringhee Theatre (Librettos of operas performed at): 7 parts: (1835). By Asiaticus (Philip Dormer Stanhope.)

Chunder (Bholanath.) Travels of a Hindoo (1869).
Compendious Ecclesiastical and Historical Sketches of Bengal (1819).
Cotton (H. E. A.) The Century in India, 1800-1900. (1901).
Crawford, Lt.-Col. D. G. (I.M.S.): Brief History of the Hooghly District, (1902).
D'Oyly (Sir Charles, *Bart.*,) and Williamson (T.) The European in India (1813).
De Rozario (M.) The Complete Monumental Register (1815).
Deville (Capt. F.) Lettres sur le Bengale, écrites des bords du Gange (1825).
Dey (S. C.) Hooghly Past and Present (1906).
Earthquake in Bengal and Assam of June 12, 1896. (Reprinted from the "Englishman," 1897.)
Eastwick (E. B.) Murray's Hand-book to the Bengal Presidency (1882).
Eden, Hon. Emily. Letters from India (1872).
Fay (Mrs. E.) Original Letters from India (1817).
Fenton (Mrs.) Journal of 1827-8 (1901).
Firminger (Rev. W. K.) Thacker's Guide to Calcutta (1906).
Graham (Maria). Journal of a Residence in India, 1812. (With views.)
Grandpré (L. de). Voyage in Indian Ocean and to Bengal (1803). (View and Plan of Fort William and of the Black Hole Monument).
Grant (Colesworthy). An Anglo-Indian Domestic Sketch (1849). *Illustrated.*
Grier (Sydney C.) Like another Helen.
Grier (Sydney C.) The Great Proconsul (Calcutta temp: Warren Hastings).
Hartly House (1789).
Hart (Rev. W. H.) Old Calcutta: Its Places and People 100 years ago (1895).
*Hawkesworth (J.) The East Indian Chronologist (1801).
Hedges (Sir W.) Diary 1681-1687 (1887-89). (Hakluyt Society).
Hill, (S. C.) List of Europeans in Bengal in 1756 (1902).
Holmes and Co. The Bengal Obituary (1851).
Holwell (John Zephaniah). India Tracts (containing his narrative of the Black Hole tragedy). 1774.
Hunter (Sir W. W.) Imperial Gazetteer of India, 1885-87. (Vol. III for Calcutta, others Vols. for places in its vicinity).
Hunter (Sir W. W.) The Thackerays in India (1897).
Hyde (Rev. H. B.) The Parish of Bengal, (1899).
Hamilton (Capt. Alexander): A new account of the East Indies: being the observations and remarks of Capt. A. Hamilton who resided in those parts from the year 1688 to 1723.
Hyde (Rev. H. B.) Parochial annals of Bengal (1901).
"Indian Review" Vol. VII, 1886. Article by J. T. Wheeler.

* *Not in Imperial Library.*

Johnson (G. W.) The Stranger in India; or Three years in Calcutta (1843).
Kaye (Sir John William). Peregrine Pulteny or Life in India (1844).
Kindersley (Mrs.) Letters from the East Indies (1777).
Kipling (Rudyard). The City of Dreadful Night (1891).
Laurie (Peter G.) Rambles in India, etc. (1859).
Life in Calcutta, by an old Military Officer: 3 series (1872).
Life in India, or the English in Calcutta. A novel (1828).
List of Tombs, Statues and Monuments, Bengal (1896).
Long (Rev. Jas.) Peeps into Social Life in Calcutta a century ago. (1868).
Long (Rev. Jas.) Selections from unpublished records of Govt. 1748-67. (1869).
Lushington (C.) History, etc., of Charitable Institutions in Calcutta (1824). *Illustrated.*
Mackintosh (William): Tracts in Europe, Asia and Africa, describing characters, customs, manners, laws, and productions of nature and art: containing various remarks on the political and commercial interest of Great Britain: and delineating in particular a new system for the government and improvement of the British settlements in the East Indies. Began in the year 1777 and finished in 1781: 2 vols. London 1782.
Martin (Sir J. R.) Notes on the Medical Topography of Calcutta (1837.)
Mitchell (Edmund.) Guide to Calcutta (1890).
Naufragus (Moffat James Horne.) The Adventures of (1827).
Newman and Co. Hand-Book to Calcutta (1892).
Parker (H. M.) Bole Ponjis (1851). Contains an excellent poem on the Adjutant Bird.
Price (Captain.) Observations.
*Rainey (H. J.) Historical and Topographical Sketch of Calcutta, "Englishman Press" (1876).
Rainey (H. J.) Articles in various newspapers.
Ray (A. K.) Short History of Calcutta (1902) (Census Report, Vol.. VII.) Maps and Plans.
Richardson (D. L.) History of the Fall of the old Fort of Calcutta and the Calamity of the Black Hole (centennial) 1855.
Roberts (Emma). Scenes and Characteristics of Hindustan (1835).
Simmons (W. J.) and Bell (J. W. M.). Municipal government in West and East Glasgow and Calcutta (1902).
Stark (H. A.) and Madge (E. W.) East Indian Worthies. (1892).
Stewart (Charles). History of Bengal (1813).
Sterndale (R. C.) Historical account of the Calcutta Collectorate (1885).
Stocqueler (J. H.) Hand-book of British India (1854).
Strong (F. P.) Topography of Calcutta (1837).
Trevelyan (Sir George, *Bart.*) The Competition-wallah (1866).

* *Not in Imperial Library.*

Valentia (Lord.) Voyages and Travels to India, etc., 1802-06. (1809.) *Illustrated.*

Wheeler (J. Talboys.) Early Records of British India (1879).

Wilson (C. R.) Early annals of the English in Bengal, 1895-1900.

Wilson (C. R.) List of Inscriptions on Tombs or Monuments in Bengal (1896).

Wilson (C. R.) Descriptive catalogue of the paintings, etc., in the rooms of the Asiatic Society of Bengal (1897).

Wilson (C. R.) Old Fort William and the Black Hole (1904.)

II.

VIEWS AND PORTRAITS.

Baillie (W.) 12 Coloured views of Calcutta (1794).

Calcutta Illustrated. 30 photo-reproductions. (Thacker.)

*Connor (Ensign James, 17th Batt. Sepoys.) Views: (Hindoo ceremony of Huson Hawson; Calcutta near the Old Fort, March 30, 1784).

Daniell (T.) 10 Coloured views of Calcutta (1786-88).

Daniell (T.) and (W.): Oriental Scenery in Hindustan. 3 Vols., 1795, etc. (Vol. I contains 6 coloured views of Calcutta.)

D'Oyly (Sir C.) Views of Calcutta (1830).

Fraser (J. B.) Twentyfour Views of Calcutta (1824).

Glimpses of India. (1904—several views.)

Grant (Colesworthy). Litho sketches of public characters of Calcutta (1838-45.)

Greene (Capt. D. S.) Views in India taken during the Mutiny—1859. (Contains 2 coloured views of Calcutta.)

Hodges (Wm., R. A.) Select Views in India (1786).

"Indian Charivari." The New Series, 1877, etc., contained portraits of Calcutta celebrities.

Jump (Capt. R.) Views in Calcutta (1837).

Route of the Overland Mail to India (1850). (Contains views of Calcutta.)

Salt (H.) 24 views in India, etc., (1809). (Contains one view of Calcutta.)

Soltykoff (Prince A.) Indian scenes and characters (1858). One picture of Durga Pujah in Calcutta.)

Vandergucht (G.) Fort William at Bengal: printed and delineated by Lambert and Scott (1730).

View of the Fort William in the Kingdom of Bengal (1794).

Wood (William, Jun). Panoramic views of Calcutta (1833).

III.

MAPS AND PLANS.

Calcutta surveyed during the years 1887-94. Surveyor-General's Office. 9 Sheets.

---

* *Not in Imperial Library.*

City, The; and Environs of Calcutta, including the Government Estate of Punchunnogram, with Alipore, Kidderpore, Garden Reach, Seebpoor, Howrah and Sulkea, 1852-56. (Surveyor-General's Office, 1861. 4 Sheets.)

Das (K. C.) and Samad (A.) Sheet maps (Nos. 1-5) of the Port of Calcutta, 1896. (Published by the Port Commissioners.)

Fac-simile plan of Calcutta in the year 1784-85, etc.

Hunton (A. S.) River Hugli, Port of Calcutta and Garden Reach, (1898). 2 Sheets.

Map of the Port of Calcutta, showing Old Fort William in relation to existing buildings. (Survey of India Office, 1903.)

Martin (Capt. Claude.) General map of the Calcutta lands (in 1760 or 1764).

Martin (Capt. Claude). Outline trace of the Calcutta lands, surveyed in 1760 or 1764.

Plan for the intelligence of the Military operations at Calcutta when attacked and taken by Suraj-ud-dowla, 1756. (Appears to have been subsequently revised by Upjohn, see *infra.*)

Plan of Calcutta (1756).

Plan of the City of Calcutta. Surveyor-General (July, 1903).

Prinsep (Capt. T.) Plan of the city of Calcutta and its environs for the use of the Lottery Committee. (Surveyor-Genl.'s office. 9 Sheets.)

Schalch (Major J. A.) Plan of the city of Calcutta and its environs for the use of the Lottery Committee, 1825. (8 Sheets.)

Simms, (F. W.) Plan of Calcutta from actual survey, 1847-49. (4 Sheets.)

Steuart, (A.) A draught of Hugley River from Calcutta to Balasore Road Channel (1767).

Territory of Calcutta (1757).

Upjohn (A.) Map of Calcutta and its environs taken in 1792 and 1793. (Surveyor-General's office (1767).

Upjohn (A.) Plan of the Territory of Calcutta, 1742, exhibiting military operations when taken by Seraj-ud-Dowla (1756).

Van Ryne (J.) Map of Fort William in the Kingdom of Bengal, belonging to the E. I. Company (1754).

Wills (Lieut. W.) Plan of Fort William and part of the city of Calcutta, 1753. 8 Sheets. (1) The above, (2) plan of Calcutta, 1889. (3) Fort William at Bengal, 1736, and (4) Port of Calcutta, 1890. All in one sheet fol.

Wood (Lt.-Col. Mark). Plan of Calcutta, reduced from the original one, executed in 1784-85. (Published by W. Baillie, 1792).

IV.

LIST OF W. BAILLIE'S VIEWS IN CALCUTTA, 1794.

[See (1) *of views and portraits.*]

1. Views of Esplanade Row, Calcutta, from the River to the Council-House.
2. North view of Fort William, from the Esplanade.

3. South view of the Council-House and Government-House, Calcutta.
4. View of Tank Square, Calcutta, from the East.
5. Military Orphan School, opposite Calcutta, for the children of private soldiers.
*6. South-East view of the New Church at Calcutta.
7. General view of Calcutta, taken near the sluice of Fort William.
8. South-West view of Fort William.
9. North view of the Water Gate and Royal Barracks, Fort William.
10. South view of Calcutta, taken near the Glacis of Fort William.
11. North-East view of the Military Orphan House, near Calcutta, for the children of Officers.
12. View of the East side of Tank Square, Calcutta.

List of Governors-General of India, Governors and Lieutenant-Governors of Bengal, in chronological order.

GOVERNORS-GENERAL OF FORT WILLIAM IN BENGAL.

Mr. Warren Hastings	1774-85
Sir John Macpherson, Bart.	1785-86
Earl Cornwallis, K.G.	1786-93
Sir John Shore, Bart.	1793-98
Lieut.-General Sir Alured Clark, K.C.B. ...	1798
The Earl of Mornington (Marquess Wellesley) ...	1798-1805
The Marquis Cornwallis, K.G., (2nd time) ...	1805
Sir George Hilaro Barlow, Bart.	1805
Lord Minto	1807-13
The Earl of Moira (Marquis of Hastings) ...	1813-23
Mr. John Adam	1823
Lord Amherst	1823-28
Mr. William Butterworth Bayley	1828

GOVERNORS-GENERAL OF INDIA.

Lord William Bentinck Cavendish	1828-35
Sir Charles Metcalfe, Bart., G.C.B.	1835-36
Lord Auckland, G.C.B.	1836-42
Lord Ellenborough	1842-44
Mr. William Wilberforce Bird	1844
Lord Hardinge, G.C.B.	1844-48
The Earl of Dalhousie, K.T.	1848-56
Viscount Canning	1856

VICEROYS AND GOVERNORS-GENERAL.

Earl Canning	1858-62
The Earl of Elgin and Kincardine, K.T. ...	1862
Major-General Sir Robert Cornelis Napier, K.C.B. ...	1863
Colonel Sir William Thomas Denison, K.C.B. ...	1863-64
Sir John Laird Mair Lawrence, Bart.	1864-69
The Earl of Mayo, K.P.	1869
Sir John Strachey, K.C.S.I.	1872
Lord Napier of Merchistoun, K.T.	1872
Lord Northbrook	1872-76
Lord Lytton, G.C.B.	1876-80
The Marquis of Ripon, K.G.	1880-84
The Earl of Dufferin, K.P., G.C.B., G.C.M.G. ...	1884-88
The Marquis of Lansdowne, G.C.M.G.	1888-94
The Earl of Elgin and Kincardine	1894-99
Lord Curzon of Kedleston	1899-1905
Lord Ampthill	1904
The Earl of Minto, G.C.M.G.	1905

GOVERNORS OF BENGAL.

Mr. William Hedges	1682-84
Mr. William Gyfford	1684
Sir Charles Eyre	1700
Mr. John Beard	1700
Mr. Anthony Weltden	1710
Mr. John Russell	1710
Mr. Robert Hedges	1718
Mr. Samuel Feake	1717
Mr. John Deane	1722
Mr. Henry Frankland	1725
Mr. Edward Stephenson (for one day)	1725
Mr. John Deane	1728
Mr. John Stackhouse	1731
Mr. Thomas Braddyll	1738
Mr. John Forster	1745
Mr. William Barwell	1748
Mr. Adam Dawson	1749
Mr. William Fytche	1752
Mr. Roger Drake	1752
Colonel Robert Clive	1758
Mr. John Zephaniah Holwell	1760
Mr. Henry Vansittart	1760
Mr. John Spencer	1764
Lord Clive	1765
Mr. Harry Verelst	1767
Mr. John Cartier	1769
Mr. Warren Hastings	1772

LIEUTENANT-GOVERNORS OF BENGAL.

Sir Frederick James Halliday, K.C.B. ...	1854
Sir John Peter Grant, K.C.S.I.	1859
Sir Cecil Beadon, K.C.S.I.	1862
Sir William Grey, K.C.S.I.	1867
Sir George Campbell, K.C.S.I.	1871
Sir Richard Temple, Bart., K.C.S.I.	1874
The Hon. Sir Ashley Eden, K.C.S.I., C.I.E. ...	1877
Sir Augustus Rivers Thompson, K.C.S.I., C.I.E. ...	1882
Mr. H. A. Cockerell, C.S.I. (acting)	1885
Sir Steuart C. Bayley, K.C.S.I., C.I.E.	1887
Sir Charles Elliot, K.C.S.I.	1891
Sir Antony Patrick MacDonnell, K.C.S.I. (acting) ...	1893
Sir Alexander Mackenzie, K.C.S.I.	1895
Sir Charles Cecil Stevens, K.C.S.I. (acting) ...	1897
Sir John Woodburn, K.C.S.I.	1898
Sir James Austin Bourdillon, K.C.S.I. (acting) ...	1902
Sir Andrew Henderson Leith Fraser, K.C.S.I. ...	1903

INDEX.

M

N

T